THE NEW FRENCH REVOLUTION

THE NEW FRENCH REVOLUTION

✻ ✻ ✻

by John Ardagh

HARPER COLOPHON BOOKS
Harper & Row, Publishers
New York and Evanston

First HARPER COLOPHON edition published in 1969
by Harper & Row, Publishers.

Library of Congress Catalog Card Number: 68-28187.

TO MY SON
NICHOLAS

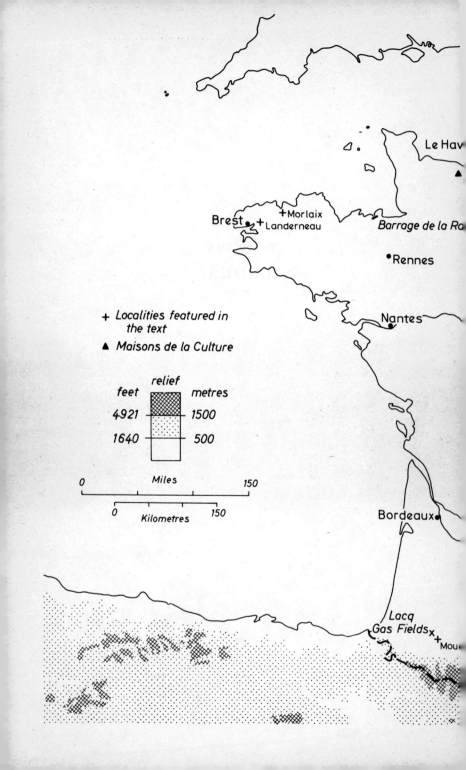

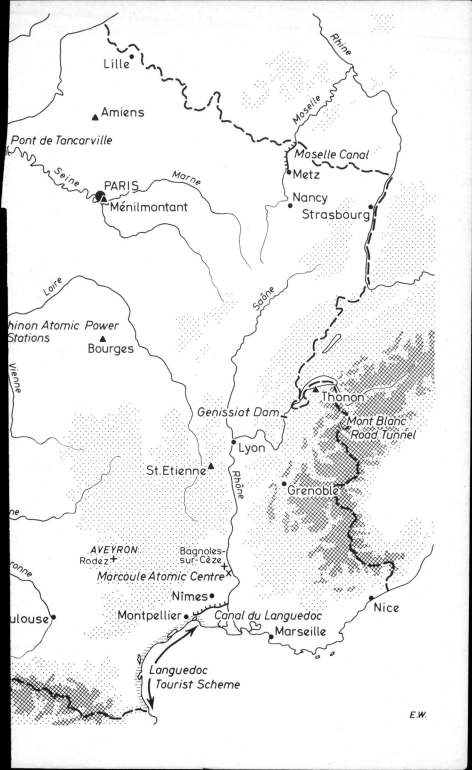

Lille

▲ Amiens

Pont de Tancarville

Seine

Marne

PARIS
Ménilmontant

Rhine

Moselle

Moselle Canal
● Metz

● Nancy
Strasbourg ●

Loire

Saône

hinon Atomic Power
Stations

▲
Bourges

Vienne

Thonon ▲

Genissiat Dam

Mont Blanc
Road Tunnel

● Lyon

St.Etienne ▲

Rhône

● Grenoble

AVEYRON
Rodez +

Bagnoles-
sur-Cèze

Marcoule Atomic Centre ✕✕

Nîmes ●

Montpellier ●

Canal du Languedoc

● Nice

ulouse

Languedoc
Tourist Scheme

Marseille ●

E.W.

CONTENTS

LIST OF ILLUSTRATIONS   xi

PREFACE—AND POSTSCRIPT   xiii

I   INTRODUCTION   1

II   THE ECONOMY: MIRACLE OR MIRAGE?   12

Decline and recovery   13
Technocrats and the Plan   17
Industry and the Common Market   25
Management in crisis   29
The Future   35

III   SOME KEY INDUSTRIES   46

The Railways: Armand pre-dates Beeching   47
'White coal' from the mountains and 'liquid gold' from the
    desert   48
Renault, Citroën, Peugeot: is genius enough?   54
Caravelles—but the Concorde?   61
Shoes and ships and sealing-wax: efficiency or prestige?   63

IV   THE YOUNG FARMERS' REVOLT   67

The Jacists, Pisani and the artichoke wars   68
Slow death of the peasant   75
Markets, Common and confused   84
The future: co-ops *versus* capitalists   92

V   THE BATTLE FOR THE RETAIL TRADE   99

A Jesuit grocer's crusade   100
Supermarkets and boutiques   105
Wanted, a French *Which?*   111

VI   NEW LIFE IN THE PROVINCES   114
Today's obsession: regional development   115
The arrogant advance of Grenoble   122
Caen and Rennes: two faces of progress   128
Languedoc, Toulouse, Lorraine   135
Factories, motorways, telephones: a dubious record   148
André Malraux's *Maisons de la Culture*   155
Prefects and mayors: State, reform thyself!   165

VII   PARIS, THE BELOVED MONSTER   175
Giant-scale planning for the year 2000   177
Romantic *vieux Paris* and the skyscrapers   186

VIII   THE HOUSING SHORTAGE:
             'NATIONAL DISGRACE NUMBER ONE'   203
The tyranny of bureaucrats and speculators   203
A painful adjustment to life in the new suburbia   212
Utopias of the new rich: 'Is Paris 2 burning?'   226

IX   NOVELTY AND TRADITION IN DAILY LIFE   231
A slow dismantling of the barricades of class   231
Families and women: femininity not feminism   239
The battle for birth-control   253
Towards an Americanised affluence   258
Leisure: from the two-hour lunch to *le week-end anglais*   265
From Escoffier to *le wimpy et chips*: '*une époque tragique*'   271
The holiday obsession: happiness is a Tahitian straw-village in
     Sicily   281
Welfare, health, alcoholism and the social misfits   298

X   YOUTH WITH A DUSTY ANSWER   306
Reform in the classroom: less humanities, more humanity   307
Universities: a crisis of growth   322
The *Grandes Ecoles*: a double challenge to 'X' from Nancy   332
La Jeunesse: not so much rebels, merely chums   339

XI   INTELLECTUALS IN DISARRAY   354
Slump in Sartre and no successor   355
The 'New Novel': from Robbe-Grillet's little puzzles to le
     Clézio's epic of hell   366
France's new dynamic: militant lay Catholicism   379

XII   ALL THE ARTS LANGUISH, SAVE ONE   391
Cinema in bloom, cinema in crisis   391
The new ciné-poets: frivolity and genius   399
Six thousand actors in search of a playwright   415
Television: the darker face of Gaullism   420
Signs of a new puritanism   430

XIII   CONCLUSION   434
Structural reform: dangers of the State as nanny   434
Birth-pangs of a new civic spirit   439
Friendliness, formalities, and foreigners   447
A decline of Frenchness?   456

XIV   POSTSCRIPT, JULY 1968   462

                BIBLIOGRAPHY   479

          CHRONOLOGICAL TABLE   482

                    INDEX   493

LIST OF ILLUSTRATIONS

The following are grouped in a separate section after page 112

Coal-miners on strike in northern France, 1963
The Rance tidal dam, Brittany
Jean Monnet
Louis Armand
Edgard Pisani
Michel Debatisse
Dauphines in production at the Renault factory, Billancourt, Paris
Agricultural unrest: demonstrators blocking a railway in the Midi, 1967
Peasant life, old style: a farmhouse in the Massif Central
Peasant life, new style: a family in a group farming enterprise in Lorraine
Morning congestion in Les Halles, "the bowels of Paris"
Edouard Leclerc in one of his grocery stores
A street in Grenoble, "France's little Chicago in the Alps"
André Malraux
Roger Planchon
A new road junction in northern Paris: the Boulevard Périphérique crossing
    over the Autoroute du Nord
Paris old and new: part of the Maine/Montparnasse development
The Métro at rush-hour
Smart new suburbia: the Drugwest "drugstore" at Parly 2, west of Paris

The following are grouped in a separate section after page 208

The earliest quarters of Sarcelles (1956): "an attempt to apply le Corbu-
    sier's ideas, without understanding them"
Some progress towards humanism: Les Courtillières at Pantin, eastern
    Paris (1964)
Pleasures and paréos with the Club Méditerranée
The Club's founder, Gérard Blitz

The old France: a *bistrot* in Brittany
The new France: advertisers' Franglais
Out of class: a street in Mourenx new town (Basses-Pyrénées)
French primary education: 'I obey'
The student mass: left-wing demonstrators in Paris
The student élite: *polytechniciens* at leisure, but still in uniform
Les Copains: Sylvie Vartan
Les Copains: Johnny Hallyday and fans
Jean-François Revel
Cardinal Veuillot
J.-M.-G. le Clézio
Alain Robbe-Grillet
Jean-Luc Godard
Agnès Varda
Alain Resnais

Photograph acknowledgements on page xvi.

MAPS

The twenty-one new Regions and their capitals page 118
The eight departments of the new 'Paris Region', showing the two parallel
  axes of the projected new urban centres page 176
Central Paris, showing the principal new roads and development areas
  page 186

PREFACE — AND POSTSCRIPT

THIS IS NOT a book about politics, nor about de Gaulle. It is a book about French society in transition. In other countries, and especially in Britain and the United States, public opinion has so often identified France with de Gaulle and his foreign policies that the rest of the complex French scene has tended to pass unnoticed. But de Gaulle is not typical of modern France. He has not been greatly interested in domestic affairs and has had little direct influence on them between 1958 and 1968 save to provide continuity of government. Only in a rare moment of crisis, like that which forced itself upon him in May, 1968, will he descend from the heights to pay much attention to the desires and frustrations of the mass French public.

I have therefore given de Gaulle little space in a book that is essentially about the lives of ordinary Frenchmen. I have also largely ignored French party politics and constitutional affairs—not because I think them unimportant, but because this ground has already been covered many times by other Anglo-American observers of France, more expert in politics than I. Instead I have tried to describe the broad sweep of post-war change at grass-roots level, economic, social and cultural.

I wrote this book in 1966–67, during a period of calm and apparent stability in France. But suddenly in May, 1968, after the book was printed and just before it was bound, that calm was shattered; and for several weeks it seemed that the word 'revolution' in my title—which refers to a long-term process of economic and social change—might acquire another, more dramatic significance. There has been no revolution in the strict sense of the term; but the social and political climate in France has changed irreversibly. And for this American edition I have been able to write a special new chapter (see page 462) which re-assesses French problems in the light of the May crisis, of the June elections, and of the Government's latest projects for reform. The rest of my book stands largely as I wrote it.

I do not claim any prescience, but the chapters that follow do, I think, explain much of the background to these recent events. They may help to show why it is that so much frustration built up—especially among students, farmers and workers, and television staff—and why so many millions of other Frenchmen nevertheless continue to vote for the Gaullist régime.

The uprising of May, 1968, was simply an acute symptom of an overall social mutation in present-day France, a traumatic but necessary mutation that is the essential theme of this book. Unlike some of the previous protest movements in post-war France—the Poujadist campaign of the mid-1950s for instance, or the OAS's battle to preserve French Algeria— this uprising was not an attempt to put the clock back but a sign of keen desire for progress and renewal. Its most positive aspect is that it may have provoked reforms which otherwise might have required decades. As many observers have noted, reform in France rarely takes place in smooth stages as in Britain, but seems to need these violent, occasional upheavals.

The uprising had negative aspects too. It may have reawakened old political quarrels, and repolarised the nation just at the moment when some national unity is badly needed if reform is to be effective. If the renewal of interest in politics, especially among young people, is in itself a healthy sign, it is no less tragic that French party politics seem farther removed than ever from the actual needs and aspirations of the French people: the electoral campaign in June was strangely removed from the problems which had provoked the uprising a month earlier, the real French problems. And the Left as much as the Right carries responsibility for this. The future is full of dangers: not only the evident economic perils resulting from the crisis (which I think can be overcome), but also the risk that the Gaullists might become more arrogant and paternalistic than before as a result of their victory, and that non-Gaullists of good faith may thus be driven into a morose opposition, refusing to cooperate in the essential work of renewal.

But there are also signs of hope. The crisis has dissipated certain old illusions, it has given new life to the movement for reform, it has offered the world new evidence of French vitality and imagination. While the French since the war have grown eager to modernise their country, they are also more aware than many Western people of the spiritual dangers underlying modern technocratic society. And the principal theme of the May uprising was just this: how to combine efficiency and social justice, how to modernise without losing one's soul. It is a vital problem for many countries besides France; but now the French, who throughout their history have shown their capacity for new ideas, have now shown once again that they may have something original to offer to civilisation.

I lived in Paris from 1955 to 1959 as a correspondent of *The Times* and have returned to France regularly ever since. During these twelve years I have seen the style and mood of the nation alter radically, though some of the changes were obscured on the surface, till the early 1960s, by the tensions of the Algerian crisis. Like other francophiles, I have developed an acute love-hate relationship with this stimulating and exasperating race: finally, love has triumphed over hate, and today I feel as emotionally committed to France as to my own country, and as much at home with French as with English people. I say this, in order to explain the spirit in which this book has been written. I have been severely critical of many things in France, but in much the way that a progress-minded Frenchman might himself be critical. The book tries to look at France from within, more from a French than an English point of view; and it takes for granted all that is great and unique and lovable about French civilisation. As the French say, *qui aime bien, châtie bien.*

In order to research this book, I travelled to almost every corner of France between 1960 and 1967, interviewing literally thousands of people: technocrats and schoolgirls, prefects and peasants, grocers and film-directors. Everywhere, except sometimes in Paris, I met with courtesy, readiness to help, and the highest degree of Gallic communicativeness; though France is a complex and difficult country to understand, and often a trying country to live in, she is ideal terrain for the note-taker. And if you meet the French on their own terms, rather than patronising them in English, they can be as charming as any people on earth. The many hundreds of people, high and low, who gave up their time to help me are too numerous to mention, but among them I should especially like to thank:

Jean Monnet, Louis Armand, Pierre Sudreau, Edgard Pisani, Simon Nora, Gilles Guérithault (editor of *l'Autojournal*), J. Cazes and other officials of the Plan, officers of the Régie Renault, S N P A, and other State and private firms; Michel Debatisse, Bernard Lambert, M. de Vauguerin, Jean Lallouët and Morley Troman (in Brittany), J. Caville and Raymond Lacombe (in the Aveyron), Professor Milhau, M. Sacarrère, Jean-Marie Crochet; Edouard Leclerc, Daniel Barrère, M. Ballerand; Philippe Lamour, M. Jaigu (of the *Aménagement du Territoire*), Robert de Caumont, Edouard Holman, Jo Tréhard, Henri Fréville (mayor of Rennes), Jean Lecotteley, Louis le Cunff, Georges Goubert (of the Comédie de l'Ouest), François Argouache, François Laffont (town clerk of Toulouse), Professors Raymond Dugrand and Jean Servier of Montpellier, M. Dupuis (of the Languedoc Canal Company), Georges Marguerita, Hubert Dubedout, M. Doublet (former Prefect of the Isère), Robert de Robert, Professor Louis Weil, Leon Chadé (of the *Est Républicain*), Professor P. Sadoul; M. Brunel (of the District de Paris), Michel Ragon, M. Taurand and other officials of the Préfecture de la Seine, M. Michaud (of the Ministry of Construction), Gilles Anouil (of *Réalités*); Georges Mesmin, Gilbert Mathieu (of *Le Monde*), MM. Lobry and James (of the S C I C), René Puiraveau, Bruno Verlet (of Mourenx), Yves André (of Bagnols-sur-Cèze).

Michel Crozier, R. Sadoun, Mr. Hagenstadt, Dr. Fabre, Gérard Blitz; Jean Capelle, Joseph Majault, J. Ozouf, Jean Joubert, Recteur Paul Imbs (of Nancy), Marcel Bonvalet, P. Danchin, Jacqueline Bertrand, Françoise Dumayet, Patrice Cournot, Michel Labartie, Michou Catzeflis, Mme. Dijol; Jean-François Revel, John Weightman, Alain Robbe-Grillet, Michel Butor, Jean-Marie Domenach, François Bédarida, Georges Suffert; Jean-Luc Godard, Jean de Baroncelli, Yvonne Baby, Jérome Brierre, Cynthia, Grenier, Jean Genet, Robert Conil-Lacoste, Pierre Desgraupes, Pierre Dumayet, Edouard Sablier, Maurice Girodias.

Finally, I should like to thank those friends and acquaintances who gave me special help with advice, contacts, or hospitality, or by reading parts of this book: in France, Claude Benoît, Claude Bonfils, Madeleine Chapsal, Estrella Pellerin, Marthe de la Rochefoucauld, Olivier Todd, as well as my French publishers, Robert Laffont, Jean Rosenthal, and Claude Manceron, and above all my translator, Bernard Willerval, and his wife; and in London, Jessica Meyersberg, Yvette Wiener, John Haycraft, Christopher Johnson, Catherine Blacklock, Virginia Makins, and Alain Jacob, as well of course as the directors and staff of Secker and Warburg who have been unfailingly kind.

Acknowledgement for the photographs is due to the following (names of photographers in brackets): Camera Press for the miners, Les Halles (G. Viollon), Métro (D. Angeli), students' riot (R. Lévy); Electricité de France for the Rance (Brigaud); Budapress for J. Monnet (Károly and Éva Forgács), *l'Express* for L. Armand (J. Roustan), M. Debatisse (D. Cande), R. Planchon (J. Roustan), J.-F. Revel (M. Bidermans); E. Pisani for the photo of himself; the French Embassy, London, for the Dauphines, A. Robbe-Grillet, J.-L. Godard (G. Botti); Agence France-Presse for the farmers' riot; Ministère de l'Agriculture for the two farming family groups (P. Bringé); Keystone for E. Leclerc and Cardinal Veuillot; French Tourist Office, London, for Grenoble (Y. Guillemaut); Documentation Française for A. Malraux, Sarcelles (J. Suquet), Bretons in café (P. Jahan), Mourenx (Yan), schoolgirls in class (P. Allard); Perceval for Paris road junction; Institut de l'Aménagement et de l'Urbanisme for Maine/Montparnasse and Pantin; Parly 2 Service de Presse for Drugwest; Club Méditerranée for the two photos of itself; Rapho for the *Polytechniciens* (S. Weiss); Salut les Copains for Sylvie Vartan and Johnny Hallyday; Gallimard for le Clézio (A. Bonin); British Film Institute for Agnès Varda; Unifrancefilm for A. Resnais (P. Toussaint).

CHAPTER I

INTRODUCTION

UNTIL VERY RECENTLY the French were often accused, with reason, of living with their eyes fixed on the past. Today they have suddenly opened them to the fact of living in the world of the late 1960s; and it thrills and scares them, like a convalescent emerging into harsh daylight from a shuttered room. Few other nations in the West are so schizophrenic about modernism: the British, by contrast, take it placidly in their stride, perhaps too placidly. With one part of themselves, the French are adapting eagerly to a new world of glamour, speed, and technical efficiency, and they show some creative flair in lending it a French flavour of its own; in other ways, they still cling for security to old habits and rituals, wary of altering the inner fabric of their lives and society. Thus, though many of the outward traits of modernism, from computers to 'pop' songs, are the same as in any Western country, the special conflicts and contrasts between old and new are sharper than almost anywhere else; and it is not always easy to tell whether France is transforming fundamentally, or only in style and mood.

Anyone returning to France today, after a long absence, will quickly be struck by the outward changes. In Paris, where almost nothing had been built for the first half of this century, the suburbs are now ringed by endless white megaliths of new apartment blocks, and the old grey house façades along the city boulevards have been scoured clean; down every street and alley, picturesque Parisian squalor is yielding to glitter. The Seine valley with its ruined abbeys and castles is filling up with big new factories. In the countryside, the peasants have bought tractors and Citroëns, and village girls in the garb of Chelsea walk beside their be-shawled, black-smocked grandmothers. In the cafés, people are less in-clined to swill litres of wine and get excited about politics; instead, they sit in the dark watching television over soft drinks. Clochemerle no longer gets worked up about a *pissotière*, but over a supermarket, or wayleave for a motorway. French advertisements, which used to concentrate on food, drink, and underwear, now devote themselves to the latest luxury gadgets, and the *lingua franca* of their snob-appeal is English. France, in short, is becoming less quaint and, maybe, less French.

Some changes go deep. Under the spontaneous momentum of economic advance, society is shifting its equilibrium. More than three million people have migrated from the farms since the war to new jobs in the towns, and the old-style peasant is slowly dying out. An artisanal economy is turning to mass-consumption. A score of provincial cities, such as Rennes or Bourges, quiet backwaters till a few years ago, are strident with new energy and activity. And a society hitherto dominated by older people and the prerogatives of age is now invaded by youth and a new cult of youth. The national mood has changed remarkably since I first knew France in the years after the war. Then, I used to think of the typical middle-class Frenchman as, say, a local lawyer or shopkeeper, sedentary and cautious, his roots deep in the town where his family had lived for generations; a man passionate in his ideological attachment to Church or Left, fond of big family reunions, heavy lunches, and ceremonial public occasions where he would make rhetorical speeches full of references to the French classics and history. Today this Third Republic flavour of life has turned fusty and is fading out, or at least is being overlaid with a different spirit. The prototype today might be, say, a salesman for an American-owned computer firm, quite ready to move across France if it means a bigger salary and a smarter flat, more likely to quote Galbraith than Victor Hugo, passionate about 'modernisation' and the enjoyment of slick new possessions and exotic holidays.

Yet dig deeper still, and many of the changes appear curiously uneven, sometimes illogical. A firm may install a costly computer, yet fail to educate its junior staff away from archaic methods of book-keeping. Small farmers eagerly buy tractors, yet shy from regrouping their farms in a way that would make those tractors effective. Everyone wants fast cars and seaside holidays, yet they cling to the tradition of going away only in high summer, thus jamming the roads and resorts. Glossy new flats with glass portals stand beside crumbling slums, protected by out-of-date property laws. France has built some of the world's finest hydro-electric and nuclear centres, but many local telephone exchanges and domestic electricity services are still crudely antiquated.

Basically, what is happening is this: an economic and technical revolution has suddenly rendered out of date the age-old social and administrative structures of France, and only very slowly and painfully are these adapting to meet the new conditions. The French may have changed their ambitions and material interests, but their basic character-traits, built round individualism, social mistrust, and desire for formalism and routine, are inevitably slower to change, and so is the legal and official framework of France which derives from the French character. The result is a fascinating turmoil and transition, rich terrain for the sociologist.

It is in the essentially economic field that the new France appears most positive and encouraging. Here the French have recovered a vitality, and a faith in their future, that many people thought impossible twenty years ago. This economic renaissance began just after the war, but for years was obscured by sloth and political crises, and did not gather real momentum until the late 'fifties. Writing in 1955, the great Swiss expert Herbert Lüthy was still highly sceptical about France's prospects of recovery.* 'The true face of France,' he suggested, appeared to foreigners and Frenchmen alike as 'that of a farmcart stuck in the mud', and he compared the French economy to a rock of Sisyphus, ever hauled up the hill by ardent technocrats only to fall down again each time, beneath the weight of petty vested interests and general apathy. Since then, as Lüthy himself foresaw might happen one day, that rock has been decisively pulled over the crest, and the farmcart is partly out of the mud. Industry and commerce have been forced to stir from their artisanal slumber and are fast modernising, even though they still have some way to go before they can meet American or German competition on equal terms.

France is in the throes of a belated industrial revolution. And so urgent and absorbing does the nation find this process that its whole energies seem to be given over to material progress and reform, and to private money-making and the enjoyment of new wealth—and the traditional French creative involvement in ideas, literature, and painting appears, for the moment, to be taking second place. Paris is no longer the power-house of European culture. Our old image of the French, fecund and original in the arts and philosophy, but financially weak and politically unstable, today needs a certain revision.

In order to trace the origins of the French recovery, we must look back to the war and even earlier: it sprang from the shock and humiliation of the 1940 defeat and the Occupation, and from the upturn in the birth-rate, which began modestly just before the war. In the 1930s, France was an extreme example of a general Western malaise: industrial production was actually on the decline during that decade, and the mood of the nation was sullen, protectionist, and defeatist, with many of the classic symptoms of decadence. The population, too, was declining—a pheno-menon unique in the modern world in time of peace—and experts today see this as a key factor in the pre-war malaise. After 1946, the French birth-rate was one of the highest in Europe; again, the experts trace inti-mate links between this and the new national dynamism.

Nowadays, when over-population in Asia and parts of Africa is the world's gravest problem, it may seem odd to regard a stagnant or declining birth-rate as a national calamity. But although for a backward country a high birth-rate is a menace, for a developed nation like France the opposite is true: a falling population usually limits investment and self-confidence. And France is still under-populated in relation to her neigh-bours and to her own territory and resources. As early as 1800 she began

* *France Against Herself*, by Herbert Lüthy (Praeger, 1955).

to fall behind her European rivals in her rate of population growth, due to mysterious factors arising from her social and political structure. In 1800, France was the most populous country in Western Europe, with 28·3 millions against Britain's 16 millions and 22 millions in what is now Germany; by 1910 France had risen to only 41·5 millions, overtaken both by Britain (45·4 millions) and Germany (63 millions). The French middle classes were seriously inhibited by the Napoleonic laws of equal inheritance, which provided an incentive against large families. And added to this were the ravages of alcoholism among the peasantry, and then the losses of the Great War, when France in proportion suffered more heavily than Germany or Britain. After 1918 the decline continued: by 1935 the birth-rate had fallen to 87 per cent, or seven births to eight deaths, and in the 1930s the global excess of deaths over births in France was 125,000. In 1939 Germany was able to put nearly twice as many men of military age into the field as France—and the results were inevitable.

During the 1930s French politicians grew increasingly worried about the low birth-rate. In 1932 a first attempt was made to remedy it, with the institution of family allowances: this was under the impulsion of the great demographer Adolphe Landry, then Minister of Labour, who is sometimes described today as 'a saviour of modern France'. The allowances were later extended, and in 1939 they were formalised in the famous Code de la Famille, basis of all post-war social legislation. By the outbreak of war they were already beginning to show results: between 1935 and 1939 the birth-rate crept up from 87 to 93 per cent, though it was still below par. Then came the wartime Pétain Government which at once promoted a strong pro-family policy, not perhaps with the noblest of democratic motives, but at least it meant that the allowances were continued; and so, in the darkest years of the Occupation, denatality was not as great as might have been expected. Directly after the war the child allowances were further extended and are now among the highest in Europe, often accounting for 30 per cent or more of a worker's income. They are certainly a major cause of the remarkable post-war demographic boom, but not the only one. The boom must be attributed also to more spontaneous psychological factors: a regaining of faith in the future, and what the demographer Alfred Sauvy has called 'a collective national conscience', a survival instinct forced into action by the shock of wartime defeat. In the middle and upper classes, where children used to be fewest, families have increased in size relatively more than in the working classes, and this may be due partly to the decline of bourgeois reliance on inherited property under the new economic conditions.

In 1945–6 the birth-rate rose suddenly from 93 to 126 per cent and then stayed at more or less that level until the 1960s. In most European countries the rate fell back in the 'fifties after an early post-war spurt, but in France it held steady for longer, although as elsewhere in the West it has tended to drop since about 1965. The annual net increase of births over deaths has stood at between 300,000 and 350,000 since the war, and thanks to this and to immigration (notably of settlers from Algeria in 1962–3), the population increased from forty-one million in 1946 to reach fifty million in 1966. This has given industry an important impulse for expansion; and the economy has proved sufficiently buoyant, at least until very recently, to be able to absorb the extra numbers that have poured on to the labour market since about 1962. France, happily for her, is still an under-populated and under-exploited territory compared with nearly all her neighbours, and could easily contain twice her present numbers without strain or overcrowding, so long as the economy stays sound. De Gaulle and his Ministers have several times proclaimed their dream of a powerful France of one hundred millions in the next century. It is not an impossibility.

'Le bébé-boom' has also brought with it a new cult of youth, and of young motherhood, in a nation hitherto addicted to patriarchal values. Baby-making is a prestige industry, and the ideal of nearly every young couple is to settle down in a new flat and breed. As for teenagers, they used to be ignored as a group in France, or treated as small-scale adults and expected to keep quiet: now they are indulged, courted, endlessly scrutinised.* *La jeunesse* has become a national slogan: every Frenchman, old or young, professes his faith in it, as a symbol of France's rejuvenated vitality. Frequently this is no more than lip-service; the barriers of age, as of class, remain, and young people have not yet achieved the same power breakthrough as in Britain (where, maybe, the revolution has got out of hand). But at least they have far more freedom and status than before the war; and younger people are now finding it easier to gain promotion through merit into key posts, in a land previously devoted to nepotism, hierarchic respect for age, and waiting for dead men's shoes.

The second fundamental factor behind the French recovery has been, paradoxically, the defeat of 1940 and the Occupation. These humiliations, coming after the decadence of the 'thirties, provided the French with a much-needed traumatic shock: it opened their eyes to the root causes of French decline, and forced a number of the more thoughtful and forceful ones to prepare action to stop it happening again. Maybe it is because Britain was spared this kind of shock that we have not developed quite the same post-war reformist dynamism as the French, the Germans, or others; we have not had to take stock of ourselves in the same way, and we have continued into peacetime with the illusion of self-sufficient invincibility.

Even the Vichy régime itself, though odious in many respects, was not without one or two incidental elements which helped pave the way for later recovery. I have mentioned the family allowances. In agriculture too, and in regional development, Vichy's corporatist policies, though fascist in inspiration, may have helped to generate a certain local awareness and self-dependence that was to prove useful later.

* See p. 339 (Youth with a dusty answer).

But much more important than this was the fact that the war gave the French a breathing-space in which to re-think the future. Under the enforced paralysis and inactivity of the Occupation, they had time to ponder, plan, and regroup, while the British were far too busy fighting. Most of the French post-war achievements and reforms can be traced back in inspiration to those years. On the land, young peasants of the Christian farming movement began to form little groups that later took the offensive to modernise French agriculture; in the Church, priests and laymen were preparing the way for a new social activism that has since transformed the spirit of Catholicism in France. Even Sartrian existentialism, the most fertile intellectual movement in France since the war, had its roots in the Occupation. Elsewhere, little groups of *Résistants* and Free French were plotting how to renovate the nation's economy and structures: the most important of these groups was formed around Jean Monnet in Washington, and out of it grew the 'Plan', which has played such a vital role in the French revival.

The Plan's greatest achievement, as the next chapter will describe, is that it has helped to instil in industry and the civil service a belief in expansion and progress that was absent before the war. The innovating technocrat began to come to the fore, in place of the conserving bureaucrat. At first, the new ethos of reform and modernisation was confined to a few pioneers in key posts, like Monnet and his team, and to local élites that sprang up sporadically around the country, like the Young Farmers. The rest of the nation stayed with its eyes on the past, protecting its *positions acquises*. Gradually, however, over the past twenty years, the new spirit has spread more widely to infect public opinion as a whole. This is the greatest change between modern and pre-war France: ordinary people now believe in progress, and accept the need for change—however much, when change actually presents itself, many of them still fight hard to defend their vested interests!

Steadily a number of diverse movements have developed, some of them stage-managed by the State technocrats, others led by private crusaders, or growing spontaneously from local grass-roots. The painful but ineluctable modernisation of factories, farms, and small shops; the remarkable rebirth of the provinces; the dawn of modern town-planning in Paris; the fiercely contested reforms in education, birth-control, and land ownership—this book will tell the story of these and other changes, and of their uneven pattern of success.

It is often assumed abroad that the French recovery has been due essentially to de Gaulle and a decade of political stability. But I doubt whether this is really so. Though the Gaullists have achieved a great deal, they have also hindered much, or have simply continued a process that was already in motion. In nearly every sector the changes were under way by the time de Gaulle returned to power in 1958, though overshadowed by the crises of colonial wars and by weak, shifting Governments. Soon after the Liberation the Plan had laid the first foundations of industrial recovery, and then a strong and stable civil service helped to provide continuity of policies despite fluctuating Ministries. And it was the Fourth Republic, not the Fifth, that prepared French opinion for the Common Market and signed the Treaty of Rome, which has done so much to stir French industry forward and to open French eyes to a wider international outlook. But, inevitably, many of the post-war improvements in France have taken years to reach fruition, and so the Gaullists have managed to steal the credit.

This is not to say that Gaullism's own record has been negative. In the first years after his return, de Gaulle was able to restore French self-confidence, and foreign confidence in France, notably by his handling of the Algerian problem and his bold financial measures of December, 1958. * And in scores of instances over the past ten years de Gaulle's strong Government has succeeded in applying vital and difficult reforms, where its weak predecessors had failed. For these various reasons, I feel that de Gaulle's credit with French history is still favourable, on balance, and I still do not regret the Treize Mai revolt that returned him to power in 1958. But in the past few years that balance has grown steadily finer. Even leaving aside his foreign policies, in domestic affairs too the same high-handedness that he shows abroad has finally alienated from him a number of the ablest and most liberal of the men who originally consented to work with his régime. Pierre Sudreau and Edgard Pisani, two ex-prefects who were perhaps the best of all de Gaulle's Ministers, both resigned in the mid-1960s in protest at his treatment of Parliament and public. At the same time, the régime has lost a part of its earlier reformist energy and idealism and has veered towards classic conservatism, in closer alliance with big business. This is one reason why the fruits of the new prosperity have not been shared more evenly in France: the peasant and working classes are still noticeably poorer and less emancipated than in Britain, and the upper classes tend to be richer. To an extent this extreme inequality is hard to avoid, as in Italy, so long as some sectors of the economic structure, such as small farms, remain so archaic. But partly it is due to the Gaullists' failure to devote more money and attention to social progress. National prestige wins the highest priorities, as any visitor will notice. The liner *France*, the Concorde, the Mont Blanc tunnel, the new Orly airport: these may be valuable achievements in themselves, but that is not the only reason why they attract public funds more easily than less eye-catching but more urgent matters such as housing, schools, roads, and telephones. And the same applies, *a fortiori*, to de Gaulle's costly nuclear policy.

In France there are two economies that uneasily co-exist: a modern one, most of it implanted since the war by the technocrats and a few big State and private firms; and below it, an old, creaking infrastructure,

* See p. 16 (The Economy).

based on artisanship, low turnover with high profits, and the ideal of the small family business. The modern sector has expanded considerably since Lüthy in 1953 described it as 'an isolated enclave inside old France', and today I would say that it predominates. But it has not yet absorbed the old system, which is strongly rooted in the traditional framework of French law and society. This society has been built up of a honeycomb of little sectional interests, each with its clearly defined rights and privileges, all mutually suspicious but carefully balancing each other in order to avoid conflict. It is a system that served France not too badly in the past: it ensured a certain stability and helped to protect the individual. But modern conditions now necessitate a different framework, more open and flexible.

Some features of the old system are gradually disappearing of their own accord, under the natural weight of economic change: many small firms and farms, for instance, find they can no longer subsist unless they merge or modernise. But other features are so powerfully sanctioned by law or custom that they cannot be altered except by legislation or other official action—this is true of the restrictive privileges of a number of professions, such as pharmacists and middlemen. Until changes of this kind are made, the modernisation of the economy can go so far but no further: improved techniques of production lose half their value if archaic and inefficient cartels and marketing methods cause waste and keep up prices. De Gaulle's Government has, in fact, put through a number of needed reforms: but there is much else it has failed to do, despite its power. It has seen its popularity slump in recent elections, and it does not dare offend too many group interests. De Gaulle is not normally a man who cares for such tactical considerations: if he wants a thing, he gets it done. But in the past few years he seems to have lost interest in domestic affairs, save to ensure that he stays in power. Some of his Ministers know precisely what needs to be done, but they are not always given the authority or the money to do it. Yet, as the French economy becomes steadily less protected, many of the problems grow more pressing each year.

It is because of the special strength of her past, and the weathered wholeness of her traditions, that France, like Britain, finds many of the structural changes so difficult, more so than a newer and more malleable nation like Germany. As the brilliant sociologist Michel Crozier* has pointed out, French society throughout its history has shown a tendency to resist change until the last possible moment, to allow an intolerable situation to build up and then, when the strain and inconvenience are too great, to change together, in a vast reshuffle, usually under the impulse of a few pioneering individuals. This is happening today, probably on a grander scale than ever before, or at least since 1789. And this attachment

---

* *The Bureaucratic Phenomenon* (University of Chicago Press, 1964).

to the past also helps to explain the fascination for the future. Even for the most dedicated French modernist and reformer, the wrench from the womb of safe tradition has been traumatic at some stage or other, and so he flings himself at tomorrow with all the more force, in over-compensation, as a man breaking an old habit discovers a new passion. If France, in de Gaulle's own phrase, is at last 'marrying her century', it is on the rebound.

The French are suddenly dazzled by new material prospects they had hardly dared trust in during their decades of archaism. Ordinary public interest in what life will be like in twenty or thirty years' time is noticeably greater than in Britain, and papers and magazines are full of optimistic articles about 'Le Paris de l'an 2000' or 'La Vie française de demain'. Some of this, in the pro-Gaullist Press, may be an astute move to distract public attention from the fact that much of France has not yet reached 1960, let alone 2000. But it does correspond to what people want to believe—that tomorrow their slums will be skyscraper garden cities, that aerotrains and freeways will banish the rush-hour tedium of Paris, and there will be smart cars, long leisure, and free opportunity for all, in a new California à la française. When the sober experts of the Plan recently produced an objective report on the France of 1985, it was eagerly read and discussed on all sides; and there may be some relevance, too, in the spectacular post-war popularity in France of Teilhard de Chardin, whose books relate older Christian humanist values to a radiant faith in the scientific future.

The French can also enjoy the feeling that their land, though ancient, is in huge areas still virgin and under-exploited, rich in untapped resources—'Europe's Texas', as someone said. They have that rare commodity in this corner of the old continent: *Lebensraum*. It is this, as much as anything, that makes planning and expansion a heady business for today's young technocrats, as new factories are implanted on the silent plains of the Béarn, or new power-dams in the lost mountain valleys of Savoy. In Britain, we look at the material future with cautious apprehension: it means the Buchanan Report, the dangers of pollution and overcrowding, the difficulties of replanning old industrial eyesores on a narrow island. France not only has more space, she was spared the full horrors of Victorian industrial growth. In many things, in architecture, décor, town-planning, industry, as well as in aspects of her economic and social structures, France is in a sense making a leap straight from the late eighteenth into the twentieth century—and though the leap is a harder one than the more continuous British process has been, there may in the longer term be practical advantages.

There is something impressive about the enthusiasm of quite a number of French, especially the younger ones, for an efficient, technology-based future. But not all of them are looking at the future quite squarely; there is a tendency to theorise about ideal solutions rather than grapple with immediate unsolved problems ahead. The Press will more readily project the millennium than criticise schemes in hand; and even the planners, though much more pragmatic than the French ever used to be, still show an over-fondness for perfect blueprints and generalisations. Some of this is simply an aspect of the French love of theorising and formalism, derived from the way they are taught to think at school; and some of it is due to the limitations on free discussion under the Gaullist régime. But I think it shows also that French society, in its present crisis period of mutation, does not quite dare look at itself in the mirror, for fear of not recognising the old familiar features. And this is one reason why so few contemporary novels, films or plays deal squarely and frankly with current social themes—the changes in the working-class and peasantry, for instance. Material change, the buying of cars and computers, is much less frightening than change of personality. And thus, while many thinking Frenchmen are excited and sanguine about France's socio-economic future, others are worried at what might be happening to French civilisation.

They are aware that France, in modernising, faces two dilemmas. The first is whether the present revolution will bring a more egalitarian and trustful spirit into French society, or whether the old barriers will simply go up again in a different form. More is at stake than solely economic efficiency: it is also a question of social justice and freedom in the widest sense. French society has always practised a certain tolerance and has based itself on respect for individual privacy and on legal égalité between all citizens. But in order to uphold these very virtues it has made itself into a closed and segmented rather than an open society: égalité has not equalled egalitarianism. So stubbornly has change been resisted that class barriers remain more rigid than in Britain today; professional advance still depends too often on having the right diplomas and contacts; and high respect is still paid to formal titles, hierarchies, and privileges. The individual's loyalties are traditionally towards family rather than community, and civic co-operation in the Anglo-Saxon sense is not highly developed. Public initiatives are expected to come from the State and the authorities, rather than from *ad hoc* citizen groups; and, even discounting the influence of Gaullist paternalism, public opinion does not have the same open force as in some countries.

Today the old groupings and loyalties are beginning to break up, under new conditions. Family ties which count for so much in France are weakening, society is becoming more exposed, and the French are having to re-assess their social attitudes. Individualist peasants are discovering the need to share their resources; on the vast modern housing estates, a new un-French neighbourliness is perforce emerging; a rigorous élitist system of education is being modified and democratised to meet modern needs; and the rigidly stratified and impersonal French pattern of bureaucracy is under agonising reappraisal in firms and public offices. Under the impulse of the reformers and modernists with their eyes on foreign models, a more open and eglitarian ethos appears to be emerging, though the process is slower than in Britain and is still heavily opposed by old reflexes of habit and suspicion. The question is whether, when the reshuffle is completed, the barriers will remain down; or whether a cycle familiar to France in the past will recur, and society will simply reclose its ranks on new ground.

The next dilemma goes even deeper, and I think it is the fundamental question to pose about France today. French and foreigners alike are aware that much of the best in France, perhaps more than in other countries, is intimately bound up with a certain traditional way of thought and civilisation, which risks being lost beyond recall in the inexorable process of modernisation. Is France fated to undergo a kind of lobotomy, which will cure many of the old economic and social weaknesses, but also kill the old turbulent creativeness and individuality? Some of the current signs are not too encouraging. While the tradition of individual craftsmanship is inevitably declining, few of the new mass-consumer industries are yet showing the same French genius for style and quality. Less time and care is spent nowadays on *cuisine*, and Paris is filling up with cafeterias and Wimpy bars. The Ville Lumière is no longer the world's art capital; her theatres are full of foreign plays or revivals, her literature has lost its human universality, her intellectual brilliance has grown stale. Above all, the French seem to have lost some of their old originality, and to have become oddly imitative, especially of their sworn rivals, the Anglo-Saxons. Their national pride cries out against the process but seems unable to stop it. While French words and phrases have for centuries been *à la mode*, even *de rigueur* in British polite society, today in France *c'est O.K., même snob*, in many circles, to speak the new hybrid language known as *franglais*; and few outward changes in the France of the 'sixties are more startling than the massive incursion of English, mainly into the vocabulary of advertising but also into some daily speech. In central Paris there is now a charcuterie called *The Little Pig* and a boutique called *Le Sweater Shop*. Anglo-American gadgets, techniques and mannerisms are all the rage. *L'Express* magazine remodels its format on *Time*, de Gaulle hires an American-style public-relations firm for the 1967 election campaign, and pop singers adopt Anglo-Saxon names like Johnny Hallyday. To be fair, the French do frequently add an authentic national flavour of their own to the things they borrow (for example, *un drugstore* is now something typically Parisian, quite unlike a drugstore). And on a more serious level, the copying of American business and industrial techniques may be healthy, if it helps towards efficient modernisation. But where will it all lead? Will the French, after their present difficult transition period, recover their old creative zest for ideas and style? Or is France fated to become a more prosperous, efficient, and contented country, maybe, but also a duller and much less French one?

Such, in brief, are the main problems and opportunities facing the French in the year 1968. In the following chapters they will be examined in detail.

CHAPTER II

THE ECONOMY: MIRACLE OR MIRAGE?

WHEN BRITAIN, at the end of 1964, came to borrow money from France and her other allies in her moment of need, many Frenchmen from de Gaulle downwards could hardly resist a twinge of *Schadenfreude*. For decades the British and others had tended to look down on France as the 'sick man of Europe', politically and economically. But now the picture was reversed. Britain's economy looked much the sicker of the two.

France's recovery had come as something of a surprise to many people abroad, since for the first years after the war it was camouflaged by recurrent financial crises and political upheavals. It was not until the early 1960s that we really became aware of a change in France more profound than the change of régime under de Gaulle. Exports and gold reserves were rising fast, industry was modernising, Caravelle and Dauphine became familiar words in many parts of the world.

Today France's economy is relatively strong, despite some enduring structural weaknesses and the unsolved threat of inflation. Statistics may give some idea of the progress. Industrial production, actually declining in the 1930s, by 1951 had regained its pre-war peak and in 1957 stood at twice its 1938 level. From 1950 to 1960 it rose 44 per cent, against 26 per cent in Britain. Gold and foreign exchange reserves, down to 10m francs in 1959, rose to 28,600m francs by the end of 1966, thanks to the Gaullists' successful devaluation in 1958 and other measures. Exports more than doubled between 1956 and 1962. The franc grew able to look the dollar in the face, and de Gaulle could even suggest a return to the gold standard. By the winter of 1967–8, his confidence in France's regained strength was all too apparent.

It is true that the German economy is stronger still, and the figures for German post-war growth even more striking. But then the Germans, as we know, are organised and methodical, and their economic structure makes sense. The French so-called 'miracle', in its French context, is the more remarkable of the two. For it has been achieved in the face of France's fundamental ailments. Some of these are now on the way to being cured: industry, for instance, has given up much of its pre-war neglect of exports and of productivity. But many structural weaknesses, rooted in old French traditions, are inevitably slower to change. Over-centralised State bureaucracy, lack of a vigorous capital market, clumsy systems of distribution, too many small family firms: these are some of the burdens that the economy still has to carry with it. Because these are such heavy burdens, France throughout the 1950s seemed balanced on a knife-edge between collapse and recovery, and many experts repeatedly predicted her downfall. Yet, with many ups and downs, she seems to be narrowly winning through.

Undoubtedly the Plan and the Common Market have played a large part in this revival. But the real causes of it would seem to lie deeper, and to be psychological as much as economic. As I have already suggested, they spring from the shock of defeat in 1940 and retrospective shame and dismay at the decadence of the 1930s. Had it not been for this basic change in outlook and in will-power, the French could never have made such a success either of the Plan or of the Common Market.

DECLINE AND RECOVERY

In the eighteenth century France was the strongest and richest power in the world. But soon after 1800 the first signs of backwardness began to appear, and, as the next century wore on, France increasingly failed to keep pace with the rapid industrialisation of Britain and Germany. Though some of the reasons for this were purely economic, the more important ones were probably human and social. The industrial revolution ran counter to the basic structures of French society, rigid, stratified, and still related to an old guild economy. An important section of the upper classes, dominated by the land-owning aristocracy and by the older liberal professions such as the law, scorned business and profit; and the huge, conservative-minded peasant class showed reluctance to move off the land in order to provide labour for industry. This, together with the stagnating birth-rate, limited not only the supply of labour but also consumer demand. Industry lacked incentives: protected from competition by high tariff walls, it grew lazily content to compensate low sales with high profit margins. Rich people preferred to invest their money outside France, where dividends swelled more rapidly; and this in turn restricted the French capital market.

During the late nineteenth and early twentieth centuries, France like Britain spent huge sums on her colonial empire, but neglected her home development. The 1920s, it is true, saw a certain revival, prompted by the need to repair the ravages of war, and helped by the return to France of Alsace and Lorraine with their heavy industries. But France survived the 1929 recession with less success than most countries, and the 'thirties were a decade of serious economic decline. A mistaken monetary policy kept her tied to the gold standard for too long; over-cautious Governments put all the emphasis on financial stability, rather than expansion, and protected agriculture with price-supports at the expense of industry. The Second World War brought less loss of life than the first, but more severe physical damage. By 1944, France's railways were shattered and their rolling-stock depleted; her ports, her northern towns, and many of her factories were devastated. And yet, as in the case of Germany, the very scale of this destruction was a blessing in disguise: it brought a chance to make a new start on modern lines. That is one reason why, for instance, continental railways today tend to be more efficient than British ones.

These opportunities might have been muffed, had not a number of Frenchmen emerged from the war with a new determination. Some, especially the younger ones, had used the enforced inactivity of the war years to think seriously about the future and to explore new ideas and techniques. That is how the Plan was born. Then, many of the older deadbeat generation came out of the war publicly discredited by their part in the Vichy régime or the Occupation. This helped new, younger men to push them aside and to fill some of the key posts of industry and the civil service, in defiance of the pre-war French *penchant* for gerontocracy.

Economists mostly agree on this view of the French revival, though sometimes with bewilderment. Professor Charles P. Kindleberger, of the Massachusetts Institute of Technology, writes,* 'to conclude that the basic change in the French economy is one of people and attitudes is frustrating to the economist' but, after examining and discounting a number of purely economic explanations of the French recovery, he declares it to be 'due to the restaffing of the economy with new men and to new French attitudes'.

Civil servants began to move from a static to a more dynamic concept of their role. Whereas before the war they had been the faceless executives of a smooth, unchanging routine, now some of them came to see themselves as animators, reformers, leaders. Together with some industrialists, they steadily discarded the pre-war notion that *regular* economic progress was impossible. This shuffling-off of the economic pessimism of the 'thirties has, of course, been fairly general in the West since the war: in France it appears most sharply, just because of the gravity of the earlier decline.

In 1946 Jean Monnet launched the First Plan, under the slogan 'modernisation or downfall'. This was a long-sighted austerity plan that gave the immediate housing crisis a much lower priority than the reconstruction of basic industries, such as steel, coal, and electricity, as the necessary basis for a lasting recovery. Then in 1947 Marshall Aid from the United States began to arrive in Europe, and in France this provided the

* *France: Change and Tradition*, p. 157 (Gollancz, 1964).

investment funds that were needed for the success of the First Plan. In fact it was largely because of her planning that France was able to make better constructive use of Marshall Aid than most of her neighbours. At the same time, the innate French flair for technology and engineering was given a new lease of life: scientist and technicians were provided with the funds and the encouragement to put France in the front rank once more in the creation of new cars and aircraft, railway engines, hydro-electric works, and computers.

By 1949, some signs of reborn prosperity were already apparent in the streets and shops. But the next years were difficult ones. Parallel with the steady, long-term rebuilding of key industries went a succession of financial crises due to the archaic structure of much of the rest of the economy. For the euphoric post-war resurgence of new ideas and new men was confined at first to a minority of planners and pioneers: the rest of France, *la vieille France*, stayed attached to its old ways, with its vested interests, its petty bureaucracy, its dislike of change. Writing in 1953, Herbert Lüthy* described the new industries, most of them State-con-trolled, as 'an isolated enclave of modernism inside old France'. The clash between the two structures produced imbalance and was one cause of inflation: it was like giving a sick man too strong a medicine, or putting too powerful an engine in a rickety car. The stabilisation policies of suc-cessive short-lived Governments (Rene Mayer's in 1948, Queuille's and Bidault's in 1949–50, and notably Pinay's in 1952) produced temporary relief from inflation, but this soon spilled over into stagnation in all but a few sectors. Every year the budget was in deficit and the balance-of-payments position grew worse. Costly colonial wars, in Indo-China and later in Algeria, did not help matters.

The Fourth Republic Governments patched over the budgetary cracks, but were too weak and too short-lived to apply the basic remedies that would have meant upsetting countless vested interests and sinecures. Yet, to their credit, these Governments did pursue two basic lines of policy that were to safeguard the future. They allowed the Plan to continue its work; and in the mid 1950s they took the courageous political decision to go into the Common Market, in face of the doubts or open opposition of most private industry.

When de Gaulle returned to power in 1958, the recovery of industry was well advanced and output was rising rapidly. But with home demand exceeding supply, and no effective wages policy, inflation and rising costs made it increasingly hard for France to export competitively, and the drain on reserves was greater than ever. The franc was trailing along as almost the weakest currency in Europe. With the first of the Common Market tariff cuts due to be made in January 1959, it looked as though France would have to suffer the ignominy of being the only one of the Six to invoke the 'escape clauses' protecting her from the shock of competition;

* *The State of France.*

and when Britain in 1958 moved to 'convertibility', it seemed that the franc would not be strong enough to follow suit.

Such prospects were intolerable for de Gaulle. He and his finance minister, Antoine Pinay, instructed Jacques Rueff, an orthodox 'liberal' finance expert, to prepare drastic remedies. Rueff did so. On 27 December 1958, the franc was devalued by 17·5 per cent to the level it has held ever since (13·65 to the £, or 11·75 since the £'s devaluation). As a psychological boost for French morale, the decimal point was shifted and a New Franc born, equalling one hundred old ones. Convertibility of the franc was allowed for non-residents; the scheduled Common Market tariff cut was respected without recourse to the escape clauses; and, most daring of all for this land of protectionism, trade liberalisation with other OEEC countries was pushed up to the unprecedented level of 90 per cent, after having been suspended altogether in the black year of 1957.

After a decade of Gaullism, these reforms can still be described as the régime's greatest economic achievement—a bold start which it has never since equalled. The results were immediate. Thanks to devaluation, imports were rapidly balanced by exports. Gold and other reserves, down almost to nil by 1958, began to climb again and have gone on doing so, at intervals, ever since. Large sums of capital, much of it French, began to return home from Swiss and other foreign banks, encouraged by the prospect of political stability and no more inflation. In ripping open the cocoon around her economy, France had indeed taken a big risk: but she was now far better prepared to face the test of the Common Market, and she was able at last to behave like a financially independent nation.

The years 1959 to 1962 were fat ones for the economy, although for the nation as a whole they were also the years of grave moral crisis over Algeria. Industry faced and survived the first shocks of German competition, and its self-confidence swelled. Production was still rising fast, and the price-advantages of devaluation were maintained. France began to show the outwards signs of a nation suddenly growing rich. Sleek new cars, like the Renault Floride and the Citroën DS 19, were filling the streets; new luxury flats, luxury shops, and holidays found a ready market. De Gaulle's political successes in those years—stability at home, assertive independence in world affairs, a final peace in Algeria in 1962—helped the economy, too, by stimulating Frenchmen's morale and the world's confidence. The Algerian war, whatever its other unpleasant effects, had not in itself done too much damage to the economy; and as soon as it ended, the return to France of nearly a million *colons* brought a powerful new contribution of skill, energy, and much-needed manpower.

But inflation, the old arch-enemy, had once again been merely curbed, not cured. By 1963 it was rampant again, and the foreign trade position was again worsening. Wages had been rising much faster in private industry than in the public sector, provoking, in March, a large-scale strike of miners and other public servants. The Government emerged from this strike with its prestige jolted, but with a determination that the upward spiral of wages and prices must stop. In September, de Gaulle's young finance minister, Valéry Giscard d'Estaing, launched his famous 'Plan de Stabilisation': it involved a credit squeeze, a wage and price freeze, and severe curbs on public spending, all of which served to cramp investment both public and private. Immediate results were satisfactory: the balance of payments again improved, home demand was cut and the budget balanced, and prices were held steady without any serious growth in unemployment. But by late 1964 the inherent drawbacks of this policy were also making themselves felt. Overall expansion slumped from a rate of about 5 per cent to less than 3 per cent, imperilling the targets set by the Fourth Plan. Industrialists grew worried at the likely long-term dangers of curbing investment, just when so many firms still needed to modernise in order to face mounting foreign competition. Workers, too, became restive at the wage freeze and at the curbs on funds for social services, while prices again began to nose upwards. France had a year of malaise in 1965, reflected in the slump in de Gaulle's vote in the De-cember presidential election. Once re-elected, he dismissed Giscard and replaced him with the ex-premier Michel Debré, much more of a re-former and advocate of expansion. Not that Giscard had been a failure: the Plan de Stabilisation had been necessary, and had done its work, though perhaps had gone too far. Giscard was able to hand over the economy in good shape, ready for a fresh burst of expansion under the guidance of the Monnet Plan.

TECHNOCRATS AND THE PLAN

Throughout these past twenty years of ups and downs and shifts of policy, the principal motor of continuity has been the Plan. This volun-tary and pragmatic association between State and industry seems, at first sight, most untypical of the formal and legalistic French. Yet its success has devolved from two other factors, both typically French: the large role of the State in the French economy, unusual for an advanced Western country, and the special position of the 'technocrat' in France. In this context, a national Plan is not such an innovation as it might be in Britain or the United States, where more of industry is in private hands and therefore less amenable to central planning.

For several centuries, so much of the wealth of France has belonged to the State, whether monarchy or republic, that large-scale private in-dustry has always had to rely on State funds and has therefore accepted a measure of State direction. In the nineteenth century, the mines, the railways, the banks, and heavy industry were all built up with the help of public capital, although they were themselves then in private hands. Even the idea of State planning is not new in France: Colbert made attempts under Louis XIV, and so did Bonaparte, while Jean Monnet's own thinking has been much influenced by the ideas of Saint-Simon, the early-nineteenth-century prophet of modern planning.

Therefore when formal nationalisation came in recent years, in 1936 and in 1944-6, it did not mark such a turning-point as in Britain. The Left-wing Popular Front Government had made a start before the war: it took over armaments, the railways, and to an extent the Bank of France. Then the idealists of the Resistance planned a more sweeping movement; and when they came to power in 1944 they found their task much eased by capitalism's taint of Nazi collaboration. They swiftly took over the Renault car firm (its owner, Louis Renault, had been a supposed collaborator) as well as Air France and the coal-mines. In 1946, electricity, gas, and some insurance firms were added to the list, the Bank of France was fully nationalised and so were the larger clearing banks.

Today about half of all French investment is controlled by the State. The big public firms, whether they are drilling for gas or making cigarettes or jet airliners, are run like private companies and usually left to get on with their own job, but always under the discreet tutelage of some Ministry. Any big new scheme, even the development of a new holiday resort or civic theatre, is usually prompted or supervised by the State. Often the Government invites the association of private capital or local interests, in its development projects, by setting up *sociétés d'économie mixte*: semi-autonomous bodies with mixed financial backing but with usually a State majority.

In this climate, it is not so surprising that private industrial firms and private financiers generally lack initiative, at least by American standards, and have grown used to regular State interference. Frequently they rely on the State for investment loans and even for policy guidance. It also follows that in France the classic conflict between capitalism and socialism, which still colours British economic thinking, has come to seem less relevant. Some civil servants even claim that France has found the ideal modern solution, with State and private industry marching hand-in-hand: but Left-wingers often retort that this is less socialism than 'State capitalism', especially under a régime such as de Gaulle's, with the third force, the workers, still having precious little say in what happens.

This economic system is natural soil for the technocrats, whose power has been growing. Today 'les technocrates' are everywhere: on the staff of the Plan, managing big firms whether public or private, even serving as Cabinet Ministers under de Gaulle. The public look on them with awe, admiration, and sometimes suspicion. Usually they are seen as benevolent sages, sweeping away past inefficiencies; but to some people, especially on the Left, they appear as more sinister and inhuman figures, like the technocrat rulers of *Alphaville*, Jean-Luc Godard's film of a nightmarish computer-city of the future.

The concept of technocracy, always stronger in France than in Britain, implies the control of policy by a disinterested élite of experts, with

technical knowledge or at least a technical outlook, differing both from
the traditional businessman and from the party politician or bureaucrat.
Their strength in France derives not only from the large role of the State in
industry, but also from the high reputation of their main breeding-ground,
the great engineering colleges known as the *Grandes Ecoles*.* Some of
these schools, notably the Ecole Polytechnique, attract many of the
cleverest young minds in France, and so help to endow technology and
technocracy with an intellectual prestige that they rarely enjoy in Britain.
The technocrat emerging from this background is often brilliant, confident, and super-rational, though he may lack the human touch. After
studying applied science in a *Grande Ecole*, he will then perhaps work
his way up to a senior policy-making job via technical posts in factories,
and so be able to back economic decisions with technical expertise. Another
type of technocrat, often to be found in the same kind of senior positions,
will have had an administrative rather than a technical training, possibly
in the new post-graduate Ecole Nationale d'Administration. Both groups
tend to share the same idealistic faith in technical progress, the same
belief in a planned economy insulated as far as possible from the pressures
of party leaders, trade-unionists, or mere capitalists. Some even elevate
this into a kind of philosophy: technology for them is a key to human
happiness, and an élite possessed of this secret will guide and save the
world. Mostly these technocrats are also men of personal culture—this,
more than anything, distinguishes them from their Anglo-Saxon managerial counterparts. France's educational system and cultural ethos endow
even her scientists with a strong feeling for the humanities, so that a
factory-manager or engineer may also in his spare time be a scholar or
connoisseur. Thus the conflict between what Lord Snow has called 'the
two cultures' is less acute than in Britain.

If asked to name the archetypal technocrat, many Frenchmen might
mention Louis Armand, a stocky, unpretentious-looking engineer from
the Ecole Polytechnique, who reorganised France's railways after the war,
led the Government's search for mineral wealth in the Sahara in the
1950s, pioneered Euratom, produced with Jacques Rueff in 1960 the key
report on French structural reform, and now in his mid sixties is rounding
off a fabulous career by heading the Channel Tunnel study group. He
told me recently: 'It's up to us in the West to prove to the Russians that
we have grown dynamic again. So we must go ahead and get the Tunnel
built—*they* certainly would'. Armand is typical of idealistic technocrats,
a man of ideas as well as of action, as alarmed at France's archaic structures
as he is proud of what he described to me as her 'ideal link between
dirigisme and capitalism'. It is hard to conceive of a mere engineer in
Britain enjoying the same kind of status as public sage and Grand Old
Man.

Other examples of *polytechnicien* graduates in top technocratic jobs

* See p. 332 (Youth with a dusty answer).

include Pierre Guillaumat, overlord of the State oil and electricity concerns, and Pierre Massé, head of the Plan from 1962 to 1966. Pierre Dreyfus, chairman and managing director of Renault, comes from the non-technical stream: he studied law in Paris, and then went into business in London before moving into public service, first in electricity and mines. But his detailed interest in technical innovation, coupled with advanced social welfare projects for his workers, are typical of the technocrat; and he seems the very opposite of the popular image of a car tycoon. Slight, reserved, very intellectual, he hates the world of Paris society, and devotes himself off-duty to books, music, and family life, or to long evenings with fellow-technocrats discussing, for instance, how technology can help developing countries.

Georges Héreil, one of the ablest of all technocrats, launched the Caravelle in the 1950s in a brilliant spell as head of Sud-Aviation, the State-run aircraft firm, and then in the mid 'sixties devoted his energies to trying to rescue Simca, the American-controlled French car firm, from a difficult crisis. A number of other technocrats have switched even more sharply than this in mid-career from civil service posts to private industry, where often they can earn more. Under a managerial revolution familiar to many countries, technocrats are rapidly enveloping private firms, as old-style family managements hand over the reins to modern-minded salaried executives.

Technocrats have been moving into Government, too. Whereas, under the Fourth Republic, Ministers were almost always party politicians, de Gaulle has appointed a number of civil servants to such posts—men like Louis Joxe, an ex-diplomat, and François-Xavier Ortoli, a former director of M. Pompidou's cabinet who became Minister of Equipment in 1967. Such men may not be 'technocrats' in the strictest sense, but nor are they ordinary politicians; they are more interested in doing a practical job than in the intrigues of party politics, and their presence in the Government has helped give the Gaullist régime its supposedly technocratic flavour. Sometimes, indeed, they find Gaullist politics too much for them, and they get out—as Pierre Sudreau did in 1963 and Pisani in 1967.

Other technocrats run the big State concerns such as Gaz de France and Electricité de France. Their technical authority and expertise in these posts is certainly one reason why nationalisation has on the whole worked better in France than in Britain since the war. The men in charge have put a premium on progress and modernisation, not simply on smooth administration and good book-keeping.

The presence in France of this network of technocrats, some of it based on old-boy college links, has played a large part in the success of the Plan. The Plan has been staffed by men with the same ideas and background as many of the key people in industry and the civil service, who have thus been able to win each others' trust and find a common language. Yet Jean Monnet himself, who inspired and founded the Plan, is not a typical technocrat at all. His origins were modest: he was born in Cognac in 1888, where his family were vinegrowers and brandy distillers. He never went through the technocrat's usual educational mill, but was brought up partly in the United States, and much of his first knowledge of the world was gained in the humble role of overseas salesman for the Monnet cognac firm. Yet he is a man of the most sophisticated international vision and sympathy; he has great personal charm, speaks perfect English, and is the kind of warm idealist who inspires high devotion in his followers.

After leaving the family firm, he spent more than twenty years in public service before and during the Second War, working for the League of Nations, the French Government, and then the Allies, in many parts of the world. He came to know the United States well, and to admire American efficiency; and during the war he and a number of friends began to plot how to pull France up to American standards—by novel, non-American methods. In 1945 he met de Gaulle in Washington, and won him over to the idea of the Plan. The following year the five-year First Plan was approved, and its secretariat, with Monnet as Commissioner-General, moved into an elegant little private house, most unlike a formal Government office, in the shadow of the St. Clothilde church on the Left Bank. And there the secretariat still lives today, though Monnet himself has long since left, and now devotes himself to promoting the cause of a United Europe and trying to undo some of what he regards as the damage done by de Gaulle's nationalist policies.

As soon as the Plan was in action, Monnet, never a conformist, broke at once with many of the taboos and formalities of French administration. Unlikely groups of people, Communist union-leaders and old-style financiers, were shoved together at short notice without form or ceremony. Instead of long, formal memoranda, there were often little notes scribbled by Monnet on sheets of pink or yellow paper while walking in the woods near his quiet home west of Versailles. Instead of long, elaborate business lunches, there were working meals of un-French simplicity in the Plan's HQ. Life there was in some ways more monastic than bureaucratic, with working sessions taking little account of office hours, weekends, or even holidays. There was even a faint air of revivalism, according to some accounts, about the inter-industry meetings of those early years, where the planners communicated their faith.

This may help to explain why a certain mystique has grown up around the Plan, both at home and abroad. The British, envious and surprised, have tried to copy some of its features, but so far without much success because our economy is so different. In France, many otherwise unexplained achievements are credited by public opinion to the Plan; there's been an element of faith-healing about it. Economists, in fact, are often dubious about how valuable it has been in strictly *economic* terms. Some of them argue that much of the French recovery would have happened anyway, and they point to Germany's even greater progress with no planning at all. Yet few of them disagree about the value of the

Plan's psychological influence on industry. It has torn some of the barriers of secrecy from private firms, helped to created a new climate of competition and productivity, and induced different classes of people to think and work together as in France they had rarely done before.

The two main facts about the Plan are, first, that it is 'voluntary' and 'indicative' rather than formally binding; and secondly, that although it is run as a Government department, it is simply a forum for drawing up blueprints and exchanging ideas, without the executive powers of a Ministry. It constantly seeks to guide the economy in a certain expansionist direction, and successive Governments have tended to use its forecasts and advice as the basis of their policy; but neither they, nor even private firms, are under any constitutional obligation to do so, and only the Government can turn the Plan's projections into decisions. It succeeds, simply because both parties, State and private industry, have most of the time agreed to collaborate with it.

Its small full-time secretariat, never more than forty strong, is an informal brains' trust of clever, mainly youngish men, drawn from the civil service, or universities, or industry. After a number of years at the Plan, they may well return to these fields; few are academic economists. Today they are still the same kind of team that Monnet first drew round him in 1946, many of whom are now well known: Robert Marjolin, now vice-president of the European Economic Commission in Brussels; Etienne Hirsch, who took Monnet's place at the Plan; and Paul Delouvrier, now in charge of planning the future of the Paris region.

The Plan's basic task is to set targets for growth, in all the different sectors of the economy, over five-year periods: for instance, the Fifth Plan, for 1966–70, was finalised in 1965. First, the staff of the Plan discuss with the Government the best overall expansion rate to aim at, basing their verdict on estimations of natural growth rather than of needs. For each industry they set three possible targets, high, low, and medium. Then, having decided on the most realistic target in each case, the Plan convenes its twenty-five 'modernisation commissions', to work out and apportion the details of growth within each sector. These commissions were Monnet's principal innovation, and their system of direct round-table confrontation marked a sharp break with French administrative practice. Within each commission, the heads of private firms, large and small, union leaders and civil servants, sit round the same table with the planners over a period of months, thrashing out in detail how to achieve their growth and their investment targets, say, in textiles, pig-breeding, or aluminium. About 4,000 people are directly involved in these talks, and each firm, or group, makes its own voluntary commitment. Then the sum of the commissions' reports—a vast dossier—is submitted for approval to Parliament and to a para-parliamentary body, the Economic and Social Council.

This system is flexible and strictly empirical—in defiance of French tradition. It is what the French call 'une économie concertée', operating a kind of working compromise between economic liberalism and *dirigisme*. Professor Kindleberger even describes it as 'in some important respects the opposite of planning',* and comments: 'The roles have been reversed from the nineteenth century when the British were the pragmatists and the French were doctrinaire.'

Yet it may still seem puzzling that French private industry, often so individualistic and suspicious of the State, should have co-operated so readily with the Plan. One reason I have already suggested: the common background of the planners and the technocrats in some key firms. Another factor has been that the big State industries obviously gave a lead in supporting the Plan, and their smaller competitors felt obliged to follow suit. Some of them were spurred by memories of pre-war stagnation; or, emerging near-bankrupt from the war, they were obliged to turn to the State for funds, and accepted a measure of planning and supervision in return. Once inside the Plan, each larger firm was encouraged to feel itself an integral part of the operation, with a democratic voice in the outcome. But of course there have been less democratic pressures, too, especially under de Gaulle. Firms' collaboration has been secured by an elaborate system of Government rewards and incentives—tax relief, tariff concessions, loans for investment, or valuable State contracts, sometimes amounting to bribery.

As the planners and the industrialists are on an equal footing within the commissions, the larger firms tend to give at least as much advice to the Plan as they get from it. 'We, and bodies like us, *are* the Plan,' I was told imperiously at the State-run Electricité de France; 'We make our own long-term forecasts, and submit them to the Plan for approval.'

It is true that the many thousands of very small firms tend to get left out of this process, and their spokesmen have often criticised the Plan as being too *dirigiste*. Inevitably it is of less value to them, individually. But its influence on larger and medium-sized firms has been considerable: simply by getting them round a table together, the planners have been able gradually to coax many industrialists out of their ingrained secretiveness and mistrust. In a France of so many family firms this mistrust extended as much to a firm's colleagues and its own professional confederation as to the State and its tax inspectors: many companies, in fact, have habitually indulged in treble book-keeping—one set of figures for the public auditors and inland revenue, one for shareholders, and a third, the real figures, to be kept a close secret among directors! But today many of the larger firms, at least, have grown readier to share details of their plans, techniques, and costs. By some Anglo-Saxon standards there is still a distance to go. For instance, one of France's giants, the Michelin family tyre-making firm, still makes a virtual fetish of its old-fashioned secretiveness. But on the whole the new atmosphere has facilitated joint planning, as well as the preparation of mergers and the sharing of

* *France: Change and Tradition*, p. 155.

research or export services. The Plan has done much to encourage productivity and the mergers of small firms, as well as investment, which in pre-war days was often regarded as a luxurious frill. All this has helped to prepare French industry for the Common Market. And over the years the Plan has also been steadily building up something that France always badly lacked: a bank of economic information and industrial statistics.

The Plan, which de Gaulle once described as 'an ardent obligation', has influenced the Government, too. One reason for its success is that Jean Monnet and his first two successors, Etienne Hirsch and Pierre Massé, were all men of the highest personal calibre, regularly consulted by the Prime Minister and his colleagues. Their prestige helped the Plan to keep aloof from the squabbles of the Fourth Republic while remaining influential.

In accepting the Plan as the basis of their economic policies, Gaullist and pre-Gaullist Governments alike came to rely less than in the past on the cautious orthodoxy that has generally held sway at the Ministry of Finance. The powerful experts there were penetrated by new ideas and influences: no longer were they dedicated solely to budget-balancing and careful economies. In periods of credit squeeze the existence of the Plan certainly acted as a brake on cuts in vital investments; and at other times, the Plan spurred the Government to give loans to the right industries. Of course there have been failures, as well. The biggest problem, still unsolved, is the permanent conflict between the long-term projects of the Plan and the dictates of the annual State budget. Sometimes the Plan has led to unbalanced growth, and it has rarely succeeded in checking inflation. But at least its forecasts have largely prevented the kind of shortages so frequent in post-war Britain. When, in 1965, a sudden early cold spell caused power cuts in Britain but not in France, an Electricité de France technocrat told me, smugly, 'Ah, if you had a Plan. . . .'

One important early success of the Plan lay in securing the co-operation of the trade unions. At first, even the Communists union leaders took part in its round-table meetings and seemed prepared to help. But this success was short-lived. It gradually became clear that most of the complex technical work of the Plan was above the union leaders' heads: they had neither the economic training nor the inside information to be able to contribute effective ideas. The largest and most powerful union, the Communist-led Confédération Générale du Travail, virtually opted out of the Plan after about 1950; and its leaders were not alone in suspecting that the invitation to the unions was a sly move to silence their opposition to capitalist expansion. Of the three main unions, only the more-or-less Catholic CFDT* (formerly the CFTC) has taken a sincere part in the Plan's committee-working, but has made no bones about its dilemma of approving of planning while disapproving of the capitalist framework. It is probably not even true that the relative infrequency of strikes in French

* Confédération Française Démocratique du Travail.

industry since 1948 has been due to the presence of the unions in the Plan: other factors have played a larger part, such as the weakness and division of the unions, and the steady wage-increases.

Hitherto, the Plan has not had too much need of the unions' active support. But, with the French economy now so much less sheltered than before, inflation has become more dangerous, and the Plan has therefore received an official brief to turn its attention towards working out an incomes policy. For this, it will need the unions' co-operation.

This is just one of the ways in which the Plan's role and position have been changing over the years. While the First Plan (1946–52) concentrated on reconstruction of basic industries, the Second (1953–7) switched the emphasis to target-setting for the whole of industry and agriculture, still its main concern. The Third (1958–61) and Fourth (1962–5) Plans widened the range to include social needs, such as welfare and housing, and to that current French obsession, regional development. Sections of the Plan are now regionalised, * and each small town is proud to have its own little plan as a segment of the national one. In fact the Plan, long accepted by Government and big business, has finally become part of the ordinary coinage of local public opinion. It is part of the land-scape, like elections or the budget. Everyone wants to plan, farmer, grocer, tinker, clerk. And yet, ironically, this is happening just when, nationally, the Plan is becoming less important, or at least when its role is becoming more difficult and uncertain.

Two developments have occurred. First, the French economy has become much less enclosed, due to the Common Market and other world influences, and is therefore now less amenable to purely domestic plan-ning. Secondly, political stability under de Gaulle has not only made the Plan less necessary as a factor of continuity: it has also, as we shall see, caused it to be identified with the Government as it never was under the quick-changing Prime Ministers of the Fourth Republic. This problem I shall look at in more detail, after examining the influence of the Common Market on the French post-war economy.

INDUSTRY AND THE COMMON MARKET

French industry is still in the painful process of adapting itself to the Common Market and to wider competition after its long years of pro-tectionism. So far, it has managed rather better than most people ex-pected, and has found to its own surprise that its earlier fears of the German juggernaut were exaggerated. It has been helped by a few inci-dental factors, notably the Rueff financial reforms of 1958: but a great deal has been due simply to the skill and energy of industrialists themselves, when they finally faced up to the choice between extinction and rapid

* See p. 119 (New life in the provinces).

and drastic renewal. The Common Market provided the shock they so badly needed.

The Plan had earlier helped to prepare the ground: by the time the Treaty of Rome was signed on 25 March 1957 several industries were modernised and reasonably competitive. One of the largest of these, steel, had already learned to face German competition under that valuable dress-rehearsal for the Common Market, the European Coal and Steel Community.* Jean Monnet, who played a leading role in founding CECA in 1951, told me: 'Back in 1946, we tried to persuade the Loire steel industry to modernise, but they refused. They began to do so only in 1953, under pressure from CECA and through fear of competition from Lorraine steel. If it hadn't been for CECA, the Loire industry would still be in the dumps today.'

The Patronat Français, the principal federation of big employers, had strongly opposed the creation of CECA, and later found to their surprise that French steel *was* able to compete! It was partly this discovery that caused the Patronat's subsequent hostility to the Common Market preparations to be rather less fierce. Yet they were still afraid and it was not hard to understand their fears, seeing how backward and cloistered much of French industry still was in the mid 1950s. The Germans easily led the field in chemicals, machinery, and metallurgy; their global production was 45 per cent higher; and they were not lumbered with the same high percentage of small artisan firms, nor with the high social welfare charges of French industry.

The Common Market was pushed through Parliament, more for political than economic reasons, by a handful of politicians on the Left and Centre, led by the far-sighted Robert Schuman. They resisted counter-pressure from the Patronat; but in order to ease French industry's problems, they did manage to extract important treaty concessions from the Germans to cover the ten transitional years. The Patronat were also being coaxed along by a few enlightened leaders within their own ranks, notably Georges Villiers, the president, who realised at an early stage how much France might benefit in the long run. So, when the treaty was finally signed, the Patronat boldly faced up to reality and switched their official policy, while many individual firms set about adapting to the new circumstances. For the Plan this was a signal victory: 'What we like best about the Common Market,' one young planner told me, 'is that it helped shock our industry into modernising.' Once again, as in 1940-4—and this time, *before* defeat, and without bloodshed—the German menace had provided a catalyst.

Today nearly everyone in industry or commerce, in agriculture or the civil service, will tell you how pro-Common Market he is. '*Moi, je suis très européen,*' is a stock phrase that has virtually replaced, '*Moi, je suis pour la France.*' The reasoning is often political or idealistic, rather than

---

* CECA in French: *Communauté Européenne du Charbon et de l'Acier.*

strictly economic: many small firms, in fact, are secretly anxious about their 'European' future, though they will not always admit it. But the general shift in economic as well as political outlook has been remarkable in this land of protectionism.

French trade with the rest of the Six began to increase rapidly even before the first 10 per cent all-round tariff cut in 1959. Since then, tariffs have come down by an average 10 per cent each year, while trade has grown at a much faster rate. Between 1958 and 1962, France doubled her overall exports and trebled her exports to the rest of the Six: a record exceeded only by Italy. In chemicals, and automobiles, French exports to Germany alone rose more than eightfold. French imports from her partners rose as well, of course, but not so fast, because of the effects of the 1958 devaluation. Of course it should be added that much of this growth of trade would have happened anyway, as a result of the European boom. The Common Market simply speeded it up and gave it a framework. The Market could not have come into existence without the boom, and in some ways it has been as much an effect as a cause.

The sectors of French industry that have fared best under the Common Market have been those already well organised—cars, aircraft, chemicals —as well as a few traditional luxury industries such as wines, perfume, and glass. Consumer durables and machinery have had a more difficult time, largely because firms were too small or ill-equipped. But in every field, the average French firm's attitude to exports and productivity has changed strikingly in the past ten years. Today the share of French national production that goes for export is as high (16 per cent) as Britain's or Germany's. Yet in 1957 France, along with Italy, had the highest tariffs of the Six, backed by a long history of protectionism dating from Louis XI in the fifteenth century. Until 1939 France concentrated on high craftsmanship and deliberately low production, leaving the big world markets to her rivals except in a few 'quality' fields. The change began after the war, led by a few pioneers. Teams of young industrialists known as 'missions de productivité', several hundred in all, went to study in the United States, encouraged by the Plan and the Government, and came back convinced at last of the need to make more, and to sell more abroad. Renault then led the car industry into the export field, invading the American market with the Dauphine.* Even today the export drive is by no means general: two-thirds of all exports come from the four hundred largest firms. But with the coming of the Common Market many smaller firms, too, have hurriedly joined forces to create new export subsidiaries, and for the first time are stirring outside their frontiers. In Lyon, I met a machinery manufacturer whose firm had not exported at all before the war, but who had paid five visits in the past year to Germany, where he now sold 15 per cent of his goods. This is not untypical. In many respects the French are now more export-minded than the British, and the

* See pp. 56–9 (Some key industries).

Government helps with reasonably generous subsidies and other incentives.

At the Plan I was told: 'We try to urge firms to feel that Germany or Italy are now part of their home market.' Exports are the first stage, but the next will be to form structural links between firms in different countries: Monnet himself set a remarkable lead some years ago when he allowed a German wine importer to buy a large share in his own family cognac business. Many French firms now conduct regular exchanges of technicians or information with their counterparts in the rest of the Six, and oblige their own executives to learn German. Robert Valentini, owner of a small metallurgical firm in Lyon, told me, 'Four years ago, at the Cologne Fair, I met the head of a similar firm in Hamburg, and we decided to work together. His firm used to be stronger on exports, but we were stronger internally, with better production. Now, by pooling our research and marketing, and standardising our products, we've both of us pushed our sales up everywhere. But our finances and capital stay separate—the links are purely personal. It works well, though there are human difficulties: our own experts think and work rather theoretically, while the Germans are more pragmatic.' Valentini is head of the progressive Centre des Jeunes Patrons (see below) and his case is hardly typical, though some other such links have been formed too. Wider progress is bound to be slow, owing to differences of language and business procedure.

In the meantime, the French are grappling with what they regard as their industry's biggest problem of all: the small size of the average firm and the lack of really large ones. This has proved the worst legacy of protectionism, and puts a strain on French competitiveness now that trade barriers are down. A much-quoted article in *Fortune* magazine in 1964 made the point that of the sixty-four firms in the world with a turnover of more than $1,000m, forty-nine were American, five German, four British, and *none* French. According to other statistics, 36 per cent of German workers and only 21 per cent of French ones are in firms with more than 1,000 employees, while two-thirds of all French workers are in firms with less than two hundred.

Government encouragement of mergers, as the simplest answer to this problem, has yielded some good results among larger firms in the past few years, notably in steel, chemicals, and heavy electrical equipment. Now the pressure is on medium-sized firms to follow suit, and many of them have at least come to accept intellectually the need for change, even though for human reasons they are often slow to take any action. The Government has been trying out various carrot-and-stick incentives: the basis of its present merger policy is a recent tax reform, of British inspiration, that aims at making it less invidious and less costly for companies to reorganise their capital when merging.

In addition to mergers, other forms of 'concentration' or 'rationalisation' have been taking place too: the regrouping of small, scattered factories belonging to the same firm, conversion away from uneconomic products, and the setting up of joint subsidiaries for research or sales, of which the star example has been the Renault-Peugeot agreement of 1966. In 1966, more than 2,000 mergers and associations of one kind or another took place in French industry, against 450 nine years earlier. Certainly this process is in the main a useful and necessary one, but in some cases it seems to have been happening too casually and hastily. A merger between two small inefficient firms does not of itself produce one dynamic firm, and now that the vogue has caught on there has been rather too much merging for merging's sake. Sheer size is not the only consideration, and it is pointed out that in some sectors even a tiny firm can be well suited to its market if it is intelligently run. I was cited the case of a specialised clothing concern in Savoy with only six workers yet with 60 per cent of the European market in its field.

This however is a rare example compared with the thousands of little firms that are quite uneconomic. Some goods, that in other countries are made in big factories, in France are still produced almost on a cottage-industry basis. This system may ensure high craftsmanship in certain fields, but in marketing and other modern techniques it is often so inefficient as to make competition difficult. Many hundreds, perhaps thousands, of such firms (figures are hard to come by) have been pushed out of business in the past ten or fifteen years, or have sold out or merged of their own accord. At Falaise,* for instance, in Normandy, a cluster of little local hosiery factories all died quietly a few years ago, to be replaced by larger modern firms making electrical equipment. But other firms elsewhere often succeed in hanging on with remarkable tenacity, frequently operating a kind of cartel arrangement with shops and wholesalers that makes it hard to squeeze them out. It is just the kind of structural defect that holds up economic progress, and yet its reform requires a more ruthless attack on vested interests than the Government has yet dared apply.

MANAGEMENT IN CRISIS

Under the impact of these changes, the world of French employers and managers is today in a state of confusion and uneasy transition. On the one hand, there are the technocrats on a broad advancing front, allied to a number of like-minded young industrialists from the Centre des Jeunes Patrons; on the other, the shrinking cohorts of the old guard, typified by some of the family firms in the textile industry, ignoring change or determined to resist it. And in the middle are thousands of small and medium-sized employers, many of them struggling awkwardly to adapt

* See p. 131 (New life in the provinces).

to changes they do not like. Huge progress has been made in French industry; huge areas still lie fallow. It is possible to be impressed or dubious, depending which way you look.

One factor that has impressed many people is the resilience of small business; or at least, the change of heart and astute change of tactics on the part of its leaders. In place of their Poujadist resistance to change in the 1950s, today these men are urging small firms to adapt quickly if they want to survive. The monarch of this world is Léon Gingembre, a handsome and eloquent needle manufacturer from Normandy, who just after the war founded the Confédération Générale des Petites et Moyennes Entreprises (PME), or union of small and medium-sized firms. He has been its president and evangelist ever since. Lüthy, writing in 1953, made Gingembre the scapegoat of all that he disliked most about the old France of selfish small interests, and several times he contrasted 'the France of M. Gingembre' with 'the France of M. Monnet'. Lüthy was right, then. But around 1958 Gingembre sloughed off his negative Poujadism (he had been a leading ally of the reactionary grocer-demagogue, Pierre Poujade), gave up his open hostility to the Common Market, accepted the inevitable, and used his immense influence for persuading his million members (nine-tenths in commerce, one-tenth in industry) to modernise and group together, or perish. Since 1958 the PME has trebled its activities, and now provides numerous services to help its members to export or make use of modern technology. It is true that Gingembre makes an ideology out of the small family business *per se*, regardless of whether a modern economy really needs it; and basically he is still acting in cunning defence of PME vested interests. This, in a sense, is reactionary. But at least he now accepts that, if a small firm is to have any *right* to survive, it must be able to compete openly on its own feet; and this is a big change from Poujade's view that State and society have a kind of duty to support and subsidise helpless little businesses. Gingembre told me: 'The Common Market has forced us to make as much progress in the past six years as in the preceding sixty, and this is fine. If the frontiers were to close again, we'd be back in a state of anarchy that would cripple us. Yes, of course I defend my members' interests, but I am also helping them to adapt to the economic revolution and to anticipate consumer demand. So we send export missions abroad, and we give loans for buying equipment. The PME are now playing a full part in the modernisation of France. And even in the most advanced economy, the small contractor will always be needed—look at the United States.'

Following this lead, a number of small firms have begun to group together. In Normandy, for instance, seven manufacturers of hand agricultural tools recently formed a joint service for sales and buying of materials, and were thus able to break into the German and American markets; in Marseille, eight coppersmiths set up a joint technical research service which led to a contract from the Atomic Energy Commission. Such examples are still rare, but they do represent the first signs of a remarkable change of heart in the traditional France of a myriad self-centred little firms, suspicious alike of each other and of progress.

This world still powerfully exists. It could even be argued that Gingembre's campaign, though sincere and valuable, has acted as an alibi or cover to protect a vast number of firms far more reluctant to change. Gingembre in effect says to the Government: 'Keep your hands off the PME! Don't worry: we *are* adapting ourselves. Give us time.' But how much time can be afforded? Some industries are still antiquated: textiles, furniture, cutlery, and watch-making are often quoted as examples. There are over 18,000 furniture firms in France, all but 1,000 of them employing less than ten workers each and happy within their home market. Here, as in textiles, firms have so far been spared the full shock of the Common Market by a kind of 'protectionism of national taste': the French consumer is conservative, and will often stick to a national product that he or she is used to, even if imports are cheaper or superior. Thus German furniture, generally better designed than French, has not yet made much headway into the French market. But this may not last indefinitely, as modern taste creeps forward.

The pleasant little country town of Thiers (population 20,000), in the green hills of Auvergne, calls itself 'the French Sheffield'. But it has no large factories: its side-streets are lined with literally hundreds of little cutlery workshops, producing 150,000 different models. They have failed to increase exports, and some firms survive only by underpaying wages and allowances: in this one-industry town they can control the labour market. A few more dynamic firms have diversified into, for instance, car accessories; but most of them cling sentimentally to Thiers' long traditions of cutlery, and the Plan has largely failed to persuade them to merge or modernise. The problem is largely a human and social one —and the same is true in the watch industry. Some two hundred separate French firms make watch parts and two hundred others put them together, while only seven firms (ten years ago it was four) do the combined operation. Some 3,000 different brands of watches are then sold by 11,000 little independent watch shops, who control all repairs and dictate the market. It is the shops' restrictive attitude, rather than the makers', that holds up modernisation. The few big firms are now beginning to control more of the market, but slowly. Short of more drastic Government intervention, which seems unlikely, the solution will depend on long-term professional education and a change of generation.

Many small firms in industries such as these continue to practise what the French call 'malthusianism': they deliberately limit production rather than risk capital on expansion. Or else they suffer from a fault common enough in Britain too: failure to study the overseas market. Especially in the textile industry, they choose colours or designs without first testing samples on the public, and then they wonder why home sales or exports do not do better.

These are some of the typical failings of the old-style family firm, once the dominant feature of industry in this bourgeois land. Not all such firms, however, are small or out of date: some are both large and efficient, such as Peugeot and Michelin. But though it still holds a larger place in France than in most Western countries, the numbers and influence of the family firm are declining. Many an owner, worried by modern competition, has retired to a chairman's desk and handed over the reins of daily management to a hired executive, the technocrat. Or else, growing more conscious today of the need for profit and investment, he has put his shares on the market rather than go on running the firm as a private money-bag. Nepotism, hitherto rife in France, is likewise on the wane. Many French owners habitually used to regard the family firm as a nice way of giving sinecures to doltish cousins or nephews. This, they realise, they can no longer so easily afford. Some may have before them the warning of Bull, the office machinery and computer firm that in 1964 suffered the fate of an American take-over, after a series of failures that appeared to have been partly due to inept family management.

The new salaried managers and executives—*cadres*, the French call them—are bringing a new spirit and approach into many old firms. Armed, very often, with a Grande Ecole training, they put a new accent on productivity and rational use of resources. Many have spent a year or two in the United States since the war, and will have brought back much-needed ideas for improving efficiency: cost-accountancy in France, for instance, is still rather backward by American or British standards.

And yet the attitude of these technocrats to modern American methods remains ambivalent. Many of them also bring home from the United States a mistrust and dislike of the American-style 'organisation man'. For even the modern-minded Frenchman remains, in many ways, an individualist, and the hierarchical structure of the average French firm still puts a premium on individualism rather than group work: this is a reason, as Professor David Granick has pointed out, * why even go-ahead French firms are often still reluctant to adopt American-style organisation charts, interview techniques, or committee work. There is a prejudice, too, against American-style high-pressure publicity. Many Frenchmen would prefer to try to work out French ways to efficiency and progress, based on the French character.

But not everyone agrees how this should be done. And nothing has shown up more clearly the present crisis in French management, and the clash of views between the old guard and the new, than the breach which occurred in 1965 between the powerful and cautious Patronat and its liberal-minded rival, the Centre des Jeunes Patrons.

The Conseil National du Patronat Français represents not only the big employers but also, through their federations, some eighty per cent of

* *The European Executive* (Doubleday, 1962).

PME members. Though it has one or two progressive-minded leaders,*
and though it can sometimes learn to bow to change (as it did over the
Common Market), it remains an incarnation of the stolider aspects of
traditional French management. Its huge and gloomy Paris headquarters
near the Etoile, with their heavy marble pillars and uniformed cohorts of
elderly *huissiers* (porters), seem a correct reflection of the Patronat's
bureaucracy and narrowness of outlook. Notably it upholds the authoritarian tradition of French industry, and it stresses unity of command.
Therefore it is not surprising that the clash with the Jeunes Patrons has
come mainly over labour relations—a field where the French, despite a
few interesting experiments, lag behind many Western countries.

The CJP, founded just after the war, includes some 3,500 owners
and executives under the age of forty-five representing about 10 per cent
of medium-sized French industry. It is stronger in its provincial branches
than in Paris, and as Jesse Pitts has pointed out,† it has helped to break
down the intellectual isolation of the provincial enterpreneur. Its inspiration, as with so many of the really dynamic forces in post-war France,‡ is
rooted in leftish, new-style Catholicism. Besides a belief in planning and
productivity, the CJP lays its own very special stress on social progress.
This is its creed: the manager has a duty to his workers; he must be their
moral leader, he must associate them with his policies, and he should
regard profit as a means for the wealth of all, not just of himself, his
family and shareholders.

This un-French ideal had already found some incarnation, just after
the war, in a Gaullist-inspired reform setting up statutory *comités d'entreprise*: each firm was to have a permanent joint committee of management
and workers to supervise welfare activities and also, more important, to
provide a forum where managers could keep workers informed of their
policy and plans and even seek their advice. But, except in a few cases,
this reform has not really worked in practice. Few managements have
accepted it willingly, while unions have generally looked on it with suspicion as irrelevant to their main objectives. 'All the *comités* do is arrange
the Christmas parties,' one union leader told me.

A further reform, in 1954, setting up *conventions collectives* in certain
key industries, had rather more success because it had a more practical
basis: managements agreed on regular annual pay rises and other commitments, while workers in turn agreed not to strike except as a final
resort. But even these *conventions* have now been rendered largely obsolete
by the speed with which wages and prices have risen spontaneously, faster
than the agreed increases. Thus French labour relations are today left
with little solid basis. The unions are weak, partly because they are
divided on lines of politics and ideology, and partly because the French

* Notably Georges Villiers, who retired as president in 1966, to be succeeded
by Paul Huvelin, who also has a liberal record.
† *France: Change and Tradition*, p. 286.
‡ See p. 383 (Intellectuals in disarray).

worker, like his boss, is an individualist and not a club-joiner. Out of an industrial working population of about thirteen million, only some 25 per cent are unionised: the largest union, the Communist-led Confédération Générale du Travail, has perhaps 1,500,000 members, the more-or-less Catholic CFDT (formerly CFTC) has 500,000, and the Force Ouvrière (Socialist) about the same number.

One of the unions' handicaps is that they do not enjoy the same legal status within a firm as in many other countries, including Britain. A shop-steward does not have the same right as in Britain to offices on the premises, nor to do union work in the firm's time. Recent moves by the Government to legalise the unions in this way were strongly opposed by the Patronat, and have not yet been ratified. It is true that one great national advantage of this union weakness is that France is not plagued by the same kind of demarcation disputes, wildcat strikes, and workers' closed-shops that result from union strength and intransigence in Britain. But if the French worker today still continues to feel a bit of a second-class citizen, it is due partly to managerial attitudes and to the unions' failures. Progress in labour relations has been left largely to individual firms' initiatives. In the public sector, Renault has set the pace; * in private industry, a few Jeunes Patrons have succeeded in carrying out their own ideals or in breathing real life into their *comité d'entreprise*, and so, notably, has one remarkable older industrialist, Marcel Demonque, manager of the big Lafarge cement firm. The *comités* in his factories work so well that even CGT workers there are full of praise, and admit to a feeling of having a real share in the running of the firm. There is close discussion between executives and workers on many issues, as well as some profit-sharing and an elaborate welfare policy.

The Patronat's paternalistic ethos, though still vigorously entrenched, is today on the defensive. M. Demonque's example has been one pinprick. Another was the publication in 1963 of a book called *Pour une réforme de l'entreprise* by a distinguished civil servant, Marcel Bloch-Lainé. He put forward the view that a firm's efficiency is in fact linked to its measure of democracy, and he proposed drastic measures to do away with autocracy and secretiveness in management. The book made a wide impact, and clearly had the sympathy of the more radical Gaullists as well as of the CJP. Then in 1967 de Gaulle revealed his own hand, and decreed a new law obliging all firms over a certain size to distribute a proportion of shares to their employees. It is a scheme that de Gaulle personally has cherished for many years, and has been called 'Gaullism's answer to Marxism'. In practical terms it may not amount to a great deal, but at least it shows that official Gaullist policy is on the side of reform.

The Patronat has been struggling to hold its position, helped by allies within the Gaullist ranks including the Right-wing Premier, M. Pompidou, who does not see eye to eye with de Gaulle on such matters. In 1965

* See p. 56 (Some key industries).

the Patronat's feud with the CJP came to a head, and it expelled the CJP leaders from their seats on its own governing board. A year later it took the unusual step of publishing a doctrinal manifesto that forcefully re-affirmed the authoritarian ideal: 'In the management of a firm,' it said, 'authority cannot be shared. Experience shows that any other formula leads to impotence.' As the old family boss gives place to the technocratic manager, so the Patronat will probably modify its attitudes in time. But the process will be a slow one, for, as in Britain, the heritage of class tension and suspicion does not make it easy for worker and employer to talk face to face.

THE FUTURE

Though France's economy is much stronger than ten or fifteen years ago it has also become more exposed, and with each year that passes it can afford less and less the luxury of its remaining built-in weaknesses. Not only the Common Market but also the reduction of world tariffs under the Kennedy Round agreements have quickened the tempo of competition; and although the initial impact of the Treaty of Rome was survived quite well, the next phase may prove harder now that barriers are down. Industrial growth has shown signs of falling off from the impressively high and even rate of the late 'fifties and early 'sixties and for the first time since the war the bogy of unemployment has appeared. Gold reserves are still riding high, but trade deficits have reappeared, and in-flation remains a threat.

There is no need to be too pessimistic for, since the war, France has surmounted worse difficulties than the present ones. But if the recurring miracle of French economic buoyancy is to continue into the 1970s, it will require a further sustained effort of modernisation, and the curing of old structural ailments. And this only the State can achieve. Though Patronat and private firms may bear much of the blame for what is still wrong with the French economy, the State, being so all-pervasive in France, carries the final responsibility for the failures as well as the successes. And many of today's remaining problems will not be solved without a strong Government lead. Shortages of capital and productive investment, lack of funds for research, the dangers of too many American take-overs and too costly a nuclear policy are some of the main issues the Government has to reckon with, and some of them can be solved only by basic reforms requiring political courage.

The first of these problems, the lack of capital for investment, has been due less to the temporary effects of the 1963–5 Stabilisation Plan than to the innate weaknesses of the French financial market. And French industry badly needs more investment, for it is still under-equipped for meeting German competition. Firms often feel obliged to seek capital from the United States, and this in turn creates difficulties of a different kind. The annual increase in industrial investment fell from about 15 per cent in 1959 to 2 per cent in 1965, and the level of self-financing dropped in the same period from 84 to 57 per cent. It seemed ironic, after the Plan's patient efforts to persuade French firms to invest, that they now lacked the money to do so. After the lifting of Giscard's austerity measures, Michel Debré since 1966 has launched a series of investment drives which have had some success. But productive investment in France is still only 21·7 per cent of gross national product against 26·4 per cent in Germany, and much of the necessary capital still has to come from State loans rather than from the Bourse (Paris stock exchange) which has been quietly stagnating for several years.

There are several reasons for the narrowness and weakness of the French stock market. The most obvious is the depreciation that has been caused by steady inflation. Another is the preference of the French public for short-term liquid assets rather than long-term savings, and the paucity of insurance—many Frenchmen, with their roots in an agricultural past, still think in terms of gold rather than paper money, and are only now beginning to learn about savings. Most important, the State's control of the big banks and savings institutions serves to inhibit private finance.

The Government, aware of the dangers of this situation, has recently begun to make serious efforts to enlarge the French capital market and to stimulate banking. In 1967 two of the largest State banks were merged and the private merchant banks were given important new incentives to increase their reserves and adopt a more dynamic policy. Symptomatically, the venerable house of Rothschild extended itself from its traditional merchant role into that of deposit-taking in order to find more money. In January 1967 France abolished most of her remaining foreign exchange controls and freed her gold market, in order to stimulate confidence in the franc, attract more capital into Paris, and revive the Bourse. These various measures seem to have yielded some results. But so long as such a large part of French banking and financing remains in the hands of the State, the Paris market will not find it easy to achieve the wealth and flexibility that French industry needs if it is to attract enough capital for investment. This is one of the drawbacks of the *étatiste* tradition which in some other respects has given so much strength to the French economy.

One of the most serious results of the shortage of investment has been the lag in scientific research. Although the State spends a fair amount in this field, notably for military purposes, few private firms are conducting nearly enough research to keep them abreast of their world rivals. French opinion has recently woken up to this with a jolt, and the papers have been full of warnings that France spends only 1·5 per cent of her gross national product on research, against 1·8 per cent in Germany, 2·3 in Britain, and well over 3 per cent in both Russia and the U.S.A. The 'balance of patents', as it is sometimes called, is severely adverse: that is, France sells only one patent to the U.S. for every five she buys from there, two-thirds of all new patents registered in France are of foreign origin, and France comes only eighth in the world 'league table' of originators of patents. Even that proud French achievement, the Caravelle, lost the chance of a large sales order from China because its electronics and pressurisation system were American patents and were forbidden under contract to be sold to Peking.

This situation is especially disturbing to French pride, as science in the past was always something she could boast about. Photography, cinematography, many early aspects of electricity and aeronautics, Pasteur, de Lesseps and the Curies: the roll-call of French inventions and inventors has been a fine one. But for a long time French public opinion has tended to rest complacently on its scientific laurels, its attitude summed up by a remark I once heard a Frenchman make to an American, 'No, we don't have pasteurised milk in France, but we *do* have Pasteur!' This, in fact, has often been part of the trouble: French science has shown itself better at pure invention than at application, and one reason why French industry fell behind that of Britain and Germany in the nineteenth century was the failure of French firms to make proper use of the inventions of the period, although many of them were French.

Yet there is clearly no lack of grey matter; and today, as ever, when scientists do get the right lead from the State or private firms, they can still produce brilliant results. After the war, the technocrat-led industrial revival inspired some splendid achievements, mainly by the big State concerns ready to invest money in research. The State-led aeronautical industry pulled itself up by its own bootstraps to produce the Caravelle (or most of it); Renault pioneered automation in France and created a new machine-tool industry; the State railways commissioned some of the world's best electric locomotives, made by French firms; Electricité de France built the world's first tidal power dam, at St. Malo, using a new type of turbine; the steel industry invented a special new non-corrosive tube for pumping the sulphurous natural gas at Lacq; and for some years Bull held its own with the American giants in the computer field. Today, in several branches of atomic energy, telecommunications, and chemicals, France has been able to move ahead without relying too much on foreign expertise. She even invented her own colour television system, SECAM, which Russia and some other countries found worth supporting.

But today, as advanced research grows more specialised and more expensive, France is faced not only with shortage of equipment but with shortage of top-level trained scientists. This is even more acute than in Britain, despite the fact that for reasons of language, and perhaps also of national loyalty, France does not suffer the same brain-drain across the Atlantic. Intellectual resources are often misused. Of the 1,298-million-franc State budget for research (in 1966), more than two-thirds was for atomic and military purposes: this stimulates a few key industries, such as electronics, but does not necessarily meet the needs of industry as a whole. Most of the rest of the State research budget is channelled to the universities, which are generally too conservative and academic to apply it to practical needs. So there is little rapport between universities and industry for research; and in their ivory towers too many scientists are encouraged to pursue theoretical lines. The lack of expensive equipment favours mathematics rather than physics or chemistry; and so it may be no surprise that no post-war French scientist won a Nobel prize until 1965.

While one need is for a reform of university science, another is to encourage more private firms to do their own research. This is something that, in France, few of them are used to doing. But there has recently been some progress, under Government pressure: private industry's research spending doubled between 1960 and 1964, and a few big firms, such as the Rhône-Poulenc chemicals giant, are producing successful results. A few companies, notably at Grenoble,* have even begun to commission universities to help them with the kind of joint work that is still much commoner in Britain or America. But few French firms are large enough to be able to compete adequately on a world scale: according to one statistic, the Bell Telephone Company in America has half as many research workers (8,000) as there are in the whole of French private industry.

Inevitably, lack of modern techniques as much as lack of capital has been driving French firms to seek American help, as in the case of the Bull take-over. And so the whole research issue has become a matter of national pride, quite as much as an economic one. There are people who argue that France must swallow more of her pride and accept the need to buy techniques and know-how from abroad, rather than pursue them herself so expensively. Atomic weapons and the space-race are the obvious examples; and it might apply also to some aspects of electronics and chemicals. And yet, an adverse balance of patents does cause a drain on payments, and therefore hurts the economy as well as prestige. And it is blatantly clear that the European reserve of scientific genius is being under-used. One solution, preached by Louis Armand and others, is for a pooling of European scientific effort, and this has already borne some fruit with the European Centre for Nuclear Studies at Geneva. But its application in other fields has been held up partly by the political teething-troubles of the Common Market.

Another direct result of the shortage of French investment capital has been the large-scale entry of American business into France. Here, as in the case of science, national pride is heavily involved. From 1959 onwards the invasion of France by big American firms increased sharply, and by 1964 was causing quite a scare. Understandably, the Americans were looking for footholds inside the Common Market, or in some cases for escapes from their own anti-trust laws; and a number of French firms, desperate for financial or technical help, were ready to accept their offers of partnership. These individual firms therefore benefited, economi-

* See p. 124 (New life in the provinces).

cally: but the Patronat and the Government began to see threats to national independence. De Gaulle, bent on escaping from U.S. military dominance in NATO, hardly wanted economic domination in exchange. The issue became far more explosive than ever it has in Britain, although the level of U.S. investment in Britain is more than twice as high.

In the summer of 1964 the notorious 'affaire Bull' hit the headlines. Les Machines Bull were the largest makers of electronic calculators in Europe, and fully French. From 1935 to 1960 the firm's record of technical pioneering had been remarkable: it was a showpiece of modern French industry. But then its progress mysteriously stopped and it began to lose money, for reasons apparently connected with its family management. General Electric, the fourth largest firm in the world, then made a bid to help Bull. Anxious to stave this off, the Government produced a counter-bid which amounted virtually to nationalisation, since little French private capital could be found. But Bull found GE's offer more commercially interesting, and the Government finally felt they could not resist. So Bull today, though it still retains some of its old family connections, has become little more than a French holding company in the world empire of General Electric.

Many Frenchmen saw this take-over as a humiliation, and not the only one they had to face. The Simca car firm is now partly controlled by Chrysler, and l'Alsacienne, the largest French biscuit firm, by General Mills. Other American companies, such as IBM, Caterpillar and United Carbon have formed their own French subsidiaries without resorting to partnership or takeover, and are extending their hold on the French market. It is a pattern common throughout Western Europe, but in France the trend has been fastest: 616 new American investments there from 1958 to 1965, against 489 in Germany in the same period and 432 in Italy.

While Americans seem to regard France as the most attractive growth area in Europe, the French Government has reacted erratically to this doubtful compliment. In one or two cases it has even encouraged American entry as a stimulant: for instance, after trying for years to persuade the archaic French fruit-canning industry to face modern competition, as a last resort in 1962 it invited Libby's* to open a tomato-canning plant near Nîmes and show them how to do it. This *is* having precisely the desired effect, and even some of the keenest anti-Americans regard this particular move as justifiable. In other cases, the Government adopted a laisser-faire policy until, early in 1965, it suddenly clamped down on all U.S. investment for several months. Remington Rand were even pressured into abandoning their new factory near Lyon, and had to switch their European typewriter production to Holland and Italy. Today the official policy is to keep some industries as fully as possible in French hands (steel and atomic development, for instance), while allowing selected

* See p. 93 (The Young Farmers' revolt).

foreign investment in other sectors, either where industry is technically weak and needs outside expertise, or where it appears strong enough to face open competition. At all events, dossiers are now studied much more carefully than before—about two-thirds of the 150 American bids for entry in 1965 were turned down.

As American investment still accounts for little more than 5 per cent of total French assets, the problem still seems to be more political than economic. But few Frenchmen, however anti-Gaullist, would disagree with the Government that some form of control is necessary, or else American flooding of the market could cause political tensions. At least it is clear that earlier fears of German competition are no longer French industry's chief external problem: the question now is how to adjust to wider competition in the world of the big combines. Even the largest French firms are too small to compete by themselves, and will have to form outside links. The answer, as many Frenchmen believe, is to create 'European' firms of American size; but one of the chief disappointments of the Common Market, to date, has been its failure to achieve this. German investment in France is only one-tenth that of the United States, and a good deal below even Britain's. The only successful inter-Common Market merger of any size, so far, has been between two non-French photographic firms, Agfa of Germany and Gevaert of Belgium; and in the car industry, attempts at international mergers or even collaboration have not yet got very far. The simple truth is that, though tariffs have come down, there are still major official barriers to the flow of capital between the Six, while national systems of taxation and company law differ so widely as to make mergers usually more trouble than they are worth. There is a pathetic tale* of the vain efforts of a Troyes hosiery firm to found a joint 'European' company with German, Italian, and Belgian partners: at first, all were keen on the idea, but after months of wrestling with the details, lawyers, tax experts, and bankers all failed to find a formula.

The only solution, if America is not to dominate the market of the Six more and more, is to create a new 'European' statute of company law, and thus encourage big mergers. Jean Monnet and others have thrown their weight behind this idea: the French Government is also keen, and has even taken the lead in opening talks on the subject in Brussels. But the Gaullist proposals for a new company statute have, needless to say, stopped short of any effective supranationalism and the EEC has not thought them adequate. It is one of the many fields in which the Common Market has yet to become an effective reality. France's industry has benefited from the Treaty of Rome and her agriculture is likely to do so even more; but Monnet and his fellow-idealists want more than this. They are pressing for the implementation of plans for a common transport policy, a common currency, harmonised taxation and social

* See *Le Monde*, 29 June 1965.

services, free movement of labour, common validity of national degrees and diplomas. Progress here has been slow and uneven. But it is only measures like these that will shake the more backward spheres of French economic life into reform.

Another problem the Government has to face concerns the future of the Plan itself. Inevitably the Plan's role is changing, as the economy grows less sheltered, and inevitably it has lost some of its *raison d'être* with the transfer to Brussels of so many long-term economic decisions. This the planners in the Rue Martignac recognise, though they point out that some of the methods used in Brussels are not so different from their own: the Common Market, in fact, has meant a greater change for the non-planning Germans than for the French. But the biggest threat to the authority and independence of the Plan comes not from Brussels but from Paris itself, where the Government seems to be allowing it to be dragged into politics. The Governments of the Fourth Republic were so ephemeral that none had time to lay its hands on the Plan, which thus remained aloof from party squabbles. Stability under de Gaulle has not only made the Plan less necessary as a factor of continuity; it has also identified it more closely in the public mind with Government policies. The Gaullists have tended to exploit it, either as a scapegoat for unpopular measures, or as window-dressing; and anti-Gaullists, whether big business, union, or Left-wing parties, have grown less ready than in the past to collaborate with the Plan, just because they see it as a Gaullist tool. The whole basis of Monnet's sacred non-party rendez-vous is now threatened. When the Fifth Plan was debated in Parliament in 1965, even the mild Christian Democrat MRP voted against it: the Left tried to produce a counter-Plan, but failed through lack of economic inside information.

It is not even clear how far the Government intends to go on relying on the Plan, which inevitably restricts the freedom of the annual budget and must therefore sometimes be a nuisance. M. Pompidou, the Prime Minister, is an economic liberal and no believer in planning; and the two successive heads of the Plan since the departure of Pierre Massé in 1966 have both been orthodox civil servants without the personal authority or the driving flair of their three predecessors. Some people see this as a sign of the wane of planning, even though Debré himself is more *dirigiste* than his predecessor, Giscard d'Estaing. The real issue is that the French have still failed to solve the basic dilemma between *dirigisme* and liberalism. The rival camps, led by Pompidou and Debré, are simply getting stronger.

Yet France still needs the Plan. Industry still needs a strong and politically disinterested hand to guide its modernisation, for the Common Market may provide an external stimulus but not the detailed guidance. No French firm is large enough to carry out its own world's-eye surveys like General Motors: they still need some central advice and direction as they face the new global markets. Under the *dirigiste* French system, private firms have all too little real freedom, and this tutelage inhibits their dynamism and drives them into sullen resentment; the Plan, by providing a democratic forum of liaison between them and the State, at least gives them some chance to help work out their own destiny.

Another argument for the Plan is that, with domestic inflation still a lurking threat, France cannot easily manage much longer without some kind of incomes policy. This the Plan alone is properly qualified to provide.

The first tenative steps towards an incomes policy have not yet moved very far, owing to the mutual mistrust of big business, unions, and State. After the severe strikes of March 1963 in the coal-mines and other public industries, the Government began to make efforts to solve one root cause of unrest: the tendency of wages in private industry to shoot shead of public ones. But this was immediately followed by the stabilisation plan, which hit workers on hourly rates much harder than salaried *cadres* and made the unions more suspicious of an incomes policy than ever. A team of experts under Pierre Massé in 1964 prepared some detailed proposals for such a policy, but unions and Patronat alike shot them down. 'It's most unfortunate for our image,' commented one planner sadly, 'that this happened to coincide with the stabilisation plan. The unions simply think that an incomes policy is a trick to limit wage increases. And the lowering of taxes on business profits, though it was aimed solely at stimulating investment, has hardly helped to convince them otherwise!' One small step has, however, now been taken: a detailed study of wages and salaries is now taking place within the framework of the Fifth Plan, and the fruits of this could provide the basis for a future incomes policy. But the process will be slow. France, for all her planning, is here behind Britain. The Patronat is suspicious both of contractual agreements with unions and of further State interference in firms' affairs; the Government, likewise, fears committing itself to bargains either with firms or with unions that might limit the freedom of the budget; and the unions are mistrustful all round. An incomes policy would require a certain weakening of the barriers that traditionally divide up French society, and for this the French may not yet be ready. Meanwhile, the past two or three years have seen a certain strengthening of union solidarity, with a new accord in 1966 between the CGT and CFDT and joint strike action in 1967. Until very recently, the steady rate of economic growth has meant regular near full employment in France, even in periods of mild recession such as 1964–5; but with the post-war 'baby-boom' now exploding yearly on to the market, there are signs that this may not continue. In 1966–7 the French expansion rate was much slower than expected, due largely to the international recession, and for the first time since the war industry found itself unable to offer jobs to all the new young labour recruits. Unemployment has risen beyond 400,000, a high figure for France. This factor might prove temporary. But it underlines more than ever the need for an effective incomes policy, and for closer consultation between unions, State and

Patronat. A new French recession might spark off dangerous strikes, especially if the unions acted together. Yet if wages and consumer demand again begin to outstrip productivity, failing an incomes policy the only way to curb new inflation might be to limit expansion: a vicious circle indeed!

The Government's management of the economy is even more directly under question in its choice of priorities for public spending. This means, above all, de Gaulle's nuclear policy. And the apparent curbs on social welfare rather than on military budgets in recent years have obviously been a principal cause of the growing Left-wing bitterness against de Gaulle. It is all a long and vexed problem: how far have France's military efforts since 1946, the wars in Indo-China and Algeria, and the nuclear programme, *really* affected economic growth and social progress? Once emotion and prejudice have been discounted, it is extremely hard to arrive at a fair answer, and statistical evidence is even harder to produce. On the Right, there are people who point out that the Algerian war (1954–62) overlapped precisely with the years of the fastest economic growth. But this was probably no more than a coincidence: 1954 happened to be the year when the post-war recovery began to gather pace. Although the active use of a large army in Algeria helped the expansion of some industries, it also promoted inflation; similarly, today, the costly nuclear policy is a boon for the electronics industry but has also been a cause of inflation.

Of the 1968 overall defence budget of 25,000m francs, about one quarter goes on nuclear weapons; in 1959, when the Army was more than twice as large as in 1968 (750,000 men against 330,000), the defence budget was 15,760m francs, of which only 1,300m was for developing the Bomb. During the same nine years, the budget for education went up from 6,510m to 20,500m francs, and for health from 1,130m to some 3,000m. It is therefore not easy to argue that the 'force de frappe' (as it is called) has *in itself* been holding back French development, any more than the Algerian war did. And yet, that money is badly needed for more valuable things. The *force de frappe* may not be stunting the growth of the economy; but it *is* preventing individual Frenchmen from sharing fully in the fruits of the nation's new prosperity. It is eating up funds that could better be spent on schools, houses, roads, hospitals.

France today in many respects presents the pathetic spectacle of a nation trying to live beyond its means in terms of prestige and power; and where individual wealth has been allowed to outstrip public services to a painful degree. Most people can afford a car, but they get caught in traffic jams through lack of modern roads; most people can afford a telephone, but the waiting lists are long and the trunk lines too few; most people can afford theatre-tickets or sports gear, but the promised new local cultural and sports centres lag far behind schedule through lack of State funds. Some of the trouble has been due to the Government's reluctance to levy higher taxes when its popularity has been waning and

elections have been imminent. But the *force de frappe* is also to blame
—and so, alas, is the fact that France cannot really afford to spend as much
as she does on overseas aid. This is certainly not money wasted, but it is
equally beyond her means. In 1966 French aid to developing countries
stood at 6,231m francs, or 1·3 per cent of gross national product, proportionately much more than Britain or the United States spends. This
aid helps to pay for French exports; but mainly it is given with a view to
winning friends and prestige, as much as for the sake of Arabs' or Africans'
blue eyes. Yet France too is in some ways a backward country—take a
look at the squalid, derelict farms of the Massif Central or the tenements
of eastern Paris. It is this kind of social progress that has been sacrificed
to de Gaulle's *politique de grandeur*. During the 1963–5 austerity period
there were severe curbs on public funds for social services and basic
equipment: these were lifted in 1966, when Debré took over, but the
funds are still far from adequate.

Much, therefore, of what is wrong with France today is due simply to
misdirection of public money. But much else is due to outmoded structures. The rapid economic progress of recent years is now, in almost
every field, coming up against out-of-date systems and practices that
prevent it from advancing much farther. The engine, as it were, has
been revved up to a fair speed, thanks to the Plan and the Common
Market; but now it cannot go faster without a decoke and a change of
plugs. Nearly everyone I spoke to in high positions is acutely aware of
this: 'la réforme des structures' has even become a parrot-cry. Pierre
Sudreau, formerly one of de Gaulle's most brilliant technocrat-Ministers
and now one of his sternest critics, told me: 'Gaullism will die unless de
Gaulle now makes some new reforms. The basic structures of France,
over-centralised and too juridical, are rapidly being made obsolete by
technical progress.'

As the Government is so all-pervasive, most reform requires its lead.
True, its record is better than that of the Fourth Republic; but it is poor
compared with the power it enjoys and with what it could and should
have done. And many problems grow more pressing each year. In 1960,
at de Gaulle's own request, a team of experts headed by Rueff and Armand
themselves drew up a vast dossier of needed reform in many fields, including such matters as the closed-shop among Paris taxi-drivers. The
Government tacitly accepted most of their ideas—but has since applied
very few. When Debré, a noted reformist, came back to office in 1966,
hopes were raised that something might happen. But with an election
due in the spring, the Government seemed disinclined to risk making
new enemies by upsetting *positions acquises*; and even when in the summer of 1967 the Government granted itself controversial 'special powers'
to act by decree, it made little use of them for valid basic reforms. Louis
Armand, when I last saw him, added another reason for the inaction,
'Politicians aren't interested in invidious structural reforms. They prefer
spectacular new projects, like the Concorde, or the Mont Blanc tunnel.

Basic structures will probably not be reformed without a new shock from outside—that is why, in my view, the answer is effective European unity. And that is my quarrel with de Gaulle.'

Some of these needed reforms touch the economy more directly than others, but most are bound up with it. In agriculture, in the retail trade, in decentralisation, housing, town-planning, and education, basic reforms are now either taking place or signally failing to take place, and later chapters will describe them. In industry itself, I have suggested that the principal need is for firms to become larger and more modern, grouping together or merging. The Government cannot do this itself, but its powers of persuasion and financial incentive are great. A start has been made by reforming company taxation; but there is still an urgent need for overhaul of the banking, savings, and insurance systems, and of the financial market as a whole, if industry is to find the French capital it needs. As I have suggested, the Government must also take the lead in promoting investment and more scientific research, in developing an incomes policy to combat inflation, and in working out just what it does really want from the Plan, the Common Market, and American infiltration. De Gaulle's recent attempts to speculate against the dollar are a dangerous prestige game, and are likely to do as much harm to France in the long run as to the Americans or British.

The administration must also put its own house in order. The Napoleonic legacy of a strong civil service and strong State economy has many advantages; but in the complex world of today its over-centralised system leads to growing inefficiencies and delays. State control was useful for rebuilding France after the war, and is still needed for running the big supply industries and co-ordinating research. But in the America-German world of mammoth private enterprise, to which France is now wedded, it could be argued that French private firms would fare better if the State allowed them more freedom and helped the capital market to develop. Thus there may have been some justice in the Patronat's cry against the steady encroachments of the State.

The French economy has come a very long way since 1945, and has startled everyone with its resilience. But its weaknesses are not cured. The next step may be the hardest.

CHAPTER III

SOME KEY INDUSTRIES

LYON, ONCE 'THE CAPITAL OF SILK', is today a capital of chemicals and engineering. Grenoble is famous no longer for its gloves, but for electro-metallurgy and nuclear research. In the Limoges area, even porcelain is beginning to seem less important than uranium and hydro-electricity. On every side, traditional French luxury products have been yielding first place since the war to modern heavy industries. This was felt to be essential, if France was to be able to compete as an industrial nation.

The policy seems to have been justified, and several industries have made striking advances, both technically and economically. As a result, this nation traditionally renowned in the arts has begun to change her colours; and some of the national pride that the French usually feel towards cultural achievement has come, since the war, to be focused instead on science and industry. Far more than in cautious Britain, public and politicians alike have responded enthusiastically, even naïvely, to ambitious or imaginative new projects; and it seems no coincidence that most of the initiative and ideas for a Channel tunnel (or bridge) have come from the French side, although Britain, having no other land link with her neighbours, would stand to gain more than France from the scheme.

The single-vault suspension bridge across the lower Seine at Tancarville, the new road tunnel under Mont Blanc, the large hydro-electric dams alone the Rhône and the Alps, are some of the post-war public works of which the French are ingenuously proud. Of course today, under de Gaulle, such grandiose schemes are sometimes conceived more with an eye to prestige than economic advantage. But this is not a charge that can be laid against France's earlier long-term efforts, in the first years after the war, to rebuild her basic industries: railways, fuel and power, iron and steel, cars and aeroplanes, machinery and chemicals.

THE RAILWAYS: ARMAND PRE-DATES BEECHING

France's State railways provide an example of the technocratic system at its best: they show just how efficient the French can be, when everything is rationally directed by one State body and nothing is left to the vagaries of private collaboration. Thanks to this, France's trains are reputed as amongst the most modern, swift, and comfortable in the world, and many nations send experts to study the Société Nationale des Chemins de Fer Français as a model of how to run their own railways.

When Louis Armand became president of the SNCF in 1946, and began to modernise, he had several advantages over Dr. Beeching, who set about a similar task in Britain seventeen years later. French railways, nationalised in 1938, ended the war with four-fifths of their engines and coaches destroyed, and a high percentage of their rolling-stock, track, and stations also out of action. But this proved a blessing in disguise: Armand could start with a clean sheet. First he closed down 6,000 miles of un-economic branch line; or rather, in many cases he simply never re-opened them. With his engineering eye on the future, he insisted that all the fresh equipment must be absolutely modern. Big new marshalling-yards, with the latest electronic devices, were built to replace the old small ones destroyed by bombing. Research technicians were given generous budgets to prepare new locomotive designs: as a result, France today not only exports electric and diesel engines in some numbers, but her trains hold the world speed records. SNCF electric engines have reached 207 m.p.h. on trial runs, while passenger trains on regular runs often cruise at their legal maximum of 125 m.p.h.

Armand also invested heavily in electrification. The electrified track has nearly trebled since 1938 and today accounts for 23 per cent of length and carries over 74 per cent of traffic. Most of the main lines from Paris to other big cities are electrified, as well as local networks in the Lille and Metz areas and in the Alps and Pyrenees. Everywhere the emphasis is on longer trains and more powerful engines. The average train in France is much longer than in Britain: British Railways, while carrying no more freight than the French, do ten times as many train-miles. This helps to give France the edge in efficiency and lower costs; and France is also helped by having a network about the right size for her country and its economy, without the obsolete bottlenecks and suburban spiders' webs of greater London and the Northern industrial belt. French freight trains, especially, benefit from being able to carry heavy loads over long distances; and although the problem of road-rail competition is far from solved, it is less acute than in many countries, and has been alleviated by a system of taxing long-distance lorries to encourage the sending of goods by rail.

The development of two-carriage diesel passenger trains for rapid cross-country connections; glass-roofed panoramic coaches, softer seats, cheap cafeteria dining-coaches, and the growth of car-carrying services for tourists; experiments with above-the-ground monorails and hovercraft-like aerotrains; advanced methods of signalling—these are some of the more recent developments on the SNCF, now that Armand himself has completed his work of modernisation and moved on to other tasks. Punctuality is secured by a system of penalties for drivers who are late without cause, and the SNCF's high record of punctuality is one reason for its low accident rate.

Thanks to modernisation and streamlining, the SNCF has been able to reduce its staff from 514,000 in 1938 to 335,000 today—compared with Britain's pre-Beeching 1963 figure of 747,000. Of course this saves money. Yet despite this glowing picture of progress and technical efficiency, the SNCF in recent years has been running up an annual deficit which in 1967 came to 1,300m francs. Several reasons are given: the continuing heavy cost of long-term investment and modernisation, the pensions paid to the many thousands of laid-off railwaymen who are still alive, growing competition from air and road transport, the Government's freeze on fare increases in 1963–6, and above all the fact that the Government tacitly helps to subsidise industry by keeping freight and other charges down. Now there is talk of drastic closures of a further 1,800 miles of branch line, and their replacement by local buses. The deficit is met by the State, but falls on the taxpayer; and until it is reduced, the SNCF will not really be able to fulfil its boast that the way to solvent finances runs through inspired modernisation. But officials are confident that the money so lovingly invested *will* soon pay better dividends, as the old costly steam-engines gently die away. As one SNCF official told me, with a certain complacent French logic: 'Our financial situation may be bad, but our economic situation is very good.'

'WHITE COAL' FROM THE MOUNTAINS AND 'LIQUID GOLD' FROM THE DESERT

The rapid growth of industry, and of private prosperity, has put a strain, as in many countries, on France's resources of fuel and power. The two main domestic sources of energy, coal and electricity, were both national-ised just after the war, and in both cases brilliant administration and technical advance have helped exploit natural assets to the maximum. The coal industry is highly modernised; and scores of new dams have been built to harness the power in France's mountain rivers. But as modern industry now increasingly prefers oil to coal, a growing part of France's energy supplies has to come from imports, notably from the oilfields of the Sahara and the Middle East. The sizable natural gas deposits found in south-west France are helping to offset this. But more probably the only long-term answer to rising oil imports will be to use nuclear energy—and after a slower start than Britain, this is what France is now beginning to do. There may also be practical benefits, one day, from the ambitious experiments in the use of solar energy now being carried out in the Pyrenees.

As soon as the State took over the coal-mines it subjected them to the same kind of rigorous modernisation as the railways. This was done so well that productivity is now the highest in Europe; by 1955, output per man was 23 per cent above the pre-war rate, compared with a rise of only 6 per cent in Britain. This has meant a useful saving in manpower in a country where labour is short. As with railways, nationalisation seems to have been more effective than in Britain, one reason being the high level of French technical progress due to the plentiful output of talented mining engineers from the three prestigious *Ecoles des Mines*.

But French coal is mainly poor in quality, and because it is hard to extract it also works out as more expensive than American or Polish coal. Therefore, though it is not plentiful (Britain produces four times as much), France soon found herself having to limit production as the coal era in Europe began to wane. Annual output had at first been pushed up after the war from forty-nine to about sixty million tons, but has since been deliberately cut back to some fifty million; even so, excess coal stocks still sometimes cause problems.

For Electricité de France, the main problem is quite different—it is simply that of trying to keep pace with a demand that doubles every ten years. The EDF was created in 1946, out of a myriad little private companies operating 14,000 different concessions. Today it is an efficient empire with a staff of 90,000, and its new glass-and-concrete HQ near the Champs-Elysées looks so futuristic that Jean-Luc Godard chose it as a location for some of the scenes in *Alphaville*. Here the élite of the EDF, including some of the cleverest *polytechniciens*, plan provisions forty years ahead, sneer at English power-cuts, and work out how to extract every drop of power from a country rich in hydro-electric resources, the *houille blanche* ('white coal') as it is sometimes called. The EDF is France's largest single investor, and has built or shared in the building of more than thirty dams in France in the past fifteen years, mainly in the Alps, Pyrenees, and Massif Central, and along the Rhine and Rhône. Of these Tignes, on the Isère, is the world's highest coffer-dam, and for several years Génissiat, on the Upper Rhône, was Western Europe's most powerful hydro-electric power dam, with a capacity of 40,000 megawatts.

These rank as some of France's most notable post-war constructions. But the most widely publicised EDF operation of all has been the construction of the world's first tidal power dam, across the estuary of the river Rance at St. Malo, in Brittany. Inaugurated in 1966, this dam uses a new type of 'bulb' turbine invented by the French, and extracts power both as the tide rises and as it ebbs. Thus it goes one better than the old tidal water-mills which worked only one way. It is a vast bulwark of concrete, 800 yards long, linking that older bulwark, the storm-washed fortress of St. Malo, to the hotels and beaches of Dinard. And yet the dam is graceful enough to fit harmoniously into the scenery of this much-visited strip of coast; what is more, a new motor road along the top of it saves the tourist the tedium of the Dinard–St.-Malo ferry, or of a thirty-mile detour via Dinan.

Tides on this estuary rise up to forty feet and are among the strongest in the world; even so, the dam produces only 0·5 per cent of French electricity, and must be regarded as an exciting technical experiment rather than as a major practical asset. It took six years longer to build than was planned, and, with new costs accruing all that time, it is unlikely to prove an economic proposition. A bolder scheme, drawn up some years ago, for a twenty-three-mile-wide dam across the whole of the nearby bay of Mont St. Michel, has been dropped as being too costly; and the EDF now say that they will not build any more tidal dams unless the nuclear development policy is held up.

After the rapid post-war expansion of hydro-electricity, the EDF is now switching its emphasis back to building new power stations using other forms of raw material. This is not because hydraulic resources are exhausted (some 30 per cent of France's river-power is still to be tapped) but because the Government wants to find other uses for France's coal, now that industry is spurning it in favour of oil.

The third principal domestic source of raw energy is natural gas. The deposit struck in 1951 at Lacq, in the Pyrenean foothills near Pau, is the largest yet found on the west European mainland outside Holland and now supplies France with a third of her gas consumption, or 700 million cubic feet a day. 'Le gaz de Lacq' is one of the clichés of modern French industrial pride, along with the Caravelle and the Rance dam—and with some justification, for the operation is impressively run and remarkable to look at. Some 230 acres in the valley west of Pau are covered with a network of brightly-painted pipes and cylinders, yellow, red, blue, and so on; each colour is for a different industrial function. At night, the security flares from the thirty-two operational wells blaze out for miles across the valley like a city on fire. This is modern industry at its best: clean, aesthetic, open to view. It is perfect, save for the pervasive odours of methyl-mercaptan and sulphur. The Lacq gas has an unusually high sulphur content, which caused problems of extraction at the outset; and the Lorraine steel industry had to invent a special new type of non-corrosive steel tubing before the gas could be successfully extracted. But the sulphur is also useful. Some of it is used locally in by-products, and the bulk is exported: the big State-backed company that exploits the Lacq concession, the Société Nationale des Pétroles d'Acquitaine, has built on the spot the world's largest sulphur-producing plant, turning out 4,250 tons a day. Everywhere you can see the great pale-yellow mounds of it.

The gas itself, once de-sulphurised, is piped direct for consumer use in the Paris region or the south-west, or else it is sold separately as propane or butane, while some of it supplies raw material for a number of new petro-chemical and plastic industries that have sprung up round Lacq. This deposit will begin to dry up after 1980; but the SNPA has just struck another one, east of Pau, that may prove to be as large, and might even enable France to cut down on imports from Holland and Algeria. There is no reason why natural gas should not become as important a national source of raw energy as coal and hydro-electricity.

But it will not prevent the steady rise in oil imports, now totalling over fifty-three million tons a year, plus a further fourteen million that are refined in France and then re-exported. The French oil industry lives in a complex political tangle of its own, partly because it is so tied up with the world market and with Franco-Algerian relations, and partly because this is the only French energy sector to remain about 50 per cent in private hands, and the Government now seems to be making a bid to extend its control over nearly the whole of it.

About 40 per cent of French oil comes from the Sahara, and the rest from the Middle East. Saharan oil is light and of high quality, and needs little refining for use as petrol: out in the desert you can just about put it straight into your car. When the French discovered it and started ex-ploiting it, during the early years of the Algerian rebellion, those who believed in 'Algérie française' saw a rosy future ahead for France's oil industry and an added reason for her not to pull out of the country. But when de Gaulle gave Algeria freedom in 1962, he knew that it would not be politically feasible to try to keep sovereignty over the oilfields. He did, however, persuade the Algerians to agree to let the French companies already installed there retain their monopoly. And this agreement has worked. Occasional fears that Algeria might nationalise the oilfields, and bring in Russian technicians, have never materialised. In fact, Algeria has good reason not to appropriate the oil industry: she does very nicely out of the agreements and especially out of a new treaty signed in 1965. This brought up to Middle East levels the royalties payable to her by the French companies, although their heavy investment expenditure is still far from amortised and production costs are way above Middle East levels. France, in effect, is now paying above the market price for Saharan oil, as one of her many forms of aid to Algeria; this was a concession the French Government made for political reasons. But it falls far harder on the private French firms who control nearly half the Sahara's production (notably the semi-private Compagnie Française des Pétroles, in which the State has a 35 per cent interest) than it does on the fully State-owned oil firms that manage the rest and can afford to run at a loss. This may have the effect of dissuading the private firms from further costly investment there, and of making them turn to the easier conditions of the Middle East. Moreover, another clause in the 1965 treaty set up a new Franco-Algerian joint governmental body to take charge of all future oil-pro-specting and subsequent exploitation in the Sahara. France is to provide most of the money and expertise for this. In other words, the Government has allotted its own State companies a virtual monopoly of the Sahara's future (with Algerian support) and seems to be trying to push the private companies out of the field.

Then in November, 1965, the Government further revealed its hand. It merged the two principal State oil concerns into a new body, the Entreprise de Recherches et d'Activités Pétrolières (ERAP), and put in charge of it an arch-technocrat, Pierre Guillaumat, whose brilliant career had included being president of the EDF and of the SNPA and Army Minister under de Gaulle. The influential Guillaumat today emerges as overlord of virtually the whole French oil world, and is obviously briefed to try to do for France's industry what Mattei did for Italy's: that is, not only to push aside the French private companies, but to challenge the American-backed giants, such as Esso, whose presence in France de Gaulle does not greatly care for. ERAP is now marketing its own brand of petrol, in France and abroad, under the trade name of 'Elf'. By making an important oil prospecting deal with the Iraqi Government, it is also carrying the challenge into the Middle East itself, where hitherto the American and Anglo-Dutch companies have enjoyed a near-monopoly.

This nationalistic policy has infuriated the big foreign oil firms. Whether it can succeed may depend partly on the attitude of France's EEC partners, who might take counter-measures against her manipulation of her oil market. By importing oil from Algeria, France does save herself dollars, and the same might apply to her new interests in Iraq; but essentially her new oil policy has political rather than economic motives. It will not alter her oil needs nor, substantially, what she has to spend on them.

Oil imports are expected to go on rising steadily over the next ten years or so, to reach maybe seventy million tons a year. They may then level off, provided that the nuclear policy develops as is now planned. France is the world's fourth atomic power (she completed her first reactor in 1956 and exploded her first bomb in 1960), but for almost a decade she has deliberately put brakes on applying this energy for making electricity on any scale. The official reason given is that she wanted to avoid the early British mistakes of hurrying uneconomic prototypes into use; she preferred to concentrate on research, so as to bring down costs and to complete the perfection of reactors that would be genuinely viable. But she knows that today she can ill afford to delay much longer, and so the brakes are being taken off. Nuclear energy, which provided only 0·7 per cent of France's electricity in 1965, is scheduled to multiply tenfold by 1970, and twenty-five fold by 1975. Several big new nuclear power plants are now being built; and it is expected that all new plants started after 1973 will be nuclear rather than thermal. By 1985, if all goes well, nuclear power may have overtaken coal and be supplying 20 or more per cent of France's energy needs.

Another reason for the delay has been that in nuclear matters France has tended to follow a strongly national policy. This has not been entirely her fault: since about 1957, the United States, for political and military reasons, has withheld from the French certain forms of nuclear co-operation which she has granted to the British. But France has done her share of rejecting U.S. help, while European nuclear progress as a whole has been slowed down by the failure of the Six to give more backing to Euratom.

Yet the French go-it-alone policy has borne some fruit. France's own scientific post-war record in this field has been outstanding, especially considering that she had to start virtually from scratch in 1945, without the wartime experience of the other major powers. The Commissariat à l'Energie Atomique (CEA) has harboured some brilliant scientists (its first high commissioner, in 1945, was Frédéric Joliot-Curie himself) and it has pioneered much important research in, for example, the production of plutonium and the use of natural rather than enriched uranium. Thanks to these efforts, France has been able to avoid having to buy enriched uranium from the United States. As the world's fourth largest uranium producer, she has enough on her own soil to last until about 1980: some 50,000 tons have been located so far, mostly in the Massif Central, where the CEA encouraged the public in the lucrative sport of taking geiger counters with them on Sunday picnics. The CEA and EDF claim that their reactors operating on natural uranium are now fully viable; but the supplies will not last for ever, and France has now completed at Pierrelatte on the Rhône an isotope separation plant for making her own enriched uranium. She is also experimenting with a fast neutron reactor so as to economise in nuclear fuel. Such projects are very expensive: in economic terms, France might benefit from closer co-operation with the rest of Europe as well as with the United States. But France's allies have been dissuaded, through dislike of her military policy, from joining with her in projects that inevitably have warlike as well as peaceful uses. Once again, the French tax-payer finds himself having to subsidise Gaullist pride.

The French nuclear budget has multiplied tenfold since 1956, to reach well over 5,000m francs a year. The bulk of this is still spent for military rather than civil ends, in so far as one can distinguish between the two when there is so much joint research. But the peaceful programme is now being rapidly expanded, and it finds a suitable symbol in the CEA's opulent new headquarters near the Eiffel Tower. The new reactor at Chinon, known as EDF 3, was at the time of its completion in 1966 potentially the most powerful in the world, with a production of 500,000 kilowatt-hours.

These energy industries are most of them, like the SNCF, good advertisements for the French system of State technocracy: streamlined central administration, with a strong accent on research and continual modernisation. Few private concerns in France achieve the same level of efficiency and forward planning.

The other leading primary industry, iron and steel, somehow escaped the epidemic of post-war nationalisation. But it is, today, closely guided by the State, and it relies heavily on State investment loans and financial concessions. Spurred on by the Plan and the High Authority of CECA, it has made great strides with modernisation since the war, and today has the most efficient rolling-mills and the most up-to-date coking methods in Europe. Steel output has doubled since 1950, and now stands at over nineteen million tons a year. The record of mergers, too, is better than in any other sector of private industry: notably, a merger in 1966 between the largest and the fourth largest steel firms, Usinor and Lorraine-Escaut, and another in 1967 between Sidelor and the Société Mosellane de Sidérurgie, has meant that 70 per cent of production is now in the hands of the four main companies.

And yet, the industry faces grave problems. Some of these are world-wide: growing competition, falling prices, excess of supply over demand as iron and steel output rises in new countries. The French industry has more difficulty than some of its rivals in coping with these factors, for internal reasons. The vast Lorraine mines, that make France the world's third iron-ore producer, are today left only with lower-grade ore that is hard to extract, and have been completely outclassed by the richer, cheaper ores from countries such as Sweden and Mauretania. This not only plays havoc with France's traditional ore exports; it puts a handicap on the big Lorraine foundries and steelworks that in the old days were purposely built close to the mines and still account for over 60 per cent of French raw steel output. If they want good ore, or good imported coke for fuel, they are badly served with transport links to the coast, despite the new Moselle canal. The steel firms that have fared best in the past few years are those near the north coast: a big new one that opened at Dunkirk in 1963 is one of the finest in Europe, and receives Mauretanian ore by ship right on its doorstep. The only answer to the industry's problems, so it is felt, is for the firms in Lorraine and elsewhere to make even greater efforts to regroup and to improve productivity. In theory, the French steel industry still has plenty of room for expansion: output per head is still about 15 per cent below the British level, and 30 to 40 per cent below that of Germany or the United States.

RENAULT, CITROËN, PEUGEOT: IS GENIUS ENOUGH?

French technical flair is no monopoly of the big State industries, as any-one knows who has tested the hydro-pneumatic suspension of a Citroën DS 19 or driven a tough Peugeot 404 for thousands of bumpy miles without a mishap. Ever since the pioneering days of Panhard and Louis Renault in the 1890s, the car industry has held a place of honour in this land of creative engineers; and today the main emphasis is still on daring new ideas of design and construction. But are these ideas enough, in themselves, for commercial success?

After the war this pilot sector of French industry rebuilt itself brilliantly, and by 1959 had secured a strong position as the world's fourth largest car-producer and France's chief exporter. In the 1960s, however, growing world competition and fluctuating home demand brought it trouble and exposed some of its weaknesses; notably its uncertain salesmanship and the wasteful duplication of resources between rival firms. In face of the German and American titans, it has been forced to regroup and rethink.

The industry bases some of its success on the average Frenchman's mania for cars, remarkable even by the usual standards of this car-mad modern world. The French have the highest level of car ownership per head in Europe, after the Swedes, * and their cars are relatively cheap. They have built a kind of popular mystique around the various national makes—the robustness of Peugeots, the bizarre ingenuity of Citroëns, the lightness and economy of Renaults, these have become legendary, along with the more recherché cult of imported Jaguars and Mercedes. With the death in 1964 of the little Facel Vega firm, France today makes virtually no luxury sports cars of her own: they are imported. Since the war she has concentrated, first, on small economy cars such as the Renault 4 C V and the curious Citroën 2 C V, and now, increasingly, on larger, elegant saloon cars such as the Peugeot 204 and the big whale-like Citroëns which, for advanced techniques, comfort, and design, have few rivals in their class.

The annual production of nearly two million cars, more than one-third of it exported, comes from four big firms, one nationalised (Renault) and three private: Peugeot, Citroën, and struggling Simca, now controlled by Chrysler. Each firm has a distinct individuality, and this gives flavour, if not always efficiency, to the industry as a whole.

Renault throughout the 1950s was the foremost showpiece of French State industry. And though today it may have lost a little of its verve, it is still a remarkable example of 'State capitalism', of a public manufacturing firm operating just like a private one, in a competitive field. It was founded in 1899 by Louis Renault, a young self-taught mechanic who in the manner of Ford or Nuffield built it over the next forty years into one of the foremost car firms of Europe. In 1944 he was charged with Nazi collaboration; the State confiscated his empire and, this being the era of nationalisation, they decided to hold on to it. They installed some inspired technocrats to run it on commercial lines, and straight away made it into a torch-bearer for French industry. Starting almost from nothing, it built up its own production of machine-tools. Its huge factory at Billancourt, in south-west Paris, was the first in Europe to use automation, in 1946. And in 1948 there began to pour off its assembly lines a remarkable new baby car, the Quatre Chevaux (4 CV, i.e. 4 h.p.), which had been planned secretly during the war by Renault technicians.

* One for six people; in Sweden it is one for 5·5, in Britain one for 7·5, in Germany one for 8, in the U.S. one for 3.

The 4 CV was a symbol of the social philosophy which has guided Renault ever since, first under Pierre Lefaucheux, and then under his successor as chairman, Pierre Dreyfus. An idealistic and humane kind of technocrat, Dreyfus regards the car as a social instrument to which every family has a right. Therefore his firm has concentrated on massive turn-out of small, cheap cars, with the models gradually growing in size only as French incomes and living standards rise. Thus in 1956 the 4 CV began to give place to the slightly larger Dauphine, one of the most brilliant and attractive small cars ever made, which has sold well over two million.

The other feature of this social philosophy is the idea that a firm owes its workers not only a wage but also as full and happy a life as possible. With discreet State backing, Renault has steadily led the field in welfare and labour relations—often to the annoyance of more staid private firms. Not only does Renault spend an unusual amount of money on social clubs, housing, education, and other schemes for its workers; but in 1954 it inaugurated a new kind of labour charter, the *Convention Collective*. This committed the firm to regular 4 per cent annual wage increases, and in return the unions agreed not to strike except as a last resort, when all negotiations had failed. The Convention also set up a compensation fund, paid for by the firm, which offsets short-timing in periods of recession.

This charter was later copied in the mines and in some private sectors. Today, as I have already made clear, inflation and expansion have made it largely obsolete, and the unions, wanting further concessions, have refused to re-sign. But the charter's spirit survives, and has had some influence on French labour relations as a whole. Renault still fulfils its own commitments unilaterally; and there is little doubt that the existence of the charter provides one reason why Renault has been virtually free from strikes since 1953; while, thanks to the compensation fund, the short-timing during the production slumps of 1960 and 1964 passed off almost without incident. With a minimum of paternalism, Renault does what it can for its workers, who often consider themselves the élite of the French proletariat. They were the first workers in France, in 1963, to be given a fourth week's statutory paid holiday, to the fury of the Patronat, who saw it as creeping socialism. And whenever there is a problem in the factory, or a change of company policy, Dreyfus sends a personal letter to each worker's home.

Renault was also a pioneer in the field of exports, in the 1950s. At a time when most French manufacturers were still slumped in protectionism, Renault's leaders foresaw which way the world car market was likely to move in the 'sixties and sensed that France could not afford to be left out of this new competition. Renault was virtually the first French heavy-industry firm to break into the American market, and by 1959 was exporting over 50 per cent of its output. Since then, its record has been rather less brilliant, especially in the American export market. But it remains a remarkable firm, generous, unsecretive, forward-looking; an object-lesson for socialists and capitalists alike. It has played a vital pace-setting role in the modernising of French industry; and although its national status has certainly influenced its social policy, it has not really had much effect on its technical and commercial ups and downs, for the management is free from active State subsidy or interference.

Citroën, its closest rival, could hardly be more different: it is a very caricature of the old-fashioned, secretive, family concern, and yet it is a nursery of mechanical genius with the best record of progress in the 1960s of any French car firm. It is controlled today by the Michelin tyre company, who bought it up in 1934 when its founder, André Citroën, went bankrupt. The Michelin family empire is the most arrogant, conservative, and fanatically secretive in French industry, and Citroën takes its colouring from them. Citroën's managing director, Pierre Bercot, is an austere soldier-like man in his sixties, and the atmosphere of the firm he rules is strict and heavy. Unions and workers are treated with a chilly paternalism. Modern commercial methods are frowned on—Citroën in France scorns advertising and publicity, takes little trouble with exports, and handles many domestic clients with cavalier contempt, while sales are still based on old-fashioned personal contact and interview. American doctrines of planned obsolescence are equally disregarded: Citroën believes in making cars that will last and can be kept in production, like the 2 C V, for twenty years or more.

Visitors are rarely welcomed at the parent factory on the Quai de Javel in Paris, nor at the big new automated plant in Rennes; and the Normandy testing-ground for new models is guarded by ten-foot walls and patrols of dogs. But the dogs have something worth guarding: Citroën's dedicated team of designers work two decades ahead of production, and the firm relies on the reputation it has created for unrivalled advance in design. This has become a mystique in France, but it is rooted in reality. Those cars with their weird shapes are solidly reliable: the internals are designed first, then the body shape is planned round them. The 2 C V may look like an old tin can, but it rarely breaks down, costs only 5,500 francs, does fifty miles to the gallon, and has been called 'the world's most intelligent car'. Born in 1959, it is still coming off the lines at the rate of 150,000 a year. The big frog-nosed Citroëns, D S and I D, are noted for their road-holding, comfort, and hydro-pneumatic suspension which makes them flop gently when they stop, like tired elephants. They are now the official ministerial car in many countries, including France itself. De Gaulle has a fleet of fifteen at the Elysée Palace, and he owes his life twice over to their excellent wheels and brakes—once, in a night storm, when a tree fell across his path, and then when he was shot at by the O A S and his chauffeur had to make a quick get-away on bullet-punctured tyres.

Though its exports are proportionately the lowest of the French Big

Four (only 21 per cent of sales), Citroën was the only one of the four to increase its overall production during the difficult years of 1963–5. This was due to technical prowess alone. But capital reserves have been falling; and in the new age of battle between giants, Citroën may be forced to modify the splendid paradoxes of its policy. Realising the dangers of its isolation, it is already reaching for ententes with more orthodox firms: in 1967 it acquired control of the Berliet lorry firm and began to form associations with Volkswagen and Maserati.

Peugeot, like Citroën, is a family firm with a good recent record. Its factory at Sochaux, near the Swiss frontier, is owned by a wealthy and clannish Protestant dynasty: six of the twelve members of the Board are Peugeots and a seventh, the managing director, is a son-in-law. There is pride at Peugeot, and some secretiveness, but little of the feudal arrogance of the Michelins. The accent is on prudence and reliability: dividends and the level of self-financing are both high, and this is the only large firm in France to pay its suppliers in ready cash. Peugeot cars, like their makers, are sober and discreet, and have a quality that might seem more English than French. They are famed, above all, for their robustness. Exports are high, and though Peugeot is still the smallest of the Big Four, its sales are rapidly catching up those of Simca.

When Chrysler were looking for a foothold in Europe, they first made overtures to Peugeot, and met with a proud rebuff. Then, in 1963, they bid for the ailing Simca; and, as in the case of Bull a year later, the Government allowed the deal, since it saw no other way of saving the firm. So today Chrysler hold 69 per cent of Simca's shares, and Fiat, linked with Simca for many years, have 25 per cent. Chrysler have brought in Georges Héreil, the brilliant former head of Sud-Aviation, to try to revive Simca. He is a man who enjoys a difficult challenge, and sympathises with American methods. So far, he has not succeeded in improving Simca's sales position; but he has time, and Chrysler are in a position to help him with export sales. Simca has always seemed a rather nondescript firm, its chief successes the Aronde, a conventional smallish saloon car, and now the interesting new 1100. It remains to be seen whether Chrysler and Héreil will be able to save Simca, or whether it will suffer the same kind of fate as Panhard, fifth and oldest of the big French firms, now entirely absorbed by Citroën.

In the first years after the war, the French car industry's task was simply to meet the needs of a hungry domestic market that in 1945 had only a million cars on the road. Tariffs were high, foreign competition was slight, demand far exceeded supply, and people wanted cars quickly and cheaply, without frills. Then horizons began to widen. When Renault attacked the American market, in 1957, success was on an unexpected scale. The Americans had never seen a car as small or as cute as the Dauphine before; they bought 200,000 in three years, often as playthings for wife or kids. But Detroit hit back by building its own small cars, the 'compacts'. Then Volkswagen arrived in the United States to challenge Renault, and after 1959 French imports there began to tumble. Dreyfus soon discovered that he had seriously mishandled the market. Whereas Volkswagen and Volvo did not open their American offensive until they had first built a proper network of agents for sales and spares, Dreyfus relied on the quick returns of a flashy publicity campaign, and soon found himself like a general who has made a brilliant armoured break-through without support troops or supplies. Shortly afterwards Italy, France's biggest regular client, also withdrew much of her custom by imposing austerity measures to deal with her own economic crisis. The proportion of exports in France's car production fell from a half to a third between 1959 and 1964. By the latter date the home market, too, was giving trouble, as saturation loomed up and the stabilisation plan cut back demand. France's car production fell from 1,520,000 in 1963 to 1,423,000 in 1965, while both Britain and Germany comfortably increased their lead over her. By early 1965, faces were long in executives' offices, and many workers were on short time.

The problem was made more serious by the growth of German competition and the entry into Europe of the American giants. General Motors already owned Opel, and the new Volkswagen-Mercedes association was larger than the whole French industry. The French began to realise that having four separate rival firms was a luxury; they must group together, with each other or with outside partners. In 1959, soon after the Common Market came into existence, Dreyfus had in fact proposed to Volkswagen and Fiat a kind of non-aggression pact, with delimited spheres of influence and no rivalry over new models. He was turned down. When Dreyfus put the same idea later to Henry Ford III, he was told, 'We'll lick you because we're stronger'. Then, while Dreyfus continued to woo the Germans, the Government began to persuade Citroën and Peugeot to link together. Citroën seemed keener than Peugeot, but in 1965 some progress was made towards a common policy on accessories and sales. Finally, on 22 April 1966, came an astonishing *coup de foudre*: Peugeot ditched Citroën and announced a new close association with Renault. Renault-Peugeot are now the world's third largest car-making combine outside the United States; they are ahead of BMC, though behind Volkswagen and Fiat. Because of Renault's nationalised status there is no financial link between the two firms, but there is now a common policy on investment, research, equipment, and exports, and agreement not to clash or compete with new models.

This was at once greeted as one of the most significant moves towards concentration in French industry since the war, and likely to *faire école*.* It came as a surprise, as Peugeot had seemed much closer to Citroën than to Renault in ethos and style of management. But Peugeot evidently felt that Renault had more to offer. Now the car world is watching to see

* Set a new trend.

what effect the new link will have on the fortunes of Renault. After the heyday of the Dauphine, this firm ran into repeated trouble. With the development of the new conditions of world competition, Dreyfus decided he could no longer afford to rely on one star model: it was too vulnerable. 'We are condemned to have a complete range,' he said. In 1962 Renault brought out *four* new models (unprecedented in Europe for one firm in the same year). They also began to phase out the Dauphine. But none of the recent Renaults have achieved the Dauphine's popularity, not even the larger new R 1600 (a rival to the Peugeots) despite its success as 1965 'car of the year'. The proliferation of models put up costs, and Renault, as one French writer put it, soon 'held the world record for fall in production'. There was even talk of de-nationalising the firm, so that it could more easily find associates; or of dismissing Dreyfus. The final blow—more a piece of bad luck than anything else—came early in 1966 when Fiat narrowly beat Renault to a contract for starting up a vast new factory in Russia. Renault won a separate Russian contract, but a much smaller one.

Fortunes change rapidly, however, in the mercurial car industry. After the end of 1965, with the relaxing of the austerity plan, sales charts began to nose upwards again in all firms and a new mood of confidence appeared. Renault shared in the new boom: in 1966 its sales were 28 per cent up on 1965's, and then rose a further 5 per cent in 1967. Overall French production for 1966 reached a new record of 1,770,000 cars, and France that year pushed Britain into third place among Europe's car producers (West Germany still easily hold the lead). Today the French industry appears more strongly based than ever before. Even so, one or two question marks remain. One of these concerns basic Government policy: by taxing petrol so highly and limiting the budget for road improvement, * it has tended to discourage French car buying, yet it urges the car firms to expand. This inconsistency annoys them. The Government will probably need to decide more clearly whether it really intends fulfilment of the Fifth Plan's provisions for nine million French cars in 1970 (there were just over seven million in 1966) or whether it should urge firms to trim their output schedules for the home market.

The Renault-Peugeot deal is already helping to streamline French production and to avoid further wasteful duplication of models. The deal is also serving to strengthen the overseas sales network, where the French still lack experience. Concentration is now more fully advanced than in any other French industry; and the French, like the Germans, are at last putting into action their conviction that the only way for European firms to stand up to General Motors is to imitate it, and unite. This, together with their technical genius, ought to enable this most crucial of French industries to weather the competition that lies ahead.

---

* See page 153 (New life in the provinces).

CARAVELLES—BUT THE CONCORDE?

The French are as proud of their Caravelle as the Russians are of Sputniks. It is a fine aircraft; and it is also a symbol of the remarkable post-war renaissance of French aviation, more striking than in any other sector of French industry. This industry was at such a low ebb just after the war that its leading firm, Sud-Est* Aviation of Toulouse, was reduced to making gas-generators and refrigerators. Eight years later it was making the Caravelle, and today the Concorde.

This is the full measure of the French triumph: to have succeeded in bringing out the Caravelle under these adverse conditions, at a time when the British and American industries with their wartime experience were still far ahead. If the French tend to boast about it rather too much, maybe it's because they know they were once the leading pioneers of early aviation, and so in this field they are even more prestige-conscious than usual. Prestige was the driving force behind the Caravelle's take-off, as it is today behind the Concorde. Fortunately, in the case of the Caravelle it made splendid economic sense too; but this is not yet certain for the Concorde.

France's aircraft industry led the world in the first part of the century; by 1945, after working half-heartedly for the Germans and then lying fallow, it was nearly derelict. All the advanced techniques and expertise were across the Channel or the Atlantic. For the next few years, French factories looking for employment had to fall back on making British or American models under licence: Sud-Est, for instance, made de Havilland fighters. The first new French national venture, the Armagnac, a heavy four-engined plane turned out by Sud-Est in 1949, was not a great success and was spurned by Air France in favour of Constellations.

But down in Toulouse, capital of the French aviation industry since the 1914–18 war, a team of gifted designers and engineers set about preparing for the real come-back. Their company, Sud-Est, was one of several aircraft firms that had been nationalised in 1936, and in 1946 the Government put at its head an exceptionally vigorous and able young administrator, Georges Héreil. He rapidly rebuilt the firm's workshops and began to plot with the Government how best to restore France's position. With over 90 per cent of the world's construction in American hands, the problem was to find a weak point, an aircraft that no-one else had yet made. The answer, it seemed, was a fast, medium-range jet. So in 1952, the Government gave Héreil the go-ahead and the funds for the Caravelle.

Hereil took a gamble that few private firms—and certainly none in France—would have dared. Believing that the Americans would not bring a similar kind of jet into service before the early 1960s, he insisted that the

* Its name was changed to Sud-Aviation in 1957, after a merger with another firm.

Caravelle be ready by 1959 in order to exploit the world market. This meant taking the unusual risk of investing 400m francs in an initial batch of fifty Caravelles before any airlines, even Air France, had placed orders. For three years the technical team headed by Pierre Satre, and known as 'la République de Toulouse', worked round the clock. The operation was almost wholly French, save for the Rolls-Royce engines, and the Caravelle's chief innovation was the placing of these in the rear, along the fuselage. The first trial flight was in 1955, and Air France had the first Caravelles in service by 1959, as planned. They were an immediate success, and other airlines such as Alitalia and SAS began to buy in some numbers. The Caravelle's speed (500 m.p.h.), its silence, its comfort, its resistance (since proven) to fatigue, put it ahead of other aircraft in its class. On a trial flight to Rome, it was personally blessed by the Pope.

Today more than 260 Caravelles have been sold, to twenty-nine different airlines—in 1963 they accounted for 77 per cent of all jet traffic in Europe. But Héreil has largely failed in his greatest ambition: to break into the American market. In 1957 he personally took a prototype on a sales tour of North and South America. The Americans were highly impressed with his wares, and with his own rare charm and persuasiveness; but they did not buy. His sole success came three years later when an American domestic company, United Air Lines, took twenty of them; but a similar deal with TWA fell through, apparently under pressure from Washington. And though Douglas in 1960 signed a contract to make Caravelles under licence, they have not taken up the option. The Americans seem to have fought shy of buying Caravelles for reasons of prestige and of military security; and also because they were planning something better themselves.

When the Boeing 727 appeared in the early 1960s as the Caravelle's expected rival, it had already sold 131 machines eighteen months ahead of its first flight! Caravelle sales at once started slipping. This shows that the Caravelle's dent in the huge American-dominated world market, though impressive by European standards, has been relatively modest.

Today, in a bid to ensure that Europe has some share in the new supersonic jet market, Sud-Aviation and the British Aircraft Corporation are building the Concorde. Prestige, once more, is at stake: and throughout this Concorde affair the French have seemed noticeably more concerned about it than the British. When in 1964 the new Labour Government, for economic reasons, wanted to cancel the project, the French, for reasons of prestige as much as anything else, wanted to go on. But French technical pride and devotion are also involved, and they amount to rather more than mere nationalistic prestige: anyone who visits Toulouse is impressed by the enthusiasm and dedicated ambition of the men at work on the Concorde. As in the car industry, the French are determined to pull out every stop of their technological genius in order to compete with the Americans.

Sud-Aviation is also preparing an 'airbus' or cheap short-range transport plane (possibly another Anglo-French venture) and is stepping up its output of helicopters, of which the firm is Europe's leading producer. But although Sud-Aviation is by far France's largest aircraft firm, it is not the only one. France is the world's third largest producer of light civil aircraft; and in the military field some distinguished jet fighters, Mystère and Mirage, have been produced by Marcel Dassault's privately owned company. The French industry in terms of output and personnel may be less than half the size of Britain's, but it is highly efficient and concentrated: 27 per cent of its budget is spent on research, thanks largely to Government help, and 35 per cent of its sales come from exports.

There are several underlying reasons for the success of the French aviation revival. The Government has not only helped and encouraged the aircraft industry to recover; it has promoted the most intensive system of air education outside eastern Europe. The aeronautical *Grandes Ecoles* are expanding fast and have high prestige. Private aero-clubs flourish, too, and there are 23,000 licensed pilots in France. Since Blériot's day and earlier the French have been an air-minded people, always ready to hero-worship *ces hommes magnifiques dans leurs machines volantes*; and the idealistic pilot Saint-Exupéry, who died while on service in the air in 1944, is still the most popular of all authors with French youth. So the success of the Caravelle stems from this background of national enthusiasm and scientific prowess. The question now is whether the Government will use prestige wisely as a stimulus, or be impelled to ambitions beyond its reach. The fate of the Concorde may provide a crucial test.

SHOES AND SHIPS AND SEALING-WAX:
EFFICIENCY OR PRESTIGE?

Almost all the big industries described so far are either in State hands or, in the case of cars and aircraft, are headed by State firms that have set the pace. And most of them have been very successful. With the older, more fragmented industries, still mainly privately owned (shipping, textiles and chemicals, for instance) the picture is often rather different.

Electronics is an example of a private industry that has done quite well; but this is largely because the State relies on it heavily for civil and military purposes and is accordingly generous with contracts and research grants. A modern, highly competitive industry such as this cannot be allowed to languish as if it were turning out *lingerie* or cargo-boats. One French electronics firm, the Compagnie Générale de Télégraphie Sans Fil (CSF), or wireless telegraph company, has made progress with radar and invented the SECAM colour TV system that has been one of the main prestige weapons in de Gaulle's armoury. Another firm, Bull, had a fine record of its own in the computer world, before its take-over by General Electric.

Today the French Government reluctantly accepts that full national independence in the electronics field is not possible, since American techniques are so far ahead. So it is operating a dual policy: the work of CSF and the other purely French firms is promoted for all it is worth, and mergers are encouraged; but the Bull take-over is also allowed, and IBM is encouraged to build up its strength in France. IBM France, with its new factory at Monpellier and its superb research centre in the hills behind Nice, is one of the most impressive firms in the country: it is fully French-run and French-staffed, with only a limited amount of supervision from its American parent. Anyone looking for an intriguing contrast between the old France and the new should go to the classical eighteenth-century Place Vendôme in Paris, where IBM has installed one of the largest computers in the world in a graceful old house next to the Ritz Hotel. Here, amid oak panelling and Louis XV furniture, assured young French scientists advise firms on their programming needs.

One of the principal State clients of the electronics industry is the space programme, conducted by the Centre National des Etudes Spatiales. France here collaborates with the rest of Europe (in ELDO and ESRO) and, within strict limits, with the United States, who in 1966 supplied the rocket and the launching-ground for the second French satellite. But basically this is a national venture; and when, in November 1965, the French rocket Diamant put the first French satellite successfully into orbit from a French base in the Sahara, all the Gaullist trumpets were sounded to proclaim France as 'the world's third Power in the space race', nicely ahead of Britain and Japan. Oddly enough, it was just ten days before the Presidential election. As with nuclear energy, the space programme has some military purposes; it will also, as the French assert, serve one day to create a global network of television satellites, capable of relaying French culture to screens around the world and so preventing an American monopoly. France spends more on space research than any other European country; even so, her programme is still so modest compared with the Russians' or Americans' that it is not clear how much useful purpose it yet serves, beyond showing the *tricolore* in space.

Charges of prestige-hunting were also levelled against the decision to build the world's longest and most modern passenger liner, the 55,000-ton *France*. This splendid ship, built at St. Nazaire and launched in 1962, is an ornate palace carefully geared to rich American tastes, with fine French *cuisine* added in. It is in fact doing good business on the North Atlantic route, and because of its speed and size is probably more economic than two smaller liners would have been. In itself, it may prove a good investment; the argument is simply whether the 400m francs of public money could not have been better spent on something less spectacular, like hospitals or telephones.

The *France*, owned by the State-controlled Compagnie Générale Trans-atlantique, is at least a rare sign of progress in the otherwise rather gloomy world of French shipping. Even more than in Britain, shipyards have been hit by the new world conditions, and several have closed recently. The main shipbuilding centres, Nantes and St. Nazaire, are two of the most depressed of French towns, where strikes are frequent. And the Government seems to have done not nearly enough to help the shipbuilding firms to retrench and modernise.

In the merchant navy and the passenger lines, the position is little better than in the building yards: whereas America and Russia are both doing all that they can to build up their cargo fleets and see that national ships carry national goods, France has strangely neglected the prestige of the French flag on the seas. The loss of Algeria and of other overseas possessions has brought a decline in traffic: France today is ninth among maritime powers, with only 4 per cent of world shipping trade. Increasingly, France's own imports and exports sail in and out under foreign flags. Shipping firms blame the trouble largely on costs and social charges, higher in France than in Britain or Germany. Oil-tankers, holiday cruises, and the North Atlantic liners are doing quite well; but elsewhere there is stagnation, and it seemed to French sea-goers like a portent of death when in 1964 the great Marseille firm of Fraissinet sold the merchant fleet that the family had built up since the eighteenth century. Onassis rides his yacht in the harbour of Cannes or Monte Carlo, and smiles; but the French Government seems to regard the whole problem as a low priority.

The chemical industry is managing a great deal better than this. It has expanded faster than any other French industry since the war, and has some good well-modernised firms such as Péchiney, Saint-Gobain, and Rhône-Poulenc. It has made a distinctive French contribution to the research development of petro-chemicals, and has so far managed to hold its own in the Common Market against the more powerful German chemical interests. But it is probably one of the French industries most vulnerable to the new world conditions, since this is a particularly competitive field, demanding expensive research and constant progress. France has to rely heavily on imports of chemical ingredients from Germany and the United States; and though there has been some successful regrouping, notably a merger in 1966 between Ugine and Kuhlmann, France still lacks really large chemical firms able to compete equally with Montecatini, Bayer, I CI, or Dupont de Nemours. Part of the industry is in State hands, mainly the part that makes use of fuel by-products. But the various State concerns are unco-ordinated, and it is sometimes argued that the State ought to set a lead to private industry by setting up a national chemical combine, maybe on the Italian model.

The Cinderella of the big French industries, suitably dressed in rags, is textiles. Here, as I have already suggested,* the old suspicious family traditions remain strongest—but without the flair of Michelin-Citroën. Many firms have modernised their equipment, but without changing

* See p. 31 (The economy: miracle or mirage?).

their attitudes. There are still 6,700 of them, and regrouping has not got far: in many areas, notably in the Vosges, firms are not yet beyond the artisan stage, and the slightest national recession will cause scores of small ones to dismiss staff or even to close down. Yet they maintain an *esprit de clocher* and refuse to unite.

It is noticeable that there are very few well-known brands of clothes, or shoes, in France; the firms and their myriad different products bear names that rarely mean anything to the public, unlike, say, Dolcis or St. Micahel in Britain. This is partly because the manufacturing firms are so many and so small, and partly because of lax French legislation about trademarks and names. Shops or wholesalers will often cheerfully replace the maker's name or the brand-name with their own. This makes it extremely hard for a good firm to build up a reputation for quality, in exports as well as in home sales. A new law has just been passed to tighten up the trademark system, and this may help the textile industry to become more competitive. It is France's second largest manufacturing industry, and the second in Europe for wool, cotton, and linen; its weaknesses are an undoubted drag on the economy.

It is evident that, with a few exceptions, the most efficient industries in France tend to be owned or closely supervised by the State. Whether this makes a case for yet more State control of the economy is an ideological question as much as a practical one. Certainly, many leaders of French private industry today are increasingly indignant at what they see as creeping State advances. If this spurs them to make their own firms more efficient, something will have been achieved.

The greatest hazard of State control, at least under a régime such as de Gaulle's, is the one that constantly asserts itself: the confusing of national prestige with more pragmatic motives. Of course pride in achievement is always a legitimate spur to progress, and in any country there is bound to be a national element in this pride. This is the spirit in which the Caravelle was born, and the great dams along the Rhône, and many other valuable post-war successes, not forgetting the tapestries of Aubusson. But in other cases, the choice of priority is more contestable. The liner *France*, the Concorde, the Rance tidal dam, the attempt to 'do a Mattei' in the oil industry, the promoting of SECAM colour TV against weightier support for the German PAL, some aspects of the nuclear and space programmes, all these are undoubtedly worthwhile projects, but possibly time will show some of them to have been an unwise extravagance.

CHAPTER IV

THE YOUNG FARMERS' REVOLT

FRENCH AGRICULTURE TODAY is an absorbing human drama, not merely a technical affair of subsidies and fertilisers. Nowhere else in the life of the nation are the human conflicts between change and tradition more acute, or more revealing of post-war France as a whole. An old peasant society is dying; and a new, surprisingly energetic one of modern-minded young farmers is painfully taking its place.

The delayed industrial revolution in France has provoked sudden transformations that in Britain or Germany were spread gently over several decades. The vast and static community of small farmers, once a source of stability to France, is suddenly an anachronism and a burden. Industrial wages and prices have risen far more sharply than food prices, so the farmers are more bitterly aware than before of their own poverty. Mechanisation of the farms has made economic nonsense of the huge agricultural population, and since the war about one-third of it (three million people) have moved to the towns where life is easier and labour short. Of those who remain on the small farms, many of the older ones are sunk as deep as ever in their seclusion and fear of progress; they are the pariahs of the nation, rather than the paragons of an idyllic and simple life. But a strange thing has happened: a new generation of young farmers, with a totally different outlook from their parents, has arisen, not from the rich estates of the northern plains but from the desolate smallholdings of the south and west. They have promoted a new creed of modernisation and technical progress, and are forming themselves into producer groups and co-operatives. They have seized from their elders most of the key posts in the farmers' unions and pressure groups; and they have even impressed some of their ideas on the Ministry of Agriculture. Whereas in industry this kind of impetus has come above all from official technocrats, on the land much of it has come from the farmers themselves. They have already done something to break down the old idea of *les paysans** as an isolated social class, and to bring the small farmers closer into the community. Even cautious scholars have described their movement as a 'revolution'. This chapter is largely the story of their struggle: of how they are trying to pull peasant farming, in one generation, from the Middle Ages to the point where it can profit from the new competitive outlets of the Common Market and meet the consumer needs of a modern urban society.

THE JACISTS, PISANI, AND THE ARTICHOKE WARS

France is the richest agricultural nation in Western Europe, and also one of the poorest. Blessed by her climate, by a fertile soil and plenty of space, her output is far greater than any of her neighbours'; yet the standards of her subsistence farming would be unthinkable in Britain, Holland, or Denmark. For in France there are two agricultures, as it is often said. On the one hand, the big wheat and cattle farms of the Paris basin and the north-east plains, which for some decades have been as modern and rich as any in Europe; on the other, the small farms of much of the rest of the country, poorest of all in the Massif Central, the extreme south-west, and most of Brittany. The pattern is diverse, varying by region and produce, and this makes it hard to generalise even about the poorer areas. In Brittany and the Vendée, for instance, there are still far too many people on the land, and few local industries to draw them away; yet in parts of the Massif Central the rural exodus is nearing its safe limits, with barely enough young people left to replace the old when they retire. The small but flourishing fruit and vegetable plantations of north Finistère and the lower Rhône Valley contrast sharply with the larger but more barren farms of upland areas, often wasting their resources on uneconomic mixed farming.

The laws of equal inheritance, dating from Napoleon and earlier, have been one main cause of the small size of farms. Even until recent years, so great was the peasant's suspicion of town and factory that a son would stay tamely to receive his share of his father's land rather than seek his fortune elsewhere. Today, the laws are still valid, but the sons move away more readily. Farms have gradually been growing larger. The average size has almost doubled since 1882, while the total number has dropped in the same period from 3·5 to under two million, but most are still too small to make economic sense under modern conditions. Four-fifths of all farms have less than fifty acres, and of these the average is under twenty acres. Yet in the United States, anything less than 200 acres is often considered unprofitable.

---

* The word *paysan* denotes the whole social class of poorer people who earn their living from the land, whether as farmers or labourers. It is a less archaic and pejorative term than 'peasant'. 'Countryman' might be a fairer translation.

Before the war, all but a small sector of agriculture lay sunk in a kind of lethargy and fatalism. The gulf between the peasant and the new industrial workers in the towns grew steadily wider; *paysantisme* was more than a profession, it was a way of life, a doctrine that nothing could or should disturb 'the eternal order of the fields'. The notorious 1892 reforms of Jules Méline, then Minister of Agriculture, had pushed up high tariff walls round France to protect the farmers from outside storms—but they simply caused stagnation. Later Governments then followed the Méline line. Agriculture was bolstered at the expense of industry, with tax relief and subsidies, so that the farmers could at least make a living. But it did not stop their discontent. In the 1930s the peasant world, hitherto dispersed and inarticulate, began for the first time to produce vocal leaders from its own ranks, mainly reactionary figures like the sinister Henri Dorgères and his 'greenshirts'. The Popular Front Government of 1936–8 realised that these were symptoms of a genuine *malaise* and helpless poverty, and so it drew up some imaginative reforms to encourage the farmers to modernise; but few were ever applied.

It was not until that weird interregnum, the Vichy period, that the stalemate really began to be broken. In agriculture, the influence of Vichy is a subject of some controversy. Led by Pétain himself, a man from a peasant family, Vichy promoted a massive 'back to the land' movement, and tried to set up a regionalised 'corporatist' structure, with the peasants forming a kind of state-within-the-State. This, by modern thinking, is pure fascism, and it had some parallels in Italy and Germany at that time; and yet in its French context it may have done some good. The system had not in practice got very far by the time Vichy ended, and the local farmers' syndicates it had set up to deal with local problems were quickly swept away by the Liberation. But even Vichy's harshest critics sometimes agree that these syndicates may have helped to sow the seeds of the practical peasant collaboration and local unity that was lacking in France hitherto and is developing, in a different way, today.

When peace came the immediate task, as in industry, was physical reconstruction. In 1945 food production was down to half its pre-war level, due to the fighting and especially to the mass deportations to Germany. The First Plan made farm machinery its top priority outside industry, and the results were striking. The number of tractors rose from 35,000 or so in 1938–45 to 230,000 by 1954, and farmers were encouraged by law to form State-aided groups for the joint buying and use of machinery. Productivity rose rapidly, and output was soon well above its pre-war level. At the same time, the much-needed rural exodus was gathering pace. It began to look as if French small farming might make some progress at last. But after about 1948 the real danger emerged: rapid industrial growth and its attendant inflation hit the farmer badly, for food prices did not keep pace. By 1950 industrial prices had risen 50 per cent higher than agricultural ones, compared with their pre-war level; by 1959, the disparity in growth was more than three to one. Yet for much of their spending, for fertilisers and machinery as well as clothes and household goods, farmers had to pay industrial prices out of a rural income. It is true that, thanks to much higher productivity, the farmers' overall standard of living did show a 25 per cent rise between 1938 and 1958. But this was most unevenly shared. In 1958, at least half the peasantry was still barely above the bread-line.

The 1950s were marked by continual rural protests and disturbances, with tractors barring the main roads. The leaders were Right-wing dema-gogues of the old school, men like Dorgères in Brittany and Paul Antier from the Massif Central. They demanded the remedy of higher price-supports and other forms of direct aid, but were utterly opposed to the real, more drastic solution of changing the structure of the small farms. Here the old peasant leaders found alliance with the rich farmers of the Paris basin who controlled the main union, the Fédération Nationale de Syndicats des Exploitants Agricoles (FNSEA). Together they formed a powerful lobby in Parliament: Antier was Minister of Agriculture himself in 1956. And so until its death in 1958 the Fourth Republic gave them what they asked for: price supports, based on a sliding scale that pegged food prices to rises in industrial ones. The farmers welcomed this system, but it helped the big well-organised farms more than the small ones, unable to compete with the chaotic system of marketing. Discontent went on, reaching a peak of violence in 1957. There were tractor blocks, the angry slogans, the mild stoppages, the burning of surplus crops, the wild-mouthed demagogues—inevitably these gave French townsfolk, as well as foreigners, a picture of the French farmer as a comic and ignorant anarchist, always complaining, his head firmly in the sand. Yet his plight was genuine, even if partly his own fault. It was time for a new outlook, and new leadership.

And it came. All this time the new young radicals were quietly mar-shalling their forces in the background. By about 1957, they began to make their presence felt. It was not a haphazard movement. Like so many of the progressive influences in post-war France, it was rooted in militant Leftish Catholicism: nearly all the young leaders came from the Jeunesse Agricole Chrétienne.

The JAC youth movement had been started by the priesthood in 1929. Its aim was to combat the spread of atheism, at an epoch when the conflict in rural France between clergy and Marxists was at its height. In the 1930s, village priests ran the local JAC branches and devoted them to prayer and Bible meetings, with a little social activity on the side. But during the war the JAC took on a different tone, more secular, but no less serious. Among the very young sons of small farmers, mostly still in their teens, there occurred one of those strange psychological changes that seem to have marked the destiny of France at that time. The danger and responsibility of their wartime activities, often in the Resistance, gave them an early maturity and seriousness. Many of them began to ponder deeply on how they could avoid a life of certain hardship and poverty, short of leaving the soil which they felt was their home. Some, deported to Germany, saw there the example of small farms that *could* be run on modern lines. But how could it be done in France?

From about 1942, little groups began to form to plan the future. The JAC's secretary-general, René Colson, an inspired young peasant from the Haute-Marne, toured the country organising meetings and firing other young peasants with his ideals. The initiative in the JAC was now out of the hands of the priests, and the accent was on learning economics, self-help, and sharing of labour. A liberal-minded priest from the Aveyron department, in the south of the Massif Central, has told me: 'Young boys who had left school at twelve or so were thinking and deciding for themselves—it was amazing, and quite new in France. The war had produced a surge of independence, both from family and from priests. The role of the priests in the JAC now changed—instead of a didactic leader, he became an equal. Most priests, of course, resented this. But for me, it was an eye-opener to meet these uneducated young Jacists who yet had far more calibre and more *sérieux* than my most gifted *lycée* pupils of the same age. They were determined to cure their sense of inferiority and make themselves articulate. One boy round here taught himself public speaking by treating his cows as an audience; another, a very rough type, kept his beret on at meetings so he could be forced to make a speech as a penalty. That was how he cured his shyness.'

One aim of the JAC in the early post-war years was to give its members something of the general culture they had missed through leaving school so young. A Breton farmer has described how the JAC 'changed his life' by introducing him to art and history, by widening his horizons outside the brutish world of the farm, and giving him some hope that the peasants *could* improve their lot. The JAC organised amateur theatricals, singing contests, and sports, for there were few cars and no television in those days, and young peasants had to find their own ways of fighting loneliness and boredom. The JAC's most important work, however, was professional. Local groups set about studying modern accountancy and the latest farming techniques—all much neglected by the older peasant generation. But the Jacists soon found that to apply these new ideas in practice was not so easy. On most farms the way was blocked by fathers who would have nothing of new methods and in many cases even tried to stop their sons leaving home in the evenings to study. In this patriarchal society the conflict of generations grew acute, and many Jacists saw little hope save to wait maybe ten or twenty years for father to retire. But the JAC was well organised nationally, with central committees and a newspaper; a rally in Paris in 1950 drew 70,000 members. The next step, so it seemed by the mid 'fifties, must be to carry their campaign into national farming politics and press for reforms of the whole structure of agriculture.

This was especially the view of Michel Debatisse, who took over the leadership of the JAC soon after Colson's early death in 1951. Debatisse, today one of the most influential farmers in all France, was typical of the

JAC of those days. He was born in 1929 in the village of Palladuc, in Auvergne, near the cutlery town of Thiers. His parents had a thirty-five-acre farm on a hill, where the soil was almost as thin as the wooded land-scape was lovely. The few dairy cows, poultry, and vegetables barely gave them a living; and in winter the family would sit round a stove in a little workshop behind the austere farmhouse, fitting handles on to knives for a firm in Thiers. Michel grew up without toys or much comfort, though he was lucky that this was one of the 25 per cent of French farms that had running water. He left school at thirteen and joined the JAC. Soon he was running a local drama group, touring the villages by bicycle on summer evenings. He was a squat, thin, badly dressed youth, but his ugly face had—and has—a fierce kind of strength, and he rapidly began to develop wider ambitions. There was little he could do, so he felt, in Palladuc, but he saw that in Paris no-one was really trying to help the small farmers constructively. He began to write articles for the JAC paper, and by 1950 was in Paris part of each week, editing it.

By about 1955 Debatisse and his friends were reaching the age when people generally leave the JAC and settle down to raising a family of their own and running a farm. Yet they felt that their campaign had hardly begun. Where could they carry it next? The main union, the FNSEA, was in the hands of much older and richer farmers from the north, and seemed hardly likely to welcome them. But the FNSEA had a moribund youth section, which the Jacists saw as a stepping-stone. When they made some innocent proposals for reviving it, the FNSEA leaders saw no objection, little suspecting what a Trojan horse they were letting in. So in 1957 the Debatisse faction took over the key posts of the Centre National des Jeunes Agriculteurs (CNJA) and began to use it as a militant and vocal pressure group. As a first step towards breaking down the isolation of the peasant, joint meetings were held with industrial workers' unions; a most unusual step in France. Debatisse toured the country, stirring up the support of young farmers, Marxist and Christian alike: though a practising Catholic, he was no sectarian when it came to farming. Other CNJA leaders were despatched to glean the latest ideas and techniques from Kansas, Denmark, or the Ukraine; today, it is rare to meet a member of that team who is not widely travelled.

The FNSEA leaders viewed all this activity with a cool suspicion, but made little move to expel the rebels. Meanwhile, and most significantly for the future, the CNJA began to form new links with the Plan and with the young technocrats who came to power with de Gaulle in 1958. Immediately they discovered a similarity of language and interest. Planners and civil servants began to consult the CNJA on what to do about farming; and Debatisse was elected one of the youngest-ever members of the Government's Economic and Social Council. The breakthrough was beginning.

Debatisse and his friends proposed that Government policy be switched from price supports to investment and structural reform. Above all, they questioned the hitherto sacred rights of property ownership, which they saw as a strait-jacket round French farming: they wanted drastic measures to persuade older farmers to retire, to take land away from unproductive hands and give it to new tenant farmers working in groups. They were still basically in favour of the family farm, as opposed to industrial-scale farming, but they saw that it must change its nature. And whereas many of the older FNSEA leaders still clung to the pre-war Mélinian doctrine that the rural exodus was a grave social danger, the CNJA saw it as necessary and good, but asked simply that it be 'humanised' to avoid distress.

The new Gaullist régime soon ran into trouble with the older and richer farmers. The Rueff financial reforms of December 1958 had stripped away many of the precious price supports, including the sliding scale. Rural discontent again grew, this time embracing even the rich farmers of the north, who were hit by the new measures: the Amiens riot of February 1960, where more than one hundred police and farmers were injured, was once of the worst since the war. But the Gaullists did not placate the old guard as the Fourth Republic had done. Michel Debré, the reform-minded Prime Minister, had an ear for the CNJA's ideas: he drew up a *loi d'orientation* partly inspired by them, and in the summer of 1960 narrowly succeeded in pushing it through Parliament, despite active opposition from the FNSEA and its allies. Above all, this law proposed a new Government agency to buy up and redistribute land; a modified form of what the CNJA wanted. For the first time, a French Government committed itself to tackling the question of farming structures, and turned its back on the heritage of Méline.

But the orientation law was no more than an outline of principle, and the Government proved very slow in applying the decrees that would put it into force. The CNJA began to suspect sabotage by Ministry officials in league with the FNSEA. The Young Farmers' rising irritation suddenly reached flashpoint at the end of May 1961, when a seasonal glut knocked the bottom out of the potato and vegetable markets in western Brittany. At Pont l'Abbé on 27 May farmers set fire to ballot-boxes in local elections and filled the streets with tons of potatoes sprayed with petrol. Then at Morlaix, a market town in north Finistère, 4,000 young farmers invaded the streets with their tractors at dawn on 8 June, seized the sub-prefecture in protest, and held it for several hours. This was the epoch of *putsches* in Algiers, and the newspapers delightedly drew the parallel. But these farmers were not terrorists: they were relatively prosperous growers of artichokes and other early vegetables, in the rich coastal plain between Morlaix and St.-Pol-de-Léon. When their two leaders, Alexis Gourvennec and Marcel Léon, were arrested by the police, sympathy riots spread throughout the west. Down as far as the Pyrenees and and Languedoc, roadblocks and banners were out in force. It was the largest and most effective peasant manifestation in post-war France, and it marked a decisive turning-point.

For the first time, French farmers were demonstrating *for* progress, instead of against it. For the first time the riots were led and organised by the new leaders, not by the old demagogues. '*L'Agriculture de Papa est morte*' read the triumphant banners in the streets of Morlaix. Gourvennec, an ex-Jacist, was only twenty-four; an arrogant, well-spoken young man with something of the looks of Gérard Philipe. He and his fellow-Bretons were protesting at the marketing system, and not for the first time: the previous year, in a rather less violent version of their famous 'artichoke wars', they had sent lorry-loads of artichokes straight to Paris to sell on the streets, after the Breton middlemen had refused them a fair price. The growers were furious because the Government had continually urged them to produce more, and yet had done nothing to reform the archaic marketing system, so that prices always collapsed in a good season. Gourvennec and the farmers of his region were highly organised and far from poor; their actual problems were rather different from those of a region like Debatisse's. But both types of young farmer shared the same dynamism and the same reforming zeal, whether the reforms they needed most were of markets or of land.

The Government responded quickly after the Morlaix affair. Gourvennec had friends in the Ministry, and it is often alleged that some of them had secretly advised him to stage the riot in order to get things moving! In August, de Gaulle dismissed the Minister of Agriculture, Henri Rochereau, a mild liberal-conservative of the old school, and replaced him with the most forceful and modern-minded figure to have filled that post in this century.

Edgard Pisani, tall, black-bearded, eloquent and flamboyant, looks something like a cross between Ustinov and Svengali. He is an ex-prefect, and very much in the new 'technocratic' mould. During his four-and-a-half years (1961–6) in the usually unwanted job of Minister of Agriculture he showed a greater understanding of the farmers' real needs than any of his predecessors. He is an ambitious man, too, and was determined to leave his mark on the scene. He at once drew up a *loi complémentaire* of decrees to activate the 1960 law, and got them approved. This Pisani Law, as it is called, established a new pension fund to encourage old farmers to retire; an agency for buying land (already outlined in the earlier law); stricter rules against absentee landlords; and measures to encourage farmers to form into groups both for marketing and for shared production. There have been a few other innovations since then (notably, in 1961, the wider extension of health insurance and social allowances to farmers), but in essence the Pisani Law is still the basis of Government policy for farming. It has often been described as the boldest and most realistic step yet taken to reform French agriculture. But in practice its application has been slow because of lack of funds and bureaucratic delays, some of them, possibly, deliberate.

The Pisani Law marked a victory for the Young Farmers, who rapidly began to infiltrate the FNSEA council itself through departmental elections. By 1961 they were so strong that one of their numbers, Marcel Bruel, a young cattle breeder from the Aveyron, was elected secretary-general of the FNSEA. Today the new leaders share the power evenly in the Federation with the big northern farmers, and the old-style peasant demagogues are everywhere falling away. But if Debatisse and his friends have won a political battle in Paris, they have not yet won the war in the fields. There is a new mood today in French farming; but, inevitably, the old structures are giving place more slowly.

SLOW DEATH OF THE PEASANT

The campaign for agriculture is being fought on two separate fronts: to modernise the farms, and to modernise the marketing system. It is no use doing the one without the other. That is why progress in one sector is often frustrated by the problems of the other. It is no good increasing productivity if the markets cannot cope with it and prices collapse; it is no good providing modern markets if the farms are too inefficient to supply them adequately.

So far, it is down on the farms themselves, rather than in the markets, that progress has been the more effective. Everywhere the old order is steadily being swept aside by new men and ideas. And some of the outward contrasts in this age of transition are striking enough to the casual visitor. In a Brittany farm kitchen a huge TV set stands by the ancient open fireplace, but there is no running water; near Avignon, one son in a farmer's family hoes potatoes while his brother goes to work at the near-by plutonium factory; in the chalky uplands of the Aveyron, an old man vacantly minds the cows while his son brings home fertiliser in a smart new Simca. Techniques and home comforts are slowly improving, from a very low level; and for good or ill the peasant's life is becoming 'urbanised', as it already is more or less completely in Britain. But the deeper changes, and the obstacles to change, are psychological. What is at stake is the peasant's rooted individualism, and his emotional attachment to his own piece of land.

Believing this to be the greatest barrier to progress, the new farm leaders have made land ownership reform the centre of their policy. They want the land to be a common tool or resource, not a property. This, in France, is a highly complex problem. Until the end of the last war the feudal tradition of land property was strong. Some small farmers clung proudly to their own ancestral acres, but many others worked on a system of *métayage*, paying their landlords a tithe, usually half their produce. Often the landlord was the all-powerful local *châtelain*, and his *métayers* were little more then serfs. If one of them gave offence, maybe by not going to Mass enough or hinting Left-wing views, he risked eviction. One of the keenest of the new ex-Jacist leaders, Bernard Lambert, who has a small farm in a very feudal area near Nantes, spoke to me with bitterness of the pre-war days: 'My father was *métayer*, and would always lift his cap to the *châtelain* and call him "*Monsieur notre maître*". Once, when my father won a radio in a raffle, the landlord confiscated it because we were in debt. No wonder there are so many Communists among farmers!'

A Socialist law in 1946 replaced the *métayage* system with a tenancy statute (*statut de fermage*) which gave much greater security from eviction and put a normal annual rent in place of the tithe. This is in force today: *métayage* has almost disappeared except in parts of the south-west. But the *statut de fermage* has created new problems. In some areas it is not applied fairly, because the tribunals are on the side of the landlords and the tenant gets victimised. In many other cases it works to the tenant's disadvantage in a quite different way. Because rents are fixed very low (they vary according to produce but average, say, forty to sixty francs per acre a year), the landlord has little incentive to keep the farms in repair or make improvements. Many farm houses are half in ruins, which harms efficiency and helps to drive the young into the towns. Lambert told me: 'I've spent 110,000 francs on new cowsheds and other improvements here, which I vitally needed but my landlord wouldn't pay for. Yet, if he chucks me out, they belong to him.' Others are luckier. In the Aveyron, I met a young man who had rented his farm from a friend, but had first made it a condition that the friend should provide new buildings.

Despite the drawbacks of the statute, most young farmers prefer to be tenants, not owners: land prices have been rising fast, and they would rather sink their limited capital into livestock and modern machinery. Probably more than half of all French farm land is rented. But many of the older farmers cling tenaciously to the idea of property. And despite the low rents, land is still considered a good investment by many non-farmers too, city speculators and others, who will snap up any good estate that comes on the market. For a variety of reasons an ambitious young farmer usually finds it extremely hard to acquire new land, whether for rent or sale, if he wants to enlarge his farm to an economic size.

So the central innovation of the Pisani Law, directly prompted by the Young Farmers, was to set up *Sociétés d'Aménagement Foncier et d'Etablissement Rural* (SAFERs): regional agencies with powers to buy up land as it comes on the market, make improvements on it, and then resell it to the most deserving, who are usually young farmers wanting to make good use of modern techniques. The SAFERs also have some rights of pre-emption, at fixed prices, thus acting as a curb on speculation. If a farmer wants to sell a plot of land, say, for 10,000 francs to a speculator, the local SAFER can step in, offer maybe 8,000 francs, and have the matter settled by an independent court.

This was hailed as the biggest blow ever struck in France against the sacred rights of property. In practice it has worked slowly so far. The SAFERs' funds are small, probably less than a seventh of what is needed. Pisani wanted more, but the Ministry of Finance said no—a typical example of a bold Gaullist structural reform spoiled by official cheeseparing. The SAFERs have also been impeded by the usual French legal delays, sometimes of up to five years for each transaction. And their powers of pre-emption are so hedged with limitations (due to concessions negotiated by the old guard of the FNSEA) that much of the most-needed land eludes their grasp. But the principle is clearly a good one, and it will probably work well in time, as the SAFERs funds increase. Success varies by region: it is poor in Brittany, but better in the Massif Central, where I was shown several useful SAFER operations.

Another grave land problem is the parcellisation of the soil, and French Governments have been trying to solve this since 1940. Fly over many parts of France, and you will see a crazy quilt of thin strips; quite a modest farmer may often have ten or twenty different little fields, not next to each other but scattered over miles. This is partly a result of the equal inheritance laws, as farms were split up between sons and then the parcels changed hands. And it often makes modern mechanised farming extremely difficult.

The policy of *remembrement*—literally, the piecing together of limbs—was initiated by Vichy and has continued ever since. By subsidising up to 80 per cent of the legal, surveying, and field costs, the Government tries to entice farmers to make rational swaps of their fields. The results have been variable: far better among the big, go-ahead farms of the north than in the sluggish south. After a long resistance to *remembrement*, farmers in some areas are now coming to accept it more easily; in fact, in some places, the policy is now held up by shortage of official funds rather than by lack of local co-operation. Even so, in the small-farm districts the process of educating the peasants to make this kind of change can still be a long and arduous one. Nowhere else does the conservatism of the older peasants show itself more keenly, or their emotional attachment to the soil show a worse side. A farmer may eventually accept the idea in theory; but when the work actually starts, he will be struck with senti-mental horror, and refuse to give up the field where his father taught him to plough, or the apple tree his grandmother planted—even if he is offered as good in return, and his costs are covered!

In the Aveyron, a poorish, upland department of small livestock and potato farms, *remembrement* was the main issue in the 1965 local elections. Several village councils that had earlier decided to go ahead with it were thrown out by the older voters. The commune of Privezac provided a *cause célèbre*. In 1963, it had voted 90 per cent for *remembrement*. So surveyors arrived and drew up a plan. Then there were protests. The village split into two clans, but *across* the traditional rural lines of Reds against Whites, teachers against priests. In the pro-*remembrement* camp, the young Catholic Jacists were led by the Socialist mayor, an ex-teacher. Against them were the older farmers led by the deputy mayor, a Catholic ex-officer. When Government officials came to inspect the crisis, the police had to protect them. And when bulldozers arrived to tear down hedges and start the regrouping, the old guard charged them on tractors and tore up the surveyors' markers. Several people were arrested, and the *remembrement* finally went ahead. Later the old guard got their revenge and toppled the mayor in the 1965 elections. Even so, the *remembrement* was not undone. Some million francs had been invested in it; and, as in other such cases, the Government swiftly applied some effective blackmail, threatening to cut off all sorts of State aid from Privezac if there was any backsliding!

One young, local farmer told me: 'I'm sure that in three years everyone in Privezac will be delighted with the results—it will be a test case round here, a showpiece. It's simply a question of breaking down old habits. Often, too, the conflicts are the fault of the officials, who reshuffle the land without tact. The job needs psychologists, as much as surveyors.' And not all the young guard are so in favour of the policy. 'Is it worth raising fire and blood in a commune just for this?' said one. 'Better, surely, to get rid of the surplus farmers first, and then regroup. After all, *remembrement* doesn't in itself make farms any bigger.'

Yet, in many areas, it has been helping to make farms more efficient and to create a more flexible rural society, less obsessively attached to its *petits coins*. And the farms *are* getting bigger, too, which is more important. In one typical Aveyron commune, their number has halved since 1911, as people sell out to their neighbours, or drift away. But the Young Farmers reckon that only one farm in twenty is large enough to be viable today. It is partly a question of waiting for the old generation to die: half of all French farmers are over fifty-five. They block not only land redistribution, but also the kind of inter-farm sharing of work and equipment that alone, as the young realise, can enable the small farm to survive. The conflict of generations within families is often bitter, and in many cases is made worse when cohabitation with in-laws is enforced by sheer lack of housing, or by the pressures of tradition. Realising this, the Pisani Law set up a fund to help old farmers retire. But its scope is modest. The pension it allows is rarely more than £150 a year, and often there is nowhere to retire to.

In the Aveyron, a hardy region that furnished the JAC with many of its best leaders, several of the most dynamic ones now seem to have persuaded their fathers to retire. Down a muddy track near the department's main town of Rodez, I went to call on a former president of the JAC, Raymond Lacombe: the man who had once kept his beret on at meetings so as to be forced to make speeches! He is a tough little man of thirty-six with coarse peasant features but a mind sharp as flint; his wife is better spoken than he and comes from the Ardennes, finds the Massif Central a bit lonely; three kids are playing on the floor; the modern farm kitchen is spotless but there are no luxuries. Lacombe said: 'I was my father's tenant till last year; now he's retired and just looks after the animals a bit. We built this house for ourselves, so we don't have to share. We're luckier than most. I've got forty acres, with cows, pigs, corn, and

barley. I've raised money to buy a tractor and I share other equipment
with friends; father wouldn't have done that. Recently I've bought a
piggery and our net income's doubled. But costs rise so fast that forty acres
isn't viable the way it used to be. If I could, I might get out, though I
love this place. On twelve farms round here, there are only four young
people left.'

It is the same story nearly everywhere in France. In Lacombe's commune the population has dropped since 1911 from 717 to 426; it could
safely lose another 200 without economic stress if the farms were fully
modernised. In many places the exodus is even more striking: in the
centre of Brittany I met a couple *all ten* of whose children had left. Less
than 18 per cent of the French now work on the land, against 35 per cent
before the war.

It is usually the girls who leave first. More than the actual discomfort,
they hate the isolation, the drudgery and sense of inferiority, and they
rarely want to marry a farmer, even a prosperous one. Then the boys
go too, in search of wives and a decent living, or because they are deprived
of all responsibility on the farm so long as father is in charge. In one recent
national survey of fifteen-to-twenty-nine-year-olds still on the land, half
the boys and three-quarters of the girls intended to leave. In the old days
they stayed out of duty or tradition; today, if they stay it is by choice.
Some men remain on alone through apathy, habit, or a kind of vocation: in
many isolated country districts the proportion of bachelor farmers is
frighteningly high, and their life must be lonely and narrow beyond
belief.

The nearest industrial town is the usual venue for the émigrés; or,
in many cases, Paris. There are more Aveyronnais in Paris than in the
Aveyron. Until recently parents often tried to stop their children from
going, and regarded the towns as wicked and corrupting. But this has
changed. Too many children have come home on visits obviously un-
corrupted and happier. And TV and other modern changes have broken
down much of the old suspicion between farm and town. One Breton
farmer with three sons told me: 'It would be nice if one of them felt he'd
like to stay, but I certainly shan't stop them going. It's really up to me,
isn't it, to make my farm attractive and viable for them to want to take
it over.'

At the same time, the older political demagogues have dropped their
Mélinian hatred of the exodus as some sinister trick of enforced deporta-
tion, and have come to see its necessity. If all farms were large and modern
enough, the farming population could well drop to 10 per cent or less (in
Britain it is 4 per cent; in the U.S., 8) without any fall in output, and this
is precisely what the Plan is working towards. It is a question of controlling
the exodus. In very few areas has it yet reached its reasonable limits; in
the Aveyron many farms are without successors, but when they fall
vacant they always find ready buyers among other farmers.

The real problem is to ensure that it is not simply the dullards who stay behind, and that enough young people of calibre remain as active farmers to carry through the modernising process efficiently. Debatisse and his friends see clearly that it is therefore essential to make rural life more attractive and varied, with more comfort, culture, education, and social stimulus.

At this point in time the French rural world, as in many Western countries, is in a bleak period of mutation between two cultures—the old folk culture, passing away, and a new modern one not yet properly installed. In the old days there was great poverty, but also a certain warmth and tradition that helped make it bearable. Many of the older people today speak of those times with feeling. In Breton moorland farmsteads young people drew round the fire on winter evenings to hear wise old women reciting Celtic legends. Auvergne had a whole world of traditional dances and music. In the Aveyron, and many other parts, there were *veillées*, where neighbours would gather in one farm to weave baskets or shred maize, and make it the excuse for a good party. And then, the harvests! In Auvergne, a farmer told me: 'When I was a boy, at harvest-time, the seasonal labourers would come up by hundreds from Clermont-Ferrand and every night in the village hall there'd be gay parties and dances. Today the work's done by two men with a combine-harvester, and the labourers work in the new Clermont factories and go to the movies.'

Today, folk culture rarely means more than putting on costumes for an annual fête to please the tourists. Even the J A C's music and drama activities of the post-1944 period have declined: the young have left the farms, or prefer to go off to the towns on their motor-scooters in the evenings. And the modern world is taking the place of the old culture, as the TV aerials sprout above the cow-byres. Some farms, where electricity is just arriving, have moved in one step from oil-lamps to the electronic age, as a TV set may be the first gadget they buy. Certainly, modern comforts and amenities are spreading: it is quite usual to see a huge new electric cooker in the kitchen of a shabby and crumbling farmhouse. Over 40 per cent of farmers have cars; often they are those charmingly ugly two-horse Citroëns that bounce so readily down any rutty track. And even health insurance and welfare allowances now embrace peasants almost as completely as industrial workers.

But the lag behind living standards in the cities, or on farms in a country like Britain, is still great. Few small farmers yet feel they can go away for an annual holiday (maybe there is no-one else to milk the cows) and many older farmhouses are in a terrible state of repair. In isolated areas there is often a serious lack of public services, too. Though the percentage of farms with running water has doubled since Debatisse's childhood, Lacombe told me: 'We're not on the mains and our well is too small. When it froze last winter, I had to fetch water with my tractor every day from a spring 400 yards away. It was tough. Many farmers round here can't build modern piggeries simply because they've got no

water. Most of them do have electricity now, but it's hard to get a telephone laid on if you want one.'

The cultural hiatus, too, means that while the peasants have lost the
old art of enriching their own lives, they often seem to be waiting for
others to bring them new commercial entertainment. One Aveyron
farmer's wife told me: 'Before the war, the families here would group
together in the evenings for *entr'aide* work-parties. Now there's just a
cinema in the near-by town, and far less real social life.' When someone
does open a local dance-hall (as a shopkeeper has done in Lacombe's village) it is usually a great success, but such initiatives are rare. Eager
people like Lacombe do what they can: he has even drawn up a project
for a new social centre in his nearest large village, with library, lecture-
rooms, etc., and he has had it scheduled in the regional section of the
Fifth Plan. But there are not so many Lacombes, and they have other
duties, too. What the countryside badly needs, and lacks, are professional
'animateurs culturels'. Early efforts after the war to build *foyers ruraux*
(village social and cultural centres) were not very successful. The present
Government has a plan to revive the idea, on a large scale; but there is the
usual shortage of funds.

It is in education that the farmer feels his isolation and inferiority
most keenly. In theory, every village child has exactly the same State
education as the most privileged Parisian. In practice, it is not quite like
that. In thinly populated areas, many children still have to walk six or
eight miles each day, and it is hardly surprising that many of them even
fail to finish their primary schooling. A Government system of *ramassage
scolaire* has started recently in some places, with buses collecting children
for school from lonely farms; but it lacks funds. Moreover, isolated schools
often have only one single class spanning the whole age-range, and this
holds back the brightest. And the teachers tend to be the dregs of their
profession. Not until rural education improves will many of the brighter
young couples feel like staying to bring up a family on the farm.

In higher and technical education, however, there have been great
strides forward. Hundreds of full or part-time agricultural colleges and
evening institutes have been opened in recent years, and France's lag
behind Germany or Holland in this field is not as great as it was. The
pressure on the Government for these has come, once again, from the
Young Farmers, who will often also form their own technical study
groups and hire specialists to come and teach them. Some of the pioneering work is rather touching: a Young Farmer's wife in the Aveyron told
me of her patient efforts to get a group of ill-educated wives in her commune to study modern techniques of farm management and accounting,
tasks that are traditionally left to the women on small farms.

In putting an accent on technical expertise, and the sharing of effort
and equipment, the younger generation realise that it may be the only
way to save the family farm. Mechanisation has spread rapidly since the
war, with tractor numbers rising today to over a million. It is true that

often the tractors have been badly used, especially by older farmers, who tend to buy them proudly as a status symbol without having large enough fields or the right know-how. A man accustomed all his life to an instinctive *rapport* with oxen or horses will often be unable to run a machine. It breaks down, or incurs heavy running costs, and the farmer grows bitter that his panacea has failed him. This was certainly one factor behind the old guard's riots and protests in the 1950s.

The younger ones have generally gone about things more intelligently. In Normandy, a Young Farmers' leader with a 300-acre cattle and wheat farm, told me: 'We formed a group of twenty-two farmers, and bought a silage machine, harvesting equipment, and several tractors in common. We share all costs. It's quite an accepted way of working now, but nearly all of us are young. You'll rarely get the old doing this.' Debatisse himself has formed a successful association with two other farmers at Palladuc.

This kind of group farming is entirely new in France, and cuts across deeply ingrained habits of individualism. More than 1,000 such groups have been formed privately, and in 1964 they were endorsed by a Government decree granting financial aid to encourage others. Besides helping with costly mechanisation, the groups bring other advantages too. Salaried labourers are scarce today, most of them preferring to work in factories; so the groups can provide a pooling of labour for many jobs, and especially the chance of a rota system for milking and minding livestock. This gives the farmer the possibility of taking a weekend off, or even a holiday The groups also facilitate specialisation of produce, increasingly necessary in the new context of the Common Market. Above all, they enable farm units to grow larger and more viable without destroying their family-farm basis or the individual's responsibility.

Some groups have failed and split up, in the Aveyron and elsewhere, either because the older members failed to co-operate; or because the principle of shared decisions was too much for the peasant spirit; or, quite often, because the women kicked against the need for joint accounting. But in one part of this district, a group experiment is taking place that could be of some significance for the poorer regions of France At Espalion, in the lovely valley of the Lot, a middle-aged farmer called Belières has grouped some twenty small farms into a *Banque du Travail*. This carries the sharing idea a stage farther: each man-hour is set a price, according to the type of work, and if a farmer spends a morning helping a neighbour, or lends equipment, he is credited accordingly in the labour bank. At the end of the season, gains and losses are paid off, like a game of poker. It is a way of getting a group to work together without anyone feeling cheated, and its success at Espalion has led to other banks springing up elsewhere in France. Now Belières has launched a more ambitious scheme: through the local SAFER, the bank itself has bought 320 acres on an empty plateau about thirty miles away, and it plans to grow crops there. Some of the younger farmers have been persuaded to move there, and have had houses built for them in the nearest large village, eight miles from the new estate. This is a first step towards an American-type solution of the isolation problem in a motor age: the farmer lives in town and commutes by car to his fields, like a city worker. Both this and the 'bank' itself may seem simple enough notions to Anglo-Saxons or north Europeans; but they represent an unprecedented breach in the French autarchic tradition. Some Aveyron farmers are sceptical: 'Will it work? People may not be ready for this kind of thing yet. Farmers are used to living close to their fields and their animals; until recently, they tended to sleep *in* the cowsheds with them.'

Although there are bound to be difficulties of this sort, it is certain that group farming will increase. It also seems fairly certain that, within a decade or two, the Young Farmers and the Government will have largely succeeded in their aims of reforming farming structures. Whole areas will have been pulled up towards the level of the big rich farms of the north. The growth in the size of farms, *remembrement*, departure of surplus population, improvement in rural culture and comfort, technical modernisation: all this is going ahead steadily, as one generation succeeds another. This battle is half won, and the new leaders are already turning to the next one: the reform of markets, the checking of over-production, the adapting of output to the entirely new and different needs of industrial buyers.

But the Jacist revolution has not touched, and will not touch, the whole of peasant France. There are wide areas where either the soil is too poor or the people too old and backward for much progress to be made. Such areas are the stark hinterland of Brittany, and the ruggedest parts of the Massif Central, much poorer than the Aveyron pasture-lands I have described. Only a score of miles from Gourvennec's smiling coastal artichoke plains, you can find grim upland hamlets where no one is left, apart from a few old people. The Lozère (east of the Aveyron), most backward and depopulated of all French departments, is in the same predicament. Here people eke out a living from useless polyculture, that inevitable curse of so much poor-soil farming: a patch of vines for the family's own vinegary wine, a cow or two and some mangy chickens, cabbages struggling to grow on a chalky hillside. Meat is a once-a-week luxury; children, if there are any, are kept from school to help with the chores, and sleep in haylofts. The working day is sixteen hours, and a family's income may be less than £300 a year. Yet the farmer is afraid of getting loans for modern improvements, for this type of peasant fears debt above all else. In a poor part of Brittany I met an old farmer who, rather than spend money on mending the broken gates and gaps in his hedges, made his wife and children stand guard in turns all day, to stop the cattle from straying.

This particular attitude is still common, and this world can only be left to die: it is too late for it to evolve. As the more desolate areas depopulate, their future will lie with afforestation and tourism—such regions are often among the loveliest. In parts of the Massif Central, large-scale

planting of new timber forests has begun, partly under the aegis of the
State, and is providing employment for some local peasants. In Provence,
and in the Cevennes, many hill-top villages are now virtually deserted
save for the tourist trade. Here, and in other lonely regions, the Government is now creating national parks, with sports and holiday centres, and
wild-life preserves. In this vast and beautiful land of France, as productivity steadily increases in the fertile zones, there will no longer be
any need for peasants to scratch at the soil of ungrateful uplands. These
can be left, as in the United States, to the splendours of nature.

MARKETS, COMMON AND CONFUSED

Despite all the signs of progress on the farms, and despite the new ideas
and energy, French agriculture today is still in economic crisis. Farmers'
unrest broke out anew in 1964 and again in 1967, led both by the old
guard and the new. There have been strikes of meat and milk producers,
repeated demonstrations in the Midi against seasonal collapse of the fruit
markets, strong FNSEA opposition to the Government in the 1965 elections, and demonstrations in 1967 by the Breton poultry and pig breeders.
The statistics appear to give the farmers just cause: their average income
actually fell in 1964–5, and though it rose again in 1966–7, it is reckoned
to be still 30 per cent below that of industrial workers. The problem of
industrial price disparities is still unsolved; and many farmers find that
their overheads and other costs have been rising faster than their productivity. Thus, though the farms may be becoming larger and more modern,
a small farm grows yearly less viable.

Linked with this is a new and growing problem of over-production in
some sectors, which puts a strain on the antiquated marketing system.
Many young farmers have found to their dismay that to modernise and
group together is not enough; they still cannot get good enough prices for
their produce. Productivity per acre has doubled since 1949; but if it
simply leads to a glut and tumbling prices, it may seem hardly worth the
money invested. If the key problem for the small farms is still one of
structures, for the larger and more efficient ones it is markets. So the focus
today is on market reform, and how to regulate production.

The chaos of French marketing is legendary. Produce often changes
hands several times on its way from the farmer to the housewife; or it
may sometimes travel hundreds of miles from its country farm to Les
Halles in Paris, only to be shipped back for sale not far from where it
came from. Les Halles is a huge blood-sucking spiders' nest of middlemen
where vested privilege, greed, and muddle go hand in hand; and some
provincial markets are hardly any better. No wonder margins between
producer and retail prices are the highest in Europe; no wonder the
farmer finds it hard to live. Even milk generally doubles its price between

farmer and consumer; while for fruit and vegetables, in summer the margins may rise to 500 or 600 per cent.

An important aspect of the problem is that the small farmer is only just beginning to acquire any effective knowledge of marketing himself. He is therefore relatively ill equipped to stand up to the skilfully rapacious middlemen. No Government, not even de Gaulle's, has had the courage to reorganise the middlemen root and branch: their lobby is too powerful. But a few gentler reforms are under way. Modern marketing centres are being built in a number of towns; and farmers are being encouraged to form into sales groups and co-operatives to gain more control of the market. The Common Market may help, by harmonising European prices and giving the French farmer new outlets; but it is unlikely to prove the panacea he has tended to think it will be.

The complexities of the marketing issue vary greatly from one produce to another, and are closely linked to the problem of over-production. Poultry, meat, and milk account for 59 per cent of the value of French produce, cereals and root crops for 15 per cent, fruit and vegetables for 11 per cent, and wines for 10 per cent. The central features of this situation are firstly, under-production of meat, especially beef; and secondly seasonal gluts of fruit and some vegetables. The Government is trying to cure the former by encouraging farmers to switch from cereals to live-stock, and the latter by developing the canning industry, reforming the markets and regulating them in periods of glut, and pushing ahead with the Common Market. Neither policy has made very much progress so far. Yet, in theory, if production were well organised, France could not only satisfy her own needs but grow rich on exports. At present, her overall export surplus in foodstuffs is only about 10 per cent. In crops and animal products it is 35 per cent, but there is a big deficit in tinned and processed foods of all sorts.

The need to regulate production is seen most sharply in the conflict between wheat and meat. Wheat is one of the very few sectors where prices are fully controlled and guaranteed by a Government Board. This was set up in 1936 by the Popular Front with the aim of helping the small farmer. In practice, it has always helped the large ones rather more. Improved techniques have sent the yields shooting up since the war on the rich estates of northern France, and their prices are protected against world surpluses and dumping. The small farmer is protected, too; but he usually has neither the soil nor the techniques to profit so much. There are frequent wheat surpluses in France, and so far the Common Market has not helped to solve this problem.

Meanwhile, the new affluent society wants to eat less bread and more meat. France, land of the *biftek* and Europe's second heaviest meat eater, shares the world-wide shortage. Yet Government efforts to turn wheat farms over to meat usually fall foul of two obstacles: the extreme corruption of the meat markets, and the farmer's distaste for the servitude and financial hazards of cattle-rearing. A go-ahead young farmer in

Normandy, with a relatively large cattle *and* wheat farm, told me how the farmers feel: 'Whatever the Government may want, *I'm* stepping up my emphasis here on wheat—it pays far better. The meat market keeps on collapsing, and prices are guaranteed only at a rock-bottom level. Wheat needs less investment, and is given better loans; if you rear a calf, you have to wait three years to get your money back, and there's often the risk of disease. But the corn harvests are nearly always good. Above all, cattle demand constant attention with never a weekend off; and hired cowmen are hard to find. Farmers nowadays won't accept this any more: they want leisure like people in towns. Group farming, with rotas, will help; but it won't solve everything.'

Other farmers I talked to felt the same. The Government has now made a start at market reform, by shifting the grotesque central Paris meat market to new and more efficient premises in the suburbs (this move will be completed in 1968), and by a law setting up a national chain of new, modern slaughterhouses. These help to standardise buying and to offer the farmer reasonable prices. But what my Norman friend described as 'the *mafia* of corrupt little dealers and local butchers' is still largely in position. The small breeder, often isolated and ignorant of market conditions, tends to get cheated left, right, and centre, and middlemen make handsome profits. A bold plan for overall market reform, put forward by the FNSEA's former secretary-general, Marcel Bruel (another Aveyron ex-Jacist), came to a halt under Poujadist pressure from the middlemen.

The farmers have, however, had some success in forming themselves, with Government backing, into marketing groups, *Sociétés d'Intérêt Collectif Agricole*. The aim of these is to negotiate collectively, and so stop the dealers from always dictating the prices. They have had good results in stopping prices from tumbling in a crisis; but they have seldom put them up in better times. In the Aveyron, Lacombe told me: 'Bruel started a meat SICA here in 1962. It certainly saves us a lot of time and trouble. We don't have to go to the market individually, a SICA lorry collects our livestock and sells it for us. And the dealers don't cheat us so much any more, because the SICA is beginning to know the markets as well as they do. But the trouble is, only 20 per cent of the breeders round here will join the SICA—there's individualism for you!—and this destroys much of its effect. If, when prices start to fall, we retaliate by withholding our produce, the non-SICA people simply jump in and get better prices. The SICA *is* growing, but it's a slow process to educate the older farmers to use it. I'd gladly switch to wheat myself, but in hilly land like this we're condemned to livestock-breeding.'

If the Government is to succeed in increasing meat production significantly, it will have to take much stronger measures, or so most experts believe. Subsidies to encourage breeders, better-planned production, and improvement of strains, more State money for research and technical development (far less favoured than in the wheat industry) are all needed.

The Common Market may help, by breaking the closed-shop of French middlemen, and raising wholesale meat prices to the average level of the Six. Hitherto, the retail price of *le biftek* has always been political dynamite, and has inhibited the Government from raising it to help the farmer. But the French housewife will clearly have to get used to paying more. The whole problem is partly caused by her: for it is her notorious choosiness about cuts that leads to wastage. The Government has sometimes made efforts to widen and educate her taste, by publicity campaigns showing that the less popular cuts are also perfectly edible; but these have not been very successful.

In the fruit and vegetable sectors, too, new SICAs have played a part in buffering farmers from the effects of seasonal gluts in some areas. Soon after the 1961 artichoke war, Gourvennec formed a SICA in north Finistère and has succeeded in imposing minimum prices on local middlemen. If prices threaten to drop lower, then the SICA withholds produce. This has been tried and proved successful, several times, with artichokes and cauliflowers Never again, after 1961, have artichokes, sold in the Paris shops for 1·20 francs a kilo, earned the Breton grower a mere six centimes. Here at least, by grouping together, the farmers have won a control over their produce that they never had before, and have grown as strong as their buyers. But the men of north Finistère are exceptionally dynamic and disciplined, and Gourvennec is an unusual leader. Some even call him a fascist: he has a commando team of local thugs, some of them paratroop veterans who fought in Algeria, and several times they have wrecked lorryloads of artichoke plants about to be sold by non-SICA members to other parts of France.

It is not certain how far his example could, or should, be followed elsewhere. Down in the south of France, in the fertile, fruit-growing plains around Nîmes and Avignon, there is no Gourvennec and the problems of glut have not yet been solved so easily. Output has quadrupled in the past ten years, notably of apples, peaches, and cherries; in a good season the wholesale price of a kilo of peaches may tumble to twenty centimes while the retail figure stays at well over a franc. The farmers, furious, resorted to riots and destruction in 1963, and in 1965 to the more sophisticated practice of offering passing motorists pamphlets and free peaches. But the farmers themselves are partly to blame for the trouble. The Vaucluse peach SICA does not work properly because 80 per cent of growers are too individualistic to join it. So the SICA falls below the 25 per cent membership needed to qualify for much-prized State financial aid.

Another problem is exports: this is a big export area, yet many farmers fail to pay proper attention to the needs of foreign consumers, and are only just beginning to adapt to modern ideas of graded and standardised quality. They will still quite cheerfully offer stunted fruit for export, and then wonder why the Italians outsell them abroad. The problem of glut can probably only be solved by improvements of this sort: by more attention to group marketing, and to graded quality. In theory, the Common Market will help to absorb some French surpluses, and will kill the high Italian export aids which the Provençaux feels give their Po Valley rivals an unfair advantage. There will also need to be much more canning and processing in France: this, too, is only just starting.

High transport costs are one main reason why profit margins are so high and producer prices so low, especially for areas as far from Paris as Finistère and Provence. This is often a reason, too, why the small farmer of the centre or south-west finds it so hard to compete with the big farms of the Paris basin. Some of this may be inevitable in a country as large as France; but not all of it. The French centripetal tradition, added to the blindness and muddle of the market, means that far too great a percentage of national produce goes to or via Paris, simply because the local dealer does not know where else, outside his own little area, to send it. And local markets' lack of mutual contact can still lead to extraordinary price disparities, with eggs or livestock of similar quality fetching 50 per cent higher prices in one town than in another fifty miles away. 'You might think we were still in the days of Louis XIV', wrote one economist, in exasperation. *

It was largely with the aim of curing these problems that the Government after 1958 started building a number of new *marché-gares*, big modern markets beside railways on the outskirts of Lyon, Toulouse, Nîmes, and half-a-dozen other provincial centres. They are linked by telex with each other and with Les Halles, and thus are able to help direct produce to where it is most needed (which may not be Paris) and to reduce excessive price fluctuations. Run as *Sociétés d'Economie Mixte*, they simply provide a new venue for the farmer to come and sell to his dealer, who will then put the stuff straight on a train. Certainly, they have enabled quicker and more open transactions and shipments than in the old congested markets in town centres. But beyond this, they have proved something of a disappointment. The dealers and the middlemen themselves are still the same, using the same methods. No one has yet succeeded in reforming the old-fashioned French system of direct wholesale buying, which is often unfair on the producer: one or two experiments at introducing the fairer Dutch auction system—*vente au cadran*, or dial selling—have collapsed for pure reasons of temperament and habit. It is partly the producers' fault, too, that the *marché-gares* have not worked better, for they have shown a certain reluctance to make proper use of them. In the Nîmes area, some SICAs have even set themselves up as rivals to the town's *marché-gare*, virtually boycotting it and preferring to use their own buildings for marketing. This simply causes an uneconomic waste of resources and collaboration.

The largest of all *marché-gares* will be opened in 1969 at Rungis, just

* *Paris et le Désert Francais*, by J.-F. Gravier, p. 157.

south-east of Paris; Les Halles will then be transferred to it, and maybe by 1970 the last ten-ton meat-lorry or barrow of carrots will have ceased to block the centre of Paris. Tourists will no longer be able to jostle with the *forts des Halles* in their blood-stained aprons, as they drink their onion soup at the Pied de Cochon after a theatre or night-club. Nostalgic tears will be shed; but a blow will have been struck for modern planning. Undoubtedly, the transfer will help Paris town-planning; it remains to be seen how far it will really improve the marketing circuits too. Their future probably depends more on how the SICAs and co-operatives de-velop. So far, there has definitely been progress. If Gourvennec's SICA is an unusually effective one, the Vaucluse peaches do not offer a fair example either. Most SICAs are in between the two. Undoubtedly they and other influences have helped to reduce the middlemen's numbers and make them group together and behave more honestly. The farmer is learning gradually to influence the market and adapt himself to its needs, just as the industrialist does. It is a two-way process: farmers cannot reasonably blame middlemen's iniquities if they themselves are not producing what a modern society needs. Inexorably, the farmer is turning himself from peasant into businessman.

This kind of trend towards more modern methods is particularly noticeable among France's 1,300,000 vinegrowers. Many of them have now formed into co-operatives, and are putting a new emphasis on quality rather than mere output. It is true that plenty of small producers of inferior wine remain stubbornly attached to their ancestral ways; but others have been following the Government's lead towards more rational policies. Wine is no longer the stormy political issue it used to be in France.

A sharp distinction must of course be drawn between the minority industry of *appelation contrôlée* vintage wines, like Burgundies, Bordeaux, and Beaujolais, and the army of growers of cheap domestic wines that rarely get exported but make up nearly nine-tenths of the total output. The first group have never caused much of a problem: they are efficient, and their sales both in France and abroad are rising happily. But the others are especially vulnerable to price-collapses in a bumper year, and their lobby is a powerful one. Until 1953, under one of the most iniquitous practices of the Fourth Republic, the Government pandered to this lobby by spending millions of francs each year on buying up and destroy-ing surpluses: wine was subsidised irrespective of quality. Then the Laniel Government introduced a less negative and wasteful policy: in an effort to curb chronic over-production, farmers were given subsidies for uprooting poor vines and replacing them with other crops. By 1958 some 250,000 acres of vines, or five per cent of all vineyards, had been uprooted, mainly in the poor-wine districts of the centre and west. But Algerian independence then altered the situation. With the inevitable decline of Algeria's wine industry, exports to France have dropped from 14 to 8 million hectolitres a year (compared with an average French yield of 60 to 65 million) and this makes France's own over-production less serious. The uprooting policy has been suspended, in most areas. Instead, the Government encourages the replacing of poor vines with 'noble' ones, and even the planting of new vineyards, so long as they are of quality. For although French domestic consumption stays remarkably constant at around fifty-eight million hectolitres a year, with prosperity the French increasingly want to drink better wines.

This vulnerable sector of agriculture is more closely supervised by the Government than any other, with a complex system of price controls and compulsory storage. Prices are fixed early each year, and the release of new wine on to the market is strictly regulated. The farmers in their modern co-operatives generally accept the need for this discipline; only a few of the older ones hanker for the old methods of subsidy and compulsory distillation. In a bumper year there are still angry murmurs about the continuing imports from Algeria. France cannot halt these imports, for they form part of her treaty obligations to support the Algerian economy. But in 1967, after some severe riots in the Midi, the Government finally decided to halt the practice of fortifying weak French *vins courants* with the stronger Algerian wines, which will now be sold separately under their own names. This decision has not pleased the wine merchants: but it will probably give French growers an added incentive to improve their quality.

Wines and vines alike are scrupulously graded and inspected by the Government; under recent measures, the very poorest wines are now banned from the market altogether and diverted for making vinegar or alcohol. The farmer is responding quite well to the call for quality, so that without any lowering of standards many acres of vines are upgraded each year to *appelation contrôlée*, or to the intermediate category between that and *vin ordinaire*, known as *vins délimités de qualité supérieure*. Even in the Languedoc, the main cheap wine area of France, where the peasants are famous for their stubborn conservatism, VDQS vines are gradually replacing the lesser breeds, as growers come to accept the economic virtues of quality rather than quantity. But farther than this they will not go; though the Government has built in the Languedoc the most important new irrigation network in Europe, the growers refuse, as I shall describe in a later chapter, to take advantage of it and replace their vineyards with more profitable crops. Many economists argue that even today France's vinegrowers are still far too carefully protected by a Government that has not the political courage to expose them to an open market.

The Languedoc is one of the few areas where the uprooting of vines is still encouraged. And, as the growers will not co-operate, there is still overproduction in some years. One solution to this recurring problem may be for France to find new export outlets in the Common Market. In theory, it should be possible to persuade the Germans and the Dutch (and the British, if and when they join) to drink far more cheap red wine, once the tariffs are gone. France is likely to benefit, though she will face heavy competition from the more cheaply produced Italian wines. Since 1958, French exports to the rest of the Six have doubled for *appelation contrôlée* wines, and quintupled for VDQS and ordinary ones. This has been due partly to a raising of quotas and partly, maybe, to the general psychological impetus of the Rome treaty.

In the present transitional phase it is hard to gauge just how much French agriculture as a whole will gain, or has already gained, from the Common Market. In theory, France should benefit more than her neighbours; but in practice this is now becoming rather less certain.

France has started off with the lowest average wholesale prices of the Six and by far the largest agricultural production: therefore it stands to reason that the gradual alignment of prices, and the dropping of barriers and national levies, should help France more than the others. France has always regarded agriculture as one of her great assets within the Common Market, a balance to Germany's greater strength in industry. Already France's trade surplus with the rest of the Six has gone up since 1958 from 121m to over 1,000m francs—due, it is true, to other factors as well as the Market—and she is gaining over one hundred million francs a year from the Common Fund. This fund taxes imports of food from outside the Six (the main importers are Germany and Italy) and uses the money to subsidise food exports from the Six (and the biggest exporter is France). This helps France with her own 1,000-million-franc annual subsidy to her grain industry. The hard-fought Community agreement on common grain prices, which came into force in 1967, will also greatly help French wheat growers—but mainly the big ones.

In other sectors, the prospects vary. Dairy products, sugar, and wine stand to benefit most. The Common Market's share in total French cheese exports, for instance, has already risen since 1958 from 10 to 68 per cent. In other words, Germans and others are possibly eating seven times as many Camemberts as before! For fruit and vegetables the position is more uncertain, as France is not yet as well equipped to deal with marketing and surpluses as her better-organised Dutch and Italian partners. Eggs and poultry will probably suffer: France has made some concessions here. And a question-mark still hangs over the meat trade: if France can only solve the internal problems of her meat industry, in theory she is much better favoured by nature than any of her partners for becoming the chief supplier for the Community's growing appetite for meat. But the task will not be easy.

French farmers themselves have tended to be starry-eyed about the Common Market, and they grew furious at the political delays and crises of 1964–5. 'We planted Common Market seeds, and look, the wretched crops have come up national!' complained one farmer after the 1965 harvest had coincided with the worst of all the Brussels farming crises. Others made jokes about *choux de Bruxelles* that were failing to sprout.

But although 'Europe verte' now seems to be moving ahead more smoothly, some French experts are doubtful how far the Common Market will really help French farmers to overcome their basic problems. It is pointed out that since 1958 France's partners have been greatly stepping up their own production to meet her challenge, so that her quantitive lead over them is not as great as it was. And whereas the Fifth Republic so wisely switched the emphasis of Government domestic aid from price supports to structural reforms, the Common Market with its rigorous accent on fixed prices could have something of the reverse effect. The farmers themselves are now waking up to the fact that the Common Market may not be all that was promised to them by the politicians and by their own leaders: Dutch and German agriculture, being better organised, can frequently offer prices that are more competitive than French ones, especially in certain sectors such as milk, eggs, poultry, and pig breeding. This also applies to some competitors outside the Six, such as the dairy farmers of Denmark or the cattle breeders of Argentina, helped by the Kennedy Round tariff cuts. More than ever, French farming will be at the mercy of its own weaknesses, on the international market.

The best hope is that closer contact with modern methods outside France (in Holland, for instance) will help shock the French marketing system into improvement, as has already been happening in industry. And as the farmer begins to understand and control his own local market, so will he be able to lift his eyes from his own farm, not only to the rest of France, but to the actual needs of dinner-tables in Hamburg or Turin or, one day, Manchester. If French farming can succeed in becoming modern and competitive, with its huge land potential there is no reason why it should not be the principal supplier of a united Europe's needs. I believe this will finally happen. But the effort required will be enormous, and painful.

THE FUTURE: CO-OPS *VERSUS* CAPITALISTS

In many Western countries today, agriculture is becoming industrialised; and I do not simply mean mechanised. I mean it is increasingly run like a manufacturing industry, dominated by big firms. The new patterns of urban living demand a massive and regular supply of standardised, well-packaged goods. Modern techniques and ways of life put a steadily growing premium on processed and frozen, rather than fresh, food.

In the United States, giant processing firms, often with their own farms and plantations, have sprung up to meet and, in turn, to stimulate this new demand. Clearly a small firm cannot do this so easily. In France, the farmer is peculiarly ill prepared for this revolution. His own values of farm-fresh quality, so closely tied up with the genius of French country cooking, are at the opposite end of the scale from the industrial values of packaged efficiency. So far, he has tended to find an alibi in the French housewife, who has been slow to accept frozen food. But change is inexorable, as cities swell beyond the capacities of local markets, and as the opening of frontiers forces France to adapt to other countries' needs and ways.

Yet today France finds herself, not only with backward farms and markets, but also with a feeble and fragmented processing industry. It is ironical that a nation that has a vast peach glut nearly every summer still has to import half her tinned peaches from America for her out-of-season needs. Several big American firms have understandably been taking advantage of this situation to establish some useful footholds in the Common Market. As with computers or typewriters, they either take over French firms or set up their own French factories. And the cries of protest are even louder than in industry, for what often seems to be at stake is not only national pride but the farmer's personal independence.

Short of buying their own land, which they usually cannot do in France, the only way these firms can operate is to make a contract with the farmer for his produce; and the firm usually demands an exclusive contract. It provides the seeds or foodstuffs, and insists on supervising every stage of production so that its own very precise standards shall be met. This, retort the Young Farmers, reduces the farmer to a peon, or at best a mere salaried worker, deprived of responsibility: it is a menace to the traditions of French farming, and all the worse when the capital is American!

This issue of 'vertical integration', as it is called, is now one of the great talking-points of French farming. Other countries are facing the same problem, whether the capital is American or domestic. In Britain, farmers accept the necessity for the trend, but try to make sure that by forming co-operatives they keep their own share of the processing industry and stop the firms winning a monopoly. In France, they are trying to do the same; but the issue has been clouded with rhetoric and passion, because the farmers are so ill prepared for the struggle, and because of latent anti-Americanism. Two spectacular new American intrusions in 1964 (a Libby's tomato factory in the Languedoc, and a Purina poultry slaughterhouse in Brittany) set French pulses racing and put war-cries like 'Alerte au colonialisme Américain!' into the headlines.

Libby's was invited into the Languedoc by Pisani only as a last resort, after he had failed to stir up the archaic French canning industry to modernise itself and so help him cope with the Midi fruit glut. There are 700 canning firms in France, most of them producing only a few hundred tons each year, yet reluctant to make mergers. Libby's was ready and eager to step right in with a minimum 15,000 tons a year. On top of this, the Languedoc irrigation scheme, boycotted by the vinegrowers, was in need of other outlets and new clients. So Libby's won its permit, and in 1964 opened a factory for tomato juice and canned tomatoes at Vauvert, south of Nîmes. At first the local farmers bristled with suspicion. 'They'll treat us like United Fruit treats Guatemala!' they said; 'Peons! That's all we'll be.' But many of the more go-ahead farmers *did* sign contracts with Libby's, including many who had not grown tomatoes before. They get a below-market price (14 instead of the usual 16 centimes a kilo); but they have security of assured sales, as well as yields two or three times the local average thanks to Libby's seedlings and techniques which they have to implement scrupulously. Despite many mistakes and errors of tact on both sides, the operation is now running fairly smoothly, and offering an Englishman an amusing picture of the head-on clash of French and American minds and methods!

In Libby's office at Nîmes I met the director of field operations, Mr. Bundy, a boyish and somewhat humourless Californian agronomist who after two years in the area spoke no more French than *bonjour*. For him, it was just another technical job in a backward country; next year it might well be Latin America. His walls were covered with scientific organisation charts of every farm: when to sow, when to water, when to harvest. The local peasantry regarded them wide-eyed with wonder.

Then I called on the president of the contractors' association (a defence group formed to negotiate with Libby's), who turned out to be anything but a peon. Roger de Flaux, a witty and sophisticated middle-class farmer with the charm and looks of Yves Montand, owned a big estate next door to his friend Lamour. A hired Spanish labourer took me on a tractor across marshy rice-fields to where de Flaux was supervising the mending of a huge combine-harvester. 'The trouble with these Americans,' he said to me coolly, chain-smoking *Gitanes*, 'is that they blindly applied Californian growing techniques without first studying the climate, the soil, or the people. Every little decision had to be referred back to Chicago. But they've learned, slowly. The other trouble is that they send people here who won't learn French and so have no direct contact with us. It causes a lot of inefficiency: three lorry-loads were lost once, just because instructions were misunderstood. And Libby's French liaison man here resigned because the whole interpreting job drove him mad.'

'But,' he went on, 'I'm basically pro-Libby's and its all working better now. At least they're quite affable, now that we've shown them we're not Puerto Ricans. We formed an association which negotiates group contracts. They didn't like it at all at first, but it helps us keep some power. I agree with Debatisse: it's very bad for a farmer to depend solely on one contract. But most of us here grow other things too. I've got 600 acres altogether.' Libby's now has 800 acres under contract, and little shortage of fresh clients. The tomato contracts are annual; Libby's' biggest test may come if and when it starts its long-term asparagus and peach contracts, about which the farmers are still wary. But the Government is pleased that Libby's *has* had precisely the desired effect in stirring up French competitors. A big farmers' co-operative in the same area has recently planted 1,250 acres of peach and pear-trees, and in 1967 opened its own factory, destined to become one of the largest fruit-canning plants in Europe, much larger, in fact, than the Libby's operation. De Flaux, and others, are under contract to both. It is just the kind of open competition between two rival systems that the Young Farmers are prepared to accept; and Libby's is now widely cited, even by Left-wing critics, as a rare example of justified and useful American investment in France.

This is much less true of the large chicken slaughterhouse opened in 1964 in a village near Rennes, Brittany, by Duquesne-Purina, a firm largely controlled by the mighty American Ralston-Purina group. Purina brought nothing in techniques or efficiency that the French poultry industry did not already have; it simply further depressed a national poultry market that was already, as in other countries, suffering from over-production. Purina is primarily a feedstuff producer, and the farmers it placed under contract were obliged to buy its feed in return for selling it their birds. By offering them above-market prices, it threatened to put the local co-operatives out of business. How Purina ever persuaded the Government to let it start the venture is still something of a mystery. Anyway, by mid-December the Breton farmers were on the warpath, and extra police were called in to protect the slaughterhouse. Bernard Lambert, the local Young Farmers leader whom I happened to see at that time, told me: 'If Pisani doesn't close the place down at once, we shall dynamite it. This is an underhand American attempt to seize the French poultry market and put our farmers in servitude.' In the event, no dynamite was used: Purina agreed to limit their output to 5,000 birds a week (one-sixth of capacity) and the affair steadily subsided. But more than Libby's, it provided the *cause célèbre* that impelled the Young Farmers to start actively planning the struggle against 'capitalist integration'.

This they are doing, as in Britain, by developing their own co-operatives. One of these now makes and sells a well-known brand of yoghourt; another has a sizable frozen-food factory. Debatisse and a few friends even essayed a chain of discount supermarkets, but more as a publicity gesture than as a way of solving the problem.

Co-operatives began in France some sixty years ago. Some are now large and well organised, notably in the dairy sector: in 1964 they had enough solidarity to maintain a national milk strike for a month. They have obvious advantages for the farmer: the danger is that in a really large bureaucratic co-operative the small farmer may feel almost as lost as when tied to a big capitalist firm. The Co-operative de Landerneau in Brittany, the largest in Europe, is often accused of being a trust in the hands of the big local farmers, where the small farmer simply hands over his produce on contract as if to Purina. Yet a smaller more democratic co-operative is less equipped to compete with the Purinas of this world; and farmers in many areas have neither the training nor skill to take on the tasks involved, nor the long leases to be able to make industrial commitments.

The Young Farmers therefore accept that perhaps at least half the new style of 'integrated' farming will have to be in the hands of capitalist firms. They ask simply that the farmers be allowed to form group contracts, as with Libby's, guaranteeing them a certain autonomy. A new law on these lines has just been passed. They also ask that the Government encourage French rather than American firms to do the integrating. This is not just chauvinism: the danger with a world firm like Libby's or Purina is that it has the power to shut down its plant tomorrow and leave its local farmers stranded, whereas the big French cheese firm at Roquefort, or the champagne firms at Reims and Epernay, all have hundreds of local farmers on contract, for ewes' milk or grapes, but are so wedded to their locality that they offer them long-term security. These are held up as models: one big sheep-farmer I talked to near Roquefort was delighted with his contract. Since the Libby's affair the Government has been trying to get French firms to set up similar contracts for canning, freezing, and so on, and is just beginning to win results.

The Young Farmers' policy towards integration ties in with their views on land ownership and group farming, and amounts to a new economic attitude to the profession as a whole. Michel Debatisse explained it to me, when he greeted me one day in his farmhouse at Palladuc:

'The farmer *must* keep responsibility for his produce—that is the basis of our *métier*. If he becomes a mere wage-earner, tied to a firm, he will be "alienated". We must try to stop farming going the way of industry in the last century and being proletarised. But of course we believe in technical progress, too, and we see the need for modern integrated markets and large-scale processing to serve the new mass-consumer needs. The only answer to this dilemma is for the farmers to group together and take charge of a large part of the processing and marketing business themselves, in peaceful co-existence with the capitalists. New farming groups and SICAs must develop, and be linked closely with the co-ops. But each farm will retain some individuality. The family or two-family farm offers the only sound moral basis; we don't want kolkhozes. What we do want is an entirely new attitude to land ownership. The peasant's implacable attachment to his own acres, even when he is no more than tenant, must be replaced by the idea of the land as a common resource or working tool, as fishermen use the sea without owning it. The right to work on the land must be utterly divorced from the right to own it.'

This revolutionary talk about land is aimed not so much against the big firms (who are rarely landowners) as against what the Young Farmers see as an almost equally serious menace, that of the *cumulards*, speculators who buy up land and then put in salaried managers and workers to farm it. In 1962, the Young Farmers in Normandy decided to make a public example of one of the most illustrious of all *cumulards*: at dawn one day, 700 of them burst in upon the actor Jean Gabin in his country home, and told him they would 'break the whole place up' unless he agreed to sell or lease the two farms he ran on this basis. Being a kind and liberal man, he apparently agreed. The farmers' argument was that many of them had farms too small to be viable, yet could not find new land. Gabin's farms, they knew, were modern and well run, and his staff well paid. But the farmers did not want to be wage-earners.

It is a quarrel of doctrine, and much of the future of French farming depends on it. Some people detect strong traces of Marxism in the Young Farmers' hostility to wage-earning and to landed property; and there are some officials in high Gaullist circles who are suspicious of them for this reason. But it seems to me, and to others, that a more serious heresy in the Young Farmers' outlook might be a kind of latent neo-corporatism. The insistence on the family farm, the dislike of capitalist intrusion, the belief in the farmer's inalienable right to his own way of life—all this, in a modern guise, brings back a faint odour of Vichy or even Méline. The Young Farmers are sincere in wanting to end the peasants' isolation from the community; and there is something admirable in their desire that agriculture's transfer into a modern economy should be more human and less brutal than industry's was in the last century. But are they being quite realistic? If a man like Gabin can prove himself a good employer, why not go and work for him? Like all revolutionaries, now the Young Farmers have won power there is a danger of them settling down to defend *positions acquises* and sectional interests. And Debatisse the fresh and eager idealist I first met in 1960 was not quite the same person as Debatisse the emphatic politician I saw six years later.

For the moment, one must retain a touch of scepticism about the long-term influence of the Young Farmers' generation. Obviously they have so far done immeasurably more good than harm, and their energy and desire for reform is far better than anything in the past. If they have not yet had more practical success in raising farm incomes to industrial levels, it has not been their fault. Much more help is needed from the Government. Edgar Faure, who succeeded Pisani in January 1966, is a tactful politician skilled at dealing with the farmers' grievances; and he won valuable extra funds from the Treasury which he used for extending the S A F E R s and for increasing price supports. He has broadly continued Pisani's policy but without developing it; and the danger is that he lacks the technocratic dynamism that today is needed more than ever, if French agriculture is to be made properly competitive. He has been criticised for spending too much money and effort on bolstering up an outmoded peasant agriculture, and not enough on developing the key sectors that can best confront international competition. He is too much of a Fourth Republic demagogue, and not enough of a modernist.

Since the war, mood and techniques have changed more than structures, in French farming. But the next ten years will inevitably bring more big changes, as the Common Market becomes reality, as farms enlarge and more people leave the land, and as the struggle between capitalists and co-operatives intensifies. The lot of the French farmer is bound to improve. and long-term optimism seems better founded here than in almost any other sector of French life. But the new ideal of co-existence between group and industrial farming will not be easy to achieve, and is fraught with difficulties. The old idyll of the small farmer with his few cows and his patch of vines is over: it was rarely such a happy idyll anyway. Now he must chart a delicate course towards a happier future, between the Scylla of the kolkhoz and the Charybdis of a billion-acre corporation run from a skyscraper in Chicago.

CHAPTER V

THE BATTLE
FOR THE RETAIL TRADE

THE DEFECTS OF THE AGRICULTURAL MARKETS, and of small industry, too, find themselves repeated throughout most of the distributive
and retail trade. With its high profit margins and low turnover, its lack
of enterprise or real competition, in this century no other sector of French
life has seemed quite so backward; and today, despite a good deal of
post-war progress, France's 800,000 shops and middlemen are still on
balance too many, too small, and too inactive for her needs. Napoleon's
jibe about Britain as a nation of shopkeepers still boomerangs ironically.

France's small-shopkeeper class emerged from the war with a muddy
black-market reputation. 'Les BOF' (*beurre, œufs, et fromages*), the
generic name for dairy shops, became a phrase of contempt to denote a
whole selfish crypto-collaborationist class of petty tradesmen, vividly
described by Jean Dutourd in his novel, *Au Bon Beurre*. After the war, the
reputation changed, but scarcely improved: in 1955 this was the class that
provided the Right-wing rabble-rouser, Pierre Poujade, with the hard
core of his support, in opposition to the growth of big industry and of
workers' salaries. Although already protected by a tax system that hit
mainly the larger stores, the small ones did what they could to resist
progress or the growth of modern rivals. The BOF mentality persisted: the
basic aim was to keep prices and profit-margins high even if it meant
selling less, and few shops stopped to consider that a reverse policy might
yield better results. In the main towns there were a number of larger
stores, mostly old-established ones like Printemps. But their margins, too,
were excessive; and the nation that had invented the department store in
the nineteenth century failed to develop it as much as her neighbours.

All this may help to explain why France often seems so expensive. And
obviously it cancels out some of the progress that has been made towards
efficiency in industry and farming. In the past few years, however, there
have been plenty of signs of change. The first French supermarket was

born in 1957; today there are more than 800. For better or worse, American methods are now creeping in, and French commerce is beginning to shown an entirely new spirit of competition and even salesmanship. Price wars, an equally new phenomenon in France, have cut some profit-margins in groceries, household goods, and textiles. And as in other sectors of the economy, the small businesses are beginning to react by grouping together, or else are slowly dying out.

A JESUIT GROCER'S CRUSADE

Government reforms, foreign influences, the growth of new suburbs and ways of living, have all played their part in pushing these changes forward. But the foremost catalyst has been an inspired young grocer called Edouard Leclerc, in a small town in Brittany. Had it not been for his persistent crusading ever since 1949, the old order would never have cracked so easily. He was the first with the courage to use discount methods, and so challenge the conspiracy of industry, shops, and middlemen to keep prices high.

Leclerc is one of the truly remarkable figures of modern France, and has variously been likened to St. Vincent de Paul, Danilo Dolci, and Rasputin. Whimsical, boisterous, conceited and religious, he is in commerce not for personal gain but with a driving sense of social mission. Today he still owns only three stores himself, all in Finistère; but all over France at least 420 others, each independently owned, use his name and apply his methods and prices under his strict control. The secret is to buy direct from the maker or producer and sell to the public at near-wholesale prices, cutting your own profits to the bone. In Britain or the United States, this might seem either quite familiar, or else some kind of sales trick. In France, applied straightforwardly, the innovation has gone some way towards forcing other shops to bring down their prices too. To the trade, Leclerc has often seemed enemy number one; to the Government he has been a blessed ally in the fight against inflation, and an alibi for not having to apply more drastic and unpopular reforms themselves.

In a land where shops are usually handed down from father to son, Leclerc could hardly have come from a more unlikely background. His father was a senior army officer, scholar, and gentleman farmer; and young Edouard, like several of his brothers, was destined for the priesthood. But after ten years in Jesuit seminaries he quit, because he could no longer face celibacy—and because his true vocation was already clear to him: to serve his fellow-men by breaking a wicked system. In 1949, at the age of twenty-three, he opened his first barrack-like little store in his home town of Landerneau, near Brest, and began by buying biscuits from a nearby factory and selling them at 25 per cent below usual prices. Soon he was dealing in the whole range of groceries. At first the local tradesmen simply laughed at this crazy young amateur. But the public flocked in, and

Leclerc's turnover shot up. By 1952 the Finistère tradesmen were alarmed, and made their first combined effort to destroy him. And they used the weapon which has been used against him and others, many times, ever since: they persuaded manufacturers and wholesalers to threaten to stop supplying him.

For the past fifty years there had been a *de facto* system of price-fixing in France, as in Britain before Mr. Heath's Retail Price Maintenance reform of 1964. Industry set the minimum prices of its goods and boy-cotted any shop that went below them. The shops themselves liked this system—in fact it was they who had instigated it, for it prevented tire-some competition. It was theoretically illegal, but never prosecuted; and it benefited everyone except the consumer. No-one for many years, until Leclerc, had dared challenge it.

Soon his supplies began to suffer from the boycott. So he wrote to the Government to complain, and to explain his aims. High officials in the Ministry of Finance had probably never heard of this strange idealist in a far corner of France; but his plight happened to chime with some of their own preoccupations for stopping inflation. In August 1953, the Laniel Government in one of its rare moments of effectiveness signed a decree that strongly asserted the illegality of imposed prices and refusal of sale. This measure, re-affirmed by the Gaullists in 1958, and again in 1960, remains the key to all post-war progress in distribution. Without it, Leclerc would have perished and the new supermarkets might have had the greatest difficulty in starting. So Leclerc was saved, and began to carry the campaign outside Landerneau. In 1955 the first of the present-day chain of *Centres E. Leclerc* began to spread across Brittany; some of them were started by former middlemen who felt their *métier* doomed and had come to Leclerc for help. Then, in 1958, two engineers from Grenoble invited him to open a centre in that city—the most dynamic and booming in France, but on that account also the most costly to live in. It seemed ideal terrain for his first real national offensive, and he agreed. Almost at once, an enterprising Grenoble business tycoon hit back by opening six local cut-price stores using somewhat similar wholesale methods. All over Grenoble, retail prices began to fall. The Leclerc centre itself, not surprisingly, did not do very well in the face of this competition. But Leclerc did not mind: he had achieved his aim. Grenoble soon became known as one of the cheapest towns in France.

So in 1959 he found someone to start his first centre in Paris, in the working-class suburb of Issy-les-Moulineaux. By now Leclerc was well known, and his campaign had caught the public imagination. In the weeks following the opening of the Issy shop, he was constantly the sub-ject of long articles or TV interviews, without having to pay a penny for the publicity. And the national grocery trade was by this time really scared. The chairman of the grocers' union came to his inaugural Press conference at Issy and heckled for an hour. 'You are a Government puppet, Leclerc!' 'No!' shrieked the journalists delightedly, 'the housewives are with you, Leclerc!' A few days later, a leader of the Petites et Moyennes Entreprises federation described Leclerc as 'a bowl of vitriol hurled in the face of French commerce to disfigure and dishonour it, to the profit of the big capitalists and international trusts'. Poujade held a rally in Paris and called Leclerc 'that defrocked priest, lackey of the Jewish-plutocrat trusts!'

By 1960 there were sixty Leclerc centres; and a few other new discount shops, such as the Grenoble ones, were daring to copy him. Now the menace was strong enough for the Grands Magasins and the chain-stores to grow alarmed, as well as the small shops. Monoprix with its 200 local branches, Prisunic with 180, and others, are the equivalent in France of Woolworth's or Marks and Spencer; and they owed much of their prosperity to the fact that, while charging prices only slightly below those of the *boutiques*, they did their own wholesale buying and so could make a double profit. This might involve a mark-up of 20 per cent on the manufacturer's price plus 30 per cent on the wholesaler's—compared with Leclerc's overall margins of 8 to 12 per cent.

These stores declared war on Leclerc. First they tried the American strategy of the 'loss leader', highly publicised shock reductions on a few obvious articles, such as detergents, while maintaining the main range of prices. This, in Leclerc's mind, is not real price-cutting at all, but clever salesmanship. But it had some effect on an ill-prepared French public. So Leclerc hit back, by extending the range of his own centres from groceries to textiles, where mark-ups in France are often appallingly high, even up to 100 per cent. Most of the big chain-stores, in fact, made the bulk of their profit from textiles; the grocery counters were simply a way of enticing customers into the shop. When a chain of new Leclerc textile centres sprang up across France, selling at 30 or 40 per cent below normal prices, they had an obvious success. Then the big stores decided to take their legal courage in their hands and put pressure on Leclerc's suppliers (who often were their own associates or subsidiaries) to boycott him. They managed to break the 1953 law discreetly, not by open boycott so much as by deliberate inefficiency: pretending goods were out of stock, sending the wrong goods, or delaying deliveries. Sometimes more sinister methods were used: in Landerneau itself a big general store was secretly subsidised by Monoprix to sell at a loss, in a bid which nearly worked to ruin Leclerc's own shop. In other cases, owners of Leclerc centres were offered bribes to desert him, and some accepted. The boycotts multiplied, and the whole Leclerc experiment looked like collapsing. So Leclerc appealed to the Prime Minister, Michel Debré. And again he was listened to. The Government was worried about rising prices; but with the Algerian crisis at its height, it was equally anxious not to stir up new Poujadist unrest with commercial reforms of a structural nature. So it simply issued, in March 1960, a loud and sharp new warning against breaking the 1953 decree; and it had the Gaullist authority to make itself obeyed.

Since then, the trade's machinations against Leclerc have changed into something nearer normal competition. In any town where a Leclerc shop flourishes, some of the near-by chain stores and new supermarkets have felt obliged to lower the main range of their prices to near his own level. So some aspects of his basic campaign are won—but only on a limited scale. Though the number and average size of his centres goes on steadily rising, they still account for less than 1 per cent of the total retail trade in their sectors. He has no ambitions to seize control of the bulk of the trade himself; he wants simply to operate stores in enough different towns to keep up a steady pressure.

In fact, it is unthinkable that his own network could ever be more than a catalyst. His own highly personal methods are more a kind of inspired free-booting than organised modern trade, and could scarcely be extended to the whole complex machinery of a big nation's commerce. He works by instinct, with a tiny staff and a minimum of paperwork, and his informal 'moral contracts' with the owners of his 420 centres are based on trust and discipline and a flair for choosing the right kind of people. In many of his ventures, his impudent charm, his verve, and his persuasiveness seem to have played as important a part as his low prices.

He holds several dogmas. One is that it is immoral for a shop to spend money on gay and expensive décor and equipment, and then pay for it by raising prices. His own new supermarket in Brest, like his original little store in Landerneau, is of an austerity that East Berlin in the late 1940s might have found it hard to beat: a big, tawdry warehouse full of packing-cases and mountains of tins and sacks of potatoes. It is true that many new French supermarkets go to the opposite wasteful extreme, and then wonder why they make a loss. But it is doubtful how far the French housewife today wants quite such grimness in return for cut prices. Now that Leclerc is facing more competition, some of his centres might do better business if they spent just a few francs on colour and brightness.

A more constructive dogma is that 'commerce' must give way to the notion of 'distribution': the tradesman exists simply to put goods on the market at the minimum extra cost to the public, concentrating on large, rapid turnover and allotting himself a fee for his services. It is a Socialistic attitude rare among small French shopkeepers. A Leclerc grocery centre will operate on a margin of 8 to 12 per cent, of which only 2 or 3 per cent will be net profit; in a traditional shop, the net profit alone may be 10 to 20 per cent. Leclerc's whisky is often 6 francs cheaper than the same brand in a normal shop, while one of his Paris centres sold 200 tins of caviare in ten days at 3·50 francs each, against the normal price of 8 francs.

In Brest, his new supermarket has stirred up the keenest price-war in France, and Brest today has the cheapest shops in the land, despite the heavy freight charges for the 400-mile journey from Paris. The branches of Monoprix, Bon Marché, and others have hit back vigorously, their losses covered if need be by their Paris offices. All down the dour main street of this big, ugly working-class naval town, gaudy posters in the windows announce 'Prix choc!' 'Réclame!' 'Sensationnel!' Veterans of the price-war game say it is like America in the 'thirties and 'forties.

A thousand small shops, mostly grocers, have closed since 1954 in Leclerc's stronghold of north Finistère; and it is not hard to see why. Whereas a small shop will perhaps buy one hundred kilos of fruit and vegetables a day from a middleman, Leclerc will bring five tons on a lorry direct from the Nantes central market and undercut the local shop by 30 to 70 per cent. This shows how much the middlemen are often still profiteering at the expense of both consumer and farmer. On one occasion, Leclerc brought in 300 tons of Bulgarian strawberry jam by boat to Brest, and sold it at far below usual jam prices. When a local chain-store manager, some time later, asked his Paris head office how they had come to miss such an attractive import deal, he was told, 'We tested that jam, and found it quite unfit for consumption.' 'But Leclerc's been selling it for a year and no one's got ill.'

It is a joke that Leclerc likes to tell. Half his crusade is deadly earnest; half is schoolboy spirits, Robin Hood against the bad barons. And he enjoys mockingly exploiting the legend he has helped to create of himself. Half the week, he is campaigning across France or the world, and the other half he spends modestly with his wife in a small house in Landerneau, his only luxury a Mercedes which he changes each year. His tiny office in a corner of the Brest shop is piled with old bottles and packing-cases, and there I called on him once. He has clear blue eyes, a cheeky smile, a soft, excited voice, and a very personal manner as if he were straight away letting you into some secret. 'No, I don't feel I'm a prophet. I run shops as a way of formulating my ideas. Maybe what I'm doing *is* close to religion, though, because it's social justice, economically viable charity. Distribution touches all aspects of man. As for Christ, I admire him as an amoral being, the first to chase the tradesmen from the Temple. I go to Mass, but don't know if I'm a Christian.' Then, voice ecstatic but eyes laughing: 'My philosophy is to be happy. In the struggle for happiness one finds the sense of eternity. Life goes past, ideas drive their course, God is a . . .' The 'phone rings. 'Yes? . . . well, cut *all* your prices, *all*, d'you hear?' Receiver down. 'Sorry, where was I? Oh, yes, God is a river of life that flows through all. It is enough to drink of this river, to live.' 'M. Leclerc, what of the criticism that you are a tool of the Government? Weren't the riot police called out to protect you when the Prefect of Finistère came to open your new Landerneau supermarket?' 'When the Government need me, they ask. The Government uses lots of people, not only me. No, I am not the Government's mistress; *une gaule me suffit*.'

Although he denies he is a missionary, a large part of his time nowadays is spent helping people in fields other than his own. He has travelled, on invitation, to advise Governments on distribution reform in Spain, Bulgaria, Gabon, and Niger. In France, he has helped fishermen to fight their middlemen by organising fish-stalls at wholesale prices outside Paris

Métro stations, simply as a way of alerting public opinion. He did exactly the same for the first of the Breton artichoke wars; but later he turned against the Breton dairy farmers and their price-fixing co-operatives, and by organising his own direct sales, played a part in breaking the 1964 national milk strike. He gave the producers 60 centimes a litre instead of the usual 38, then sold to the housewife at 63 instead of the usual 70, cutting out the co-ops' profit of some 30 centimes. Yet most of the farmers, out of solidarity to their own organisation, refused to supply him. 'I try to help the peasants, but they won't listen,' he told me with his usual mocking arrogance. 'I give them circulars and tracts. It'll take ten years to sink in. As for the Spaniards and Africans, they are still too backward for my ideas.'

Brilliant publicist, sharp businessman, genial fanatic, Leclerc has had an influence out of proportion to the size of his sales. Sometimes, the mere threat of a new centre in a town is enough to send prices down. Once, stopping overnight in Tours, just for a joke he called on a house-agent and said he was looking for ten local premises for shops. The price-cutting panic was widespread, and for a few days the public benefited.

Conversely there is the danger that if a Leclerc centre closes down in a town, prices simply go back to their former level. The main question, therefore, is this: has there been any true change of heart and method on the part of the other stores, or have they simply adopted new expedients to deal with a common enemy?

SUPERMARKETS AND BOUTIQUES

When the Bon Marché opened in the Rue de Sèvres in 1852, it was the first real modern department store in the world. Soon it was followed by Printemps, Galeries Lafayette, Samaritaine, and the other Paris giants that are still there today. Gradually they began to form branches in the provinces, and chains for cheap consumer goods—the Prisunic chain belongs to Printemps, and Monoprix to the Galeries Lafayette. But the big stores and their chains were soon overtaken in scope and efficiency by their Anglo-Saxon counterparts. Their growth was stunted by their high-price policy, by their *ententes* against competition, and by the general stagnation of the French economy until the 1950s. Encouraged by the housewife's conservatism, nearly all the food trade remained in the hands of small independent shops—even the early Leclerc centres were all small ones.

Then in the late 1950s the growth of new suburbs and spending power gave a cue for the appearance of a few self-service supermarkets, first of all in the Paris region. Though they were influenced by the struggle against Leclerc, and though they sometimes tried to follow his prices, their main ideas and techniques were borrowed not from him but from the United States. In 1955, the Paris branch of the National Cash Register

Company began to invite groups of leading French shop executives to its headquarters at Dayton, Ohio, to attend the famous sales courses given by Bernard Trujillo. The aim was to inspire the modernising of French shops and so push up the sales of cash registers. It succeeded brilliantly, and Trujillo has possibly had even more influence on French commerce than Leclerc. His Latin oratory and flamboyance struck a sympathetic chord with his French audience. Over 3,000 Frenchmen have been to Dayton, many of them three or four times, and 300 from Prisunic alone. France has provided Trujillo with 30 per cent of his foreign pupils—far more than Britain.

He teaches the doctrine of rapid turnover, of large shops with a wide range of goods, and of the loss-leader or, as he puts it, 'islands of loss in an ocean of profit'. It is all within a general motive of profit, and therefore not quite the same as Leclerc's more radical philosophy. Trujillo's French pupils, especially the younger ones, listened in amazement to this gospel, so different from the old French traditions; and back home some of them began to try to apply it.

The change started to make its impact around 1959. This was about the time that Leon Gingembre of the PME (nine-tenths of whose members are tradesmen) was breaking with Poujadism to face up to the Common Market, so it all fell into place. An extreme example of the change is a man such as Hubert Delorozoy, owner of a new chain of stores in outer Paris and one of the most vocal figures in the world of French commerce. Until about 1958, he was a strongly Poujadist believer in the old small shop. Then he went to Dayton three times. Today he will proudly show a visitor his big new supermarket at Corbeil with its gaudy lighting, its crowds, its rows of clicking registers, and its prices not far above Leclerc's. The aggressive sales atmosphere is reinforced by megaphones blaring details of the latest bargains. It all seems centuries removed from the old *épicier du coin*; yet, regrettably or not, its noisy materialism seems as typically 'French' as the quiet, unambitious order that is passing away.

Delorozoy is one of those who have applied Trujillo's ideas intelligently. Many others, however, have failed to do this; and in general the super-market movement has not yet had a great success in France. Though the numbers have risen since 1957 from nil to 800, their share of overall trade is still no more than 3 per cent—in the United States there are 30,000 supermarkets and their share is 72 per cent. Many of the new French supermarkets belong to the 'integrated' combines such as Prisunic, who have simply added a self-service format to their existing chain-store methods, and have not really applied the basic techniques of fast turnover and low costs. Many of them are simply too small, with too narrow a range of goods; or they stay fixed to the idea of high profits; or they spend too much on costly prestige overheads of décor and large staff. Then they wonder why they fail to do good business, and why the customers will just as soon stay with the old shops or go to Leclerc and the discount houses. In some cases, supermarkets practise the loss-leader tactic too blatantly, and the housewife sees through it. And sometimes supermarkets have been crippled by shop-lifting, which is rampant in France. One chain succeeded in bringing it down to less than half its normal level, but only by costly outlay on detectives and concealed mirrors.

The most successful supermarket chain, Carrefour, is in fact the only one that closely follows Leclerc's price methods, though it has borrowed some ideas from Trujillo, too. Its largest store is a bleak hangar at St.-Geneviève-des-Bois, near Orly, where it has amortised its installation costs within three years with a $2\frac{1}{2}$ per cent net profit on an annual turnover of sixty million francs. It has the advantage of being outside a town, with room for a large car park, and people come from miles around, spending on average 50 francs a visit. One class of regular customers are Leftish intellectuals, from the new colleges and science centres south of Paris, who disapprove of ordinary 'commerce'. Another class, very different, are local tradesmen who find it cheaper than buying from their own wholesalers, partly because they can avoid tax declarations. One café-owner buys eighty bottles of Pernod a week, and never asks for receipts.

Needless to say, Carrefour has suffered from something of the same persecution as Leclerc. Even today, so its manager told me, many firms find excuses for not supplying him. And worse, in several towns his building permits for new stores have been blocked by municipal councils under pressure from the local trade. Many rival firms resent Carrefour's success, which they do not understand. It is this kind of thing that makes it very hard to assess how much progress has really been made in French commerce. Certainly, there is a new spirit of competition in many quarters; but it is still held up by secret *ententes* between some of the biggest chains —between Monoprix and Prisunic, for instance—that are sometimes based on intermarriage. Only where there is direct conflict with Leclerc or Carrefour have prices come down appreciably. Elsewhere, they may have dropped a little, but are still higher than in most countries. The Common Market is now beginning to help to promote further competition, notably in fields such as electrical goods where French prices have been artificially high. But it is too soon to say how far there has been a real change of heart in large-scale French commerce.

Most of the large firms have at least been reacting positively to the modern challenge. Among smaller shops and middlemen, there tends to be a sharper contrast between a minority who are also adapting, and a majority who are not. Some middlemen have gone out of business; others have reacted by grouping together in face of Leclerc and the combines. In the grocery trade, their numbers have dropped strikingly since 1945, from 3,000 to 720. A few have even started their own supermarkets, while others have succeeded in grouping retail shops into 'voluntary chains', bound to them by contract. This facilitates bulk buying, and helps both parties to survive; but the shops and their turnover are still so small that they may not be able to stand up long to modern pressures.

As for the myriad little shops of France, a minority of intelligent owners realise that, if they want to maintain their place, they will probably have to adapt to fulfil specialised needs. Since Delorozoy opened his Corbeil supermarket, the near-by grocers have floundered, but a little quality leather shop has done a roaring trade, sharing some of Delorozoy's clients but not competing with his goods. It is the same story at St. Geneviève: nearly all the little general stores near Carrefour have closed, and been replaced by coiffeurs, dry cleaners, or house agents.

Gingembre is trying to push as many of his flock as possible in this kind of direction: 'There will always be some things,' he told me, 'that the small shop can do better than a large one—keeping late hours, personal repairs and deliveries, or specialised luxury goods where economies are not important. American experience proves this. It is simply a question of adapting French commerce to it without too much hardship. My job is to goad the shops to change, but to protect them while they are doing so.'

He will have a hard task. The majority of France's small shops are slipping gently into decline, but not into death. Even more than the farmer, the small tradesman tends to cling tenaciously to his dying business, neither modernising it nor moving to something else. The setady growth of population and spending power is artificially prolonging his life, but without curing his rooted obsolescence. There are more than 700,000 shops in France; yet despite the growth of the new large ones, the total went down by only 35,000 in 1954–60, while in 1960–4 it actually rose again by 11,500, mainly due to the rapid development of new suburbs. In France there is one shop per 56 inhabitants, against 86 in Britain and 100 in the United States.

Only in the shadow of a good supermarket, or in a few special places like Brest, are shops dying out in any numbers. Elsewhere, especially in depopulating villages or older suburbs, it is easy to find an extreme example of the malaise: the dingy general store that ekes a bare living by selling everything from tin-tacks to poor-quality fruit, and often acts as a café for its few faithful clients. It is true that the superficial outward picture may in other cases be rather different. Even in out-of-the-way places, many little shops parade new glass fronts, neon signs, and fresh paint, thanks to a system of loans that enables them to make some concessions to changing public taste. But this and the laden, well-dressed windows, may simply be masking old-fashioned attitudes to sales and profits, and a primitive lack of accountancy that serves mainly as an alibi for the shopkeeper in his staple occupation of tax-evasion.

Some 80 per cent of shops are family affairs with no employees. Often they are run by the wife while her husband has another job; this helps the family to live, but does not make the shop itself any more viable, nor does it seem to cure the average owner's apathy, frustration, and Poujadist resentment. Poujade himself was a grocer from one of the poorer country towns of south-west France, St. Céré in the Lot; and though he is spent as a political force, his attitudes linger on. A Government sociological survey carried out recently among 300 average small-shopkeepers showed that nearly all of them were quite satisfied with their own methods, and blamed their difficulties on the State and on the big shops who 'got all the advantages'. Although pessimistic about their long-term future, nine out of ten were hostile to forming into groups in order to survive; each hoped to 'last a little longer than the others' by developing personal contacts with clients and counting on their loyalty. 'We are sellers, not mere distributors,' some of them said proudly. 'The French housewife likes us to advise her—happily she's not yet Americanised.' In most cases it was the women who showed the most negative attitudes, typical of the older French *petite bourgeoisie*: suspicion of State and community, reliance on family links and habitual loyalties, miserliness, hatred of change.

As on the farms, there is often a difference of outlook between generations, save that in commerce the percentage of brighter sons who stay is even lower. They leave for industry or management, while the dull ones remain to inherit a family concern that needs no qualifications. And the average age of shopkeepers is fifty-five. Leclerc hates them, and has publicly suggested they should be forcibly retired and turned over to road-building. More probably, they will be left to die out, and the Government will make increased efforts to train the new generation to a different outlook.

Education is a problem for the larger firms, too. The main training-grounds for executives, such as the Haute Ecole Commerciale, have high academic standards and some prestige. They are turning out a new élite; but they are sometimes accused of producing scholarly statisticians and economists rather than practical salesmen. It is noticeable that the commercial world has failed to produce, from within its own ranks, the same kind of dynamic new leaders and ideas as agriculture has, or even industry. Almost all its pioneers have come from outside—Leclerc from a seminary, Leclerc's early rival at Grenoble from engineering, and André Essel in the electrical trade (see below) from journalism. Whether the only or the best solution for France is to breed a professional corps of aggressive American-style salesmen begs other questions; as in so many fields, the problem is how to borrow the good ideas from America and to avoid the faults.

The Government has one other weapon it can use to modernise commerce, and that is fiscal reform. In 1965, after six years of delays, it found the courage to push through Parliament a much-contested Bill that revises the French profits-tax system in such a way as to penalise the firms with large margins.

Hitherto, manufacturing firms and wholesalers paid a *taxe sur la valeur ajoutée* (T V A), or value-added tax, of some 20 per cent of their gross profit margin on each article, while shops simply paid a 2·75 per cent local tax on their sales turnover, irrespective of profits. A shop with an average 50 per cent mark-up would therefore pay only one quarter more tax than one with 20 per cent on the same range of goods, and this encouraged high profit margins. Shops could, if they wished, use the TVA system instead, but only the Leclerc centres, Carrefour, and one or two others had low enough margins to make it worth it; and as a result Leclerc was branded, quite unjustly, by the rest of the trade for being 'privileged' by the wholesalers' tax system.

The new Bill, in force in 1968, does away with the turnover tax and extends the TVA to the retail trade on a scale varying from 20 per cent for cars and TV sets to 6 per cent for most ordinary foodstuffs. Propelled by Leclerc, the Government first put the idea forward in 1959, but the trade fought it every inch of the way, and with some success: the final Bill contains striking concessions to the small shopkeepers, who would have been hit hardest. Those with a turnover of less than some 20,000 francs a year (about 400,000 shops and servicing firms) are *altogether exempt* from the TVA, while a similar number of others in the medium range will be assessed for a modified tax on a lump-sum basis. The reason put forward for this is that small shops have such archaic methods of accountancy that this new tax on each article sold would be far too complicated for them, whereas the old tax was on overall turnover. There is some truth in this; but it is even more true that the Government finally funked a reform that would have spelt rapid death to many shops and caused widespread unrest. So the small shops, protected already under the old system that gave such an alibi to tax evasion, will now benefit even more. The firms that will be affected are the 200,000 larger ones, including all chain-stores and supermarkets. By providing them with some new incentive to sell more cheaply, the reform may succeed in its aim of getting them to cut profits and streamline services and management; but in some cases it might have the opposite effect of forcing prices up, to offset higher taxes. The TVA reform is in line with similar new legislation in other Common Market countries; it is clearly a good idea, but may prove to have been applied too half-heartedly in France to have the necessary effect.

And there are still some specialised corners of the French commercial world where vested privilege and restrictive practice are far more iniquitous than in the general retail trade, yet nothing has been done to cure them. The worst case is pharmaceutics. Any visitor to France will have noticed that in this land of high prices the chemists' shops have the highest ones of all. This is because the chemists cling on to an old privilege that forbids the sale of their goods in other kinds of shop; and they exploit this through a price-fixing cartel with minimum mark-ups of 52 per cent. Cases have even been quoted of the same drug costing four times as much in a chemist's shop as when sold wholesale for medical purposes. The Rueff-Armand Report in 1960 proposed that the monopoly be removed, and a number of ordinary chemical goods and medicines be authorised for sale anywhere, as in many countries. But the Government has not yet dared act: the chemists are powerfully organised, and are in close league with the industry, which also profits from the price-fixing. Watch-sellers and butchers pose similar problems. All three trades have this in common, that they demand some special expertise: watch-shops do repairs, a butcher has to know how to cut meat, and a chemist needs a diploma to prepare medicines. They can therefore easily dig their heels in whenever anyone tries to reform them. 'They represent the worst aspects of the medieval guild spirit,' an official in the Ministry of Finance told me, 'and I'm afraid they'll be the last strongholds of the bad old France to be swept away.'

WANTED, A FRENCH *WHICH?*

It is partly the consumer's own fault that French consumer prices are not lower. After the war, the housewife grew so used to the steady rise in prices that she ceased to question them, and in a land so snobbish about quality, anything cheap came to be regarded with suspicion. Soon after the war the Government carried out an experiment that consisted in cutting cheeses in identical halves in a number of shops, and giving them different price-tags: most people chose the dearer halves. With price-fixing so widespread, the notion of a valid 'bargain' never really developed. In the past few years, however, the influence of Leclerc and the new competition has helped to make the housewife more price-wise, at least for ordinary goods. But there are still few firms that have succeeded in putting across the idea of quality *plus* cheap mass-production in the manner, say, of Marks and Spencer; and amid the welter of new goods and their myriad different brand-names in the shops, the buyer is handicapped by the relative lack of disinterested advice from consumer bodies.

The various French consumer associations are too small, too poor, and too split by petty rivalries to have much effect. The largest of them, the Organisation Générale des Consommateurs, has only 15,000 private subscribers for its monthly bulletin—against *Which?*'s 500,000 in Britain. It gets a little money from the Government, too, but neither it nor its rivals can afford to undertake much of the regular scientific testing that alone gives teeth to consumer protection. Perhaps this is not very surprising. The French are notoriously bad at this kind of civic initiative, and are changing only slowly. The consumer bodies find that they cannot get subscribers.

In one specialised field, however, that of photography and household electrical goods, an inspired kind of consumer venture has produced remarkable results. In 1954 a bold young man called André Essel founded a body with the snobbish-sounding name of Fédération Nationale des Achats des Cadres (executives' shopping federation) This is primarily a discount shop, in a field where mark-ups are exceptionally high—often 50 per cent for TV sets or cameras. By buying wholesale, Essel was able to undercut other shops by 20 per cent or more, and has played a big part in forcing prices down elsewhere. The Grands Magasins and the older TV and electrical shops hate the guts of this debonair and thrusting ex-journalist; but they have not been able to destroy him, and his turn-over has risen more than a hundredfold in ten years. The FNAC is also a kind of club, with a matey atmosphere in its big, three-storey store in the centre of Paris: most of its clientèle are *cadres*, 75 per cent of the record sales are classical music, and you can sit down for a snack or a drink while selecting your new Leica camera or Marconi pick-up. The FNAC has 140,000 subscribers to its monthly consumer magazine, *Contact*, which exists partly to publicise FNAC goods, but manages to be objective too; it does much testing in the photo and electrical field, and recently advised members against buying the FNAC's top-selling photo flashgun, when it detected a fault.

The FNAC, though valuable, is not a true consumer body. As usual in France, the initiative for founding a strong and wide-ranging one will have to come from the Government, which is now setting up a national Consumer Institute. This will provide funds and facilities for regular testing. It will publish a *Which?*-type monthly magazine, and will also make use of the State-run television channels. Its ruling council will include representatives both of Government and industry, but only a minority of independent consumer delegates: it is therefore not certain that it will have the same integrity and independence as the Consumers' Association in Britain. The Government plans at the same time to strengthen legislation against phoney advertising. A cinema advertisement for sweets once featured lorry-loads of milk and butter, but the sweets were found to contain neither. The advertising industry is not as well organised as in Britain to check this kind of excess, and the Government wants more power to do so itself.

One task of an effective French consumer organisation will be to help to ensure that the new mass-market does not bring with it too great a loss of quality and variety. This is a problem in many countries today, but especially in France, and many Frenchmen are aware of the danger. I have already suggested that, in certain industries, the old French traditions of individual quality and craftsmanship are not adapting easily to the new mass consumer needs. In commerce, there is the same dilemma. It may be sentimental to shed a tear about the passing of the old corner grocery; and the new supermarket, if properly run, may well be cheaper and more efficient—but will it make life pleasanter? One of the arguments flung against Leclerc is that he is bringing in an un-French uniformism.

In the long term, this may prove a more fundamental problem than the more practical and immediate one of modernisation. And it gives less cause for optimism. I am quite confident that before too long the ideas of Leclerc and Trujillo will prevail over the *ancien régime* and commerce throughout France will become efficient and progressive. The present movement is irreversible; it is simply a matter of time. The transformation is a necessary one—but what kind of world will it bring in its place?

Coal-miners on strike in northern France, 1963

The Rance tidal dam, Brittany (in the background: St. Malo)

Jean Monnet

Louis Armand

Edgard Pisani

Michel Debatisse

Dauphines in production at the Renault factory, Billancourt, Paris

Agricultural unrest: demonstrators blocking a
railway in the Midi, 1967

Peasant life, old style: a farmhouse in the Massif Central

Peasant life, new style :
a family in a group farming enterprise in Lorraine

Edouard Leclerc in one of his grocery stores

Morning congestion in Les Halles, "the bowels of Paris"

A new road junction in northern Paris: the Boulevard Périphérique crossing over the Autoroute du Nord →

A street in Grenoble, "France's little Chicago in the Alps"

André Malraux

Roger Planchon

Paris old and new: part of the Maine/Montparnasse development →

The Métro at rush-hour: "an exciting city to visit,
a cruel city to live in . . ."

Smart new suburbia: the Drug-West "drugstore" at Parly 2, west of Paris

To the surprise of many experts, the old idea that the French housewife could never be wooed away from her familiar local shops and buying habits has now been disproved. In fact, she is proving more adaptable than the shopkeepers, and will readily follow American methods when they are properly applied. Inevitably, some human quality will be lost, at least in the larger and more impersonal supermarkets. That is the price of efficiency. But an experience like that of FNAC, or Leclerc's shops, suggests that it might still be possible to combine a personal style, and attention to quality, with modern methods. In commerce, as in other fields, the issue for this nation is how to modernise without losing the essential French qualities.

CHAPTER VI

NEW LIFE IN
THE PROVINCES

UNTIL VERY RECENTLY, the French provinces were second to none in
Europe for lethargy and bourgeois narrowness of spirit. Bourges, Reims,
Dijon, and a score of other towns, with their soaring cathedrals, their
graceful old streets, and their calm reflection of history: how delightful
they were to visit, and how tedious to live in. Ipswich or Nottingham
might be far uglier, but were never quite so dead.

In no other country was the contrast more striking between the
dazzling capital and the rest, '*le désert français*', as it was sometimes called.
Nowhere was 'provincial' quite such a term of contempt as in Paris—even
the Larousse dictionary defined it as 'gauche, undistinguished'. French
literature is rich in monuments to Parisian writers' hypnotised love-
hatred of their home towns, from Flaubert's Rouen to Mauriac's Bordeaux; for it is a French paradox that the deadness of the provinces has
gone hand in hand with strong local attachments, and many a Parisian
would proclaim 'Moi, je suis Auvergnat', or Angevin, or Limousin, but
would never dream of going back to make a career there. In this most
centralised nation on earth, Paris over the centuries sucked the blood
out of her provinces. Their intellectual life, their talent and initiative,
their powers of decision on the smallest matters of local government, were
all drawn to Paris. Even heavy industry settled in Paris, or in a few
favoured regions in north-eastern France.

Since the war, this situation has been slowly changing. The rural
exodus, and the growth of new industry, prosperity and mobility, have
brought a new liveliness and self-awareness to many provincial towns and
their regions. This time, Paris has been unable to hog all the new wealth
and progress as she did in the nineteenth century: in fact, the unplanned
post-war overgrowth of Paris has made it such a nerve-racking city to
live in that some sophisticated Parisians are reversing their age-old scorn

and beginning to move out to the provinces. New factories and theatres, new university institutes and town-planning schemes, are making provincial life more tolerable. Regional development has become today's obsession, a pillar of Gaullist policy: 'la grande affaire de la nation,' Pompidou called it.

But France still has a long way to go towards real decentralisation. Though in two respects—in industrial development, and in social and cultural animation—there has been definite progress, in local government there has not been much effective change. That is why her larger towns, such as Toulouse or Lyon, are still far from becoming true regional capitals in the manner of Turin, Munich, or Edinburgh—or even of Birmingham and Manchester, which also suffer from the magnetism of an over-privileged capital. Though the French machine of State is handing out new money to the provinces, it still keeps a tight control on how it is spent, and has not given up one drop of real sovereignty. True regional revival, based on local powers of decision and financing, must under these conditions remain limited.

TODAY'S OBSESSION: REGIONAL DEVELOPMENT

Some of the roots of French centralisation go back deep into history, to the Capetian monarchs and even to Roman times. For more practical modern purposes, they date from Napoleon. Before his day, under the *ancien régime*, France's thirty historic Provinces were governed by *intendants*—rulers centrally appointed by the king, but with large local powers of decision. It was a system of decentralised administration that worked perfectly, without being federal. Then, in 1793, a violent conflict between the two main factions of the Revolution led to a victory of the Jacobin extremists from Paris over the milder provincial Girondins, and a few years later Napoleon with Jacobin aid decided to impose the authority of Paris more sternly. He carved up the provinces and replaced them with ninety-one arbitrary 'departments', named after often obscure rivers. Brittany, for instance, now had no legal existence; Rennes, its chief town, became the capital of Ille-et-Vilaine. And in charge of each department Napoleon placed a Prefect, a strong ruler answerable to Paris for everything. This is the Jacobin heritage under which France still labours today. The system has many advantages, and not solely political ones, for the Government of the day; but it has hindered the regions from developing their own personality, and the process of adapting it to modern economic and social needs has only just begun.

Throughout the nineteenth century the political dominance of Paris encouraged other forms of centralisation too. When the railways were built, for political and strategic reasons their network was traced like a spider's web round Paris with few good cross-country lines, so that even as late as 1938 it was quicker to go from Toulouse to Lyon via Paris

(683 miles) than direct (340 miles). When heavy industry grew up, some of it settled near the coal and iron-ore mines, in Lorraine, Flanders, and the upper Loire; but much of it went to Paris, to be near the sources of finance and the vital lobbies of Ministries. Yet at this time the growth of new techniques and transport were, in other countries, encouraging decentralisation.

Gradually all the big banks became centred in Paris, while the snobberies of the literary salons joined with the hold of the Sorbonne over the State university network to deprive the provinces of much of their intellectual resources. And the ordinary population came too, hungry for work. The great Parisian building programmes of Baron Haussmann in the 1860s saw little counterpart in the provinces, and this helped draw to the capital hundreds of thousands of destitute peasants, for the rural exodus was now beginning. The statistics are astonishing. From 1851 to 1931, the population of greater Paris went up by 4·4 million, that of Flanders and the Lyon-St.-Etienne region by 1·8 million, while that of the rest of France went down by 1·2 million. Paris's share of the French population rose in this period from 5 to 15 per cent, and by the 1931 census many lesser provincial towns were smaller than they had been in 1800. In Britain, London saw a similar growth, but it was at least shared by many other towns too. No wonder that France, even today, has far fewer large towns than Germany, Britain, or Italy, despite a national population only slightly below theirs. Only Paris, Marseille, and Lyon are over the 400,000 mark, against fifteen towns in West Germany, ten in Britain, and eight in Italy.

Far more than the actual size of the towns, it is the imbalance that matters, and the consequent waste of resources. By 1939, a high percentage of the private wealth of France was concentrated in Paris, or in country châteaux belonging to Parisians; and workers' salaries in Paris were 40 per cent higher than in the provinces. All this time, France had been investing eagerly in countries like Morocco or Senegal, where the legacy of her inter-war colonial development still catches the eye. But she neglected her own provinces, notably the south and west. The notion began to grow up of 'two Frances', with the country divided diagonally from Caen to Marseille. To the east of this line, Paris and 85 per cent of the industry, the big modern farms, and Parisians' rich playgrounds on the Riviera; to the west, a territory more thinly populated than Spain (except in Brittany), with backward farms and towns without industry. This division is still the basic problem—but only since the war has it really caught public attention.

Since the 1930s several forces, some spontaneous and some in the form of Government action, have been helping to revive the provinces. First, the pre-war decentralisation of a few car and aircraft factories, for strategic reasons, may have had a little influence. And even the natural pull of Paris was beginning to wane, so the demographers tell us, due mainly to the overall industrial stagnation and population decline. Then came those ubiquitous blessings in disguise, Vichy and the Occupation. A number of dynamic leaders and firms withdrew from Paris and the occupied zone in the north to the 'free' Vichy territory. Thus it was, for instance, that two brilliant scientists from Strasbourg, Professors Néel and Weil, settled at Grenoble University and have since helped make that town the most go-ahead in France. Cut off from Paris for two years, the southern provinces under Vichy were forced to act and think for themselves. And right up to the Liberation, the straitjacket of the war put a curb on the usual procedures of central bureaucracy and gave local initiatives, whether Résistance or collaborationist, a chance to flourish. Lack of transport crippled the circulation of national newspapers outside Paris, and gave the provincial daily Press a chance to build up a strength it has since managed to maintain.

After the war, the sudden up-swing in the birth rate took place everywhere, not just in Paris, and gave a new psychological impetus to stagnating provincial towns. There was also the renewed rural exodus, this time faster than ever. Paris was still the immigrants' chief target, and its population swelled rapidly but so did that of other towns. Between 1939 and 1954, for the first time since 1890 Paris's population increased less than that of the rest of France. Since the war, Greater Paris has grown from six to eight million; but many other towns have almost doubled in size and Grenoble has trebled. In a world overpopulated with the billions of Asia, this may seem a dubious achievement; but France is still underpopulated for her size and resources, and the smallness of her towns has been a reason for their dullness as well as a curb on her own economic strength. Paris is the only town to have passed its optimum size: its appalling traffic, its shortages of housing and every form of public service, contribute to its current neurosis and are beginning to drive some people away. Engineers, professors, and executives begin to see that life in some other towns, in the warm south, or near the sea or mountains, may be more human and pleasant, even if less intellectually exciting. So they stay or move there, rather than seek the conventional road of promotion to the capital. And the provinces are the richer for them.

The growth of car-ownership, of faster trains, and domestic air services, all have helped to make a life away from Paris seem less like exile to a cultured family used to its stimulus. With a working week in Nancy or Toulouse, and then a weekend in the capital, a cake can be had and eaten. This new mobility has had its effect on staid provincials, too, and so has the growth of television and tourism. Towns have slowly been coaxed out of their isolated slumber, and made more aware of each other and of the outside world. All this is common experience, in any modern country, but in France with its long neglect it has been especially striking. Finally, the post-war rise of industry has been so great that there physically was not room for it in Paris alone.

These changes have been largely spontaneous. In the general context of post-war France, some degree of provincial revival has been inevitable,

whether encouraged by Governments or not. But the State has closely
supported it—with varying success—and is increasingly trying to channel
and control it.

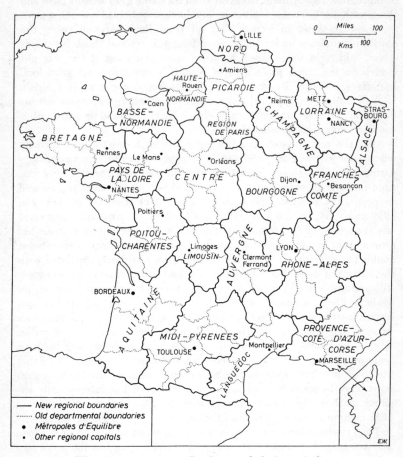

The twenty-one new Regions and their capitals

'*Aménagement du territoire*' as the French call it (regional development
in the widest sense) was almost unheard of before the war. After 1945 it
soon became a major preoccupation of Monnet and his planners. In 1947
Jean-François Gravier, a young geographer attached to the Plan, published
his famous book, *Paris et le désert français*, which brilliantly analysed the
economic aspects of the problem. He showed how the neglect of the west
wasted the country's resources, and how the congestion of Paris and other
key areas led to inefficiency and high costs. France, he said, could not
become a modern nation unless she remedied these faults. The rural

exodus was right and inevitable, but new jobs must be found for these people within their own home areas, not the other side of France.

The warnings of Gravier and his colleagues deeply impressed the civil service and politicians, and many of their proposals became accepted as the basis of official policy. Soon after the war, the Government began to encourage the formation of local 'expansion committees', and in 1950 it instituted the first scheme of subsidies and tax concessions for firms prepared to shift their factories from Paris or open new ones in the backward areas. Other measures managed to narrow some of the gap between Parisian and provincial wages.

These steps met with a few successes—for instance, a big new Citroën factory at Rennes—but in general they were too weak and haphazardly directed. So, in 1955, rules were imposed to prevent the creation or enlargement of factories in the Paris area. Soon afterwards, a start was made with regionalising the Plan; and the ninety departments were grouped into twenty-one new economic regions, roughly corresponding to the old provinces. The department kept its existing functions; but the region had a new super-Prefect in charge of economic co-ordination, for the department was now clearly too small a unit for this.

At the same time, the subsidies for new provincial factories were increased, especially for the west and south-west. But these incentives have not been very successful: most factories have preferred to move out to somewhere nearer the capital. In more recent years, the Government has come to accept that in the more difficult and unpopular areas it must take the lead itself. Therefore it has initiated such schemes as new atomic and spatial centres in west Brittany, the development of the Landes forests, and irrigation and tourist projects in the Languedoc.

The Government has also accepted that the only valid way to counter the appeal of Paris is not by setting prohibitions against it, but by stimulating rival centres of attraction. Therefore it has designated eight of the largest towns* as *Métropoles d'Equilibre*, and has declared the aim of building up their populations to between 500,000 and a million. Though this policy in itself may not be more than gesture, at least it officially emphasises the need to endow other towns with some of the same amenities and metropolitan qualities as Paris.

In the intellectual field, a chain of new multi-purpose arts centres— *Maisons de la Culture*—are being built in towns large and small, while one or two of the *Grandes Ecoles* are being transferred from Paris, and provincial universities are being developed much faster than the Sorbonne. Finally, a new reform of State administration regroups the Government services in each department under the authority of the Prefect rather than of their respective Ministries in Paris.

These measures are certainly stimulating regional growth, and may be promoting efficiency, too. But there is no decentralisation of power:

* Marseille, Lyon, Toulouse, Bordeaux, Nantes, Strasbourg, Lille, and Nancy/Metz.

public services, and universities, remain in State hands. In other respects as well the Gaullist régime's regional policy is running into criticism: the checks on the growth of Paris industry have recently been relaxed, while eastern France is still being developed fast, partly at the expense of the west, in order to compete with German industry. Nevertheless, within these limits, and within the context of their own *étatiste* ethos, the Gaullists' enthusiasm for *aménagement du territoire* is patent enough. It has been elevated into a science and a doctrine, the subject of endless speeches, books, and conferences; a new Government department has been created to take charge of it, under one of the most powerful and loyal of de Gaulle's *aides*, Olivier Guichard. And Guichard's close associate, Philippe Lamour, pioneer of the Languedoc, has proclaimed, 'Regional development is France's fundamental problem. It is the condition of her remaining a modern nation.'

For all the failures and delays in the application of policies, there is something well founded about this enthusiasm. France today presents her planners with some of the exciting challenge of a virgin land. It is one of the few parts of Western Europe where there is still the space, and the resources, for really ambitious possibilities. And as one talks with Lamour about the future of the Languedoc, or with eager young technocrats about the new industries of the Béarn or the Rhône-Rhine canal, one gets just a glimpse of the vision that inspired the early developers of the New World. Whereas in Britain, it is a question of patiently rebuilding the town-centres of old eyesores like Birmingham and Newcastle, in France only Flanders and the pre-war Paris suburbs present this kind of congested mess. Elsewhere, Corbusier-style ideas can have their fling: linear cities on virgin plains, factories in the depths of unknown valleys, tunnels under high mountains. True, there is the usual French chasm between theory and achievement; but at least a start has been made. Since the war, this freedom of space has favoured the harmonious siting of new factories, such as the gleaming blue-and-white power station beside the Oise near Beaumont, which must strike any tourist on the road from Calais to Paris. And France is lucky to be making her real industrial revolution in this age of mobility and clean fuel. One has only to contrast the sparkle and cleanness of Grenoble and its modern industries with smoky nineteenth-century St. Etienne in its coal-grimed hollow, virtually the only large French town as dour and as ugly as its score of English industrial counterparts.

The new enthusiasm is beginning, in some places, to percolate from the technocrats to the local organisations—chambers of commerce, municipal councils, departmental *conseils généraux*.* Their preoccupations are changing, from the details of their own little budgets and the jealous guarding of their own interests, to a wider co-operation with the State,

* A form of local government with very limited powers.

and with each other, in schemes of expansion. It is a slow process, and there is plenty of obstruction; but gradually the relations between State and citizen, on a local level, are evolving beyond the old questions of political doctrine and privilege towards economic and social matters. Often the arguments are as bitter as before, but they are rather more practical. Recently I happened to overhear an animated conversation in Caen between a group of local *conseillers généraux* of the Calvados department. A decade earlier, their debate might have been about, say, the Church schools issue, or conscription in Algeria, or the wickedness of Mendès-France in attacking the local *bouilleurs de cru* (home distillers of apple alcohol). This time, they were discussing whether a new international airport should be built at Caen or at Deauville, and whether the new motorway to Paris could be ready in two years or three. These were matters for the State to decide, finally, but the local dignitaries were determined to have their say.

A new kind of regional spirit is beginning to appear, notably among the younger generation now pushing their way to the top in many local councils. It is a very different spirit from the old sentimental attachments of 'Moi, je suis Auvergnat'; in fact, it is quite the opposite, for it is based on a new mobility. The dynamism and the keenest local pride often come from young citizens who have moved in from elsewhere, who are prepared to put down roots but will still want to keep in touch with the rest of France. This is different from the outlook of the old Breton whose pride is never to have ventured on to foreign soil east of Rennes.

This new spirit has been awakened partly by the decline of French nationalism and the rise of Europe. Behind de Gaulle's misleading façade, the average Frenchman is far less of a nationalist than he used to be, and he believes in Europe. He knows too that, if Europe is allowed to move towards closer integration, the regions will grow in importance as nations fade. This will happen in the economic field, even if there is no more political progress. It is already happening, as Lorraine with its new Moselle Canal to Coblenz feels the pull towards the Ruhr and the rise of a new economic Lotharingia. Gravier, Lamour, Armand, all the prophets have emphasised that Europe is the great chance of the French regions, just as without regional revival France will be lost to Europe. Armand has written: 'The regions can renew their personality through European union *without having to do it through the monster that is Paris.* If Lyon were a little more Milanese, Toulouse a little more Spanish, Lille a little more Flemish, we would all be the better for it.' But will de Gaulle ever allow any such thing? Will the State, anxious to revive the provinces so long as it can choose the terms, ever allow them their own political and spiritual rebirth in a wider context?

In the past few years, the pattern of regional development in France has come into a steady focus. All the larger towns that ring Paris (Caen, Evreux, Rouen, Amiens, Reims, Orléans, and others) are doing well. Some are sites for new overspill universities; all are favourite spots for new industry. But to the north and east, the already highly industrialised regions of Flanders and Lorraine are now in some difficulty because of the nature of their industries: coal-mines and textiles around Lille, impoverished iron-mines around Metz. In the west, a few key spots are now flourishing, thanks to special efforts—Rennes, Toulouse, the Pau-Lacq area—while even decadent Bordeaux is at last seeing a revival. But most of the rest of the west is still in trouble: 'It may be too late to save Limoges and the Limousin,' say the planners, like doctors at a death-bed.

The main expansion area is now the south-east, thanks to its climate, its tourist delights, its natural resources, and its good geographical position between the Mediterranean and the heart of Europe. Massive new oil refineries at Marseille, big power dams and factories in the Rhône and Durance valleys, the rapid growth of a luxury tourist industry throughout Provence, the Languedoc coastal development, all these are on the move. And the brightest star of all in the south-east is France's 'little Chicago in the Alps', site of the 1968 Winter Olympics and winner of every French gold medal for post-war regional development: the astonishing city of Grenoble.

THE ARROGANT ADVANCE OF GRENOBLE

A young nuclear scientist took me up in the funicular to the old fortress on the cliffs beside the city. We watched, as the sun set over the jagged Vercors massif, and the ranks of new skyscrapers below us glimmered from pink to grey. There it sprawled in its flat valley within a ski's-leap of the high Alps, France's little answer to the New World, *ville-pilote*, terrestrial Sputnik, showpiece of a nation's future.

'My wife and I are hard-core Parisians,' said my friend, 'and we were rather dubious when we first moved here eight years ago. But very few of the thousands of Parisians who've settled here recently want to go back. It's not like moving to the provinces, it's living in the France of tomorrow.'

In the 1820s, Stendhal wrote of his native town: 'What could I add, if I were God?' He was referring to the landscape; Grenoble itself was little more than a sleepy village. Some things have not changed since Stendhal's day: the Alpine freshness in the air, the close backdrop of snow-peak or steep forest behind every street, the hardy traditions of the mountain people of the Dauphiné. But man has added plenty else, without waiting for God. The valley of the Isère beneath its toothy rocks pullulates with some of the most advanced industries in Europe, electro-chemicals, electro-metallurgy, heavy machinery, and nuclear laboratories. The population, 80,000 in 1945, will probably reach 400,000 by 1972. Seven people in ten are immigrants to the town; one in eight is a student or scientist. The crowds in the streets are youthful and cosmopolitan, and there is a new social informality still rare in the provinces. 'You can wear ski-clothes in a smart restaurant,' I was told, 'and no-one minds or notices, as they would in Lyon.' There is even an air of self-assertive brashness that some people find more American than French.

It is this unusual marriage of touristic setting and intellectual and economic dynamism that sets Grenoble so far apart either from a more conventional French town like Dijon, or from the average British industrial centre, even from a so-called boom town like Coventry. Since the war, Grenoble has become something of a legend in France; and the open-mindedness and enterprise of its new élites have made it a pace-setter in many diverse fields. What Grenoble does today, France does tomorrow. In 1960 the first French family-planning clinic opened here, in defiance of the anti-contraception laws; Edouard Leclerc here started his first centre outside his Brittany home base; the university is the least provincial in the provinces, with the highest percentages both of non-Dauphinois and non-French students; as a nuclear headquarters, Grenoble is second only to Paris; and in 1965 it became the first large French town to stage a 'municipal revolution' by electing a young mayor from the new technocratic class, rather than from the traditional élites of bourgeois *notables*. And these recent achievements were preceded by others, mostly more fortuitous, dating back into history: the first funicular in France, the first *Syndicat d'Initiative*, the first scheme of family allowances, the pioneering of hydro-electricity, the most courageous Résistance fighting (in the Vercors, 1944), and even the origins of the French Revolution.

What has made Grenoble so special? It has not been due to any particular Government pressure, nor, until 1965, to municipal dynamism. The twofold answer lies in its surrounding mountains. Grenoble's industrial strength originates from the near-by invention of hydro-electricity in the last century; and today it is the skiing, above all, that attracts the young élites from Paris and elsewhere, for no other big town is so near the mountains. The rest is a snowball effect: the more factories and intellectuals come, the more others tend to follow.

Grenoble was no more than a quiet burg noted for its glove industries when, in the 1860s, some French engineers experimented with a new idea of drawing electric power from the high waterfalls of the Belledonne and Chartreuse mountains. Thus the age of 'white coal' (*houille blanche*) was born. Factories large and small came to settle near the new sources of power—some of them were little paper mills which you can still see today clinging to the sides of steep clefts in the Chartreuse, for the electricity at first was not on the grid. And Grenoble has never looked back. The population doubled between 1872 and 1926, at a time when most of France was stagnating. By the 1950s the largest firms were Merlin-Gerin (electro-metallurgy) and Neyrpic (turbines and hydraulic research), both among Europe's leaders in their fields. The university was also developing fast, especially in science, spurred by the presence of Professor Néel and other outstanding physicists. It was this that persuaded the Government, in 1956, to choose Grenoble as the site for France's principal nuclear research centre, which today has a staff of 2,000, a third of them specialists.

Since then, industry has taken a new direction. The older metallurgical firms, based on the *houille blanche*, seem to have passed their prime; Neyrpic and another big one, Bouchayer et Viallet, have been taken over by outside companies. But some equally large and more advanced industries have arrived to work closely with Grenoble's reservoir of research scientists, Pechiney, one of France's leading chemical firms, is opening electro-chemical research laboratories also with a staff of 2,000. Grenoble's industries are today thriving more than ever.

This town offers the only really successful example in France of close and fruitful co-operation between the university and local industry. In the United States, or even in Britain, this is not so uncommon; but French professors with their ivory-tower traditions have tended to scorn practical work, and hence the lag today in French applied research. Grenoble even eighty years ago managed to create a different outlook, when pioneering electrical industries first began to settle in this remote university town. In 1892, the world's first university course on industrial electricity was held here, and the links have steadily strengthened ever since. Today, the firms give little in the form of direct grants but they constantly commission the Science Faculty for special jobs of research, while, in return, the university specialists make full use of the firms' laboratories and practical experience. This situation helps to entice brilliant scientists from Paris, as well as the kind of advanced industries that especially rely on research. As one example, Professor Néel's invention of a new form of powder magnet has led to the creation here of two factories specialising in this.

The Dean of the Science Faculty, Professor Louis Weil, as ebullient and engagingly conceited a man as most leaders of this city, took me on to the roof of the Nuclear Studies Centre and showed me his and Néel's kingdom—a 300-acre site beside the Merlin-Gerin works where thirty million francs' worth of new reactors and cyclotrons were taking shape. 'It's the human contacts,' he told me, 'that are so much easier here than in most towns. We seem to be creating a new sort of open society, unusual for France. I'm sure the skiing has a lot to do with it. It's easy to settle thorny problems of liaison with some top industrialist or civil servant when you're up in a funicular with him. Everyone here goes skiing.'

Weil, Néel and the firms wanted the liaison to go farther. They set up a new association for joint research which the firms would pay for— but the Government clamped down on it. The Ministry in Paris feared that it would give the university delusions of autonomy and encourage higher salaries than elsewhere.

Even so, these links are one main reason why Grenoble is the best example in France of what economists call the 'multiplier effect': investment breeding further investment. Whereas in some places—such as Lacq or Rennes—new industry has implanted itself as an alien growth, here it perfectly animates its region and is animated by it. This, plus the tourism and the large cosmopolitan university, are creating a new kind of social ambience that offers pointers to the way the rest of France may be about to move. In most other towns, despite the new liveliness, the old bourgeois hierarchies are still largely in place. Here, the original nucleus of conservative Grenoblois are being pushed aside by the flood of immigrants, and a certain new classlessness is emerging, unusual in a land where class divisions are still much more rigid than in Britain. People in Grenoble are judged for themselves, rather than for being 'Monsieur le Président' of this or that. But though the old barriers are down, a new organised pattern of society is only just beginning to emerge and many of the newcomers feel a bit rootless.

One of the largest new firms, Caterpillar, the American tractor-makers, say they chose Grenoble for their main European plant because its pioneering spirit was so familiar; but in fact the town's marriage of brashness and *finesse* seems rather more Milanese than American. Grenoble shares something of the Milanese obsession for hard work, and Italians predominate among the city's large foreign minority. The streets have the animation of the Midi, and the people in their bizarrely assorted clothes look as if they have come from everywhere—the coal-mines of Lorraine, the farms of Auvergne, the Mezzogiorno, Texas, the Champs-Elysées. It is a town of youth, and of *cadres*: at least 35,000 people earn their living directly off science or studies. But there is not much organised culture— 'people are too busy working, or skiing', I was told—and traditional social clubs are badly attended. Though it has more character than most boom towns, Grenoble, like many of them, is still in the process of finding its soul.

The State's direct contribution to the boom has been largely confined to the nuclear centre and to the university's handsome research grants. But now the Gaullists, in order to show the flag, have built the most splendid modern Préfecture in France, all glass and marble and fitted carpets. The Prefect arrived as a somewhat phlegmatic civil servant but soon became infected with Grenoble's fire and energy; certainly his staff of young technocrats from Paris have a cool arrogance which I did not find equalled elsewhere in France, and which perhaps they feel is needed for dealing with Grenoble.

Today the Prefect watches warily over the most remarkable municipal situation in France. Throughout the boom years of 1945–65, the *mairie* remained, surprisingly, in the hands of the old guard of Grenoble-born *notables*, in turn Socialist or Gaullist by label but reactionary by temperament. And the new immigrants were not yet sufficiently organised or civically aware to dislodge them. During those years, almost nothing was done for town-planning. The city spread its tentacles along the valleys, and rents and land-prices shot up unchecked. I remember admiring a new ring of peripheral skyscrapers in southern Grenoble in 1959, and coming back six years later to find that other rings had grown outside them, like the layers of a tree, and the city centre had virtually transplanted itself in that time from the old town to the southern 1959 periphery. It reminded me of the posters in Texas, 'Don't park your car in this lot: there'll be a new building in an hour.' This was all very exciting for boom-worshippers, but inconvenient for people living in a city that had vastly outstripped its public services.

Then in 1964 a certain Hubert Dubedout of the Nuclear Centre found that his water supply kept failing in his fourth-floor flat. Thousands of others were in similar plights, for the mother city of hydro-electricity was served by a water system unchanged since 1883. Dubedout launched a public campaign to get the mayor to do something, and he succeeded. Encouraged by this, he and a few young friends from the city's scientific *élite* formed a non-party group to contest the local elections of March 1965. Allying with the Socialists, and helped by Communist abstention in the second ballot, they succeeded to everyone's surprise in dislodging the Gaullist-conservative ruling coalition from the *mairie*. The intellectual immigrants of Grenoble had found their force at last; nearly all of them voted for Dubedout.

Today he is mayor of Grenoble. He is an ex-naval officer and electronics engineer from Pau, in his early forties, slim, good looking, and disdainful in manner: a man generations apart in spirit from the usual mayor of a large French town. When I first met him, at a pompous lunch in the Préfecture for the mainly elderly *conseillers généraux* from near-by villages, he winked at me in front of the Prefect as if to say, 'I feel as much an outsider here as you'. He is the prototype of the new French technocratic pragmatist, a kind that normally steers well clear of the intrigues of municipal politics. He has no party-political views or ambitions, is neither for de Gaulle nor against him, but simply wants to get a job done. His victory had a few echoes in other towns in the 1965 elections, and was greeted by the political observers in Paris as a national portent. Pierre Viansson-Ponté, political editor of *Le Monde*, wrote: 'This success proves that the current French mutation is giving birth to new styles, to unprecedented forms of political action. With men like Dubedout, public life is no longer the same.' It seemed that at last the sterile alignments of the old political parties might be about to crack before a new outlook and and new generation. Grenoble had set the pace once again. And it was the success of Dubedout and his Left-wing alliance that led Mendès-France to choose Grenoble South as the constituency for his political come-back in the 1967 general election.

Dubedout and his energetic team have revitalised the *mairie*, and then worked flat out to get Grenoble ready for the Winter Olympics. Besides preparing a huge new ice rink and improving the skiing facilities at Chamrousse, Alpe d'Huez, and Autrans, this involved a complete overhaul for the town as a whole. New airports and motorways had to be built, a new railway station and post office, a big modern theatre, and an Olympic village to house 4,000. Three-quarters of the total cost of 1,000 million francs was borne by the State; the town had to find most of the rest, and some of the burden fell on ratepayers. But the lasting benefits will be enormous: Grenoble has got in two years the modern infrastructure that would otherwise have been spread over twenty. The Olympic village, for instance, will now be used to provide two thousand flats and houses, and the Maison de la Culture will be a considerable asset. For though this is a town of science more than of culture, in France the two go hand in hand more than in Britain, and the existing small theatre was always packed out and quite inadequate for the town's needs.

Thanks to the happy coincidence of Dubedout and the Olympic Games, Grenoble now has the town-planning policy it so badly needed. Yet all did not go so smoothly. First, several of the smaller communes on the edge of the town used their powers of veto to hold up the general projects. In one case, a Socialist mayor refused to let a road to the Olympic village pass over his territory because he feared it would bring new housing, and he did not want his village to change.

Then, the defeated mayor, Albert Michallon, waged a vendetta of comic-opera extravagance against Dubedout. Michallon, a doctor from an old Grenoble family, is a witty, flamboyant playboy who had been elected mayor in 1959 on a UNR ticket but was always something of an embarrassment to the Gaullists. Careless of civic management but a fanatic for prestige, it was he who secured the Games for Grenoble, and when he lost his seat as mayor he remained chairman of the Olympics organising committee and refused to stand down. He and Dubedout proceeded to block each other's plans, and Dubedout said the *mairie* would boycott the committee until Michallon resigned. Faced with the prospect of the world's athletes turning up in a half-ready town, the Government took to action and in February 1966 virtually nationalised the preparations for the Games. Six weeks later, Francois Missoffe, the Minister of Youth and Sport, somehow succeeded in reconciling the two rivals, and Michallon even said publicly, in his own fruity style, 'Dubedout and I are henceforth *cul et chemise. Lui, c'est le cul.*' When the Dubedouts have replaced the Michallons throughout France, perhaps municipal politics will be more efficient—but less colourful.

Grenoble's expansion seems all the more remarkable in the light of its geographical position, 350 miles from Paris and off the main communication routes. The lack of ideal transport had been setting local industrialists a problem; but matters will now be improved by the Olympic legacy of motorways, jet airport, and better trains. Even so, it seems uncertain that the town's growth can continue indefinitely. Some economists now talk of 'saturation', and soon there will be little building space left in the confined plain. Lyon, sixty miles away, may lack Grenoble's zest, but is far better situated as a natural capital and still has more than twice its population. In the new eight-department 'region' of the Rhône-Alpes, Grenoble is merely the capital of one department (the Isère) while the super-prefect is at Lyon; and if the notion of regions and *métropoles d'équilibre* gains in importance, this will benefit Lyon more than Grenoble.

The question therefore is whether Grenoble will keep its unusual pioneering spirit if its growth is slowed. So far, it seems to have offered the best example in France of success breeding success, of mystique and achievement linked in a chain reaction. It is something of a Californian phenomenon, with new human energy responding to environment. Grenoble also, most significantly, affords some glimpse of what the French can do once their natural talents are released from the conventions and structures of the past which mostly still weigh on them so heavily. Above all, it is an example of spontaneous growth and private initiative, with the State for once playing a secondary role.

In other parts of France, this is less often the case. But since about 1960 some other towns have been growing livelier, too, and the contrast between Grenoble and the rest is less striking than it used to be. The spirit is catching on, whether it be due to the dynamism of a few local people, to special Government efforts, or to unplanned social or economic factors. I shall now describe a few typical areas where change, or the forces resisting change, are especially interesting—Caen, in Normandy; Rennes and the rest of Brittany; the Languedoc coast; Toulouse and its struggling hinterland; and Lorraine and its capital, Nancy.

CAEN AND RENNES: TWO FACES OF PROGRESS

Five hundred miles from the Dauphiné Alps, on the rolling plains of western Normandy, Caen, like Grenoble, is a thriving university and industrial city. It has been growing faster than any French town except Grenoble, but not simply of its own accord: the special efforts of a dynamic team of civil servants have made it one of the few really striking successes of the Government's decentralisation campaign.

Caen is the regional capital of Basse-Normandie, comprising the three departments of Calvados, Manche, and Orne. This is an average French region with some industry and much agriculture, marked by an even higher level of rural overpopulation than in Brittany. There has been a steady rural exodus since the war, most of it towards Paris rather than local towns. In 1946–62, net emigration from the region accounted for 110,000 and was barely compensated by the high local birth-rate. So the Government decided to try to develop Caen as a local counter-attraction to Paris.

Almost totally destroyed in the 1944 fighting, Caen was one of the towns to benefit from special reconstruction grants in the late 1940s, and this helped to give it an early impetus it has never lost. Whereas the rebuilt quarters of Le Havre or Calais, amongst others, are impressively hideous, Caen carefully restored itself in something like the old style, with gabled roofs and harmonious local stone; and today the pale ochre façades leading up from the Pont Winston Churchill, along the Avenue du 6 Juin, are a rare architectural success. The university has been elegantly rebuilt on a hill behind the castle, and its numbers have swelled from 800 in 1958 to more than 10,000 today. All this, together with the port facilities in the Orne estuary and the good transport links over the 140 miles to Paris, have made Caen a relatively attractive bait for new industry, provided that new labour could be persuaded to settle there too.

When the Gaullists came to power and the regions were created, a fanatical young *sous-préfet* called Robert de Caumont was appointed to co-ordinate the economic development of Basse-Normandie; and he made it his vocation to build Caen into a great metropolis. The conservative city council of stolid Normans, despite their architectural taste, were even more lifeless than in pre-Dubedout Grenoble, nor did Caen have the spontaneous magnetism of Grenoble: so the State had to make the running. De Caumont, then still in his twenties, is an extreme example of the new school of young French technocrat-civil servant, energetic, apolitical, obsessed with expansion and forward planning, concerned to find human solutions but often too over-educated to possess the human touch, the sort of person who in America would rapidly rise up in a giant corporation, but in France tends to go into public service via the Ecole Nationale d'Administration. De Caumont spent four years in Normandy coaxing or bullying mayors and businessmen into action, and visiting Paris to entice factories down to Caen or to wheedle extra money out of Ministries.

Rarely can one civil servant have done so much for an area. He brought new firms, he had new suburbs built, he helped animate this poorer western half of Normandy with a new regional awareness—hence the councillors I heard arguing about airports. In 1964, he and the Prefect launched a 'return to your homeland' campaign by writing to young émigrés and local boys away on military service, telling them that the region had changed and there were now new factories offering work. Several hundred positive replies came in: rather more, in fact, than there were suitable new jobs. Today the industrial drive is beginning to bear fruit more rapidly, however, and Caen and its region lead France in the growth of fresh employment. There are new Renault and Citroën factories at Caen, and others making television sets, electrical machinery, and steel; and the exodus of youth has been slowed right down. Caen's population of 130,000 is twice its pre-war figure, and is expected to reach 180,000 by 1975.

Firms are attracted by the fact that they get some subsidy for the transfer, yet are still not too far from Paris. The chairman of the newly arrived Gramont television firm told me: 'The Government wouldn't let us extend our three little Paris factories. I went to see my old friend Massé, head of the Plan, and proposed Amiens. He said 'No, we're keeping Amiens for the rubber industry, go to Brest! I thought Brest was much too far and its workers far too Communist. After a lot of palaver, we fixed on Caen as a compromise. It suits us all right, as there's plenty of unskilled female labour, which we need. The only trouble is that the girls are green and tend to get exploited by unscrupulous union leaders.' He and some other firms admitted that an added attraction of a town like Caen is that you can still get away with paying lower salaries than in Paris. But the young director of the new Jaeger car-dashboard plant stressed to me that there are other advantages too: 'We chose Caen because we have to keep fairly near our headquarters and our clients in Paris. The Government first suggested Bayeux, which was too small; or Le Havre, which was too Left-wing. Caen is fine—the university, for instance, will be helping us with research and makes the town a livelier place to live in. Of the forty executives and technicians we invited to transfer from our Paris works, half agreed to come, more than we expected, and most of them like it here. As for me, I was glad to leave Paris with its ghastly traffic— life's impossible there nowadays. Here I've a house and garden near the sea with my wife and four kids, and our Paris friends come down for weekends. We've lots of lively new friends, too, many of them teachers at the university, and the Maison de la Culture keeps us occupied with modern plays, concerts, and lectures.'

De Caumont and his colleagues have been trying to make Caen as active and well endowed a place as possible. Links between town and gown, or gown and firms, are much less developed than at Grenoble, partly because of the reticence of many of the more senior professors; but on a social level the new Maison de la Culture is providing a lively point of juncture for students and immigré *cadres*. As in Grenoble, or elsewhere, much of the local dynamism comes from the new arrivals. The native Caennais are a sedate, conventional breed, old-style Catholics, and famous like most Normans for their refusal to commit themselves. Their own temperament, and the opulence and neat style of their rebuilt city, give it very much the air of a modern German town.

Many of the older citizens are suspicious of the new expansion, despite the prosperity it brings; and the mayor, M. Louvel, a typical Caennais diehard on the Right wing of the MRP, has been waging a feud against de Caumont. Here, as in several such towns, the problem is antipathy between central and suburban communes. Caen's own territory is almost full up, so de Caumont is building a satellite town of 35,000 in the Socialist-led suburb of Hérouville. But Louvel refuses to help pay for it, and neither he nor the mayor of Hérouville will accept any integration of their communes through fear of loss of autonomy or even electoral defeat. It makes the task of the Préfecture much harder. Last time I saw de Caumont, he was in his flat at Caen on a Sunday, composing a speech spiced with anti-Louvel innuendoes for the mayor of Hérouville to make at the inauguration of a new housing estate.

De Caumont has his protégés in other parts of the region, too. Twenty miles south of Caen lies the little town of Falaise, where William the Conqueror was born and Rommel made his last doomed stand against the Allies. Today under its Gaullist mayor, Edward Holman, Falaise is a remarkable example of what a town of a mere 8,000 people can achieve if it has the right dynamism and friends in the right places. Holman, a local lawyer, shares de Caumont's *panache* and his ethos. When he became mayor in the 1959 Gaullist landslide, the town had nothing but three decaying little hosiery factories. Holman got them to close, made a special study of local labour resources, and managed to convince two larger firms that it was worth setting up local plants: the Sumé mining equipment company from Paris and Moulinex, the makers of electrical vegetable-mincers. 'In fact, there used to be under-employment here,' he told me; 'for instance, the clerk in my office was really a skilled machine-tool operator. Now he's found suitable work with Sumé. And we've persuaded plenty of other former Falaisians to come back from Paris and work here. Of course, the Government helped the firms to move, but I sold them the sites cheaply.' Today Falaise is humming. Holman drove me excitedly round the town in his Citroën and showed me what he had built since 1959: a new civic centre, a hospital, a library, a youth club, a theatre, a big modern slaughterhouse, several housing estates, an enormous new lycée, sports centres, and a swimming-pool. If all the towns in France. . . . 'Of course de Caumont's helped me with funds,' he said, and added with a grin, 'and when I visit Ministries in Paris, it helps to be UNR.' But it would not be fair to dismiss Holman as an opportunist. His Gaullism may be naïve and the aid he gets excessive; but his keenness to develop his town and his region is real enough. 'Look!' he said, brandishing at me the 250-page regional *rapport* of the Fifth Plan, 'We've drawn this up *here*! We've got our own budget now. The regions are coming alive at last! We shall work hard and we shall win!' No wonder, I felt, that precisely 900 years ago poor King Harold found a Falaisian too much for him.

From Caen a main road runs south-west through the hilly *bocage* country, passes Avranches where Patton's tanks made their decisive breakthrough, skirts the bay of Mont St. Michel, and finally arrives at Rennes, the capital of Brittany. This hitherto sleepy city is today no less active than Caen, but in a very different style. Far more than at Grenoble or Caen, or almost anywhere, its revival has been sponsored from within its old self, and draws its spiritual strength from the culture and pride of this most nation-like of French provinces. Though the Government is keen to help economically backward Brittany, at Rennes the re-awakening has been led and animated by its exceptionally vigorous and progressive mayor, Henri Fréville. Not only is he operating on a much larger scale than Holman at Falaise, he is also *anti*-Gaullist. Yet he has been able to prove that even in centralised France a mayor of a large town, given the right courage and energy, can get some things done without having to be a stooge of the Government.

Rennes, which survived the war almost intact, is a dignified, unsmart, animated town of old grey buildings, with a less complacent and a more metropolitan atmosphere than Caen. Where the Normans are phlegmatic and almost Teutonic, the Bretons are humorous and individual—the Irish of France. For centuries their capital was a great centre of army, law, and learning; but it had no industry at all, and by about 1950 seemed depressed and poor. Yet émigrés kept arriving from the desolate, over-populated hinterland, and this being mother Brittany, they were less keen than in many parts of France to make straight for Paris. It was essential to find new work for them in Rennes.

This was the situation facing Fréville, a middle-aged, bespectacled history professor from the university, when he won the *mairie* in 1953 on an MRP ticket. His first and biggest *coup* was to persuade Citroën that Rennes was just the place for the big new factory they wanted and could not build in or near Paris. From that day, the Rennais began to recover confidence in their future, and Citroën today has 8,000 workers there. A few other industries have since arrived, too, and efforts are being made to develop Rennes as an electronics centre in collaboration with the big new Science Faculty. It is not easy, for most firms are reluctant to move 220 miles westwards from Paris, despite the 20 per cent installation subsidies. But since the war the population of Rennes has been able to rise from 100,000 to 170,000 without any unemployment. Fréville, a radical ideal-ist, has made exceptional efforts to provide cheap but good-quality housing and to endow the new estates with the kind of social and cultural equip-ment that usually is so conspicuously lacking in the modern French dormitory suburbs.* He also concerns himself with mental hospitals, and has done a great deal to help the local experimental repertory company, which has become one of the best in France. Under Fréville, Rennes was the first big French town to take town-planning seriously and provide itself with a master-plan.

Thanks to Fréville, and to many other less discernible factors, there has been a marked change in social atmosphere in Rennes since the early 1950s. The director of the theatre company told me: 'There's a totally different spirit, a revolution. The older Rennais haven't changed much, but they've been submerged by the new ones—the student generation, the technicians from Paris, the peasants arriving with the open outlook of émigrés. It used to be a dead town where, as they'd say, "Nothing ever catches on except fire" [there was a big fire here in 1720]. Today, there's a new kind of curiosity and sense of adventure: you can see it in the growth of the ciné-clubs, the popularity of composers like Schoenberg, or our own success with plays by people like Brecht and Osborne.' A university lecturer told me: 'Rennes has been transformed completely. It used to be dead after seven at night; now some cafés are still full well after midnight. Twelve years ago, the shops were seedy, and their window-dressing hadn't changed since 1910. Now, though it's sad in a way, the Breton *coifs* are gone from the streets, and the girls wear Paris dresses.'

Any visitor could see he was right about the cafés and the dresses. It is a town with a thriving cultural life, and a more evident student atmosphere than most—though inevitably this may change when the big new campus is completed outside the town. For the moment, the large *Brasserie de la*

* See p. 226 (The housing shortage).

Paix on the river, and the chic little Angelus café by the *mairie*, are both
crowded much of the time with rather more sophisticated and interesting-
looking students than one often finds in the provinces. With its northern,
misty, Celtic flavour it seems to have something in common with, say,
Bristol, or Exeter, its own twin-town; and today it is also the centre of a
modest Breton cultural revival, though this is due more to the enthusiasm
of a few local intellectuals and folklorists than to wide popular feeling. As
the coifs and handicrafts die out in the villages, so the Breton culture and
language clubs grow in the towns.

This may be a bit phoney and not especially significant. Nevertheless,
Rennes has the vocation to be a more authentic regional centre than
almost any town in France, and is already the capital of a 'region' comprising the four Brittany departments. More spontaneously than Caen in
Normandy, Rennes is providing a magnet for the province's rural exodus,
while its new factories and housing-estates offer the sociologist an absorbing study in peasantry transformed overnight into city-dwellers. Behind the pleasant blue-and-purple façades of the blocks of flats in the new
suburbs, Fréville has deliberately tried to jumble the classes together—
Breton peasants and Parisian technicians. The Parisians are said not to care
for this much. But the Bretons with their maritime toughness and their
native intelligence seem to be adapting better than many peoples to the
modern revolution of sudden urbanisation.

Rennes' revival is well ahead of that of the rest of Brittany. It stands
on the province's eastern frontier, half turned towards Paris; to its west
are 150 miles of a rugged and ill-developed peninsula, one of France's
worst 'depressed areas'. Long distances to Paris and poor transport services, backward farms and too-numerous peasantry, declining traditional
industries and lack of modern ones, crisis in the St. Nazaire shipyards and
slump in the naval roles of Brest and Lorient: all these factors work
against Brittany, and now, to add to them, the Common Market has
brutally pulled France's attention farther eastward. But the Bretons are a
demanding, resourceful people, used to struggling against odds, and they
feel that their economic problems, like Ireland's or Cornwall's, are not
entirely their own fault. In 1951 they founded an important pressure-
group for regional expansion, the CELIB, led by René Pleven, deputy
for Dinan and a former Prime Minister. This has continually been urging
the Government to do more to help Brittany. If the response of Paris has
so far seemed a little half-hearted, it is partly because of the immense
cost of the operation, and partly, so it is argued, through fears of a revival
of Breton separatism if the CELIB were given the power and funds it
asked for. In reality, however, nationalism is a less lively issue today than
in Wales or Scotland and on a political level attracts only a few extremists:
the Bretons' new regional spirit is based much more on economic practicalities than on political hopes or on the Celtic traditions of this mysterious
land.

The Government has done some things. It has begun to provide Brittany with its own sources of energy, through the Rance tidal dam and a new atomic centre in Finistère. It has built an important space-communications station near Lannion, and browbeaten the CSF electronics firm into setting up a big plant at Brest—for the Government wants Brittany to have 'an electronics and atomic vocation'. But though Pompidou tours the region saying, 'We must help to rid you of your complex of isolation,' he and his Ministers have not been too successful in persuading other factories to move in. The level of industrial employment is little more than half the French average, and it is the all-too-brief tourist season and the rich market-gardens of north Finistère that provide the surest revenue.

Some parts of Brittany do better than others. North Finistère is traditionally adventurous and dynamic: this is the land of Leclerc and the artichoke wars, where young Gourvennec has now set up a Société d'Economie Mixte to develop the whole area and has enlisted the help of Philippe Lamour and the mayor of Brest. It is an inspired and unusual move by a farmer to integrate agriculture into an overall planned economy; but it will need a lot of outside help. In contrast, the Morbihan department of southern Brittany is one of the three or four poorest and most lifeless in France. Tourists in summer find it so lovely, with its golden beaches, its abbeys and menhirs, its graceful walled capital of Vannes. But when the tourists have gone, there is not much left save the decaying farm-houses, the under-employment, the struggling shipyards of Lorient. From 1954 to 1962, the total of industrial jobs in the Morbihan actually fell by over 3,000.

In Brittany as a whole the picture is better: it is creating new industrial jobs at the rate of 5,000 a year. But this, so the planners say, is not nearly enough to bring prosperity. One solution for their problems which the Bretons much favour themselves is to develop links with Britain. If Britain were to join the Common Market, the centre of gravity would shift westwards again and Brittany would have a big new natural outlet on her doorstep: her isolation would be relieved. The hope is that Britain should buy Brittany's food, and also set up factories there on favourable terms, whether she joins the Market or not. So the CELIB has opened a Breton Centre in Sloane Street, London, and puts out glossy brochures in English, 'Industries of the Future have chosen Brittany', with gleaming new factories beside the beaches and the cows. It is touching to find an area where the British today are so popular and sought after: a British Week in Rennes in 1966, with the help of a team of guests from Exeter, was a great success. But on the economic level, the attempt at *rapprochement* between what Bretons modestly call '*la petite et la Grande Bretagne*' has met with a cautious response in Britain. Firms have shown little interest in settling there, and recent official British moves have tended to cut, rather than increase, the food imports.

This reaction, like that of Paris, has disappointed the Breton leaders, who are anxious to march with the times. Industrialisation is *à la mode* there today, and every little town wants its own expansion committee or *zone industrielle*. If the province had more autonomy and powers of decision, it might be able to move ahead faster or even turn elsewhere for help: its great seaports jutting into the Atlantic make it a natural point of contact with the Americas as well as with Britain. But Brittany has to wait upon Paris, and there the neo-Jacobins are not keen on the provinces managing their own destiny.

LANGUEDOC, TOULOUSE, LORRAINE

At the other end of France, the Languedoc presents the opposite picture: a sluggish area with little local pride, where the State has had to take the initiative. This coastal plain between the Rhône and Catalonia has much the same climate as Provence; and with its good soil, thick population, and strategic position astride the main routes into Spain and the south-west, it seemed ideal for development. But its race of lazy vinegrowers clearly needed a strong push from outside. So the Government chose the Languedoc for two of the most important development schemes in modern France: the canal, biggest irrigation network in Europe; and the largest State-sponsored tourist project in world history. It all seemed like a technocrat's dream: *carte blanche* to make bold new strokes across the map. But the Government was anxious not to repeat the mistakes in some countries of alienating the local population. To carry out both projects it set up Sociétés d'Economie Mixte, directed by the State but associating local municipalities and some local business interests. They have had some success in terms of public relations—except when it came to uprooting the vines.

The vine has been described as 'the Languedoc's sole wealth—and its greatest tragedy'. This province, named after its ancient dialect, the 'tongue of *oc*', was the most powerful in France in the days before Napoleon, and stretched to the west beyond Toulouse, then its capital. Today the Toulouse area is strictly the 'upper Languedoc', but in practice the word Languedoc is now usually applied only to the eastern coastal part of the province, with its capital at Montpellier. In the early nineteenth century, factories were flourishing along this coast, and one of the first railway lines in France was that from Montpellier to the port of Sète. But the vine killed this brief era of industrial expansion. When French wine consumption rose rapidly in the nineteenth century, the Languedociens found they could produce plenty and cheaply on their sunny slopes and it was much less trouble than building railways. Today the thick vineyards roll for scores of miles on every side, and life is easy when the grape grows fat on the red earth and needs little attention. The region produces over half of France's *vin ordinaire*; wine accounts for over a third of local revenue, but this revenue is up to 35 per cent below the national average, for these are not the lucrative vintage wines of Burgundy or Bordeaux. The vines and the climate have united to produce a slow, conservative, unenterprising temperament. Only when their prices or markets are threatened will the growers get excited and take action: in 1907, and again in the crisis year of 1953, they staged some of the worst farming riots of the century. Even today, they are still most defensive about their interests: big posters along the main roads announce, 'Pasteur says, wine is the healthiest of drinks!' After all, they have to do something to counter the Government's anti-alcoholism campaign.

The monoculture of cheap wine was dangerous for the region's economy. Yet it could not really be diversified unless there was water for growing other crops. In 1940 Philippe Lamour, novelist, man of action and Left-wing farming leader, escaped from the Occupation in the north and bought an estate at Bellegarde, south of Nîmes, at the eastern edge of the Languedoc, near the fertile, fruit-growing zone of the lower Rhône. There he settled, and after the war gave himself the mission of rescuing the Languedoc. 'We must save the "French desert" before it is too late,' he wrote—and he persuaded the Fourth Republic to build the canal which had lain dormant as a project since 1851. The Government agreed, and put him in charge of it. Lamour is an unusual and striking personality, a kind of freelance technocrat and man of ideas, but neither civil-servant, politician, nor academic expert. He is versatile, charming, and human: it amuses him to disconcert romantic-minded girl secretaries by announcing his surname most seductively to them down a telephone. 'Vous cherchez l'amour, mademoiselle? Me voilà.'

He formed a company that dug a wide master canal from the Rhône to Montpellier and built dams in the Cévennes behind Béziers. Soon a network of little canals began to transect some of the vineyards. Lamour and two or three other local pioneers uprooted their own few vines and proceeded to demonstrate that the same acreage of apple- or pear-orchards could earn six times as much as vines, if properly irrigated. The vinegrowers were invited to follow suit. And how did they react? They formed 'committees of defence against the canal', they rioted in the streets of the big towns with banners saying 'Death to Lamour!', they behaved, in short, like farmers a hundred years ago afraid those new-fangled trains would run over their cows. Agitation finally subsided, once the farmers realised they would not be *forced* to uproot their vines; but today hardly a single vinegrower has yet destroyed a single acre. The canal simply ran into debt through lack of clients, and Lamour has had to sanction what at first he had regarded as intolerable: use of the canal to irrigate vines. This is allowed only for the higher-grade V DQS or eating grapes, and so to some extent it is helping the campaign for more quality, but so far, only 7 per cent of the 35,000 acres actively using the canal's water are under vine. The water is used mainly in the non-vinegrowing plain south of Nîmes, where yields of fruit, asparagus, and tomatoes have risen sharply.

But it is in the foothills behind Béziers, far to the west, that the vine-yards are the the poorest, with soil often unsuited for VDQS, and here the farms could benefit most from transformation, using the water from the Cévennes dams. Yet it is here that the small farmers are most stubborn. France's leading viticultural expert, Professor Milhau of Montpellier University, explained to me: 'You must remember that this irrigation project was launched long before Algeria became free: uprooting of vines is less essential now, so the project's *raison d'être* has really changed. Even so, a lot of those vineyards up behind Béziers are on quite the wrong soil and ought to go. But vinegrowing has been in those lazy farmers' blood for centuries—it's a religion. The young ones will listen to us, but it will take a generation for much to happen. The other big problem is that many of the vines are hired out on a *métayage** basis by absentee land-lords, middle-class people who live in the cities. And they can't be both-ered to make changes—you see, the vine round here is considered *un métier noble*, it's not ungentlemanly like pig-breeding.'

Despite this considerable failure with the vines, the canal in itself has been a technical and administrative success. Several foreign countries have copied the ideas that underlie it: Rumania has even signed contracts with the canal company for technical aid. More than a third of the irri-gable area is now actively using the canal's water: the proportion is highest in the fruit-farming region south of Nîmes, and so long as the problems of marketing and fruit surpluses can be solved, the areas not under vine will probably succeed in becoming, as is planned, a 'French California'. The growth of ventures such as Libby's and its rival co-operative shows that a new dynamism, linked with the canal, is beginning to have the desired influence on the region, at least around Nîmes. But it will certainly take a generation or more before the 'tyranny of the vine' fades to the right proportions in the areas to the west, where it is strongest. And not until then is the canal likely to become economically viable: it is a scheme that cannot be fairly judged for another twenty or thirty years.

The tourist project, like the canal, was Lamour's original idea, though its official endorsement, in 1962, must be credited to the Fifth Republic, not the Fourth. Between the mouth of the Rhône and the Pyrenees lie one hundred miles of splendid sandy beaches, hitherto largely unexploited because of the mosquitoes, the marshy lagoons just inland, and the flat, relatively unbeautiful scenery. But Europe's tourist hordes are growing each year, the Riviera and the Costa Brava are saturated: where are the extra crowds to go? And how is France to halt the steady worsening of her tourist balance, due partly to the lack of space and high prices in Pro-vence?

As the Government pondered these problems, it seemed that the ideal

* See p. 75 (The Young Farmers' revolt).

solution might be to build a chain of new popular resorts along this coast, and so help re-animate the Languedoc too. First the Government made war on the mosquitoes, successfully, with a chemical process that killed their larvae. Then it prepared a master-plan for six resorts, and in 1963 began buying up land at key points. This was done secretly, through third parties, to avoid sudden speculation. Surprisingly, the secret was actually kept, and nearly 7,000 acres were acquired on the cheap before the project was revealed at all, whereupon prices shot up all along the coast, sometimes a hundredfold. But round its own little enclaves the Government has marked out wider zones, where under a new law it has given itself the right to regulate prices and, if it wishes, pre-empt land at its own figure. Thus, in the places that matter, speculation that might have ruined the whole project has been kept right down; and even the severest critics of the régime admit that this part of the operation has been a great success. 'No Left-wing Government in France could have done it,' a Marxist professor at Montpellier told me: 'It needed the connivance of the big financiers.'

A special new inter-ministerial committee in Paris master-minds the project, while a series of locally constituted Sociétés d'Economie Mixte are in charge of providing the infrastructure and public services for each resort. When the land is ready for building, most of it is sold or leased to private firms who will then construct the hotels, villas, and casinos and run them on a profit basis as anywhere else. But they have to adhere closely to the architectural master-plan, which is the charge of Georges Candilis, the brilliant Greek who was le Corbusier's assistant for ten years. This is capitalism, but controlled. 'We want to avoid the anarchy of Florida or the Costa del Sol,' I was told.

Another important aim is to keep rents and hotel prices down and to encourage rather more 'social' and 'popular' tourism than on the Riviera. This has been a main reason for the anti-speculation measures. It is linked with the official campaign to dissuade quite so many Frenchmen, and others, from preferring the beaches of cheaper lands like Spain: France, by tradition a great tourist country, today earns no more from foreign visitors than French tourists spend abroad. So the Touring Club de France, the Club Méditerranée, and other such bodies, have been encouraged to buy land in the Languedoc for holiday camps and modest villas; and some low-cost flats will be subsidised by using them out of season as lodgings for Montpellier students. All this makes good sense, in an age of mass tourism. Unfortunately, the Government is finding that the policy conflicts with other realities. Under the Fifth Plan alone it is investing 350m francs in the project, and it is under heavy pressure from its financial partners, the State and private banks, to amortise its costs quickly. It finds it can get far higher and quicker returns by encouraging luxury flats and hotels than it can from 'social' tourism; and it now seems that more of these will be built than was planned originally. In their final form, the resorts may have more in common than was intended

with the rich new development around Cannes, even if, with their Corbusier-style sun-terraces and garden-cities, they show little visual re-
semblance to a traditional seaside town.

Thousands of acres of cypresses have been planted to act as wind-
breaks, new roads have been built, and dredgers have worked on preparing
pleasure-ports. Although the usual disputes and shortages have set everything behind schedule, in the summer of 1968 the first tourists will
begin to arrive at the first of the resorts, la Grande Motte, south-east of
Montpellier, and le Barcarès, near Perpignan. Finally, maybe in ten years
or so, it is planned that there will be 600,000 new tourist beds, as many as
on the whole Riviera.

The technocrats here face one of their sternest trials. More than any
other single project in France, this complex venture is a test of whether
such bold and imaginative planning can really succeed in practice, when
faced with the hazards of multilateral collaboration and financial pressures. So far, the auguries are fair, despite the delays. The local population, at first sceptical, are now quite enthusiastic. And they are being
coaxed forward by the team in the Préfecture who look after the growth
of the Languedoc region, the five departments from the Pyrenees to
the Rhône and the Massif Central. With typical Gaullist majesty, this
team describe themselves as a 'mission', and have something of the outlook of a Peace Corps unit in central Africa. My local Marxist friend,
Professor Raymond Dugrand, leading expert on the Languedoc's economic
geography, told me: 'I abhor Gaullism, but I've chosen to help this lot
here all I can, because I accept their good faith, and they're the most
dynamic and effective administration I've ever seen. You see, we're
becoming more pragmatic in France at last, and less doctrinaire.'

The team are also preparing a national park in the Cévennes to complement the coastal project, for tourists who want mountains as well as
beaches. And they are beginning to have some success in attracting new
industries to the Languedoc: IBM has built a big factory at Montpellier,
and chemical works are growing at Sète. Under the impact of all the new
influences, Montpellier itself is a place of curious contrasts. The ancient
kernel of the city, with its steep, Spanish-style little streets and graceful
courtyards, is as delightful as Toledo or Cordoba; the rest of the town is a
hubbub of traffic far too heavy for it. Conversely, the sluggish Right-wing
municipality is still dominated by the bourgeois society that grew up round
the wine industry; but the streets, old and new, are full of lively youth, for
the university is growing fast. Montpellier at present combines the natural
out-of-doors animation of any Mediterranean town, with the newer and
more urgent bustle of economic resurgence. It will need the most skilful
planning for the two to be properly integrated.

Sète, twenty miles away, also has intriguing contrasts. Home town of
Paul Valéry, where he wrote his finest poem, *Le Cimitière marin*, it is
the world's largest wine-trading port and the only port of any size on the
long coast from Marseille to Barcelona. Fishing-boats, pleasure-yachts, and

big cargo vessels lie delightfully cheek by jowl in its picturesque canals. And the Communist town council, controlled by dockers and sailors, works hand in glove with the Right-wing Chamber of Commerce, for it accepts that they both have the same interests, the expansion of the port. But Sète's politics have meant that Paris took an unduly long time giving it the funds necessary for enlarging and modernising the port.

There is one other development that in some ways has done more than anything, so far, to reanimate the Languedoc—and that is the arrival of several hundred thousand repatriate *pieds noirs* * from Algeria. Some 25,000 settled in Montpellier alone in 1962–3, swelling its population by one-fifth. The absorption by France of over 800,000 *pieds noirs*, most of them in the Midi, has been one of the great unsung achievements of the 1960s, and bears witness to the elasticity of the economy as well as to the Government's astuteness and the tolerance of the French. There has been remarkably little friction of any sort, and though there was some initial hardship in the refugee camps of Marseille, Government resettlement grants have helped virtually all the *pieds noirs* to find new homes, jobs, or businesses. Some who at first settled in the north found they did not like the climate or the local temperament, and many of them have drifted back south where they find closer affinities. The ones in Montpellier are mostly Oranais, either of Midi origins themselves, or else of Spanish descent like many Montpelliérains. This and the climate make them feel at home, even though they no longer have flocks of Muslim servants. Though in Oran or Algiers they produced the thugs and diehards of the OAS, back in France those same characteristics of toughness and perseverance show the bright side of their medal: they have bought up dying farms or businesses and are making them buzz. In the Languedoc, their hard-working vitality acts as a catalyst on the local rhythm of life, especially in commerce. In some parts of the Midi, especially around the Garonne, they have helped to stimulate agriculture by importing a new outlook as well as the modern techniques they used on the much larger estates of North Africa. As someone said, 'They see the Midi as the kind of challenge to them that Africa was in the last century.'

Socially, they tend to stick together, make a lot of noise, and stay out far later on café terraces than the Midi people. Every town of any size has its 'Cercle Mostaganem', 'Amicale de Sidi-bel-Abbès', or whatever. In one vinegrowing village near Montpellier, the sole local café had been quietly stagnating for years; then some *pieds noirs* bought it up, modernised and enlarged it, and now it is full every night with young ex-Oranais playing with the juke-box and pin-tables. In Montpellier I had an intriguing experience. It is today a town of quite exceptionally pretty girls, with brown skins and bold figures, dressed in gaily coloured slacks. Sitting near an animated nest of them, in one of the student cafés in the town's

* When the first French settlers arrived in Algeria, the barefoot Muslims called them after their black shoes—and the nickname has stuck.

main square, a memory came into my mind that I could not at first identify. Where had I seen girls precisely like these before? Then I remembered. These girls were like the hysterical crowds of *Algérie française* youth in Oran in the May 1958 revolution. And Oran, in the days before Ben Bella, had the loveliest European girls in the world. Later that day I was told: the café I had been sitting in was the *pied noir* student headquarters.

With this double infusion of new blood from Oran, and new leaders and ideas from Paris, the future of the Languedoc looks promising, and of all the more backward regions of France it is now the one changing the fastest. It will benefit, too, from being so close to the current industrial development of the lower Rhône Valley and the Marseille area. Whether the local people of the Languedoc will become revitalised too, or whether they will gradually get pushed aside and submerged, it is probably too early to say.

A hundred miles or so to the west, the sprawling region known as Midi-Pyrenées is one of the poorest and most neglected in France—save for its turbulent capital, Toulouse. This oasis of noise, industry, culture, and driving local pride is one of the key points in the policy of building up the *métropoles d'équilibre*, and its rapid post-war progress has been due in roughly equal parts to spontaneous growth, civic initiative, and Government action. Today it is a fascinating example of a medium-sized provincial town beginning consciously to realise its vocation as a big city, rather as Manchester did in the late nineteenth century. Since 1939, Toulouse's population has doubled to reach 400,000 and it has overtaken Bordeaux as France's fourth largest town. In that time, it seems to have crossed that mysterious theshold where an ordinary town begins to take on the atmosphere and habits of a metropolis: the suburbs grow larger than the city itself, townsfolk become commuters, Parisian quick-lunch bars and night-clubs spring up, and you can no longer reach the open country in a pleasant walk from the centre.

Toulouse might never have become an important industrial town had not aircraft and explosives factories been shifted there for strategic reasons in the Great War. Today it is the main centre of aircraft construction and headquarters of the State-run nitrogen industry. But it is badly placed geographically in relation to Paris and the Common Market nerve-centres, and is finding it hard to draw new industries, even with State subsidies as high as in Brittany. Its own ambition is to turn its face south, not north, and instead of trying to compete with Lyon or Strasbourg to become a rallying-point for new links with Spain and Africa. Toulousians remember with pride that their city, in the 1920s, pioneered the first air postal services from Europe to Africa and across to South America, led by those great aviators, Jean Mermoz and Antoine de Saint-Exupéry. In the new supersonic age, Toulouse wants to be in the lead again; and not solely by building Caravelles and Concordes in its workshops. The town clerk,

François Laffont, an excitable visionary, told me: 'Toulouse is the avant-garde of Europe towards Spain and Africa, and those are the countries of the future. The world is changing fast, and Toulouse must be a springboard. We want to build the great economic *axes* of tomorrow, Toulouse to Madrid and the Sahara. The Pyrenees are a fake barrier.' If Spain continues to develop, and is able to associate with the Common Market, this dream might be realised. It would be helped by the building of a tunnel under the Pyrenees, a project often discussed but inevitably slow to take shape.

In the meantime, the Government is trying to develop the city on the basis of its own traditions: the two leading aviation *Grandes Ecoles* are being transferred there from Paris, and the new National Centre for Space Research is to be built there. The new science faculty, now being completed, will be the largest in the provinces. Like Grenoble, Toulouse is to be made into a great capital of advanced industry and science. It is a worthy effort of regional development in a difficult and isolated corner of France, but Paris will keep the real power.

Toulouse, on the wide plain of the Garonne, is rather different in looks and atmosphere from Grenoble. It is strident and dusty, full of heavy lorries, and yet is a fiercely impressive place, not only because of the mellow grandeur of its rose-brick classical buildings. Its rough pride seems a blend of the modern working-class and the cultural-historical, and it knows it is now recovering some of the strength it once enjoyed as the old capital of the Languedoc. Though there are not many new factories, the immigrants flood in, and they find work somehow, often in the building trade. Many come from the villages of the region, which are rapidly losing their population. Some 40,000 new arrivals are *pieds noirs*, who have joined forces with the 25,000 Spanish exiles from the Civil War. It is a city with a strong immigrant tradition: a quick-tempered Latin melting-pot, utterly different from its sedate and bourgeois rival, Bordeaux.

To provide for the influx, the city council is building one of the largest new suburbs in France, Le Mirail, for 100,000 people. The architect, as in the Languedoc, is Candilis; and he is closely applying some of his master's doctrines,* with towering blocks of flats amid lakes and gardens, whole districts free from traffic, and intersecting motorways. But the construction work advances slowly, because the State is niggardly with its funds and in France local taxes are too low for a town to be able to carry out a project like this on its own. 'Paris penalises us, because the council is anti-Gaullist,' complained Laffont; and like Fréville, he made a snide remark about Chaban-Delmas' advantages in Bordeaux. There may be some truth in this, today, though until recently much of the impulse for developing Toulouse did come from the State. Though Toulouse has always nourished a strong civic pride, it has also habitually indulged in

* See p. 214 (The housing shortage) for le Corbusier's delayed influence in France.

violent party politics, and until about 1963 the councillors were often too taken up with brawling about Algeria or clericalism to pay much attention to town-planning. Today, however, all the non-Communist parties save the Gaullists are in coalition, with a Socialist mayor and a right-wing deputy-mayor. 'The parties are far less intransigent nowadays,' said Laffont; 'We haven't got time for ideology any more, practical matters are too urgent.' Even so, de Gaulle is not popular. Working relations with the Prefect are tolerably smooth, because of the common desire to develop the town; but they are based on an uneasy mutual *rapport de force*, and Toulouse's pride is offended by its lack of real autonomy. As a sign of its desire to do things its own way, it has built its own civic cultural centre, without waiting to fit into Malraux's national network. But such initiatives must remain rare while Paris holds the strings; and Toulouse's vocation as a real provincial capital, in the German or Italian manner, must remain limited.

Another and very different problem is that Toulouse's growth may create a 'desert' round it, almost as bad as the old *désert français* caused by Paris. Instead of radiating and animating its rural hinterland, Toulouse simply drains its population: several departments round here, notably the Ger, the Lot, and the Ariège, are among the poorest and emptiest in France. The rural exodus may be necessary in itself, but it is dangerous if it simply creates a void for miles around; and in some parts of these departments there is not enough labour or resources left for repairing roads and buildings or fallen telephone wires. In some areas, tourism might help to provide a solution; but it will need heavy investment in new services, and in creating and staffing the national parks now planned there. The real answer, so the technocrats believe, is to develop the medium-sized and smaller towns, especially the capitals of departments, and build some of them up as counter-poles of influence to Toulouse, just as Toulouse is to Paris. In many such towns, the local artisans and cottage-industries have died away, and not much has yet taken their place. It is usually hard to persuade new industries to settle in a small out-of-the-way place, if it is far from Paris. Sometimes, on main roads in the Massif Central, one sees hopeful hoardings on the edge of little towns: 'Industrialists! Choose Noirétable for your new factory! We shall be proud to welcome you!' One wonders how many enquiries they receive.

The Aveyron, north-east of Toulouse, in the south of the Massif Central, is an example of a department literally fighting for its life. It is on a knife-edge between considerable new prosperity and further decline, with strong forces pulling in both directions. Its population, now 283,000 over 3,426 square miles, has dropped by a third since 1886, and on many of the chalky upland *causses* the villages are dying. But the Aveyronnais are an unusually tough and enterprising people, more prepared for an uphill struggle than the soft plainsmen of the Languedoc. Their young farmers, as I have shown, are already fighting with some success to improve and modernise agriculture, the Aveyron's main industry. But they cannot operate in a void. They need flourishing local centres, for markets, shopping, schools, social and cultural life, especially if the next generation is to find a life on the land congenial. The nearest big town, Toulouse, is one hundred miles away over difficult winding roads.

The Aveyron's one real industrial town, Decazeville, collapsed into irremediable depression a few years ago when its coal-mines wore thin and ceased to be competitive. When the State began to close them down, 800 miners protested by staying at the bottom of a pit for several weeks over Christmas 1961. The miners were offered resettlement in State mines in other parts of France, but they stubbornly wanted to stay in their own area, and demanded that new industries be provided. Yet no industry wanted to come to a dying coal town on a remote branch railway line.

It was a new blow for the Aveyron. Fortunately its capital, Rodez, has fared much better, and today is an unexpectedly thriving and go-ahead town of some 30,000 people. All around, for scores of miles, there is nothing but chalky plateaux, and brown hills with straggling farms. But Rodez itself, in the valley of the river Aveyron, is an oasis of modernity with its Parisian shops, newly decorated hotels, and many new blocks of flats. It benefits from its position on one of the main tourist routes through the Massif Central, and also from being the marketing capital of a large agricultural area, although not a rich one. Another secret of its success is that though people emigrate from the Aveyron they do not forget it. Its boundaries are much the same as those of the old province of Rouergue, and so it is less artificial than most departments and keeps its own regional pride. Many of its émigrés make their fortune in Paris but keep up the old links: men like Marcellin Cazes who founded and ran the famous literary café, Chez Lipp, at St.-Germain-des-Près, and then came back to die at his old home in Rodez in 1965. Similarly when a big Paris chemical factory had to be evacuated for strategic reasons in 1939, its managing-director chose Rodez of all remote places, because that was where he came from. Today, with 800 workers, the factory is one of the causes of Rodez' prosperity. Another cause, oddly enough, is the town's vocation as a centre of boarding-schools: 'It's really our chief local industry,' I was told. 'There are 10,000 schoolchildren here.' Because the air is so fresh, and venial distractions so few, many parents would rather send their children away here than, for example, to Cannes with its fleshpots. And so the streets of this unlikely backwoods Seaford are regularly full of crocodiles of uniformed pupils, led by nuns or priests or young State *surveillants*.

Finally, Rodez has succeeded in reviving its local artisanal industries. Woodwork, furniture, packaging, decorative ironwork—a score of little firms of this sort have sprung up or expanded since the war, whereas in the smaller towns of the Cévennes, to the south-east, the old silk and hosiery industries are dying. Rodez is just large enough, and sufficiently enterprising, to benefit from the new urban trends in France, and so act as a catchment centre in a region of heavy rural exodus. The problem is to help the lesser or feebler towns to do the same.

Of the other *métropoles d'équilibre* besides Toulouse, the one now changing the fastest is Bordeaux. Until about 1958, it had the reputation of being the least active of France's larger towns, and after the war it fell from fourth to sixth place, overtaken in size by Toulouse and Nice. Its narrow-spirited mercantile ruling class, straight out of the pages of Mauriac, still clung to the illusions of Bordeaux as a great seaport. They rebuilt the damaged harbour after the war, only to find that half its cranes stayed idle. The end of France's colonial links, the decline of the shipping trade for coal and wood, the relative loss of ground by Bordeaux wines to those of Burgundy and elsewhere, all spelt stagnation to the city and its port, which, apart from the wine, and the wood of the Landes forests, had no industry or prosperous hinterland on which to depend.

But the ambitious young mayor, Jacques Chaban-Delmas, was a Gaullist of exceptional influence, and after 1958 his hour came. Using his new prestige as President of the National Assembly, third highest post in the land, he persuaded the snobbish and cautious burghers to accept a change of course. More important, he could now secure the right funds and decisions from Ministries. Over a hundred new factories—most of them small ones, admittedly—arrived in Bordeaux from 1960 to 1965. Today, large areas of the city are being rebuilt or extended, new bridges and motorways are nearing completion, the university has grown into one of the largest in France. Bordeaux is now catching up with the rather more spontaneous success of Toulouse. It is true that Chaban-Delmas is often accused of prestige-hunting; and it might be wrong to suggest that the older Bordelais businessmen have experienced a real change of heart. But the new activity is patent, and is supported by the younger generation. One youngish Bordelais told me, 'Ten years ago, it was such a dead town. All that people would talk about was the port, the wood trade, and the wine. The theatre was lousy, and even to get one ciné-club going was hard. Today, people talk about new factories, the space-research centre, the international arts festival . . . and there are lots of ciné-clubs. It feels like being in a metropolis, at last.'

Marseille is a much greater port, with an even greater mayor, Gaston Defferre, but he is not exactly a Gaullist. Despite his difficulties with the State administration, his record of housing and other public works in the city has been striking: the latest, and grandest, is a tunnel under the Old Port to help cure traffic jams that are among the worst in Europe. Though some of the city's traditional sea-trade and industry have declined, oil refineries and other modern works have grown rapidly in the vast new industrial complex between Marseille and the Rhône. With its population of one million, this brash, torrid, proletarian town is the second in France, and the first seaport of the Mediterranean. If only because of its strategic position, where the great axis of the Rhône valley meets the sea, it has prospects as bright as that of any large French city. Lyon, too, benefits from a pivotal position and is booming, though some of its thunder has been stolen by near-by Grenoble. Strasbourg has been stimulated by its European role and by the new trade along the Rhine. It has attracted more than its share of new industry, but is beginning to feel the pressure of German competition. At Lille, the difficulties of textiles and coal are balanced by the rise of the Nord steel industries; the town is doing all right, but not brilliantly. In the west, the graceful city of Nantes has many of the outward signs of new prosperity, with bustling streets and some fine modern shops and buildings. But this is something of a façade: at heart, Nantes remains one of the most conservative of French towns, and like St. Nazaire and Lorient it as affected by the malaise of the shipping industry.

The eighth and last of the *métropoles* is a hybrid: Nancy-Metz, twin capitals of Lorraine and inseparable rivals. Nancy is the aristocratic university town, Metz the energetic centre of heavy industry. They complement each other well, and their province was, until very recently, one of the most prosperous and successful in France. The 'French Ruhr' it was sometimes even called, and is well placed at the heart of the Common Market. But today Lorraine has run into trouble. It has become one of the few regions of France where the problem is that there is the wrong kind of industry, not a lack of industrial activity. The great iron-ore mines, basis of Lorraine's wealth, are beginning to wear thin; even on the home market they can no longer easily compete with higher-grade imported ore. Recession has also hit the Moselle coal-mines and the outmoded Vosges textile firms, both typically vulnerable sectors. Of the major local industries, only the steelworks are still doing quite well, but they are being obliged to level off production as world competition grows. Since about 1963, Lorraine's firms have found that they can survive only by cutting labour costs and improving productivity. Yet this is an area with a high birth-rate, and is now showing signs of unemployment and unrest. In the frontier districts, people are increasingly having to find work in the Saar or Luxembourg.

The irony is that, until 1961, new factories were discouraged from settling in Lorraine. The local iron- and steelworks wanted to keep a monopoly of industry in the Moselle area; unlike the Ruhr firms, they would not allow the steel to be used on the spot by manufacturing industries, fearing that this would lead to shortages of skilled labour. But now, with 60,000 new jobs urgently needed by 1970, Lorraine is crying out for just that sort of new factory, and finding it hard to get them quickly. 'The trouble,' I was told, 'is that the Government regards us as a "developed" area, and won't give us any priority aid. So we're trying to attract German firms here: a few have come already.' The Lorrains also feel they are handicapped by lack of good canals and roads: the new Moselle canal from Coblenz to Metz helps the Germans more than the French. The Lorrains are unusually hard-working, skilled, and resourceful—just the kind of labour that industry likes. This makes them all the more indignant about their present troubles, but it will probably help them to win through.

Lorraine was an independent duchy until 1766. It is one of the least French parts of France in character, with a northern tone to its cold winters and scarred landscapes, and a people who are stolid, reserved, reliable, not very typically Gallic. Yet in the past century they have manifested a stronger French patriotism, almost mystical, than any other region of France. Verdun is here, and the *Colline inspirée* of the nationalist writer Maurice Barrès, and, as a living reminder, Joan's Domrémy. From 1871 to 1918 the hated Germans ruled Metz, and Nancy was a French military frontier town. Today, the anti-German feeling has almost disappeared, Nancy is enthusiastically twinned with Karlsruhe, and national patriotism is yielding ground to Lorraine regional pride which has always been strong too.

Nancy, the historical capital, has something of a royal air with its superb eighteenth-century squares built by Lorraine's last duke, ex-King Stanislas of Poland. But Metz, a slightly smaller town, showed so much more dynamism after the war that the Government awarded it the regional Préfecture, to Nancy's indignation. Probably the Government was right. Nancy is yet another French city where the senior townsfolk and the council have shown little civic initiative, and the impulse for renewal has had to come from other elements—in this case, mainly from the university and from youth. Nancy, until recently, had an *esprit de petit commerçant*: its councillors would not allow industry within their borders for fear of building up Left-wing voters. Like Michallon at Grenoble, its Right-wing mayor was less keen on civic progress than on prestige operations—hence the big notices at the gates of the town, 'We are twinned with Karlsruhe, Liège, Newcastle upon Tyne, Padua!'

But the university has been growing fast, under some exceptionally vigorous leaders,* and though they have received scant aid or encouragement from the council, they have succeeded in infusing the city with some new spirit. Nancy has led the way in France in adult education and university drama: thanks entirely to the initiative of a young law lecturer, Jack Lang, it now has the world's leading annual international student drama festival. The mayor, Dr. Weber, and his team, are shamefacedly proud of the renown this has brought their town, and they are now beginning to take more interest themselves in town-planning and improving cultural life. Despite the region's economic difficulties, Nancy has a far less narrow and inactive social and cultural existence than ten years ago.

Nancy and Metz are bound to remain two separate towns, so that their designation as one *métropole d'équilibre* seems a curious sort of compromise. Elsewhere, too, the choice appears arbitrary. Nantes is on the list,

---

* See pp. 336 and 351 (Youth with a dusty answer).

but not Rennes, a smaller but more important centre. Grenoble does not figure either, and nor does Nice, fifth town of France and one of the wealthiest. If the *métropoles* are to receive priority funds and equipment at the expense of other towns more dynamic and fast-growing, it could lead to a waste of resources. More probably, the policy behind their designation is merely a gesture of good intention towards the provinces as a whole. But how real are the Government's good intentions? It remains to analyse more critically the aims, achievements, and limitations of the Government's regional policy, in the three principal fields: industry, the arts, and local administration.

FACTORIES, MOTORWAYS, TELEPHONES:
A DUBIOUS RECORD

This survey of a few typical towns and regions may have shown how uneven the success of the policy of industrial decentralisation has been. The growth of industry in the Paris region has been slowed, but not halted; many hundreds of firms, like Citroën, have set up new subsidiary factories in the provinces, but very few have actually transferred their plant from Paris; and though the graph of new development in the provinces rose steadily until 1963, the rate has since fallen off sharply, for a number of reasons.

The figures also show strikingly that a Paris firm will put a new factory within 150 miles of the capital, but will rarely go farther out. Grenoble, Rennes, or Bordeaux are exceptions. On the whole, towns like Reims and Amiens are faring best. Their revival is at least one step forward, for in 1950 the 'desert' began at the edge of Paris; but it does not help the general imbalance and waste of resources. Official incentives do not seem to be enough. Subsidies for new factories' installation costs are nil for the towns within 100 miles or so of Paris, but rise to 25 per cent for the main towns of the west and south-west, and cover 60 per cent of costs if you are actually transferring a plant *from* Paris. But other factors usually seem to weigh more heavily with firms when deciding where to settle. The need to keep near the Paris financial and commercial world, the fear of not finding enough skilled labour in the backward areas, the high transport costs over longer distances, are important considerations. And though a Parisian executive may enjoy the ski-slopes of Grenoble, he feels he would be less happy in Nantes or Limoges.

Often, firms simply lack the courage to take the plunge. Indeed, most of those that *have* moved to somewhere pleasant in the south are pleased with the results, in human as well as economic terms. IBM has had a trio of successes: at La Gaude (near Nice), at Montpellier, and nearer home, at Orléans. For a few others firms, the mountains and lakes of Savoy have been almost as great a draw as Grenoble: 'I've had two nervous breakdowns in Paris, and now I'm happier here,' said an executive of a new electronics factory, on the balcony of his chalet overlooking the Lake of Geneva at Thonon.

According to one recent survey, over 50 per cent of Paris professional people say they would rather live in the provinces if they could find the right kind of job and conditions. But relatively few are yet prepared to act on it. Often it is the wives who are most cautious about moving; or there is the worry of finding a good *lycée* or university for the children (it is significant that the towns that do expand fast, like Caen and Grenoble, nearly always have universities). And even when the *cadres* are prepared to decentralise, the skilled workers of a firm are often much more stubborn. For although the educated classes and the emigrating peasantry are increasingly mobile, the third section of the nation (the urban workers) still tend to be sedentary in their outlook. Like the miners of Decazeville, they will rarely move to find work elsewhere, and especially not from Paris.

In the light of these problems, it is perhaps not very surprising that fewer new jobs than was officially hoped have been created in the areas where they are most needed. Statistics can be misleading here, as they often make no distinction between real decentralisation and the enlargement of existing factories. Official figures claim that the Paris region's share in the total number of new jobs created each year fell from 32 per cent in 1949–54 to a mere 6 per cent in 1961. But the 1,031 operations of claimed 'decentralisation' in that period yielded only 114,500 new jobs outside Paris, at a time when the population and economy were expanding rapidly. In few areas have the regional development societies set up so hopefully after the war had much real success, though it is noticeable that wherever there is a really dynamic local initiative, as at Rennes or Falaise, it usually bears some fruit.

If the overall policy has not worked better, it is partly the Government's fault. Left-wing leaders often accuse it of not being tough enough with firms, or of yielding to pressure from the Patronat who want to keep the *status quo*. Citroën has spent years successfully resisting official efforts to persuade it to shift its huge main factory from the centre of Paris; on the other hand, it is reliably reported that in order to get the CSF to set up its electronics plant in Brest, the Government resorted to tough threats of suspending its valued State contracts. It is therefore hard to pass a hasty judgement; but it seems that the Citroën case is the more typical. The Government will use enticement, but rarely anything more, and often allows its own rules to be broken. Nor has it done all it might to decentralise its own industries. New refineries and power stations, certainly, are placed near ports or the sources of raw energy, and several State aircraft firms have been moved out of Paris recently. But it is partly the State's fault that most of the car industry is still in the Paris area: Renault still has its main factory at Billancourt, and, though it has decentralised several smaller plants, few of them have moved far from the capital.

There may even be an element of truth in Left-wing allegations that the Government campaign for developing the south and west has now become slightly two-faced. The growth of the Common Market and of German competition has made it more imperative than ever to build up French industry where it is strong—in Paris and the east. Heavy firms in the Rhône Valley, in Alsace or the Nord, have been allowed to expand at full tilt. This may be right and necessary in the short term; but the Government knows there are just not the resources to carry out both policies at once. Therefore its endless speeches of sympathy and encouragement for the west are partly electoral eyewash. As one anti-Gaullist put it to me, 'The two main planks of the régime's industrial policy, concentration of firms and deconcentration of their plants, often contradict each other.' And in the longer term it is possible that the waste of money and resources caused by the congestion of Paris and the east may begin to tell, as they do in the case of north and south Italy, in face of the better-distributed German economy. All basic costs, for new industry, housing, and services, are some 30 to 40 per cent higher in Paris than in an area such as Brittany.

There have also been signs that the restrictions on the growth of industry in the Paris area have been eased since 1963. That year, the Government changed its town-planning policy for Paris:* instead of trying in vain to check its population growth, they decided to accept it and plan to cope with it. Though the rules have not been formally changed, industries are now finding it a little easier to get permission to expand in Paris. 'De Gaulle feels he needs a Ruhr to keep up with the German one,' said someone. 'The Lorraine Ruhr isn't working too well, so he's trying Paris again.' This may be a caricature: but the new policy is certainly one reason for the slump in the decentralisation figures since that year. Other causes were the Plan de Stabilisation, and the fact that most firms who wanted to move had by now done so.

Between the 1954 and 1962 censuses, the population of Paris grew faster than the national average (14 against 8·1 per cent) but slower than that of most larger provincial towns (e.g. Lyon 20 per cent, Marseille 17). Since then, it seems to have been moving ahead faster again. According to official statistics prepared for the Plan in 1965, at the present rate Paris will have increased by 2·6 million between 1963 and 1977, to reach over 11 million; a quarter of this will be due to natural growth, and the rest to French and foreign immigration. Paris by 1977 will account for 20·6 of France's population, against 18·3 per cent in 1962. In the same period, the Lyon-Grenoble region will go up by 830,000, Provence by 630,000, and the Nord by 670,000, but in areas such as Brittany, Auvergne, and the south-west, natural growth will be almost equalled by emigration. Assuming these alarming forecasts to be sound, the Government will have to act fast and vigorously if it wants to prevent such a situation.

* See p. 181 (Paris, the beloved monster).

It could be argued that not all areas can prosper equally all the time, and that the demographic decline of some of them does not matter so long as their resources are used efficiently—which does not necessarily require a large population. *Le Monde*, commenting in 1965 on the figures I have just quoted, wrote 'Regions like Champagne, thought to be poor in the nineteenth century, have become rich a century later. The south-west, and even the centre, envied in the last century for their prosperity, can no longer keep their population because it feels economically and socially frustrated on its native soil. So one is tempted to feel reassured: each region has its chance according to the epoch.' But the writer added: 'There is however a threshold below which a region risks becoming poor beyond recovery, and it can be all the more rapid when balance between regions is delayed by local forces of inertia.'

In the areas where rural emigration is inevitable, and large towns do not exist, it is therefore essential, as I have already stressed, to try to strengthen the smaller ones. And few of the smaller towns are as fortunate or as vigorous as Rodez or Falaise. The planners and sociologists feel that, in rural areas, small towns must be used as a buffer for emigration between farm and big city, for otherwise peasants flung straight into big factories and housing estates risk 'alienation' and 'sub-proletarianisation'. In a small town in their own area, they can still live on a scale they are used to. But for this, the towns will need new light industries, or a conversion of their artisanal ones. This was a major preoccupation of the Ministry of Agriculture under Pisani; unfortunately, the Aménagement du Territoire staff have shown more concern with life and industry in larger towns, except in a few special zones such as the Languedoc. In 1965 an eager young man on Pisani's staff told me: 'The Government must do more to help these towns find industry, or they will die. In one little town in Anjou, where M. Pisani happens to be mayor, we're developing factories linked with local agriculture: one for making wine-bottles, one for tractor parts. But that's an isolated case, and Pisani can't be mayor of everywhere. In general, there's a terrible neglect. The Dutch, British, and Germans are far ahead of us with this sort of planning.'

It is often argued that, if the State wants industrial decentralisation to succeed, it should help by moving some of its own central services to the provinces. This applies, above all, to banking. It is because the big State banks and powers of financial decision are all in Paris that many big firms tend to keep their head offices there even when their factories are elsewhere. Centralisation of the banks is a late phenomenon that was still going on even in the 1930s, and though today the process is halted, it has not yet moved into reverse. One of the largest State banks, Credit Lyonnais, bears the name of a city that before 1914 was a great banking centre but today, as one Lyon financier told me indignantly, 'is no better than a village in terms of banking autonomy'. He added, 'It is this, as much as anything, that stops Lyon from becoming a real capital like Frankfurt or Turin. At least, civil servants today are becoming more aware of the problem, and you can discuss it with them without being thought some sort of Girondin terrorist. But real reforms don't seem likely: it would upset the whole State system.'

A few big firms, with family roots in a town, do try to keep their head offices by their works: Michelin at Clermont-Ferrand is one, and the Berliet lorry firm at Lyon another. But it entails incessant tiresome journeys to the capital. Another large firm, Pont-à-Mousson of Lorraine, was always especially proud of keeping its offices at Nancy near its plant; but when I called there recently I was told, 'Sorry, there's no one you can talk to here. The top staff have all just moved to Paris.' They had finally given in. Sometimes this happens because, if you want influential directors on your board, you must choose Parisians. Not only the banks are there, but the Ministries, and foreign clients for sales. What foreign importer bothers to tout round the provinces? Yet if this vicious circle were broken, the cities with their new liveliness and prosperity could become centres of decision as well.

Finally, the State must provide and maintain an efficient modern structure of transport and communication, if regional development in the widest sense is to succeed. Here, the pattern is uneven. Although rail and air services are good, funds for new motorways and especially for telephones are not enough to keep pace with growing needs. Possibly de Gaulle's expensive nuclear policy is again partly to blame, or so a Frenchman tends to think as he waits two hours for a trunk call, or for release from some traffic jams on the N7 road from Paris to Marseille. It can be argued that some priorities have been selected too much in terms of prestige. The Mont Blanc road tunnel, opened in 1965 at a cost of 100m francs, is a marvellous piece of engineering and a useful new link with north Italy; but the investment will remain partly wasted if the roads leading to it in that part of France are not improved. The Pont de Tancarville, the Moselle canal, the new Rhône and Rhine dams, all these are noble and valuable feats, but more is needed—a Pyrenean tunnel, a Channel tunnel, above all a canal for heavy barges linking the Rhône and the Rhine via the Moselle. This project is today keenly demanded by Lorraine, Lyon, and Marseille: it would help Lorraine's harassed industries to trade with the Mediterranean, and Lyon's with Germany, while giving Marseille a better chance to compete with Rotterdam for the commerce of the Ruhr. After much argument, and jealous counter-lobbying by the SNCF, the Government has now agreed to the plan in principle, but has not yet set a date for it. It would cost at least 1,300m francs. The trouble is, there is not enough money for everything in this 'virgin land' where so much is to be done and funds are so questionably distributed.

Railway links between Paris and the main cities are among the fastest and best in the world; but inter-town services, though improved since before the war, are still inadequate. Internal air services are now improving rapidly after a slow start. Throughout the 1950s they were held back by narrow-sighted objections from the SNCF, whose interests are not lightly cast aside by the Government because of the money so heavily invested in it after the war. But soon internal air traffic could be neglected no more. The lack was even holding up the factory policy: at least one firm selected Savoy for its plant largely so as to be near the international air link from Geneva to Paris. Since about 1960, Air Inter, the State-run domestic affiliate of Air France and the SNCF, has expanded rapidly—its passenger traffic doubled in 1964–6. Toulouse, for instance, is now linked to Paris by five Caravelles a day. But it was only in 1965 that Toulouse, Lyon, and Bordeaux became linked with each other at all.

The road network is today a sore subject of debate in this car-mad country. Critics of the Government are always ready to point out that although France has the highest petrol taxes and some of the highest other motoring charges in Europe, yet among advanced Western nations its record of motorway construction is as poor as that of Britain: there are some 600 miles of motorway in France and 450 in Britain, against 2,100 in Germany, 1,380 in Italy, and 510 in Holland. But this criticism can be misleading. France still enjoys the legacy of about the best network in Europe of secondary roads and traditional main roads: they are straight, well surfaced (except in cobbled Flanders), well engineered in hilly areas, and a delight compared with most roads in Britain. In most places they are still quite adequate for their traffic. The problem, however, is that in a few key places, mainly on the edge of big towns, or on certain trunk routes in summer, the traditional network is rapidly becoming inadequate, and not enough is being done about it. It is thus quite usual to be able to drive for scores of miles at top speed between towns, and then get stuck for hours in some bottleneck.

After long delays, a motorway from Lille to Paris has been laboriously completed, and work is well advanced on the Paris–Lyon–Marseille motorway which eventually will remove the notorious summer jams at places like Vienne in the Rhône Valley. But work has only just begun on the much-needed motorway through the Languedoc. The present main road there is the only route linking Spain and Toulouse with south-east France and beyond, and in summer the bottlenecks of Béziers and Montpellier are a congested mass of infuriated tourists. The problem in a populated district like this is that essentially the French system of land ownership makes wayleaves and expropriation a desperately slow and costly business, taking up to four years. This is why, though France may have better roads linking towns than Britain, she has fewer modern by-passes. Reforms* of land-ownership are now planned; but they are likely to take a long time.

For many years the Government would neither spend much money on

* See p. 210 (The housing shortage).

motorways itself nor hand them over to private enterprise. An exception was allowed for the new Autoroute de l'Esterel from Nice to Fréjus, because it was 'touristic': it was built at great speed with private capital, and is a success. Elsewhere, roads are considered a public service, which means they advance slowly at the whim of State budgets, even when the problem of wayleave is solved. Since about 1965, however, the Government has suddenly taken more notice of the road problem, realising that the bottlenecks might hamper industrial traffic or even keep foreign tourists away. Funds have been sharply increased, loans are at last being floated, and the Government now claims to be building motorways at a faster rate than Germany or Italy. But, unlike nearly all the rest of Europe, it insists on levying tolls to help pay for them, even though the ensuing partial boycott keeps some of the old roads clogged up and destroys part of the value of the investment. The highly taxed French motorist possibly has some right to feel aggrieved.

With the Post Office telephone system, matters are very much worse. In no other public service is France more backward. In Britain, telephones tend to break down or yield wrong numbers; in France, they work rather better mechanically, but there are just not enough of them. Nearly 500,000 names are on waiting-lists for telephones, and it is estimated that another two million would apply if they did not consider it hopeless. The number of lines, one for every sixteen people, is half the average for a modern country, and the lowest in the Common Market, below Italy. And trunk lines are so inadequate that nearly 40 per cent of long-distance calls fail to get through at the first demand. Amsterdam can dial Paris in a flash; a Paris caller may have to wait an hour for the operator to get him Amsterdam. The dismal queues waiting to make trunk calls in almost any post office are a disgrace for a nation that calls itself modern; and many new factories and offices, especially in the provinces, have to survive for months with no telephone. This situation wastes thousands of business man-hours a day, and in a number of cases it has dissuaded firms from decentralising their plant from Paris.

The root of the trouble is that the Postes, Télégraphes, et Téléphones is something of a poor relation among Ministries, and is given little chance to run the telephones on a proper commercial basis. Subscribers' dues are regarded as Government taxes and not all of the money finds its way back to the PTT, which nevertheless has to pay for all improvements out of its own budget and is not allowed to float loans. Added to this are its own internal problems: the vested interests of its petty-bureaucratic staff, the poor quality of many of the firms it has to rely on for equipment, and the cost of keeping up village exchanges and wires in a country as scattered as France (there are ten times as many miles of overhead wires as in Germany, for half the number of telephones).

Governments in France have shown a curious tendency to regard the telephone as a bourgeois luxury rather than an essential tool of modern business. The early Plans totally ignored the subject. More recently, however, there have been signs of a change of heart. Annual investment quadrupled in 1958–66, and in 1967 the Government promised that the telephone would get 'top priority'. The current rate of progress is now about enough to keep pace with growing needs, but not enough to remove the backlog. And there are still few signs of a change in structures and methods. While many millions of francs are spent on the prestigious new space-communications centre in Brittany, most local exchanges are still on a pre-automatic system, and in thousands of villages you cannot put through a call when the operator is away for her two-hour lunch, or at night. Reform needs not only money but a basic administrative shake-up, which is blocked by the hostility of the PTT staff and their fear of change. French telephones present a classic example of how the State often prejudices its own policy of modernisation, through failure to take measures that would lead to unrest within its own ranks.

ANDRÉ MALRAUX'S *MAISONS DE LA CULTURE*

The gulf between Paris and its 'desert' has nowhere seemed so wide in the past as in the arts and intellectual activity. Today in France, as in Britain, the bridging of this gulf is recognised as an essential part of regional development, especially if the new *élites* are to be content to live in the provinces. In the past few years, many towns have begun to develop a new cultural vitality, even though Paris intellectual cliques often choose to ignore it and retain their contempt. University expansion, the arrival of young professors and industrial *cadres* from Paris, the growth of leisure and affluence, have all helped to shatter the local stagnation. Provincial drama, dead between the wars, has revived astonishingly in a number of towns; led by Aix and Avignon, scores of summer arts festivals have sprung up. In some cases, town councils have helped, but in many others they have acted as a damper on local revival. Therefore the State is intervening; for though there has been plenty of vigorous private initiative too, in France this never manages to make much public progress without official help.

The Fourth Republic aided the drama renaissance, and kept up the traditional subsidies for local opera and music; but it did little else. When in 1959 that visionary philosopher, André Malraux, became de Gaulle's Minister of Culture, he soon embarked on a more ambitious policy.

Malraux is an enigma. Novelist and Left-wing revolutionary in the '20s and '30s, aloof and mystical historian of art in the '40s and '50s, he has spent the '60s as an emotional public apologist of Gaullist nationalism; and many people who admired his early career now regard him as unbalanced, a bit of a crank, even a crypto-fascist. But this mandarin is more complex than that, and the change may not be so great as it appears. His unswerving personal loyalty to de Gaulle dates from the war years, when Malraux was a leader of the *maquis*. Today, he is closer to de Gaulle than almost any other Minister; and while he shares something of his master's didactic and authoritarian approach, his actual ideas, like de Gaulle's, are often liberal and unorthodox. Within the régime, his influence has been consistently liberal, notably in defending films and books from censorship. Whatever he does, he does fervently and with an ideal in view; and all the strands of his past thinking are still evident in his present actions, notably in his scheme for a national chain of multi-purpose arts centres, the *Maisons de la Culture*.

Some eight of these are so far in action. Eventually, there are plans for nearer a hundred. The State has set the pattern, but in each case the local council is required to go fifty-fifty with it on building costs and annual subsidies. The first purpose of the centres is to present only works of quality and to spread Paris standards through the provinces: 'In ten years' time,' claimed Malraux, opening a new *Maison* at Amiens, 'this hideous word "provincial" will have ceased to exist in France.' His second aim is to destroy the notion of culture as a bourgeois preserve, and to draw a new social class into theatres and art galleries. Here speaks Malraux, man of the Left, where his ideas are close to those of a far less highbrow 'Minister of Culture', Britain's Miss Jennie Lee. But Malraux, mandarin of art, goes much further than Miss Lee. For him, art is a means whereby the soul attains to God, * and with a Gaullist missionary zeal he seeks to colonise the French desert with this divine truth. It is therefore a matter of doctrine that the *Maisons* should be highbrow, and should not find a place, as many people want, for local amateur or popular activities.

In practice, his ideals are not working out quite like this. The mainly Left-wing directors of his *Maisons* have to take a more pragmatic approach, as they struggle with low budgets, local snobberies, and philistinism, and lack of available top-line talent.

Each *Maison*, once built, is supervised by a board of local and State nominees. They appoint a full-time director, usually in practice chosen by Malraux; and the success of the *Maisons* so far has been due more than anything to the quality of the men he has found. They are mostly young men of the theatre with social ideals, closer in spirit to Peter Hall or Arnold Wesker than to a civil servant. Malraux has backed them in their local battles, and while encouraging them to keep standards as high as possible, he has had the sense to accept tacitly some of their working compromises. One important function of the *Maisons*, quoting Malraux again, is to provide for the 'interpenetration of the arts'. Under one roof there should be three or four different halls, with facilities for plays, concerts, film shows, library, cabaret, lectures, art exhibitions. Thus it is hoped that a film lover, once drawn inside, might begin to take an interest in sculpture, or an opera fan in poetry. But this sensible idea is prone to difficulties. The Malraux policy poses the question: where does 'art' end and mere 'entertainment' begin? And how do you keep up top-level standards, when

* See either of his main works on art, *La Métamorphose des Dieux* or *Les Voix du silence*.

so many local people want something more easy-going and so much local cultural activity is inevitably amateur? Jennie Lee, too, believes in 'interpenetration' for her arts centres; but she and many people in Britain would cast the net wider, and allow that the staging of pop concerts, amateur drama, or even handicrafts, might be a way of initially enticing a mass audience into the centres and destroying the popular fear of 'culture'. The French, especially the young, are probably less wary then the British of the avant-garde or highbrow: the problem exists nevertheless, and has given rise to some fascinating local conflicts, notably in Caen.

This was one of the very first of the *Maisons*. In a sense, it pre-dates them, for it was designed in the 1950s as a municipal theatre to replace the one destroyed in the war. Jo Tréhard, a lively young man running the town's 'rep' in a converted Nissen hut, was in those days already thinking in terms of arts centres; but he failed to convince the council, mainly elderly and Right-wing, that this was what Caen needed. They wanted a classic bourgeois theatre, like the old one, and in terms of design they got their way, for this was before Malraux's day. When the building was ready, in 1963, the State (which had paid for half of it) designated it *Maison de la Culture*, and Tréhard was appointed as the obvious man to run it. He found himself with a palatial foyer and a fine modern stage and auditorium, but little space for other activities. Nevertheless, he pushed ahead with the Malraux policy, which he agreed with; he aimed his programmes at the 'new wave' of Caennais, the hordes of university students and the technicians and *cadres* from Paris, and he won a big success. Avant-garde plays, concerts, and debates, unusual in a staid town like Caen, picked up eager new audiences. But the older townsfolk were furious. Their idea of theatre was light operetta, and boulevard comedies on tour from Paris: that was what they'd had before the war. The council supported them, partly for electoral reasons, and began to plot Tréhard's removal. The council juridically owned the building itself, and in theory shared with Malraux a power of veto over the director. In the winter of 1964–5 the crisis was acute, and Tréhard was saved only when a pressure group of *amis de la Maison* formed itself and rallied enough signatures to convince the councillors that his policy had best be left alone. Today there is an uneasy truce, but Tréhard has basically won. 'I'm still having to go slowly,' he told me; 'I even put on *The Merry Widow* once, to appease the council, though I'm ashamed of it. But there are signs at last that the bourgeoisie are unfreezing: they're beginning to come to my programmes.'

This dark, monkey-faced little Norman, with a quicksilver, most un-Norman temperament, has progressive Leftish ideas about art and society. 'I hate this airless, monumental block of stone,' he told me; 'an arts centre should have open windows on the world, inviting people in. I want to build an annexe of glass, with little halls for intimate events like poetry recitals—but the council aren't keen, and the State are short of funds. For some events, the auditorium is far too large and formal—I've crammed 500 people into the foyer for a reading of Brecht or Lorca but I can do this only on evenings when the theatre's not in use. I'm limited to one event a night—crazy for a building that cost eight million francs.'

Room nevertheless has been found for a small reading-room and art gallery, and a most attractive bar; and on any evening the *Maison* is an animated social centre. French universities are generally lacking in clubs and extra-mural amenities, * so the *Maison* has provided the students with a focus they badly needed. It has done at least as much for Caen as the Playhouse has for Nottingham, where some of John Neville's problems have been strikingly similar to Tréhard's! The *Maison* has 12,000 signed-up 'members', just over half of whom are students. They pay a small annual fee in return for reduced admission rates and a handsome monthly journal. Tréhard's local drama company has tried its hand at Sophocles and a Britten opera. Other plays are imported from Paris: Madeleine Renaud in Beckett's *Oh! les Beaux Jours* played to full houses. Besides film shows and recitals, Tréhard holds lecture-debates, inviting from Paris film-makers like Alain Resnais or philosophers like Roland Barthes. He is trying to break with the highly conventional and reverential French attitude to culture, and to build up more informality and audience-involvement. It is not easy, especially in Caen: some of his fiercest opponents have been the older university literature professors who, as he puts it, 'think French drama ended with Victor Hugo and have barely heard of Brecht'.

At Bourges, where there is no university, the *Maison de la Culture* has had even more influence than at Caen. It has completely revitalised the life of what used to be a sleepy old market town, as dead as its cathedral is lovely. Bus companies have now revised their timetables to take villagers home at night from the *Maison*; and some touring variety-shows have decided to give Bourges a miss in future through lack of support. The centre is housed in a converted pre-war public building, not very modern or elegant but large enough to contain several different halls and therefore well suited for 'interpenetration'. The director, Gabriel Monnet, is a young man of the same stamp as Tréhard, but with standards a little less restrictive. Cutting his suit according to his cloth in a city with little in-tellectual tradition, he gives shelter to local painters, amateur actors, and folklore enthusiasts in the corners of his ample premises. But they are not allowed to prejudice the professional programme, which is quite as highbrow and ambitious as at Caen. Monnet has staged the French prem-ières of new experimental plays, run them for fifteen performances (remarkable, in a country town) and won enthusiastic notices from the Paris critics. Every night there are several activities, and the *Maison* has 9,000 members, including more from the working class than at Caen. A network of unpaid 'delegates' in suburbs and near-by villages try, with some success, to persuade workers and country people that the new centre is not just for the educated.

* See p. 330 (Youth with a dusty answer).

A third *Maison* has been set up in a converted cinema at Ménilmontant in the poor eastern quarters of Paris, an area quite as much part of the cultural 'desert' as Bourges. Modelling itself on the Théâtre National Populaire in western Paris, it has succeeded rather better than Theatre Workshop did under Joan Littlewood in wooing local working-class audiences to classical and modern plays. At Amiens, the centre that opened in 1966 was the first to be fully built and conceived as a *Maison de la Culture*, with the proper equipment; it cost 12m francs, and had 7,000 members before it even started. There are other smaller *Maisons* at Le Havre and Thonon; big ones have just been completed at Grenoble and Rennes, and several others are planned.

It is obvious that these centres answer a real need. With a few reservations they are a success, but there are not nearly enough of them. Under the Fourth Plan, 1961–5, twenty were scheduled and six built. It is not the towns' fault (more than 90 municipalities have put in demands) so much as the usual problem of lack of State funds. On top of building costs, the larger *Maisons* each get an annual subsidy of about 1·5m francs, of which the State pays half. One or two towns, such as Toulouse and Rouen, have built their own modest centres without waiting for Malraux's help. But in France, local finances do not easily stretch to this kind of initiative, and it is frowned on by the Ministry, who want to keep centralised control. The State's interference here does seem justified: there is no doubt that Malraux has more idea of what a *Maison de la Culture* is all about than someone like the mayor of Caen, and as one intelligent liberal in the Ministry put it to me, 'If we left these councils to their own devices, half of them would run their *Maison* as a glorified Rotary-club-cum-fun-fair, with an eye on their own re-election. We have to keep a close watch.' Yet the *Maisons*' legal constitution marks at least a gesture towards a kind of autonomy and delegation of power. Once each centre has been set up on the pattern approved by Malraux, its board of administration is composed of three delegates appointed by the Ministry, three appointed by the council, and a majority, usually seven or nine, elected by a public meeting of members. At Caen, because of the special tensions, all the delegates are officially chosen by State or council; but elsewhere, the planned democratic constitution appears to be working. If the majority did anywhere fall into the hands of some clique wanting to use the *Maison* for its own ends, no doubt the Ministry would find ways of intervening.

In practice, all the programming is left to the directors: most of them are Leftish non-Gaullists, hand-picked by the arch-Gaullist Minister. Tréhard told me: 'One of my troubles here is that the Catholic bourgeoisie think I'm an atheist or a Communist because I like modern drama, and some of the Left and intellectuals think I'm a Gaullist because I work for Malraux. I'm no admirer of *étatisme*, but I've the highest faith in Malraux himself—politically speaking, we're left entirely free in our choice of material, so long, I suppose, as we don't gratuitously satirise the régime.' In the matter of programming, it is 'brow', not politics, that sets the problems. Tréhard has made many enemies by refusing to have any truck at all with local arts clubs: 'Une Maison de la Culture, ce n'est pas un garage,' he says scornfully. Also, he generally refuses to make the kind of popular concessions that might win larger audiences and so help eke out his subsidy. Under the Malraux umbrella, this is normal practice both in the *Maisons* and in the State-backed drama companies: you give people enrichment rather than entertainment. This policy is accepted more easily than it would be in Britain, because people are accustomed by their education to a high degree of cultural spoon-feeding, and because among young people, even in the provinces, there is enough enthusiasm for experiment and depth of ideas. In the provinces, it is essentially a conflict of generations between two very different conceptions of culture. The older people, even if they really prefer André Roussin, will at least pay lip-service to Molière, Racine, and the classics they were brought up, on: this is *la vraie culture française*, as opposed to that dangerous modern or foreign stuff from Paris which the young enjoy. And this attitude is shared by many highly cultivated older people. The rift is much sharper than in Britain, where classical culture does not enjoy the same status in the bourgeois ethos.

In the single month of October 1964, Bourges presented plays by Tchekov, Pirandello, Rilke, and Shakespeare, as well as ballet, concerts, films, and lectures. In November 1965, Caen had a calendar of eighteen different events, from the Modern Jazz Quartet to an evening with the avant-garde playwright Jean Vauthier. The quality, of course, varies. Not all is up to the Paris standards that Malraux wants, but much of it is. Some material is provided by the *Maison*'s own repertory company, or local professional musicians; the rest comes from Paris. The Ministry has set up a national agency to help supply directors with a steady stream of material. It is not yet working very well, but it will soon be badly needed, when there are more *Maisons*.

The drama renaissance pre-dated the *Maisons de la Culture* and helped pave the way for them. It is a striking phenomenon. Of the sixty-two regional 'reps' in France in the 1870s, almost none survived the 1914 war, and the inter-war years were dead. Then, after 1945, a few young actors tired of Paris began to form their own little groups in the provinces— another token of the spontaneous French rebirth of those days. At first the struggle was tough, but soon the State and a few councils began to provide grants. Today, at least a dozen fixed companies are flourishing, in addition to the *Maisons*; and some of them, notably Roger Planchon's Théâtre de la Cité in the Lyon working-class suburb of Villeurbanne, have won international fame. Jean Dasté at St. Etienne, Maurice Sarrazin at Toulouse, Hubert Gignoux first at Rennes and now at Strasbourg: these and others, equivalents of John Neville at Nottingham, forwent a career on the Paris boulevards to stay and animate the provinces. And a town like

St. Etienne can hardly have seemed promising ground at first. This kind of private initiative is still rare in the arts outside Paris; but it is growing.

The Comédie de l'Ouest at Rennes, now led by Georges Goubert, has had an amazing success. It has patiently created an audience for serious theatre, in a region with no modern dramatic tradition. Today it tours thirty north-western towns each year with near-capacity houses for Sophocles, Brecht, Strindberg, Beckett. In the tiniest Breton upland villages its posters are everywhere; eight towns have even built themselves new theatres to house its tours. It has also presented seasons in Paris, Brussels, and Geneva. On its home ground, Shakespeare is by far the most popular author (in the provinces with their insular Racinian standards, Shakespeare often represents a modern break with tradition). Another British play, *Look Back in Anger*, caused something of a storm in Brittany, and set older Catholics distributing tracts against it. The clash between cultures, in fact, is almost as strong as at Caen. Fréville, the mayor of Rennes, has helped the company a lot, and now he and Malraux have rewarded it with a large new *Maison de la Culture* which Goubert will direct. Until now, the company has not had its own theatre; its offices, scenery storerooms, and rehearsal stage are in a converted warehouse in a back street, and for its performances in Rennes it has to borrow the old municipal theatre which is really the preserve of the antiquated local opera company. Goubert told me: 'They haven't changed their décor since 1870. Our audiences are twice the size of theirs, and far younger. But it's a tradition in a town like this to go on croaking out *Faust* and *Carmen* year after year with third-rate singers; and Fréville can't really get rid of them, though he'd like to. As a result, we run for only three nights in Rennes, though with all these students we could do far more. But,' he grinned, 'if it hadn't been for this, we probably wouldn't be getting our *Maison de la Culture*.'

Planchon's problems are much worse. This ascetic-looking, bespectacled young man, still in his mid 30s, was able to develop his astonishing experimental theatre partly because he was helped by the Left-wing municipality of Villeurbanne. With social views on the arts that outshine Wesker's, he has gone all out to build up a working-class audience. Aided by a few local industrialists and works committees, he has staged lunch-hour excerpts in canteens and on factory floors, while in the evenings a fleet of buses bring workers to the theatre on its hilltop above the yellow tenement-skyscrapers of unlovely Villeurbanne. The operation is a success and the theatre has 150,000 season-ticket subscribers.

The rich theatre-goers of adjacent Lyon, snobbiest city in France, at first took no notice of this young Bolshevik crank. When he became famous and began to do seasons in Paris, the Lyonnais, surprised, would go and watch him there; but few of them would venture in their evening dress to sit among the workers on their own doorstep. Today, Planchon is an obvious candidate for a *Maison de la Culture*, and the Government wanted it to be a big one for which rich Lyon would have to pay as well as poor Villeurbanne. But Lyon was still suspicious of Planchon, and the two municipalities failed to agree on site, financing, or administration. Planchon threatened to walk out, and five other cities made him offers. Today, Lyon is still posing conditions, one of them being that the *Maison* should not be allowed to harm the city's existing bourgeois theatres, and long negotiations seem to lie ahead. If Planchon leaves Lyon and moves to Paris, as he has been sorely tempted to do, it would be a grave defeat for the cause of provincial revival. At St. Etienne, Jean Dasté has been facing exactly the same problem: a *Maison de la Culture* has been built for him, but the municipality consider him too highbrow and have been trying to limit his powers as artistic director. He in turn has threatened to resign if they succeed.

Such are the growing pains of a cultural scene that is rapidly changing in the provinces. In Lyon itself, despite bourgeois stuffiness and the lack of a *Maison de la Culture*, the growth of sheer activity in the past ten years has been striking. The number of art exhibitions was twenty-four in March 1966, against seven in March 1965; of concerts, thirty-three against thirteen; of theatre performances, one hundred and five against nineteen. This suggests that well-to-do people are now much readier to find their culture on the spot, rather than save it for their visits to Paris where some of the arts are anyway in decline. Not, however, that all the new provincial culture is of high quality. Reviewing the work of a subsidised company in Nantes, *Le Monde* wrote, 'Is decentralisation worth it at any price? The movement is fine, but why back the good and less good without selection, and so risk putting people off the theatre?' It is music that fares worst. The thirty provincial *Conservatoires* are mostly moribund, and few of the eight traditional opera-houses have much vitality left, apart from Marseille. In the Lyon figures quoted above, it is significant that opera performances alone went down from twenty to thirteen. The brilliant summer festivals, at Aix, Besançon, Royan, and elsewhere, are exceptions in the provincial musical field; but they are brief, and are nourished largely by visitors and performers from Paris and abroad. The overall position of music in France needs drastic revision.*

It hardly needs repeating that the development of the universities has played a key role in the awakening of the provinces. The four large towns that have grown the fastest, Grenoble, Besançon, Caen, and Rennes, all have universities. The student population in such towns is often five to ten times higher than before the war, and is growing on average about twice as fast as that of the Sorbonne. Though the pull of Paris remains strong for the more brilliant students and professors, an increasing minority of them are beginning to realise that working conditions are often easier in the provinces.

The students animate the streets and cafés, and provide audiences for

* See p. 419 (All the arts languish, save one).

the new arts and drama centres. But it is characteristic of French youth that they do not, except in rare cases, take much public initiative themselves as they do, *ad nauseam*, in swinging Britain. An exception is Nancy, where a group of students and young local graduates have given an entirely new cultural impetus to a hitherto lethargic town. *

If the students are generally so passive, it is partly the fault of the State. The Ministry of Education is at pains to 'decentralise' numerically, but has not allowed the universities one jot more sovereignty. If a professor wants to modify his curriculum, or even if a group of students want to form a club in a university hostel, formal permission is needed from Paris. There are funds for splendid new laboratories and lecture-halls; there are new universities opening or planned in fifteen towns; there is even the beginning of a policy to remove some of the *Grandes Ecoles* from Paris. But these moves will remain of limited value so long as the whole structure is so heavily bureaucratic.

The tendency is the same in another State-run sector, radio and television. In 1963 the highly centralised ORTF† began to develop regional TV news and magazine programmes, largely in order to combat the influence of the provincial Press, most of which is anti-Gaullist. Today there are daily fifteen-minute TV bulletins, and weekly half-hour news-magazines, in twelve regions. These may be doing something to stimulate regional interest, while in some cases the ORTF studios give useful work and publicity to local drama companies or musicians. But the stations have none of the organic links with their region of the British ITV companies or even, say, of the BBC in Scotland. Their political tone is carefully controlled from Paris; and real local controversy rarely enlivens their screens. The charming and otherwise liberal Gaullist who runs the Brittany station tried to disarm me: 'With only fifteen minutes a day, do we have time to air local criticisms of Government policy? We, the Government, are doing all we can to promote regional progress. The time isn't ripe to let people here in Brittany criticise us openly, just when we're really doing something for them. They're too immature.' I had rarely heard a more succinct résumé of Gaullist philosophy.

The regional Press itself at first sight presents an encouraging contrast. Here, for once, the influence of Paris on the provinces is minimal. The Occupation, and the wartime restrictions on transport, destroyed the pre-war circulations of the Parisian Press in the provinces, and allowed the local papers to build up a relative strength that they have since maintained and even increased. Since 1939, sales of provincial dailies have risen from 5·2 to 7 million, while sales of Parisian ones have dropped from 6 to 4 million. After *Le Parisien Libéré* (790,000), the French morning paper with the highest circulation is *Ouest-France* in Rennes (720,000), with forty-four editions covering twelve departments, and third comes *Le Dauphiné Libéré* of Grenoble with 520,000. There are eighty-eight

* See p. 351 (Youth with a dusty answer).
† See p. 420 (All the arts languish, save one).

provincial dailies, and the larger ones are solid empires with fine, new offices and presses, making many of the Paris dailies look like struggling poor relations. In Caen, which is little farther from Paris than from Rennes, *Ouest-France* has three times the sales of all the Paris papers together!

All this, however, is not quite the evidence it might seem of a thrusting new regional spirit. Most of these papers are editorially feeble, and parochial. In many cases they have built up their strength by killing off smaller rivals and have established a virtual monopoly in their area. They feel that, in order to keep this, they must appeal to everybody and not risk alienating any section of readers by flaunting bold opinions. Though in a general sense they are mostly anti-Gaullist, with a few courageous exceptions (*La Dépêche du Midi* in Toulouse, *La Voix du Nord* in Lille) they rarely take a strong editorial line on anything that matters; they deal objectively but dully with national news, and worst of all, most of them dismiss international and foreign affairs on a page or two of poorly edited agency messages. For most local people, this is their sole source of news and political comment, apart from the Gaullist radio and TV and perhaps the Europe No. 1 radio bulletins; the intelligentsia take *Le Monde*, one of the few Paris papers to have much sale in the provinces, or weeklies like *Nouvel Observateur*. Far more than before the war, the big local papers put their whole accent on pages and pages of local news; and opinion surveys show that this is what the readers turn to first—they no longer care much about politics. The coverage is thorough, and reasonably objective, and no doubt it has helped a little to promote the new regional awareness; but alongside the very occasional article on a real public issue, there are endless columns of accounts of civic banquets or what the French call *histoires des chiens écrasés*, trivia of the silliest sort. When the commercially aggressive *Dauphiné Libéré* staged a battle-royal with the staid *Progrès de Lyon* recently for circulation in overlap districts, the Grenoble paper won by exploiting trivia, and by every kind of gimmick such as big prizes for quizzes and full pages in polychromatic colour. Even the wide circulation areas of the larger papers give a misleading idea of their coverage, for the multiple editions are so localised that there may be no news at all of the regional capital in an edition sold in another town thirty miles away. Most of these papers appeal to the lowest common denominator, and they pander to parochialism rather than encouraging true regionalism. The new regional movements in France are taking place in spite of them, rather than through them. They have the power to be leaders, but they abuse it.

Chiens écrasés, culture snobberies, reactionary mayors, villages that reject town-planning schemes or *remembrement*: the *esprit de clocher* is still far from dead in France, despite the decline of the old ideological factions and the undoubted progress of the new generation led by the Dubedouts and de Caumonts, the Lamours and Tréhards. There are still plenty of intellectuals who find life isolated and stifling in the provinces—

especially those who have not yet lived in Paris. But change is coming fast, and the real test will be to see how many of the ambitious leaders of the new generation renounce the traditional path of Julien Sorel. Jack Lang of Nancy, the young local graduate who founded its world drama festival, is the sort of talented person who could make a good career in Paris tomorrow; but he told me, 'I'll stay here. This is the place to achieve things now.' It might not have been his attitude thirty years ago, or even ten. People are beginning to realise that Paris is often the parochial place; at home and abroad, for good or ill, its legend is waning. It is the hard core of Paris writers and intellectuals, with their heads firmly in the sand, who are often most to blame for the gulf of suspicion between capital and provinces, and theirs will be one of the last bastions to fall. They still prefer to live or gather round the parish-pump of St. Germain or Mont-parnasse and will rarely leave the capital save for a villa or a beach in Provence. They know nothing of the provinces and, unlike writers in England, they will not live in them. Mauriac, who for all his love-hate keeps his provincial roots, once wrote: 'An artist out of touch with the provinces is also out of touch with humanity.' Precisely. Post-war French novels are not noted for their humanity.

A few younger artists and writers are beginning to resist the lure of Paris when they win recognition, and to remain in the provinces. J.-M.-G. le Clézio, one of the better young novelists, lives in Nice not that Nice exactly typical. Several young little-known writers in a symposium held by *Arts* magazine stressed how much more 'real' and 'deep' they found life in the provinces; and if any renaissance emerges to take French creative writing and art out of its present sterile phase, it might well come from the provinces, as it did, in a sense, in Britain a number of years ago. For the present, the new cultural activity in towns like Caen inevitably takes its tone from Paris. The provinces have not yet found a creative style of their own, apart from the somewhat self-conscious and backward-looking folklorism of Breton, Provençal, or other groups.

Are French provincial towns livelier than English ones? Oxford and Cambridge apart (which have little equivalent in France), on a cultural level there is possibly more activity in a French town, certainly more highbrow activity. But it tends to be carefully organised and formalised, as in the *Maisons*, rather than spontaneous. It is likely to be a long time before Bordeaux produces its Beatles. On a wider level, social and civic as well as cultural, there is not the same range of community activity and interest as in Anglo-Saxon towns. The reason lies partly in the French character, and partly in the prefectoral system which makes it hard for a town to be master of its own destiny.

PREFECTS AND MAYORS: STATE, REFORM THYSELF!

There are many people in France today who look longingly at the German Länder, the Swiss cantons, or the English boroughs and county councils, and wish they had something similar. There is a whole school of thought, led by people like Louis Armand and Pierre Sudreau, which holds that France will never properly be able to modernise its structures and its habits unless it develops a more genuine regional democracy. On the other hand, there are plenty of civil servants in other countries who admire the strength and lucidity of the prefectoral system, and envy the projects that a powerful central administration has been able to carry out in its regions.

In terms of practical results, no less than of ideology, it is extremely hard to draw up a fair balance-sheet of the present French system. Though a town with a vigorous mayor, like Rennes or Marseille, could certainly benefit from more autonomy on the English model, yet in an area like Caen or the Languedoc all the driving force and ideas seem to have to come from the State; or rather, they come mainly from a few dynamic individuals, prefects or others, who are serving the State without necessarily sharing the Government's views. Though the prefect is still the political servant of the Minister of the Interior, under modern conditions his daily functions are inevitably becoming more economic than political. Often his working relations even with anti-Government mayors and communes are perfectly good, whenever they share the same aims of progress and expansion.

Prefects and mayors in fact are frequently victims of the same common enemy: a centralised State machine that despite some recent reforms is still too slow and bureaucratic for modern needs. This is one of today's two main problems of local government. The other is much more fundamental: a century and a half of State tutelage over local affairs has sapped the spirit of civic initiative. No wonder the State has to make most of the running, not only in a big town like Caen but in ten thousand smaller communes; no wonder the reaction of so many of them is wary or apathetic. And this is a vicious circle. So long as the State nanny holds its children so tight, they will not break their legs—but they will not learn to walk either, and they will not feel any incentive to try. Why bother with civic or regional initiatives, when the State decides all? This is often the attitude. The communes do have a kind of autonomy for some local matters, within strict budgetary limits; but on the wider departmental or regional plane that is now the main unit of economic and social planning there is still very little effective democracy. This the French must find, so it is argued, if they are to reach civic maturity. But the present Napoleonic system seems tailor-made for the Gaullist nanny.

This system is based, today, on an uneasy balance of power between State and commune, with each possessing a virtual veto on the other's projects and often using it. There are over 37,000 communes, most of them small villages, while others are towns like Lyon or Marseille. Unlike the departments, they are real traditional entities, often with strong local pride. Each has a mayor and council, local men locally elected

in the normal way; but the mayor, once elected, becomes a servant of the
State, responsible to the prefect. The council's own budget, and many of its
decisions, require formal approval by the prefect, who also has the right
to suspend mayor or councillors from office, or take over some of their
duties. The council derives its modest budget from local taxes and State
subsidies, and spends it on local services and public works. This system
depends on good relations between mayor and prefect; and there is no
doubt that a wealthy commune with a good mayor can initiate a great deal,
if he has the prefect's backing. But a great many local services, for which
in Britain the council is autonomous, in France require the collaboration
and aid of the relevant Ministry in Paris or of its local officials acting in
liaison with the prefect. For instance, the council has to help pay for
building new schools, but the State runs them. Much the same is true of
hospitals. Council housing, main roads, and bridges, and larger civic projects such as a *Maison de la Culture*, are usually built or maintained
jointly by commune and State, and though the commune can in some
cases go ahead on its own, it will rarely feel it has the money for the
luxury of forgoing State aid. So the commune is dependent on the endless
delays and muddles of the Ministries, or on arbitrary last-minute budget
cuts by the Ministry of Finance. Or if it has *mal voté*, it may even face
Government vengeance or blackmail. Many communes, especially the
smaller ones, feel either powerless or resentful; and sometimes they in
turn will block State projects for their area. In theory, the State may have
the right to override such obstructions. In practice, for obvious political
reasons, it is generally more cautious, whether it is dealing with *remembrement* in the Aveyron or Lyon's *Maison de la Culture*; and it will
prefer the carrot to the stick. So the *status quo* of mutual vetoes remains,
wasting endless time and effort.

On the level of the department, a locally elected *conseil général* acts as a
kind of enfeebled county council, with its own little budget for some
services such as secondary roads, public assistance, drainage. It meets only
twice a year, its budget has to be approved by the Ministry of the Interior,
and in practice it usually does what the prefect tells it. It is elected on a
'rotten borough' basis, heavily weighted in favour of villages rather than
towns, and its members are usually elderly. If rejuvenated, it would have
the constitutional power to wield more influence than it does. As it is,
people tend to forget about it.

So the department is run by the prefect and his staff, in themselves an
admirable institution. Prefects are high civil servants of at least the calibre
of senior ambassadors. They are usually men of culture, personal presence,
and impartiality, with little personal concern for the intrigues and
squabbles between Government politicians and communes, though inevitably they get caught up in them. A prefect has a luxurious flat in his
préfecture, he wears a blue and gold uniform on official occasions, and if
he dies in office he is buried with full military and civil honours. He is
appointed by the Ministry of the Interior, and like a diplomat he is moved

from post to post every few years, partly so that he should not get too involved with his 'subjects'. As conceived by Napoleon, his first task is to maintain law and order and to keep his Minister informed of local opinion and possible trouble. This system has served the State well in stormy periods, from Napoleon's own to the great strikes of 1948 and the crises over Algeria in 1958–62. Today, the prefect still controls most of the police forces, and, whether he is a Gaullist or not, he is expected to act as a 'spy' for the Government on local political developments. But the bulk of his work is elsewhere. Besides supervising the communes and the *conseil général*, he has to co-ordinate the ever more complex activities of the various Government services within his borders. He is assisted by a staff of sub-prefects and specialists, of whom the brighter younger ones have usually come from the Ecole Nationale d'Administration, the post-graduate civil service college founded in 1946. This college is placing a new emphasis on economics and sociology, as opposed to the more legalistic civil-service training of older days. It has strengthened the already high prestige of the civil-service élite, previously recruited direct into Ministries or other State bodies from various faculties or *Grandes Ecoles*. The ENA has served to build up a powerful old-boy network among brighter civil servants in the twenty-five to forty age-bracket, who in earlier days often did not know each other. This has certain practical advantages: an ENA man in a *préfecture* can often short-circuit the usual Ministerial delays and disputes by ringing up an old college chum in a Paris office and saying, '*Écoute, cher camarade*, can't you help . . .?' This can be most useful, in a land where personal contact is everything and a stranger, even in the same line of duty, is often an object of suspicion.

The danger of ENA is that it is helping to create an arrogant caste of brilliant but sometimes inhuman technocrats, and risks enlarging the psychological gulf that already separates the prefectoral corps from ordinary citizens. This might grow worse, as the new graduates reach the top prefectoral positions and ENA men come to rule France as Old Etonians once ruled India. Many older local people, councillors, mayors, and others, are suspicious of the new young technocrats who speak a language they do not follow. The younger generation in the communes are more sympathetic to them, and this will mitigate the danger: even so, it remains.

Prefects and their senior staff are clearly the source of much dynamism and progress in France. But it became increasingly clear, as the post-war years went by, that in terms of administration alone some changes were badly needed. The department had become too small a unit for modern economic planning; and as the problems of local development became more complex, there were increasing failures of co-ordination between the prefect and the specialised services of each Ministry in the department. In 1964 a double reform, regional and prefectoral, sought to apply remedies.

First, the departmental services of the Ministries were regrouped and placed under the authority of the prefect. This has helped quite a lot to harmonise local administration. Previously, the *préfecture's* own technical and specialised staff frequently duplicated the work of local officials of, say, the Ministry of Health or Public Works; and the prefect as he went about his department might come across a new hospital or bridge, for instance, that Paris was building without having informed him. Now, the prefect is a channel for everything, and though many technical matters still have to be referred to Paris, at least he has the authority to settle the simpler ones. Gravier quotes the case, in 1957, of a Ministerial decree being needed to authorise the social aid bureau of a small town near Dunkirk to accept a legacy from a local widow; and often, before 1964, local mayors would complain to me, 'I can't put up a monument or change a street-name without consulting Paris'. Now that these matters can be settled locally there are not only fewer delays; they are now decided by officials with some knowledge of local factors, instead of by grey men in Paris who might never have heard of the commune in question. To cope with all the extra work requiring his formal attention, the prefect is allowed to 'delegate his signature' to local officials of Ministries acting in his name.

This reform has helped shake local bureaucracy out of some of its inertia and routine. It has given an opportunity for certain procedures to be modernised—to move in one jump, as it were, from quill-pens to computers. And it has certainly helped the work of a man like de Caumont in Caen. But it causes problems. In many cases, the *préfectures* do not have the staff to carry out the new work properly, and many petty officials are either unable or unwilling to adapt themselves to the changes in routine. In many other cases, it simply means that the same people are dealing with the same things, though in the name of the prefect, not of Paris.

The most serious criticism of the reform, however, is that it has been fanfared by the Government as a great feat of decentralisation, when it is nothing of the sort; it is merely deconcentration. By reinforcing the prefect's powers so strongly, the State has probably increased its own influence over the communes, which previously might play off one inefficient Ministry against another. Some Left-wing critics even see the reform as a sinister move by the Gaullists to extend their hold over certain spheres of the civil service. Local schoolteachers, for instance, a notoriously Left-wing breed, were previously appointed by the university rectors (often men of similar Leftish sympathies) in conjunction with the Ministry of Education. Now, the nominations pass via the prefect. There is no positive evidence yet that this is leading to the selection of teachers with different views; but several rectors are highly indignant about it. Probably this particular issue has been inflated; and there is no doubt that, in general, the prefects use their powers wisely and moderately, and the new system is more efficient than the old. But it is not democratic.

Some of the same conflicting arguments are true of the regional reform. This has grouped the ninety departments into twenty-one regions purely for the purposes of economic planning; in other respects, they keep their old functions. The departments are all much the same size, though their population may vary from over a million (Bouches-du-Rhône) to the Lozère with 81,900. Their size was conceived in Napoleon's day so that an official in his capital could travel by stage coach to any part of his domain and back 'between sunrise and sundown'; but the motor-car has killed all that. The departments have also remained artificial, without acquiring the emotional significance of the old provinces, so that when a man from Avignon says, 'Je suis du Vaucluse', he is stating a legal fact, but when he says, 'Je suis provençal', he is making an emotive statement.

It was however the economic rather than the human artificiality of the department that prompted the reform. In many areas, big new projects such as the Languedoc canal cut across departmental boundaries and caused problems of liaison; and the economic future of a region such as Brittany, or the Auvergne, clearly could no longer be considered only at the level of their impoverished departments. So the prefect of whichever department contained the chief city was named *préfet de région*, with a sub-prefect beneath him specifically charged with co-ordinating economic growth. In each region, a new consultative body was set up to advise the prefect, a *Commission du Développement Economique Régional* (CODER). A quarter of the members of each commission are designated by the Prime Minister, a quarter are delegates from the *conseils généraux*, and half are delegates from local bodies such as trade unions and professional and commercial associations. Often their president is a leading politician of the region, as Antoine Pinay (Rhône–Alpes) or René Pleven (Brittany). The Plan now has a special chapter for each region, which the prefect and his staff draw up in consultation with the CODER and in close liaison with the Commissariat in Paris. Finally, some aspects of the annual State budget are now regionalised, so that instead of the spending of every franc being decided in Paris, the regional and departmental prefects are given lump sums in certain fields such as housing or roads, and are allowed to decide the details themselves. Major projects, such as inter-regional motorways, of course remain in central hands.

This reform, like the prefectoral one, marks a definite step forward. Most of the new regions do correspond roughly to the old provinces— Brittany, Burgundy, Auvergne, Provence, Lorraine, and so on. Therefore they mean something to people, and their creation has done a good deal to stimulate the growth of the new regional spirit. They show that at least the Government is interested in the regions, even if it wants to keep total control. Any mayor or other local individual prepared to co-operate with the regional prefect may find himself caught up in an excited atmosphere of dynamic activity: witness the enthusiasm of the mayor of Falaise or of Professor Dugrand at Montpellier. In Lower Normandy, de Caumont has enlisted teams of students and young councillors to work together for regional progress within the context of the new reform, and so has given it real life.

Politically, the situation is very paradoxical. In practice, you may find people of various views working together in the field: Gaullists and Socialists, Catholics and Marxists, unite in their work if they are more interested in progress than ideology. There is plenty of discussion, and the prefects and their staff are often ready in private to take notice of criticism and advice of a practical kind. But the Gaullists are extremely reluctant to formalise democratic opposition and decision; they fear this would give a cue to the old 'corrupt' party system and give old doctrinal quarrels a chance to re-assert themselves against the new technocracy. The CODERs are a façade: they meet only twice a year, they have no proper funds or secretariats, they are not properly elected, and there has been little evidence so far that either the prefects or the Fifth Plan have taken much notice of their advice. The town clerk of Toulouse complained to me: 'The CODERs have to accept a *fait accompli* from the prefect. The trouble is, in France, the opinion of the opposition isn't respected. Our old regional expansion committee here went off at half cock, because the local people felt that all the decisions were taken by mysterious hidden technocrats and it wasn't worth their trying.' And when Pinay, Pleven, and other anti-Gaullist CODER leaders urged that they should be given more power, Michel Debré, a reformist but an arch-Jacobin, said: 'Perhaps their responsibilities and composition can be improved. But there are limits: we don't want the French parliament rivalled by twenty regional ones.'

Yet if democracy *were* encouraged, if more power were given to the CODERs or more autonomy to the communes, in the short term it might lead to anything but practical progress, at least in many places. Among the older guard of mayors and other dignitaries, the *esprit de clocher* and sectarian, non-expansionist attitudes are still entrenched. Many Gaullists argue that it might be wiser, before trying to revive local democracy, to wait for the new generation to establish its take-over; and in so far as they are not just making excuses, they may have a point. The mayor of a small town is often an elderly lawyer or doctor with a sense of political tact, but without economic ideas or the desire for change. Many communes will refuse to fit into any general project unless they feel certain to benefit: some on main roads have been known to veto plans for a new motorway or bypass through fear of losing trade. One notorious case concerns the Electricité de France, which despite its splendid new power dams and reactors is still forced to use an antiquated system of tariffs and charges that varies from commune to commune and thus makes computerising of accounts impossible. This is simply because each commune feels it has some special advantage to maintain, and refuses to help the EDF to harmonise its tariffs. And the EDF, like most other organs of State, prefers patient persuasion to an imposed system that would cause an outcry.

Some anti-Government mayors and councils tend to be against progress just because it is identified, in their minds, with the State. Maybe, if they were given more power to make their own progress, this attitude would change. But if communes became more autonomous it might, in some places, raise the problem of Communism. Several large towns are in

Communist hands, notably Le Havre and Nîmes. In practice, their municipal control of affairs works quite smoothly, because they know they have to co-operate with the State—and because, to be fair, they often do have a progressive civic policy. But if they had more power and money of their own, they might form virtual Communist enclaves which, in the case of a port like Le Havre, could do some damage to the national economy.

Another problem is that the municipal election system, a Gaullist creation, tends to produce homogeneous single-list councils with no opposition. A party wins all seats, or none. This hardly stimulates democracy and free discussion. In Caen, where the passive Centre-Right faction under Louvel has a virtual monopoly, de Caumont has tried to stimulate interest in civic problems through a public campaign that he calls 'Caen Demain'. He holds public debates and study groups, distributes articles, and so on. A number of young people have responded. But although an élite is now actively interested in regionalism and town-planning, this has not yet spread to the man-in-the-street, perhaps in part because of the failures of TV and the local Press; and the general public level of civic awareness and responsibility in a town like Caen is rather poor by British or American standards. In Nancy, a local journalist told me: 'The municipal council here is old and mediocre, and the Chamber of Commerce has an average age of seventy. There are lots of lively young people, engineers, teachers, and so on, who are interested in the problems but won't try to take part in public life—they feel it's too difficult to dislodge the old ones.' In other areas, the picture is brighter, and the assumption of power by a new generation really seems to be happening. Dubedout of Grenoble is the star case, but there are other lesser Dubedouts appearing in other parts of France, especially in some country districts where the JAC revolution in farming has had its repercussions in many local elections. In the elections in the Maine-et-Loire in 1959, the average age of councillors fell at one swoop from sixty to thirty-five. Almost everywhere in France, the traditional position of the *notables* is declining; though they may still hold on to the formal positions of power, their influence and prestige is falling. The transfer to a new generation with a quite different outlook is ineluctable; it is simply a question of whether it can happen democratically, and with the right people.

One minor, but significant, change that is needed is the grouping or merging of the smaller communes. There are 37,000 communes in France, more than in the rest of the Common Market together. Over 3,400 have less than 100 people; one has three people, and most of its statutory municipal council of nine live elsewhere! Obviously the villages must pool their resources if they are to afford or justify modern equipment; and the planned expansion of larger towns is often held up by the fact that their suburbs form separate communes. But the communes are proud of their identity, while the mayors and councillors fear losing their positions and are therefore generally against mergers. Rather than make itself unpopular by forcing them to merge, the government encourages associations of communes in the countryside and urban 'districts' in the main towns. In each case a joint committee is formed with a common policy and budget for roads, water, housing, and so on, while each commune keeps its mayor and some say in its own more parochial matters, a little like the Greater London Council. Nancy, for instance, has a district that works well, though two of the more Left-wing of its fifteen suburbs have refused to join. And Lyon, Bordeaux, Lille, Strasbourg, and their suburban communes are now being regrouped into new 'communantés urbaines' somewhat on the lines of the GLC.

Since 1962, 8,700 communes have associated or formed districts, and 253, mostly tiny ones, have merged. Real mergers in towns are rare. One at Tours has been a bit of a failure because the Prefect pushed the communes into it; another at St. Chamond has done rather better, partly because its prestigious mayor, Antoine Pinay, put his weight behind it. The whole movement has still hardly started, and in some big towns the failure to achieve even a 'district' is a serious handicap: at Caen, as I explained, the Right-wing town and its Left-wing suburbs refuse to collaborate. Rich Caen therefore does not pay a sou towards the development of the new satellite towns which, when populated, will add greatly to its own trade and prosperity; and the planning of an area in rapid expansion is rendered difficult. At Grenoble, the preparation of the Olympic Games was even prejudiced by the attitude of some peripheral suburbs. This is most un-British and shows how sharp local tensions can still be in France. It is a paradox that this powerful and elephantine State cannot, or will not, deal with the flea that tickles its ear. But when there are 37,000 fleas you have to be careful, and the communes' jealous exercise of their legal rights is one price they exact from the State for its constant intrusion on their privacy in other respects.

Five principal reforms, as I see it, are needed in French local government. First, the State should take stronger measures to encourage the regrouping of communes in suburbs and isolated areas. Under existing legislation, it has the right to enforce a merger or an association when two-thirds of the local communes are in favour; but even this right is often unused. It is true that the commune is one of the few genuine civic entities of France and should not lightly be destroyed. But while some communes are very much alive, others are dying of their own accord, either through depopulation or the reverse, absorption by a big town. It is these that need to be reshuffled.

Secondly, the 'live' communes, the growing towns, should be allowed stronger finances of their own and stronger powers of deciding on their use. For instance, it is absurd that Lyon and Marseille, both now building badly needed underground railway systems, should be dependent on the State for every phase of their construction. Some general improvement is possible from the new local tax reforms, which will remove the old levy on trade turnover* and replace it with a tax on salaries as the main source of local revenue. This, and a new system of property taxation, will encourage local expansionist policies and may slightly increase local budgets. But they will still be as subject as ever to State supervision.

Third, the State should make its own bureaucratic system less rigid: the 1964 reforms have not gone far enough. State regulations are far too monolithic and inflexible, and do not take account of the varying needs of different regions. In agriculture, for instance, an otherwise useful reform like the SAFER or the SICA has fixed rules which apply easily in some areas but not in others. The Prefect is often empowered to use his discretion, but there are limits to which he can bend written dogma. If there were more regional autonomy, flexibility would follow automatically.

Fourth, a new broom needs to be taken to the whole world of petty officialdom: I have quoted the PTT and the telephones as a bad case, but it is not the only one. In many Ministries, prefectures, or other Government offices, one is struck again and again by the contrast between the vigour and efficiency of a small élite at the top, and junior employees whose muddle or lethargy simply sabotages the technocratic effort. This is a common problem anywhere, but especially striking in France. These officials are usually very badly paid. The answer, in theory, is to raise their salaries, reduce their numbers, and bring in modern business methods and machinery—an operation whose initial investment would probably soon be recovered in improved 'productivity'. But any shake-up of this sort meets with such stubborn staff resistance, even from those likely to benefit directly, that not even the Fifth Republic has dared attempt it on any scale.

Finally, an attempt must be made at real regional democracy, either by strengthening the CODERs, reforming the *conseils généraux*, or creating something similar. A certain void is appearing at the moment on a local level, between the decline of the old political forces, partisan, doctrinal, aggressive, and the rise of a new technocracy mainly imposed from outside. This could be dangerous: if the void is not filled by a new kind of democracy, the only answer will be yet more State control. But democracy cannot be imposed in a day: it needs careful nurturing over a long period. Plenty of technocrats working for the régime are fully aware of these problems. Lamour told me: 'Our projects are useless unless they are followed by valid local initiatives. Once we have given the impetus, we want to be able to leave them in local hands.' But Lamour's masters, in practice, seem unprepared to take the political risk this involves.

Many people, Louis Armand among them, see Europe as the answer to the problem. As Europe unites and the power of Paris fades, so France's centralised structures will crack under outside weight, under the force of economic reality and of influences from France's more decentralised neighbours. This at least is the theory. It is still rather hard to see it happening in practice under the present régime.

* See p. 110 (The battle for the retail trade).

CHAPTER VII

PARIS, THE BELOVED MONSTER

WHILE DULL PROVINCIAL TOWNS turn into lively ones, Paris, lively already, has become something of a madhouse. Frenetic and congested, it has been ill prepared either physically or psychologically for the new pressures of growth and prosperity. Parisians, a restless and self-willed breed at the best of times, find their nerves stretched taut by the traffic jams, the noise, the bad housing, the lack of space and services. People are late for appointments, snappy down the telephone, or choking back an irritation that the plumber will not come or the shops are over-charging. Life is much simpler in the provinces.

No wonder that Parisians' feelings have grown so fiercely ambivalent towards a city that has always inspired deep loyalties and whose personal spell, even today, is not lightly broken. 'Paris, what a monster!' is a phrase I have continually heard people use, almost lovingly. And so the two Parises co-exist: the unpleasant modern town of practical daily life, and the strong, secret personality of a city whose insidious beauty and vitality still manage to survive the odds against them and even to renew themselves. For these reasons, many foreigners like myself find Paris a fascinating and exciting city to visit for a month or two but we no longer want to live there, as so many francophiles and expatriates did in the decades before the war.

Even Parisians are coming to realise that their city has lost some of its old uniqueness and lustre, though opinions may vary as to why this is so. One explanation is political: Paris, far more than the provinces, bore the brunt of the upheavals and humiliations of the past thirty years, from Nazi parades on the Champs-Elysées to the last sickening months of the Algerian crisis in 1962, with their terrorist bomb-attacks and armed police raids all over the city. And Parisians, despite their new wealth and stability, have not quite emerged from the shame of these events. The present mood of Paris is also coloured by a *malaise* in French intellectual and artistic circles that I shall try to analyse later.*

* See pp. 354 (Intellectuals in disarray).

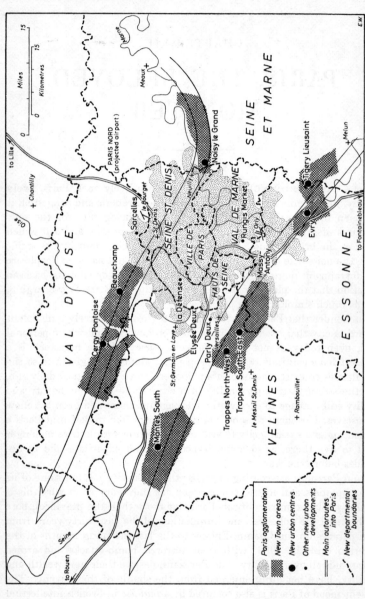

The eight departments of the new 'Paris Region', showing the two parallel axes of the projected new urban centres

But some of the trouble at least is purely practical. Paris is today paying the price of nearly a century of neglect of town-planning. The Ville Lumière that the tourist sees is bright with new paint and whitened façades, but it hides realities: the hideously congested commercial districts, the lack of parks or even car-parks, the crumbling tenements, and, outside the old city gates, the sprawling wilderness of pre-war suburbs, ill equipped with hospitals, schools, public transport, or even water. As the population swells, these problems grow too, and they sour the life of the whole city.

Just at the moment when greater Paris has seemed to be on the verge of seizing up like an engine without oil, at last the problem is being tackled seriously. First of all, in the past ten years the grave housing shortage has been checked if not cured, and today the outer suburbs are ringed with a white phalanx of new blocks of flats like some vast Stonehenge: many of them are unbeautiful and ill planned, but at least they provide essential roofs. And now, since the early 'sixties, the Gaullist master-planners have been at work on the whole shape of the city, eagerly colouring the maps in their offices with grandiose designs for garden cities and urban freeways. The French do not do things by halves: after years of total disregard, the future of Paris has now become a public obsession, the subject of scores of books, reports, and conferences. Several of the projects are imaginative—and some are even beginning to take shape. Up through the waste land of the old slums and suburbs, the first shoots are appearing of a new, daring, possibly very beautiful city, worthy of the heritage of the Place des Vosges and Versailles. But, with the population and its needs growing so fast, the whole operation is a race against time.

GIANT-SCALE PLANNING FOR THE YEAR 2000

When Baron Haussmann, prefect of the Seine department in 1853–70, drove his broad boulevards through the congested bowels of the old city, he turned Paris into the best-planned and most elegant modern capital in Europe. Today the boulevards are still her most distinctive feature, and until very recently they have enabled the growth of traffic to be kept virtually under control. But they never cured the problems of the archaic and densely packed quarters in between them, nor was Haussmann's planning extended to the new industrial suburbs that after 1870 grew up higgledy-piggledy outside the old city gates. Aubervilliers, Les Lilas, Issy-les-Moulineaux, lovely names for ghastly places—these and a hundred other townlets arose while Paris was sucking the blood from the rest of France, and they became, as the planning expert Peter Hall puts it, 'a vast, ill conceived, hastily constructed emergency camp to house the labour force of Paris, presenting almost the limit of urban degeneration'. *

* *The World Cities* (McGraw-Hill, 1966).

Auguste Renoir's pastoral canvas of the Seine at Argenteuil, painted in the 1870s, was soon blotted out beyond recognition.

After 1918 this industrial growth slowed right down. But, with land prices so low, a different type of excrescence now appeared in the suburbs, the individual *pavillon*. The Parisian *petit bourgeois* found that he could afford to realise a dream that he has always cherished as dearly as the Englishman: a suburban cottage with a garden. But instead of the English ribbon-development of that period, there was anarchy. Some 80,000 little red-roofed *pavillons* spread their ungainly rash of assorted shapes across the outer suburbs, and were among the few new buildings put up in greater Paris between the wars. Then after 1945 the city's population again began to grow rapidly, and new blocks of flats were flung up piece-meal to cope with it, slowly at first, and after 1954 at a faster rate rising to 70,000 or more new flats a year. Nearly a million have been built in greater Paris since the war, to house or rehouse a third of the city's eight million people. In sheer numbers, this is some achievement, even though the old slums are still far from cleared. But only very recently has much attempt been made to plan the new suburbs coherently. At first, stray blocks of flats were planted anywhere, usually in vacant gaps between the old suburbs where land was cheap because of lack of public transport. Then a few dormitory towns were created, on the edge of the Paris conurbation, but these have been heavily criticised.* London's solution of new towns out in the country was rejected, partly because it was thought that Parisians could never be persuaded to become thirty-mile commuters, and partly because of the difficulty in France of attracting new light industries quickly to the areas.

Thus, in the past decade or so, actual achievement has been limited largely to keeping pace with the bare essentials of new housing. The wider structural town-planning problems of the Paris region remain unsolved, and are only now being approached systematically.

Inside Paris itself, the over-riding problem is congestion of every sort. By 'Paris itself' I mean the municipality of twenty *arrondissements* within the old city gates, known as the Ville de Paris. Since 1911 its population has steadily declined from 2·9 to 2·75 million. But the people are still packed more densely than on Manhattan: 114 to the acre, against 43 in the equivalent area of London. Green parks cover 6·9 per cent of the Ville de Paris, against 15·4 per cent of London and 17·3 per cent of New York—and the only Paris parks of any size are at either extremity, Boulogne and Vincennes. The open spaces by the Seine in the city centre are deceptive; and the patch of dusty scrub that bears the royal name of Tuileries is not of much practical use as a park.

In the eastern and northern districts, thousands of antiquated little factories and depots lie cheek-by-jowl with residential tenements, pol-luting the air, and blocking the traffic with their lorries. Apart from the

* See p. 213 (The housing shortage).

boulevards, most streets are narrow, and there are more cars in the city than parking spaces for them, so that it becomes a major exploit to find room to unload a van. The noise of the high-pitched French car engines reverberates in the chasm-like streets, and, though drivers are not supposed to use their horns, they do. Compared with much of Paris, even a poorish London district like Fulham or Lambeth seems a haven of space and calm. Offices have spread into old-fashioned residential districts quite unsuited for them, while Paris holds most of the records among major Western cities for poor housing. At the 1962 census, nearly a third of the dwellings inside the Ville de Paris were classified as decaying or insanitary. Some 80 per cent were built before 1914, and some 30 per cent have neither lavatory nor washing-place.* Large family flats are especially scarce: the average size of a Paris flat is 2·2 rooms, against 3·1 in London and 3·3 in New York.

The well-known character of Parisians seems to me to aggravate this situation, in a kind of vicious circle. It is their egotism and lack of civic spirit that have helped to get their city into this mess; equally, their intolerance and hypertension seem peculiarly ill suited to putting up with the results. A Londoner is tempted to observe, smugly, that a more phlegmatic or community-minded people would have found more effective ways of living with their difficulties, if not of solving them.

One of the troubles is that local government in the Paris area is notoriously weak and divided. The municipal council of the Ville de Paris has even less autonomy than an ordinary French commune: it is allowed no mayor and is governed directly by the prefect of the Seine. This is because the State is haunted by memories of 1789, 1848, and 1871, and will allow little power to the dangerous Parisian populace. So the council has neither the scope nor the resources to tackle the problems on the scale needed. *A fortiori*, for the same political reasons the State has never encouraged it to fuse with the hundreds of suburban communes into an effective co-ordinating body in the manner of the Greater London Council. And these communes, many of them Communist, have proved equally reluctant to co-operate or to merge their identities.

For a hundred years now, these communes have been quite inadequate for their tasks. The late nineteenth-century urban growth engulfed existing village communities that at once became paralysed by what faced them—how could the mayor of a peaceful townlet, like Asnières or Montreuil, cope with the needs of the new flood? And the State did little to help. Hence the ugliness and physical chaos of these suburbs has been matched by their lack of public equipment; only very recently has much start been made on providing them properly with hospitals, sports centres, theatres, university colleges, or even adequate *lycées*. All the culture for which Paris is famous has rested within a small circle between

* Current estimates based on recent surveys.

Montmartre and Montparnasse; the rest was *la banlieue,* a melancholy hinterland of shacks and seedy cafés where children play in the weeds of vacant lots.

Nearly all the main offices, too, are in central Paris. Yet to travel there for daily work or an evening's enjoyment can be hard, because of the shortages of public transport. The Métro network barely extends outside the Ville de Paris, because of jealous rivalries with the SNCF at the time of its building, in the 1900s; the SNCF's own local services radiate effectively from the central stations, but with very few inter-suburban ring lines, while suburban bus services are equally rudimentary. In the 1950s, when the housing shortage was at its worst, some workers would have to get up at five a.m. to make a two-hour journey into central Paris and out again to their factory, arriving back home at 8 p.m. This is now less of a problem, since it has become easier to find a flat near one's work; but the average time spent commuting a day in the Paris area is still seventy-seven minutes, and could be much reduced if transport were less centripetal. For those with a car, there is rarely anywhere to park in Paris, while the rush-hour traffic jams at the main exit-routes are worse than in London.

Such are the main problems still facing the planners today. The Fourth Republic made little effort to solve them: its few early post-war schemes all fell foul of bureaucratic and political disputes and muddles. And this failure is one reason why the Common Market preferred the more manageable city of Brussels for its headquarters, and Paris, as someone has put it, 'muffed her chance to become the capital of Europe'.

In the mid 1950s, however, a project finally began to take shape for actively limiting and controlling the growth of Paris. This the Gaullists took over, and published it in 1960 as the PADOG (*Plan d'Aménagement et d'Organisation Générale de la Région Parisienne*). Linked closely with the provincial decentralisation policy, the PADOG's aim was to cut down immigration to Paris from 100,000 a year to 50,000 or less, by putting severe curbs on new offices and factories in the Paris area. The inner city was to be renovated and thinned out, but the Paris conurbation was to be contained within its existing limits.

This plan was at least a step forward—but it ran into criticism. Many people argued that to check the economic growth of Paris like this, and especially the building of offices, would hinder it from competing with other Western capitals; big new international concerns looking for a base would turn instead to London, maybe, or Rome, or Frankfurt, and this would not be in France's interests. These views were largely shared by Paul Delouvrier, the brilliant civil servant and former delegate-general in Algeria who in 1961 was appointed head of a new Government department charged with planning and supervising the city's future: the *Délégation Générale au District de la Région de Paris,* usually known as 'le District'. The census of 1962 showed that Paris was growing even faster than had been thought: its population had gone up 1·1 million since 1954. This further convinced Delouvrier that sharp limitation of growth was going to be not only economically undesirable but also very difficult, and in 1963 he won de Gaulle's support for a change of policy to one of planned expansion. Two years later he pushed through parliament the grandiose Schéma Directeur, or directive outline, that forms the basis of all today's activity.

The Paris area had by now become one of the twenty-one new 'regions' * of France; it comprises the Seine, Seine-et-Oise, and Seine-et-Marne departments and part of the Oise, 5,000 square miles in a radius of thirty to sixty miles from the city centre. The Schéma deals with the whole of this area, thus allowing planning on a sweeping new scale. Delouvrier anticipates that the Paris region, 8·5 million in 1962, will grow spontaneously through birthrate and immigration to 12 million by 1985, and 14 or possibly 16 million by the year 2000, nine-tenths of it within the Paris conurbation. But this estimate also assumes that other big French towns will double or treble their size in that period: it is not that the provinces are again to be bled white by Paris, rather that France's delayed urbanisation and rise in population are both happening so fast. The issue, as Delouvrier sees it, is not how to prevent the growth of Paris but how to prevent it from happening chaotically. The Schéma takes over and extends the PADOG's unquestioned plans for central renovation, and complements them with titanic new suburban projects.

The basis of its thinking is that Paris will be asphyxiated unless it is made polycentric. The Schéma has rejected one much-canvassed solution, for a kind of Brasilia fifty miles west of Paris, on grounds that artificial cities of this sort are rarely successful and would not be suitable in France. But although the main centres of power and wealth are to remain inside Paris, the Schéma plans eight new cities on the perimeter, each with a population rising by A.D. 2000 to between 300,000 and 1,200,000, and each with its own complete social, cultural and commercial equipment, unlike the present suburbs. The 'new towns' solution, hitherto rejected, is now espoused fanatically, but not quite on the British model. Instead of radiating round Paris, these cities are aligned on two parallel axes astride the Seine and Marne, pushing towards the sea. On the south side, Tigery-Lieusaint and Evry (near Corbeil), two cities at Trappes (west of Versailles), and Mantes; on the north, Noisy-le-Grand (on the Marne), Beauchamp and Cergy (both next to Pontoise). These towns are to have their own light industries, for two million extra jobs will have to be found in the region by 2000, mostly in the tertiary sector. By early 1968 work had begun on the building of two of these towns, Evry and Cergy.

Not all the new population will go to these cities. The smaller existing towns of the Paris region, such as Senlis, Meaux and Etampes, most of them so lifeless and dreary in the 1950s, have already been revitalised

* See p. 169 (New life in the provinces).

in the past few years as commuter and light industrial centres, and this policy will continue. Other new towns of medium size will be built in the gaps of the existing conurbation, as is happening already. And here is the crucial point: the planners hope that if these towns can be built in the right way, with the right amenities, then gradually they will be able to absorb and wipe out the older suburban chaos in between them. But it will take a very long time. To start by razing to the ground the existing mess and then rebuild from scratch would be too costly, and would arouse too much hostility. At least the planting of new towns in the middle of the mess will help to provide the needed services and will ease the suburbs' dependence on central Paris; and this is already happening in some places. Nanterre, for instance, west of Neuilly, boasts a new theatre and embryo university among its modern housing estates. There are even plans for the formal zoning of the decongestion of central Paris, with the business *milieu* extending itself westwards from the Champs-Elysées to beyond Neuilly; some Government offices will move south-west to a site at Villacoublay, now a military airport, and parts of the Sorbonne will move out, possibly to the south or the north-east.

The Schéma also plans new networks of intersecting motorways, and 60-m.p.h. express Métro services far into the suburbs. Some of these projects are earlier ones already under way. A new ring motorway outside the city gates, the Boulevard Périphérique, is now partly in use and due for completion by 1970; access motorways have been built since the war towards Fontainebleau and Compiègne, while others are planned towards Chartres, Meaux, and Pontoise. These, as well as ring motorways in the outer suburbs, are urgently needed as traffic grows. Le Bourget airport will eventually be closed, since it is too near the new suburbs, and a large new jet airport is now being built six miles farther north-east, to share the traffic with Orly.

The Schéma Directeur at least shows boldness and imagination, and has been welcomed by most of those who accept its premise about the inevitability of the growth of Paris. Even the Marxist writer Michel Ragon, a leading architectural critic, has said, 'It is thanks to courageous and clear-sighted civil servants like Delouvrier that Paris will perhaps be saved.'* But plenty of other people, on the Right as well as the Left, have criticised the Schéma as being far too grandiose, technocratic, and in-human, as 'a pipe-dream of polytechnicians' or 'a Gaullist attempt to revive the "royal myth" of imperial Paris'. Much of this opposition is purely political, but some is more objective. One fear is that the publicising of plans on this giant scale may simply encourage more immigration than ever. And what about the size and siting of the new cities?—why, it is asked, first reject the British or Brasilian models for their artificiality, and then make this *volte-face* with projects ten times the size of Stevenage

* *Arts* magazine, 10 June 1964.

and without even the political *raison d'être* of Brasilia? How can such growths ever find real humanity? Might it not be wiser to enlarge existing towns, like Orléans, Reims, and Rouen, which are much farther from Paris but will soon be less than thirty minutes away by 'aerotrain', no more than Pontoise by rail today?

There may be some force in these arguments. Much therefore will depend on the manner in which the new cities are built, and on whether from the outset they can be turned into more than mere dormitories. In theory, the aim is to provide them with civic centres, theatres, and such like, even in advance of the building of most of the flats. But this will need special funds, and the most resolute supervision, and it is still far from clear where these are to come from. For the *District* itself has only a small budget of its own: it is a brains-trust for study and co-ordination, rather like the Plan, while execution depends on the Ministries (notably those of Construction, Public Works, and Finance) and on the communes.

This is the central dilemma: the ideas and the spirit of the planners are decades in advance of the cumbersome French legal and administrative machine, and of the habits and attitudes of most ordinary civil servants and local councillors. Many of the Schéma's warmest supporters are therefore sceptical about how far it is realisable, in the present French context. The planners have done their part: now it is up to the executive departments, where already the Schéma is up against the gravest difficulties: lack of co-ordination, lack of funds, bureaucratic and legal delays, human and political oppositions. For instance, work on the big urban project at La Défense has been held up by the failure of the Government's bridges and highways department to start widening the Pont de Neuilly; on several matters, the SNCF is still caught up in rivalries with the Paris public transport authority; and the slow, tortuous process of granting building permits, though designed to favour planned development, often simply has the effect of inhibiting private initiative.

In order to meet these problems, the *District* has now been complemented by a more powerful co-ordinating body, the *Région Parisienne*, similar to the economic prefectures in the other regions. Delouvrier is the regional prefect as well as head of the *District*; and the three departments of the region have been redivided into eight smaller but more logically shaped ones. Hitherto the small Seine department with Paris at its centre has formed an island in the middle of the Seine-et-Oise, and this concentric pattern has hampered administration in a period of rapid growth. But the new divisions have a patent political motive, too: they will involve constituency changes, and will help to break up the notorious 'Red belt' of the Seine suburbs. This has simply aggravated the suspicions and hostility of many of the Left-wing communes towards the Government's overall plans for the region. Yet the *District* badly needs the co-operation of the region's two thousand communes, whose powers of obstruction are the same as elsewhere in France.

A number of mayors, on the Right as well as the Left, have complained loudly that the *District* failed to consult them adequately when drawing up the Schéma. And they may have some justification. It is true that the *District* does have a kind of advisory committee, something like the provincial CODERs, and this was consulted occasionally, as were some individual mayors; but it was the State officials, even more than in the provinces, who did all the real thinking and decision-making. As one *District* planner put it to me, in typical Gaullist tones, 'How on earth can you expect the mayor of some wretched suburb to grasp the kind of problems *we* are facing? Their arguments would simply have held things up.' But the State may have to pay the price later, if the communes remain resentful. Clearly the planning of the Paris region would benefit from some kind of union of communes, as in London; but this, as I have explained, is out of the question.

While the larger urban communes resent State officialdom for political reasons, some of the smaller ones outside the conurbation oppose the Schéma simply because it threatens their rural peace. In the village of Le Mesnil St. Denis, eight miles south-west of Versailles and barely a mile from the bounds of tomorrow's megalopolis at Trappes, I paid a call in 1966 on the Right-wing mayor, Raymond Berrurier, a local solicitor and a most fruity character. He received me with old-world courtesy and talked charmingly and plausibly: 'Here, we're trying to keep the human scale and save the landscape from these skyscrapers. I've formed a national association for preserving the Ile-de-France, and we're at war with Delouvrier. What we need in France are more civic trusts and commissions of enquiry. That's what I admire about Britain. In this country, people's opinions aren't consulted. Even so, my association's managed to make some progress. For instance, when Citroën were planning a new factory at Bièvre, a village near here, we fought them, and managed to get the authorities to reduce its planned size—it would have spoilt the village. Here at Le Mesnil, there are three little factories; but each of them signed a contract with me, before it arrived, promising not to get too big. So, when one firm later wanted to expand, I obliged it to move elsewhere. Instead of building up the Paris region, the Government should force people to stay in their rural provinces, and build scattered little factories for them there. The other menace we're fighting is land expropriation. Why should the planners buy up our villas and estates for their new towns? You see, I don't want my village to change.'

I bade him farewell, reeling before his mixture of civic good sense and reactionary nonsense. One cogent argument against his point of view is that there is little in the unlovely Ile-de-France worth 'preserving', apart from the *châteaux* in their great parks, which the Schéma will not touch. Le Mesnil itself has little charm or character. Though Berrurier himself died in 1967, his outlook and his pressure-group are still very much alive, and have some influence in the Paris region. But the Government is likely to find ways of dealing with this opposition, and most of the larger communes do at least accept the basic need for change, even when resenting the *District* politically. Some of them are trying to go ahead with their own development schemes: the big north Paris suburb of St. Denis, Communist-led, is building one of the largest skyscrapers in Europe.

But however progress-minded a commune may be, the task of creating a sizable new town on its territory* is generally quite beyond its power or resources. How can Trappes, population 9,700, build itself a city the size of Marseille? The French are now actively considering the British solution of new-town development corporations, with local powers of control. Without some such bodies, there are dangers of the new suburbs growing up in piecemeal chaos, as already seems to be happening in some places where private speculators have set to work on their own schemes. As a first step, the Government has been trying to check speculation, with new laws blocking the sale of land in the development zones; but in France this is not easy.

If the Schéma's various projects are now to pass from theory to action, firmer legislation will be needed, but also vast new funds. Lack of money is, needless to say, the biggest obstacle of all in the Paris region, and has been for years. Private capital is still reluctant to invest in cheap housing, where returns are so low; the communes are starved of revenue; and the State still gives housing and other public services a relatively low priority. Now, if the Schéma is not to remain a dead letter, the State must urgently launch massive loans or find other ways of enticing private investment. The *District*'s own annual budget has been rising steadily but is still no more than 425m francs, used mainly to stimulate selected projects. Thanks to this, and to a general rise in public spending in the Paris region, at least some progress has been made recently in renovating the suburbs: for instance, whereas no new hospitals at all were built in greater Paris in 1954–60, ten are now under construction and two have just been completed. New theatres, university colleges, swimming-pools, and libraries are at last beginning to enliven *la triste banlieue*.

But the advance is painfully slow. The urgently needed Boulevard Périphérique moves forward at only two and a half miles a year: its cost, seventy-two million francs a mile, is ten times higher than for a similar road in open country largely because of the price of land expropriation in Paris. Huge stretches of outer Paris today are *en chantier*: it all looks impressive, yet for months on end the same site may stay half-completed, for lack not of labour or techniques but simply of cash. The years taken over the admittedly impressive new multi-level road junction at the Porte de la Chapelle contrast with the relatively fast work on new flyovers and underpasses in London.

Yet the population of Paris swells by almost 200,000 a year, the traffic

* As there are no 'rural districts' in France, the whole national territory is divided into communes, and an isolated village will generally be the head-quarters of a commune covering several square miles.

jams mount up, and the schools, clinics, telephone exchanges, even the cemeteries, are full to bursting. 'Are you really in control?' I asked a smooth young *District* technocrat; 'Will you be able to stop the whole thing seizing up?' '*Théoriquement, oui,*' he replied with French precision: 'We have the blueprints and the technical means. But we need the authority, and the cash.' It will be a race against time, to save the Ville Lumière from the twilight of asphyxia.

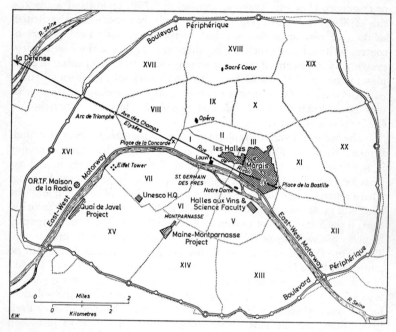

Central Paris, showing the principal new roads and development areas
(the roman figures mark arrondissement numbers)

ROMANTIC *VIEUX PARIS* AND THE SKYSCRAPERS

The Schéma Directeur has little to say about the Ville de Paris itself. This is because decisions here belong, in theory, to the municipal council; and although this body is a weak one, the State is generally careful not to upset it by poaching its prerogatives. In practice, this uneasy stalemate of power between city council and State is one of the main reasons why effective town-planning inside Paris has remained so paralysed since the days of Haussmann. City councillors are indignant at their lack of a mayor and their direct dependence on the prefect: yet they have usually proved too sheepish, divided, and conservative a body to make proper use even of the power they do have. Thus an essential priority project like the removal of Les Halles central markets, first mooted in the 1920s, was repeatedly contested and shelved by the council right up until the 1960s, and this has added hugely to the city's mounting congestion.

For many years the city fathers rejected nearly every imaginative proposal, by Le Corbusier and others, for the future of Paris. But today the council is Gaullist-dominated, and therefore at least is inclined to fall in with Government plans, so that a more dynamic approach has at last emerged. Les Halles *are* finally under transfer to the suburbs. Other big schemes, too, are under way, some of them admittedly pre-dating the Fifth Republic in their origins.

The underlying policy is to keep a working balance between aesthetics and practical needs, in a city where so much is worth preserving and yet so much will have to be wiped out. So far, this seems to be succeeding. One positive aspect of the council's past immobilism is that at least, with a few exceptions, they have preserved the city from desecration; and this is now continuing, even under a more active régime. Any visitor from London is impressed by the relative lack of ugly piecemeal rebuilding of central office areas in Paris. Historic districts like the Marais and the Latin Quarter are being restored rather than pulled down; and the big new skyscrapers are all, or almost all, outside the city's beautiful centre.

The most important of the new skyscraper projects—at La Défense, two miles west of the Arc de Triomphe—lies slightly outside the bounds of the Ville de Paris, but its character is metropolitan, not suburban. Here a State organisation is carrying out what has been called the most ambitious and exciting urban renewal scheme in the world today. A towering cluster of office and apartment blocks will act as overspill for the saturated Champs-Elysées area and may soon come to rival it as the city's main business centre. Thus it will sharply accentuate the historic tendency of Paris, like London, to shift its centre of gravity steadily westwards.

The area chosen is a 1,700-acre site astride the tip of the straight axis that runs from the Louvre up the Champs-Elysées to Neuilly. Work started in 1958, and is due to end in the mid-'70s. The existing mess of tenements and seedy little factories is being cleared; and several new sky-scrapers have now taken their place. The most original feature is that all traffic will go underground. The main road here carries the heaviest traffic in all France, being the principal route from Paris to the north-west suburbs and eastern Normandy, and in order to cope with this, a magnifi-cent five-level junction network has now been built deep down in the bowels of La Défense, where the roads divide for Pontoise and St.-Germain-en-Laye: a subterranean Los Angeles. Up above, in an airy precinct, will stand the thirty skyscrapers, one of them (700 feet) the tallest in Europe. There will be offices for 40,000 employees, flats for 80,000 people, and underground parking for 20,000 cars.

The project was agreed in 1950, and as a first step a big triangular single-vaulted exhibition hall was completed in 1957. A year later, just before de Gaulle's return, a public body was set up to finance and build La

Défense. This associates the State with the three communes concerned, Nanterre (Communist), Puteaux (Socialist), and Courbevoie (now Gaullist), and it might well provide a model for the corporations that will be needed to develop the Schéma's new cities. When it took over by decree some of the local powers of the communes, Puteaux and Nanterre were at first furious and used what rights they had left to obstruct the process of clearance and expropriation. But today they seem to have acquiesced and are even enthusiastic. Indeed, most of the present delays on the building programme have been due much more to inter-Ministerial disputes, technical trouble over tunnelling the new express Métro, and shortage of clients to provide advance financing for their new offices.

At first a number of leading firms leapt at the chance to move from the cramped Champs-Elysées: several, notably Esso, are already installed at La Défense. But others now seem to be hesitating, and the consequent lack of funds has been slowing down operations. By late 1967 only three of the towers had been completed. It is sad to see a scheme of such imagination held up by the usual troubles, but no doubt it will all be finished one day. There are even plans to extend it westwards into the slums of Nanterre, where there will be a university and cultural metropolis, including a 'Museum of the Twentieth Century' commissioned by Malraux and designed by Le Corbusier before his death. Thus one of the nastiest of the pre-war suburbs will be 'absorbed'. The towers of La Défense will crown the sweeping townscape of Haussmann's western boulevards, and the Champs-Elysées, as Michel Ragon has put it, 'will become in comparison old-fashioned and provincial, a mere corridor for cars'.

The architecture and the siting of La Défense have few serious critics: but the same can hardly be said of the next largest project, at Maine-Montparnasse, which is far nearer to the centre of Paris and therefore far more likely to spoil its harmony. Here a *société d'économie mixte* formed by the State, city council, and private interests, has implanted some monolithic edifices on the site of the old Maine and Montparnasse railway termini, which have been shifted southwards down the line. Two huge rectangular blocks have already been built, each 780 feet long and 200 high, forming an ugly backdrop of concrete behind the Invalides and the Ecole Militaire; and they are to be joined, in 1970 or so, by a 600-foot skyscraper in similar style, much the tallest building in central Paris after the Eiffel Tower. The three blocks together will contain 1,000 flats and 8,000 office rooms (Air France's new HQ is already installed there) as well as parking for 5,000 cars and, in the tower luxury hotel, a Press club and swimming-pool.

The promoters' main argument in favour of the tower has been a financial one, as in Manhattan, due to the soaring costs of land in Paris. But there was strong criticism on aesthetic grounds, led by a number of city councillors and a section of the Press. The critics objected less to the tower's height than to its shape: it was to be 240 feet wide and risked looking like a huge replica of the much-loved Shell building on London's

South Bank. Finally the project has been modified and the planned width reduced to 200 feet. With its surrounding gardens and fountains, the ensemble may in itself achieve a certain elegance, like the skyscrapers of Milan or the area round Victoria Station in London: but on such a vast scale it risks dwarfing the historic monuments of this part of Paris, notably the Invalides and the Ecole Militaire.

Gradually the whole of the cramped and slummy district south-west of Montparnasse, the fifteenth arrondissement, is to be renovated. Already a second ensemble of smaller skyscrapers is beginning to take shape there, along the Seine at the Quai de Javel downstream from the Eiffel Tower. The planning in this case appears to be rather more aesthetic: there will be a dozen or so slender and carefully spaced 275-foot blocks, set on various levels amid gardens, and they can hardly fail to improve this ugly stretch of the river. But progress is strangely slow: some investors and buyers have been frightened off by high land and expropriation costs, local factories such as Citroën have proved hard to dislodge, and there have even been hints of financial scandal. Farther upstream, piecemeal development is moving ahead much faster: the old sports stadium, the Vélodrome d'Hiver, has been pulled down and a number of impressive new buildings put up nearby, notably the Atomic Energy HQ and the 500-bedroom Paris Hilton, the city's sole large post-war hotel.

And so, after an even slower post-war start than in London, the familiar skyline of Paris is now changing fast. Inevitably, this is provoking the usual modern debate about skyscrapers. The majority view is that a big city, even Paris, *is* enhanced by having a few really tall buildings, even if they are not very beautiful in themselves. The Eiffel Tower caused fury in its day, but today few lovers of *vieux Paris* want it pulled down; and even the wedding-cake pomposity of Sacré Cœur has come to seem acceptable because of its gleaming hill-top position. But a skyscraper, especially a broad one, does pose more delicate aesthetic problems than a church or a slim spike of steel. Indeed, many modern architects see Paris's vocation as essentially a feminine city of slender towers and spires, and not of square blocks. The planners and authorities seem to have accepted this too. And on the whole, apart from the lapse at Montparnasse, they have shown more sensitivity than their colleagues in London. First, they have tried to group the skyscrapers in clusters, or in some harmonious relation to each other, rather than let them sprout piecemeal as in much of London outside the Barbican. Secondly, the skyscrapers are being kept away from the historic city centre. There are strict rules about the height of new buildings—100 feet for central Paris, 120 for the outer districts, such as the fifteenth—and exceptions are rarely granted in the centre.

Of course there are plenty of Parisians who object to skyscrapers or modern buildings in any form. They want the city to stay unchanged. Their point of view generally exerts less influence than in Britain, partly because of the weakness of public opinion in France as a whole, especially in terms of Press and television. It is hard, for instance, to imagine in France the kind of public debate that for years centred round the Oxford road schemes. But there have been exceptions: when in the late 1950s the Ministry of Agriculture planned a ninety-foot (nine-storey) new office block in the Faubourg St. Germain, a Press campaign did for once have some effect, and the authorities agreed to reduce the plan to five storeys, the same height as the rest of that graceful old quarter. On the other hand, officialdom itself is more alert than in London to the need to avoid desecration: you cannot so much as cut down a tree without permission of the prefect. Both Malraux's ministry and the city council have active preservation committees: often they do not agree—and Malraux wins—but always they have some power. Designs are carefully examined; and modern building in Paris has certainly been more elegant than before the war, when the monstrous white Medical Faculty extension was allowed to implant itself close to St.-Germain-des-Près.

One of the most successful post-war buildings is the Y-shaped UNESCO headquarters opened in 1958 near the Invalides. It has some functional shortcomings; and a number of critics have objected to its stylistic clash with the adjacent eighteenth-century Ecole Militaire. But with its elegant *salle des pas perdus*, its conference hall by Nervi in bare, fluted concrete, its Japanese garden, and its commissioned works by Picasso, Moore, Miro, Arp, and Calder, it is one of the highlights of a tour of modern Paris and as much a contemporary art museum as Coventry Cathedral. When UNESCO later needed to expand, the French authorities refused to let it build a new block upwards on the site; and so Bernard Zehrfuss, chief architect of the original building, created in 1964 an ingenious three-storey *underground* block, air-conditioned and miraculously sunny.

Other impressive new buildings in Paris include the ORTF's circular Maison de la Radio in Auteuil and the Electricité de France headquarters near the Parc de Monceau. Two rather more dubious achievements, however, are the barrack-like new Science Faculty block that brashly affronts the romantic old quays of the Ile St. Louis, and the new international artists' centre just across the river in the Marais. This centre marks a not very inspired attempt to keep to a traditional style, whereas French architects are usually more successful when being really modern with plenty of glass and steel. So modernistic, in fact, are some corners of Paris today that Jean-Luc Godard was able to use actual Paris locations for the entire filming of *Alphaville*, his satire on a computerised city of the future.

I have already stressed that the over-riding problem of Paris today is congestion of every sort. And the challenge is how to cure this, within a limited budget, without either spoiling the city's character or hampering economic growth. It requires the most careful policy on such matters as new offices, slum clearance, road improvements, and restoration of old buildings.

The policy on new office buildings has been haphazard. In theory, they are not allowed in the city centre, where much commercial activity is already far too cramped, especially in the teeming areas round the Bourse. If a landlord pulls down a block of flats, he can put offices in the new one only if it also includes the same residential space as before. But in practice offices have been creeping, often clandestinely, into old residential blocks quite unsuited for them, in bourgeois districts such as the sixteenth and seventeenth. The Government has now finally accepted that to limit Paris office-space artificially will harm the economy as a whole: if there is no more room for it in the centre, and if there are social and aesthetic arguments against pulling down old houses to make way for offices, then the only solution can be to press ahead faster with decentralised projects such as La Défense.

Slum clearance is another matter that has been approached somewhat half-heartedly. A number of 'insanitary zones' have been designated, mostly in the poor and overpopulated quarters of east and south Paris, and notably in the thirteenth and nineteenth districts a number of streets have been torn down and replaced with better-spaced municipal housing; but not more than about 25 per cent of the worst of the Paris slums have been cleared since the war, and new ones fall into decay each year. Any tourist can find these slums if he looks, stinking alleys with crumbling façades and dank courts, where large families live huddled without water and sometimes without electricity—the 'other Paris' from the chic of the Avenue Montaigne or the Opéra with its new Chagall ceiling. Just as wartime destruction helped France's post-war railways to become more modern than British ones, so do Paris planners sometimes envy London's East End for the Blitz! But this can hardly excuse the delays in Paris, which are largely due to lack of public funds, sometimes aggravated, it is true, by the slum-dwellers themselves. Many of the older ones resist being uprooted: the Parisian is often strangely attached to his filthy but warmly human *quartier*, and he resents the fact that his new home will probably be in some lonely suburb while his own street, because of land prices and profiteering, will be replaced by bourgeois housing.

Another principal cause of congestion has, for years, been the concentration in Paris of the nation's central food and wine markets. The latter, the Halle aux Vins, was finally removed in the early 1960s. Under the Fourth Republic, the authorities had repeatedly failed in their efforts to winkle the wine-traders out of their ancient stronghold near the Jardin des Plantes: their political lobby was too strong and their legal resistance too cunning. Then de Gaulle came to power, and simply banished them by decree: it so happened that the Sorbonne Science Faculty badly needed more premises, the wine market seemed the only suitable site, so an ugly new science block was erected, literally on top of the old wine vaults. The traders have since then been gradually transferring themselves to the suburb of Bercy, where a new market is being built. It is one of the most notorious Gaullist victories for rational planning, if not for aesthetics.

The central food market, Les Halles, has taken longer to shift. Zola called it 'the bowels of Paris' and every morning it blocks whole square miles on the Right Bank with its lorries. Whereas London's little Covent Garden is mainly a market for samples, and the bulk of the goods it buys and sells stay in the docks or stations, Les Halles physically handle a large part of the nation's food. Some 6,000 tons of fruit and vegetables, in addition to meat, are brought into the heart of Paris each day, some of it at peak business periods, and this total rises yearly while the rest of the city's traffic grows too. But the rich middlemen of Les Halles were always strongly opposed to change: they made fat profits out of the organised chaos, and they had built a powerful lobby to defend their interests, with plenty of allies on the City council. Thus it took many years of pressure and persuasion by Government and planners before the city fathers finally agreed, in 1963, to the transfer of Les Halles. The meat market is now being regrouped at La Villette, in the north-east suburbs, and in 1968–9 the fruit and vegetable sections will move to a huge new *marché-gare* now being built for them at Rungis, near Orly. Here marketing will certainly be more efficient and honest. No wonder the middlemen are angry.

The future of the eighty-six-acre site to be vacated by Les Halles is now being decided. It is surrounded by a network of squalid little streets, with little of value in them save the church of St. Eustache; and if these were wiped out, too, the renovation of the whole area could provide a splendid opportunity for imaginative modern city planning. Several rival projects have been considered; the city council set up a commission to select the best, which now requires State and municipal approval. On one point all are agreed: at least part of the zone will be made into a park, for at the moment there is no greenery at all in this grimy and teeming corner of the city. But there agreement ends. A Right-wing lobby wanted luxury flats and a few smart shops round a small park, while the 'modernists', led by a number of famous architects and town-planners, preferred the renovation of Les Halles to be just one part of a much wider scheme to remodel this region of Paris, notably the drab district to the north towards the Gare du Nord, which has been steadily sinking into squalor. A third group, the compromisers, were ready to settle for a small new business centre round a garden, with some hotels and flats, a library and theatre, and underground car parks. This solution appears to have won official support and is likely to be formally adopted during 1968. There will probably be a large office block (partly reserved for the Ministry of Finance) as well as an international commercial centre, flats for 3,000, and other amenities. The only question undecided (at the time of writing) is whether the style will be traditional or ultra-modern. Though it seems that space will be severely cramped, this development project is clearly better than nothing and might not preclude a wider one later on.

The removal of Les Halles and the lorries will ease, but it certainly will not cure, an overall congestion of traffic in Paris that is now on average worse than in London; or at least, it is much worse in certain places and at certain times. As on main roads in the provinces, the motorist's progress tends to be either very fast or not at all. You may sweep majestically down the Champs-Elysées, and then get stuck for half an hour in the bottle-necks between Concorde and the Opéra. Except at peak hours, traffic moves at a spanking pace along the new Seine embankment roads and the main boulevards: but just you try negotiating one of the main exits from Paris, say the Porte de St. Cloud, at 7.30 on a wet evening, caught for hours in a slow-drifting sea of horn-blowing Gallic frustration. And parking is a nightmare, almost everywhere.

This is the legacy of Haussmann and after: a few broad roads masking a honeycomb of narrow ones, ill served with exit routes and ill adapted for the building of modern traffic islands. Until the early '60s the city authori-ties did somehow manage to keep abreast of the problem, and in 1960 traffic was still moving as fast as ten years earlier, despite a doubling of volume. This was achieved by the building of underpasses on the Boule-vard Extérieur and along the Seine, by widening some streets and by creating the most extensive one-way system in Europe: even major thoroughfares like the Boulevards St. Germain and de Sébastopol are now *sens unique*. But by about 1960, *ad hoc* improvements of this sort had reached their physical limits, short of much more drastic and expensive rebuilding. Yet traffic has gone on growing by 10 per cent a year. In greater Paris there is now one private car to 4·5 people, and in the past few years a dangerous saturation level at peak periods has been reached. The Prefect of Police would like to restrict or ban private traffic far more severely in the city centre; but the shortage of adequate alternative public transport makes this difficult.

At last, a more drastic and expensive road-building programme is now under way. Tunnels have been carved under the Louvre and the Place de la Concorde for a fast new east–west motorway across the city centre near the Seine, which has been completed in record time—a remarkable achievement. Another urban motorway, north to south, will probably be built along the line of the disused Canal St. Martin. And there are vaguer plans for the valuable new Boulevard Périphérique to be complemented by an inner ring motorway along what are known as the 'boulevards of the generals', via the Places de l'Etoile, de Clichy, de la Nation, d'Italie, and Denfert-Rochereau. But surface roads of this kind involve so much expropriation and rehousing that many experts believe that tunnels would be both quicker and cheaper to build, and that a new underground road network should be carved out, similar to the Métro.

Although fast new roads may speed up through traffic, they do little to solve the worst problem of all, that of parking. More cars are now owned in Paris than there are kerbside or garage spaces for them, and many Parisians thus have no option but to keep their cars outside the city limits. During working hours, a 'blue zone' covering all the central districts limits parking to ninety minutes: there are no paying meters, but the motorist adjusts a cardboard disc inside his windscreen that shows the time he is due to leave. This system requires some honesty, and brings in no public revenue apart from the fines: it was adopted as the lesser of two evils, as it was feared that Parisian cunning would rapidly find ways of robbing or cheating meters, and Parisian pride would never abrogate the citizen's 'right' to free public parking. Four times the city fathers have rejected police proposals for paying meters, and Paris is now the only major world city without them. The present system does work quite well in its way for daytime business purposes, even though many fines are never collected. But it has done nothing to solve the worsening problem of evening or overnight parking in residential or entertainment districts. To go to a dinner-party in Passy, or a café or cinema in Montparnasse, involves the most acute parking problem that is not yet shared anywhere in London, after six p.m., except round Leicester Square and Soho. After circling around for anything up to an hour, one arrives late, furious, and apologetic, vividly reminded of the basic statistics: 114 people to the acre in Paris, 43 in London.

Inevitably, the official solution now is to build car parks underground. Since 1964 the first of a series of big ones have been opened in the city centre: one of them, on six levels beneath the Avenue George V, has 1,200 places and has given the police an excuse for banning surface parking on the near-by Champs-Elysées, to the fury of the big shops and cafés. 'We'll lose so much trade, we'll have to sack half our staff,' moaned the manager of Fouquet's. In order to find the money for these expensive new caverns, the city council took the unusual step of calling in private firms to finance, build, and run them. These are allowed to recoup their investment quickly by selling a third of the spaces on long leases, and hiring out another third by the month or year. A thirty-year garage lease at George V costs about 20,000 francs. The remaining third are for general use at two francs an hour; but even this small number of spaces are often not fully used, for the Parisian, spoilt by the free disc system, still has a rooted objection to paying for his parking. Yet he regards the daily use of his car as an inalienable human right: individualistic to the last, he will often spurn public transport even where it is adequate, and insists on taking his car into town in the imprudent hope that he, unlike the next man, will succeed in beating the jams and will find a parking-space.

This prejudice might be overcome more rapidly, if public transport were to be made more efficient and comfortable. The low green buses move splendidly fast whenever the traffic is clear, and their system of numbered queuing-tickets, based on a supposed Latin refusal to queue democratically, is actually far more just than the London rush-hour free-for-all. But the buses are infrequent, especially in the suburbs, and often full. Some English-type double-deckers are about to be introduced, experimentally; but there is opposition, as Parisian conductors object to climbing stairs, and the public retains a curious notion that they are likely to topple over.

Buses are at least acceptable to the bourgeoisie; but the Métro, with its nostalgic stench, its prison-like automatic barriers, its long Kafka corridors and its sad ticket-punchers like *tricoteuses* at the Guillotine, is still defiantly a working-class institution. 'So sorry I'm late,' says Marie-Chantal, the archetypal French deb, in a well-known Parisian joke, 'but my brother Claude had taken the Jag, brother Pierre had taken the Mercedes, so I took the Métro—do you know it?' London's debs have been cheerfully boarding trains at Sloane Square since the days of W. S. Gilbert. But London tube-trains, with their plushy seating, are a cut above even the first-class carriages of the Métro.

In the past few years the Régie Autonome des Transports Parisiens has at least brightened up a few central stations, such as the Opéra, with chic modern décor. It even tried to remove the familiar, acrid smell by introducing perfumed trains, but this experiment was short-lived. If the smell has grown less with the years, it is simply because Parisians now wash. But most of the basic problems of discomfort and over-crowding remain, while passenger traffic increases. A number of platforms have now been lengthened to allow longer trains, while the introduction of rubber tyres on a few lines has helped a little to increase speed and reduce noise. The only real solution, however, is to press ahead faster with the plans for a deep-level de luxe express Métro network embracing both city and suburbs. The first line, from La Defénse across the city centre to Boissy-St.-Leger, has suffered from serious technical hold-ups: the expensive new tunnelling machinery literally broke its teeth on the hard chalk of the Paris sub-soil, and much of the work has had to be done by hand, at a slower rate than for the original Métro in the 1900s! This line will perhaps be ready in 1969. In the meantime, Marie-Chantal and her business friends use their cars. Or they take taxis, if they are lucky enough to find any.

Taxis in Paris are in theory more plentiful, but in practice more scarce, than in New York or London. There is one for 360 people, against one for 677 in New York, and one for 1,350 in London. Yet at least a thousand stay locked up in their Paris garages each day for lack of drivers. This is because Paris taxi-drivers operate one of the most effective closed shops in France, and refuse to admit new recruits. When a driver dies or retires, his taxi-licence changes hands on a private black market for some 30,000 francs. The Rueff-Armand report in 1960* criticised this as one of the 'structural defects' in need of reform, and proposed the massive issue of new licences by the police. The 15,000 drivers replied with threats of a strike. In the end, in 1961, the police did persuade them to accept a small increase of 1,000 licences; but the rest of the reform, including a suppression of the black market, has never been applied. A new attempt to

* See p. 44 (The economy: miracle or mirage?).

apply it, in 1967, simply met with another strike. And as the city grows, the shortage of taxis becomes yearly more acute. Incredible as it may seem, there are far fewer taxis in Paris today than in 1931 (13,500 against 21,000) despite a huge increase in population and business. Moreover, the drivers exploit their control of the situation by sticking to rigidly conventional meal-times, so that taxis are scarcest when they are most needed, between noon and two p.m., or between six and eight p.m. 'In New York or London,' Art Buchwald has written, 'taxis drive their clients towards their destination; in Paris, you accompany the *chauffeur* towards his garage or his restaurant.' Drivers will rarely bother to learn the names of minor streets, or keep abreast of changes in the one-way system, thus involving the client in costly and time-wasting detours.

The drivers try to justify their closed shop, and their attitudes, by pleading that the traffic-jams are slowing down their turnover and reducing their earnings. More taxis, they say, would mean worse jams. But this is illogical: in fact, if there were more taxis, there might be far fewer private cars on the streets. Clearly, the only long-term answer to the Paris traffic problem is, first, to improve public transport, especially by providing more buses, while at the same time taking stricter measures against street parking, and building more underground parks. Only then, so the police feel, might it be possible to smash the taxi lobby. But in a city like Paris, there is always some private group in every sector of life, be it *chauffeurs* or Champs-Elysées café-owners or marketing middlemen, ready to defend their own interests against the public one. And the Government is reluctant to make more political enemies. So the public suffers, and the economy, too, through time wasted in trying to get to business appointments.

If Parisians still have to live in a congested city, at least it is a whiter and smarter one than some years ago. The official aesthetic policy today is to clean and restore old buildings, as much as to prevent new eyesores; and of all recent changes in France, the whitening of Parisian façades is often the one that first strikes the casual visitor. Some people, though not all, see it as a symbol of the French revival under de Gaulle.

Fifteen years ago, this capital of European gaiety and chic gave an overriding impression of greyness and lack of paint. It was sometimes picturesque, as in parts of Montmartre and the Latin Quarter, but more often just depressing, as in the dour commercial quarters around the Rue Lafayette or the Gare St. Lazare. Then in the mid 1950s a large number of shops and cafés began of their own accord to modernise their fronts, with glass, chromium or marble, and fresh paint. Owners found that their new boom in trade made them able to afford these changes, and their clients were beginning to expect it. By 1958 the glittering transformation was remarkable, even in many poorer streets. But it was very superficial: on upper floors, house façades were still black and peeling, while passages and courtyards behind the chic shops were often a morass of decay, grime, and bad sanitation. Landlords, of course, lacked the direct trade incentives of their business lessees.

Then came Gaullism. In 1958 Pierre Sudreau, the new Minister of Construction, issued a solemn public warning that the decay was not merely unaesthetic, it was also eating at the fabric of the city. But he found it hard to act, because ground-rents of most older buildings were still fixed so low that landlords had a valid excuse for not making improvements.* So in 1959 a law was passed allowing phased rent increases, so long as part of the money was spent on cleaning façades *and* courtyards and other basic repairs. At the same time, a forgotten law of 1852 was cunningly revived, that had made the *ravalement* (literally, 'scraping') of façades compulsory every ten years. Then Malraux, whose Ministry is responsible for the upkeep of State buildings, set an example by cleaning, first, the Marine Ministry building in the Place de la Concorde, followed by the Foreign Ministry on the Quai d'Orsay and others. And a few private landlords were induced to follow suit, along eye-catching streets such as the Champs-Elysées.

At first, most people laughed at Malraux and Sudreau: 'What! Get Parisians to clean their houses? It's the kind of law you just can't apply, in France.' But surprisingly it has worked. Today more than a third of the city's façades have been *ravalé*, many of them in poorer districts, and the work goes steadily ahead. Each year a number of streets in selected areas are designated by the Seine préfecture, and notices served on landlords. Fines for failing to comply within a given time are 1,000 francs; but full *ravalement* may cost up to 100,000 francs, so at first it is cheaper to pay the fines. That is why, in many streets, you can often see an odd black sheep that has failed to copy the new whiteness of its neighbours. But this happens surprisingly rarely. Public opinion has accepted *ravalement* more readily than anyone expected, in a city not famed for its individual house-pride, and it is one sign of the big psychological changes in France since the war. Very often, landlords are under strong pressure from their tenants to comply; and if they feel unwilling or unable to afford it, sometimes they sell the building to an association of tenants who then get the work done. For buildings in poorer streets, where rents are still pegged low, the authorities offer subsidies of up to 15 per cent of the cost of *ravalement* and 40 per cent of the cost of mending roofs and drains. In such areas, the sanitation and basic repairs have priority; in the smarter, more prestige-conscious streets, *ravalement* is usually done first.

While the town council devoted forty million francs in 1960–4 to assisting private *ravalement*, the State spent ten million francs in the same period on cleaning public buildings. Private stone buildings, most of them nineteenth-century, are generally scoured by a form of wet sand-blasting, while the more delicate stones of older or more precious buildings, such as

* See p. 205 (The housing shortage).

the Louvre or Invalides, are treated with a special process of pressurised water jets, which takes time and is costly of labour. Today, though no-one has yet risked touching the sensitive façade of Notre Dame, nearly all the other famous buildings are now restored to their original pale sand-stone hues. Most Parisians approve the results, though some do not. 'The Opéra's like a wedding-cake,' they complain. But earlier fears that the cleaning might cause damage seem to have been unjustified; and when the first newness has weathered a little, the effects may be even finer than they are already. With the exception of the *Maisons de la Culture*, the *ravalement* of Paris has probably been Malraux's foremost achievement as Minister, and is now being extended to the provinces.

Malraux has also set about restoring the neglected historic quarters of Paris, and notably the Marais, rather more forcefully than any Minister of Culture before him. Before his arrival, the public authorities and a few rich individuals had both done something, with limited means, to purchase and restore a few of the thousands of lovely old *hôtels particuliers* in Paris. But many others were falling gently into ruin. Then in 1962 Malraux initiated a law that obliges landlords to play their part in the work and cost of restoration, under pain of expropriation, and thus enables the authorities to tackle whole areas rather than just individual buildings. Armed with this law, the city council made a modest start by selecting a nine-acre pilot zone in the centre of the Marais for intensive restoration.

The Marais, between the Hôtel de Ville and the Bastille, was in the seventeenth century the most fashionable and aristocratic quarter of Paris. Since then it has slipped steadily into decline, and today much of it is a slum area, insanitary and overcrowded. Hundreds of its elegant six-teenth- and seventeenth-century houses are still standing; but many of them have been carved up internally into tenements or even depots and workshops, or covered over with ugly superstructures. A few, such as the Hôtel de Sens and the Hôtel d'Aumont, had been rescued by the city council in earlier years. Now the plan is to work outwards from the pilot zone and gradually restore the whole Marais: slum-clearance without demolition. The traditional artisan activities of the area, jewellery, leather-work, and toy-making, will be encouraged to remain or return. Some of the modern additions, including garages and a chemical depot, will be cleared away, and a quarter once famed for its greenery will be given back its gardens.

State, city, and landlords are each to spend some seventeen million francs on restoring the pilot zone in the next five years. It will involve removing about a third of the zone's present population of 1,200, mostly poor people, to new homes in the suburbs. Some working-class people will be allowed to remain: but landlords, in return for their share of the costs of the scheme, will be allowed to charge what rents they like once the houses are restored, and though the authorities claim that they want the area to be socially mixed, it is easy to see it becoming largely a *quartier de luxe*, as it was in the days when Louis XIII held court there in the Place des Vosges.

Many people on the Left strongly resent this solution, although they are otherwise in favour of restoring old Paris. But with public money so short, it may be the most realistic answer. Several areas besides the Marais urgently need attention, and it will all take a very long time: it is therefore essential to appeal to private capital and private snobberies. In the Marais, the authorities are merely exploiting the already marked vogue on the part of rich Parisians to return to live in the city's historic centre. The adjacent Ile St. Louis is the focal point of this movement. Its *quais* have been fashionable for many years; now the equally lovely old stone buildings in the island's interior, hitherto working-class slums, are being restored privately at great cost and turned into bijou flatlets, smart antique shops, and modish candlelit restaurants in ancient, vaulted cellars. Precisely the same trend is engulfing the old hill-villages of Provence and, as if to underline the point, the food in the new 'bistrots' is fashionably '*provençal*'! In the Marais, slum-clearance is less easy; but people like Zizi Jeanmaire and the Prince de Broglie have already moved there, to privately restored buildings; a two-room flat in the Place des Vosges may now fetch 180,000 francs; chic boutiques are opening up all round; and there is now a fashionable Marais arts festival every summer.

These are not the only parts of the city which are changing, socially, under modern economic conditions. Although certain areas, such as Passy and much of the seventh, have for many years been strongholds of the *haute bourgeoisie*, most of Paris has hitherto tended to be rather more socially intermixed than London, partly because of the way the Haussmann-era blocks were built, with flats of varying size and quality under the same roof. This was later intensified by the housing shortage: middle-class people took flats where they could find them, and if the controlled rent was low, they felt disinclined to move. So one might often find quite smart people living at a poor address, behind the Gare de l'Est, for instance, or in the nineteenth. This simply increased their notorious reluctance to entertain at home.

Today all this is gradually changing, as the housing shortage eases and areas are rebuilt. While some rich and fashionable people move into the ancient city centre, others, possibly as rich but less fastidious or cultivated, move out to glossy new luxury housing estates towards Versailles, with names like Résidence Elysée and Parc Vendôme. Steadily the Parisian prejudice against living in *la banlieue* is being eroded, and a nation of commuters is arising. Inside Paris, rents and leasehold prices have been rising so fast, especially for new flats, that many working people too are moving out to the suburbs; and previously humble districts, notably in the thirteenth and fifteenth, are rapidly growing more bourgeois, just as Camden Town or Islington are. But in Paris this is due mainly to new middle-class blocks of flats, and rarely to the conversion of older houses as in London. Communists and Socialists even see the trend as a deliberate move by the authorities to reduce the city's Left-wing vote, and are demanding that more cheap State housing be built inside Paris.

The central districts of culture, café life, and entertainment are also slowly altering their character or their fashions. The Champs-Elysées grows steadily more brash and commercialised: it is now the stronghold of the rapidly expanding new trades of advertising and public relations, and of the fashion-model world, the movie business, and a good deal of organised gay-Paree tourism. As the Edwardian elegance of Fouquet's dims into the past, so the giant new car showrooms rise up beside it, and so do the quick-service beefburger bars with their oddly Americanised names. The stately private homes around the Etoile have mostly been transformed: one of them now houses the very latest Champs-Elysées gimmick, 'le Sir Winston Churchill Pub,' a plushy and amusingly phoney imitation of London.

Perhaps not too many tears need be shed for the Champs-Elysées. More disquieting is the rapid 'Champs-Elyséefication' of St.-Germain-des-Prés, a quarter that up till now has always provided such a contrast to the materialistic glitter of the Right Bank. This enchanted kingdom of literary cafés and old street markets, satiric cabarets, bookshops, art shops, and plain working Parisians, has always been something of an intellectual madhouse—but on its own authentic terms. Now it is being colonised and exploited, and is under massive invasion from a new commercialised, trend-conscious arti-smartiness, the Parisian close equivalent of some of the more dubious aspects of swinging London. Op-art boutiques in weird styles are swarming down the boulevard; yé-yé discothèques blare from the bowels of quaint old houses; in the Rue St. Benoît the modish new faux-bistros crowd thicker than in Chelsea; a leading bookshop on the boulevard has suddenly become a Wimpy Bar; and if parking anywhere in Paris is difficult, here at night it is hysterically impossible, as the big smart Citroëns slither on to the pavements of alleys built only for handcarts. To crown it all, in 1965 a new multi-storey 'Drugstore' of laughable brashness planted itself at the very heart of St. Germain, right next to the distinguished old Café Lipp and opposite the Deux Magots. Its gaudy lights blaze out at night like Blackpool pier, and its multiple shops, snack-bars, and cinema, all open till after midnight, attract crowds of goggling visitors, Parisians and others, who have little kinship or sympathy with the milieu of Aragon and Sartre they are supplanting. Over the decades, Parisian artists and intellectuals have remained remarkably loyal to the cafés on this square; but now they are giving up the unequal struggle.

The death of Lipp's owner, Marcel Cazes, has ended an era. Sartre, too, has recently moved from his flat above the Café Bonaparte to a new home in Montparnasse. And so, as St. Germain's glory fades, Montparnasse seems to be coming back into favour again as a haunt of artists and writers, after its long eclipse that followed the heydays of Hemingway and Modigliani. Though the Rotonde has been turned into a cinema, the other historic Montparnasse cafés, notably the Dome and the Coupole, seem now to be attracting a more interesting and genuine clientèle than those of St. Germain—and this was certainly not so in the 1950s. But when the new 600-foot skyscraper is built, 300 yards west of the Coupole, will it kill the quarter's tentative cultural renaissance, or give it added lustre?

The Fifth Arrondissement, around and behind the Sorbonne and the Panthéon, I find the most attractive part of Paris nowadays. Modern change is adding to its vitality, but without yet spoiling it. Some buildings, down by the river facing the islands, are being expensively restored, notably on the initiative of an architect who owns property there, Jean Daladier, son of the former Prime Minister. Just inland, the Rue de la Huchette and other quaint and narrow old streets teem excitingly with students, bohemians, and foreigners of every colour; and here is the best selection in Paris of really cheap restaurants, especially Levantine and Oriental ones. Up on the hill, in a strange bohemian hinterland, picturesque squalor, cheerful modernity and academic traditionalism go hand in hand. Risqué cabarets and off-beat bistros stand close to the walls of the greatest of all French colleges, the Polytechnique and the Normale Supérieure; in the crumbling Rue Mouffetard and the Place de la Contrescarpe, Champs-Elysée-style cafés merge with old shops and stalls that evoke the Medina of Fez. And in the peeling old stone-floored houses of the *quartier*, impoverished artists and writers co-exist with working-class families, and with a few young émigrés from smart Passy homes who find it fun to deck out the romantic little attics as stylish modern flatlets. Here the Paris of Mimi and Rudolf whispers its last enchantments.

Montmartre, on the other hand, today seems hardly worth a mention. Artists no longer live there, and though the Butte with its steep steps and streets retains some of its visual charm, the whole area is in the grip of a grasping and vulgar tourist racket. The Parisian folk-songs in the cafés, the comic local characters, the careful folksy décor, are all calculated, down to the last franc, to entice the tourist; and Montmartre has lost nearly all of its old authentic life.

With their glittering neon lights, and glass and marble, the streets of central Paris have changed astonishingly in their outward aspect since the mid-1950s; and, as befits a Latin city of terrace cafés, the style is superficially more dazzling than in London. It is by no means confined to Paris: in the smallest village today, you can find shops with new plate-glass fronts, a blaze of light half the night. Around 1955, the hitherto conservative French commercial world suddenly went overboard for modernism and modern design: much of it is unoriginal and imported and some of it is vulgar, but, on the whole, it shows a better sense of harmony and stylistic gaiety than its counterparts in Britain, America, or Germany.

In theory, the authorities try to supervise the new developments. In the Place de l'Opéra, for instance, the colour scheme for electric publicity signs has to be blue-and-white. On the Champs-Elysées, too, no red signs are allowed, in an effort to avoid the worst horrors of Piccadilly Circus or Times Square. Yet a new gaudiness seems to be creeping in. In Paris you need a building permit to modernise a shop or café, and the designs are scrutinised; but permits are given far too easily, and there have been some serious lapses of taste. How did the St. Germain Drugstore get by? According to one account, the promoters originally submitted designs as horrific as possible—a familiar trick—and then accepted modifications. It is also pointed out that one of the promoters was the Rothschild Bank, of which the Prime Minister, M. Pompidou, was formerly director.

Paris today is a stimulating place for the visitor lounging in a boulevard café and watching the world go by. But it is a tiresome place to work in. Certainly, the mood is less ominous and sour than in the Algerian crisis years when the streets were full of sten-guns; but peace and stability have brought an upsurge of materialism and have not done much to ease the Parisians' hardness. *Odi et amo.* I love and hate the Parisians for their ruthless intelligence, their bitter-sweet sophistication, their zest and their cruelty, and I grow tearful at the cabaret-song clichés about the chestnut-trees and the dear little bistros, because I know their tarnished magic is still real. But I do not want to live there. Some of Paris, mainly the Latin Quarter, I find as invigorating as any city in the world; the rest is strained and unacccomodating. In Paris, people often seem to lack the time or the self-discipline to be generous or fully human: many of the more sensitive ones are today acutely aware of this and of what Paris does to them, and so they try to insulate themselves within their home lives and small circle of friends, or they leave.

But these are difficult years of transition for Paris, after the decades of upheaval and neglect. Maybe, if and when the practical problems are solved and the renovation is done, then a calmer, easier, less self-destructive city will arise, blending the best of old and new. It would be unwise to underestimate how far the *malaise* of Paris today has purely practical causes. But there is something else, which cannot be solved merely by ending the traffic jams or clearing the slums. Paris no longer appears as the world's unrivalled generator of art, ideas, and *douceur de vivre*. To find out whether this is really so, and why, we must first look at some of the underlying social, intellectual, and cultural changes in post-war France.

CHAPTER VIII

THE HOUSING SHORTAGE: 'NATIONAL DISGRACE NUMBER ONE'

—————

ANYONE RETURNING TO FRANCE TODAY after fifteen or so years' absence might be surprised at the rows of new blocks of flats in every town and suburb—a common enough sight in most parts of the world today, but quite an achievement in its sorry French context. The French have finally been shocked out of their long neglect of housing by the pressures of rapid urbanisation; and the nation that built almost nothing from 1914 to 1954 has somehow managed since then to house or re-house over ten million people. New dormitory towns are rising up, where the traditional French way of life is painfully adapting itself to the very different needs and patterns of modern suburbia. But the housing shortage is still far from solved: it is still often described as 'national problem number one'. And neither the private temperament nor the public administration of the French are lending themselves at all easily to the perfection of today's suburban utopia.

THE TYRANNY OF BUREAUCRATS AND SPECULATORS

It often used to be said that the French submitted to bad housing because they preferred to spend their money on other things. I do not think this is nearly so true today: the French are even becoming quite house-proud, when they get the chance. But the millions who still look in vain for better homes are finding out the hard way that nations, like people, have to suffer for their past. The backlog of neglect will take decades to cure; and even today the building programme is inefficiently organised and well below what is needed.

Whereas Britain and Germany began massive rehousing right after the war, the French (perhaps wisely) gave priority to industrial recovery. In 1952, France was still producing only about 75,000 new flats a year. The annual rate then began to shoot up fast, and in the '60s it has been running at about 400,000. But Germany has built over half-a-million dwellings every year since 1953; and Britain, with less war damage than France and a far slower population increase, has completed five-and-a-half million since the war, against France's four million. The scandal in 1966 over the television film *Cathy Come Home* has suggested that even in Britain the crisis still endures; but it is far less general than in France. For one thing, the French are having to fight against the appalling archaism of much of their existing housing. Certainly there has been progress: between the censuses of 1954 and 1962 the percentage of homes without running water fell from 42 to 22, and of those without inside lavatories from 73 to 39, while in the same period the proportion of homes with bath or shower rose from 10 to 25 per cent. But the 1962 census (the last complete one) classified one flat in four as 'overcrowded' (that is, with more than four or five people in three living rooms) and found that 60 per cent of all French houses dated from before 1914, many of them in shocking repair. And though the quality and amenities of the newest flats are steadily improving (few today are built without bathrooms) on average they are still less well finished and well equipped, and with smaller rooms, than their counterparts in northern Europe.

The social problems and hardships caused by the housing crisis are obvious enough. According to one survey,* one in four of the 800,000 annual abortions in France is directly connected with it. Often it may disrupt a marriage, or dissuade a worker with a family from moving to a better job in another district. The Press is full of horror stories: especially I remember the case of a young Paris hospital orderly and his wife and baby, who could not find lodgings and finally were granted a room inside the hospital. But the baby cried at night and disturbed the patients. Terrified lest they be thrown out, the witless parents resorted to putting sticking plaster across its mouth—and it suffocated to death.

For workers, there are State-built flats with low rents, but these are still hard to find. For people with higher incomes, not eligible for this cheap housing, the problem is not scarcity but cost. There are plenty of smart flats around, but rents and prices of new ones have soared fantastically, especially inside Paris. Many professional people have to choose between moving far into the suburbs, spending much more of their income on housing than they wish, or living with in-laws. I know one French journalist who lives with his wife in a modern five-room flat in an unsmart part of the fifteenth, for which they pay 1,450 francs rent a month, unfurnished. To buy, it would cost about 500,000 francs. 'We're living above

* For this and some of the other statistics in this chapter, I am indebted to Gilbert Mathieu's excellent book, *Peut-on loger les Français?* (Editions du Seuil, 1965), and to his regular articles on housing in *Le Monde*.

our means,' he told me, 'but I have to live in Paris for my work, and it's hard to get anything much cheaper, unless you're lucky enough to find an old flat with a rent still controlled.'

It seems absurd, in a country where private affluence has been rising steadily ever since the war, that housing should remain so deficient. A working-class family may have a car and TV, but live in an old tenement, or else in a new flat that may yet be dingy and cramped by many modern standards; a middle-class family may dine out extravagantly and take holidays in Greece, yet be ashamed to invite their friends to their home. In the past, such things were attributed to the French disregard for home comforts, and preference for food, clothes, and pleasure. But today many Frenchmen would gladly spend more on improving their living conditions, if only they could do so at an economic price.

The problem today lies not with French domestic habits but with Government policies and the crazy structure of the property markets. This is one of those typical sectors of French public life where State investment still gets a low priority because it offers few returns of productivity or national prestige: the proportion of the Gross National Product spent on new housing (4·5 per cent in 1964) is lower than in most European countries, and is not keeping pace with overall economic growth. And not only is the Government niggardly with its own funds for 'social' housing; it has failed to entice enough private capital into the building indsutry, or to set up a proper mortgage system. It has allowed speculation to flourish, and has not simplified its own bureaucratic tangles which make the building of a block of flats as much as exercise in paperwork as in bricks and mortar. Although the Fifth Republic has built at a faster rate than the Fourth, and although it has passed a few well-intentioned land reforms, there has not been much basic improvement. Some French observers, in fact, still speak of the housing crisis as 'our number one national disgrace', or as the biggest single social and material problem facing France today.

Much of the trouble stems back to August 1914. On the outbreak of the First World War, one of the Government's first actions was to freeze all rents, in order to protect soldiers' families from profiteering landlords. It was a fair wartime measure. But in the difficult post-war period it was maintained as a permanency, and no inter-war Government had the fore-sight or the electoral courage to lift it. Thus developers and financiers had little incentive to promote new building; new rents, too, were blocked. No more than 1,800,000 homes were built in France between the wars, a quarter of them simply reconstruction of war damage, while Britain and Germany each built over four million. The stagnant birth-rate made the neglect supportable. But it had other, less immediate consequences: the low rents gave landlords a valid excuse for making no improvements or repairs, so that gradually many houses fell into premature decay. This helps to explain why, even today, so many buildings in France look woe-begone.

After the Second War, the upsurge in the birth-rate and the rural exodus soon brought the crisis to a head. Many privileged people were living practically free, at 1914 rents shrivelled away by inflation; many others were homeless. So in 1948 a coalition Government passed a bold law. This permitted gradual long-term rent increases for existing flats, so long as part of the money was spent on repairs; and it freed rents henceforth on new private building. The law was vigorously applied by the excellent Socialist Minister of Construction, Claudius Petit, and was partly successful in its twofold aim: to encourage both repairs and new building.

But the controlled increases in pre-1948 rents have been far outstripped by the rapid rises in the newer ones, caught up in the spiral of inflation, and there is still a wide price gap between flats of similar quality in the two groups. Moreover, the 1948 law did not repeal one crucial clause in the 1914 law that grants a tenant virtual freedom from eviction, even on expiry of lease. Families, often quite wealthy ones, will thus cling stubbornly to relatively cheap flats they may have occupied for generations; and this severely limits the market, especially for the people who need it most, the young couples with growing families. The market, instead of being flexible to suit demand, is still artificially divided into three sectors: old controlled rents, new cheap State housing (also controlled), and new uncontrolled housing which is often unreasonably expensive.

If the cheap State housing were more plentiful, the problem for many people would be eased. This is the equivalent of 'council housing' in Britain; the categories are many and complex, the commonest being the *Habitations à loyer modéré*, built by public agencies (led by the State, but partly municipal) with money from long-term Treasury loans at one per cent interest. Some 127,000 HLMs were completed in 1966, four-fifths for rent and the rest for ownership; and over 120,000 other cheap flats received other forms of public aid, partly derived from a regular housing tax on firms to the tune of one per cent of their wage bills. These figures rise steadily each year (in 1959 only 90,000 HLMs were built) but they still fall well short of needs when set against the urban growth, the immigration of *pieds noirs* and others, and especially the collapse beyond repair of at least 100,000 old houses a year. The fixed HLM rents are not high—around 200 to 250 francs a month for a three-roomed flat excluding heating—and the quality of the newer ones is generally fair. But waiting-lists are often full for years ahead, and are subject to some graft and political intrigue: your own political views may or may not help you find a flat, depending on who controls the local HLM office. Moreover, though the HLMs are supposedly reserved for lower-paid workers, they are frequently infiltrated by junior *cadres* and civil servants, who would rather sink their social pride than pay the prices of the open market. This does not ease working-class resentment.

Rather than increase the burden on the Treasury, the Gaullist Government has been stepping up its efforts to woo more private capital into building investment. But the response has benefited the luxury market far more than the 'social' sector. Inevitably, financiers and developers are still reluctant to invest in low-rent flats; they prefer free rents and quick returns. So the early 1960s saw an extravagant boom in new luxury housing, especially in Paris and on the Riviera, with ready buyers among the newly rich. And the losers have been the middle-income groups as well as the poor; for not only are middle-range flats over-priced, but mortgages are scarce.

Before the war, urban flats were mostly rented. Today there is a growing trend towards owner-occupation of new flats, especially by middle-class people with some capital. It satisfies their property-owning instincts, it provides developers with quick dividends, and it suits the Government for political as well as economic reasons. But not everyone can raise the money. The State has its own generous mortgage system for a small number of owner-occupied HLMs, but funds for these are strictly limited. Outside this cheap range, State mortgages are negligible, and there are no building societies in France. A buyer without capital must try to borrow from the banks: if he is lucky, they will lend him up to 60 per cent, but at 10 to 15 per cent interest, repayable within ten years. This puts an average flat, costing, say, 100,000 to 120,000 francs for four rooms, in the suburbs or provinces, outside the means of many young middle-class families.

The Government is now at last making tentative efforts to create a mortgage market, inspired partly by foreign models. In 1966 it authorised the deposit banks and insurance companies to institute twenty-year loans at 8 or 9 per cent interest; but it is still not clear where the capital is coming from. It also launched a modest new savings-bank scheme for housing, with some initial success. But it has not yet tried on any scale the solution to the housing crisis practised in Britain and elsewhere, that of massively enlisting private savings. It is true that the French are not great savers: their average per head, 1,073 francs a year, is half that of the British or Germans. But there are signs that this could easily change, given the right incentives, now that the franc is at last strong and stable. This would seem to be the best financial means of solving the housing problem, unless the Government greatly increases its own direct aid.

And yet, any progress is likely to remain slight, so long as the Government fails to check the flagrant abuses of speculation on land and property. This is the biggest obstacle of all to cheaper or more plentiful housing. This, more than anything, has sent the free rents soaring; this, too, limits the number of HLMs, simply because so large a part of their precious funds has to be spent on the initial buying of land.

It may seem a paradox that a country with so much virgin open space should suffer from the kind of speculation usually associated with land shortage. But the French have generally rejected the policy of commuter towns deep in the countryside, and even the planned new Paris satellites mark only a modified new departure. The French urban tradition is one of close city living, and this has pushed up land prices all round the perimeters of towns, as well as inside them. Prices in urban areas rose twentyfold in 1945 to 1957, far more rapidly than overall inflation. They jumped a further 350 per cent in 1958–63, and were still adding a steady annual 50 per cent to their value a year later. This is a paradise for any-one wanting to make easy money. In an area scheduled for massive development, such as La Défense or the western suburbs of Toulouse, prices have risen anything from twenty-five- to a hundredfold in a few years. Today, a square metre of land may cost 10,000 francs on the Champs-Elysées or in parts of Nice and Cannes, 5,000 francs in a smart suburb like Neuilly, and 1,000 francs or more in many other parts of greater Paris or the Riviera. No wonder that the HLM agencies have abandoned the Ville de Paris to bourgeois housing; no wonder that in Nice no new HLMs at all were started between 1961 and 1965.

Scarcely less grave than land speculation is profiteering over property, which often is allied to corruption or embezzlement. There are proven cases of officials being suborned by developers to push through the build-ing permits for some dubious luxury-housing project; or of the real financing and conditions of a scheme being dissimulated by its promoters in order to allay suspicions. To be fair, one must add that only a minority of developers are dishonest and unscrupulous. But corrupt practices are so widespread that the State tends to turn a blind eye: to make a purge might implicate too many of its own officials, or might deter the business world from investment in building. Sometimes, however, a scandal bursts into the open of its own accord: in 1961, a fashionable and gifted architect, Fernand Pouillon, was imprisoned for embezzling funds for a smart new block of flats in Paris; and in 1964 a highly respected Marseille develop-ment company, the Urbaine Immobilière, was found guilty of massive tax evasion and of cheating its own contractors and clients. In many other cases, less illegal but scarcely less immoral, speculation takes its most obvious form, with people buying new flats not for their own use but solely in order to resell them at a profit. New laws now forbid this traffic in the case of State-aided building, but not in the free sector.

And so, with demand exceeding supply, rents and prices went on rising in the early '60s until, in 1965, the high-class market finally saturated itself. Many flats began to remain unsold for months, and some prices even began to fall: even the new-rich began to kick against having to pay 400,000 francs or so for quite a small flat in central Paris or Cannes. This brought a temporary curb to speculation, but has not killed its roots.

In theory, the Government has plenty of legal means to take stronger action than in fact it does. One of the first Gaullist measures, in 1959, was to pass a law giving birth to the *Zones à urbaniser par priorité* and the *Zones d'aménagement différé*: sectors of private or public land marked out either for immediate public development (ZUPs) or reserved for future use (ZADs). In these zones, the authorities have the right to forbid sales of land, to pre-empt, and, if they consider the price demanded too high,

The earliest quarters of Sarcelles (1956): "an attempt to apply
le Corbusier's ideas, without understanding them"

Some progress towards humanism: Les Courtillières at Pantin,
eastern Paris (1964)

Pleasures and paréos
with the Club Méditerranée

The Club's founder, Gérard Blitz (left), an athlete with a vision

The old France: a *bistrot* in Brittany,
where some men still drink a gallon of wine a day

The new France: advertisers' Franglais (cuttings from *Elle*, *l'Express*, etc.)

Out of class: a street in Mourenx new town (Basses-Pyrénées)

French primary education: 'I obey'

The student élite: *polytechniciens* at leisure, but still in uniform

The student mass: left-wing demonstrators in Paris

Les Copains: Sylvie Vartan

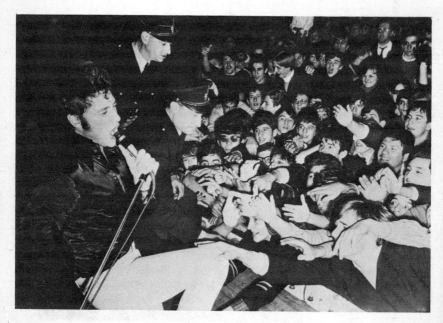

Les Copains: Johnny Hallyday and fans

Jean-François Revel

Cardinal Veuillot (died 1968)

J.-M.-G. le Clézio

Alain Robbe-Grillet

(above) Jean-Luc Godard
(top right) Agnès Varda
(right) Alain Resnais

to have it fixed by a tribunal. The idea is an excellent one, as with the
SAFERs in agriculture; and in France, where so little land is municipally
owned and where the rights of private property tend to be held sacred, it
is probably the only way to make coherent town-planning into a reality.
But the ZUPs' funds have so far been too small for much effective pre-
empting: 150 zones were created in 1959–65, covering eighty-one square
miles, but by the end of 1965 only 50,000 flats had been built on them.
Another limitation is that details of a town's development policy often
leak out in advance, and by the time a ZUP or ZAD has been officially
created, the speculation has already taken place. The secret preparation
of the zones for the Languedoc tourist scheme* was a happy, but rare,
exception. Another new measure, passed in 1964, authorises the landowner
to be associated in the development of an area rather than be forced to sell
or be expropriated. The aim is to encourage low-cost building by cutting
out the initial costs of land purchase; but many critics fear it will simply
give rise to worse speculation after development, when the owner too
will demand his share of the profits.

The ZUPs and the ZADs were the creation of Pierre Sudreau, who
made great efforts during his four years as Minister of Construction
(1958–62) to lay the foundations of a stronger and more liberal housing
policy. This remarkable man ranks beside Pisani as one of the best of the
'technocrat' Ministers of the Gaullist era. In 1952, aged only thirty-two
he was prefect of the Loir-et-Cher department, where he had the distinction of inventing the art form known as *Son et Lumière*, in the château
of Chambord. Then he became housing commissioner for the Paris region
before being appointed Minister, where another of his achievements was
to push through the policy of the *ravalement des façades*,† along with
Malraux. But in 1962, after six months as Minister of Education, he left
the Government through dislike of de Gaulle's authoritarian ways. He is a
liberal from a Leftish Catholic family, and a rare combination of thinker
and man of action; and it is a measure of his personal calibre that, although
not a career politician, in 1965 he was the Democratic Centre's first choice
of presidential candidate. He declined, so they turned to Lecanuet.

Sudreau's reforms were not effectively followed up by his successor at
the Ministry of Construction, Jacques Maziol, who lacked the personal
authority to resist pressures from the Ministry of Finance for economy
cuts. In 1965 Sudreau told me with some bitterness, 'The ZUPs and
ZADs today are like a gun without bullets. Funds are too small to be
effective, and even an operation like the Languedoc, which I began, would
no longer be feasible now.' He felt that some general Government measure
to block land prices was essential, if the housing crisis was to be solved.
And his views were shared by Edgar Pisani, who in January 1966 moved
from Agriculture to a new overlord post as Minister of Equipment, with

* See p. 138 (New life in the provinces).
† See p. 197 (Paris, the beloved monster).

housing as part of his domain. Pisani at once put forward a plan to combat speculation by a series of new taxes. The Government at first shelved his project, but finally laid it before Parliament in 1967, and after much modification it has now become law. It provides for a new tax on high-density building, and for an 'urbanisation tax' (to come into force in 1970) that will penalise those who own vacant unused land in urban areas. This law is better than nothing: it may help to provide new funds for social housing. But in its final watered-down form it may prove to have little effect on speculation: there is no sign of the land profits tax that Pisani pressed for, before his resignation. The Pompidou Government appears once again to have compromised with its big business allies.

Another factor often advanced as a cause of France's housing problems is the state of the building industry itself. Lüthy in 1953 gave a vivid picture of the 'idyllic chaos' of the average building site at that period: * 'Work-men may turn up today or perhaps tomorrow, but they will probably have to go away again without being able to do anything because the wall in which they were going to lay a pipe, for instance, is not yet ready. France still builds as she did in 1900.' Since then, matters have improved, and the industry is now better co-ordinated and less artisanal: a flat that would take 3,600 man-hours to build in 1949 needs 2,100 or less today. But the rate in Britain, Germany, or America is much faster still, and the reason lies not in techniques but organisation. Technologically, French engineers and builders—men like Camus and Barets—have played as large a part as any in pioneering modern methods of prefabrication. But, as with Le Corbusier, their ideas have had more influence outside France than within it. Only 4 per cent of French building is prefabricated, against 10 per cent in Britain and 15 in the U.S.A. There is also an alarming multiplicity of different prototypes of material used in France—300 different types of door, for instance, or 1,000 different taps—all adding to the high costs of building. And if France's 250,000 building firms still have a long road to travel towards proper efficiency, the archi-tects themselves are equally to blame. Architects in France belong to a jealous and reactionary guild: they consider themselves 'artists' above all, and few of them deign to learn modern engineering requirements. With the contractor and his technicians they carry on a dialogue of the deaf, yet their formal signature on a design is usually required by law.

An even graver cause of inefficiency is the bureaucratic rigidity of Government building regulations. HLMs and other subsidised housing have to adhere to a complex system of norms, and building permits of all sorts often take years to be granted. This, more than anything, deters the more enterprising developer from risking his money. Then there are the legal complications: expropriation may take several years under the French system, while even the simple buying or exchanging of a flat is hedged

* *The State of France*, p. 309.

about with all sorts of red tape. An official agency exists to arrange exchanges of cheap housing (when a worker, for instance, wants to move into a larger flat), but its practical value is strangled by its own bureaucracy.

Government regulations are responsible also for the artificial division of French rents into three categories, which frequently leads to injustice. In the same street in an average town, a middle-class pre-1948 block may have three-room flats controlled at around 100 francs a month, while similar flats in a post-1948 HLM block next door might be 200 to 250 francs, and scarcely superior ones in a new block down the road might have 'free' rents of 400 to 700 francs. It is even possible to find rich businessmen in smart flats in Passy who are paying the same rent as workers in the eastern suburbs. And these privileged pre-1948 rents give rise to all kinds of rackets. Sometimes, for instance, a family in a large flat will sub-let one room furnished for as much as their whole rent. Or a big Paris flat may remain virtually unused, rented by a rich widow on the Riviera who comes to Paris only once a year and yet has legal security of tenure. Or an outgoing tenant may succeed in extracting key-money (supposedly illegal) from his successor, of maybe up to 100,000 francs. Or a Paris flat may be sub-let furnished to foreign diplomats or other visitors, at a colossal rent. This practice, too, is illegal; but it flour-ishes, and few foreigners in Paris have not suffered from it. How well I remember Madame C. in Passy, coming round each month for her 800 francs *in cash* for my simple three-room flat (that was 1958; the price might be double now), always seeming a little nervous that I might call her bluff and report her, which I never dared to do.

Some economists believe that the housing problem will never be cured until all rents are freed and allowed to find a unified natural market. They argue that the artificial divisions are causing a scarcity of new middle-range housing and pushing up its prices abnormally. One expert, Georges Mesmin, an *Inspecteur des Finances*, has brilliantly drawn an analogy with the car industry. Could this ever have developed after the war, he asks, if the Government had blocked second-hand prices so that owners would not sell, and subsidised graceless utility workers' cars? The natural middle-class market of Citroën I Ds and Peugeot 404s could never have expanded viably on any scale; and what French housing needs today, he says, is the mass equivalent of the 404. But Mesmin is a liberal economist, and there are those on the Left, such as Gilbert Mathieu of *Le Monde*, who feel that a free, unified market would simply lead to other abuses. They want more State money for social housing, paid for by taxing the rich; and they want partial municipalisation of the land, in order to halt speculation. Very little land in France is publicly owned.

One thing is certain: there can be no solution unless the Frenchman agrees to spend more of his income on housing. Since the war the figure has risen from 3·4 to 7 per cent of the average family budget; but in Germany and Britain it is over 9 per cent, and in the United States over 12 per cent. Because of the contortions of the market, many Frenchmen spend only 2 or 3 per cent, and many others, no less well housed in proportion to their incomes, 10, 15, or 20 per cent. Millions therefore could spend more without hardship; and there are signs that the nation as a whole would accept this, for the French today do care about their homes. It is a problem, therefore, not of individual poverty but of organisation; and only the Government can provide the answer.

Its failure to do better is a symptom of the weakness of social justice and civic morality in France. Despite the urgent efforts of men like Sudreau and Pisani, the Fifth Republic as a whole has not tackled the problem at its root. This is partly because a régime preoccupied with prestige and industrial progress sets a low priority on housing; but it is also because so many of the Government's allies in big business have been profiting from the present sitation. 'The State's connivance at land speculation,' wrote *Le Monde* in 1965, 'shows a crisis of morality in high places.' Though the Fifth Republic has built at a faster rate than the Fourth, the Fifth Plan in 1965 admitted that the housing shortage is not getting any easier. Many experts consider, in view of the rising population and the rate of obsolescence of old buildings, that the volume must go up from 400,000 to at least 550,000 new dwellings a year, if there is to be any chance of solving the shortage within the next twenty years.

A PAINFUL ADJUSTMENT TO LIFE IN THE NEW SUBURBIA

Approaching Paris from the north, from Chantilly, you see a sign to the left, 'Sarcelles, Grand Ensemble', and the eye follows it down to the forest of grey-and-white rectangles stetching across the plain below. To many Frenchmen, that signpost reads 'Brave New World': this is the largest and most notorious of the new French suburbs, and has given its name to a new 'disease': sarcellitis, or new-town blues. Its criss-cross streets bear names like Allée Marcel Proust and Avenue Paul Valéry, but there is little poetry in the flat utility façades of their buildings; the town has 50,000 people, yet there is no *lycée*, and the planned civic centre is still a pool of mud. In the noisy, perfunctory cafés, young *pieds noirs* and slum evacuees play with pin-tables or argue about racing bets; in the Parc J. Kennedy, beside the new flats, children scrabble at sand in the playgrounds; a notice in a shop window pleads with lonely housewives to join some religious fellowship. For students of Harlow or Stevenage, it is all very familiar—and yet different. In many ways, Sarcelles is a paradise of fresh air and modern plumbing after the old slums—and yet, what opportunities have been missed! Today to the French it seems more than a town, it is a portent, an emotive concept like St. Tropez or Verdun: a victory in the grim battle for more housing, but at what cost to the human spirit?

The French woke up late to the social problems of modern mass suburbia, but now they are fascinated and disturbed by them. At last they realise that to build enough new flats is not the only answer to the housing problem: there must also be rational, human town-planning. But the French social temperament, still family-orientated and unneighbourly, adapts ill to these new conditions. Without some community living, the new suburbs will remain lonely and soulless: yet steps to promote it are often resisted in the sacred name of French privacy and individualism. This is the drama of Sarcelles, and of many towns like it.

In the first decade after the war, while the British were fast at work on their New Towns, in France virtually the only concerted new building was the reconstruction of the ravaged centres of towns like Caen and Le Havre. Elsewhere, housing was simply thrown up piecemeal, block by block, wherever there was a suitable gap or land was cheap. But by the mid 1950s, as the building programme at last gathered pace, a more coherent approach was clearly needed. So Pierre Sudreau launched the policy of the *Grands Ensembles*, self-sufficient suburbs each with its own shopping-centres, *lycées*, theatres, and so on. In some ways they are not so different from the British models, save that they are usually closer to existing cities, they consist of flats rather than houses, and because of the usual French administrative tangles they are taking shape with less efficiency. The French usually recognise this, and papers such as *Le Monde* carry envious and reproachful articles whenever reporters visit somewhere like Stevenage.

Sarcelles, the largest of the *Grands Ensembles* and the archetype, was started in 1956 and is due to house 80,000 when completed. Others, not so large and rarely as ugly, are growing up in other parts of the Paris region and elsewhere. They were born of necessity, and at least they have fulfilled their basic aim of rehousing: in Sarcelles, for instance, one inhabitant in three has come direct from the Paris slums, while most of the others never had a home of their own before, but were sharing with relatives or living in cheap hotels. But the rehousing has created new problems in turn, and the *Grands Ensembles* have come in for heavy criticism. Why cannot even low-cost housing be more attractive? Why are the suburbs not provided with better social and cultural equipment, more transport, and local industries? Why are their citizens not leading happier and fuller lives? These are the questions posed and analysed without cease in a stream of books, theses, conferences, and sensational newspaper articles. A former Prix Goncourt winner, the novelist Marc Bernard, has written a whole book about Sarcelles, after going to live there for three months. The French, so conservative about their living patterns, seem to be finding the new-town experience far more traumatic than the British. The *malaise* of some inhabitants is therefore not so surprising, nor is the excited amazement of some officials and sociologists that new towns should appear in France at all. Life there is scrutinised as if it were the planet Mars, or some new biological discovery.

The first main criticism, of Sarcelles in particular, is of crude architectural planning. Unlike the wide-spreading new towns of England, the French ones are usually built with higher density, in the usual south European urban manner. This may not in itself be a drawback; in fact, it may promote a feeling of urban warmth and animation, whereas the long, tidy lanes of English suburbia can often seem lifeless and depressing. But at Sarcelles the density has become a fearsome geometry. Its central quarter, dating from the 1950s, is an austere gridiron of straight avenues and grey box-like blocks, mostly five storeys high, some rising to sixteen. There is a fair amount of space, with trees and gardens, in contrast to the ultra-high density of most of central Paris; but this does not really atone for the rectilinear concept which horrifies so many visitors. Ian Nairn of The *Observer* has castigated 'the intellectual arrogance and paucity of invention of this loveless, pre-cast concrete desert'.* Sarcelles, in fact, sprang from a clumsy attempt by French architects to apply some of Le Corbusier's ideas without properly understanding them. They were also reacting obsessively against the chaos and anarchy of the inter-war and early post-war years, and were trying to return to the great French axial traditions of Versailles and the Paris of Henri IV and of Haussmann. But the axial sweep of a royal route cannot be the same as that of rows of cut-price HLMs; and this ideal, cross-bred with the Corbusian concept of towers amid trees, yielded bastard results at Sarcelles and elsewhere, which Sudreau and others now admit were a great mistake.

Modern town-planning, neglected and misunderstood in France for so long, has fortunately made great strides in the past eight years or so, since the early days of Sarcelles. At last the French are beginning to realise what le Corbusier has been preaching at their deaf ears since the 1920s. Was ever a prophet so not without honour save in his country of adoption? When the great Swiss died in 1965, one of his French devotees told me, 'Good: *now* perhaps the French will take him seriously!' But even before his death there were signs of a thaw. Two of his closest disciples and former assistants, Candilis and Wogensky, are now very much *à la mode* in France; and since about 1960 Georges Candilis in particular has been entrusted by the Government with some vast operations, much nearer to the true spirit of the Master than Sarcelles. Candilis, a vague, genial Greek, told me, 'All architecture is "social" today. In the old days they planned the roads and squares first, then fitted the houses round them. Now we do the reverse. I try first to think out the buildings in relation to each other, to meet human needs.'

This evolution of thinking is noticeable even inside Sarcelles. Its newer quarters, built in the mid '60s, are markedly less monolithic than the old ones, and the new blocks are grouped in some harmonious relation to each other. The design and quality of individual buildings and flats shows a similar improvement: whereas the older ones have severe barrack-like

* The *Observer*, 3 January 1965.

façades of stone and concrete, the new ones are much gayer, with balconies, larger windows, and façades made of coloured synthetic materials. Though costs must always be kept very low, improved techniques and productivity have finally made it possible to add a few frills for the same relative price. Likewise the newer workers' flats now have larger rooms, the luxury of a small bath in place of a shower-tub, and sound-proofing that is still imperfect but less of a farce than it was in the days when *les bruits des voisins* were major causes of un-neighbourliness and 'sarcellitis'.

Slowly but surely, therefore, French cheap-housing standards are creeping up towards north European levels. After the horrors of the early period, some of the newer estates and suburbs are beginning to show quite a pleasing sense of landscaping, design, and detail. Among low-cost developments, I am thinking especially of Aillaud's ingenious pastel-coloured serpent-shaped ensembles at Pantin (eastern Paris) and Forbach (in Lorraine); of the new suburbs of Rennes; and of Mourenx, in the Pyrenees, and Bagnols-sur-Cèze, near Avignon. As for the smarter bourgeois estates, some of those just west of Paris, around Marly, Meudon, or Vaucresson, are as elegant of any of their type in Europe.

And yet the French have a habit, often baffling or irritating to foreigners, of leaving even some of their best-designed new projects with an untidy, unfinished air. A smart new building may remain for months surrounded by rubble or weedy waste-land; sleek flats will co-exist cheerfully with shacks or rubbish-heaps which no-one seems to be bothered to remove. Sometimes this is due essentially to delays over expropriation of adjacent land. At Sarcelles, for instance, where the streets are kept neat and tidy by the firm that is building the town, a few scattered privately owned sheds and villas nevertheless manage to survive incongruously amid the new geometry, defying the lawyers' efforts to remove them. But in many other instances, the cause of this untidiness seems to be a kind of aesthetic blindness of the French to surroundings that do not interest them: thus a smart restaurant often does not bother to decorate its *toilettes*. Once the main job has been done, people worry less about clearing up the bits: it is a typical facet of that slapdash French perfectionism that puts more stress on form than on detail. Notice how the French love elegant new cars, yet often leave dents and scratches unrepaired. I think this national trait, at all levels, is partly a hangover from the defeatism and lethargy of pre-war decades, and is certainly on the wane today under the impact of the new technocratic thoroughness: the success of the *ravalement de façades* campaign is one sign of this, and the new concern for personal hygiene may be another. But the trait still exists, especially in aspects of public life such as building and town-planning; and though many Frenchmen may not notice the results, others are affected at least subconsciously. Like the other forms of ugliness, it may add marginally to suburban *malaise*.

The aesthetic failings of the *Grands Ensembles* are slight, however, compared with their administrative troubles. The French system of local government, and the economic structure of the housing industry, are both of them peculiarly ill suited to this kind of venture, so that two inter-related difficulties arise. First, when the houses are built there is little money left over for the social equipment that alone can turn a dormitory into a living town. Secondly, civic progress is often frustrated by conflicts between the new town and the old semi-rural commune on to whose territory it has been 'parachuted'. The two largest new towns in the Paris region, Sarcelles and Massy-Antony, both afford striking examples.

At Sarcelles, the main operation of building, renting, and upkeep is carried out with impressive efficiency by a body known as the SCIC (Société Centrale Immobilière de la Caisse des Dépôts). The Caisse des Dépôts is a huge State finance house; and the SCIC, its subsidiary, is France's leading building promoter, with a record of over 130,000 low-cost flats completed since the war. Its own work is scrupulous, and free from any breath of scandal. But its official brief is simply to provide houses quickly and cheaply, and the Government has neglected to insist that it also be given the funds for the next stage. Of course, basic shelter must be the first priority: but the inhabitants, deprived of their fair share of schools, sports grounds, or public transport, are quick to point out cynically that it is the flats, whether rented or sold, that bring back the investment.

Responsibility for providing public equipment is divided rather vaguely between the SCIC, the relevant Ministries, and the local municipality: and here the trouble begins. In June 1964, in the middle of Sarcelles, I noticed a splendid hole in the ground, some 200 yards square and fifteen feet deep: 'That,' I was told proudly by the SCIC, 'will be our civic centre, with a big *Maison de la Culture*, library, skating-rink, scores of shops including a giant Prisunic, 40,000 square metres of offices, and under-ground parking for 2,500 cars. Any day now, work will begin.' I came back *two-and-a-half years* later: the hole was quite unchanged, a bit muddier in the January rain. What had happened? First, there were municipal elections, bane of the new towns. The *Grand Ensemble* is adjacent to the old townlet of Sarcelles, population about 4,000, which until 1965 held most of the seats on the communal council. But the afflux of new working-class votes produced an inevitable swing to the Left, and in March 1965, Sarcelles elected a council with a Communist-Socialist majority, most of its members from the new town. (This has been a common pattern in many such places: one alleged political motive behind the Gaullists' rehousing policy, that of breaking up the mono-lithic 'Red Belt' of the older suburbs, seems to have been a complete failure!) The new Communist mayor, M. Canacos, a technical worker, was damned if *he* was going to help the State with its *Maison de la Culture*. For a long time, he refused to commit his 50 per cent of the needed funds. Finally, in 1966, some kind of agreement was reached; but neither commune, nor SCIC, nor private business found themselves prepared to sink capital in so ambitious a project as the civic centre, and in 1967 the hole was still filling up with rainwater.

At Massy-Antony, over in the southern suburbs, the problems are worse. The State authorities deliberately planted this *Grand Ensemble* astride two communes in different departments (Antony in the Seine, Massy in the Seine-et-Oise) in order to provoke maximum administrative difficulties and so draw the fullest lessons for the future. And they've certainly got what they wanted. The town is being built by a Société d'Economie Mixte comprising State and private interests plus the two existing communes, which already were quite populous; but the communes' role has so far been largely obstructive. First, the Socialist mayor of old Antony rejected plans for a new separate commune for the ensemble: it would have deprived him of some territory and power. Then the mayor of old Massy began systematic opposition to the new town. Most of the ensemble is in Massy, not Antony; but the burghers of the sleepy old market-town of Massy, most of them small tradesmen, farmers and *rentiers*, are ill equipped to cope with the growth of a big modern suburb. They fought it: and building might never have started at all, had not the State, in 1958, made rare use of its ultimate right of veto over communal obstruction and sent bulldozers out over the cornfields while the farmers were in the act of harvest. This incident has not made for happier relations. Today the council is still controlled by old Massy; and the mayor, an old-style reactionary Socialist, sees little reason to spend his precious budget on the new town. For some years he succeeded in blocking the *dossiers* of joint projects that needed his formal support, notably for a sports centre. And so, even today, the young slum evacuees in the new town are condemned to play football on improvised pitches amid car parks and vacant lots. The irony is that the mayor derives much of his electoral support from those who suffer from his policies, for most of the new Massiens are left-wing.

Such conflicts do not augur well for the projected new cities of the Schéma Directeur. If these are to succeed, it seems imperative for the State to devise some entirely new local structure, with special financing and new separate communes, possibly on the lines of the British New Town development corporations. The present French system aims, hopefully, to breathe life into a *Grand Ensemble* by grafting it on to the living tissue of a traditional town. But is it reasonable to expect these old communes to take civic and economic responsibility for big new suburbs? Is it not like putting a car factory down in a cornfield, and then compensating the farmer by making him managing-director? And even though the political problems are often ephemeral, the financial ones remain. However co-operative a mayor (and few are as tiresome as at Massy), his own resources just do not stretch to the vast task of providing a new town with what it needs. A commune's finances derive mainly from taxes on local shops and factories: yet these are the very things that the new towns initially lack. And the State has shown little willingness to be flexible and provide special funds: it sticks to its own formal rules, that the commune must pay its routine share, 30 per cent for new hospitals and schools, 35 per cent for sports facilities, 50 per cent for *Maisons de la Culture*, and so on. The delays and shortages are therefore often the fault of the State (Massy is an exception) and can be due to inter-Ministerial rivalries, if the Ministry of Health, say, or Education, refuses to come to the relief of one of the Ministry of Construction's new schemes. Hence the results. At Sarcelles, for instance, though the SCIC has provided an impressive home for the elderly and a hostel for bachelor workers, work is only now beginning on a sports centre and swimming-pool, while for 7,000 schoolchildren there are a mere eight primary schools, and the building of a *lycée* is held up by land expropriation problems. So the *lycéens* must get up at six or so to make tedious journeys to schools in St. Denis or Paris. Fortunately both for *lycéens* and workers, Sarcelles is on a main line to the Gare du Nord; but the trains are fearsomely overcrowded at rush-hours, and the SNCF has refused to provide this town of 50,000 even with a covered station, claiming that the SCIC should pay for it. At Massy, transport links with Paris and the factory zones are a good deal worse: one Métro line to the Luxembourg, and a few inadequate, crowded buses. Most people, it is true, have cars, but not all can park near their work. Throughout the Paris region, there has been a disgraceful lack of effective liaison between the town-planners and the transport authorities.

The consequent fatigue and waste of leisure-time hardly needs stressing. A worker in a new suburb spends, on average, two hours on travel each day; he is away from home twelve or thirteen hours, and may be too tired in the evening to do more than watch TV, which helps to explain these towns' lack of social animation. And this is aggravated by the housing shortage, which often makes it hard for a worker to move to a new flat nearer his work. A remarkable article by Boris Kidel in *l'Express* in May 1963 compared the lives of three typical skilled car-workers and their families, from Renault, Opel (near Frankfurt) and Ford (Dagenham). The article showed that the Frenchman's lot was tougher than that of his counterparts simply because he lived on the wrong side of Paris from Renault. The German bicycled for twenty minutes through open country to his work; the Englishman had a thirty-minute motor-bike ride from his Hornchurch bungalow; the Frenchman struggled for ninety minutes each way in train and Métro, from his flat in north-east Paris to the Billancourt works, leaving home at 5.30 a.m. and getting back at 7 p.m. Yet, having acquired his precious HLM in the days when you accepted what you could get, he now had no right to a transfer. Maybe this is an extreme case, even a piece of special pleading by the (then) left-wing *l'Express*. But it has some general truth.

This kind of situation would be eased, for many people, if the projected policy of providing the *Grands Ensembles* with their own local light industries had ever been carried out. This is perhaps their most striking deficiency when compared with the British new towns. Desperate to solve the worst of the housing crisis by any means, the State dumped people where it could, without providing either local work or better transport. Then, until 1963, the official ban on new factories in the Paris region put a halt to plans for industrialising the *ensembles*. Today, at long last, this is easing. In 1965 Massy got its first factory, seven years late; but Sarcelles', now a decade late, have not yet arrived. The situation is in some ways harder on the women than the men: having homes to run, they often cannot spare the same long days away at work, yet there are few suitable jobs for them near at hand, despite efforts to create new office employment in some ensembles. And when they have finished the chores in their easy-to-run little modern flats, they spend much of the day in boredom.

These failures of planning and development simply aggravate the psychological difficulties of the French in adapting to this new suburban life. If the lack of local jobs is one cause of housewives' boredom, another, much greater, is their relative lack of Anglo-Saxon neighbourliness or of any tradition of women's clubs and associations, and their wariness about making friends or pooling resources with strangers. Much has been said and written about this in France, and about other aspects of the new towns' so-called *malaise*.

Sometimes the picture painted is too black. The inhabitants' reactions vary immensely: certainly, many of them feel a sense of incompleteness, and yet without any doubt the majority *are* happier than in their old slums. A little flat with all mod. cons. where the family can bolt the door and build its nest, a playground outside for *les gosses*, blue sky with no smog—these are their first priorities, and these at least they find. Few consciously object to the grim geometry of Sarcelles; some even yearn to go and live there. 'That's a true City of the Future for you!' enthuses the teenage working-class heroine of a sensitive novel* about life in the HLMs, on her first visit to the place: 'kilometres and kilometres and kilometres of houses houses houses houses—and sky, and sun, houses full of sun . . . and green spaces, enormous, clean, superb, like carpets, with a notice on each one, "Respect the Lawns and Trees and See they are Respected", notices which seem to have some effect here as the population are no doubt progressive like the architecture.' Ian Nairn should meet *her*.

After some initial problems, such as learning how to use baths and refuse-chutes and modern lifts, many families settle down devotedly to their new domesticity and soon develop what has been called '*le réflexe petit-bourgeois*'. This means, first, an avid materialism, a buying spree of furniture and electrical gadgets, usually on hire purchase and sometimes beyond their real means: the new towns are rife with skilful sales-touts,

---

* *Les Petits Enfants du siècle*, by Christiane Rochefort (Grasset, 1961).

who can often persuade wives into rash commitments while husbands are at work. Poor families also tend to be feckless at first with gas and electricity, unused to the new luxury of meters on deferred payment. Some households thus find themselves paying up to 60 per cent of their income on fixed charges, including rent; and the rents, though reasonable for what is offered (200 francs a month is the HLM average), are usually much higher than their old ones in the slums and not always so easy to meet on a worker's salary. * Many budgets are helped out by State housing allowances, averaging seventy francs a month; even so, the sharp change in spending habits and living standards, with no immediate corresponding rise in salary, often spells recurring financial crisis during the first months in a new home. This has been reckoned as a common cause of nervous breakdowns in the *Grands Ensembles*; and according to some reports in the Left-wing Press, it even drives a number of respectable wives and mothers to part-time prostitution in a desperate effort to make ends meet.†

Possibly this whole issue has been exaggerated. Though the financial difficulties are often real enough, it is partly a question of learning how to adapt to new middle-class ways of being budget-wise, and this the workers usually manage in time. But the other aspect of the petit-bourgeois reflex goes deeper, and derives from one of the strongest traits in the French character, the attachment to family rather than community. In their old slums, for all the discomfort, people were close to friends and shops they had known for years, and often were surrounded by relatives too. Put them down in a new setting, and they draw in their horns. Their first reaction is to close the door, enjoy the new privacy and comfort, and cling to what still remains that is familiar: the immediate family cell. Friendly calls by neighbours are resented, or are assumed to have some ulterior motive. However much people like their flats, they show a deep emotional wariness towards regarding the *milieu* of the *Grand Ensemble* as 'home'.

Sometimes this reaction takes a violent or hostile form. Some people strongly resent their enforced removal from the slums; others, whose old homes are still standing, retreat back to them after a few experimental months in a *Grand Ensemble*. Women find the adaptation hardest, and sometimes, as the lonely days drag on, they will take to making special journeys back to do their daily shopping among the old friendly faces. In a few cases, the *ennui* of the new towns can lead even to illness or suicide, or, among teenagers, to a kind of listless petty vandalism. But, though the newspapers enjoy building up sensational scares, most sociologists and social workers deny that the level of delinquency or nervous illness is in fact much higher in a *Grand Ensemble* than elsewhere; it is simply that the causes are different.

Most inhabitants react more placidly, and their *malaise* is more subtle

---

* See p. 260 (Social).

† See *Nouvel Observateur*, 23 March and 4 May 1966; also Jean-Luc Godard's film, *Deux ou trois choses que je sais d'elle* (1967).

and less conscious. They vaguely resent the lack of social warmth and ambience, but they answer this by retreating into their own ambience rather than by working together to create a public one. At Massy, a complacent middle-aged clerk in an HLM told me: 'Some newcomers here were unhappy and suspicious at first, but now they're getting to like it. Here we sunbathe on our balconies at weekends, we watch TV, or we drive into the countryside, which is only ten minutes away. Yes, we'd like more sport, but we don't need more clubs or social life, the French are too individual and *renfermés* for that. Personally, I don't see these new towns creating a new collective spirit in France.'

The inhabitants do resent a shortage of utilitarian facilities that they could use as individuals: schools, clinics, transport, jobs, sports fields. But when it comes to general social or cultural amenities, or even entertainment other than sport, they often fail to patronise what they are given. And this is true even of that noble French institution, the café or brasserie. The rarity of pavement cafés is one of the most striking lacunae of the new towns, at least to the casual eye. It is due partly to a new anti-alcoholism law, that limits cafés in new suburbs to one per 3,000 people, but also to the reluctance of most cafetiers to try their luck in this strange new milieu. Massy, with 30,000 people, has only three cafés, one-third of its legal ration, whereas a traditional town of its size might have a hundred. The cafés that do emerge in the new towns are mostly overlit, functional places with stone floors, bare walls, and a vaguely listless atmosphere: juke-box or TV blaring, a few youths playing with pin-tables. Usually there is not enough traditional café warmth to tempt the locals away from their own TV sets. In one sense, this is a sign of progress: the cosier their new flats, the less need the French feel to visit cafés.*

There are plenty of shops in the new towns: Sarcelles has five separate *centres commerciaux*, each one grouped round a traffic-free precinct, cheerful and pleasantly designed, strikingly similar to their English counterparts. But, though the housewives gladly use them for their daily needs, for the 'serious' buying of clothes, furniture, or other such items they still prefer to go off to shops in a real town, be it Paris or St. Denis. It is all part of their reluctance to put down roots. Hence, the specialised shops that help to give a town an air of pride and prosperity have trouble in making their way. It is the same with entertainment. Most people, understandably, prefer to go off to central Paris for their cinemas or theatres. In Sarcelles, the one makeshift commercial cinema does bad business, and even the ciné-clubs, usually all the rage in post-war France, have had difficulties.

And yet, within each new town there is always a small minority of people who think and react quite differently from all this, and who create little cells of extreme animation. These are the pioneers, usually the more

* See pp. 269–70 (Social).

educated ones, who instead of drawing in their horns are inspired by the challenge of turning the concrete desert into a spiritual flower-garden. Sometimes they are militant Catholics; or eager Communists; or social workers with a sense of mission; or cultural enthusiasts. However opposed their ideologies, they usually find that they have a lot in common.* It is them against the rest. Thanks to them, Sarcelles has its evening courses of drama, German, and basket-work, its high-powered visiting lecturers from Paris, its ciné-clubs, its youth centre, and its large public library run by a young bearded campaigner who treats the civilising of the city as a military operation, and can tell you at once from the coloured pins on his wall-map how many people in each block have discovered Dostoievsky. The only trouble is that these manifold socio-cultural activities are often badly attended, and are kept alive by the same little band of loyalists who circulate from one to the next.

As far as culture goes, this is perhaps not so surprising, and not so different from the pattern, say, in Stevenage. After all, Sarcelles is hardly a university town like Caen, with a ready-made audience for its *Maison de la Culture*. But in another respect the French experience does seem to differ significantly from the British: the pioneers have not had much success even in promising obvious civic self-help activities. Baby-sitting, crèches, help for old people or invalids, youth movements, courses in domestic science or civics—good works of this sort are carried out on limited budgets by various official or semi-official bodies, but usually in a rather formal, juridical manner, and without over-much public response. Even in a middle-class setting, a young housewife in a prosperous new suburb west of Paris told me that she was treated with some suspicion by the neighbours when, purely as a public service and without asking for payment, she tried to start up a crèche. 'She must be a Communist—she's trying to get at us,' was the initial reaction of many bourgeois mothers who really would have liked nothing better than to be able to leave their small children in safe hands for an hour or two. Because the woman was not someone they knew, and because she was doing something 'unofficial', and was not a paid social worker, she was suspect. Finally, the crèche did get going, and was a great success, but it took great patience. A nation with little tradition of voluntary public service, where most welfare work tends to be institutionalised, is naturally finding it hard to adapt to the informal community living that life in the new towns demands. Slowly, new habits are forming. But in the meantime, where officialdom fails to provide what the citizens need, they show little initiative for taking remedies into their own hands.

You must travel 400 miles and more from Sarcelles, to the Pyrenees and Provence, to find the two most successful examples of new-town pioneering. Mourenx, fifteen miles west of Pau, is the only case in France

* See p. 385 (Intellectuals in disarray).

of a *Grand Ensemble* all by itself in the open country, unattached to an older community. It was built to house the workers of the new industries of near-by Lacq; and the big State company that exploits the gas-fields has co-operated closely with the SCIC in trying to ensure that Mourenx is as much a showpiece of modern French town-planning as Lacq is of French industry. Aesthetically, this policy has paid off. Set in the gentle green foothills of the Pyrenees, Mourenx with its white towers, lawns and piazzas, and Béarn-style flower-boxes, looks quite beautiful, especially on a summer night; and though there is much the same rectangular pattern as at Sarcelles, the effect is far less monolithic. Socially, the town has been through the usual crises. The workers arrived here from all corners of France, notably from the mines of the North, and many at first were lonely and *dépaysés*: 'Maman isolée! ne restez plus seule au foyer, venez chez nous,' was the significant appeal, by a religious club, that I saw in a shop-window on my first visit, in 1960. But gradually the families settled down and found content, seduced by the warm southern climate, the scenery, the sea and mountains close at hand: all school-children are taken for skiing classes once a week in winter. It is a town made up almost entirely of young married couples with children, and nearly every family has a car, for the workers of Lacq are quite well paid. Civically, too, it is ahead of most *Grands Ensembles*. In the early years, the SCIC and the Lacq company (SNPA) made the mistake of running the town as their own private operation in which the inhabitants had no say: there were even uniformed SCIC wardens to keep people off the lawns. But in 1963 the population rebelled, led by their mayor, a school-master from Normandy: tired of being treated as 'minors', they de-manded control over their own local affairs, as in any other commune. The SCIC backed down, gracefully; and today the Mourenxois, thanks to their show of public spirit, seem to have achieved a kind of civic maturity that is still rare in the new towns. The mayor co-operates vigorously in the development of Mourenx with the two giant State firms, who have even coaxed priority funds out of the Government for providing Mourenx with better-than-average equipment: it has a splendid municipal swim-ming-pool and holiday centre, and a fine new *lycée*. Not that life is all roses. The symptoms of *ennui* and withdrawal so common in Sarcelles are still evident in Mourenx too; and although the rank-and-file workers are content to stay, the prosperous executives and scientists of Lacq have mostly shown a reluctance to settle in the chic villas built for them at Mourenx, and are tending to drift away to Pau and elsewhere. But at least Mourenx is proving that it *is* possible for a *Grand Ensemble* to overcome its teething troubles and become civilised and congenial.

The same is being proved, more effectively, at Bagnols-sur-Cèze in the Rhône valley, twenty miles north-west of Avignon. Here, in a lyrical Provençal setting of vineyards and blue-grey hills, a new dormitory for the workers and scientists of the big Marcoule atomic centre has been cun-ningly grafted on to the ancient and beautiful little market town of

Bagnols, through the talents of the architect Georges Candilis. The three medieval towers of the old city are carefully balanced by three white towers of flats in the new town; the modern buildings with their gaily coloured sun-blinds and shutters blend as easily with the landscape as the weathered stone of the old Gothic churches; and in a space between the two towns, a new shopping-centre forms a meeting-point for the two populations. The harmonious result won Candilis, in 1959, the first official French *Prix de l'Urbanisme*.

Bagnols has architecture, scenery, and climate on its side, and more besides. The town is composed of two rival élites. On the one hand, the 5,000 'vieux Bagnolais', who like all Provençaux have history in their blood, and have been used since pre-Roman days to welcoming and as-similating successive waves of newcomers to their epic homeland. They are eagerly proud of their old town with its fine museum, its ramparts, its Roman tower; and, unlike the burghers of Massy, they are almost equally proud of Bagnols' new pioneering, modernistic role. The other élite are the 12,000 'nouveaux Bagnolais', known as 'Marcoulens', technicians and skilled workers from all over France, mostly well paid, and generally happy to settle in this sunlit valley. Their lives are subsidised by their employers at Marcoule, the Commissariat à l'Energie Atomique, who are anxious to help make the Bagnols experiment a success by putting money into its cultural centre and its manifold sports clubs. At the large and handsome swimming-pool and lido in the new town centre (where the French team trained for the 1964 Tokyo Olympics), the sons and daughters of physicists and farmers flirt and splash under the white light that seduced Cézanne, and life seems far nearer to St. Tropez than to Sar-celles. And yet, even this idyll is not perfect. The ideal of the planners for a fusion of 'old Bags' and 'new Bags' (as my scribbled field-notes describe them) has not yet been realised. Although many of the 'old Bags' have been rehoused in the new flats among the newcomers, the two groups still practise, not so surprisingly, a certain *apartheid*. It seems to be largely the fault of the Marcoulens: aloof and clannish behind the prestige of their *Grande Ecole* diplomas, their top-secret nuclear work, and their keeping-up-with-the-Duponts society, they tend to look down on the old Bags as 'paysans'. And the old Bags in turn resent what they regard as patronising pretentiousness. Real friendships between the two are not common: the case of a Norman at Marcoule, who married a local artist and learned Provençal, is a rare exception. Yet the mutual coolness is usually masked by civility and rarely develops into conflict. And the new generation are breaking down their parents' barriers. One technician told me, 'At home, my son plays only with other little Marcoulens; but at the *lycée* and the lido he makes friends with Provençal children too, and doesn't seem to differentiate.'

Bagnols is such a success in other ways that this one unremarkable failure, of social integration, achieves undue local prominence. In many other respects, adaptation to the new suburban living has been swifter and easier here than in less privileged *Grands Ensembles*. But nearly everywhere in France, and not only in Bagnols and Mourenx, a certain thaw is now beginning to be felt in the new towns. In Sarcelles, in Massy, in a score of other such towns, families are slowly and tenatively breaking with age-old habits and forming new loyalties, almost despite themselves. *Natura abhorret vacuum.* The influx into the new working-class suburbs of a certain number of *cadres*, and of energetic and gregarious *pieds noirs*,* is beginning to produce a new social ferment and class fluidity that is still rare in Paris and other older towns.† And though the family *foyer* is still generally held sacred against intrusion, on neutral territory the barriers of unneighbourliness are beginning to come down; neighbours who, for the first year or two, do no more than exchange a wary 'Bonjour, Madame' on the staircase, may finally meet at some local fête, find that they share the same problems, and become quite friendly. At Mourenx, a young social worker, Mlle. Auger, told me of her efforts to promote basketwork and pottery classes for housewives, and voluntary baby-sitting: 'Women here feel a lack of something, they're not sure what. Their new homes are so easy to run, it leaves them with leisure—for what? I believe they come to my classes in order, above all, to meet new people and form new links that they don't seem to manage to do on their own doorsteps. It's hard going but, willy-nilly, a new mentality of participation is emerging here—a new life is being created, despite itself.'

Mlle. Auger also referred, as others have done, to the 'new French élites' that the *Grands Ensembles* are throwing up: the pioneers, the do-gooders, the apostles of community-living, people like herself. The new suburbia seems, in fact, to bring out the best and the worst in the French: this new, uncharacteristic social spirit, and an atavistic petit-bourgeois egotism and withdrawal. And these two are now in battle for the soul of France. Or rather, that is one way of putting it: there is also another point of view. Some people claim that the *Grands Ensembles* are leading towards a dangerous collectivism, alien to the glorious tradition of French privacy and individualism. Marc Bernard in his book on Sarcelles‡ writes: 'Some of our animators inveigh against this passive, closed-door spirit and condemn it; I'm not sure that they're right. I fear that by trying to improve things they may make them worse. There's such a powerful current drawing us towards collectivism these days that anything that slows it down and blocks it should be desirable, even to be encouraged. It wouldn't be a bad thing to hold courses on individualism in all the Sarcelles of the world.'

But this seems to me to ignore the facts of a town like Sarcelles, where usually it is the active ones who are the individualists. The answer must be to strike a balance. New towns are inevitable, and if the French are to

* See p. 140 (New life in the provinces).
† See p. 239 (Social) and p. 445 (Conclusion).
‡ *Sarcellopolis* (Flammarion, 1964).

live in them happily they cannot afford not to develop some kind of community living. It is a question not of stifling their individualism but of providing it with new kinds of social outlet—without running to the un-French extremes of the *kibbutz* or *kholkhoz* or, worse, of the undiscriminating conformist good-neighbourliness of American 'organisation-man' suburbia.

For the *Grands Ensembles* to flourish in this way, it seems to me that initially the State and the communes will have to play a large part. They will have to provide the equipment and a staff of 'animators' to make the towns congenial, for in officialised France these will not easily appear of their own accord. And this will need a change in the powers and finances of the communes. It is significant that one of the few successful examples of 'animation' in the new suburbs of a big town is at Rennes, where the new housing estates all happen to be *inside* the prosperous and go-ahead commune of Rennes, led by its vigorous mayor, M. Fréville. He has set up a 'social and cultural' office for the city, grouping various State and municipal services, with animators in each new suburb who have succeeded in creating local civic units to run their own arts clubs, crèches, and so on. But this is still rare in France: it demands a large unified commune and a strong official lead. And ideally it should be only a first step towards a more spontaneous kind of community life. The real question it poses is whether the State in France will ever wither away, whether a crèche will ever be an informal circle of housewives, instead of a unit in some *Fédération Nationale*, governed from Paris by complex legal statutes dating back to the law of 1901.

UTOPIAS OF THE NEW RICH:
'IS PARIS 2 BURNING?'

If you've money in the bank, then the dilemma of collectivism *versus* individualism loses much of its force. For poorer people wanting a new home, there is little choice but an HLM amid rows of similar HLMs; but for a few, there is all the glory and diversity of the open market: a chic new town flat in Neuilly at half a million francs, a modern 'maison de campagne, style anglais' in the woods of the Ile-de-France, or a bijou apartment with sun-terrace and built-in barbecue on one of the modish little estates west of Paris, with names like 'le Parc Montaigne' or 'le Résidence Vendôme'. Some of this type of housing lies inside Paris; but Parisian prices and rents have soared so high, for new property, that most of those with middle or upper-middle incomes are obliged to move out of town. The Parisian business man is being forced to learn the Anglo-Saxon habit of commuting.

The Ile-de-France is thus rapidly changing its social character. Until very recently, civilisation was regarded as ending at the gates of Paris; outside, there was only the despised 'banlieue', and beyond that, little but the empty plains and forests of the Paris basin, broken only by the royal *châteaux* in their great parks. The Ile-de-France had never known much equivalent of the stockbroker belt in Buckinghamshire, the tea-shops of Tunbridge Wells, or Betjeman's mid-Surrey with its colonels and tennis-girls. Towns like Etampes and Senlis, thirty miles from Paris, were closed and lifeless. A few film-stars and writers, it is true, owned smart villas in discreet villages like Montfort-l'Amaury; and it was just socially acceptable to live, say, in St. Cloud or St.-Germain-en-Laye. But for most of the bourgeoisie, Paris alone counted.

Today, while the rich commute at weekends to their *châteaux*, say, in Normandy, or by Caravelle to the *Côte*, thousands of not-quite-so-rich Parisians are developing a new craze for weekend country cottages.* And throughout the middle classes, by force of necessity the old snobbism against *la banlieue* is dropping away, and a new counter-snobbism is being carefully fostered, for a certain style of smart Americanised suburban living. Out to the west of Paris, around and beyond Versailles, the spare land is rapidly filling up with these chic little housing-estates and their tennis-courts, *piscines*, and boutiques. A small flat or *pavillon* here may cost 130,000 francs or more, with poor credit facilities, but at least that will be no more than half what it would be inside Paris. And in this suburbia the young short-haired executives are basking in a new, un-French ideal. Some drive their Peugeots or Citroën I Ds across the Bois to their offices; others sit reading *Le Figaro* on early trains to the Gare St. Lazare as if on the 8.44 from Sevenoaks. And France will need her John Betjeman to hymn the tennis-court life of this new world.

The most apparent difference between all new housing in France and in Britain is still, of course, that the French build flats and the British build houses. But even this is now changing. The French do not live in flats by choice; flats were thrust upon them. 'In the heart of every Frenchman there slumbers a *pavillon*,' writes Marc Bernard, and opinion surveys reveal that 82 per cent of Frenchmen yearn for nothing better than a little house with a garden, just like an Englishman. The anarchic rash of *pavillons* built outside Paris in the inter-war years shows how far the French will go towards realising this dream when they get the chance. But, to meet the post-war housing crisis, officialdom leaned towards flats rather than rows of houses because they were cheaper and quicker to build. There was also the French tradition of in-city living, countering and frustrating the secret dream of the *pavillon*. Today, however, conditions are changing. The housing crisis has eased a little, affluence is growing, the middle class has caught Anglo-Americanisation like the measles— and the decline of pro-Paris snobbery means that people are readier to move right out to where land prices are still low enough for the mass production of little commuter villas with gardens. Even the Government is

* See p. 267 (Social).

now sponsoring a few English-style HLM estates of this type, at Essonnes and at Creil. As for private building, you will find full-page advertisements in papers like *Le Monde* offering '*la joie de vivre authentique et profonde*' of modern five-room villas '*à la manière anglaise*' with lawns and crazy paving. At Le-Mesnil-St.-Denis, south-west of Versailles, the American firm of Levitt and Sons is building an estate of 520 villas of this type, ranging from 108,000 to 165,000 francs each; no more expensive than their equivalents twenty-five miles from London. In the first three weeks, the 'show' villas had 35,000 visitors, and the whole estate was subscribed twice over. Buyers were *cadres moyens*, engineers, doctors, older people wanting to get out of Paris or newly-weds with some capital.

The most interesting factor is that on this type of estate, and at this social level, a most unprecedented neighbourliness soon develops. Often there are no hedges between the gardens and no one minds; yet these same people, in their old Paris flats, often never got to know their neighbours. Of course flat-dwelling is far less conducive to neighbourliness than house-dwelling (this partly explains the difficulties on the *Grands Ensembles*) and when there is no too-close neighbour to make a noise through the ceiling, or mess up the communal stairways, he no longer need be shunned.

The experience of these garden-estates in France is still far too recent for any firm conclusions to be drawn; but it seems that their new American-style communal spirit may bring with it some American-style dangers. In their old flats the French at least tended to be tolerant towards and uncompetitive with neighbours, so long as each left the other in peace; you could be rich or poor, black or yellow, living in sin or addicted to drugs, and no one cared so long as you were discreet. On the new estates, people show signs of being more choosy about their neighbours, less tolerant of social non-conformists, more envious of the next man's smarter car or niftier spin-drier. This has not yet reached American proportions; but it might be moving that way.

Preoccupation with material status, *le standing* as the French call it in their charming *franglais*, is growing inevitably in the newly affluent middle class, and housing is one of its first considerations. Someone put it to me: 'An executive can ask you to his office, where his surroundings reflect his standing; or he can entertain in a smart restaurant; but his flat may give him away.' House-agents and promoters are now playing skilfully upon these snobberies and these desires, and in the past few years a publicity campaign unique in France has gone into persuading people that a new earthly paradise of ease and elegance awaits them beyond the western gates of Paris. '*Le murmure des Eaux Vives au sortir de Métro!*' promises one advertisement for an estate with its own park and fountains at the end of the Métro to Palaiseau. Another full-page spread, rich in house-agents' *franglais*, plays on the theme of Californian-style luxury at Le Parc Montaigne, near St. Cyr: '*Les tennis-quick . . . avec*

*des amis; piscine . . . pour goûter la détente d'un "crawl"; centre commercial,
lieu plaisant du shopping; barbecue chez soi . . . été comme hiver; dressing-
room en acajou; cheminée . . . une joie intime . . . dans une atmosphère de
vacances.'* Or again, '*Il prend son drink au Drugstore . . . ils vont au club
de bridge.*' I am not making this up. This is France 1968. Luridly the
glossy colour-ads offer a world of mahogany and fitted carpets, of parasols
and wide sun-terraces amid beeches and poplars; and the public follow.
The show-flats in their nouveau-riche way are often almost as enticing
as the advertisements have suggested, and visiting them has become a
popular Sunday afternoon sport, a sort of window-shopping enjoyed
also by workers who couldn't possibly afford to buy. But others can and do
buy: starved by decades of poor housing, and seduced by the agents'
slogans of '*la luxe à la portée de tout le monde*', many young couples readily
take the risk of signing away their capital and committing themselves to
larger monthly payments than they can easily afford. Payment is usually
demanded in advance of building, in order to help the promoters'
financing, and certain extras are often artfully concealed in the contract,
so that final costs may be fearsomely high.

The most striking of these estates so far completed is Elysée Deux,
at La-Celle-St.-Cloud, the work of a sharp and ambitious young promoter,
Robert de Balkany. Here the five-storey blocks of elegant flats (many
with two bathrooms) are set amid pine-trees on a hill-side, and surround a
shopping-centre whose chief features are a luxury first-run cinema, a
sauna bath, a night-club whose metallic décor has been designed to harmonise with modern Courrèges fashions, and a 'drugstore' roughly
similar to the new ones in central Paris. It is called *Le Drugwest*, and it
serves Franco-American dishes to the sound of Western music, amid a
jazzily sophisticated décor of glass, dark wood, and huge yellow and orange
Chinese lanterns. It is immensely popular, lively, plushy, modernistic,
and I can think of nowhere else I would sooner take a foreign visitor to
show him what the new France is like. Though Elysée Deux as a whole,
and the Drugwest in particular, owe a lot to America, they do retain a
curiously French flavour, sharp, brashly chic rather than vulgar, that I
cannot help finding attractive and stimulating. De Balkany's policy—a
sound one, that needs copying more effectively in the *Grands Ensembles*
—is to entice people out to suburbs like this by trying to *recreate* the chic,
the appeal, the amenities of central Paris. Hence the Courrèges night-
club, the first-run cinema, the Drugwest; and hence the name, Elysée
Deux, a new little Champs-Elysées. Even the local coiffeur has transferred
from the Champs-Elysées. This policy has not worked ideally; some of the
promised amenities, such as youth centre and swimming-pool, have
arrived late or have not been properly looked after. But on the whole
these '*banlieusards de grand luxe*' are happy with their new home.

The success of Elysée Deux did, however, go to de Balkany's head.
In 1966 he began work on a much vaster project: a luxury city for 20,000
people on a 250-acre site just north of Versailles, complete with theatres,

churches, smart hotels, exotic gardens, night-clubs, a new Drugwest open all night, and 'the largest shopping-centre in Europe'. And this Xanadu he baptised, inevitably, *PARIS DEUX*. 'The idea is not new,' proclaimed a four-page advertisement in *Le Monde*, with touching modesty: 'Louis XIV once transported Paris to the countryside. He, like us, felt the imperious need to do so. And so, 300 years later, on almost the same spot, we shall build a quintessence of Paris and recreate an art of living unique in the world.' True to his policy, de Balkany first built the new Drugwest at Paris Deux as a 'magnet', before any dwellings were finished. Then a giant publicity campaign, costing 3,500,000 francs or more, drew in the crowds and the clients: 200,000 came in four weeks to see the Drugwest and the show-flats. But the Left, the Press, even the Government grew restive. Would de Balkany be able to honour his contracts and his promises? Suppose he failed to sell enough flats in advance and his project collapsed, half finished? Was it all a confidence trick? And anyway, why spend the nation's resources on these snobbish absurdities when millions of workers were still homeless or in slums? *Le Nouvel Observateur* sharply attacked Paris Deux, alleging that its publicity was phoney and its information to clients misleading: '*Paris 2 Brûle-t-il?*' the paper enquired hopefully in a front-page banner headline. (This was the time of the première of Clément's film on the Liberation.) Delouvrier at the *District* was also hostile, and wanted to see the whole project go up in flames: it was just the kind of development that might sabotage the careful long-term planning of his Schéma Directeur. But de Balkany had influence in high places, and the Right-wing Pompidou intervened in the rôle of von Choltitz, if hardly for the same reasons. All the Government did was to induce de Balkany to modify the scale of Paris Deux—and to change its name to 'Parly Deux', after the Paris municipal council had threatened legal action over the 'sacriligeous' abuse of the city's name!

For the moment I feel we should suspend judgement on Parly Deux. It is true, the luxury-housing market has become over-saturated since 1965, prices have risen too high, and many smart flats are not finding buyers. For these reasons, de Balkany may run into trouble, and it appears that his sales have not been as high as he had hoped. But if he can ride this storm, and if Parly Deux *can* live up to its promises and repeat the success of Elysée Deux on a larger-scale, then many of the partisan attacks on it will seem to me to have been unjustified. One fact is certain: even if this Parly Deux fails, there will still be others in the future. This new-affluent bourgeoisie has now found what it thinks it wants: all-night drugstores, built-in barbecues, mahogany dressing-rooms, and the rest. And whatever the sins of speculators, the trend in France towards this 'new art of living', this 'authentic and profound *joie de vivre*' seems irreversible.

CHAPTER IX

NOVELTY AND TRADITION
IN DAILY LIFE

——————

THE NEW FRANC (one hundred old francs) was introduced in 1959: eight years later a large percentage of people, educated people, still felt unable to calculate in anything but old francs, and not through want of arithmetic. It is just one example of the way that personal habits and rooted methods of thinking are still slow to change in this ancient country, even under the impact of economic revolution. In preceding chapters we have seen how the French are adapting unevenly, often bemusedly, to change forced on them by technical advance and sheer modern necessity: new gadgets like tractors or built-in barbecues they may seize on eagerly, but basic changes involving social attitudes often seem harder to accept. In their private and daily lives, and in their new leisure and spending habits, the same is equally true, and in this chapter I shall trace how certain modern styles of life are being seized on with frenzied appetite, while certain others, in practice more necessary, are being shunned. The formalism and stratification of French traditional society does not easily adapt itself, and today the French are often the unwilling prisoners of their own rigidities.

A SLOW DISMANTLING OF
THE BARRICADES OF CLASS

These rigidities can be seen especially in French social divisions. Despite the tradition of civic *égalité*, this is still a less egalitarian society than the United States or Scandinavia, or even the Britain of today. Britain has often been regarded as the land of caste, second only to India: but in practice, though the British are far more class-conscious than the French, I think they are today less class-divided. In Britain, with its new social fluidity, the classes are fascinatedly aware of each other on a personal, everyday level. In France, class distinctions are taken very much more for granted and are rarely discussed with the same passionate human interest—it would be hard to imagine a French *Look Back in Anger*. Though most children go to the same primary schools, and though there is certainly more fluidity than before the war, yet there is still little sense of a classless meritocracy where a worker's son can rub shoulders with a banker's or a general's. The bourgeoisie retains much of its aloofness, its ignorance of the lives of workers or peasants, and the different strata mix surprisingly little.

You have only to wander round France to notice how the working classes, despite their new prosperity, are less assertively emancipated than in Britain. There are some parts of central Paris, notably around the Faubourg St. Honoré, that still have the air of elegant upper-class preserves in a way that is true of no part of the West End of London. Or contrast the democratic hubbub of Heathrow airport with the chic, expensive atmosphere of Orly. Workers in France, even when they can afford it, are reticent about thrusting their way forward to share in the bourgeoisie's own public world of smart shops, theatres, and airports, and their own tastes are not publicly catered for on the same scale as in Britain. It is one reason why there is less vulgarity in France than in Britain today, but also less justice.

The causes of these abiding class rigidities lie deep in French history and character. The desire to avoid open conflicts between groups has led to a protective formalisation of French life which over the centuries has pushed each class into its fixed place. Animosities are often bitter, but they are oddly depersonalised. Conflicts take the form of economic pressures, political demands, and attitude-striking: the taking of pot-shots from behind sheltering barricades, rather than the British hand-to-hand jousting. A French worker may resent and fear the alien bourgeois world: but when he meets a bourgeois, he is likely to treat him naturally as a simple fellow-citizen, without the chip-on-the-shoulder awkwardness common in Britain. For, paradoxically, there is a real and strong ethos of *égalité* and mutual respect between all individuals, when regarded as citizens rather than as members of a class. And this *égalité* produces a kind of legal fiction that the gross inequalities of income, opportunity, and way of life do not exist.

Class patterns are certainly changing in France today, but less through a merging of different classes than a blurring of the outward distinctions between them. Under modern conditions their interests and habits are drawing closer. A skilled worker may own the same kind of car as a bourgeois, and off-duty he may dress the same way; like Lancashire mill-girls, the new working generation is giving up its old class 'uniform' and is dressing like the middle class, so that it becomes harder to tell them apart. But the real barriers remain, despite progress towards integration in the *Grands Ensembles*.

One reason often put forward for Britain's post-war social revolution is the enforced mucking together of wartime; the French did not have this kind of experience, being split up and paralysed by the Occupation, even though in other ways this was a catalyst. But the social rigidity is due more than anything to the way the bourgeoisie has managed to retain virtual control of the secondary and higher education systems. Strange as it may seem, education in France* is in many ways even more closely divided on class lines than in Britain with its public schools. The State *lycées*, though in theory free and open to all, are in practice still largely a preserve of the middle class, and they alone provide a passport to higher education and the best jobs. The percentage of workers' children who go to university is slowly rising but is still little more than 1 per cent, much less than in Britain. And inside the middle class, the cachet of a *Grande Ecole* diploma produces a further distinction, separating the higher professional élites in industry from the lower bourgeoisie. These gradings stay for life: once a *cadre* always a *cadre*, and there is less opportunity than in Britain for an able man to win promotion from the shop-floor or from junior clerical ranks. According to one recent survey, of the 2,530 most famous or powerful people in France today, from de Gaulle to Sylvie Vartan, only 3 per cent have come from working-class homes, while 68 per cent of France's ruling élite is recruited from the top 5 per cent of the population.

Much of this is due not only to bourgeois opposition but to the reluctance of humbler people to push their way forward via the *lycées* into an alien world. There is still a feeling of 'us' and 'them': the feeling that used to be much stronger in Britain than it is today. A worker's son will sometimes enter the white-collar middle-class by training to be a primary teacher or a *fonctionnaire*; but he will rarely aspire to be an engineer or doctor. Within his own lifetime a man does not change class; and though his son may do so through the right education, his social mobility remains restricted. His accent may not give him away so quickly as in Britain; but his family background will cling to him more closely.

Inside these barriers, the character and the influence of each individual class have been changing considerably. And nowhere so much as in the aristocracy. In the days before 1914 the French nobility set the tone in France and in all Europe for taste, gallantry, and prowess. Unlike their often-so-Philistine counterparts in Britain, they were the guardians of national culture, and gifted young bourgeois like Marcel Proust were drawn to their *salons* as the natural forum for their talents. But in the past decades the nobility has been pushed into the sidelines of national life, though not extinguished. Few young writers or artists seek their patronage today: French culture has changed its form and passed into other hands, those of a bohemian wing of the bourgeoisie. More recently, the aristocracy has suffered a new blow through the loss of another of its

* See p. 309 (Youth with a dusty answer).

fiefs, the army. Since the end of the Algerian war the army has been stripped of much of its prestige and power and reduced to an instrument of modern technological warfare: no longer does it seem able to offer, as it once did, a glorious and dignified career to the sons of the provincial nobility.

Yet many of the great families, the de la Rochefoucaulds, the de Cossé-Brissacs, and the rest, are managing to keep their identity and their pride, by coming to terms with the modern economy. If they had done this sooner they might have kept more influence today: but in the nineteenth century their lordly code of values led them to scorn business and vulgar competition, and so they let the new empires of banking, industry, and technocracy fall into the hands of the bourgeoisie. Today, late though not quite *too* late, they are taking up salaried posts in industry, in banks, in the senior civil service, as the only answer to financial ruin. Economically, they are thus merging into the upper bourgeoisie, just as, socially, in the last century and earlier many bourgeois families succeeded in merging into the nobility and prefixed the lordly 'de' to their names.

With their landed fortunes eroded by inflation, taxes, and social changes, aristocrats often have to devote part of their new industrial incomes to the upkeep of their cherished family *châteaux*, if they want these to remain habitable. Other *châteaux* are falling into ruin, or have been sold; a few, the historic ones, are helped along by State grants. A family may spend weekends and part of the summer in its *château*, and most of the year in its flat in Paris, usually in one of the dignified older quarters such as the Faubourg St. Germain. Here the great families for the most part live unflamboyantly and discreetly, clinging together in their own exclusive social world, inviting each other to formal cocktail parties or to an occasional ball or banquet with echoes of past glories. And the rest of France tolerates and ignores them. For although the French public adores foreign royalty or the idea of an English *milord*, it cares not a jot for its own nobility whose doings find little place in French gossip-columns. It is one typical facet of the stratified privacy of French society. Snobbishness certainly exists, but not in the national limelight: it is provided by those bourgeois social-climbers who do still hanker for *la noblesse* and who make a pastime of collecting invitations to the right homes. '*Mais je suis reçue par les de Rohan-Chabot!*' said one insecure middle-class girl I know, in tones of pride. But if the rest of France lets them be, if they are not constantly Hickeyfied like the Duchess of Argyll, perhaps this privacy has helped the aristocrats' own true qualities of *finesse* to endure. Many of them seem to be cultured and gentle people, less grasping than the bourgeoisie. Many are liberal, though they rarely feel the desire or need to renounce their titles publicly like a Wedgwood Benn. The aristocrat's pride in his family name remains deep. Though the big clan-like family is on the wane in France, the nobility is one of its last strongholds, and the emotional security of their pedigree is still powerful.

Family influences are declining in the upper-middle class: the *grande bourgeoisie* and, just below it, the *bonne bourgeoisie*. This professional and money-making class retains much of its strength as the central ruling élite of France: de Gaulle is a typical product of the *grande bourgeoisie* and Michel Debré, a lawyer and son of a professor, of the *bonne bourgeoisie*. But the bourgeoisie's nature is changing as France changes. Traditionally its power was based on property, passed down through family hands and so necessitating close family loyalties and careful marriages. Today, the bourgeois family firm is yielding place to the managerial corporation, and bourgeois property like that of the nobility has been hit by economic change. So instead, the upper bourgeoisie now relies increasingly on income from élite salaried positions; and as it still controls the higher rungs of the educational ladder, a near-monopoly of these jobs is well within its grasp. The new technocratic power groups, whether in public or private services, are mostly from this class; and the general rise in prosperity has poured new money into the pockets of successful surgeons, lawyers, architects, and others of the professional bourgeoisie. These economic changes tend to weaken family links by making individual members of the class more self-sufficient.

The 'arranged' marriage has now almost disappeared, and so have large dowries. And with this has come greater personal freedom. The stifling world described by Mauriac and others, where family honour was placed way ahead of individual happiness, is relaxing its bonds. A grown-up son or daughter can today more easily escape from the family orbit without being treated as a rebel and outcast. But, by English standards, this is still relative; and even in Paris, the smart bourgeoisie of Passy or Neuilly remains rather more formal and conventional, rather less open to bohemian or other outside influences, than its London counterparts. Not only is there stronger social pressure to *sauver les apparences*; but, except in the small and artificial socialite world of *le tout-Paris*, one is much less likely than in London to find people of different interests and intellectual *milieux*, Left-wing thinkers and go-ahead bankers, young technocrats and way-out artists, mixing together naturally at the same parties and gatherings.

The upper bourgeoisie still makes strong efforts, largely successful, to preserve its social *milieux* against *parvenus* from lower down the middle classes. However, a new middle-middle class is arising in its own right, and its numbers and influence have been growing fast without necessarily bursting through the barriers above. Economic expansion, especially of the new tertiary services, has thrown up from the ranks of the lower bourgeoisie a new property-less but affluent group: sales and advertising executives, skilled technicians, *cadres moyens* in industry and public service, and those shopkeepers, craftsmen, and small industrialists who have managed to adapt to the times. This is an aggressive status-seeking world of new social mobility, still in the process of forming its own standards and tastes. These are the people who aspire to share Elysée Deux and

Parly Deux with the older *bonne bourgeoisie* (the *grande bourgeoisie* and the intellectuals keep well away).

Elsewhere in the middle classes, the rise of prosperity has been spread most unevenly. Many older people especially, their savings or investments eroded by inflation, and no longer able to count so much on help from their families, are living in genteel poverty. And a large part of the traditional *petite bourgeoisie* has slumped into decline, notably the millions of self-employed artisans and small traders now outclassed by the new consumer economy. Even the *petits fonctionnaires* in public service (postal workers, clerks, primary teachers) have seen their wages rise much less fast than in the private sector. Their ranks are now being infiltrated by the sons and especially by the daughters of the peasantry and of some workers— young people who prefer soft jobs as clerks or typists to the drudgery of farm or factory. The change gives them the status of *classe moyenne* rather than *paysan* or *ouvrier*, but in the case of a worker it may not benefit him financially.

Most of the three million peasants who have left the land since the war have joined the ranks of industrial workers, though some have penetrated the middle classes, becoming tradesmen or, as above, office employees. And the gap that these and other rural émigrés have left behind them has caused class structures in the villages to alter far more radically than in the cities. In the old days, as Henri Mendras has pointed out, * the village was ruled by an élite of local *notables*—the *châtelain*, the curé, the school-teacher, the lawyer—who acted as intermediaries between the peasants and the rest of the nation. But since early in this century, these *notables* have begun to drift away or lose influence: *châtelains* today often have jobs in Paris, while the calibre of local teachers has declined and so has the role of the curé. And the peasants, fewer in number but more edu-cated and forceful than before, have begun to take affairs into their own hands and produce their own élites. Laurence Wylie† has described how the village of Chanzeaux, near Angers, was ruled on semi-feudal lines till 1939 by the *châtelain* (who was also mayor) and the priest. But when the old *châtelain* died, the land was split up between heirs, many of them absentees, and the estate began to fall into ruin. The priest retired, and the village was left without leaders. Finally, the villagers elected one of their own number, a former cartwright, as mayor, and began to form committees to run the commune themselves, which they are now doing with great success. In recent elections, the new *châtelain* received fewer votes than any of the twelve other council members: top of the list was his own *fermier*! And the *châtelain's* children, who in the old days would address the local carpenter and his wife as *le père X* and *la mère X*, now respectfully call them *Monsieur* and *Madame*. The *châtelain*, a pleasant and liberal man, runs an insurance firm in Paris and uses part

* *Sociologie de la campagne française*, pp. 72–87 (P.U.F., 1965).
† *France: Change and Tradition*, pp. 181–9 (Gollancz, 1963).

of his profits to keep up the *château*, as I was told on my own visit to Chanzeaux recently. But other neighbouring *châteaux* have been closed or sold: one has been bought by a new-rich Parisian family, and another by a garage-owner in Nantes who has put in a manager and runs it as a farm. Not far away, in another corner of this highly traditionalist region of western France, the Young Farmers' leader, Bernard Lambert, told me how his own relations with the local gentry had altered since the days when his father, a *métayer*, was victimised by his landlord. 'Some of them are quite human nowadays,' said this fiery young Left-winger: 'You should meet my neighbour, the Comte de Cossé-Brissac!' To prove his point, he lifted the 'phone, '*Écoute, mon vieux, je t'envoie un journaliste anglais—d'accord?*' Astonished by the *tutoiement*, I took my leave of the Lamberts in their ugly, squalid little farm-slum, and drove under cover of truce through the social barricades to the baronial hall where the young gentleman-farmer count and his charming wife gave me *un scotch* on a Louis XV sofa: '*Oui, c'est un brave type, Bernard—un peu excité, un peu farfelu, mais il est bien.*'

Perhaps these are extreme examples. In some other parts of France there is still a good deal of conservatism and suspicion between rich farmers and small ones. But the trend is in the direction of Chanzeaux, and Mendras predicts the day when 'new peasant élites' will have entirely taken over from the old *notables*, when the small village will have lost its social importance save as a farmers' co-operative centre, and the new hubs of rural life will be the country towns, thriving with culture and agricultural technocracy. Increasingly, as transport and education develop, farmers are using the local towns rather than the villages as centres for marketing, shopping, and entertainment; and as the farmers become more urbanised, so the townsfolk penetrate into the country, buying up old houses and villas for weekend or summer visits. In Provence, and to the south and west of Paris, as many as half the houses in some villages are used for this purpose.

Thus one of the sharpest of French class distinctions, that between *paysan* and *citadin*, is beginning to fade as the two grow closer in styles of life and knowledge of each other. But the other sharp distinction, that of *ouvrier* and *bourgeois*, may prove harder to erase, since it derives not from mutual ignorance but from the direct economic and social subordination of one class to another, whose urban conditions of life may not be so very dissimilar.

The workers, as I have suggested, are becoming more bourgeois without necessarily assimilating into the lower bourgeoisie. Nowadays they watch the same TV programmes, sometimes go on the same kind of skiing or camping holidays, even dress the same way. And they are beginning to develop the same property-owning instincts and material aspirations, at least when they move into new flats. A university professor near Toulon told me: 'My *femme de ménage* is a practising Catholic and a good Communist and her husband is a dustman. When she comes tomorrow we'll have a good chat about the TV play we'll both be watching tonight. Her young daughter is a *coiffeuse* and one of the most elegant girls I know—her wedding photo was all over the local papers.'

Together with this goes an inevitable decline, as in Britain, in the old working-class emotional solidarity born of hard times. Someone said to me, 'People aren't so willing any more to spend their Sundays selling *Humanité-Dimanche*. They'd rather take the family off into the country in their new 2 CV.' Though they still vote Communist by tradition, and though a political rally in Paris or some other towns may still draw out the crowds, the class is beginning to lose some of its old sense of pride and self-identity. It is also becoming less homogeneous as its better-paid upper échelons, such as the envied 'métallos de chez Renault' and other skilled workers, develop new proletarian élites who, without becoming middle class, often find that their interests are closer to those of their own factory *cadres* than of low-paid workers in the old artisanal firms.

This new unrevolutionary passivity of the working class is reflected in the weakness and mildness of French trade unions, to which only 25 per cent of workers feel the urge to belong. And yet, despite the outward picture of regular wage-increases and relatively few industrial strikes, it cannot be said that labour relations are based on harmony. It is a cold-war stalemate and suspicion, more than co-operation. Nowhere else are the class barriers so evident as in industry. As compared with the turbulent, troublesome, but very human situation in Britain, in most French firms there is an absence of direct discussion between employers and workers. The sociologist Michel Crozier, who has closely analysed this problem,* regards it as initially the fault of directors and *cadres* in most cases: in all aspects of labour relations, and not only in times of dispute, they prefer to keep their distance through fear of losing authority. The failure of the *comités d'entreprise*† is one symptom of this. The workers resent the barriers, but are too proud or class-inhibited to make their own efforts to break them, and instead they plough their grievances into voting Communist. Bargaining therefore is usually done collectively, on a national level with the Government as arbiter, rather than within the individual firm. It is another example of the French tendency to formalise and depersonalise inter-group relations, in order to avoid awkward conflict.

If I have drawn a somewhat severe picture of French class divisions today, it is because change has been so much less apparent than in Britain. But change has begun, and the French themselves are very aware of it and of a break in the icepack after the long 'alienation' of workers and peasantry from any control of the nation's destinies. 'The working class is much less isolated than it used to be, the insertion of groups of workers in French society has probably started', wrote Georges Suffert in *l'Express*.‡

* *The Bureaucratic Phenomenon* (University of Chicago, 1964).
† See p. 33 (The Economy).   ‡ 26 December 1963.

On the *Grands Ensembles*, newly prosperous workers and middle-class families are beginning to make personal contacts that they never knew in their older homes. The new young generation, less bound than their parents by family conventions and appearances, are also strikingly less concerned about class distinctions; and, as at Bagnols, a teenager who at home has friends only from his parents' *milieu* will mix easily at school with children of all sorts. This is likely to develop as more workers' children enter the *lycées*. But often in past French history change has proved deceptive: society has shown a talent for regrouping under pressure of new conditions and then simply hardening its ranks once more. It is too early yet to say whether the new suburban contacts, the new youthful friendships, will produce a new climate or be absorbed into the existing system.

FAMILIES AND WOMEN:
FEMININITY, NOT FEMINISM

France has often appeared *par excellence* a land where the family reigns supreme, focus of the individual's loyalty and affection, of his economic interest—and even of his legal duty, for the rights and obligations of family ties were clearly defined in the still operative Code Napoléon of 1804. Many a Frenchman has spent his youth in a world where he was expected to regard cousins, uncles, and grandmothers as more important to him than friends of his own age, and where the family's needs and demands were put before those of the local community or even of the State: 'I cannot pay my taxes: you see, I've a duty to support Aunt Louise,' has been a stock French attitude.

Today, when set beside the waning of family life in Britain or America, France at first sight appears much its old self. Once I called up a girl I knew in Paris who lived with her parents. 'Do come round this evening,' she said, 'I'm giving a little party.' Of the thirty people present I was the only non-relative, and it was not any special family occasion. Admittedly, this was *la noblesse*, where family still rules most strongly, and therefore it was an extreme case. Lower down the social scale, there are plenty of signs of change at work, and especially in the bourgeoisie. The focus of loyalty is steadily narrowing from what sociologists call the 'extended family' to the 'nuclear family': from the big multi-generation clan to the immediate home cell of parents and children. The trend varies from class to class. In the property-less lower bourgeoisie the nuclear family has for many decades held more importance than the clan, and therefore the change is less marked. But in rural areas the big patriarchal peasant families are steadily losing their influence as young people drift away to the towns. And in the all-important upper bourgeoisie, as property gives way to income, as family managements disappear and sons disperse to new salaried careers in other parts of France, so does the close network of the big family gathering, subject of a thousand bitter novels, become less necessary for the individual's future and security, and also less easy to maintain. Many young couples are today likely to prefer pleasure motoring, or foreign holidays, or the privacy of a weekend cottage, to the old traditional family reunions on Sundays and in August. It is hard to be precise on this subject, for French sociology though abundant with data about working relations and economic habits shows a typical French reticence about invading family privacy: therefore I cannot state for sure that the average French bourgeois, say, meets his uncles and cousins 5·7 times a year against 13·8 times in 1938, though this might be so. But even this putative 5·7 would still be near the European record. 'I had to cancel my holiday in Greece this summer,' a sophisticated girl teacher of twenty-five told me, 'because, you see, my grandmother got ill and my mother was worried.' I doubt if her English equivalent would often display such a sense of duty.

On another occasion, a friend of mine who is a successful young civil servant invited me to spend Sunday in his parents' prosperous country home near Paris. There I met four generations of them, from his grandmother of ninety-two to his own children and their hordes of little cousins, twenty or more people, and myself one of the only two outsiders. It was delightful, relaxed, and very French. In other words, though clan loyalties towards more distant relatives may be fading, an adult's ties with his own parents and even with *their* parents often remain surprisingly close; and though between teenagers and parents there is less deference and formality than there used to be, children usually still live at home until married. Obsessive relationships between adults and their parents, especially between sons and mothers, are still a constant theme of French novels, and show how much this subject still preoccupies the French: witness Marguerite Duras's *Des Journées entières dans les arbres*, about an old woman's destructive love of her worthless son, or Jacques Borel's 1965 Goncourt winner, *L'Adoration*, about a man's inability to break the umbilical cord of emotion, or Robert Pinget's *Le Fiston* which treats of an old man's tragic mooning about the son who has left home without trace. If many younger French people today are trying to lead more emotionally independent lives, it is often not without a sense of guilt, or an awareness of the pain it causes to their parents who cling for security to a different family tradition. This may be so in any country: it is especially sharp in France.

The rise in the birth-rate, *le bébé-boom*, has perhaps done more than anything to strengthen the prestige and social importance of the young nuclear family. This rise has played such a key psychological role in the post-war French recovery that today, after more than twenty years, baby-making and baby-rearing are still regarded as a kind of prestige industry, as in Russia. The young mother filling her HLM with cots and nappies is now saluted as of more value to the nation than the old family patriarch holding up the pillars of society. Stimulated by the large child-allowances, the average size of families has swelled since the war, notably in the work-

ing class: on a small income, once a first child has arrived and the wife
has given up her own earning-power, it is often more economic to go on
and have two or three more, so large are the allowances. And in the middle
classes too, now that property counts for so much less, the laws of equal
inheritance are no longer such a disincentive to having several children.

These economic factors, plus the typically Latin adoration of small
children, have led to a veritable _culte de l'enfant,_ as it is called. 'Mais
comme elle est mignonne, la petite!' you hear them drooling in parks and
streets. The French are usually generous and truly kind to their small
children, and though a Frenchman may still react with narrow selfishness
towards neighbours and officials, he will often make big personal sacrifices
for his own children. More than in many countries, the golden ideal is to
get married young, settle down, and breed: the pregnant woman enjoys a
privileged social status, special stores for her like Prénatal ('tout pour la
future maman!') proliferate in every town, and the new suburbs pullulate
with the kind of images of fecundity that Agnès Varda satirised in her
film _Le Bonheur_. Some others, like her, suspect uneasily that this sacred
cult has gone too far; and when another director, J.-C. Averty, defied it in
a surrealist TV series in which babies were peeled, sliced, minced in
machines and sold in butchers' shops, the public giggled in embarrassed
outrage, some of them inwardly relieved to see a taboo exposed and the
Baby-King ridiculed. It was rather like _TW_3 satirising the Queen.

The rise of the nuclear family has brought an increased element of
sincerity and comradeship to married life. Couples are marrying younger
than before the war, and are freer to make their own choices: arranged
marriages have disappeared except in a few older provincial families.
This does not mean that every match is a love-match: French girls can be
shrewdly practical as well as romantic, and often have an eye for the
character, position, and prospects of their fiancés. Nor does it mean that
bourgeois parents do not still fight much harder than in Britain, and often
with more success, to prevent their daughters making 'unsuitable' marriages across the barriers of class or religion. When she meets her Jimmy
Porter, the bourgeois French girl may well have a secret affair with him,
but is still most likely to heed parental advice not to marry him. But this
is becoming less so, and Jesse Pitts reports: * 'An upper-class girl graduat-
ing from _Sciences Po_ wants to marry a young Jewish man who works in
movie-producing. Her parents offer her the alternatives: stop seeing the
young man or leave their home. She leaves their home and goes to work
for 750 francs a month in an advertising agency. Before the war nobody
would have employed her; ten or twelve years ago the job did not exist.
In 1962 she can live her own life long enough for the parents to capitu-
late.'

The increased sincerity of marriages has its counterpart in an easier

* _France: Change and Tradition_, p. 296 (Gollancz, 1963).

attitude to divorce, which is still highly disapproved of in theory but has become so prevalent that in practice it is often socially acceptable. 'Je n'approuve pas ce qu'elle a fait, mais je peux la comprendre, la pauvre,' is how an elderly Catholic bourgeoise might speak of a niece who had just left her unkind, unfaithful husband. The divorce figures, after a steady rise in the post-war years, have now levelled off at about one for every ten marriages, some 25 per cent above the British rate but below that of some countries. In this secular State, divorce poses few of the legal problems that it does in Italy. Although it is expensive, it is now almost as common in the working class as in the bourgeoisie—and twice as common in Paris as in the provinces. According to the opinion surveys, religious conviction or fear of scandal or family dishonour are no longer the main factors inhibiting divorce, when a marriage is on the rocks; fear of harming the children, or of financial stress, or of loneliness, rank higher. Depending on your views, you can see this as a decline in morals, or in social hypocrisy.

A Bill passed in 1964 removed most of the last remaining legal inequalities between husband and wife, as regards property-ownership and grounds for divorce; and this was claimed as one of the final steps in a series of post-war measures for the social emancipation of women. But the most significant fact about Frenchwomen today is that, apart from a small and untypical band of feminist pioneers, they are not really interested in this kind of equality. They care for femininity, not feminism; and all the foreigner's silly clichés about the Frenchwoman, chic, seductive, flirtatious, and sexy, derive from this one abundant truth.

Women in France have rarely been segregated or treated as inferior, in the manner of Spain or Italy. The Frenchwoman regards herself, and is regarded, as the equal of man—*equal, but quite different*. Given an opportunity to play the *same* rôle as a man, legal, professional, or social, she will often shy away in fear of losing her femininity, and the men will cheer her for it! France is still the land, cliché or not, of *la petite différence*: it is not the land of suffragettes, nor of the women's clubs beloved of Anglo-Saxon amazons. Women's rôle in the family, and in society, is a powerful one; but she lives and sees herself in relation to that family and to individual men, not to other women or the community as a whole. This is splendid, save that, today, this profound psychological orientation finds itself under pressure from all sorts of new factors, economic and social: women are being pushed and tempted towards a different kind of emancipation, and they feel deeply torn between this and their traditional feminine rôle. All the sociologists speak of this as an 'age of transition' for the Frenchwoman. Let us look at her dilemma more closely.

Frenchwomen were given the vote in 1945, by the reformist Liberation Government under de Gaulle (not himself noted for his feminism). But they have not done much with their new rights: 80 per cent are said to vote the way their husbands suggest, and if the rest have any political influence of their own, it is towards conservatism. De Gaulle, because he stands for peace and stability, has a higher vote among women than men, and this may have helped to keep him in power, so he need not regret his post-war feminist gesture. Women today are not legally barred from any office of State. But they seldom appear on political platforms; and after an initial burst of post-war feminist enthusiasm, their numbers in the National Assembly have dropped steadily, from 30 in 1945 to 11 in 1967, compared with the 26 British women M.P.s. In the 1967 French elections, only 2 per cent of the candidates were women, nearly all of them Communists or Socialists: only 1 per cent of the staff and committees of the Plan are women, and in all the shifting ministries of post-war years only three have reached even junior office. This state of affairs is due more to women's own disinclination to enter public life than to male bias against them. They prefer to wield influence behind the scenes (Madame de Pompadour is their prototype, not Jeanne d'Arc) and I suspect that Madame de Gaulle has had more influence on France's internal affairs than all French post-war women politicians together.

In ordinary working life, however, women have not shown the same reluctance, and in several careers there is now virtual equality. A girl of good family is no longer expected to lead an idle life at home before marriage: she goes out and gets a job. And in the universities, the proportion of girl students has risen from 25 per cent in 1930 to over 42 per cent. In the liberal professions, women's numbers have also been rising, and now account for about 15 per cent of the whole—20 per cent of university professors, 18 per cent of lawyers, 9 per cent of doctors. The editor of the current-affairs weekly *l'Express* is a woman, Françoise Giroud, and the world's leading woman film director is French, Agnès Varda. Only in industry and big business is there still often a masculine bias against women on boards and in directors' chairs; but even here, too, they are infiltrating.

Conversely, in the poorer classes, where for decades wives have habitually gone out to work, the rise of prosperity has now enabled many of them to give up their jobs and devote themselves to the home: in this *milieu*, to have a wife who does not work is often a status symbol. Because of this trend, the total number of women at full-time work, 7,500,000, is actually no more than it was in 1900, despite the growth of population. But women still account for a higher proportion of the total labour force in France (34·3 per cent) than in Britain (31 per cent), though less than in Germany (37 per cent). And France is nearer than most countries to achieving the ideal of equal pay for equal work: when the Treaty of Rome was signed in 1957, the gap between men's and women's salaries for the same work was 20 per cent in Germany and Italy and 9 per cent in France, and if France's gap has increased slightly since then, it is solely because she has been obliged to harmonise with her partners.

The main point to draw from these figures is that, in the educated classes, far more women are at work than before the war. And yet relatively few of them emerge as actively career-minded. A woman will work before she is married, and maybe again when her children are grown up or if her marriage collapses; but there is still a certain prejudice in bourgeois France against the young housewife, however gifted, who leaves her small children with a nanny or *au pair* girl and continues a full-time job. In Britain, we know the problem of the young graduate wife by the kitchen sink, full of guilt at wasting her expensive education; in France, the guilt tends to be the other way round. And even before marriage, as one feminist at the head of a big agency put it to me, 'These young girls come with their degrees looking for jobs, but there's nothing they really want to do, they're just waiting for the right man.' It is all a sign, in the eyes of some indignant feminists, that Frenchwomen are not yet fully emancipated.

The same hesitance to share a man's privilege was noticeable during the campaign for the 1964 matrimonial Bill: this finally abrogated the old laws whereby a wife had to obtain her husband's permission to open a bank account, run a shop, or get a passport, while much joint property was legally the husband's and the divorce courts were obliged to regard a wife's infidelity as more serious than a man's. The feminist pioneers and their male accomplices fought successfully to push the Bill through, but it was not particularly popular with women as a whole. As one leading feminist said to me, 'Many women felt that the Bill implied a mistrust of the husband. They felt they did not need legal equality, but would rather use their charms on a man to win their way.'

To live for one man, to use charm or guile to woo or persuade him, to devote feminine skills to pleasing him, feeding him, rearing his children —this may be a woman's instinct anywhere, but especially in France, and the French male provides her with an enthusiastic alibi. It exasperated Simone de Beauvoir, and in *Le Deuxième Sexe* (1949), a book that has less meaning in an Anglo-Saxon context, she gave her compatriots some tart precepts on how to escape from their self-imposed 'inferiority'. That famous book had some influence in intellectual circles, and in the first post-Liberation years there was even a small upsurge of feminism, linked to the existentialist movement. But since then, de Beauvoir and her co-militants have seen their influence wane, just as the numbers of women in Parliament have waned; and feminist themes, except for birth-control, have largely disappeared from the trend-setting women's magazines such as *Elle* and *Marie-Claire*, which owe their huge post-war success to their articles on fashion, beauty, home, the arts, and love.

There has never been much of a suffragette movement in France. Men and women alike have a fear and contempt for the independent, no-nonsense, masculine type of woman so common in England, and those Frenchwomen who do emerge as leaders of their sex are usually subtly and exquisitely feminine people such as Hélène Gordon-Lazareff, editor of *Elle*. Another such person, Christiane Collange, the mildly feminist but highly seductive assistant editor of *l'Express*, told me: 'Whenever I go to make a speech about the rights of women, I'm always especially careful to look soignée and appealing. Feminism here gives people the willies.'

So there is not much feeling of solidarity among Frenchwomen, and consequently very little of the club-activity of women's institutes and guilds in Britain or the legions of American sororities. Until recently, the strength of family links made up for this lack of clubbiness and in fact was a cause of it. But with the dispersal of families and the move to new suburban homes, the French housewife is beginning to feel her isolation. 'Put the young bourgeoise down in a new flat,' said one critic of this mentality, 'and what'll she do? Still spend half the morning telephoning to Maman to discuss what to cook her husband for dinner.' Or else she may overwork herself trying to do a job and run a home all at once, yet fail to ease her burden by linking with neighbours in self-help. I have described this problem on the *Grands Ensembles*, and how new attitudes are gradually emerging, born of necessity. In other aspects of life, too, changing conditions are compelling women into a different realisation of themselves. The new opportunities for higher education and careers, new forms of leisure, greater social tolerance about sex and birth-control*—these are opening wider horizons and providing escapes from what de Beauvoir called 'the slavery of the female condition'. And, consciously or unconsciously, women are faced with the problem of reconciling this new kind of emancipation with their prized femininity and emotional urge to depend on a man's world. This is their central dilemma. It is a confused question, much debated in France today, especially in the form of 'le foyer contre le travail'. A spate of articles, seminars, and lectures deal with it every week—and I quote from one of the best known of the many recent books on the subject, *Le Métier de femme*,† by the sociologist Ménie Grégoire: 'The feminists of the early 1900s who fought to snatch away from men some of their privileges would be very disappointed to see how much the equality that they demanded embarrasses women today. It is time to give a clear picture of the formidable confusion in which most women of the present generation find themselves: they try to reconcile everything while sacrificing nothing. We are in the century of the feminine *mauvaise conscience*. Every mother who keeps on with her professional job knows this perpetual feeling of duty ill performed. She lives by stealing time away, from her children, her employer, herself.'

This desire to depend on a man's world, on happiness brought by a man, may bring its ecstatic rewards, but also it makes Frenchwomen especially vulnerable and subject to strain. For there is no doubt that Frenchmen, those notorious egotists, exploit their advantage both emotionally and in practical ways; they even refuse to help with the chores because it is considered unvirile. Both before and after marriage a woman usually has to fight harder than in most countries to keep her man's interest in her;

* See below, p. 253. † Plon, 1965.

and though this is certainly one reason why in their forties and even fifties Frenchwomen often remain so chic and sexually alert, it may also explain those tense, sharp expressions, the hard lines around the mouth. They lack the puddingy relaxedness of English matrons.

My own subjective reaction is just this: often I find Frenchwomen ill at ease and brusquely defensive compared with men. Why is it that French secretaries, when telephoned by a stranger, are usually so much more curt and unhelpful than their bosses? 'Il n'est pas là—moi, je n'en sais rien, rappelez,' they snap, without offering to take a message. Yet when you do finally contact the boss, he is often charming and ready to help. Why, at a dinner-party, does the conversation even of a clever and educated woman often appear conventional and slightly stilted? Why are women, rather than men, the chief guardians of French formalism, less prepared than men to modernise a business or adapt to new office routine, or to get on christian-name or *tu* terms with friends instead of the endless *madames*? Why does the natural feminine reserve of a Frenchwoman so often have an uneasy edge to it, as if she wanted to assert herself but was not quite sure how, lacking either the passive shyness and sweetness of a Mediterranean or oriental woman, or yet the assured and emancipated ease of a northerner?

For the answers, *cherchez l'homme*. If anyone is still unemancipated, it is the French male, in his attitude to women. He may behave with gallant charm to a woman he loves, or desires, or wants to flirt with; he is still backward at treating a woman as an equal, as a social human being, when there is no sexual undertone. Possibly that is why at the dinner-table a clever Frenchwoman does not always feel at ease in men's conversation; and I am certain that it is often because French bosses are tiresome and inconsiderate that secretaries vent their irritation on outsiders. The qualities of the Frenchwoman—warmth, subtlety, finesse, loyalty—often lie buried, and they expect *you* to make all the effort to woo them out of their defensiveness. After all, they have much to endure: they bear the brunt not only of Frenchmen but also of many of the practical strains of living in a city like Paris today. And it is only fair to add that there are plenty of unprickly exceptions, especially among the younger generation, who are beginning to develop a new ease and confidence. Among the middle-aged middle classes the rudeness and strained defensiveness are worst.

It is in her sexual attitudes that the unresolved semi-emancipation of the Frenchwoman appears most clearly today. Generally she is *sérieuse* and romantic, though not necessarily virginal before marriage; and with part of herself she welcomes the growing climate of freedom and frankness between the sexes. But another part of herself is still under the shadow of all kinds of complexes and conventions, the legacy of a traditional Catholic society. She is often unsure whether she really wants sexual freedom, or what to do with it. And this is true of Catholics and agnostics alike.

Of course the idea of the Frenchwoman as *légère*, or of France as the land of unfettered *amour*, has always been one of the silliest of foreigners' clichés. It sprang largely from the tourist's inability to distinguish between the strict codes of French domestic life (which usually he never saw) and the manifest tradition of public tolerance which readily sanctioned conspicuous minority activities such as Montmartre night-life or the free-living world of the Left Bank bohemia. If you are on your own and outside society, then the guardians of morality ignore you—and so for many decades Paris has been a favourite refuge for foreigners wanting privacy and freedom. Even today, many of those couples living so romantically in sin on the Left Bank are expatriates. But if you belong to one of the rigid compartments of French society, than you must obey its hypocritical rules.

The tourist is often misled, too, by all the charming billing and cooing that goes on in cafés, parks, and buses. But this, too, is an aspect of *public* tolerance: so long as there is no one around who knows you, then no one minds or stares, as they do in some countries. You virtually do not exist, and so you can do what you like. And anyway, demonstrative flirtation is all part of the French romantic game, with men expecting women to be coquettish and women expecting men to be *galant*. But how often, among the unmarrieds, does it end up in bed? Much less, nowadays, than in London, where far more young people live on their own away from parents.

Certainly there is more sexual freedom among the young than there used to be, though the revolution in post-war Britain makes France look mildly puritan. On the one hand, French parents now more easily allow their daughters to go out with boys; young people have more leisure and more money for getting away on their own together; and the younger clergy are now much more liberal about sex. In some student and working-class circles relations have become very free, and some teenage girls are developing the complex, familiar in Britain, that they *ought* to lose their virginity. But though she may no longer be so chaste, the French girl of any age or class remains strikingly *sérieuse* in not giving herself unless she thinks she is in love: she rarely goes in for the kind of promiscuity common in Scandinavia and rapidly spreading in Britain. And all the evidence suggests that French unmarried girls as a whole, especially in the provinces, are still among the most virginal in Europe, outside Italy and Spain. There is a true story that when, in Lyon, a dead baby was found recently in a hostel for working girls, and all 144 inmates agreed to a police request that they be medically examined to see who could be absolved from suspicion, all but seven were found to be virgins. And according to the one serious Kinsey-type survey* in France, in 1960, over 72 per cent of married women under thirty claimed that they were still virgins on their wedding night.

* By the *Institut Français d'Opinion Publique*.

In some respects the social codes are becoming more tolerant. Not only has divorce become more acceptable, but the *fille mère* with an illegitimate child is no longer such a social outcast: her title has been officially changed to *mère célibataire*, she can legally call herself *Madame* if she wishes, and there are plenty of State and private organisations to help her with her problems or look after her child. Even pre-marital sex, according to the IFOP survey, is no longer regarded by most women as a dishonour or a crime but simply as 'rather a pity' or 'rather stupid'. Yet when family respectability is directly at stake, the codes still hold firm. It is still the ideal of almost every family in France, Catholic or not, to lead its daughter a virgin to the altar (or *mairie*); and one Frenchman told me he was deeply shocked when he visited friends in West Germany and 'The parents gave me the impression they wouldn't really have minded if I'd slept with their twenty-year-old daughter'. According to IFOP, more than half French women think a girl should not be allowed out with a boy till she is nineteen, and many still act on it. And only 27 per cent of girls under thirty say they approve of pre-marital sex even between fiancés, while few admit having practised it. Yet figures from another source reveal that 32 per cent of first children in France are conceived before wedlock, which suggests either an amazing level of fertility or, more probably, that girls do not tell the truth to opinion polls on a subject like this, nor practise what they preach.

Again according to IFOP, two men in three want to marry a virgin, or at least get engaged to one. Jean-Pierre Mocky in his shrewd and witty film *Les Vierges* (1966) suggested that modern French girls are inhibited by male taboos about virginity, above all else. He gave a satirical account of five young Parisiennes all longing to leap into bed but frustrated by various social hypocrisies and especially by their boy-friends' terror of deflowering them: 'I do not accept shop-soiled goods,' says a snobby playboy to his fiancée. As in any Latin or Catholic country, virginity in male eyes is still something of a sacred property, and the most dedicated womaniser will often draw back when confronted with *une jeune fille*: virgins are for marrying, not seducing. Mocky's portrait was deliberately overdrawn, but I think there is some general truth in his point that many French girls are at heart readier for sexual emancipation than society, and especially male society, will let them be.

There are still many strong conventions and *idées reçues* about sex which are only gradually being eroded by changing practice. The most damaging result of this climate is that there are still prejudices against proper sex education. Under pressure from parental opinion rather than from the Church, sex education is still banned in schools (though some teachers give clandestine lessons under the heading of philosophy or biology), and most mothers are too inhibited to explain anything directly to their daughters. The new nation-wide debate about birth-control is making some breach in this wall of silence, but slowly. And because they are told so little, many Frenchwomen carry throughout their lives a burden of superstition and guilt about sex. I admire French girls for their romantic *sérieux* and, when it is a true choice, for their chastity: but often it is not a true choice, it is muddled up with fear, inhibition, and convention.

While the pre-marital 'affair' may be rarer than in many countries, after marriage the pattern changes and I suspect that adulterous intrigue is as common in France as anywhere. Many French people resent this national image, fostered in ten thousand novels and films from Flaubert to Jean-Luc Godard: when in 1964 Godard made a film about a modern Bovary with the title *La Femme mariée*, the Gaullist censors sprang to defend French marital honour and forced him to change '*La*' to '*Une*'. There are many people who argue, rather more to the point, that adultery has grown less common, now that fewer marriages are arranged and divorce is easier. On the other hand, the growth of travel and prosperity has probably tended to encourage infidelities, at least in the bourgeoisie where adultery is more widespread than in the working class. There are no statistics: I can only suggest that, in a land where so many women are still torn between Catholic ideals of chastity and the impulses of hedonistic romanticism, the extra-marital affair is more likely to prove the norm than the pre-marital one.

I am also impressed by how very discreet, indeed secretive, the French are about their love-affairs—even when both partners are unmarried and it is not a question of trying to preserve appearances or to avoid hurting someone else. Except in a small Parisian bohemian *milieu*, lovers rarely live together openly, and, however free you both may be, it is considered vulgar to 'flaunt' your liaison by moving as a couple in your own social circle. London has now become more permissive about this than Paris, where even the very young go about together in couples much less than in some countries. Nor will a Frenchwoman easily confide her private life even to her nearest and dearest: a French friend of mine told me she once shared a flat with her most intimate girl friend who all the time was having a serious affair with a married man in the same town yet never dropped a hint of it, and my friend only found out afterwards, accidentally. And when on another occasion I told an emancipated upper-class Parisienne how disconcerting I found it, when with a group of young French people, even quite bohemian ones, that one could never tell who was involved with who, she said, 'Don't worry, nor can we. In France, we like to keep people guessing. I was shocked when I went to London as a young girl and everyone asked me who my boy-friend was. I said, "In France we don't have boy-friends." When I am with my lover and our friends, no one knows we are lovers. We each go out with other people sometimes too, and trust each other to be faithful. My private life is my own. I'd hate other people to know what I was up to, they'd simply gossip and make it seem cheap. And then it would get back to my family, who'd be mortally upset, so why should I cause them needless distress?'

You can call this a sign of civilised delicacy in a society—just as you can call the relative lack of discussion of sex and sexual morality a token of French maturity when set beside the endless naïve self-analysing of British and Americans who, as someone once said, 'have sex on the brain and that's not the right place for it'. In France *il y a des choses qui se font mais dont on ne parle pas*: de Gaulle is a good Catholic and some of his Ministers have mistresses; *bien sûr, c'est normal*, but a public man's private life is his own affair so long as he's discreet—except maybe in an extreme case involving criminal conduct, such as the 'Scandale des Ballets Roses' in 1957, when the elderly Socialist President of the National Assembly, M. le Troquer, was involved with some friends in orgies with girls under sixteen. But as for John Profumo's little fling with a high-class tart, the national crisis *that* affair caused in Britain was greeted in France with hilarious amazement: it is hardly conceivable that a French Minister's public career would be judged by peccadilloes of that sort, or that the French public would be surprised or outraged to learn of them, or that he should be expected to answer questions in Parliament about them. Even the divorce cases of well-known people usually take place in private in France, and though they may cause gossip among their friends, they are rarely reported in the newspapers.

This may be a sign of civilised delicacy, but I cannot help feeling that on the ordinary social level there is also a good deal of hypocrisy involved. Just as the lack of discussion of sex might be as much a sign of taboo and refusal to face facts as it is a sign of maturity, so the concealing of a love-affair is often part of a social pretence that restricts the freedom of people's lives. 'Ah yes,' sighed my upper-class Parisienne, 'of course it would be nice in a way if we could be together more openly as a couple, maybe live together. Of course having an affair under these conditions *is* a strain in many ways, with all the subterfuge it involves, often it's hard to spend the night together when we'd like to. But you can't have everything. Things just aren't like that in France.'

This climate of intrigue does at least help to keep the French romantic temperature running high, with the titillation of *fruits défendus*. It relates closely to the French male attitude to women, which is still at heart very Latin: women are prized feminine possessions, to be courted and desired but also to be protected from other men. Therefore, as an essential alibi of a masculine society, *amours* must be discreet. For all the apparent freedom and equality for women in France, there is still a slight hangover of this Latin mentality. Women who break the rules, by being too assertive or self-dependent, by trying to live on their own terms or develop their own morality, are not approved of and, much worse, are not found attractive. And most women accept the *status quo* because what they treasure above all is French male appreciation of their femininity. This they are given, abundantly.

It might even be claimed that the French have found the ideal balance between Italo-Spanish female subservience and America-Nordic destruc-

tion of the prized *petite différence*. Many women, at least, think so. An
English girl who has lived and worked for some years in France told me:
'In England when you're working in an office with men, they either
treat you as just silly, or if you're good at your job they forget you're a
woman. In France, they manage to treat your work seriously *and* flatter
you as an attractive woman, and I prefer that.' A French girl married to
an Englishman and living in London said, 'For all the difficulties of being
a woman in France, at least one is supremely a *woman*, and I find that
more deeply satisfying than English comradeliness.' And several other
Frenchwomen who have lived in Britain or America have told me, in
effect: 'In your country, couples are bound by affection and respect, but
they seem to remain a bit separate; in France, there's a sort of *complicité*,
a forming of a unit against the world, and perhaps that's why so many
marriages don't work, because romantic aims are pitched too high.'

The Frenchman's demonstrative delight in female company is therefore the Frenchwoman's greatest compensation for her various difficulties
—and she relishes it, even when she knows it is no more than skin-deep.
It gives to relations between the sexes a certain romantic tenderness and
intimacy, a subtle pleasure in being together, that is not always equalled
in more emancipated but less philogynous countries. The Frenchman
may often be a sexual egotist, but his egotism is not brutish or in-turned.
Partly to flatter his own vanity and sexual power, he is more sensitively
concerned than most males to see that the woman, too, is fulfilled; and
donner le plaisir is for him as important a part of love-making as his own
satisfaction. Hence his reputation as a lover, which according to Jean-
François Revel* is far better justified than the Italian's.

So the Frenchwoman is offered an atmosphere where she is easily
tempted to indulge her deep-seated romanticism, in a land where words
like *plaisir* and *séduire* have overtones of emotional delicacy that are lost
in literal translation. In a recent interview in *Elle*, a middle-class divorcée
of twenty-four says, 'On a envie de savoir si on séduit . . . de se confirmer
un petit peu vis-à-vis des hommes. Beaucoup de femmes font l'amour
uniquement pour sentir qu'elles plaisent. Ce qui est important dans
l'amour, c'est de séduire, et puis d'être limpide brusquement à quelqu'un;
de le rencontrer vraiment; c'est la chose la plus belle qui existe . . .': and
séduire means something not easy to translate: to win power over someone through the giving of pleasure.

There are drawbacks, however, to this tender idyll between the sexes.
Not only are women made vulnerable and sometimes strained by the
emotional dependence on male egotism; but men are not easily prepared
to treat them as friends or ordinary social equals. Many Frenchwomen
regret this lack of easy-going camaraderie: in France, a close friendship
between a man and a woman does not so often develop without ceasing
to be platonic or at least giving rise to gossip. A girl who knows both

* *Pour l'Italie* (Julliard).

Paris and London said to me, 'In London, if a man takes me out to dinner, I know I can ask him up to coffee in my flat afterwards, out of politeness—and it needn't mean any more. A Frenchman will always take it as *une invitation*.' In England, in ordinary conversation you can use carefully ambiguous terms like 'boy-friend' and 'girl-friend' which have no real French equivalent: *amant* and *petite amie* have much more precise connotations and cannot be used so casually. 'Mon amant et moi . . .' would cause raising of eyebrows; 'My boy friend and I . . .' does not. And a woman who in England might be described as 'having an affair with' or 'involved with so-and-so' in France would be 'la maîtresse d'un tel', with its subtle indication of male ascendancy. These verbal nuances indicate the national differences of attitude.

The Frenchwoman today is often unsure which male attitude she prefers. In a way she is pleased to be reminded so continually of her femininity—she regards a suave pass as rightful *hommage*, and the English approach she may find boorish and unflattering. But she is also beginning to look enviously at the more easy-going and emancipated Anglo-Saxon world; and that is the direction which younger French girls, students and teenagers, are now following. Among younger couples, for instance, a wife now does expect her husband to help her with the chores, and she no longer so easily accepts a man who will not take her own views and ambitions as seriously as his own. A very young divorcée told *Elle*: 'I lived for two years with a boy. He saw it as a one-way exchange. I agreed to share his life, take an interest in his work. Not he. My concerns were unimportant to him the moment they were mine. So I left him.'

Thus a new kind of attitude is now emerging among the post-Bardot, post-Sagan generation—a new assertiveness, but still very man-orientated. The present age is indeed one of mutation for the Frenchwoman: the old pattern of 'femininity, not feminism' is certain to be modified, though how fast or far remains to be seen. Some emancipation on Anglo-Saxon lines is inevitable. But male exploiters of the present *status quo* are not the only people who feel that the French ideal of womanhood contains much that it would be sad to lose. Françoise Giroud, herself something of a feminist, told me that she thought the French version of *le couple*, intimate and equal but different, might prove a stronger bulwark than other styles of marriage for protecting the warm human cell of parents and children against the forces that in some modern countries are threatening to destroy it. So the issue for the Frenchwoman today is how to become happily emancipated (in her relations with men both social and sexual, in her community relations with other women, in her career and intellectual interests) without sacrificing *la petite, et précieuse, différence!* She wants freedom, but her own kind of freedom. She doesn't want to be an amazon in the Crusades. At heart, she would rather stay at home and be wooed by a troubadour. And France would be the poorer without its troubadour spirit:

Bertrans, En Bertans, left a fine canzone:
'There is a throat; ah, there are two white hands;
There is a trellis full of early roses,
And all my heart is bound about with love.' *

THE BATTLE FOR BIRTH-CONTROL

There is one domain where Frenchwomen have especially lacked emancipation hitherto, but where suddenly a revolution is now taking place, in a climate of controversy bordering on national crisis. Until a very few years ago, birth-control was almost as taboo from public discussion as in Italy: now it is debated without cease, even on State television. Since 1920 this secular State imposed anti-contraception laws which liberals often described as scandalous, criminal, or 'medieval, when compared with the family-planning policies of Tunisia, France's former protectorate'. And it has seemed that nowhere has the Frenchwoman suffered so much from society as in the privacy of her own married life.

In the past ten or twelve years the campaign of a small group of pioneers has forced a breach in the veils of social prejudice, brought the whole issue into the open, and has finally driven the Government to accept a partial repeal of the 1920 laws. Public opinion is changing fast, But the campaign is not yet won: the pioneers still face a number of obstacles, of which the Roman Catholic Church is probably the least implacable. The most serious are the reticence of the medical profession, and the high level of ignorance, fear, and inhibition among a large part of the ordinary female public.

The aim of the law passed in 1920 was not religious but demographic: to help repair the human losses of the Great War. It prohibited all publicity for birth-control, including advisory clinics, and it banned the sale of contraceptives except for certain medical purposes. Since then it has frequently been side-stepped and long been overtaken by most educated public opinion; but only since 1967 has it begun to come under reform, and over the years it has caused untold hardship and frustration, especially to poorer people who could not afford the luxury of trips abroad to foreign gynaecologists. Most French couples still resort to the time-honoured methods of *coitus interruptus*, uterine washing, or periodic abstinence. Or they practise abortion; and, this being also illegal, they often do it themselves. There are about one million abortions a year, more than the number of live births, and five times the British figure; deaths from clumsy self-abortion, estimated at 10,000 a year, exceed those from road accidents. And most doctors have hidden behind the 1920 law. In 1964 a woman in Chartres died giving birth to her twenty-third child; after her

* Ezra Pound, *Near Périgord* (Faber and Faber, 1928).

fifteenth, her doctor had said, 'You mustn't have any more, do something about it,' but would give her no advice as to what. In another case, a woman of thirty-nine who had had four miscarriages, four still-births, and seven live births, four of them producing abnormal children, had great difficulty in persuading the doctors to sanction an abortion (which by then would have been legal) when she was pregnant for the fifteenth time and acutely ill.

A few thousand rich and informed women can avoid these problems. They go off regularly for their diaphragms or abortions to private doctors in London, Geneva, or Morocco: '*Elle va en Suisse*' is a stock whispered joke at smart Paris parties. But most couples have neither the means for this nor, more relevant, the degree of knowledge or initiative to take other, less costly steps themselves, such as finding one of the few French doctors who will help with birth-control. And millions of working wives, faced with the horrors of raising a large family under French housing conditions, come to regard sex and their husband's desires with panic, and greet the menopause with relief. So the lack of birth-control is one main reason why the sex-life of the French, despite their romanticism, despite their warmth and skill as lovers, has not always been the paradise of fulfilment that foreigners often imagine. But few novelists have ever dared say so.

This was the picture until recently. Today, all is in flux. In 1956 a courageous young Jewish woman doctor, Madame Marie-Andrée Weill-Hallé, was the first to declare war on the 1920 law by founding with a few colleagues the Mouvement Français pour le Planning Familial. Its first advisory clinic was opened, in avant-garde Grenoble, in 1961. Today the Movement has some 180 clinics and has been spreading steadily, with discreet support from the International Planned Parenthood Federation to which it is affiliated. The Government turned a blind eye: though the clinics could well be regarded as illegal under the 1920 law, Ministers have been anxious to avoid a showdown with informed public opinion that might make them look ridiculous. So a kind of tacit truce has existed between Movement and Government: but the former, in order to keep its side of the bargain, has had to resort to the most bizarre procedures in order not to flout the law too openly. When a woman visits one of its clinics, she is put in touch with one of the 1,500 or so French doctors who have agreed to work with the Movement, and he will probably fit her for a diaphragm. But the sale or import of these has been supposedly illegal. So, by an arrangement with the IPPF, the woman sends a ten-franc postal order and her prescription to a British clinic in south London, which then posts her the cap in a plain envelope. Sent singly, by letter post, they usually escape customs checks; an initial attempt to import them in bulk packets often led to seizures. Dr. Pierre Simon, one of Dr. Weill-Hallé's most militant colleagues, told me: 'Whenever I go to London, I bring back dozens in a suitcase for my patients. Once, the customs officer at Orly inspected my case, and they dropped out all over the floor. All the women near me giggled sympathetically, and then the officer laughed too, and told me to clear out quickly or he'd get into trouble.' And to show how contemptuous he was of the whole farcical business, he added, 'You can print that story, too'. It has never been quite clear whether the actual manufacture of diaphragms in France has been also illegal, and the Movement has been trying to persuade one or two firms to take the risk. In the meantime, at the Walworth clinic I was told, 'We wish our French friends the widest possible success, but if this postal traffic grows much more, we shan't be able to cope.' And it seems to me a sign of the changing times that London should today be providing Paris with aids to sexual pleasure.

This has been by no means the only example of the Government's hypocritical handling of the 1920 law. On the pretext that they limit syphilis, male condoms have always been freely on sale on chemists' shops (some forty million are bought a year, or just over two for each adult male); and even the pill is now beginning to be available, on prescription —officially, it is for curing a variety of obscure diseases. A number of officials at the Ministry of Health have privately encouraged the Movement, and so have some Ministers, though they could not say so in public: when the Movement invited the Minister of Health to the opening of its first Paris clinic, in 1961, the reply came back, 'He cannot of course appear openly on such an occasion, but he sends you his best wishes.' Hypocrisy is at least preferable to repression, and one might be tempted to argue that the law has been so cleverly turned by usage that it has scarcely needed reforming. But this is not really so. Not only has the law greatly added to the hesitance of doctors and manufacturers, but the Movement has never dared publicise its clinics openly. It has had to rely on 'bush telegraph', mainly among the bourgeoisie; and class barriers and female reticence to talk about sex are such that most working women still do not know of their local clinic. The Movement is a remarkable and rare example in France of effective unofficial civic action on a national scale; but, lacking official funds, it has to rely mainly on voluntary staff working in pokey and obscure premises.

Since de Gaulle, his wife, and many of his Ministers are loyal Catholics, official Vatican policy has counted for much in the Government's reluctance to end hypocrisy and reform the law openly. Just as the easing of Vatican attitudes in 1964–5 helped to bring reform much closer, so the stiffening of Pope Paul's position in 1966 had a parallel influence in Paris. The French hierarchy, like Cardinals anywhere, are divided and confused about the subject; but among rank-and-file French Catholics there has been a massive change of heart in recent years. Priests no longer come to the Movement's meetings to heckle and protest, as they used to in its early days: many of the younger ones even advise their penitents to use its clinics. Several Catholic bodies are now taking an active part in birth-control education, while many of the Movement's own leaders, and a high proportion of its clientèle, are practising Catholics.

The Communists are a little more hostile. Many of their leaders still cling to the old Stalinist belief that birth-control is a bourgeois subterfuge to win over the working class and weaken its numbers. Municipal opposition has so far prevented the Movement from setting up any clinic in the Paris 'Red Belt', nor has it yet succeeded in enlisting Communist trade-union support for its efforts to make contact with working-class women. But there are now signs of a thaw in Communist attitudes; and the rest of the French Left has been openly in favour of birth-control for some years. When in 1966 François Mitterand put repeal of the 1920 law into his presidential election programme, the Gaullists saw that they could ill afford, electorally, to stay silent or inactive any longer: and so they promised, and actually set up, a commission of enquiry into the use of the pill, but its findings they afterwards discreetly ignored. However, the national conspiracy of silence on birth-control has been firmly broken ever since 1965, and the past two or three years have seen a crescendo of discussion—in the Press, in long polemical articles by people like Ménie Gregoire in papers like *Elle*, in films such as Autant-Lara's *Journal d'une femme en blanc*, and even on State TV, where admittedly the evidence is sometimes carefully slanted in favour of the *status quo*. Public opinion has been moving steadily in favour of repealing the law; and most demographers and economists, although insistent on the need to keep up the birth-rate, doubt that the 1920 demographic arguments against birth-control are valid under modern conditions.

But the Government, for electoral reasons, remained wary of offending the old-guard Catholics: they are numerous and vocal, and they include Madame de Gaulle herself, who is said to have had some influence in these matters. So until after the 1967 elections the Government continued to sit on the fence, trying to give an impression of concern without actually making any changes, and clutching at straws of medical doubt about the pill or the coil as alibis for inaction. Finally, however, it did allow a progressive-minded Gaullist deputy, Lucien Neuwirth, to put forward his own reform Bill which with discreet official support was approved by the National Assembly right at the end of 1967, and will gradually come into force during 1968. This new law legalises the sale of all contraceptives by chemists, on medical prescription only, to those over eighteen (others will need parental as well as medical agreement). It will also set up a national centre for birth-control advice and information. These are broadly speaking the measures that the Movement itself has always advocated, and they mark a big step forward. The legal situation is at last catching up with liberal public opinion, and the Movement will now be able to function more openly, even though direct publicity in favour of birth-control is still to be forbidden. But in order to work effectively the new Act will clearly need the active co-operation of French doctors. And in very recent years the greatest obstacle to progress has been neither the Church nor the law but the medical profession itself.

Often her own doctor is the only person a woman knows to whom she can turn for expert advice: and she turns to him in vain. In 1962 and again in 1966 the Council of the Order of Doctors, the supreme French medical body, declared formally that contraceptive advice, and changes in the 1920 law, were none of a doctor's business; most older practitioners, whether Catholic or not, have been bound by a strong professional instinct that they had best keep out of the whole controversy, and many of them have never bothered to learn anything about modern birth-control methods. Of France's 40,000 doctors only 4 per cent actively co-operate with the Movement, while perhaps a thousand others give contraceptive advice privately. These numbers are rising (the list of doctors on the Movement's books quadrupled between 1965 and 1967) but most GPs, when consulted by a worried and ignorant patient, still tend to give her a lecture on the joys of motherhood and refuse to offer advice, even to tell her of the existence of a clinic. Fortunately, birth-control has at last become part of a medical student's formal training, and young doctors are becoming more interested in the subject. Now the law is formally repealed the situation will probably evolve more rapidly, for many doctors are cautious and legalistic and it is this that has been holding them back. But if there is no large-scale change of attitude, the Neuwirth law with its insistence on medical prescription does not make much sense.

This law, though it bars the under-18s except with parental agreement, draws no distinction between married and unmarried women—this will be left to each doctor's discretion. Here again the Act follows the lead of the Movement, which in this respect has always been more liberal than its larger British counterpart: marital status is irrelevant, so long as the girl is not under age. 'Nowadays,' one of the staff told me, 'you don't preserve virginity by keeping girls away from contraceptives: that simply encourages abortion, illegitimacy, and unhappy marriages.'

And yet Frenchwomen, wed or unwed, have proved curiously slow to take advantage of the Movement's offered liberation from anxiety, pain, and restraint. Though there is now a clinic in nearly every major town, only 120,000 women frequent them and no more than about the same number get medical help elsewhere. Although, according to one survey, even back in 1962 some 57 per cent of women were in favour of the sale of contraceptives, and of the rest only one in four was opposed for religious or moral reasons, when it comes to applying these views to their own personal lives they are far more hesitant. It is true that many women do not know about the clinics and some suppose, wrongly, they would be too expensive; but very many are scared. Old-style, anti-sex Catholicism may be receding fast in France, but has left behind it a widespread legacy of semi-conscious guilt, superstition and prudery about sex, even among women who have rarely been inside a church in their lives. And this is one of the greatest obstacles to birth-control. Dr. Weill-Hallé told me: 'If we are still far behind Britain in family-planning, the reasons are much less legal or religious than social or psychological. The first task of our staff at the clinics is usually to try to *déculpabiliser* a new client, to rid her of her complexes about coming to us.'

Attempts in a few schools to initiate education in sex or birth-control have nearly always been blocked by a hostile minority of parents or teachers; many girls even today enter marriage with the haziest ideas; and as recently as 1964 an expert survey revealed that 92 per cent of women were ignorant of modern birth-control devices. A woman who ventures to try out one of the clinics and is satisfied (as they nearly always are) may still be unlikely to recommend it to her friends; it is almost as if she had discovered some secret opium-den, a source of guilty delight. These prejudices are commonest in the working class, where there is often a political element too: because the clinics are not a State welfare service but a bourgeois-led private enterprise, many women, or at least their husbands, tend to ask themselves, 'What financial trust is drawing the profits from this new trade? Is the Patronat behind it all? Watch out, it may be another capitalist trick.' And this, allied to the traditional Communist suspicion of birth-control, is often a serious deterrent.

These attitudes have been changing under the impact of the publicity given to birth-control in the past year or two, though it is difficult to say how far. They seem to me to illustrate, once again, the lack of solidarity among Frenchwomen—were it not for this, one might have expected the bush-telegraph to spread more rapidly, even though the Movement cannot advertise. They illustrate, too, the Frenchwoman's personal conservatism and fear of change, even when offered change for the better. Were it not for this, the sheer weight of some kind of grass-roots movement of opinion might have broken down legal and medical resistances more quickly.

This affair seems typical of the manner in which many social and economic changes are taking place in France today. First, an intolerable situation is allowed to build up without anyone taking action. Then a handful of pioneers set to work, and progress slowly follows, haphazard, empirical, unauthorised, usually resisted by the strong social forces always at work to protect the harmony of the *status quo* against conflict. Then, finally, legal or structural reform is sanctioned, not so much to facilitate change as to regularise changes that have already taken place.

TOWARDS AN AMERICANISED AFFLUENCE

Material change is rarely so traumatic as psychological change; and if in their family and private habits and social attitudes the French are still uneasily torn between old and new, they show fewer complexes about adapting to the more practical aspects of modern affluence. After some initial consumer resistance, they are now throwing themselves into *la civilisation des gadgets* with a hearty materialist appetite; and two decades after the austere 'forties, modernity is as much the rage in France as in any Western country—modernity with an increasingly Americanised flavour.

The statistics suggest that individual prosperity has risen faster in France since the war than in almost any other part of Europe (except perhaps north Italy), though admittedly from a lower starting-point than in some countries such as Britain. But are the French today as prosperous as the British or Germans, or more so? It is a question often asked, and not easy to answer—especially in face of the seeming discrepancies in the French standard of living. A casual visitor, seeing the smart cars parked outside the tenements, the drab-coated workers emerging from glittering boutiques, and other perplexing contrasts, may conclude either that criteria of wealth are different from in Britain or that distribution of it is more uneven. And to a degree he will be right, on both counts.

The real purchasing power of the average French worker's salary is stated* to have risen by 85 per cent between 1950 and 1966; and in the middle and upper income-groups it has certainly risen faster still. According to other figures, overall private consumption rose by 88 per cent in 1950–63. One may therefore conclude that average real incomes, taking inflation into account, have virtually doubled since the late 1940s, the date by which they regained their 1939 level. Foreign comparisons are as follows. According to OECD figures for 1965, France and Germany have an identical annual production per head ($1,850), lower than that of Sweden ($2,280—the richest nation in Europe) or of Switzerland or Denmark, but above Britain ($1,700) and well above Italy.† From this we must next deduct the differing proportions of national production that are ploughed back into investment (26·4 per cent in Germany, 20·9 per cent in France, and only 17·6 per cent in Britain) to arrive at figures giving the Frenchman an income per head (including allowances) 7 per cent higher than the German's and 4·6 per cent above the Englishman's. Differences in the cost of living must then be taken into account. If this is roughly the same in France as in Germany, it is 10 to 20 per cent higher, perhaps more, than in Britain. So, if the Frenchman is more affluent than the German, he is still marginally less so than the Englishman. But even this calculation does not fully answer the question about living standards, which depend not only on purchasing power but on factors inherited from the past, notably housing: a man who owns a cottage may rise to the same level of income as his neighbour in a mansion, but without thereby having the same standard of living. This is why French families often seem to be less well-off than their English counterparts, despite equal spending power: they are less well endowed with a legacy of good housing and other such amenities. And they still spend their money in

* Statistics are from official and semi-official French sources, and from OECD.

† Since devaluation, the French, German and Swedish leads over Britain will of course have greatly increased, but the cost of living in Britain will have dropped correspondingly.

different ways. Although the styles of living and spending habits of the two countries are moving steadily closer, it is still true that the French spend more on pleasure, whether it be food, leisure, or holidays, and less on comfort and possessions. But the gap is narrowing, and if they can improve their housing, the French will probably overtake the British in standard of living within the next decade. Their expansion is steadier, swifter, and more firmly based. Many experts predict that by 1985 they will be the richest people in Western Europe, outside Scandinavia.

But will they, by 1985, have also succeeded in distributing their wealth more fairly? The fruits of new prosperity have been spread more unevenly than in post-war Britain: especially in the past Gaullist decade the rich have been getting richer proportionately faster than the poor. Expansion under a liberal economy, and the shortage of technicians and skilled workers, have tended to favour those with higher salaries or running their own businesses. And in periods of retrenchment such as that of 1963–5, it is the workers who have come off worst, notably through loss of overtime.

The French upper bourgeoisie today are probably better off, on average, than their English counterparts: one reason is that they rarely inflict on themselves the same burden of private school bills for their children, and so they can often afford two long, expensive holidays each year, and plenty of smart meals and clothes—especially if they live in a flat with one of the old controlled rents. The group faring next best in the race for prosperity are probably the skilled workers in growing industries: under conditions of full employment, they have seen wages rise fast without their having to fight for it. Even so, the gap between them and the *cadres* has been growing. From 1956 to 1964, *cadres'* average spending power rose 39·4 per cent, that of foremen and technicians 26·6 and of workers 25·4 per cent: today a *cadre supérieur* (senior executive, engineer) earns on average 3,690 francs a month, a *cadre moyen* 1,812, a qualified worker 955, and an unskilled worker 588.* These disparities are certainly greater than in Britain. And several other groups have failed much more obviously to share in the new affluence, whether or not through their own fault: older middle-class people living on fixed incomes, old people living away from their families, many small farmers and shopkeepers, *petits fonctionnaires* in Government offices, and workers in declining sectors such as the small textile firms. The official minimum legal wage, which aims to protect more than a million of the lowest-grade workers against exploitation or sheer starvation, has done no better than keep pace with rising costs and barely exceeds two francs an hour. And so today, if one Frenchman in ten is really well off, something like a quarter of the rest of the population are still close to real poverty—and disgracefully so, for a country that calls itself advanced and democratic.

But what of the others, the mass of better-paid workers and junior or middle employees—*le français moyen?* With the help of family allowances,

---

* French Government statistics, December, 1966.

and in many cases of a second income from wife or grown-up child, the average net revenue of a household in this bracket is today around 1,350 francs a month; and, provided they can find a decent home, most of them could be considered reasonably prosperous. The working classes are eating far more meat than before the war, and, another sign of prosperity, are even beginning to adopt the middle-class habit of saving part of their earnings. Cars, television, summer holidays by the sea, and other middle-class privileges are changing their lives. The percentage of homes with refrigerators has risen since 1954 from 7 to 64 (in Britain, it is 47); with washing-machines, from 8 to 45 (in Britain, 59); with television, from 1 to 53 (Britain, 88); with cars, from 21 to 48 (Britain, 44). After years of resisting a mass-consumer economy in the name of individualism, the French are now embracing it more eagerly than the economists expected. You have only to notice, as you drive through France, how the old faded house-wall advertisements for things like Byrrh apértifs have been giving way to strident new hoardings for the latest household gadgets.

Food and drink today account for no more than one-third of the average family's budget, compared with one-half before the war. Spending here is still rising in absolute terms, at nearly 2 per cent a year, but not nearly so fast as in other sectors. For instance, private spending on transport, travel, and telephones has risen 130 per cent in real value since 1950, and its share of the family budget has increased in this period from 5·4 to 8·2 per cent. Over the same years the sector described by the statisticians as 'health and hygiene' has risen by 140 per cent, from 5·9 to 9·3 per cent of the budget—in other words, the French are getting cleaner. Consumption on clothing, home equipment, and leisure activities has seen similar increases, and within the sector of leisure, café and restaurant-going are in relative (but not absolute) decline compared with the rapid advance of television, cars, and sport. These dry statistics confirm that affluence is pushing French spending habits closer to the British or American models. There is still, relatively, a greater emphasis in France on enjoyment, but the gap is closing, and the former reluctance of the French to spend their money on useful possessions is now sharply waning. And the patterns of pleasure-spending are changing, too: the old traditions of occasional lavish ceremonial expenditure, on a big annual banquet or family outing, for instance, are giving way to more routine and private activities, such as weekend motoring trips or visits à deux to bistrots. And some will feel that this is making France a duller and a less French place.

Another symptom of this change: the French now spend not much less money on their homes and making them comfortable (17·3 per cent of their budget) than the British do (21·9 per cent). In each country, about 40 per cent of this sum goes on rent or mortgages, and the rest on fuel, furnishing, and decoration. Le bricolage (do-it-yourself odd-jobbery), which used to interest the French so little, has now become a major pastime, linked especially with the new middle-class vogue for buying up derelict country villas for weekends. And even in respectable suburbs, a bourgeois husband is no longer so likely to consider it undignified for the neighbours to see him painting his own front door on a Sunday. In equipping the home, a family will pay less attention than before to the formal *salon* and more to smart new gadgets for the kitchen—somewhat paradoxically, seeing that the housewife puts less emphasis these days on serious cooking. But in working-class homes a big refrigerator is usually a better status-symbol than smart chairs, and many of them keep their *frigo* or washing-machine in the *salon* for show.

Armed with these luxuries, the housewife spends far less time than before on household chores, but they still take her three times as long, according to one estimate, as in the United States. The main reasons for this, obviously, are that the French housewife still has far *fewer* gadgets than the American and still takes her cooking far *more* seriously; also, as I have noted earlier, the Frenchwoman gets much less help from her husband, and is shy of collective self-help with other wives. It is noticeable that launderettes have caught on far less widely in France than in many countries: literally as well as metaphorically, the Frenchwoman has a distaste for washing her dirty linen in public, nor does she feel the same urge as an Anglo-Saxon for a neighbourly chat.

In one or two other respects, the French seem not quite sure how to deal with their new domestic affluence. Take furniture and décor, for example. Many sophisticated couples with a smart modern flat show a bias against filling it with modern furniture, and go out of their way to install antiques, often with incongruous results. Modern designs, readily accepted in the office or restaurant, are still regarded by many people as cold and inhuman in the home—witness Jacques Tati's horrified satire on this style of living in the film *Mon Oncle*. I think that this bias is now declining, and many well-to-do people now have new flats most elegantly furnished in a modern manner, often with Scandinavian influences. But the French are still drawn more strongly than the British to their own classic tradition, to those spindly straight-backed Louis XV chairs and formal settees that decorate so many bourgeois salons. The French have little equivalent of the comfy vulgarity of English pre-war style: their taste is either for the classical or the ultra-new. Neither in furniture nor in domestic décor have they yet found a satisfactory modern style of their own. Influences have frequently been foreign, either Scandinavian or Italian. But today they are now beginning to try harder, and with more success. The most fashionable decorator of the moment, a suavely enigmatic and bearded figure called Slavik, has forged ahead on his own with some rococo innovations that can be seen, in Paris, at the St. Germain Drugstore, the Elysée 2 Drugwest, the Bistrot de Paris in the Rue de Lille, and the Sir Winston Churchill pub near the Etoile. Many people find the results outrageous; others are intrigued and stimulated. Parisian décor is at its best when using glittering surfaces of glass and metal, and then in its flamboyant way if often achieves an elegance and lightness that far outclasses London.

In the important French domain of clothes and fashion, affluence has brought with it an increase in the general level of public taste—paradoxically, just at a time when Paris has been losing its pre-eminence as world trend-setter. But the true *milieu* of Parisian *haute couture* has always been restricted to a few thousand rich society women. And although it is true that this little *milieu* has lost some of its importance, and that there are fewer supremely elegant women to be seen in Paris these days, at the same time good taste has become more democratic and has spread much wider. Many of the simpler of the new fashions are nowadays quickly copied and mass-produced by the big stores like Le Printemps, at prices within the reach of secretaries and even of some factory-girls; and, ever since the war, papers such as *Elle* and *Marie-Claire* have been drumming notions of elegance into the heads of ordinary Frenchwomen who, as a general breed, never used to have any special claim to be so very well dressed. More recently, men as well as women have been strongly influenced by the new fashions from Italy, Scandinavia, and especially from London, and in 1966 the mini-skirt and the trouser-suit began to invade the French teenage market.* French fashion experts are quick to point out that this English invasion is strictly limited to the very young and to daytime clothes: in clothes for more adult women, and for evening or formal wear, the French claim to be holding their own. But wherever the influences may come from, there is no doubt that the ordinary not-so-rich French girl dresses more carefully and elegantly than even ten years ago, let alone before the war.

Elle, Marie-Claire, and one or two similar women's magazines can take much of the credit for this, and for the improvements they have prompted in décor, housekeeping skills, and especially in hygiene. Just before the war, when Frenchwomen were among the dirtiest and smelliest in Europe, *Marie-Claire* took the lead in a public campaign to get them to wash more. After the war this developed further, other papers joined in, the public responded, and the post-war rise in the sales of soap, toothpaste, and cleansing creams has been phenomenal. If the provision of bathrooms in the new flats has been one factor in the new cleanliness, the women's magazines can claim a share in the triumph too. Marcelle Auclair, founder and principal columnist of *Maire-Claire*, told me: 'French girls used to disguise their dirt with powder and make-up on top of it. Now they wash properly, and clean their teeth. Haven't you noticed how the Métro stinks much less than it used to?'

'The aim of my paper, as of *Elle*,' said Madame Auclair, 'is to show girls that "le bon goût ne coûte rien".' Both these magazines sell about a million copies a week; their appeal is mainly to the young middle-class housewife or unmarried girl, but they are read also by a number of older women and increasingly in the working classes too. They have little direct equivalent in England, being much more sophisticated and literate than *Woman's Own* but not as exclusive or glossy as *Nova* or *Vogue*. Stylish

* See p. 346 (Youth with a dusty answer).

articles on home and beauty alternate with brilliantly presented features
on the arts: these may be simply what Catherine Deneuve thinks of her
husband, David Bailey, or something more searching such as a five-year-
old's reactions to the Picasso exhibition or a long interview with the
Goncourt winner, Edmonde Charles-Roux. The papers tacitly draw their
readers into sharing a charmed world of modernism, success, and intelligent glamour; rarely are their Candidean pages troubled by social-
conscience articles about poverty or suffering, save in matters directly
touching their readers' lives such as birth-control. And though Marcelle
Auclair and Hélène Lazareff have worked wonders to bring more brightness, confidence, and sense of style into women's lives, they are under
fire on the Left for surreptitiously importing an Americanised ethos of
success and materialism.

Flip through these pages, or even through those of a more intellectual
glossy such as *l'Express*, and the same pattern of phrases will strike you
again and again from the advertisements: 'Apres les sweaters d'hiver,
voici les fully-fashioned des beaux jours. . . . New! Smart! c'est Dacron!
Votre Shopping Club. . . . Le véritable wash and wear. . . . Le drink des
gens raffinés. . . . Les chips Foder. . . . Night Cream pour la nuit. . . .
Sneakers mode 1966. . . . Pour les bébés, Baby Relax.' These, and many
others, I culled at random from single issues of *Elle*, *Marie-Claire*, and
l'Express. Whatever is happening to the language that Proust and Pascal
spoke? In the past few years there has been, understandably, a great
intellectual outcry against this invasion of French by Anglo-Saxon words:
franglais it is called, and in 1964 a professor at the Sorbonne, Etiemble,
wrote a whole book denouncing it. But I think that the invasion has sometimes been misunderstood. It is not that ordinary French people are
voluntarily abandoning their own language; rather, they are the victims
of a commercial conspiracy. Modern techniques of advertising, publicity,
and public relations are very recent arrivals in France, but now they are
sweeping through the land with hurricane force, and were seen at their
most spectacular in Louis Bongrand's American-style management of the
Gaullists' election campaign in 1967. Men like Bongrand inevitably get
many of their ideas from America, and adapt them cleverly to suit French
reactions; and this *milieu* has decided that the French can be conditioned
to accept a commodity as new and smart if it is given an Anglo-Saxon
name. The entire clothing and cosmetics world have now virtually
adopted English as their *lingua franca*, and house-agents and others are
doing the same. Some of this inevitably spills over on to journalists and
others who pick up the new habits of speech, but only to some extent.
Though the advertisements may talk about *un drink* and *le shopping*, a
Frenchman is still more likely to invite you to *prendre un verre* and his
wife will *faire les courses*. If they do use the English words, it will be
only as a kind of joke. Of course, words used first as jokes do have a habit
of ending up fifty years later in the dictionaries.

The alleged and much-discussed Americanisation of France, and the new craze for all things English, are matters I shall return to more fully in the final chapter. In the context of modern domestic living and affluence, I would merely make the point that Americanisation is not necessarily the same as modernisation. Because the Americans happened to do it all first, any other country that tries to modernise may appear to be aping America. But though the French may naïvely describe their new *brasseries* as 'drugstores' and their new *salons* as 'living-rooms', the flavour often remains recognisably French.

LEISURE: FROM THE TWO-HOUR LUNCH TO *LE WEEKEND ANGLAIS*

The French are a hard-working people, in their own not-always-so-constructive way; and though they have traditionally set high store by *le plaisir*—self-indulgence in brief intervals between toil or duty—only now, with their new affluence, are they facing up to the different modern concept of *le loisir*. 'Leisure used to be synonymous with idleness, at least for the working classes,' writes the sociologist Joffre Dumazedier, 'but today it has acquired the status of a *valeur*, like work.'* And it has won official recognition as such. Since the war, in France as in Britain, Governments and local bodies have shown a new concern with the need to help people use their free time positively: the Plan has a *commission des loisirs*, and the huge development of holiday travel, sport, and the mass media is accompanied by official attempts to promote popular tourism and to build centres for youth, the arts, and recreation.

In their new leisure habits, as in so much else, the French are steadily becoming more like other people. The Englishman who deserts his darts in the pub or his cricket matches, and the Frenchman who tires of his *bistrot* or *boules*, both of them turn today to watching much the same kind of T V programmes, or listening to the same records, or driving their little cars to the same kind of crowded beaches and camping sites. 'Modern leisure will be uniform and mutually imitative,' Dumazadier told me: 'In New York, they are copying Parisian terrace-cafés; London is filling up with coffee-shops, *bistrots*, and *discothèques*; Paris is building "pubs" and "drugstores".' Yet there are still some respects in which the French attitude to leisure differs noticeably from the British, especially in the way they like their free time divided up: that is, in the French preference for longer annual holidays rather than for shorter working hours.

The French take the longest holidays in Europe. Just before the war, workers won the legal right to two weeks' paid annual leave, a third week was added in 1956 and a fourth, under union pressure, in 1965. Now there are even demands in some industries for a fifth week. Holidays have

* *Vers une civilisation des loisirs?* (Seuil, 1962).

become a major national obsession. Nearly one-third of the population take more than five weeks away from home each year, and in the middle classes it is perfectly usual to spend all August by the sea or abroad, and then go skiing for a fortnight in winter. Added to this, the number of official public holidays (July 14, November 11, VE Day and the rest) has been growing with each new victory to celebrate, and now accounts for eleven days a year. And whenever one of these falls on a Thursday or Tuesday, many a *cadre* will *faire le pont* by taking the Friday or Monday off as well, to give himself four free days in a row. And yet, this does not mean that the Frenchman fails to work hard. It is simply that he works differently. Executives will frequently stay in their offices from 9 a.m. till 7 or 8 at night, while in the average factory the working day is from 7.30 a.m. to 5.30 or 6 p.m. The legal forty-five-hour working week is frequently extended by voluntary overtime, which makes it in practice as long as it was forty years ago. Given the new transport problems in many suburbs, the working man's effective week-day leisure time may even have declined since the war in a number of cases—and this helps to explain, as I have suggested, the dearth of evening activity in places like Sarcelles. Yet two workers in three, asked to choose between more weekday leisure and more money, say they prefer the latter—a sign, according to the sociologists, that the French have not yet achieved real affluence.

I think there may be several reasons for this emphasis on annual rather than daily leisure: the relatively low standards of housing, and the rarity of private gardens, both give the French less incentive than the British to stay in their homes; and despite the decline of family ties there are still very many people who regard leisure as best spent visiting parents or relatives in the country. There is also, in the moneyed classes at least, a new spirit of restlessness and wanderlust. Nor do the French have much tradition of indoor hobbies, in the English sense: the only French word for 'hobby' is the quaint *violon d'Ingres*, which implies not so much an amateurish pastime as a secondary professional pursuit at which one excels.

There is, however, one important respect in which the French are moving closer to the British pattern: they are giving up work on Saturdays, and as they have no word of their own for the Saturday-plus-Sunday leisure unit, they are forced to borrow ours. *Le weekend* is growing in social significance. More and more factories are closing on Saturdays, and the unions have now switched their main demands from longer holidays to the universal five-day week. In Paris ministerial offices, an experiment began in 1966 to give up Saturday morning work in favour of longer daily hours, and it seems to have been welcomed. The middle classes go away for the weekend far more than they used, and some workers are beginning to follow suit. Many more families in all classes would certainly do so were it not that the French still inflict on themselves the illogicality of State schools closing on Thursdays, not Saturdays. There are pedagogic reasons for this, and apparently 70 per cent of parents are in

favour of the *status quo*: although the middle classes might welcome a
reform, in poorer homes where there is rarely the money for weekend
trips, parents are often quite glad to have their children out of the way on
Saturdays.

You have only to stand beside one of the main roads out of Paris, at
7 or 8 p.m. on a summer Friday, to see the extent of the new weekend
vogue. Even as long ago as May 1958, at the height of the crisis that
brought back de Gaulle, the sight of that army of cars, piled high with
suitcases, cots, and children, misled a *Daily Mirror* correspondent into
writing a scare story about the threat of civil war: 'Mass flight from Paris
begins' ran his front-page headline, and the Pflimlin Government all but
expelled him for it. Today, as in 1958, it is not the threat of paratroops
from Algiers, but the growing strains of daily life inside Paris, that incites
a steadily increasing number of people to make for the weekend quiet of
the country, and as likely as not they will go neither to a hotel nor to
relatives but to their own little country cottage. The *résidence secondaire*
has become something of a cult among middle-class Parisians in the past
few years. Today they own over 200,000 of them within an orbit of 100
miles of Paris; and in the Yonne department, around Sens and Auxerre,
17 per cent of all housing falls into this class. Many are old farmsteads,
left empty by the rural exodus and now made over to the new bourgeois
sport of *bricolage*. Others are new weekend villas for the well-to-do. Some
35,000 of these are built a year in France, using resources that might
otherwise go towards new housing for those who lack even a *résidence
primaire*.

If there is not more evening leisure in France, it is partly because so
many people still prefer to keep to the old tradition of the two-hour family
lunch. This has always been the principal meal of the day in France;
and although in Paris the habit is dying under the *force majeure* of suburban commuting, in the provinces everything still tends to close down
from 12 till 2, and husbands come home from office or factory and children
from school. The Frenchman still regards lunch as something of a necessary human right; and even when pressed for time on a long car journey,
rather than snatch a sandwich he will probably insist on stopping for a
full-scale meal, and think you odd if you suggest driving straight through.
In Paris, professional or upper-class people who live centrally invite
friends home to lunch during the week almost as much as to dinner. And
foreigners, such as diplomats and journalists, easily pick up the lunch
habit too: living in Passy, half an hour door-to-door by Métro from my
office at the Opéra, I used to go home to lunch as a matter of course.

It is a practice that can be pleasant in one's own life, but is irksome
when everyone else is doing it too. Even today in Paris it is still hard to
get a hair-cut, or collect laundry, or go shopping, or do anything else
constructive during the lunch-hour except eat, and it is much harder still
in the provinces. Only in the past few years have a few of the larger banks

and stores begun to stay open, or close more briefly. But the French with their new American business influences are now coming to realise what a drag this two-hour break can be on a modern economy. At the same time, change is being forced on them, willy-nilly, by the drift out to the suburbs. The past few years have thus seen quite a revolution in greater Paris, where the percentage of employees who go home for lunch has dropped from 60 to 25 since 1958: most factories and many larger offices have opened canteens, while snack-bars and cafeterias have been springing up fast in central Paris to cater for those with limited means. Many firms have finally changed over to a uniform one-hour break, usually welcomed by a majority of staff, which enables them to close an hour earlier in the evenings or, more probably, to cut out Saturday work. The conservative world of the Ministries finally made this change, after much internal resistance, in 1966; but many small private firms or their employees are still resisting, especially in the *milieu* of family shops and businesses where old ways die hard. The conflict has often been acute: many firms delayed the change-over for years simply because it was strongly opposed by those employees who did live fairly close, and the staggering of hours to suit both sides was not possible. So those of the staff who lived in the suburbs found a cheap lunch where they could, and then had to spend an hour or more killing time. Or else, in defiance of sense, they still made a long trek home, often spending three hours or more each day on their four bus or train journeys.

It is usually the younger people who accept the change most easily. A journalist on *Réalités* told me: 'I live near St.-Germain-en-Laye. I have a big English breakfast with cornflakes, and hardly any lunch—this is still rare, but it's catching on. Our office is too small to have a canteen, but the girls bring sandwiches, and most of us seem quite pleased with the new system.' But older people often grumble at having to change their habits: 'It's upset my whole family life,' said a saleswoman in her forties; 'I used to get home in time to cook a big hot lunch for my husband and children, who go to school near-by, and we'd have a cold meal at night. Now, I have to stay at work and eat in the canteen, my family get the maid to cook them lunch, and I have to prepare a hot meal for myself in the evening.' In some other cases, curiously enough, it is the senior executives who have opposed the change most strongly: they hold dearly to their three-hour business lunches (either as a necessity or a useful alibi!) and they want their secretaries' lives to be accommodated to theirs. One manager told me: 'I usually stay here till 7.30, but my young secretary who lives in the suburbs leaves at 5.30 now we've switched to the one-hour break. Luckily, there's another secretary here who's old and lives quite close, and she doesn't mind staying till 7.30, so long as she can keep her two-hour lunch. If it weren't for this, I don't know what I'd do.'

The pressure for earlier office closing has not been nearly as great as one might have expected, even from young people, and the French often seem not to know what to do with extended evening leisure when they get it. They are almost as conservative about the time of dinner as about lunch: it is usually set for 8 or at earliest 7.30, and they will rarely shift it earlier in order to spend a full evening doing something else. Evening events, whether club meetings, cinemas, or theatres, therefore do not start until 9 or possible 8.30, and as so many people have to get up early for their work, inevitably most serious leisure activity is left for the weekend.

Thus it is not surprising that the main post-war trends in leisure habits and expenditure have been towards sport and recreation rather than culture and *les spectacles*. I doubt if the French as a whole, despite their reputation, are today any more culture-minded than the British, except for the educated minority of cinémanes and frequenters of the *Maisons de la Culture*. On the other hand, they are possibly more prepared than the British to find their own individual recreation, rather than be passive recipients of the new mass-media. Almost as much money is spent today on camping and sporting equipment as on cinema-going, which is in decline as in many countries; television* has fast been taking its place, but is still less dominant than in Britain or Germany.

Personal expenditure on leisure activities has risen by 250 per cent in real terms since 1950, and its share of the average budget has grown from 9·7 to 14 per cent. Of course the rise has not been even: a *cadre*, with three or four times a worker's salary, will spend eight times as much as a worker on leisure and seventeen times as much as a farmer. But workers and even farmers are today aspiring towards leisure spending as never before. One symptom is the immense development of horse betting, known nationally as *le tiercé* (three-horse bet): though still less of an obsession than in England, its turnover has nevertheless reached seventeen francs a week per head. The mysterious letters 'PMU' outside a café mean that it houses one of the 3,000 branches of the *Pari Mutuel Urbain*, the semi-public body that controls all betting in France and draws in annual profit of more than 800m francs.

Another trend towards the British pattern is that leisure money is now spent increasingly on possessions and equipment, rather than on more transitory, if intense, enjoyments. The French are buying thirteen times as many music records as in 1950, eight times as much photographic and film material, three times as many toys and musical instruments: yet the share of café-going in the average leisure budget has dropped from 40 to 26·4 per cent. Thousands of little old *bistrots*,† formerly haunts of alcoholism, have gone out of business. Even the larger, modernised terrace-cafés and brasseries, though they still do a brisk trade in most places, have lost some of their old importance as centres of social life and gossip: people

---

* See p. 427 (Arts).
† In England this word, without its final 't', is taken to mean a small French-type restaurant; in France, it is more correctly used to mean a little café selling wines.

tend to spend more of their time at home, at least in the new suburbs. Many cafés, faced with a relative decline in their trade in wines and spirits, are now trying to diversify their appeal. Some sociologists have suggested that what France needs are 'café-clubs', with some existing places turning themselves into a cross between a café and a youth-cum-arts-cum-social centre. It sounds a noble idea: but for the moment, cafés are adapting rather more haphazardly and with less sense of social purpose. Many have introduced juke-boxes and pin-tables (known as *le baby-foot*), and so manage to fill themselves with strident youth, even at the risk of driving away staider clients. Others, in parts of southern and south-eastern France, are becoming mainly venues for games of *boules* or *pétanque*, both a type of bowls. The French have not yet caught up with bingo, which is probably too much of a community game for their temperament—and, dare one suggest, too fatuously unintelligent? But many cafés, especially in poorer areas, have installed TV as in Italy, and the clients sit hushed all evening in the semi-dark: what a change from the old days of public chatter! They drink less, argue less, and have become, you might feel, more docile and less picturesque.

So are we to infer that the French are growing less sociable, or simply that they are transferring their sociability from the café to the home? And if so, does this mean a decline in the notorious French trait of domestic inhospitality? I am quite certain that younger professional or upper-class people, freeing themselves from some of the formal standards and obligations of their parents, are today becoming more casual and informal in entertaining friends as well as relatives, and are therefore readier to do it more often. Often they will extend you a casual invitation to supper at a few hours' notice, although they may add, apologetically, 'ça sera à la fortune du pot', half ashamed at betraying the old ceremonial standards. How much they entertain may depend on where and how they live. Generally people are more hospitable in the provinces than in Paris, where daily and professional life is so hectic that many families prefer to hug their privacy to themselves. The deeper you go into country areas the warmer the welcome, and once or twice I have found young farmers almost embarrassingly hospitable, as in Greece: 'Mais restez chez nous jusqu'à demain, vous pouvez coucher dans le grenier.' In Paris, on the other hand, even more than in London, a friend is likely to greet you with, 'Il faut que tu viennes dîner à la maison, on te fera signe,' and then do nothing. Bourgeois families who cling on to unsmart flats, because the rents are low, will often prefer to dine their friends in restaurants. Conversely, those who move out to expensive new suburban homes may find that they cannot afford to entertain much, or else that their old friends are now too far away and they do not make new ones easily among neighbours. Especially in the working classes it is still rare, through social tradition as much as economic necessity, to entertain people at home except relatives and a few close friends.

Among the bourgeoisie and the nobility, the old tradition of formality is still quite powerful. And though, today, there is more impromptu entertaining *à trois* or *à quatre* than there used to be, a curious gulf seems to exist between this and the formal dinner or *réception* with everyone in their best clothes and everything just so: the Hampstead or Kensington norm of regular little dinner-parties for six or eight, elegant but informal, is still infrequent. I think that the 1939–45 War, just as it produced a greater loosening of class barriers in Britain than in France, also prompted the English to relax their formal standards, whereas in France, conversely, formality was a means of maintaining national pride under the Occupation, of showing a stiff upper lip to the invader. This might be one reason why the convention still lingers so strongly that, if you are to give a party in your own home, then it must be done perfectly or not at all. Another reason is that far more bourgeois families still have servants than in England, and this makes formality easier: 'I cannot have anyone to dinner this month,' a leisured housewife once told me; 'you see, my maid has hurt her leg.'

'A la fortune du pot' may mark a breach in this tradition, but anything more involves, at least at a certain social level, champagne buckets and waiters in white coats, and workmen called in to redecorate the *salon*. And so, unless you are hailed in the street and bid to supper that night, you probably won't be asked for a year. In Parisian 'society', dinner-party habits are still Edwardian by most London standards, with printed invitation cards, probably evening dress, white-gloved hired waiters, rigid conventions about serving the correct food and wines; and, very possibly, much of the expensive silver, glass, and china will have been borrowed for the occasion from relatives! When it comes to giving a drinks party, if it is not one of the noisy *surprise-parties* of the very young when left on their own, then it will probably be the opposite extreme—a prim little *cocktail* or *vin d'honneur*, always with the same neat *canapés* and conventional talk, a style that still epitomises most social gatherings among the well-to-do over-forties and has set the tone for diplomatic receptions all round the globe. Younger people, it is true, are trying to desert this tradition. Sometimes they now give *saucisson-et-vin-rouge* buffet suppers where you eat off your lap. But the French often contrive to appear ill-at-ease when trying to be informal like this, and except in very modern flats this casual style rarely seems suited to their furniture or décor. Consequently, they do not give parties very much.

FROM ESCOFFIER TO *LE WIMPY ET CHIPS*: 'UNE ÉPOQUE TRAGIQUE'

In almost every subject I have touched on so far, from farms and factories to family-planning, I have suggested that the changes now emerging are imperative and fundamentally for the better, and that if some of the old subtle quality of French life is being lost in the process of modernisation, this is a price that France must pay, for the time being. But there is one sanctum of French civilisation, dear to all our hearts, where change is much harder to welcome and where today's modernisation may not be worth the price it entails.

The shiny new snack-bar, the quick-grill, and the deep freeze, having conquered half the free world, are now infiltrating the last and most cherished of citadels, *la vraie cuisine française*, which is not in need of reform save that it demands too much time and trouble for a modern nation in a hurry. Foreign influences, which have done so much to raise standards of eating in post-war Britain, are in a different way having quite the reverse effect in France; and so the quality of restaurants, once uniformly high, has been growing erratic and unpredictable.

This decline, it must be stated, is very relative: you still eat better in France than anywhere else. The malaise has not yet spread widely beyond Paris and a few leading tourist centres. In the ordinary provinces, *la vraie cuisine* manages to stand fairly firm. And even though French standards may be slipping, this nation continues to eat with a great deal more seriousness and discrimination than any other in Europe. Older people in particular still talk and think about food to an amazing extent, comparing in detail this week's *poulet à l'estragon*, say, with last week's in a way that the English, even today, might find boring or in bad taste. Eavesdrop on a conversation in street or bus, and there is still a large chance it might be two men enthusing over the flavour of the *quenelles de brochet* in their favourite *bistrot*, or working wives comparing the subtleties of ten different cheeses. And although the younger middle class with its 'drugstores' may be growing more indifferent to gastronomy, both the peasantry and the workers are affording to eat better than before the war and are helping to keep up the traditions. So the situation is not yet desperate. But there are clouds blowing up, larger than Mr. Charles Forte's hand.

I have often thought that, in the difficult years before, during, and just after the war, the Frenchman clung to good eating partly as a compensation and a constant in a shifting world: his *cuisine* went on tasting the same, it did not turn sour or betray him as so many ideals of liberty and patriotism had done; and its near-aesthetic pleasures did not, like the enjoyment of art or books or women, make spiritual or emotional demands on him in return. But today he may feel less need for this kind of solace, or if not, there are so many other material compensations available too. Television, cars, foreign holidays, smarter flats, and other possessions, have all developed huge new rival claims on the Frenchman's attention and budget—and especially on his wife's time. In the middle classes, fewer wives have servants than before the war and more have jobs, and life has grown more hectic. So today the *bourgeoise* will as soon toss a couple of steaks under her new electric grill as spend hours over a *plat mijoté* as her mother or her mother's *bonne* would have done. Many younger middle-class people even take a conscious pride in reacting against their parents' self-indulgent gourmandise, and some young wives feel the need to assert themselves by refusing to be a slave in the kitchen.

So I doubt if today the average young middle-class family really eats any more excitingly at home in France than in Britain (where standards have risen so much). They will still, however, eat a little differently: table wine is still far cheaper, fresh French bread is uniquely and compulsively chewable, the French are still much more likely than the British to know how to dress a salad or cook vegetables, and there is a wider variety of fresh foods available in shops open everywhere until eight or after. But the family *pot* of which you are invited to *prendre la fortune* will probably be no more than a conventional roast veal or chicken dish, followed by cheese or fruit; and the housewife rarely troubles herself with complicated sweets or puddings. When she entertains more deliberately, just as in Britain a young hostess may now tend to desert traditional recipes for 'amusing' foreign experiments.* She may prepare a *paella* or *moussaka* discovered on summer holidays, or adopt the modish new American barbecue habit, or even acquire one of the widely advertised Japanese *hibacki* kits. English breakfast foods like kippers and cereals have been creeping in, and one shop near the Opéra called *Produits Exotiques* turned out to be full of goods from Kelloggs and Crosse & Blackwell.

These trends horrify the gourmets—and so does the fact that, after a long resistance, housewives and shopkeepers finally show signs of thawing towards frozen foods. For many years after the entry of frozen foods into Europe, in France the gastronomic tradition prevailed: shoppers shunned goods which they felt lacked flavour and freshness, so grocers did not stock them and the habit barely caught on. Even today, the French eat only a fifth or a sixth as much frozen produce as the British or Germans. But the figures are now creeping up: several of the more advanced farmers' co-operatives are now doing their own frozen processing, deep-freezes in the modern supermarkets are at last growing larger than token size. You can even, if you wish, buy frozen snails or frogs' legs.

This decline in gastronomic fervour among the younger bourgeoisie has inevitably affected not only home cooking but also restaurants, which have suffered from this and from other new economic and social pressures too. Before the war, food was exceptionally cheap and many people ate out a lot as a matter of course; but by 1950 the number of meals served daily in Paris restaurants had dropped from a million in 1939 to 250,000, due partly to rocketing prices (these went up twice as fast as the overall cost of living) but largely to the wartime development of office and factory canteens. Many restaurants closed. Since 1950 this tally of daily meals has crept up again to 400,000, but the number of really good restaurants has not increased. Instead, the shortening of the lunch-break, together with

---

* I am not referring to formal Parisian parties, where the conventions remain.

other modern trends and foreign influences, has thrown up a rash of new snack-bars and self-service cafeterias quite alien to the French tradition.

The snack-bars are a good deal less successful than the cafeterias. The latter sometimes adopt absurd *franglais* names like *Le Self des Selfs* (just off the Champs-Elysées), but at least the food they offer bears some relation to French classic dishes (you can get an *andouillette* for about 2·50 francs, and maybe a *choucroute* or a *petit salé aux lentilles* for a little more) and though mass-produced it is quite edible. The cafeterias are crowded, cheerful places, popular with office-workers at lunch-time, and compare favourably with their English equivalents such as Lyons or the ABC. They now account for one in four of the restaurant meals served in Paris.

But the new counter-sevrice snack bars and light-lunch places seem to me a hybrid failure—an attempt to adapt the New York coffee-house or the Forte's or Wimpy formula, while keeping something of the style of a French terrace-café. An energetic and very American-minded young caterer, Jacques Borel, has even started up a small chain of Wimpy Bars in association with J. Lyons: you can get *un wimpy* for 1·65 francs or *avec chips* for 2·50, *un super-wimpy king-size* (3 francs) or *un breakfast anglais* (5·25 francs), flavoured with ketchup from an authentic round red squeezy Lyons flask and washed down, if you wish, with something as out-of-place as Beaujolais. This kind of bar is beginning to catch on with young French people, not merely with tourists; but prices are high by English standards, for the French catering trade is not yet geared to this kind of eating, any more than French bakeries are suited to producing Wimpy buns or sandwich loaves. And the French public still find it very hard to get the kind of cheap but edible snack that for three or four shillings you find everywhere in Britain, in pubs or snack-bars.

It seems inevitable and not necessarily regrettable that the French should want to move over to the snack or light-meal habit for at least one of their main meals of the day. France has always been a nation of over-eaters, where the middle-aged *crise de foie* has been an occupational disease, and where too much stress has probably been set on the tradition that a meal must, *de rigueur*, contain three or four full courses. In theory, it ought to be perfectly possible for the light snack and true gastronomy to co-exist, each for different occasions, for J. Lyons to lie down with the *carré d'agneau aux herbes* and with the *cuisine* of Lyon.

Today, both in restaurants and at home, people are tending towards smaller and less complicated meals, with fewer rich sauces and *plats mijotés* and more emphasis on good-quality meat cooked simply or on expensive but unelaborate dishes, such as oysters whose consumption has risen enormously. With the nervous speeding-up of life, far more care is now being given to dieting, and those who can afford to lunch each day in classic restaurants will often take only one or two courses—a remarkable break in tradition. But the catering industry is not adapting easily to these changes. Not only is it failing to provide suitable snack-bars to meet the new needs; but its economy has been threatened by the public's move to smaller meals. Many restaurants have seen their profits die right away, now they can no longer sell so many *hors d'œuvre* or desserts, or so much alcohol—and they have retaliated either by pushing up prices, or by slapping on large cover charges to dissuade the meagre diner. But the Government in 1966 partly foiled them by prohibiting cover charges, which had been making it more difficult than ever to eat cheaply and had begun to discourage foreign tourists.

For some years there has been a malaise among many of France's 50,000 or so ordinary restaurants. A minority are still doing very well— the new cafeterias and brasseries catering for cheap lunches, the smart expense-account places such as (in Paris) Ledoyen and Lasserre, the two thousand or so really good classic restaurants still patronised by gourmets (over 600 have one star or more in Michelin), and the new 'amusing' haunts in Paris or in tourist centres, frequented by French gay young things and by some foreign visitors. And so, if you stroll through St.-Germain-des-Prés or St. Tropez, or around any business district at lunchtime, you may get an impression of crowded prosperity: but the ordinary *bistrot du quartier* of the average suburb or town, hitherto the backbone of the French tradition of good eating, is far less likely today to be full of customers, and has been letting its standards slip. So the industry is being dramatically polarised towards strictly functional modern eateries, Anglo-Saxon style, and specialised restaurants of various types, for gourmets, tourists, or tycoons.

One of the worst of the new problems facing the restaurateur has been the immense rise in labour and other costs. Before the war nearly all restaurants were family concerns or else they exploited under-paid labour, and in either case their own costs were slight. But today, staff are protected by new social insurance schemes and working regulations, and this is a main reason why restaurant prices have risen faster than the general cost-of-living. Clientèle has consequently fallen away, and many owners have reacted short-sightedly to this by pushing their high prices even higher and inflating themselves out of the market. There is also a growing shortage of good young chefs, even though they can usually command good pay. Many a son of an old *patron-chef* decides that he would rather work in an office or factory, where the hours are easier, than follow in his father's rigorous footsteps; and so the old family *bistrot* dies or falls into less worthy hands. And in the smartest restaurants, an increasing proportion of the most brilliant French chefs have been wooed away to better-paid jobs in New York or even London. At a small French restaurant in Hampstead, the Parisian chef in his early thirties is earning £70 a week. Waiters, it is true, are in less short supply domestically than in Britain, for the young Frenchman is still much less likely than the Englishman to feel he is demeaning himself in this job. But here again, factory and office jobs are a lure, and the French are now beginning to import foreign labour.

Another hazard is the increasing normalisation of foodstuffs, inevitable *quid pro quo* of the modernisation of French agriculture. Here once again the French are beginning to copy American methods, with mixed feelings. The broiler has begun to oust the farm-reared chicken; fertilisers and machine-sowing are helping to make potatoes, vegetables, and fruit larger and more handsome, but not always more succulent; bread, so it is thought, has lost some of its old flavour; and Charente butter, instead of being dumped on the table in a rich golden lump, now tends to come in tiny, wrapped packets. Though the supply of fresh and non-synthetic food is still far wider than in Britain, it is easy to see which way things are moving.

There is an even more dangerous American import, too: the tourist. Many French gourmets claim that the biggest single cause of decline in restaurant standards, at least in Paris, is simply this: some chefs are corrupted by not having to work hard to please the new hordes of wealthy foreign visitors, notably Americans, who do not understand French cooking and sometimes are scared of it. Once I saw a newly arrived couple in the Franco-American Pam-Pam restaurant near the Opéra, gamely exploring a dozen *escargots* each and washing them down with strawberry milk-shakes. On another occasion, some French people I know were lunching at France's best restaurant, the Pyramide in Vienne, when an American party came in, ordered their meal from the great Monsieur Point, and then asked for Cokes to drink with it. 'Get out!' said Point, and he threw them out. My friends cheered him for it. Maybe the British and even the Germans are often as barbaric—'All foreigners accept just what you give them, without complaining,' said one French gourmet, a common if unfair French generalisation. But the Americans are the worst. And they enable some shameless restaurateurs to make a fat living out of French *cuisine* that is as phoney as a mock-Tudor pub.

All these new influences have combined to make restaurant standards far more erratic than they used to be. Some *patrons* are resisting them with heroic success, others are not. And so today, whether in a smart or a simple place, you often have no idea in advance whether or not you will get a classic dish correctly cooked and served, and whether or not you will get value for money. This never used to be so before the war. And I think this is why the fat red *Michelin* is no longer such a reliable guide: it has been betrayed by its own standards. Its elaborate system of grades and symbols worked ideally in days when standards were firm and unfluctuating: but today it is beginning to face the same kind of hazards as *The Good Food Guide* in Britain, and has not yet really succeeded in adapting to them. Its tastes are formal and expensive, like those of some elderly, rich uncle; and its small corps of inspectors, with such a vast field to cover, are often slow to spot the decline in an established place or the arrival of a better new one. In many towns I find that *Michelin* simply does not include the best restaurants, at least in the lower-middle price range, and today I prefer to use *Julliard* (for Paris) and the *Auto Journal* (for the provinces). These like the GFG include some personal description, and can therefore point the way through today's gastronomic jungle with more flexibility and precision than *Michelin*.

If the young French bourgeois cares less about gastronomy than his parents, this may not mean that he cares less for dining out. His tastes are shifting: today he may want his restaurant to be 'also something of an amusing spectacle', as one gourmet said with scorn. Until recently, nearly all the good restaurants popular with Parisians for dinner were sober, brightly lit, ordinary-looking places, either conventionally elegant (like Fouquet's) or plain and shabby (like many of the greatest *bistrots*). But now, in the wake of London, a new atmospheric modishness is creeping in. To meet a new public demand, a number of restaurants have modernised their décor in a rustic or arty-crafty style, probably installing canned music or even a guitarist. And frequently they recoup these expenses by skimping the quality of their food, hoping their new clientèle won't notice. The vogue now is for small 'intimate' restaurants with the accent on *ambiance*, open very late and probably helped along by dim lights or candles: yet in the old days the French thought it barbaric not to be able to see clearly what they were eating.

Just as in London, a number of new restaurants have opened in beautiful old historic buildings, artfully converted, and frequently run not by professional restaurateurs but—heresy in France—by moneyed amateurs. They like to specialise in such *à la mode* dishes as *viandes aux herbes de Provence grillées au feu de bois*, which you might regard as today's French cult equivalent of *steak Diane flambé* in an English country pub. This trend is most obvious around St.-Germain-des-Prés and the Latin Quarter, on the Ile St.-Louis, and in parts of Provence itself. At the Tassée du Chapitre, for instance, on the Ile St.-Louis, a young American architect and his French wife have opened an antique shop on the ground floor of an old house, and converted its exquisite vaulted cellar into an ultra-modish restaurant where young Parisian smarties cram tight at rough wooden tables, their ears assailed by canned Vivaldi and their nostrils by those aromatic herbs. Les Brochettes, across the river near the Sorbonne, pursues the same kind of ambience in a Greek style, while the charming little Maravedi near the Panthéon tries it *à l'espagnole* and the new Bistrot de Paris cultivates Slavik's *fin-de-siècle*. And all around St.-Germain-des-Prés, in new haunts with names like Le Bistingo, Le Steak House, or La Brocherie, the candlelight flickers on well-bred young faces and 'Provençal' décor, the peasant cuisine is what the Guide Julliard calls 'style camping élégant'—and who could ever guess he was not in Chelsea?

One obvious aspect of this vogue is that hitherto despised foreign cuisines are now coming into their own in Paris. The French (who rarely get as far as Peking) have always been acutely and chauvinistically conscious of other nations' inferior cooking, and gourmets would seldom accept even the best Italian, Russian, or Tonkinese dishes as anything more than quaint or amusing. But today, amusement and quaintness are just what many people want. Of course, there have always been some foreign restaurants in Paris, notably those nostalgic little Russian ones that arrived after 1917; but until recently they formed a kind of ghetto, patronised by their own national exiles or by a few tourists and curious intellectuals. Now foreign food is becoming *à la mode*. First in the late 1950s came the wave of *pizzerie*, all Chianti-flasks and Amalfi posters and waiters in Neapolitan costume (many of them Corsicans) singing *Torna a Sorrento* as they flicked their *pizze* into the oven. Now Spanish, Greek, Danish, Arab, and even Japanese restaurants are spreading in Paris, while the *pieds-noirs* have imported *couscous* and *mechoui* to scores of menus throughout France, and a few Tonkinese and Italian ventures are appearing even in provincial towns where till now foreign food was unknown.

Many of these new places are perfectly authentic and of reasonable standard, run by their own national chefs. Others, notably the slick new quasi-Anglo-Saxon ones, have a good deal less to do with gastronomy but are quite funny. The glossy St.-Germain-des-Prés Drugstore, for instance, offers a mixed Franco-American menu that includes barbecued spare-ribs, 'club sandwiches', hamburger steaks, and *Chien Chaud dit Hot Dog*—and this for its French public, not just for tourists. As for the British, for decades our island cuisine was a stock topic of mirth in Paris, and for years after the war the only English restaurant in Paris was The Tea Caddy, a discreet little teashop on the Left Bank serving Welsh rarebit and scones to sad expatriates and a few curious Parisians. But now the Parisian passion for mimicking all things English has scaled new heights: to observe this, go to Slavik's extraordinary new Sir Winston Churchill pub near the Etoile, run by a young couple from Auvergne with help from Watney's and Fortnum & Mason. Here, amid an implausible baroque pastiche of a Victorian pub, a well-dressed Champs-Elysées crowd (French, mind you) can be seen gobbling up *le London Lunch* (*rosbif et Yorkshire pudding*, 9 francs), *le Soho salad, le rice crispies*, and *l'Exotic cup* (pineapple ice-cream), and maybe washing it down with one of nine recherché blends of tea at three or four francs a pot, just like in an English pub. And it's open from 8 a.m. to 3 a.m., just like an English pub.

Some Parisians take this place with a snobbish seriousness, others enjoy it as a bizarre joke. In either case its appeal is very different from that of the less outrageous new restaurants from the Orient or Mediterranean. French tourists on their foreign holidays have been discovering that Spanish, Greek, Italian, or Austro-Hungarian food is not always as coarse or unsubtle as they had been told; and so, back home, they carry these new tastes into their own Parisian dining-out. And although these new foreign restaurants inevitably fill a far less crucial need than in Britain, I do feel they have added some variety and liveliness to Paris. True gourmets will still have none of it: they claim that younger French palates are simply losing their discrimination. Partly this is true, and no one can dare pretend that French cooking at its best has any near rival in Europe.

All the same, I am glad the French are beginning to bury their own myth that foreign cuisines thereby have no worth at all.

The true gourmets are still numerous, and they are now staging a kind of counter-offensive against the general decline in taste and standards. Many well-to-do people, and especially older ones, have developed a passion for hunting down and cultivating little unsmart, out-of-the-way *bistrots* where the cooking and the wines are still superb. Before the war, this was more a matter of spontaneous routine and there was no need to be so selective: now it is becoming a cult, a retort to the un-gastronomic cults of the gay young smarties. But whereas in Britain the restaurants that we Postgatians track down in this way are mostly new arrivals, in France it is obviously the other way round: the really good cuisine is generally found in the old-established family places, which in Paris tend to be run by provincial émigrés with their roots still deep in the soil of the Lyonnais, Provence, or the Périgord.

There are still enough serious eaters to ensure that these really good restaurants do stay full and prosper, at least for the time being. And I must stress that the new modishness has not yet affected the provinces much, where cooking is usually more authentic and cheaper than in Paris. And although value-for-money may have declined in the smarter restaurants along tourist routes, there are hundreds of small out-of-the-way hotels and *bistrots* throughout France where you can still eat superbly for ten or fifteen francs. Another encouraging factor is that the working classes still seem to care about their food: though a young Parisian bourgeois may today have little better taste than a similar Londoner, at a lower social level the gulf between standards in the two countries is still immeasurable. Witness the French *relais routiers* for lorry-drivers, and the British transport 'caffs'. Working families now have the money to buy much more meat and fresh vegetables than before the war, and meat consumption is the highest in Europe after Belgium. As the working-class wife, unlike the bourgeois wife, is less likely than before the war to have a job, she may spend more time on elaborate dishes. Henri Gault, co-author of the *Julliard* guides, told me: 'Wives in this class still cook *pot-au-feu* or *bœuf en daube*, and their husbands expect it. At the small factory near where I live, workers bring dishes like *petit salé aux lentilles* or *bœuf bourguignonne* in canisters for their picnic lunches, cooked by their wives, and they heat them up in the factory. But at Sarcelles, where the working class *s'embourgeoise*, all that is disappearing.'

Although many French may have now become negligent about gastronomy, they still have it in their bones: in Britain it is still something of a self-conscious minority interest, often verging on the chi-chi or vulgar. Scratch an Englishman guzzling his *tournedos Rossini* in a plushy Midlands roadhouse, and you will find a ketchup-and-chips man, even a Wincarnis man; scratch a Frenchman in his 'drugstore' or candlelit vault, and you will often find a gourmet playing truant. Recently in

Grenoble I went to an ordinary routine luncheon in the Préfecture for some local councillors: we had *lotte à l'armoricaine* followed by *pintadeau farci aux morilles*, with superb cheeses and *profiterolles*—all of it memorable and magnificent. Does an English county council ever entertain like that?

But how long can it last? What will have happened in France in ten or twenty years' time? Frozen foods, packaging, snack-bars, and industrialised catering will sweep their way forward through sheer necessity and economic momentum. Jacques Borel, the clever young tycoon in the vanguard of this movement, told me: 'In France, as elsewhere, the future is with the big chains. Individual restaurants just won't be viable any more—all but a few. Restaurants today should be run by accountants, not by *patrons* who see themselves as artists. I'm now opening a chain of *de luxe* steak houses with a small menu of grills, London or New York style. Not many people ask for elaborate sauces any more, so sauces can go to hell, they're too much trouble. And if Paris today is copying New York ten years late, be sure that in France the provinces *always* copy Paris, twenty years later still. I'm not saying that gastronomy will die: but it'll end up confined to just 200 or so expensive restaurants, as in Britain.'

Borel, who now owns more than 100 cheap restaurants in addition to his Wimpys, has the convincing air of a man who knows what he is doing. But there is one possible alternative to the picture he gives of little islands of real cooking in an ocean of hamburgers. It might be possible to make industrial labour-saving techniques into the ally of classic recipes, not their enemy. Methods of dehydration and deep-freezing are still far from perfected: and one day, a *coq-au-vin* mass pre-cooked in this way by an expert might taste almost as good as the real thing, whatever we purists now fear. And by then it might seem as unusual to order a freshly cooked dish of this kind as it is today to buy hand-made clothes or furniture. It will not be beyond the wit of the French to pioneer in this field, allying science to traditional quality.

Even so, something will be lost, and the individual restaurateur will become a rare craftsman like the designers of hand-printed fabrics or leather-bound books. Nearly all gastronomes sadly agree with Borel that the present polarisation is bound to proceed and that the number of 'serious' restaurants will fall drastically. They will continue to find clients —but how long, in practice, will they keep up their standards? For centuries, the greatness of French cuisine has depended on its grass-roots tradition: it has belonged to workers and peasants as much as to the rich, it has not been imposed from outside by an élite as in Britain. Its genius has grown from the marrow of the nation, like music in Germany, sport in Australia, art in medieval Italy. Cut away these grass-roots, replace them with snack-bars, push gastronomy into a ghetto for specialists, and it might well wither. So the French will sacrifice their high level of daily cuisine on the altar of modernism, and a new generation will grow up, not noticing what has been lost. Borel is sending sauces to hell—and

Pierre Grobel, a leading gastronome, laments, 'La base essentielle de la cuisine, c'est la sauce. Mais la sauce se meurt. Nous vivons une époche tragique!'

THE HOLIDAY OBSESSION: HAPPINESS IS A TAHITIAN STRAW-VILLAGE IN SICILY

If cuisine is ceasing to be national indulgence number one, it is easy to see what is taking its place. *L'Express* wrote recently: 'Is not the myth of holidays a specifically French phenomenon? We are the first to have made it a national institution, a collective dream. Psychologically, the French think about holidays all through the year.' Of course, others do so too: the post-war growth of tourism is not confined to the French, and the number of people who take holidays away from home is still lower in France than in Britain. But *l'Express* may be right in a way: there are few countries where the annual urge to get away from it all has grown quite so powerful, or where failure to do so is quite such a cause of discontent. In London, many of us work peacefully through all the dog-days of summer: in Paris, by the end of June people are talking of nothing but *les vacances*, and their irritation with the city has grown visibly near breaking-point.

Before the war the well-to-do took long holidays but few others did so too. Now French wage-earners have secured for themselves the longest annual paid leave in Europe, and the numbers taking holidays away from home each year (50 per cent of the population) are twice as great as in 1939. Many workers now leave home for the sea or mountains, and many others would do the same if they felt they could afford it: they stay idle and envious in their HLMs. Even farmers, who account for nearly half of the 50 per cent of stay-at-homes, are beginning to dream of the holidays they've never yet had in their lives: *Nous aussi, nous voulons voir la mer*, are the placards you sometimes see in summer along the routes to the crowded beaches. Only 9 per cent of farmers, and 12 per cent of farm-labourers, take holidays.

The strongest element in the new holiday cult seems to be an urge towards a 'return to nature'. Previously the French city-dweller often felt ill-at-ease in the deep country with its despised, alien peasantry: he preferred urban resorts like Biarritz with casinos and promenades, or else the orderliness of some family *château* or villa. But today the vogue is all for going native, and millions are happy to lose themselves amid the lonelier mountains or beaches of this huge and still unspoilt land. Hotels and *pensions* with their mounting prices have lost ground heavily to the new craze for cheap camping holidays: the numbers who practise *le camping* have risen since 1950 from one to well over five million a year, and though in August it may look as if all of them have flocked at once to the Côte d'Azur, in fact there are plenty elsewhere too. Skiing, sailing, swimming, cycling, and other holiday recreations have also increased hugely in popularity. And whereas the less sophisticated Englishman usually likes to recreate his own home environment on holiday, in his well-equipped caravan, his Butlin's camp or his jolly boarding-house, the modern Frenchman tends to prefer as complete a change as possible, to wear as little as weather and decency will allow, and to scrabble amid pine-needles in a tent. Caravans are still rare, and have very low social prestige.

Maybe this return to nature marks a sub-conscious national desire to compensate for the desertion of agricultural traditions. Certainly it is a reaction against urbanisation, to which the French are not adapting easily. Sociologists are therefore unsure whether the frenetic urge to escape to a new life is a token of healthy adventurousness or of maladjustment. One of them, Michel Crozier, blames the holiday mania on the rigidities and tensions of French society and office life where, he says, 'no one is truly at ease or in his right place, and so the French *need* holidays more than, say, the Americans.' * Many Frenchmen are thus looking not only for change and relaxation on holiday, but for a social liberation they do not find in their own lives. Many of them, it is true, still take the long, quiet, traditional family holiday amid lots of relatives, in grand-mère's villa in the Dordogne or tante Louise's *château* in Burgundy: but this habit is declining, and instead there is a new emphasis on holidays at once more collective and more individual—on the *colonie de vacances*, the holiday village or big skiing party, where everyone is democratically equal, yet liberated from the emotional ties *chez* tante Louise.

Most surprisingly, the French are now touring outside their own frontiers as much as the sun-starved British, and this never used to be so. The reasons may be partly economic (Italy and especially Spain are both cheaper than France, and not far away) but they are also psychological. The rise of Europeanism and the decline of French nationalism† mean that the French, although still chauvinistic, are much less insular than they used to be, or than the British still are: at least, they have grown much more aware of other peoples and curious about how they live, even though they still feel highly competitive and touchily superior. The growth of air and car travel have obviously played their part too. The foreign travel allowance has nearly always been more generous than in Britain, and restrictions have now been lifted altogether. French tourist spending abroad rose sixfold between 1950 and 1959, and today more than one French holiday in seven is spent abroad, a higher proportion than in Britain, where the tradition of foreign travel is much greater and the climatic incentive for it much stronger. And so the nation that has always ranked beside Italy as one of the two leading tourist countries of Europe now finds itself, since 1965, on the verge of deficit: although revenue from foreign visitors to France is still rising, French tourists now spend as

* *L'Express*, 25 July 1963.
† Despite de Gaulle—see p. 450 (Conclusion).

much money abroad as the industry earns from foreigners in France. Three million go annually to Spain for a night or longer—excluding those who cross the frontier on day-trips—and a minority venture much farther, to Israel, Morocco, Russia, or Greece (now flooded with French philhellenes). These are usually the more educated French, and on holiday abroad they often give the impression of being more culture-conscious than other Europeans. In the south of Spain the beaches are crowded with reddening Teutons and Britons, and the churches and museums, relatively, with Frenchmen in shorts absorbed in academic guide-books. This impression may be misleading: there are plenty of Frenchmen who also want to redden on beaches, but for obvious reasons they are still relatively more likely than a northerner to stay in their own country. Even so, Frenchmen by virtue of their rigorous education still seem to pay higher attention than most peoples to cultural sight-seeing: some through snobbery or a sense of duty, many with real feeling and scholar-ship. Even house-agents in France, advertising villas in Spain, consider it a useful selling-point to add when they can, 'Fascinating medieval abbey near by'.

All that I have said about the new French holiday ideals could be summed up quintessentially in one magic phrase: Club Méditerranée. This is the Great French Dream made reality, sorely deserving its French Scott Fitzgerald. It is probably the most remarkable organised holiday venture the world has yet seen, and its success reveals a great deal about the spirit of the French today.

It all began in 1950 when Gérard Blitz, a tall blond athlete from Antwerp, founded a small informal holiday-camp on Majorca with a set of U.S. Army surplus tents, and was surprised when as many as 2,600 people answered his advertisement to join him there. The idea snow-balled and became a permanent holiday club with a current membership of half-a-million; and today Blitz and his co-director Gilbert Trigano operate a score of those famous little straw-hut summer 'villages' around the sea that lends the Club its name, together with a dozen others in winter ski-centres. Like Edouard Leclerc, Blitz is something of a visionary at work in a cut-throat competitive field, and his Club applies skilful organisation and packaging to his own philosophy of human happiness. 'Today's luxury,' he has written, 'is not comfort but open space. Adven-ture is dead and solitude is dying, in today's crowded resorts. But if you can no longer go on holiday alone without finding yourself in a crowd, it ought to be possible to go off in a crowd in order to find yourself alone. The individual has a horror of promiscuity, but he does need community. And so he needs a very flexible holiday community where at any moment he can join in, or escape—a strange cocktail of *la vie de château* and *la vie de sauvage*.' And the Club's villages have been carefully developed to satisfy some of the deepest French desires: individualism amid camara-derie; sophistication amid primitive return-to-nature; a blend of sport, sensuality, culture, and exotic foreign settings; a harmless once-a-year escape from the barriers and tensions of French society into a new kind of never-never-land fraternity. Today this is still the formula even though, victim of its own success, the Club has inevitably been veering from spontaneous towards pre-packaged primitivism.

Borrowing the enchanted model of the Polynesian village as the most 'natural' human social unit, Blitz built up his colonies on the tracks of another no less romantic tradition, the Odyssey—the pearl of them all is at Corfu (Corcyra) near to Ithaca, others are on Djerba (authentic island of the lotus-eaters), at Foca not far from Troy itself, at Palinuro and Cefalù beyond the Sicilian straits of Scylla and Charybdis, at Al Hoceima in Morocco towards the Pillars of Hercules, as well as in Israel, Spain, and Yugoslavia, while there is even one in the Tahitian motherland itself (for those who can afford to get there).

In all the Mediterranean villages you sleep down by the beach in little round Tahitian thatched huts, two or three to a hut; and many of the more dedicated Club members go around all day in next-to-nothing but a *paréo* (gaudy Tahitian sarong), uniform of the new utopia. In some villages you can also wear flower-garlands. Phoney and embarrassing? Possibly, to some people. But the appeal to the imagination, especially to a real craving for a kind of comradely naturalism, is genuine enough. Virtually no money changes hands within the village, save in the form of pop-art beads, worn like a necklace, for buying bar drinks or cigarettes. Meals, served in elegant open-air patios, are plentiful and excellent; and wine is unlimited and included in the basic fees. Everyone, staff and members, calls everyone else *tu* and by first-names (astonishing, for France); and the staff, known as *Gentils Organisateurs* (GOs), help discreetly to imbue the *Gentils Membres* (GMs) with *le mystique du Club* in which many of them apostolically believe. Yet (unlike in some holiday camps) no attempt whatever is made by the staff to force individuals to join in activities. You can skulk in your hut all day, or wander alone into the hinterland, and no one will mind or notice. And there is plenty to do for those who wish it: nightly open-air dancing and sing-songs, sports from water-skiing and snorkelling to judo and volley-ball, all included in the basic fees. There are also daily open-air concerts of classical records, as well as lectures and debates in some villages and, in response to members' demands, an increasing supply of live culture in the form of touring dramatic groups (such as the Belgian National Theatre) and chamber orchestras performing under the stars in bathing-trunks or jeans. The Club's appeal is essentially middle-class, and it is as different from Butlin's as Rupert Brooke from Tommy Trinder.

Et in Arcadia ego. Bleary-eyed, I cross Arcadia's frontiers one Saturday morning at seven, at the Gare de Lyon. Our first rendezvous is a café opposite the station. Parisienne secretaries with rucksacks, heavy forty-ish Belgians with moustaches, a few stray English clutching dictionaries, we emerge like insects from the chrysalis of our city selves, warily greet each other and begin to unfurl our new wings. The Italian train rattles south: we are bound for Cefalù in Sicily, fourth largest of the summer villages (1,098 beds). In my compartment, a young woman who works at IBM-France, a petite Brussels ballerina, and an engaging curly-haired Parisian student who's already 'done' Cefalù the year before and is an expert on ambiance. By Turin, we are on *tu* terms; by Naples, we know each others' jobs. In the high season, the Club runs special *trains-dansants* across Italy, where GMs can vociferously break the social ice in the bar and rock the train almost off its rails; but, this being September, there is no bar and no dancing. Even so, the time passes as gaily as a thirty-five-hour, second-class train journey reasonably can. (It is probably more sensible to go by one of the chartered air flights, but I wanted to be initiated in the Club's mystique the hard way.) At Palinuro, south of Naples, a party from another village climb aboard: they are on a five-day Club excursion to the Lipari isles, where they will clamber down inside volcano craters and live like the Swiss Family Robinson. They are singing, and happy. The train is ferried across the straits, then swings along the built-up north Sicilian coast, past the new oil refineries and the heart-rending slums. Finally we tunnel under Cefalù's unmistakable Gibraltar-like rock, the train halts, a bevy of lovely *hôtesses* rush up to help us with our suitcases, a man in a comic hat is blowing a trumpet (all new arrivals are greeted, traditionally, by fanfares), and the village's *animateurs* are standing around on the platform in weird fancy dress. It's all happening! In the village, I am allotted a hut called Sagouin (it means 'filthy wretch') which I share with a solemn Milanese technician. It is underneath an ancient floodlit tower inhabited by a GO sailing-instructor from Dublin. Other GMs have huts with names like Vinaigre and Hula-Hula. The next morning, we new-boys and new-girls are given a pep-talk in a pine-grove by Charly, the young *chef de village*, clad in the lowest-slung *paréo* I've ever seen, kept up by will-power. He tells us that the aim of the Club is that we should all be very nice to each other (which the French need to be told, as they aren't normally nice to people they don't know, but here they seem to manage it). Charly, twenty-five, tells me that he trained as an accountant, then joined the Club after visiting Corfu as a GM one year and falling in love with it and a GO there, now his wife. And so, under his aegis, our Sicilian days and nights slip by.

Here is a typical day. I wake late, after a night partly spent fighting a mosquito (the village boutique sells aromatic *insecticcido* spray, but it's probably more effective to sleep wrapped up in a sheet, or ask a GO to get your hut fumigated). A quick visit to the communal ladies'-and-gentlemans' *lavoirs*, where it's slightly unnerving to shave while a very luscious blonde in a bikini beside me is cleaning her teeth with an electric brush. Breakfast (nearly everyone in swimsuits) is an odd meal: you help yourself from a long buffet laden with melon, yoghourt, smoked fish, strong local cheese, semi-hard-boiled eggs, and orange juice. Then a bathe, and sunbathe: this is Cefalù's weakest point, for though the village is beautifully situated and landscaped on a slope full of flowers and lemon-trees, in another sense the site is badly chosen, for there is only a small, mediocre sandy beach and most beach-lazing has to be done on rocks or a concrete jetty. But we make do. The more enterprising ones are having sailing-lessons, or Yoga instruction from a blonde called Yogush who attracts large classes. Lunch in the lovely patio with its blue and red parasols is a lavish meal: twice a week there is a vast help-yourself *hors d'œuvre* buffet, Provençal style, stretching about thirty yards. Today for our first course there are excellent *quenelles de brochet*, not an easy dish to cook well for 1,100 people. All tables are for eight, and conversation is general, without introductions. Today I find myself sitting with four young Parisian doctors and their girl-friends, typical hard-core GMs, swapping anecdotes about previous Club holidays like veterans telling campaign stories ('Moi, j'ai fait Djerba en '62—c'était sensass!') but, significantly, not saying a word about France or their other lives back home. They do not exactly greet me as a long-lost friend, but at least they turn to include me in the conversation, which they probably would not have done in any other setting. After lunch I laze in the sun on the wide dance-terrace beside the circular straw-roofed bar, swapping jokes and money-beads with the Sicilian barmen, and offering *espresso* to a handsome girl psychologist from Abbeville while the hi-fi pipes out Jacques Brel and Pete Seeger—'I'm not too young to try for the sun.' Waves of happiness lap over me. This is Arcadia's solstice. At six there is more music, this time a recorded Bach concert in an area known as 'le Forum', an alfresco theatre on a cliff where we gaze at the silent sea as the sun sets and the Brandenburg Concerto finds a more perfect setting than any concert hall. After dinner, the mood is rather different. Hundreds of us crowd round the bar and terrace as the nightly sing-song and *animation* begin. The GO *animateurs* embark on various carefully rehearsed pranks, and at last Billy Butlin seems to be present as well as Rupert Brooke. One GO, a picturesque bronze-bearded Israeli called Czopp, mimes film-titles which we have to guess. He and another GO (male) waltz sexily in each others' arms. '*Le Conquistador (les-cons-qui-s'adorent)*' shouts out one cinélogue. Full marks. English GMs express irritation that they can't follow the French dirty jokes. But other jokes don't need language. Volunteers from the audience are called for, and this brings out some of the unpaid GM *animateurs* who have appointed themselves the-life-and-soul-of-the-party and without whom no village is complete. Like little Néron, a tubby forty-year-old so called because he habitually wears his *paréo* toga-style and a laurel-crown. Czopp gives him a pink tutu and makes him do a nutcracker waltz as a *petit rat de l'Opéra* which has us all rolling about. Néron is hugely popular at Cefalù, and we wonder what he is in real life: a respectable bank manager maybe from some sleepy town in the Charente, or a commercial traveller from the Paris Red Belt whose inner personality comes alive for three weeks each summer by the old *mare nostrum.* Or there is René, a gigantic, vociferous wizard-prang type with a big ginger moustache, always clapping his hands and singing 'Ooh-la-la', who tonight is made to lie on the floor as a squalling baby while a lady GM changes his nappies and powders his fly (an old Club classic, this). 'The ideal Club holiday,' remarks someone, 'is a return to childhood.' After this, we go through the nightly ritual of belting out the Chanson Village (every village has its own song), its tune borrowed from a Sicilian folk-song and its words strictly non-Sicilian: 'Il y a le soleil et la mer à Cefalù-oo-ooo-oo-oooo! Mais aussi le ponton et les cailloux'. Then there is dancing, non-stop. The boring French band has gone and tonight we have a new one, a Sicilian long-haired pop group, Mick Jaggers every one, whom someone claims to have seen practising down town in Cefalù cathedral—odd place, Sicily. This new group is excellent. *Ca chauffe, carrément,* and no one chauffes more than pretty fourteen-year-old Jane from Inverness, beset by eager Latins: 'Och, when I tell them about all this back home, they'll just nae believe me.' Her parents look on, tolerantly. After midnight, the dance-terrace packs up (there are huts close by, and some people seem to want to sleep), but dedicated night-lifers make their way down the slope to a makeshift alfresco cabaret on the beach, where with our beads we buy *moules marinière* or barbecued spare-ribs, and under the Tyrrhenian moon to the strains of the Beatles' *Sergeant Pepper* on the pick-up we release one or two of our remaining inhibitions. We are cupped in a narrow cove below high rocks; Czopp is handing round *moules*; young couples sit round in tiers on the steps, talking softly, or dance slowly to the music; the mood is dreamy and intimate, Lucy is up there in the sky with diamonds, tender is the night. Alain, my student train-mate (whose romantic career at Cefalù I've been watching with interest), is having his curly hair stroked by Mary from Hammersmith. Pretty Marie-Laure from Boulogne-sur-mer tells me, 'Every man I've danced with tonight has asked me to go back to his hut with him'. Which brings me to the question you've all been waiting for me to answer. Well, Alan Whicker in a BBC film shot at Corfu claimed that the Club was entirely given over to the four S's, of which three are Sun, Sea, and Sand; but Gérard Blitz back in Paris had told me, 'I assure you that there is no more and no less *libertinage* than on any other kind of seaside holiday,' and I rather fancy he is right. After all, the logistics of the situation are not easy. Married couples have a hut to themselves; but if you come on your own you share with a stranger of your own sex, and hut-swapping isn't easy unless your hut-mate happens to hit it off with the hut-mate of your own girl, which by the law of averages can't happen often. In an ordinary hotel with single bedrooms, things are much simpler. It is true that at Corfu, Cefalù, and other villages, a towel folded just so over a hut door is an accepted Do Not Disturb sign, but for how long will your hut-mate be generous enough to stay away? Personally, I find the Club's sensuality operates a law of diminishing returns, and the proximity of so many near-naked female bodies all day makes me feel like a sweet-shop owner who doesn't want to eat sweets. So, when the *Sergeant Pepper* record ends, I go back alone to my Milanese and my mosquito. And the next day with fifteen other GMs I leave for a mule-back trek through the Sicilian mountains—one of the many unusual excursions that are possibly the Club's strongest feature. (From Cefalù you can also do a five-day tour of the main sights of Sicily; at Djerba, you can go on a Saharan safari; and at Corfu you can take a Robinson Crusoe trip to a near-by desert island, where you are cast away for several days with nothing but knives and fishing-tackle.) Sicilian guides takes us in Fiats up to the hill-town of Castelbuono where we are treated to a 'typical Sicilian banquet' and chant bawdy French student drinking-songs over much Marsala; then we dance by candlelight in a pine wood and doss down in rough dormitories in a country shack. At dawn, the mules arrive and for hours we zig-zag high into the lonely hills while the muleteers with their Tito Gobbi voices parade their folk-song repertoire and offer us terrible local cheese, tasting like sickly chewing-gum. After more dancing, and a *méchoui* and a siesta, we descend again and are given more Marsala in an ex-monastery-turned-night-club. The trip has been exhilarating and sympathetic, and by now I am firm friends with the girl psychologist from Abbeville, the Parisian electronics expert, the Linotype operator on *Le Parisien Libéré*, and freckled Judy Hillman, Town-Planning Correspondent of the *Evening Standard*, whom I have sold to one of the muleteers for two million lire after much haggling. Back in Cefalù, it is almost time to return to Paris, and my last image of the Club is of Czopp like a pied piper leading us all in a galloping chain-dance as, impelled by the pop group, we re-echo

'Nos soucis et nos peines loin derrière nous,
Nous reviendrons Un Jour à Ce-fa-looo-oo-ooo-oo-oooo!'

Of what value is this never-never-land for the future of France and of French society? This might sound a ponderous question to ask about a harmless summer frolic, but it is not an irrelevant one. The clientèle is almost entirely middle class: one-third *cadres* and the rest petit-bourgeois down to clerks, typists, and artisans, but with very few real proletarians. This in its French context is not surprising, even though the prices would be within the means of many workers nowadays (roughly 1,100 francs for two weeks including air travel, or for three weeks off-season). As a social catalyst the Club therefore has its limits: but within its broad middle-to-upper range it does seem to have managed some shaking-up of the usual class barriers and inhibitions, however superficially. Its officials enjoy telling the story of two men who struck up a friendship of rare warmth over Samos wine and deep-sea diving in one of the Greek villages: only on the way home did they swap names and adresses, to discover that one was a director and the other a night-watchman in the same factory.

But we are not told what happened to this friendship when they got back home; and one managing-director GM has been quoted as saying,

'At one village I got friendly with one of my clerks: it was all right down there, where everything's so free and easy, but it did make it harder to keep up *les convenances* back in the office.' At Cefalù I found it noticeable that the French GMs, much more than the foreign ones, preferred to remain anonymous and not discuss their jobs or backgrounds with each other. They wanted to forget about France. Nor has there been any pressure from members for Butlin-style winter get-togethers in Paris: one or two Club attempts at these failed because they simply showed up the social differences that were masked in the villages, and Blitz himself told me with disarming frankness, 'The success of the Club is due to its divorce from daily life: if French barriers dropped, the Club would become less attractive. We found that trying to hold meetings in Paris simply lost us the credit we had won in the villages; French barriers are too rigid.' So this is a kind of compensation-world, almost a Jean Genet territory where men and girls act out the fantasy rôles they cannot manage in their own lives: classless democrats, cultured pagans, noble savages, high-spirited friends-to-all-the-world.

I think that the French do, at a certain level, feel a genuine urge to escape from the rigidly stratified society in which they have imprisoned themselves, and therefore the Club is a kind of therapeutic. It also provides a forum where strangers can be naturally nice to each other without the usual French mistrust. This, in a French context, is important: the atmosphere of the villages is genuinely and unforcedly friendly and co-operative, free from the usual French tendency to split into rival factions. Whether this mini-lesson in civism makes it any easier for GMs to go and spread the same spirit in their tougher lives back home is another matter. But I think that, to a small degree, it might.

The traditional bias against *les vacances collectives* is still quite strong in France, so that many people join the Club with initial misgivings. But most of them seem delighted with what they find. Of course there are plenty of things to criticise, which are largely a matter of individual taste. At Cefalù, our main complaint was of a certain claustrophobia due to the siting of the village on a built-up strip of coast beside a main road and railway with no open sandy shore: Blitz's boast that with the Club you can 'go off in a crowd in order to find yourself alone' fell a little flat. But most of the other villages are in much more isolated spots, with beaches where you can wander away for miles. Some people might also dislike the *animation*, the fanfares and the singing, the schoolboy jokes and the few fanatics who wear their *paréos* even on the ski slopes. Actually, this is only a small part of Club life and obtrudes only in the evenings; and I think a holiday community of over 1,000 would feel a certain emptiness if there were none of it at all. Therefore I was grateful to the public-spirited volunteers like René and Néron as well as to the GO *animateurs*. I felt at Cefalù there was not, in fact, enough professional *animation* to give the village a strong cohesive atmosphere.

The successes of the Club, in addition to the food, the sport, and the cultural excursions, are a certain basic good taste and lack of vulgarity in the way the whole thing is conceived and run. The hundreds of straw-huts, for instance, are dotted irregularly among trees in a way that pleases the eye: many foreign holiday-camps are far more monolithic in appearance. I agree with what one of Blitz' officers told me: 'Only the French could have succeeded with a holiday formula like ours. In Italy, the position of women would have made it impossible, while the Germans or British would have turned it into jolly boy-scoutism for adults. Our French individualism saves us. Lots of foreigners are members, but the Club's style is entirely French. And our aims are quite different from Butlin's. He tries to flatter workers by treating them as bourgeois; we take people right out of any social context. Butlin gives them cinemas, bingo, and such-like; we remove urban life totally, and we certainly don't allow transistors, or washing hanging outside huts.' Considering what hell holiday-makers *en masse* generally are, especially British or Germans, the Club's members *en masse* are surprisingly unirritating and pleasantly behaved. I think French reserve and lack of clubbability saves them too: put people together in a setting like this, and anything above a certain level of clubbability rapidly becomes insufferable.

But the Club's basic structures are today developing and changing fast, and there is possibly a danger of its unique ethos becoming overlaid. Numbers rise each year (membership doubled between 1963 and 1966) and success has tempted it to diversify its activities. It is now part-owned by the Rothschild Bank and has become a public company with shares quoted on the Bourse. Gilbert Trigano the businessman is today as important a figure in the Club's affairs as Blitz the man of instinct. There are now sea-cruises, select guided coach-tours, sedate new camps in France itself for families with small children, and new all-season luxury village-hotels at Agadir and Caesarea made—heresy—of actual houses. What is more, the Club has now set its cap at the American mass market. With eager Government support, it is building a new chain of village-hotels inside France, to cater mainly for American and other foreign tourists. Other village-hotels are opening in Mexico and the Caribbean, mainly for Americans, and in these the language will be English. Blitz has opened an office on Fifth Avenue, and talked excitedly of his vision of five million American Nice Members: 'We have *proof* that our particular holiday formula will appeal to the Americans as much as the French, given a few alterations of comfort and language. America's an under-developed country in its methods of tourism, the style of the hotels is so old-fashioned. So we shall export our techniques to them, just as France has imported American techniques in other fields. The Club will be an authentic French penetration into the America sphere, just as IBM or Libby's penetrate into France.' And in a sense, why not? The new installations will retain many of the essential Club features—*animateurs*, free sport, beads, and *paréos*, if not the straw-huts—and so long as the Mediterranean villages do not become Americanised, perhaps one should not object. But, even within its own French context, the Club's spirit has been changing under the impact of wider success. Inevitably, it has grown more conventional and comfortable, and less of a mad pioneering adventure. Today the plumbing is better and the *paréos* fewer: some new GMs even dare to be seen in cocktail dresses. The back-to-nature veterans of the early Majorca days are being joined by a more sedate clientèle who want their primitivism to be carefully streamlined—and the gap between the Club and other types of holiday is narrowing. It would be sad if the true originality of the Club were to be too far diluted: for Blitz created something rare and inspired, no mean feat in the overcrowded jungle of today's tourism, and his claim is not far-fetched that the Club is 'the pilot-organisation of Europe's leisure, laboratory for the holidays of the future'. I hope that this leonine, latter-day Ulysses will long continue to find new ways of wooing his followers as they sip their *ouzo* or Marsala beside the wine-dark sea—

> The lights begin to twinkle from the rocks:
> The long day wanes: the slow moon climbs: the deep
> Moans round with many voices. Come, my friends,
> 'Tis not too late to seek a newer world.
> It may be we shall touch the Happy Isles . . .

There are echoes of the atmosphere and ethos of the Club in some of the ordinary public camping-sites in France, especially along the Côte d'Azur: on the Côte des Maures and the Ile de Porquerolles, in the rocky coves near Cassis, and notably around La Capte, south of Hyères, where everyone is bronzed and youthful and the gaudy blue-and-orange tents fill the pine-forests for miles. This is modern, post-Bardot mass tourism with a vengeance, utterly different from the mood of the classic resorts farther east. The whole trend on the Riviera today, for rich and not-so-rich alike, is away from the Edwardian sedateness of Cannes or Monte Carlo and towards the St. Tropez* or La Capte pattern—film-stars with sand between their toes, pine-needles in your *soupe de poissons*, nudists among the rocks, a juke-box idly blaring Mireille Mathieu in the sun, and all the paraphernalia of *le camping élégant* which the French are able to manage with a lithe Latin flair.

In a rather more contrived and showmanlike genre, I can recommend two or three new-style tourist ventures on this coast that reach bizarre heights of Hollywoodian flamboyance and ingenuity—notably at La Brague, north of Antibes, and on the Ile de Bendor near Bandol. La Siesta at La Brague is a huge beach-club-cum-night-club that holds 3,000 people and was created in 1962 by a local cement tycoon. It has every gimmick you could ask for, down to a special restaurant for dogs, and a set of old gipsy caravans tarted up to make a smart boutique and hair-stylist. The

* See p. 341 (Youth with a dusty answer).

real beach was shingle here, so tons of sand were specially imported by Air France from Acapulco, Tahiti, and Sussex: and a real Chinese junk was brought from Hong Kong to lie offshore and serve as a Chinese restaurant. After dark, when the lido is deserted, the night-club takes over, and the network of little open-air bars and dance-floors with their illuminated waterfalls are lit by a myriad flaming torches; you can dance on big metal water-lilies in a pool full of flowers. 'Our image,' the *petite* blonde manageress told me proudly, 'is the marriage of fire and water.' La Siesta is hugely popular, with minor film-stars and lesser smarties who pay sixteen francs' daily entrance fee; and for all its artificiality I do find it rather lovely in a *Great Gatsby* kind of way, even though these 'men and girls who come and go among the whisperings . . . and the stars' are drinking *le scotch*, not champagne. On this very Riviera where Fitzgerald found the night so tender and pursued his strange ideal, is it possible that forty years later the French, or some of them, are now in thrall to the same *mystique* of spiritual fulfilment through glamour and wealth? Are those flaming torches, for some people, the same as Gatsby's green light? There are signs of it today in romantic, glamour-dazzled, new-rich France—and not only at La Siesta.

A hundred miles to the west, an experiment on the tiny island of Bendor recalls another fictional American tycoon, more notorious than Gatsby. Until recently Bendor was a rocky wilderness; then it was bought by Paul Ricard, the imperious apéritif king, who a stately pleasure-dome decreed. His island Xanadu is a weird fun-palace dedicated to new-style social tourism and also to his own self-projection, and *Le Monde* has written, 'Why doesn't Orson Welles hurry up and film *Citoyen Ricard?*' Starting life as owner of a modest bar in Marseille, Ricard built up an industrial empire that sells anisette and many other drinks to half the bars of the world: his feudal paternalism is prodigal of strange ideas, and one of them was to make Bendor a shrine of the questing human spirit, where like Polycrates on Samos he would draw into his charmed circle the finest poets and athletes of his day. Anyone is welcome: one day I took the boat from Bandol, and was greeted by an exceptionally smooth resident PRO and uniformed hostesses who showed me the sights—a small zoo with gorillas, a little phoney 'fishing-port' rather like Portmeirion in Wales, a sailing and water-skiing school, a glassworks and art gallery (full of M. Ricard's own appalling paintings), a museum of wines and spirits (very impressive), a rather lovely restaurant and café-terrace by the sea's edge, a night-club, and a big hall used for business congresses, and for such events as poetry festivals. At one recent festival the Great Man, who has a villa on the island, turned up in a red-and-black cape looking like Mephistopheles and proceeded to recite his own poems. If you raise a query about the island, the staff in reverential tones will tell you of the master's wishes: I was reminded of *The Loved One*. Ricard has said, 'I have never worked for any end save the good of the common people.' His two hotels on Bendor are pretentious and expensive places, one of them a mock-Venetian palace, the other aggressively ornate with each room in a different imitation classical style, Renaissance, Louis XV, or Empire. Bendor is *sui generis*, non-typical, a millionaire's folly: but it has its niche in the new French cult of the life-giving Mediterranean.

The French are increasingly drawn to the seaside (40 per cent of all holidaymakers went there in 1965, against 23 per cent ten years earlier) and to the mountains (18 per cent in 1965, 10 per cent in 1953). This means that fewer holidays are spent in the spa towns like Vichy, or with relatives in their country homes. And sea and mountains provide the main settings for the post-war growth of sport in France. The number of private sailing-boats and motor-yachts rose from 20,000 in 1960 to 120,000 five years later: today the Côte d'Azur is so jammed with yachts in summer that some ports such as Beaulieu have instituted ninety-minute parking-discs for them as for cars. Of all sports, sailing is the most popular, followed closely by skiing: more than a million go to the ski-slopes each year, mainly to the French Alps but also to the Pyrenees and Vosges or abroad. Grenoble owes its fantastic post-war boom partly to its proximity to the skiing resorts, while the building of new ski-lifts and hotels in smart centres like Mégève and Courchevel has meant big business for financiers and developers. Some well-to-do Parisians are now picking up the New York habit of long trips for skiing weekends; they drive all through Friday evening the 380 miles from Paris to Megève and return early on Monday. But if you want to see the most vivid illustration of the new French skiing mania, go to the Gare de Lyon at the start of the Christmas school holidays, when the crammed Alpine expresses are leaving every few minutes and the whole vast station is a marching forest of upturned skis.

Probably the French are today more *sportif* than the English; or at least they are relatively more devoted than the English to participation-sports rather than spectator-sports. True, the annual *Tour de France* cycle race is essentially a mammoth spectator-sport, and so are the great car races and league football. But France's 66,000 sporting clubs and associations claim among their three million members nearly a million and a half *licenciés* or certified active participants, and these include 440,000 footballers, 62,000 judoists, and 37,000 racing cyclists. Fishing and hunting are both more popular than ever for not solely sporting reasons, despite the waning of gastronomy. *La chasse* is generally conducted with a rifle, not horse and hounds: in the old days it was the preserve of peasants and gentry, as in Renoir's *La Règle du jeu*, but today it has spread more widely, and in fact so many urban amateurs have taken to the woods on Sundays with their guns that the accident-rate has soared and new licensing laws have had to be enforced.

In international competition the French show up better at individual than at team sports, as you might expect. They did poorly in the 1966 World Cup at Wembley, and their post-war summer Olympics record has been consistently disappointing, due partly to failures of team training and morale. At Tokyo in 1964 they were placed eleventh, and their only Gold Medal was for the most aristocratic and individual sport of horse-jumping. Front-rank French athletes are rare; but when they do emerge, like the runner Michel Jazy and the swimmer Christine Caron, they are lauded as national idols. And in the case of skiing, it does seem that all the widespread grass-roots fervour has thrown up its due crop of outstanding talent, as with football in Brazil or cricket in the West Indies: the young Goitschell sisters, Olympic Gold Medallists, are as popular as any film-stars, and so is the 1968 Olympic winner, J.-C. Killy. One fan told me, 'In a way, they're our Beatles.'

Millions more people would take an active part in sport if there were more facilities. Though the Government has recently increased its efforts to provide better equipment, there is still a serious backlog. Its annual budget for sport was increased almost fourfold between 1958 and 1965, to reach 422m francs: but the shortage of sports grounds and swimming pools is still a leading local grievance, especially on the *Grands Ensembles*, while sport in schools is still much under-provided for, and there have been sinister Ministerial delays over plans to build a big new stadium in greater Paris to replace the now destroyed Vélodrome d'Hiver. In many areas, sport remains largely the preserve of those who can afford it: 13 per cent of *cadres* against 1 per cent of workers go skiing, yet in France this is supposedly a mass and not a minority sport, with the ski-slopes sometimes within sight of the factory windows. The past few years have seen some interesting new ventures ('snow classes' for poorer children, and cheap State-subsidised skiing holidays for young workers) but funds are very limited, and there are frequent complaints on the Left that all the best ski-runs are falling into the hands of property tycoons who charge high prices and are at pains to keep out *hoi polloi*.

Some of these arguments apply to holiday-making as a whole. One person in four in the eighteen-to-thirty-four age-bracket has still not yet been away on holiday in his life, and often it is because he feels he cannot afford it. The Government, it is true, has been making growing efforts to create cheap holiday-villages and hostels in deserted rural areas, and to develop *colonies de vacances* under trained monitors for poorer children, whose parents cannot afford holidays *en famille*. More than 400,000 children visit these *colonies* annually: you find them all along French beaches in summer, a touching and slightly pathetic sight. But far more public money is needed for what is called 'social tourism', and, as in the housing industry, the Government needs to take a sterner line with the property developers who will always, when given the chance, prefer luxury tourist projects. *

If only the French public could be induced to spread its holidays over a longer period of the year, fuller and more effective use could be made of

---

* e.g. the Languedoc project: see p. 138 (New life in the provinces).

such cheap tourist amenities as do exist. Many of the hostels and camps within the range of modest families are over-subscribed in August and at Christmas, and empty most of the rest of the time. Yet many a Frenchman will stay at home rather than change his habits. Holiday-making in August is typically one of those rooted French traditions that is proving hard to alter, however unrealistic and irksome it grows as the tourist numbers swell each year. Some 91 per cent of French summer holidays are taken between July 15 and August 31 against 70 per cent in Britain and 61 per cent in Germany.

Anyone who has lived in Paris knows how the city goes to sleep that month. It is the time that tradesmen in particular choose for their annual bolt to the country. You can stroll pleasantly in empty streets and even park your car, but your favourite *bistrot* will probably have closed, and in some districts you may find it hard to get a hair-cut, or shoes repaired, or even to buy food. In the prosperous classes, mothers and children generally depart for six or eight weeks at a stretch, leaving breadwinners behind for part of the time in silent flats, possibly up to no good. The nation's business slows to a crawl, and those who are still at work often pretend to their friends they are not there. Until recently, in the upper bourgeoisie it used to be such a sign of failure to stay in Paris in August that spinsters in genteel poverty would sometimes spend the month like hermits behind closed shutters rather than show that they could not afford to leave.

Meanwhile the summer traffic-jams and casualties mount up on the tourist routes, and hoteliers faced with spiralling costs find they can no longer balance their budget with so short a season. This is probably the gravest of the problems facing the French hotel industry, which has been in crisis for several years. It has been affected also by staff shortages, by new competition from cheaper countries like Spain, and by the camping vogue. Even foreign tourists in France spend more nights in camps than in hotels. To meet this vicious circle the Government has given hotels extensive loans for modernisations, and thousands of them have carried this out: but they have also used it as an excuse to double or treble their prices, and the Government has failed to stop them. Though French hotel prices (at least for shared rooms) are still well below the absurd English ones, they are equally well above the Continental average.

A State-led campaign for the wider staggering of holidays has made a small amount of progress in the past few years, and some of the burden has been shifted from August to July. But the results of the campaign have been disappointing. Although a few big firms have been induced to close their plants in July rather than August, most others, notably Renault, have refused to do so, for apparently valid commercial reasons, and hardly any will follow the foreign pattern of keeping plants open and staggering their own staff holidays. The Ministry of Education has recently instituted staggering in State schools: previously they all closed at the end of June for nearly three months, but now holidays begin ten days earlier in the

North than the South. And independently of any State initiative, in central Paris itself an increasing number of theatres, shops, and restaurants have come to realise what lucrative tourist trade they lose by closing all August: in 1965, no less than twenty-six of the city's forty-odd theatres were still open that month. But in the suburbs, where there are no tourists, the blinds are still down.

The Government has also persuaded more than 300 resorts to keep their full tourist amenities going in June and September, but with lower hotel prices. Apparently this has had some influence on a public whose chief objection to these months was the fear of finding the joyrides, clubs, and casinos closed or bleakly deserted. The remaining obstacle now is purely that of habit. The unions are not against staggered holidays: some of them are co-operating with Government and Patronat in trying to arrange for the fourth week of paid holiday to be taken, in some cases, in spring or winter. Even the public, according to the opinion polls, would not object to a change so long as the weather was still good; and this is less of a problem in the Midi than in Britain. But as usual they are cautious at responding to official prodding or even to appeals to civic common sense. The French are individualist about nothing so much as the right to share the same herdlike conventions and habits.

Hitherto the French have always seemed a sedentary people, each attached to his *petit coin*, seldom venturing to live and work in a new town, returning year after year for holidays in the same quiet places, and rarely touring outside France. Now they are smitten with a new restlessness. The holiday craze is one symptom of this; another is the much greater readiness of *cadres* and even workers to migrate to other parts of France, so long as they can find a flat. Many professional people are becoming, like Americans, unable to stay in the same place for two days together. Ring up a businessman, even quite a lowly one, and he is sure to be just back from Toulouse, or just off to Geneva, or on the point of driving his family 200 miles for a short weekend. Partly it is that Paris needs to be escaped from periodically, and partly that France is still so centralised that a constant *va-et-vient* between Paris and provinces is unavoidable. But much of it is sheer nervous energy, the near-hysterical discovery of the joys of a mobile society.

This can be seen, too, in the French passion for their cars. Few people in Europe are so car-mad. Not only do they have the highest level of car-ownership in Europe after Sweden, but they react emotionally to cars as to women: 'Une voiture, Monsieur, est comme une femme,' my *garagiste* once told me when I complained that my Dauphine's performance was varying mysteriously from day to day. The French like to drive fast when they get the chance, using their brakes a lot and taking chances. The price they pay is 10,000 deaths a year, nearly twice as bad as the British fatality rate per car-mile and about the same as Germany's. Drink is a frequent cause, and big posters of the national road safety campaign re-

mind motorists along main roads, 'L'alcool tue—surtout à 100 à l'heure'
—but the penalties against drunkenness while driving are less severe than
in most countries. If France had the same density of traffic along average
roads as Britain or Germany, one hesitates to think what the accident
figures might be. But the French, though great car-owners, are not such
great car drivers: the average private vehicle travels 25 per cent less distance a year than in Britain. This can be ascribed partly to the high cost of
petrol in France and to the excellence of long-distance trains. Farmers
generally make little use of their cars except for short trips to market; and
in the working class, a car is often a status-symbol more than an object
of utility. But the wealthier classes, though only a minority of car-owners,
partly redress the balance by adoring to drive great distances whenever
possible. You don't have to be a racing-driver in a Ford Mustang in love
with Anouk Aimée to motor non-stop through the January night from
Monte Carlo to Deauville. 'Where are you going this Easter weekend?' I
asked a Parisian journalist recently. 'I'll drive to Spain, I think,' he said,
while ten years ago it might have been Fontainebleau—'and my dentist
is driving to Prague for Easter, and my lawyer's taking his mini-bus to
Nice.'

Snobberies about certain makes of car go deep and have their own
elaborate and shifting scales of values. Foreign cars are smart: their share
of the market has been rising steadily to over 14 per cent, and reaches 30
per cent in some areas like Passy and Neuilly. British cars have the highest
snob-value of all, especially Rollses, Bentleys, Aston Martins, and
Triumphs; Jaguars are now a shade vulgar. In a more conventional range,
Mercedes also score high, and have ousted Cadillacs and Chevrolets as the
prestige family saloon car. Among French cars, Citroën and Peugeot have
most cachet: de Gaulle and plenty of other top people are not ashamed to be
seen in a Citroën DS, while at the other end of the scale the little old tin-
can Citroën 2 CV maintains its unrivalled mystique of inverted snobbery,
but its owner should preferably be young or a bit bohemian. Though
Panhard and Renault were among the greatest of pioneers, the French
today care little for veteran cars, a hobby they leave to the quaint English.
They prefer modern cars: and though they often do not bother to keep
them properly polished or to repair scratches, they are fascinated by speed,
power, and elegance of line. The buying of sports cars is now number one
craze among the rich. All these are imported, as the French car industry
is still strangely wary of taking risks in this specialised market. Alfa-
Romeo, selling 4,000 in France in 1965, is the most popular make, followed by Triumph, Ford Mustang, Porsche, Ferrari, and (for a very rich
few) Maserati. It seems no coincidence that the hero of that archetypal
modern romantic French film, *Un Homme et une femme*, chief French box-
office success of recent years, was a Mustang racing-driver. It all fits in
with the world of *Elle* and La Siesta's flaming torches, the pursuit of
heart's-ease, through glamour, to the far side of paradise.

WELFARE, HEALTH, ALCOHOLISM, AND THE SOCIAL MISFITS

And so this society goes racing ahead in its Citroëns and Alfa-Romeos, towards the millennium and limitless new horizons of Mediterranean holidays, weekend cottages, emancipated birth-control, amusing new restaurants, and fashions from *Elle*. But what of those who are not in the race? Even in the United States, there are plenty who fail to compete in the drive for prosperity—the aged, the ill, the misfits, the hopelessly poor. In France, as in most Western countries, the State has now formally taken upon itself responsibility for its weaker citizens: it performs this duty with uneven results. In some sectors, Social Security has made huge strides forward since the war; in others it lags, and so do several aspects of social justice.

In the early part of this century France was slower than some of her neighbours to develop social legislation. But there was progress in the 1930s, culminating in 1939 in the *Code de la Famille* and the famous family allowances that have played such a part in French post-war resurgence. This policy was continued and extended in 1945 in a Social Charter that laid the foundations of a modern welfare State. On paper, France's Social Security today looks extremely impressive: its budget accounts for 18·9 per cent of national income, a slightly lower figure than in Germany but much higher than Britain's 12·6 per cent. Yet in practice the French welfare State probably works a little less efficiently than the British: it was conceived on too ambitious and theoretical a scale, and since then has been frequently obstructed by vested interests, such as doctors and rival private insurance schemes. But the Gaullists must take the credit for having greatly improved and extended social security in the past decade. Its budget has been rising much faster than national production, and due to a mixture of State over-generosity and bureaucratic mismanagement it was even allowed to build up a serious deficit, which the Government finally tackled in 1967 with a series of measures to increase contributions, pare down benefits, and streamline office routines.

These economies have not however altered the general framework of the Social Security system, of which the family allowances are still the strongest feature. So great is the Government's desire to keep the birthrate high that if you have only one child you get no help; allowances start with the second child, and run at about fifteen to twenty francs a week for each. In addition, a wife and mother gets a generous allowance if she forgoes a job and devotes herself to the home. Over three million families comprising eight million children benefit from these bonanzas, and 1·3 million families also receive State housing allowances, financed by a direct levy on employers. One typical home I visited in a new H.L.M was drawing 90 francs a week in allowances, equal to nearly half the husband's

NB

wages: 35 francs for the two children, another 35 because the wife did not work, and 20 francs rent subsidy.

Since the nations of the Six are committed to harmonising gradually their various Social Security schemes, where possible at the level of the highest, France's partners have been struggling to improve their family allowances while France tries to make up for her lag in unemployment benefits and pensions. There has been so little unemployment in France since the war that the low level of benefits has not been a great issue, save to those unhappy few who *did* find themselves out of a job. Now a National Employment Fund, set up in 1963, helps to retrain, resettle, and compensate redundant workers in declining industries. Its *raison d'être*, like that of the family subsidies, is forward-looking and economic as much as humane; if, however, you are very old and so have little value for the nation's economic future, you do much less well out of Social Security.

Old-age pensions are the worst of any advanced European country. The Gaullists have increased them significantly since 1961, but from such a low initial level that today millions of people over sixty-five are still living on the official minimum of 150 francs a month. Traditionally, old people are provided for by their children in France, and often live with them; but for obvious reasons this tradition is dying, except in some rural areas. Big families are breaking up, and younger people are too busily engaged in their own struggle for better homes, jobs, and children's education. According to one recent survey, only one person in ten now around sixty expects help from his relatives in his final years; and of those over sixty, 30 per cent are living quite alone and only 24 per cent with their children. In Britain, although the sense of family is less strong, as many as 40 per cent of old people are living with relatives; and the State does far more, too, to help the rest.

Some 2 per cent of French old people are living in State or charitable homes for the aged, where conditions are often horrific; many others eke out an existence on their own, often obliged to keep on part-time jobs well beyond sixty-five or seventy in order to supplement their pensions. Those who live on their pensions alone can rarely afford meat, or new clothes, or proper heating, or any kind of entertainment. In terms of Social Security, the crux of the problem is that a proper pension insurance scheme started only in 1945, and today's aged have therefore paid few contributions. It is the formerly self-employed who have had least protection of all, and only after a public enquiry in 1961 had revealed the full depths of their misery were their pensions raised to the present 'adequate' minimum. Only recently, too, were pensioners brought within the national health service; previously they either had to pay, or else throw themselves at the mercy of a public assistance system that treated them as second-class citizens.

Occasionally an article in a Left-wing paper describes in lurid terms what it is like to be old and poor in France. But on the whole this is not a problem that troubles the public's conscience greatly, apart from that of a few religious and charitable bodies who do what they can with limited means. There is still this ominous gulf in France between individual and State responsibility: if a man cannot solve a problem himself, then he feels it is up to 'them', the public authorities, to do so, and he has little of the English sense that 'them' in a democracy is also 'we'. * I do not deny that the Government has some conscience, and has been making efforts; but although France's five-and-a-half million over-sixty-fives all have the vote, they do not form an organised lobby like vinegrowers or small shopkeepers, and so their problems are not a high electoral priority.

The national health service began, as in Britain, just after the war. Its basic difference from the British system is that the patient pays the doctor direct for each consultation, and has to apply afterwards to his local Social Security *caisse* for a refund, like paying your garage for repairs and then claiming from insurance. And throughout the 1950s this gave rise to growing abuses, as doctors began to charge three or four times the admittedly very low sum of 3·2 francs that the *caisses* were authorised to refund. In 1960 the Gaullist Government agreed to revise this figure, by now quite out of touch with economic reality; and it tried to get the doctors on their side to agree to a new fixed scale of charges. The powerful medical union said no. So the Government, to its great credit, sidestepped the union and began to fix agreements with individual doctors, threatening that any doctor who did not honour the new charges would not have them refunded by the *caisses* and would thus risk losing most of his patients. Enough doctors collaborated for the Government to be able to win its trial of strength with the union, who backed down except in the Paris and Lyon regions where about half the doctors decided to boycott the health service and to rely on private practice. Today some 80 per cent of all French GPs belong to the service (the rest have private patients), and they are allowed to charge the quite handsome fees (in Paris) of thirteen francs for a surgery consultation and twenty for a bedside one—it is a little less in the provinces. Eighty per cent of this, and of prescription charges, is reimbursed by the *caisses* after a delay of a week or two.

The health service in France is therefore not entirely free, but this extra 20 per cent does possibly dissuade people from consulting their doctors unnecessarily. Even so, though they are well paid, most doctors today are frantically harassed and overworked, and they complain that their prestige has dropped now that they are little more than civil servants, with most interesting medicine in the hands of a few specialists. All this will be familiar enough to an English GP's ears. Though France does not face the British problem of emigration, the intake of new recruits into the profession is slipping seriously, and it is feared there may be a shortage of some 10,000 GPs by 1975. Many of them today work a sixty- or seventy-hour week, and France has only eighty-six doctors per

* See p. 446 (Conclusion).

100,000 people, far fewer than Russia (181), the United States (133), or even Spain (100), but more than in England and Wales (42).

This is probably the gravest of the French medical service's deficiencies. Another is that the building of new hospitals has not kept pace with urban growth, especially in the Paris area: many hospitals are old-fashioned and overcrowded, and standards of nursing and of hygiene are not always as high as they might be. French nurses, who, like doctors, are in short supply, are not famous for their bedside charm. But this cannot be blamed entirely on the Government, which in other sectors has made real efforts for medicine in the past ten years: notably, the sum devoted to research increased ninefold between 1959 and 1964.

As in other countries, improved living conditions and medical care have brought a reduction in infant mortality, tuberculosis, poliomyelitis, and similar diseases; and there has also been a certain decline in that most notorious of all French social scourges, alcoholism. A vigorous official campaign against alcoholism ever since 1954 appears to have borne some results, but it is extremely hard to tell just how much. On the one hand, there are several encouraging signs: the huge increase in the consumption of soft drinks, the apparent disaffection of the younger generation for their parents' style of heavy drinking, and the decline in inveterate alcoholic café-going. On the other hand, deaths from cirrhosis of the liver or sheer alcoholic excess still run steady at about 20,000 a year, though as these are nearly all old people, it can of course be argued that this figure relates more to past habits than to present ones. The more disturbing fact is that French alcoholic consumption per head declined only 5 per cent between 1951 and 1964, and now appears to be holding steady: it is still the highest in the world, 26·8 litres of pure alcohol per adult per year, with Italy coming second at 24 litres and no one else seriously in the running— the American with his Bourbon and dry Martinis downs only 8·2 litres of alcohol a year, and the English beer-drinker a mere 7·1. The best that can be said of the French statistics is that prosperity has at least brought an improvement in the quality of what is drunk: consumption of champagne, whisky, and vintage wines has soared, while that of the old liver-rotting strong coarse wines and *eaux-de-vie* has dropped.

It was Pierre Mendès-France who as Prime Minister in 1954 first gave official status to the anti-alcohol campaign, and won himself a good deal of derision for his milk-drinking image. But the High Committee he founded for 'study and information on alcoholism', attached to the Prime Minister's office, is still very active and seems to have done something to wean the new generation away from the traditional French ideas that wines and spirits are actively good for the health and that not to drink is unmanly. The Committee prompted the distribution to schoolchildren of five million blotters, and much other literature, which did not advocate teetotalism but warned against excess. The blotters almost led to civil war in winegrowing areas like the Hérault, where even today the anti-anti-alcohol lobby puts up posters on the main road, 'Wine is the healthiest of drinks, said Pasteur'. But the campaign may have made some impact: according to one recent survey, only 38 per cent of young people still think wine is essential to health.

Meanwhile, several anti-alcohol measures have been pushed through Parliament recently. One, strongly fought by the wine lobby, forbids the sale of strong drink in public to children under twelve: it is frequently winked at, notably in the case of wine served with meals, but it does limit the kind of thing that horrified me when I first lived in France, the sight of babes of two and three being encouraged by their fathers in cafés to drink whole glasses of undiluted wine. Another Act restricts the frequency of cafés in new suburbs and in the vicinity of factories and schools. Heavy drinking in cafés is certainly declining in France—but this may not in itself solve the problem, if people simply transfer their drinking habits to their homes.

The problem is still huge, mainly in older slum districts and in backward rural areas such as Brittany. You see few merry drunkards on the streets in France, because wine and eau-de-vie do not have that kind of effect, they strike deeper; and the French are heavy drinkers not through neurosis or unhappiness like many Anglo-Saxons but from sheer ancestral habit. It is reckoned that a million French adult males, or one in fifteen, drink more than two litres of red wine a day, and another three million drink more than the litre a day that the doctors generously concede as a safe maximum for a manual worker. Some 1,700,000 adults are medically classified as alcoholics; two-thirds of the nation's 450,000 mentally handicapped children are born of alcoholics; and 75 per cent of Parisian delinquency and 50 per cent of road accidents are said to be due to alcoholism or excessive drinking. The annual cost of alcoholism to the State, in terms of medical and social care and loss of production, has been put at 2,500m francs, three times what the State earns from taxes on alcohol. And yet, in a land where four million people derive their living from the wine and spirits trade, every step towards reform, whether by raising taxes or cutting production, is frantically opposed. Often the wine lobby will invoke the most lofty national sentiments to defend its interests. 'It is wine that enabled the French private soldier to win the Great War,' said a deputy in Parliament, while in the same debate a duke from the Armagnac region claimed, 'Wine is the glory of our civilisation—vine leaves adorn the capitals of our cathedrals.' Such speakers always invoke the idyll of the innocent small farmer, whose livelihood they say the Government is threatening.

One dubious idyll is now definitely ending—that of the bouilleurs de cru or home-distillers. These are the two million farmers who have traditionally had the right to produce for their own consumption up to ten litres of tax-free eau-de-vie each year, from fruit-trees on their property or from the marc (pulp) of their wine-harvest. Many have always distilled secretly a great deal more than ten litres, and a total of some 400,000 hecto-litres (ten million gallons) is believed to have found its way illicitly on to the market each year, bringing tidy profits both to farmers and to racketeering middlemen. Mendès-France was one of those who tried, in vain, to bring the *bouilleurs* to justice: he found the lobby against him too powerful, and in some of the wilder apple-growing regions of Normandy and Brittany it seemed that everyone, even policemen, priests, and politicians, was involved in the racket.

But in 1960 the Gaullists managed to steamroller through Parliament a law that empowered them to act by decree: and they decreed that henceforth the home-distilling privilege would no longer be passed on by inheritance or sale of property, but must end with the death of its possessor and so gradually die out. *Bouilleurs* are now dying off at the rate of some 50,000 a year. This will not automatically end the illicit distilling, but will make it easier to detect. Some *bouilleurs*, seeing which way the wind is blowing, are even jumping on the anti-alcohol wagon and have agreed to turn their trees over to producing apple-juices. *Calvados* and *vieux marc* should gradually disappear in France, and one of the causes of alcoholism may thus be eradicated.

However, 70 per cent of alcoholism in France is due not to *eau-de-vie* but to red wine. And it is worst, strangely enough, not in the wine-growing regions of the South but in Brittany and Normandy, and in some wild upland areas such as Savoy. In Brittany the alcoholic death-rate is eight times the national average, and many men drink a gallon of red wine a day. One of the problems is that, in poorer districts, much social and even economic life revolves round this habit: business transactions are regularly conducted over a litre of *rouge* in a café, and in one fishing port a merchant navy doctor had to set up his dispensary in a café. There are Breton villages where the coinage for repaying small services is often a bottle of wine.

Alcoholism is therefore a quite different kind of problem in France from Britain or America. It is essentially connected with social backwardness in rural and slum areas, and is nourished by the extreme cheapness of strong red wine and of crude brandy. Among sophisticated people, excessive drinking of whisky or cognac through stress or neurosis or social habit is probably much less common than in many countries. The best hope therefore is that urbanisation, education, and improved housing will gradually limit the evil of their own accord. Already, in the middle classes, the convention that no meal is complete without wine is beginning to fade, and often in restaurants you see people sitting down with their *quart de Perrier* or just plain *eau nature*. From 1952 to 1960, consumption of mineral waters rose 85 per cent and of fruit juices 341 per cent; fruit juice is two or three times as expensive per glass as wine, which limits its sales in the poorer classes, but in the middle class this gives it a prestige appeal. Vermouth sales are lower than fifteen years ago; but anisette, after a decline in the 1950s, has been making a come-back, thanks to Citizen Ricard's sales-drives. Cider is dropping in popularity, and beer is increasing. But the biggest advances have been made by the smart drinks—champagne, and especially Scotch whisky, which is now drunk almost as widely as in England.

The sum of these trends suggests that the French, although they may not be drinking much less than before, are at least turning away from fire-water to more sophisticated and less destructive drinks, without having yet taken to that nastiest of all fire-waters, gin. The wine industry, too, is now devoting itself under Government policy to improving the quality of ordinary wines. No one, or hardly anyone, demands that the French should become teetotal—this has never been the aim of the anti-alcoholism campaigns. No one denies that the great wines of Burgundy, Bordeaux, and Champagne are among France's foremost gifts to civilisation. But there is a difference between half-a-bottle of Vosne-Romanée, enjoyed over a good meal, and the Breton hospital wards overflowing with cirrhosis cases and mental defectives.

Along with combating alcoholism, the Government has been making efforts to clear up shanty-towns and vagabondage, but is finding the task Sisyphean. The growth of shanty-towns (*bidonvilles*) is quite a new phenomenon of the past decade or so, and is due almost entirely to the arrival of foreign workers.* France's own sub-proletariat, despite the housing shortage, usually manages to find some tenement or attic with a semblance of bricks-and-mortar; but workers pouring in to labour-thirsty France from Iberia and North and West Africa often cannot find proper homes, and so they have been settling in encampments of shacks and disused vehicles outside the main cities. Fifty thousand of them now live in these *bidonvilles*, four-fifths in the Paris area, most of them Portuguese or Algerians. One camp, in the suburb of Champigny, houses 10,000 Portuguese, many of them women and children. They live without drains or electricity, on waste land deep in mud. The Government has been making efforts to resettle them, and claims to have rehoused about 1,500 a year since 1965 in special communal hostels. The families are often glad of the chance to move, but the single workers consider it an affront to their pride, and many prefer to stay where they are.

The tramps or *clochards* present a different kind of problem—save that they, too, proudly resist attempts to integrate them into society. There are some 3,000 in Paris alone, it is reckoned, who are *clochards* by choice, liking the life, hating regular work, and hating above all to sleep in a bed; only a minority have become tramps temporarily through unhappiness, breakdown, or unemployment. Usually they despise society and want it to leave them alone; they rarely steal, and are too proud to beg. Really they are quite innocuous, apart from their lack of hygiene and their unsightliness, as they lie huddled on the pavements or slouch along the *quais* tippling their bottles of *rouge*. Many are alcoholics. One Paris *clochard* was a Foreign Legion officer, another a Tsarist colonel, a third

* See p. 454 (Conclusion).

an intellectual who even as a *clochard* would give *alfresco* lectures on philosophy in the Latin Quarter for the price of a bottle of wine. Many have been poets or artists. One recently came into a legacy of 100,000 francs but preferred to remain a *clochard*. The police periodically round them up and take them off to an official hostel where they are deloused and forcibly given a shower—a supreme affront to their dignity. This happens to the average tramp about twice a year; but if he can prove means of subsistence, as he usually can (from pensions or odd jobs), the police have no right to hold him. Recently some Right-wing deputies made moves to suppress the *clochards*: they argued that it was demoralising for youth, and bad for the image of France, for these filthy, besotted old men to be seen lying around outside smart theatres and restaurants. But the Bill that would have made vagabondage in itself a crime was narrowly defeated. The life of blissful monotony can go on.

But for the rest of France there is no blissful monotony. Unlike the *clochards*, the French are being compelled to march with the times, and, as this chapter has tried to show, it involves the upheaval of some of the oldest French traditions and possibly the loss of some of those things most precious about France. The dilemmas are acute: how to adapt to the new while preserving the best of the old—and nowhere is this so apparent as in the changing rôle of French youth and in the struggle now engaged between reformers and conservers over the proud and classical French concept of education. This is the subject of my next chapter.

CHAPTER X

YOUTH WITH A DUSTY ANSWER

IT WAS IN THE CORRIDORS of the new Préfecture building near the Bastille, one day in 1965, that I had my own Gibbonian moment of awareness of the rise of a huge new generation in France. Usually one expects French public offices to be filled with shuffling, elderly bureaucrats and messengers, spun about with the cobwebs of the Third Republic, and nothing is more typical of this than the old Préfecture in the Hôtel de Ville. Suddenly in this new annexe, as the clock struck noon for lunch, I was besieged by hundreds of chattering clerks and typists, few of them over thirty. Visibly I saw confirmation of the statistics: there are more than twice as many people under twenty-five in France today as in 1939, although the population has risen only 15 per cent. In many offices the old *huissiers* with their stained suits and sad faces are being replaced by sleek young *hôtesses* with public-relations smiles; and it is easy to find scores of other symptoms, too, of France's demographic facelift and of the new national emphasis on youth.

Every Frenchman today professes his faith in *la jeunesse. Une France jeune—soyez jeune—il faut l'esprit jeune*—the phrases tumble daily from the mouths of politicians and the pages of glossy magazines, as though youth were synonymous with virtue. In a country previously dominated by the prerogatives of age and hierarchy, this marks a striking change of heart. '*We* may have failed—but *les jeunes*, they are serious, they are made of good stuff, they will do better than us': this is a comment you sometimes hear from older people still ashamed of the defeats of recent decades. Often this kind of sentiment seems to be based more on hopeful thinking than on reason: few older people, even parents and teachers, claim to know what this reticent and elusive new generation is really like. But at least they are given more public attention than ever before. In their name a great national debate on education is now raging, and the highly traditional structure of French schools and universities is being remodelled to an extent unparalleled since Napoleon.

REFORM IN THE CLASSROOM:
LESS HUMANITIES, MORE HUMANITY?

'In *Andromaque*, did Racine respect the rule of the three unities?'A sixteen-year-old at the back of the room, in tieless shirt and informal jersey, stands up and gives the perfect formal answer, with four carefully numbered logical points, exegesis and peroration, just the way he's been taught. The rest of the class, also in a motley of informal dress, listens quietly; the boy sits down, and the teacher resumes his own brilliant didactic performance, tripping his way through the subtleties of literary analysis as only a Sorbonne *agrégé* can. Outside, the sun falls on an austere and silent courtyard. It could be any *lycée*—and you can be sure that if one *lycée* class is studying *Andromaque* at a given hour of the week, then a thousand are doing so at the same moment, throughout the French cultural empire from Tahiti to South Kensington.

Much of the best and the worst in the French national spirit can be imputed to this concept of education as inspired academic pedagogy limited to the classroom walls. Teaching is deductive, rhetorical, formal, preoccupied with style and expression; the teacher seldom has real personal contact with his pupils, and his concern is to train their intellects. The *lycées* have traditionally provided a bourgeois minority with the loftiest academic disciplining in the world; they have moulded a cultured élite where technocrats can turn to any problem with the same clarity they were taught to apply to Racine, and where literature and the arts have flowered naturally in a society indoctrinated with belief in their supremacy. Scientists and classicists alike in the *lycées* get such a strong dose of the same 'culture générale' till the age of nineteen that in later life they can always find a common language, and so the divorce of the two cultures is less serious a problem than in Britain. Even poorer children, though largely absent from the *lycées*, are put through sufficiently rigorous mental hoops in their junior schools for a foreigner to be frequently impressed by the French working man's articulateness and grasp of ideas.

But every classroom is now a battlefield of reform. The old system has increasingly come under criticism since the war for being undemocratic, over-classical, and generally unsuited to the broader needs of a technological age; even the excellent principle of 'culture générale' has come under fire for its old-fashioned syllabus and didactic methods. Since 1945 a group of progressive and liberal-minded experts in the Ministry of Education have managed to push some valuable innovations between the Scylla of State parsimony and vacillation, and the Charybdis of teachers' conservatism. Some of these measures have been frankly utilitarian (to provide the economy with more technicians) but others have been humane: to broaden access to the *lycées* and technical colleges, to modernise teaching methods, and to lighten the severities of the fearsome examination system. They culminated in the somewhat incoherent but basically liberal and far-reaching Fouchet reforms of 1965–6 (Christian Fouchet was Minister of Education, 1963–7). Eighty per cent of French schools are run by the State,* on the same highly centralised civil-service basis as préfectures or post offices; this makes reform much easier to decide in principle than in Britain but often harder to apply in practice, for it has to be imposed from above rather than proceeding naturally by ground-swell movement from area to area. And the teaching profession, who mostly vote Left but in practice are hostile to change, have not taken kindly to measures imposed by a Rightist government without consulting them properly. It has therefore proved much easier to make purely adminis-trative changes, concerning new types of school or examination, than to alter the spirit and attitudes of French teaching. Many individual teachers are now aware that change is needed, not only towards less academicism, but towards a more human teacher-child relationship; but many are frightened at the same time of a drop in their cherished intel-lectual standards. And in the consequent running battle between teachers and State, there seems a lot to be said on both sides.

Much of the State's effort since the war has been concentrated on the largely material problems of trying to keep pace with the post-1944 baby-boom, with the growing public thirst for more education and with the nation's need for more specialists. Outwardly, the record looks quite good, although there are many on the Left who rightly complain that the nuclear programme stops it from being much better. The State budget for education has grown nearly sixfold since 1952, in real terms, to reach 20,500m francs for 1968; over two million children are today in secondary schools, against 300,000 in 1939; and some 30 per cent of French children are still under education at eighteen, three times the British figure. Even the inevitable shortage of teachers has eased a good deal in the past few years, at least in primary schools, where classes are smaller on average than in Britain or most countries. There are plenty of gaps to be filled, however, notably in junior technical education. And although the Government is now belatedly struggling to fulfil a nine-year-old promise that by 1967 it would raise the minimum leaving age from fourteen to sixteen, it looks very much as if there will not be the classes or teachers to carry this out coherently before 1970 or so. In prac-tice 75 per cent of children do now stay at school beyond fourteen, against 53 per cent in 1955, and 58 per cent stay beyond fifteen. But plenty of not-so-bright children are still being thrown into jobs at that age without vocational preparation, through lack of the means of training them.

A deeper-rooted problem is that education is still based strikingly on

* The remainder are still mostly in the hands of the Church, and one of the most remarkable developments of recent years has been the cooling of the old feud between Church and State on this issue, which is no longer a serious educa-tional problem—see page 382 (Intellectuals in disarray).

class distinction. And the barrier is not so much one of money as of custom. Though the *lycées* offer mainly free tuition and in theory are open to all, in practice the most distinguished of them such as the Louis-le-Grand or the Jeanson-de-Sailly in Paris are as much a preserve of a certain class as the £600-a-year English public schools. There has been far less democratisation than in post-war Britain, where at least the grammar schools (which correspond largely to the *lycées*) are now full of workers' children; and as only a *lycée* or a private school prepares for the *baccalauréat* or university entrance exam, higher education remains a middle-class near-monopoly too, and only 12 per cent of French university students are from workers' families against 30 per cent in Britain. In some *lycées* it is the teachers who maintain a snobbish bias against admitting workers' children, but more often it is the workers who exclude themselves, whether for social or partly financial reasons: a worker may feel, with reason, that his son will lack the right kind of cultured home background to be at ease in the rarified *lycée* atmosphere, and even though tuition is free, there are always extras such as books, meals, and transport, and the loss of a valued extra bread-winner for the family.

There have always been brilliant exceptions, it is true, including a recent Rector of the Sorbonne, who worked his way up via the *lycée* stream from a humble home. And today, certainly, as the better-paid skilled workers develop new aspirations, so the number of working-class children in *lycées* is far greater than fifteen years ago. But social barriers of this kind are always hard to crack in France without an official helping hand. And so, in an effort to hasten the equalising process, the Government in 1963 adopted the most controversial of all post-war school re- ‖ NB forms: in future, it decreed, there would be only one type of State school for all children, rich and poor, between eleven and fifteen.

Hitherto, though children from all social backgrounds have attended the same State or Church primary schools, at the age of eleven the *lycées* have taken their own privileged stream while the rest have gone to junior secondary schools where they either leave at fourteen or fifteen or, if they are lucky, go on to some kind of technical college. The reform, still in the process of being applied, involves gradually abolishing most of the junior classes in *lycées* and merging them with the old junior secondary schools into thousands of new comprehensives known as Collèges d'Enseignement Secondaires. Selection from these for entry to the *lycées* at fifteen is not by exam but by teachers' recommendation and general school record: thus a bright working-class child has four years' more time and probably more serious encouragement than before to make the jump to a *lycée*. And the rest will have a choice of a variety of technical and vocational schools, of which a few already exist and others are being built.

There are now more than 1,100 CESs, and if they can build up a new corps of the right kind of teachers, they will probably work quite well. I visited one in a suburb of Montpellier that impressed me a lot: the headmaster, a vigorous young ex-*lycée* teacher, was excited by his experiment and said he expected about half his children, from varying backgrounds, to go on to *lycées*: 'We're out to destroy the social snob status of the *lycée*, and that's a good thing.' The school was co-educational, unlike most of the older *lycées*, and the thirteen- and fourteen-year-olds looked more informally relaxed and happy than in the strainedly cerebral atmosphere of the average *lycée*. The principal had managed to attract a good staff, most of them qualified *professeurs de lycée*, but he knew it was partly because sunny Montpellier was a sought-after posting, and that many CES in other parts of France would have to rely on lower-grade teachers.

Like the comprehensive schools in Britain, and for similar reasons, the CES have run into strong opposition—mostly from the *lycées* and from bourgeois parents. Many of the latter are scared that *lycée* entrance will now become harder and less automatic for their less bright children, who will be streamed into despised technical careers. And many *lycée* teachers are alarmed that the bright children now coming to them only at fifteen will not have been taught properly in the new schools and that standards will drop. They are also asking: who will teach in the CES? There has always been a rigid professional gulf in France between the *professeur de lycée*, a graduate and often an *agrégé*, and the 'inferior' *instituteur* in a secondary or primary school, often a peasant or worker's son who has been through teacher-training college but not university. Yet the two will clearly have to work side by side in the CES, as they are now doing perforce; or else, as seems likely, a new grade will have to be created with some special training. The rigid hierarchy of teachers' privileges and status has always been a big obstacle to school reform in France, and any change is a slow and painful business. Meanwhile, some *lycées* are hoping that they will be able to hold on to their junior classes, under a compromise system now proposed whereby the junior part of a *lycée* may be turned into a CES with a wide social range but remaining under the *lycée*'s control. In the Ministry's eyes, this will obviate the building of so many extra schools, and so is likely to find favour. In the case of some of the more brilliant *lycées* in large towns, it may also help to ensure higher teaching standards and more continuity for the cleverer children. But it could lead to continued social discrimination. Whatever the general success of the CES, it is hard to believe in France that the upper bourgeoisie and its teacher allies will not find ways of preserving some of their class strongholds.

Another feature of French education has been the emphasis set on written examinations, on class marks awarded weekly for academic progress, and on sheer brain-slogging even at a very young age. A child has been under pressure from his teacher and maybe from his parents to outshine his rivals, and when he falls a few places down the class's ladder, he is in disgrace. It is a system that often inhibits the less bright child, and though it may encourage the clever ones to achieve their very best, it can also induce intellectual snobbery. It has even been held responsible for some of the rivalries and discords in French adult society.

In the years after the war an experiment in less severe and old-fashioned teaching methods was carried out by a remarkable lady called Madame l'Inspectrice-Générale Hatinguais, who might be described as the Jean Monnet of modern French education. The post-Liberation Government, influenced by American and other thinking, gave her *carte blanche* to try out her ideas at a special centre in Sèvres, west of Paris, and in pilot classes attached to a few schools. The basis of her scheme was to do away with written exams as far as possible for young children. And so great was her influence that in 1957 the Government pushed one jump ahead of Britain on the path to modernism and abolished the French equivalent of the Eleven Plus, the *lycée* entrance examination at eleven known as the *entrée en sixième.* * This exam had been much criticised for its academicism and for the level of abstract intelligence it expected: one question in the general paper of 1956 invited eleven-year-olds to comment on the philosophical significance of a passage from Gide in which he described how, as a boy, he once let a favourite marble roll into a crack in the wall, so he grew one finger-nail to a huge length to be able to winkle it out again, only to have lost interest in the marble by the time the nail was long enough, so he bit it off again.

Since 1957, eleven-year-olds have been selected for *lycées* by their teachers in consultation with parents, and only borderline cases now take a written test. This may have relieved some of the traumata of primary schooling, but it has not in itself made *lycée* selection much fairer. In many cases it has simply masked the intellectual inequality of social discrimination. However, the exam-free system is now being extended to the CES, where children for all their four years go through a *cycle d'observation et d'orientation*: a careful dossier is kept of their record, and they are streamed either towards *lycées* or technical schools, with plenty of flexibility to allow for late developers. Those whose studies end with leaving the CES will take a *Certificat de Fin d'Etudes*; others will pass on to their next school without exam if their record is good enough. It is a system that depends on having smallish classes and capable teachers, and so far it appears to be working reasonably well and producing a more relaxed atmosphere. The danger is that, in the hands of a pedagogue of the old school, it can simply increase the pressure on French children to please teacher and accept didactic authority.

Madame Hatinguais also elaborated a number of direct and audio-visual teaching methods, using film, tape-recorders, and so on. Many of these have won official blessing, but attempts to introduce them widely are not proving easy, so alien are they to the French academic tradition. Teachers in France are notoriously stubborn, and often, when a decree arrives from the Ministry telling them to use some new method, they find ways of quietly ignoring it save when an Inspector is around. The progressive headmaster of a primary school near Paris told me, 'I've tried to introduce

* French classes are numbered the other way round from English ones: *sixième* is the junior class in a *lycée* and *première* the top one.

new methods here, but my staff, young and old alike, aren't interested. They'd rather go on in the old ways. They don't even like making use of the TV programmes for schools because it means a break in routine. I've got a handsome new tape-recorder, but I'm the only person who uses it for teaching.' It is the usual French problem of a small number of pioneers fighting against general apathy or conservatism. A major difficulty is that, though primary teachers are in reasonable supply, their calibre and their prestige has been falling. This profession used to be the summit of ambition for a bright working-class child, and the best way of entry into the white-collar middle class via the *école normale*; today he is more likely to try for a better-paid technical job in industry and often regards teaching as a last resort. The same headmaster told me: 'Primary teaching only attracts the dregs nowadays—and what do you expect, with the salaries they get? One of my staff left recently to earn twice as much as a travelling book salesman; another resigned because he was earning much less than his wife, an anaesthetist, and felt humiliated.' This embittered idealist was exaggerating the picture a little: primary-school salaries have increased in real terms by over 50 per cent in the past ten years, and now run from 737 to 1,542 francs a month according to age. But that is no more than half what an *agrégé lycée*-teacher gets. And the decline in teaching quality is one reason why the Government's well-intentioned reforms have not yet been more effective.

Although the academic burden of the under-fifteens has now been lightened, in the senior classes of *lycées* it is still oppressive, for here every minute of life is still lived in the shadow of that most sacred and imperious of French institutions, the *baccalauréat*. Taken at eighteen or nineteen, *le bac* is a far more rigorous and brain-searching exam than its rough English equivalent, A-level GCE, and even more essential a passport to success. With the *bac*, a student has traditionally had the right to enrol in any faculty of any French university; without it, all the gates of higher education are barred. As more and more middle-class people come to prize a degree, so more of them try for the *bac*, and the faculties swell uncontrollably. It has been described as the national obsession of the middle classes, dividing the French into two camps, *bacheliers* and non-*bacheliers*; and though the exams are controlled as fairly and strictly as possible, there have been notorious cases since the war of parents paying high prices to bribe examiners or secure advance copies of papers. The French word for cramming is *bachotage*; and hundreds of private fee-paying *boîtes à bachot* have sprung up to cram those who find the large *lycée* classes too impersonal. And of course, the more people of mediocre intelligence try for the *bac*, the higher the failure rate, aggravated by larger classes and declining teaching standards in some *lycées*. Failures now average 40 per cent, reaching 71 per cent in the Paris region in 1966. Those who fail have not only acquired a stigma and possibly a complex for life; they have spent three or four years on an unvocational academic syllabus that leaves them untrained for anything else and with few other educational outlets. They are lucky to get much more than a mediocre job, as clerk or salesman. And this sheer wastage of national resources has prompted growing demands for reform of the *bac* from many people, except those *lycée*-teachers whose heads are in the sand.

In an earlier age, the rhetorical classicism of preparations for the *bac* was possibly ideal for training a ruling élite of lawyers, technocrats, and men of letters. Even today, given the right kind of teacher, its syllabus has many noble virtues as a mental grounding for the more gifted child. And the greatest of these, in principle, has always been its insistence on a high level of 'culture générale' rather than early specialisation. This was so whether you took a classical or a scientific option. Prior to the current Fouchet reforms, the main option on the arts side, known as *le bac philo*, contained a severe dosage of some nine hours' philosophy a week but also no less than five hours of science; and the principal maths and science options ('math-élém' and 'sciences-ex' in *lycée* jargon) each had nine or more hours a week of philosophy and other arts subjects, as well as a rigorous thirteen to seventeen hours of physics, biology, or higher mathematics. While a typical essay subject in the *bac philo* exam might be, 'Do we find anything in perception that assures us about the reality of its object?', even a *sciences-ex* candidate in his philosophy paper might be expected to tackle, 'Can liberty be conceived when there is no reasonable choice?' It is not so easy to see an English science sixth-former coping with this kind of question. No wonder the French scientist or engineer is often a man of such high personal culture, more so than his Anglo-Saxon counterpart.

But the syllabus, and in particular the rhetorical and deductive methods of teaching, tend to develop a turn of mind that is conformist, theoretical, and often uncreative, schooled to think and verbalise with great clarity along predetermined lines. And although a brilliant pupil may be able to master the system and contribute his own originality, others get submerged. Doubts have been growing as to whether this pre-*bac* pressure-feeding is the best way to train the imagination, and whether a classical diet of logic and moral philosophy (Descartes, Plato, Kant) is the right initiation for the entire élite of a modern nation. 'I am horrified,' writes one *lycée*-teacher, 'at the hatred that today's young people feel for Racine and Corneille. And oh! those November mornings we spend crossing the Alps with Hannibal.'

For the past ten years the air has been heavy with reform. But everyone has a different idea of just how the *bac* should be reformed, while many *lycée*-teachers are passionately in favour of the *status quo*. In the early 1960s measures and counter-measures flowed from a vacillating Ministry in a bewildering stream, alienating even those teachers who were sympathetic to change. The syllabus was altered three times, ostensibly with the aim of lightening it. Then in 1964 the *premier bac*—which is a sort of weeding-out exam taken at sixteen or seventeen—was abolished altogether, but not so much to help the student as to save money and relieve pressure on examiners. Finally in 1965 the Minister, Christian Fouchet, announced wide-sweeping reforms which appear to be definitive and coherent, and are coming fully into force in 1968. Their aim is to make the *bac* more vocational and less encyclopaedic.

The syllabus and the options are being re-arranged and modernised. Economics, sociology, and statistics are at last recognised as subjects worthy of a *lycéen*'s study, and they go into a new 'modern' option together with maths, history, and geography. In the *bac philo*, where classical literature has tended to be taught from the standpoint of philosophy, there will now be less philosophy, and more literature for its own sake and modern languages. French literature will no longer stop at 1900: it will reach to Sartre, Camus, and beyond. There will also be a new purely artistic option, to include drama and music, while the ration of science for classicists will be more applied and less theoretical.

This up-dating of the syllabus on the arts side has been generally welcomed by students themselves and by the more liberal teachers. But on the science side in particular the changes carry a more controversial corollary: earlier specialisation. The science and maths options are to be shorn of some of their philosophy and arts teaching, and no longer will any option grant entry to any faculty: if you take the *bac philo* you will now be unable to enrol in a science faculty except with special permission. Thus, although the first two years of the *lycée* syllabus (fifteen to seventeen) will remain fairly general, at seventeen a student will have to decide almost irrevocably what path he wants to follow for life. The aim of the reform is not solely to lessen the range of encyclopaedic study and bring the *bac* closer to modern life: it is also frankly utilitarian, to force scientists to get down to their own subjects earlier, and to oblige students to be less dilettante about their choice of university work. It is a step towards the English model and away from the tradition of 'culture générale'—and for this it has been heavily criticised. Plenty of older teachers, of course, are opposed outright to all the changes: they want to go on teaching about *Andromaque* and Hannibal's elephants just as they were taught in their own youth. But others, who approve of the introduction of modern subjects, are nevertheless worried that some of the old universality of French élite education is being sacrificed to narrow expediency, to the need to get more scientists quickly and cheaply. As this old élite system adapts to the new mass needs of education, clearly something will have to go overboard. But even with a modern syllabus, is not 'culture générale' still a valid ideal? If the French abandon it, may they not risk a divorce of the 'two cultures'? And is it not the teaching methods much more than the syllabus that really need modernising—the magistral discourse, the lack of inductive enquiry, the reliance on set texts? This French tradition produces results that in many ways are most attractive: a verbal finesse, a sophistication of thought and language, so that young people discourse easily about abstract ideas, and make natural use of words like *spiritualité, sensibilité, poésie* that embarrass an Englishman. But it can also lead, especially among intellectuals * and bureaucrats, to a frightening orthodoxy. However, the reform of pedagogic methods can come only with a change of generation.

Another change in the *bac*, less controversial, institutes a new lower-grade pass certificate for those who average 40 per cent in their papers but fail to reach the 50 per cent that will still be needed for university entrance and for the title of *bachelier*. This is clearly a right step and should reduce the wastage, so long as employers can be persuaded to regard the new pass as some kind of qualification. At present, even the full *bac* rarely opens many office-doors in itself, unless followed by a degree or technical diploma. This may change as the syllabus becomes more vocational. And the pass will probably be used for admission to some of the new technical colleges that are springing up to meet the economy's need for more lower-grade specialists.

This shortage of technicians may seem paradoxical when set beside the high prestige of the technologist in France and of the *Grandes Ecoles* that train him after the *bac*. But this prestige belongs only to an élite and ends abruptly below a certain level. An upper-bourgeois family will be proud for their son to take the *bac math-élém* or *sciences-ex* if it leads the way to a *Grande Ecole* and a noble career as engineer or technocrat; but they will turn up their noses at his going instead to one of the few *lycées techniques* and taking the *bac technique*, a far more practical work-shop exam leading to a middle-grade technical career. Yet the failure rate for the prestige *bacs* and for *Grande Ecole* entrance is fearfully high, and few of the throw-outs are trained for much else. At a big *lycée* in Paris I visited a class immersed in the final strained weeks of cramming for the *math-élém*, and their teacher told me: 'Most of these poor kids will fail. They'll end up in clerical jobs or small commerce. Few of them have the minds for this high-quality theoretical work: they'd have done better in a technical stream, if only their silly parents had let them.' Then the school's *censeur* or disciplinary assistant, a woman from a modest family, told me, 'My son went happily to a *lycée technique* and from there to an electronics college, and now in his blue-collar job he's doing better than most of these kids ever will.' So the bourgeoisie is caught in its own snooty trap. But the human wastage and disappointment is great, and the official aim now is to stream more of the beta-plus minds at an early age away from the élite obstacle race and into technical education, where they will still receive a certain amount of simple 'culture générale'. As the new CESs dissuade the less academic children from entering classical *lycées*, so the bourgeoisie may be obliged to modify their prejudice against the only valid alternative. Lack of facilities has prevented this expansion from taking place more quickly; but a number of new technical schools are now at last being built for the fifteen- to eighteen-

---

* See pp. 362–4 (Intellectuals in disarray).

year-old children, while new higher technical colleges at near-university level are being created to fill the gap below the *Grandes Ecoles*.

Nearly all these new reforms are still in the process of being applied, and it is too early to assess results. At least the present régime is now reshaping the whole basis of education, as no-one has dared to do before in this century, and is trying to adapt it to a changing society. And the bulk of the teaching world has, in the past few years, come to accept the need for reform, even if many of them still dig their heels in when it comes to applying the details in practice. If there were more trust between the State and the teachers, the reforms might be more effective. But the Gaullists, typically, in order to avoid argument and obstruction, usually decree new measures high-handedly without consultation and without a field commission to discover first whether they are feasible. It is a short-sighted policy that sometimes defeats its own ends. But the teachers are warily accepting that, however clumsily applied, most of the Fouchet reforms are a move in the right direction.

Anyone who has visited an average French school may have been struck by the rarity of informal human contact between teacher and child, and by the relative absence of a sense of warm, human community where the full personality can be developed. You don't have to be an Arnoldian character-building devotee to be worried by this: the French themselves are becoming more aware of it, and of how over the years it has aggravated some of the negative traits of their national character. But it's something even less amenable to legislation than the deductive *ex cathedra* teaching methods that are closely bound up with it. Efforts at change run into various obstacles: the ingrained disconcern of many teachers for anything but their pupils' intellects; the monolithic State system, painfully ill suited to a matter as delicate and personal as bringing up a child; and the swelling size of many schools, which increases their bureaucracy.

In any State school the smallest departure from routine, such as an extra half-holiday, cannot be fixed without written orders from Paris; and the precise duties of each member of staff are governed by a statute from the Ministry that cannot easily be departed from to suit individual needs, except by the usual French methods of subterfuge.* In the large *lycées* the civil-service atmosphere reaches its height, where teachers stand on rigid ceremony and are called by their formal titles—'Oui, Monsieur le Proviseur', 'Non, Madame la Censeur'—by pupils and colleagues alike. Inevitably most teachers tend to lack initiative and to behave and think like the civil servants they are. Sometimes an energetic or liberal headmaster will succeed in infusing his school with a certain personality of its own without actually defying the Ministry. But this is becoming harder as the *lycées* swell in size, to 2,000 pupils or more: 'just pedagogic fac-

---

* *Débrouillardise* or *le Système D*—see p. 441 (Conclusion).

tories', as someone put it. And because they are now so much larger, it is often felt that the average *lycée* today has even less community spirit and humanising influence than before the war.

I visited a superb-looking new girls' *lycée* at Nîmes, a real showpiece, with modern sculpture and gay murals, sunny, attractive rooms and fine equipment. No child, I felt, could fail to benefit from such a setting. But the atmosphere! The Directrice, a plump, elderly tartar of the old school, a Queen Victoria in looks and outlook, disapproved of the Fouchet reforms and resisted efforts by some of her younger staff to introduce clubs or hobbies or social activities, or give the girls any responsibility for disciplining themselves. They were there simply to be taught, and kept in order. The largest hall in the school held 350, but numbers had swelled to 1,500, so that any ceremony, such as prize-giving or a school concert, that might help to give some community feeling was virtually impossible. The girls arrived in the morning, received their dose of academicism, and went back home. And the teachers did likewise.

Lycée-teachers work hard, to be sure, and may have to spend several hours each evening in term-time correcting pupils' essays, so rigorous is the academic routine. This leaves few of them with much time, or incentive, for sponsoring out-of-class activities. For the average *professeur* it is a kind of office job: he arrives, delivers his series of lectures, maybe with donnish brilliance, and goes home. Discipline, or the children's out-of-school lives, are not his business. Discipline in a *lycée* is in the hands of a non-teaching and usually not highly educated member of staff, the *censeur*, a sort of sergeant-major, assisted by a team of *surveillants*, usually unqualified youngsters of twenty or so earning a little pocket-money while they complete their own studies. They see that the boarders keep out of mischief, but it is not their job to inculcate group spirit or help with character-building.

Usually therefore a *lycéen* will have no-one at school to whom he feels he could turn for personal advice or comfort; and if his home life is not easy, this may be a real lack. In primary schools, the pattern is much the same as in *lycées*: teaching is scarcely less magistral, and classroom discipline is strict but negative. A class has to line up in order at the end of each lesson before it can leave the room or be dismissed. Only the exceptional teacher will try to break through the wall of formality dividing him from his class, while the bad ones resort to petty tyranny: Truffaut's semi-autobiographical film *Les 400 Coups* gave an extreme but not impossible account of what life can be like for a sensitive child (with an unhappy home) at a bad primary school. The obverse of this solemn picture is that at most schools French children are really made to work, and they spend less time than in many countries ragging their masters or being given an amusing time. But these are rarely the happiest days of their lives. For what it is worth, a scientific opinion survey* conducted in

* Published by the *Institut Français d'Opinion Publique*, 1961.

Separation bet. teacher + students in lycée + primary schl.

1960 among fourteen-year-olds in several Western countries found that the percentage of those who 'did not like school much' was 26 in France, 14 in Britain, 9 in the U.S.A., and of those who 'liked it a lot', 23 in France, 34 in Britain, 33 in the U.S.A. Whether the purpose of school is to make children happy or make them learn is a matter for the educationists: it seems to me, as a layman, that both should be possible, given the right sort of teacher.

In France the failures are largely the fault of the teachers and the system. French children are not especially different from any others, and many of them privately hanker for some more personal encouragement and human contact at school. One eager young *professeur de lycée* told me: 'I find that when I do make the running and express warmth they are very responsive. It's usually the teacher's reserve that drives children to become afraid and suspicious of them.' The American sociologist Jesse Pitts has analysed this problem: 'The French teacher makes relatively few allowances for the interests and fantasies of youth. Typically, he ignores his students' needs as children. He often talks to pupils of eleven or twelve years old on a level which supposes an intellectual maturity that they are far from having reached.'* Pitts goes on to explain that the children react by outwardly accepting the teacher's authority but secretly developing among themselves their own 'delinquent community' which rejects and fights against the adult world. The school system represses the child's character, or forces it into private rebellious paths rather than encouraging it to grow as part of a community. And it hardly needs Mr. Pitts to tell us how this marks the French for life. Much of the egotism and friction, the lack of civic feeling, and the private loyalties among sectional interests, spring from attitudes inherited at school. Perhaps the main cause of this state of affairs is that traditionally it is the family, not the school, that is supposed to train character and personality. Parents look on school as a facility, which is not supposed to compete with them as a centre of loyalty; and when a school does try to encourage group activities, or when a teacher goes out of his way to help a child, they often resent it as an intrusion on their own sphere. Yet there is little evidence that parents are better educators in France than anywhere else.

family as chr. for character training

More than sixty years ago a teacher called Edmond Demolins, founder of the famous *Ecole des Roches*, the one French private school run on English public-school lines, wrote a book, *A quoi tient la supériorité des Anglo-Saxons?*, which answered this loaded question with classic Arnoldian arguments in favour of team-games and prefects. The French never took much notice of Demolins' views, any more than they have accepted the British adage about why we won Waterloo. And yet, in the past few years, a nagging feeling has grown among the educationists that some kind of change *is* needed—not towards the English cold-showers-and-

* *France: Change and Tradition* (Harvard University Press, 1963).

fagging system (in its way, almost as austere as the French), but at least towards more out-of-class activities, towards making school life gayer and more varied.

For a start, practical steps have been taken to encourage more sport in schools—more, it is true, for reasons for health and fitness than for Arnoldian ones. All *lycées* now have four hours' compulsory sport and physical training a week, and the *bac* itself contains an obligatory gymnastics test. But many schools are still handicapped by lack of suitable playing fields or gymnasia, and the sports staff generally have low prestige compared with the academics, so that unless the instructor is really good the children use the classes as an opportunity to fool about. And in primary schools there is still virtually no sport. At one school I was told, 'An instructor comes to give classes once a week, but the kids treat it as a joke and prance around the courtyard with him.' I thought of that hilarious scene in *Les 400 Coups* where the boys slip off to play truant in the streets of Montmartre behind the back of the daftly prancing gym teacher.

A more interesting development, though still limited in scope, is the *classes de neige*. Every winter some 50,000 children aged about ten or eleven, mostly from big cities, are transported for a month with their teachers to hostels or cheap hotels in the Alps where they carry on with their normal school work mixed in with afternoons on the ski-slopes. The initiative and the finance has come mostly from town councils rather than the Government: some towns, notably Communist-controlled Le Havre, have even built special centres in the far-distant Alps, to use in winter for snow classes and in summer as workers' holiday camps. The operation is a great success and the children, many of whom would not otherwise have holidays, benefit hugely. Another experiment, which the Ministry is conducting in a few schools, is to reshuffle the timetable so that children go home much later but spend part of the afternoon in organised recreation, outings, and games. It is a success with junior *lycée* classes, but not easy to combine with *bachotage* in the senior ones. Few other schools have yet shown eagerness to adopt it, so the Ministry has not made it compulsory. But at least these changes show the signs of a crack in the old formula of all work and no play. Sport has increased so rapidly in popularity since the war that even teachers and parents are beginning to accept it as not such a waste of school time after all.

Tentative attempts are also being made to introduce more clubs and cultural activities into some schools. But this faces opposition from older teachers who regard such things as frivolous and a threat to academic standards. In one of the most distinguished of Paris *lycées*, the Henri IV, the staff prevented the students from forming an orchestra because it might make noise during school hours, and a drama club in the same school foundered after two months because none of the staff were prepared to help run it. French schoolchildren live in such awe of their teachers that they generally lack the initiative to start such things themselves, unless helped officially. And a teacher who shows too much interest in clubs is often *mal vu* by his headmaster. Fortunately, some of the younger ones are going eagerly ahead: at the girls' *lycée* in Nîmes, an enchanting young woman classics teacher told me, 'The Directrice disapproves of clubs—but I did finally persuade her to let me form a kind of literary society. I asked the girls to prepare an exhibition on Camus. They were absolutely thrilled; they wrote to firms in Paris for books, films, and cuttings, and one of them, a *pied noir*, went to immense trouble to collect material about Camus' Algerian background. It proved to me, conclusively, that French children do enjoy this kind of extra-class activity, so long as their teacher gives them a lead.'

The disparity between such activities in France and elsewhere is astonishing. According to the survey I quoted earlier, in France 11 per cent of fourteen-year-olds have a drama group in their school against 76 per cent in Britain and 78 in the United States. For a school orchestra, the percentages are France 8, Britain 46, USA 83; for a newspaper partly edited by the children, France 4, Britain 34, USA 64. 'But,' the French may retort, 'just look at the difference between French and American academic standards in schools.' Surely it should be possible to strike a balance?

Teacher opposition is one part of the problem: lack of funds is another, for the State, needless to say, puts out-of-class activities near the bottom of its priorities. *Lycées*, even good ones, usually lack even a proper library: the headmaster gets no special funds for the purpose, so new books can be acquired only through parents' donations or the children's own modest subscriptions. And many teachers are quite glad there should not be too many foreign or modern classics around to distract pupils from their real work. Better Kant and Molière, who are on the syllabus, than Pasternak or Faulkner. I am also amazed, in this land of culture, at the lack of time devoted to music and visual arts in the curriculum. Every *lycée* has its music room: as often as not it is locked and silent, in contrast to the sounds of piano and part-song that echo round schools in Britain or Germany. No wonder that French musical life is in crisis and Malraux is forced to admit that the French are not a musical nation. Art, in the land of the Impressionists, the adopted land of Picasso, scarcely fares better. The number of hours devoted to it in *lycées* has been falling, and few pupils over sixteen study any art at all. In one large Paris *lycée*, where the art-room in midmorning was totally deserted, I was told: 'There used to be three art teachers here, now there are two and one may soon be sacked.' As art and music feature hardly at all in the *bac*, they can safely be neglected. The new reforms have now ordained a new specialised arts option, a superb idea in theory; but it will probably be restricted in practice to a few of the more cultured *lycées*, and some people I spoke to doubt whether it will really come to fruition. In junior schools, where there is no *bac*-fever, a little more attention is paid to these subjects, but less than in many countries. Teachers, when criticised, usually lay the blame on parents' lack of interest. Parents merely want their children to pass exams, and will not press for more art and music until these play more part in exams. And the victim of this vicious circle is French creative culture, now in such ominous decline.*

My final lament is for the lack of practical training in democracy or leadership in French schools; either on American lines where a school becomes a parliament-in-embryo, or as in Britain where seniors are responsible for the discipline of juniors. There are classroom lessons in civics and government, but, as one teacher said to me, 'Though we teach them about the Council of State, and how Parliament and the communes work, we give them no chance to try it all out in practice. We tell them about Prefects; you *make* them into prefects.' Each form elects its *chef de classe*, but his duties amount to little more than collecting the exercise-books for teacher: all actual discipline is left, in class, to the teacher, and outside, to the *surveillant*, and is not concerned with more than stopping mischief.

This problem, too, has been worrying the pioneers in the Ministry, and the glimmer of a new movement is beginning to emerge. As a first tentative step, each school now has a kind of committee made up of staff and a few 'delegate' pupils elected by their fellows—much on the paternalist lines of the worker-management committees in industry! The committee is allowed to discuss such matters as clubs and outings, and pupils' criticisms of food, heating, or equipment. But the masters are very much in charge, and in stuffier schools the delegates are told sharply, 'Your place here is to listen, not to talk'. However, one or two of the more liberal *lycée*-headmasters have won State approval to go a stage further. One of them, in Provence, has even allowed the boarders to elect a committee among themselves: 'I want them to become aware of their responsibilities,' he told me proudly. But instead of granting it any practical tasks of self-government, the brief he gave it was to draw him up a document on 'What should be the right conditions for boarding-school life'. And this shying-away from practical delegation of authority I thought quintessentially French.

At Briançon, in the Alps, a much more ambitious scheme† was attempted recently in a *lycée* with a high percentage of boarders from difficult home backgrounds: the headmaster tried to create a more human and easy-going atmosphere by doing away with formal punishment, putting the boys on their honour to behave, and appointing each senior boy as a kind of 'moral tutor' to three juniors, to see that they dressed and behaved properly and were happy—an inspired kind of fagging system in reverse! The scheme was welcomed by the boys at first and worked quite well for three or four years. Finally it broke down because too many seniors abused it and showed little aptitude for this kind of responsibility. The

* See pp. 419–20 (All the arts languish, save one).
† Described in *Le Lycée impossible* by André Rouède (Editions du Seuil, 1967).

parents, too, were sceptical and often hostile. It is often because parents object to this, as to other usurpation of their own duties, that moves towards self-government or leadership-training make little headway in schools. Many a parent would find it intolerable for his little Pierre to be bossed around at school by the son of a neighbour, possibly considered socially inferior. All French children are equal in law; therefore all must have equal status in the same school—however unequal the opportunities of getting there!

An inspector in the Ministry told me: 'I feel that in England your prefects have too much power; here, children aren't given enough.' Many of them would probably welcome a move in this direction. At a *lycée* in Caen, after a lecture on English education, the whole school voted for adoption of the prefect system. But, failing an extraordinary change of heart on the part of French teachers, the trend is much more likely to be in the American direction—towards greater freedom and casualness, more sport and entertainment and discussion, but not towards complementing the teacher's formal class discipline with any other kind. Already, even in the years of *bachotage*, school weighs a little less heavily than it used on the average child—far fewer exams for the very young, a little more skiing and outings and clubs devoted to Camus, and now even the prospect of less Descartes at eighteen. It is a slow progress, but probably a right one. And yet, as they reluctantly dismantle parts of their perfectionist academic assault-course, have the French really thought out what kind of humane education, in the broadest sense, they want to put in its place?

UNIVERSITIES: A CRISIS OF GROWTH

When, in February 1964, the Government was about to show a distinguished State guest, President Segni of Italy, round the Palais de la Sorbonne, the national students' union theatened to seize the building *en masse* and wreck the visit. And it took strong counter-threats from the police to induce them to call off the embarrassing gesture. The students had nothing against poor Signor Segni, nor was it simply a rag: they were protesting in deadly earnest against the high-handedness of their professors and the meagreness of their study conditions.

Over 160 students were arrested that week in various scuffles with the police around the Latin Quarter. It was the worst of the many post-war battles between students and State, and it underlines three points about the present crisis of growth and mutation in French higher education. First, that students in France feel obliged to form a pressure-group that has often been as militant in its discontent as the peasantry. Second, that uneasy and distant relations with the teaching staff are at the root of the problem. And third, that the sudden explosion in university numbers has not been adequately matched by the rise in funds or change in methods:

students live on pitiful grants or jostle for places in overcrowded lecture-rooms and canteens, and plenty of them should probably not be at university at all.

Apart from a few private colleges, all higher education is in the hands of the State. And, under this State umbrella, there is a sharp division between the dozen or so élite *Grandes Ecoles*, each with some autonomy and strictly limited entry, and the swollen, amorphous faculties of the twenty-three universities where anyone with the *bac* can enrol. The carefully chosen *polytechnicien*, aloof behind the high walls of his noble college near the Panthéon, considers himself in a different world from the struggling, anonymous student down the road in the Sorbonne's science faculty. And so he is, in terms of prestige and training. Even within the faculties, there is a gulf between the utilitarian degree-hunting of the new student proletariat, and the rarified academic milieu of professors and post-graduates. As in the *lycées* but even more acutely, today's problem in higher education is how to adapt the rigid élitist traditions of the past to modern mass needs, without too great a sacrifice of quality. Reform has hardly touched the *Grandes Ecoles* yet: but the universities are involved in complete overhaul.

The overall student population has risen from 122,000 in 1939 to 247,000 in 1960, and then 514,000 in 1967—more than twice the British figure. Numbers at the Sorbonne are now at least 160,000; at Caen they have multiplied tenfold since 1939, and at Grenoble they have grown since 1952 from 3,800 to over 16,000. More and more middle-class people have come to want degrees, and there has been no legal means of denying any *bachelier* entry to any faculty in any town. University teaching, always less individual than in Britain, has become a mass industry, and the faculties, as someone put it, are 'no more than student broiler-houses'.

By 1960 the shortage of staff and equipment was at its worst. Since then, the Gaullists have made a big effort and have just about managed to keep pace with the growth. The massive appointment of new staff has reduced the student-teacher ratio, though it still stands at more than twenty to one, much higher than in Britain. Seven new universities have been opened recently, four of them within range of Paris (at Rouen, Amiens, Reims and Orléans) in an attempt to reduce pressure on the Sorbonne. Several of the older universities are being virtually transplanted from their cramped buildings in the centre of towns to huge new American-style campuses on the outskirts. At Grenoble, Toulouse, Montpellier, and elsewhere the rehousing is impressive, and has helped a lot to ease conditions of work.

In Paris as well, new faculty centres have appeared in the suburbs, at Orsay and Nanterre; but the great bulk of the work at this elephantine university still goes on within the charmed circle of the Latin Quarter, Mecca of so many young foreigners and provincials, and quintessence of the conflict in modern Paris between turbulent intellectual excitement and tedious physical congestion. A lecture-hall seating 500 is sometimes crammed with twice that number, and some students will even sit through a lecture in a course outside their subject in order to be sure of a seat for the next one. Scientists often fail their exams because study laboratories are too overcrowded. Lodgings and hostels are in short supply, and even a meal in a cheap student canteen may involve a long wait in a queue. So Mecca's glory has been tarnished, and thousands of provincials have come to accept that it might be wiser to stay on their home ground, whatever the excitements of Paris.

Overcrowding is the biggest and most boring problem, but not the only one. The universities are also having to face the issue of whether they are providing the right kind of training and to the right people. More than 70 per cent of those enrolling in the faculties withdraw without taking a degree; though the number of students has grown fivefold since 1918, the number of annual degrees has merely doubled; and no more degrees are awarded than in Britain, for twice the number of students. This flagrant wastage of time and resources suggests that many of those who enrol should be going straight into jobs or some other kind of training. One reason for the high fall-out is that, although tuition fees are very low, many students are obliged to earn their keep. About 50 per cent get some help from parents, and 10 per cent draw a pre-salary from the Ministry if they are training to be teachers; but only 22 per cent have ordinary grants, and these average a mere 2,350 francs a year. This helps to explain why so many poorer families hesitate to launch their children into the *lycée* stream. Over 30 per cent of students have regular jobs, and mostly these are full-time, for part-time employment is hard to find in France. Some act as sales touts or even night-porters at Les Halles; the largest percentage are *surveillants de lycée*, a job that is intellectually undemanding but a strain in other ways. Studies suffer severely.

Thousands of other students are not 'serious'; they enrol as a kind of status-symbol, or in order to be able to make use of the subsidised canteens and hostels, or (if their parents are well off) as a way of passing a pleasant, dilettante year or two before settling down to marriage or a post in the family firm. *Etudiants fantômes* they are called, and they infuriate their teachers. At Montpellier, where the problem is especially serious, a professor told me: 'Some 150 students signed up for my class in October, but I've no idea how many will seriously sit the exams. They drift casually in and out of lectures, as they feel like: go down to the beaches in summer, and you'll find them in hordes. It's a racket, a waste of our limited resources, and demoralising for those who *are* trying to study properly.'

Even among the more dedicated and responsible students, many simply feel out of their depth in a university course. After the close academic supervision of the *lycées*, they enter a world where there is virtually no personal contact between teacher and student: they feel isolated, adrift, bereft of real intellectual guidance in their studies. Many of them suffer breakdowns, or give up, or go on trying and failing the same examination. In most faculties, the course for a *licence* (the standard degree) has hitherto lasted three years, punctuated by a series of intermediary hurdles of which the most important has been the *propédeutique* exam at the end of the first year. The aim of the *propé* has been to weed out those not really suited for a degree course, and this it has always done: of the mass of students who leave without a degree, four in five stumble at the *propé*, so that two-thirds of those who survive it do finally pass their *licence*. But so imbued with liberalism is the traditional French system that each student has been allowed up to four attempts at the *propé*, spread over four years. Many people fail all four and then, having wasted two years, are thrown on to the labour market with no qualifications save the *bac* which is curiously regarded as not much use in itself.

This whole structure is now under urgent reform, after years of mounting criticism. Some professors have wanted the pass-mark of the *bac* to be raised, or a *numerus clausus* imposed with selective entry on the British model. Marc Zamansky, forceful and outspoken Dean of the Sorbonne science faculty, took matters into his own hands in 1965 and declared he would start applying his own selection methods to bar *étudiants fantômes*: but he was answered with a students' strike, and a rap from the Ministry for exceeding his functions. The ordinary mass of students do not want to give up their franchise, but they have not been alone in opposing a *numerus clausus*. Many of the most progressive-minded professors, anxious to improve the present situation, have nevertheless felt that entry based on the *bac* is the only fair one, and that any other might lead to regional inequalities or the personal bias of selection boards. 'I know we get a lot of unsuitable students,' a young professor at Rennes told me, 'but at least the *propé* and the first year's work do give the student a chance to *prove to himself* that he shouldn't be there, rather than be told so in advance by some board.' It is an admirably liberal approach, if an expensive one. And this prescriptive right to higher education, for all who pass the same exam, is a rooted French tradition that it has not proved easy to adapt to the new conditions. Therefore the sweeping university reforms announced in 1966 made only relatively minor changes in the system of entry. First, it would no longer be automatic for those who pass the *bac* only at a second attempt: they would then have to go before a board. Secondly, students with the *bac philo* would no longer be able to enrol in a science faculty except with special permission. This was one of the changes Zamansky had urged, aimed at weeding out 'amateur' science students who arrive without much knowledge, and tying in with the measures to make the *bac* more specialised. But since 1966 numbers have continued to swell ever more dangerously especially in the arts faculties (which generally attract the weaker students, as providing a softer option than science) and a growing number of professors as well as Ministry officials have come to accept that some more rigorous form of initial selection may be unavoidable. The present Minister, Alain Peyrefitte, has promised to act, and it now seems that under sheer pressure of events the *bac* will soon have ceased to be an open-sesame to the doors of French universities.

Once a student has been admitted to the faculties, he faces a completely revised system of courses and exams under the 1966 reforms. The *propé* has been abolished, and so has the *licence* in its previous form. Instead, a new and sharp distinction is established between 'short' and 'long' higher education. Everyone entering a science or arts faculty will initially take a two-year course ending in a new kind of diploma: there will still be a weeding-out exam after the first year, at least as hard as the *propé* and able to be taken only twice. It is hoped that many will decide to end their studies after these two years—so long as the new diploma can be established as valid for certain jobs and careers such as junior secondary-school teaching. This is still being worked out. Other students will continue, either into a one-year course ending in a *licence*, or into a two-year cycle culminating in a new exam, the *maîtrise*, which will open gates to research or post-graduate work. One aim is to bring French degrees a little closer to those of other countries, with the *maîtrise* corresponding roughly to an MA in some places. But the principal motive of the reforms is to provide a short, easy course for weaker students and so reduce the wasted effort of those struggling beyond their abilities. At the same time, some twenty colleges of an entirely new type have been created, University Institutes of Technology: they require only the new lower-grade 'pass' of the *bac*, and their purpose is to fill a much-needed gap just below *Grande Ecole* level by providing some kind of vocational higher education for future middle-rank technicians. They will relieve pressure on the faculties, so long as the would-be students they are aimed at can be persuaded to go to them. The plan, eventually, is that of every 100 passing the *bac* at any grade, some 35 should go to universities, 25 to the new institutes, and 40 straight into employment.

Basically these are utility reforms, to adapt university courses to the teaching of much larger numbers; and inevitably they have been criticised as 'trying to get graduates on the cheap'. Professors and students have also complained that the Ministry has not yet made it clear just what the new diplomas and degrees will be valid for, especially as teaching qualifications. No doubt this will be sorted out in time; but, as with its secondary-school reforms, the Government has pushed out its decrees piecemeal, with a typically high-handed disregard for public relations and without consulting the teachers in advance. Had it consulted them, maybe the reforms would never have got through, for the university world as a whole is still cliquish and suspicious of change, a great deal less liberal than the planners in the Ministry or rare figures like Zamansky. And the reforms, though far from perfect, are clearly a necessary step in the right direction: therefore the Ministry's autocracy may well have been justified. But the Gaullists rarely bother to ease matters by sugaring the pill, and they have left the teachers angry and confused.

Many professors who accept the need to alter the ordinary degree courses are nonetheless worried at the effect the changes may have on academic standards at a much higher level. The initial two-year cycle is compulsory for all. Will this not, they ask, hold back the more brilliant? And what of the future of that most cherished of élite exams, the *agrégation*, which Fouchet in a rash moment recently threatened to abolish? This is a competitive *concours*, based on a thesis, prepared each year by a few hundred of the ablest post-graduates and corresponding roughly to a B.Litt. Most *agrégés* then make a career in the academic world, either as teachers in the senior classes of *lycées* or as university assistants and lecturers, and they develop a very special mentality. Once he starts preparing his *agrégation*, a student enters that élite academic stratum where values are so very different from those of the 'broiler-house' he has left behind. His contact with his professor at last becomes real, and he sits an exam where only a predetermined number each year are allowed to pass. And this is because the academics who control the exam, themselves all *agrégés*, do not want to devalue the exclusive prestige of their fraternity by widening the gates. Yet the demand for qualified *agrégés* in *lycées* and faculties has been growing fast; and since the numbers who wish to sit the exam has also been growing, it should be possible to grant more titles without a drop in standards. The professors pursue the argument that 'more means worse'; but in reality many of them simply want to keep their own little academic world intact. It is a familiar problem, with much to be said on both sides. And so far not even the Gaullists have yet dared to lay their hands on this inner sanctum of French scholarship, despite the Minister's threats.

Many of those who pass the *agrégation* then try to move on to the next and most fearsome hurdle of all, the *doctorat d'Etat*, essential qualification for a university professor's chair. But whereas the thesis for an *agrégation* is a relatively slight affair, the *doctorat* involves up to ten or fifteen years' work preparing an exhaustive document of maybe 1,000 pages on a highly specialised subject. This usually has to be combined with a teaching job in a *lycée* or faculty, and many people emerge at thirty-five or forty quite worn out. But the final prize is great. A *docteur* who then manages to get elected to a professorship can do exactly what he likes for the rest of his life. He gets a pleasant salary, maybe 60,000 francs a year, and need not write another word. All he has to do is give the odd lecture. Many professors still work hard, but others abuse their freedom. Today there is a growing movement, among younger *agrégés* and in the Ministry, in favour of lightening the *doctorat*, for letters if not for science, and increasing the number of *agrégés*. This would enable more people to give more of their time to the actual job of teaching, and would make for closer contact between staff and students. In science, there may be a case for leaving things as they are, for here the *doctorat* is often a valuable piece of original research. But in the arts it can be absurdly academic and encyclopaedic: what the examiners demand is often little more than an exhaustive bibliographical résumé of every published text on the subject, with little original thought involved. But the examiners, themselves *docteurs*, do not want to 'lower standards' or 'devalue the quality of research' by simplifying the thesis: that is, they want others to go through the same mill, and they don't want to share their privileges too widely.

Although the reformers have changed the ordinary degrees so radically, they have not yet touched the *doctorat*. And though university professors have mostly come to accept the need for change at the lower level, they will fight to the last hieroglyph to defend their own purist traditions. There is much to admire about this high standard of scholarship. The *agrégés* are schooled to a formal clarity of thought and expression which has no equal, and which many of them later pass on in the *lycées* to other future *agrégés*, like monks on Mount Athos handing down their secrets. Sometimes one of them leaves the monastery, like Jean-Paul Sartre, who began life as a *lycée* teacher. His implacable intellect bears the stamp of this training at its best, but also of its limitations; even he, with his belief in *engagement*, is marked by that divorce from everyday reality that typifies the French academic élite.* Whereas an Oxford don nowadays will readily appear on television, dabble in business, or sit on commissions of enquiry, the average Sorbonne professor maintains a steady scorn for the world of industry, journalism, or practical politics. Raymond Aron, who broadcasts, writes for *Le Figaro*, and is something of a public figure, is an exception; but people are often surprised when they learn that he also happens to be a Sorbonne professor. Conversely, academics are highly resentful of any intruder from outside, however distinguished: when Pierre Massé, a brilliant *polytechnicien*, gave up his job at the head of the Plan and broke all precedent by giving a course of lectures at the Paris law faculty, the reaction of many law professors was, 'But how *can* he? He's not a *professeur en droit*!' Everyone must abide by his *titre*, no one must poach in another's preserve. This attitude is also making it difficult for the Common Market to progress towards its ideal of harmonising European degrees and diplomas. French professors are not the only ones at fault, but they are even less interested in equivalent foreign titles than their German or Italian colleagues. And the almost total lack of contact or sympathy between Europe's two greatest universities, on Seine and Isis, is if anything more the fault of the French than the British.

It is true that a growing number of younger professors and lecturers are coming to think differently and to form contacts more easily outside their own academic circle: with colleagues abroad, with non-university people in France, even with their own undergraduates. I quote the example of a lecturer in English at Rennes, Jean Lecotteley, who finds time also to be a municipal councillor and the city's effective PRO, to pay frequent visits to its twin-town, Exeter, and play a large part in Anglo-Breton links, and even to stage an annual drama production in

* See p. 358 (Intellectuals in disarray).

English with his students. Lecotteley of course has no ambitions for a doctorate; he would hardly have time. And undoubtedly research and scholarship would suffer if all behaved like Lecotteley; that is the excuse that many professors give for staying in their ivory towers. But a simple broadening of outlook need not necessarily take up a great deal of time. The tragedy is that this deliberate abdication from the affairs of the rest of the nation, on the part of most university teachers, deprives French public life of much of the country's highest resources of talent.

The immediate victims of this self-seclusion are the students. They have even less informal human contact with their teachers than in the *lycées*; and many a professor who lectures to the same class twice a week for a year may get to know the names of no more than a handful of them. A professor at Nancy once talked to me eagerly for an hour about the academic curriculum and its problems, and when at the end I asked, 'And your students—what do they feel about it all? What are they like?' he looked at me in surprise as if I were asking about Martians: 'Oh, *them*: I wouldn't know. You see, they're very secretive.' It is true that most students are individually secretive and corporately suspicious and aggressive in their attitude to their teachers—but whose fault is it largely? Students are thrown back on themselves: if they want to voice their feelings on any subject, instead of being able to stroll across the quad into the Dean's study for a chat over sherry (as at Oxbridge), they are forced into unionised protest action as if they were metalworkers wanting more pay. It is another of France's famous barriers. The crisis at the time of Segni's visit to the Sorbonne was typical: faced with overcrowded lecture halls, many students nowadays prefer to buy roneoed or printed copies of lectures, but the professors refused to modify their right to charge high royalties on these, and the students, instead of being able to discuss it face to face, staged a demonstration. Paradoxically, students in France as elsewhere on the Continent enjoy quite high social prestige; and this makes them all the more resentful at being in practice 'treated as minors' by the authorities. They want to be consulted on matters affecting them. The leftish Union Nationale des Etudiants Français goes on campaigning for better privileges including 'pre-salaries' in place of grants, although, admittedly, it is nowadays less militant and powerful than it used to be in the days of conscription for the hated Algerian war. Visit any UNEF campus office, its walls covered with big printed posters, 'Etudiants, Défendez-Vous! Continuons la Lutte!' and from these and the tone of discussion you might think you were in the underground HQ of some Castroist liberation movement.

Many of the younger university staff would like to modify a system of which they, too, are prisoners. A few do make real efforts to get to know their students or even to develop Oxbridge-type pastoral links. A sociology professor at Montpellier told me: 'I try to be a kind of moral tutor to some of them in my spare time. I feel they do need me. Sometimes my wife and I have them to dinner.' In some faculties, *groupes de travail* of about thirty to forty students have now been established under young assistant lecturers, who have a much better chance of making personal contact than the professors with their crowded *conférences*. But the rate of growth of the student population has made it impossible to develop any kind of tutorial system, as some would like: it is not until the *agrégation* that a student works under the regular guidance of a professor.

Even in their leisure time, many feel a similar isolation. The paucity of clubs and organised social activity is another feature of French universities that marks them off from Redbrick, let alone Oxbridge. Each university has its student club centre, usually little more than two or three shabby rooms with a bar, a UNEF bureau, a ping-pong table, a pick-up for *sauteries* (hops) on Saturday nights, and a notice-board covered with appeals for digs, part-time work, or free lifts to Paris. Students tend to live private lives with their own little group of friends; few have the time, money, or inclination for such a luxury as founding an arts or drama club. There are one or two striking exceptions to this pattern: at Nancy, notably, the students have recently set up a most ambitious cultural network of their own, with encouragement from the Rector. But in most places the authorities make little effort to help by providing premises or leadership. In the provinces, where most students are local and have family or friends close by, the sense of isolation is not always so acute, and the same applies at the Sorbonne for students with homes in Paris or for a few in the friendlier hostels. But for tens of thousands of others who come to Paris, whether from the Côte d'Or or the Côte d'Ivoire, from Carcassonne or Casablanca, the obverse of the prize of freedom is to be anonymous in the lonely crowd, unable to find any congenial social context. Several of the more shy ones have told me of their acute difficulty in making friends or finding somewhere to belong to except, maybe, devotional or politically activist circles.

The building of the big new provincial and suburban campuses is at least providing the challenge to create something different. These are the student equivalents of the *Grands Ensembles*, with some of the same social problems. Their inmates no longer live and work in town centres with cafés, shops, and cinemas to hand; they are out on their own in the more artificial setting of vast *cités résidentielles*, and the authorities are beginning to accept that something must be done for them. Grenoble, in its usual pioneering role, is now the scene of a fascinating attempt to move towards the Anglo-American college system. The local branch of an official national body, the Œuvres Universitaires, which has a general brief from the Ministry to look after the physical and moral welfare of all students, has persuaded a few young professors to go out and live on the campus among them. This began in 1965. Men and girl students live in separate hostels, with strict rules about visiting; but they have a joint cultural and social centre, built with public money and well equipped with a theatre for films and plays, a record library, music and photograph rooms, and so on. It is open day and night: the evening I called, the music room was packed with a cosmopolitan crowd listening to a Turkish student at the piano and a Canadian guitarist. Everyone seemed happy. The students are encouraged to run their own community life, under the friendly guidance of the resident professor. Already after six weeks they had founded a drama club, and arranged their own lecture society with visitors coming to talk about such extra-curricular but relevant topics as birth-control.

All this may seem stale and obvious to a British reader: but it marks the most revolutionary improvement in the social conditions and atmosphere of a French student's life. And clearly, once they are given some lead, they welcome it. One student at Grenoble, a Béarnais, told me: 'I was in the Cité Internationale at the Sorbonne before, and I was horribly lonely. You can't think what it means to have a young professor with us on the campus here, instead of the wardens they usually put in charge of hostels. We can actually *talk* to him.' This experiment is possible because the local director of the OU, and the Dean of the Science Faculty, Louis Weil, are forceful men who talked the Ministry into letting them try it and providing some funds. It might not work, yet, in a less unusual university than Grenoble. Most of the older student hostels are controlled by the Ministry on a strict legalistic basis, and at one I was told, 'Paris would not allow us to hold dances on Saturday night, because the *statut* of our resident students' association had not been formally recognised as correct by the Ministry.'

This is just one example of the absurd centralisation and bureaucracy that plagues the universities as much as the schools. Though provincial faculties have some power to select their own staff, all their appointments have to be approved by the Ministry, and are sometimes overridden; and the same applies to any of their changes in routine or administration. A university's rector thus has a role quite different from that of an English vice-chancellor: he is a kind of *préfet*, appointed by Paris to administer not only the faculties but all the State education in his *académie* or region, down to and including the primary schools. And while some rectors are men of considerable presence and vision, others are little more than ciphers. A university has little corporate existence or distinctive personality of its own; it has often been said, 'There is just one big university in France, with groups of faculties scattered around the provinces, all following the same courses'; and if one university happens to outshine the others in a particular subject (as Lyon for medicine, or Grenoble or Toulouse for science), it is due usually to the heritage of some pre-Napoleonic tradition, or to the prowess of some local personality, or to deliberate Government policy. Within each university, the faculties have no organic connection with each other: they are responsible via the rector to Paris, and there is hardly any of the interdisciplinary penetration now all the rage in Britain. The rector's own freedom, too, is circumscribed, especially if he is known to be critical of Government policies: when Rector Martin

of Caen, an outspoken critic of the Fouchet reforms, was about to set off to
take part privately in a conference in Tokyo, the Ministry sent an official
car to Orly airport and stopped him from boarding the plane under threat
of dismissal. He was not considered a suitable ambassador for French
education.

In the past years there has been much deconcentration from Paris to
the provinces, but not any derogation of power. The regional universities
have been encouraged to grow much faster than the Sorbonne, and have
been given most of the new funds; with their new equipment and their
easier living conditions, they now attract a growing share of the best
teachers and students. No longer does a gifted professor at Lille or Dijon
feel that his career has failed if it is not crowned with a chair at the
Sorbonne; no longer does a bright *licencié* of Besançon or Bordeaux feel it
so necessary to move to Paris to study for his *agrégation*. But this is not at
all the same as decentralisation. In fact, for the very reason that the Sorbonne has always traditionally been allowed a certain autonomy by the
Ministry, the recent decline in its influence and prestige has simply served
to increase the hold of the State over the network as a whole. It is hard to
assess fairly the good and the harm of this Napoleonic system. As in the
case of local government, the Ministry's ideas for reform are frequently
more dynamic and liberal than those of local professors; but as with local
politics, if the universities are kept in this tutelage, they cannot develop
the initiative and personality that would help them to progress. It is a
typically Gaullist vicious circle.

THE *GRANDES ECOLES*: A DOUBLE
CHALLENGE TO 'X' FROM NANCY

The dozen or so great colleges known as the *Grandes Ecoles*, most of them
devoted to engineering or applied science, do not suffer from State centralisation to nearly the same degree as the sprawling monolith of the
universities. Each is allowed a certain autonomy, and each keeps itself
proudly apart for its own chosen élite. The *Grandes Ecoles* account for no
more than one in twenty of the numbers in higher education, but they
turn out a very high proportion of France's top administrators and
engineers, and they enjoy a very special mystique. One or two are privately run; most belong to the State but not all to the Ministry of Education. The *Ecole Polytechnique*, for instance, comes under the Army
Ministry. And one of their main differences from the universities is that
each controls its numbers with its own fiercely competitive entrance exam,
requiring two or three years' special study after the *bac*. Entry is thus a
prize of the highest prestige.

There is much that is very fine about the *Grandes Ecoles*, that few
reformers want to change. They have built up an *esprit de corps* that
has served France well. The prestige they impart to their graduates has

helped the technocrat or engineer to enjoy higher status and influence than he does in Britain, and this has played some part in France's economic recovery. There are some advantages to a modern nation for its key industrial executives to possess an engineering background; and although the old-boy network of some *Ecoles* is encrusted with favouritism and arrogance, this has created a unified and efficient élite, frequently able to join hands across the restricting barriers of French public life, both in private industry and public service. Without this, the Plan could never have worked so smoothly.

All this is true, supremely, of the proudest of the schools, the *Ecole Polytechnique*, often known as 'X' for short because of its badge of two crossed cannon. By origin this is a military college, founded by Napoleon to train engineers for the armed forces. Today it is still run on the lines of an officer cadet school, with a serving general at its head: its pupils, *les X*, wear full-dress uniform with fantastic curly hats. They attend parades, and are allowed outside their gates for less than three hours each weekday, in contrast to the freedom of the ordinary student. But only a minority of *polytechniciens* today enter a military career; most go into the civil service or the big State industries, or they are allowed to buy themselves out of their commitments and join a private firm. Louis Armand, Pierre Massé, Jacques Rueff, Pierre Guillaumat, and Valéry Giscard d'Estaing* are just a few of today's great names among *les X*. And not Eton nor Balliol can equal the power of the freemasonry among the graduates of this mighty *alma mater*. Once an X, always an X: in a land where informal contact between strangers is normally so difficult, all X high and low call each other *camarade* whether they have met before or not, and *tu* if they are fairly close in age, and the lowliest X can write out of the blue to a famous colleague and be sure of help and sympathy. Private firms traditionally fall over each other to entice *les X* on to their staff.

But, and it is a big but, is this arrogant apparatus substantiated by the actual quality of the teaching and training? Many people feel increasingly that it is not. They argue that the whole structure, and the syllabus and selection methods of the 'X' and the other *Grandes Ecoles*, badly need revision—despite their qualities. If *les X* still rise to so many of the top posts in the land, frequently it is due less to their training than to the school's prestige and their own innate brilliance. For there is no doubt of the quality of recruits.

The same applies, to a lesser degree, to some other *Grandes Ecoles*. Yet this is one of the few sectors of French education which the Fouchet reforms have not yet touched. In 1964 a Government commission headed by a former Socialist Minister of Education, André Boulloche, proposed some radical measures. They have remained a dead letter. Attempts at reform stumble on that most powerful of political obstacles: nostalgia. Several members of the Government are ex-alumni (Pompidou himself

* For all these names, see Economy and Industry chapters, *passim*.

was at the *Normale Supérierure*, next in prestige to the 'X') and their old-boy sentiments make them want to keep things unchanged.

The first argument against the *Grandes Ecoles* is that methods of entry are far too rigorous. The two- or three-year preparatory courses for the entry exams take place in special post-*bac* classes in *lycées*, known in slang as *khâgnes* (for the *Normale*) and *taupes* (for the other schools). So fierce is the competition that many students work a crippling seventy- or eighty-hour week over the whole period, turning into pale swots and driving themselves and their parents mad. 'Those who come out top for entry to the *Polytechnique*,' one professor used to tell his class, 'do not smoke, do not drink, and are virgins.' The work in these *lycée* classes is of a far higher standard than in the average university faculty; in many ways, they represent the intellectual pinnacle of French education below *agrégé* level. But for all except the most brilliant it is an unnerving obstacle-race, with a large prospect of failure at the end. The Boulloche Report proposed lowering the hot-house atmosphere by integrating the classes into the more easy-going university system. Boulloche also wanted a simpler and more flexible entrance examination, based less exclusively on written papers and more on interview and school record. But Pompidou personally opposed this and so did others: they argued that it would lay the way open to graft and personal bias and was less in the democratic French tradition than a written exam. However, the recent Fouchet reforms, though they do not alter the *khâgnes* and *taupes* nor the methods of entrance, do at least equate them with the new initial two-year faculty cycle: anyone who fails *Grande Ecole* entrance but gets a reasonable mark can move straight on to the *licence* or *maîtrise*, instead of having to start again at the beginning in a faculty, as before. This will save immense heartache and wastage of labour.

A more serious objection to the *Ecoles* is that, after the gruelling business of entry, once you are there work is too easy. This applies especially to 'X': its failure-rate for the passing-out exam is almost nil, and even with a low placing you are assured of a cushy job somewhere for the rest of life, so great is the school's snob-appeal and old-boy solidarity. It breeds an arrogant caste of *rentiers*. 'They're a bunch of spoilt, immature Minou Drouets,' one law student told me, spewing out his sour grapes. *Les X* have little incentive either to work hard or to develop originality: they receive an encyclopaedic general education at a high level, with plenty of thermodynamics, astrophysics, logic, and economics, but their minutely detailed timetable is the same for everyone and leaves them hardly any scope for individual specialisation or initiative. They emerge, as Pétain once said of a *polytechnicien*, 'knowing everything but knowing nothing else'. The system produces fine administrators, but not great creative thinkers, and has sometimes been held responsible for the lack of top-level research scientists in modern France.

There is also a need for closer liaison between the *Grandes Ecoles* and the universities. However much the schools cherish their exclusiveness and restricted numbers, they as well as the faculties do in fact suffer from the rivalries and lack of contact between them. For instance, only the faculties are empowered to grant *doctorats* and are not keen to extend the privilege; therefore it is not easy to prepare to be a *docteur* on the staff of a *Grande Ecole*, and this is one reason why the schools are weak on higher research. Conversely, the faculties cannot always make the best use of their handsome research funds because the calibre of their students is not high enough: the best ones are in the *Ecoles*. Each *Ecole* lives in its own little world and sets its own exams, unrelated to public degrees: except at entry stage, they are not really competing either with each other or with the faculties, and so it is difficult to assess their calibre or results. Some are simply living on their reputation. At the 'X', the teaching of mathematics was, until recently, so old-fashioned that it was reckoned that many students would have failed the maths *licence* if they sat for it, despite their brilliance.

Although there has been no general reform, some changes are now happening piecemeal: for instance, the *Ecole Supérieure d'Electricité* has agreed to share some facilities and staff with the new Orsay branch of the Paris science faculty. The *Ecole Normale Supérieure*, too, has been drawing closer to the Sorbonne and encourages its students to sit for Sorbonne exams. The *Normale*, concentrating on the humanities as much as on science, is rather different from the other *Grandes Ecoles*: its primary role is to prepare university and *lycée* teachers via the *agrégation*, although in practice nowadays, as with the 'X', many graduates prefer to buy themselves out of this obligation and go into administration or a literary career. The *Normale* is a superior kind of Balliol, the supreme citadel of French scholarship: Sartre was a *normalien*, and so were Blum, Jaurès, Herriot, Giraudoux, Soustelle,* and many other great figures besides Pompidou himself. Like the 'X' it lies close to the Panthéon—in the Rue d'Ulm— and like the 'X' it is residential. But unlike the 'X' it is bohemian in spirit and largely free from discipline. Its students can wander about in jeans and are trusted to work as they choose. In the past few years it has even increased this freedom, and has modernised its curriculum, hugely improved its science research facilities, and generally brought itself up to date. Although its entry system (via the *khâgnes*) may still be open to criticism, in other respects it appears the very model of a great classical college that has managed to move with the times yet retain its old genius.

Even the *Polytechnique* now shows signs of movement along the same kind of path. In the past few years the syllabus has been made a little less encyclopaedic and more research has been introduced, to encourage the training of scientists. A further modest reform is promised for 1969, including the establishment of maths and physics 'options' that might well

* Soustelle I consider 'great' as an anthropologist, not as a politician.

encourage a higher quality of research. These reforms have been due to pressure from younger professors and graduates, many of whom would like to see much more radical changes: an updating of the curriculum, lightening of the military routine, and modification of the entry system. But the board of ex-alumni who control the school's policy, many of them senior serving officers, are generally opposed to innovation. Yet if the 'X' does not modernise itself, and soon, its power and prestige are likely to slip seriously, as already they have begun to do. Since the war the civil service's own post-graduate Ecole Nationale d'Administration* has arisen as a potent rival and has reduced the hold of *les X* over the best executive careers. The 'X' old-boy network, though still powerful, is not what it was twenty or thirty years ago; and State and private firms are increasingly learning to their cost that not all the school's cherished products can prove themselves equal to complex modern tasks.

ENA's challenge is limited to public administration; but in technology, too, the traditions and techniques of the Polytechnique are now coming under threat from several newer-style schools, and notably from two in Nancy. There the Ecole Nationale Supérieure des Mines, one of the grandest of the *Grandes Ecoles*, was reformed on American-inspired lines in 1957 by its vigorous director, Professor B. Schwartz. He has done away with examinations and most lectures and divides the students into small study-groups, which allows them far closer contact with their teachers than is usual in France. There are also close working links with local industry; and whereas at Grenoble these are confined mainly to joint research, at Nancy they extend into the college's daily training, with Lorraine industrialists taking part in seminars, and students going on practical courses in near-by firms. This is usual enough in the United States and even in Britain; in France it marks something of a break with tradition. It has come in for some criticism, and has not always worked smoothly: Schwartz had to back-pedal recently, after finding that he had given his students too much freedom and some had not been able to cope with it. But his system is beginning to influence other schools. It may not be ideal for training research workers, but has advantages for turning out practical engineers and technical executives.

An engineering school that opened at Nancy in 1960, the Institut des Sciences de l'Ingénieur, has embarked on an even bolder and more unusual path, under its fanatical and messianic young director, Marcel Bonvalet. It is not a *Grande Ecole* at all, for it takes students directly after the *bac*, and is really closer to the new technology institutes set up by Fouchet. But this has not deterred Bonvalet from the most startling innovations, nor from aiming very high, perhaps too high. His experiment is open to many criticisms; but I do not think I have come across anything in modern France, of any kind, that has impressed me more.

On a hill outside the town, it shines out into the night, floodlit, with

* See p. 168; the ENA takes graduates from places such as the Ecole des Sciences Politiques ('Sciences Po') at the Sorbonne.

gay polychromatic glass façades of red, purple, and gold. Nothing could look less like the grey old walls of 'X'. As I arrived, Bonvalet bounced up to me, sat down in his sleek office with a bottle of malt whisky, and then excitedly propounded his gospel at me non-stop for four hours, while three of his young staff sat by as mute, admiring disciples. He is a *pied noir*, born in Bizerta in 1928, a short, tough-looking man with the *pied noir*'s usual brash energy and contempt for red tape. After speeding through his *doctorat-ès-sciences* at the Sorbonne, he went back to Tunisia in 1956 under a technical aid programme to help Bourguiba set up crash-courses for technologists. There he forged his basic methods of inductive, empirical teaching: later, back in Paris, he persuaded some of the more progressive educo-technocrats in the Ministry to let him try them out in France as well. They built the new school in Nancy for him. There he has kicked nearly every French pedagogic precept out of his wide windows, and especially the deductive method. Unlike Schwartz at the Ecole des Mines, he claims he is trying to produce researchers, not men of action; but, like Schwartz, he starts from the belief that in an age of swift, technological change you need to teach not facts but principles and methods of enquiry. His pupils are not told; they are made to find out for themselves. It is a blow in the face to the *cours magistral* of the *lycées*, the faculties, and the 'X'.

Bonvalet takes nineteen-year-olds straight from their mathematics or technical *bac* and puts them through an intensive and imaginative four-year course. From their first day they are encouraged to 'share the creative joy of the inventor' by exploring inductively every channel of enquiry and knowledge. Second- and third-year students act partly as monitors and study-leaders for the juniors in order, so Bonvalet told me, to help them with their own revision and to provide a kind of leadership-training. Nearly all study is in small groups, with elaborate use of closed-circuit TV to link the many small classrooms with the central lecture hall. And most important, in the senior years the accent is increasingly on operational research and experiment: students are given handsome funds for making their own equipment, with impressive results. I was shown several computers and other advanced gadgets they had built themselves. 'We've got two closed-circuit TV networks now,' said Bonvalet; 'the first, I admit, we bought, but the second the boys made—after all, it's so much cheaper.' The lighting, the panelled electric signs, the whole interior style of the building seemed more lavish and imaginative than in the average, fund-starved French college. 'Simple,' said Bonvalet; 'we made a lot of it ourselves. Saves money.'

Were his teaching methods, I asked, inspired by the United States, like Schwartz's? 'Christ, no! *We* are inspiring them! Several American teachers and students are working here now to learn from us. Van Karman himself, greatest of all American aeronautic scientists, said just before his death that he thought my school was the world's finest pioneer of the future, in its field. All our methods we work out empirically.' It is clear

that his arrogant enthusiasm carries the devotion of his staff and pupils—
and he claims to know personally all 300 of them. He reminded me of
some hearty team-spirited English housemaster, with technology in
place of muscular Christianity—a refreshingly incongruous figure compared with the usual drily bureaucratic head of a French college. He said,
'The Sorbonne got my goat with its medieval, superficial academicism
and lack of human contact. The "X" is just as bad, in its own way. It's out
of date, and the first really strong Government in France will be the one
with the courage to close it down. Of course it still attracts the best brains
because of its legend. But we're catching up. Our influence is growing,
and we'll win. Much of our intake now is as brilliant as the X's. Till now
there's been a prejudice in France against inventive research. That's
what we're trying to break down.'

But the argument against Bonvalet is that in trying to pit himself
against the Goliath of the 'X' he has overstepped his brief and exceeded
his resources. His is not a *Grande Ecole*; and, despite his claims, his students
are rarely brilliant enough to benefit from the magnificent chances he
gives them. It can also be argued that he lays too much stress on gimmicks,
like his TV feed-back system; and that in avoiding the wide-ranging
'culture générale' of the 'X' he swings too far in the opposite vocational
extreme—the teaching of languages, economics, and history he airily
dismisses with, 'They've not the time for that. Let them read books in the
holidays.' But at least he is a man with fire in his belly, the kind of
trouble-shooter that French officialdom can do with. The reformers in the
Ministry look on their *enfant prodigue* with an anxious indulgence, aware
of his value and of his limitations; and now there is talk of transferring
him to take charge of a real *Grande Ecole*, better suited to his ideas and
ambitions. Wherever he goes, and whatever happens to the school at
Nancy, his influence, like that of Schwartz, seems likely to spread. Already
some of his methods are being taken up by *Grandes Ecoles* at Rouen,
Toulouse, and elsewhere. And the Ecoles, including 'X', are more likely
to be reformed by the gradual percolation of new ideas in this manner,
than by the kind of formal legislation that Boulloche tried and failed.

There is much in the *Grandes Ecoles'* tradition of polyvalence and
public service that it would be tragic to lose. A swing too far to Bonvalet's
opposite extreme might yield a far narrower outlook, and prejudice the
training of the kind of technocrat who has been one of France's greatest
sources of strength. France may need more scientists, but she also still
needs human beings. It ought to be possible to combine the positive elements of the Bonvalet and Schwartz reforms with the traditions and ideals
of the present *Grande Ecole* framework. This is what the moderate reformers want. But amid the clamour of the diehards and the revolutionaries, it is not so easy to achieve.

LA JEUNESSE: NOT SO MUCH
REBELS, MERELY CHUMS

'*Mais que pensent les jeunes?*' ask the headlines in a constant stream of magazine articles: '*Nos jeunes, qui sont-ils?*' And few of them can find an easy answer. What are they like, this mysterious new generation, for whom all the educational crusades are being fought? Ostensibly, they are following much the same paths as modern youth in other Western countries, though less aggressively than in Britain. They have their own powerful new consumer market for music, clothes, and cars; their own world of young singing idols like Johnny Hallyday and Françoise Hardy, their own fringe minorities of delinquents and beatniks with hair-styles imported from London. All, or nearly all, have far more freedom from parents than cloistered French youth had before the war. Many are conscious of the gulf between their own morality and that of the older generation.

And that older generation in turn has become aware of youth as never before. *La Jeunesse* is now a slogan, a doctrine of faith in the future, a symbol of France's recovered vitality. For more than a century this used to be an adult-dominated country, where teenagers were treated as small-scale adults and were not expected to exist as a national group in their own right. Now the grown-up world has woken up, as it were, to the existence of a neglected minority in its midst, with its separate values and needs. Youth is solicited, analysed, indulged (except by its teachers). But this parental lip-service to the new cult of youth is not always accompanied by actual understanding of individuals. And in some ways the youthful revolution *à l'anglaise* is more apparent than real in France; or at least, it has not yet found proper expression.

In the first decade or so after the war, many of the most important changes in France were due to a new generation rising against the standards of its elders—from the young farmers of the JAC to the cinema's *nouvelle vague*. And other phenomena (St. Tropez, Françoise Sagan, the early existentialists) gave the world a popular image of French youth in open revolt. Today, in the late '60s, that image has become strangely deceptive. As often as not, older people nowadays complain, 'But the young, they're so docile, so conformist'. While Britain's youth have now leapt ahead in precocious emancipation, the French are still, relatively, under the shadow of school and parents. Seduced by prosperity and placated by adult acceptance, many of them seem to be tamed into a listless submissiveness, or else into a feeling of impotence.

The climate of 1945 was very different from today's: more austere, but also more adventurous. The upheavals of wartime had broken down some of the barriers that previously kept youth in its place, and an idealistic new generation was able gradually to make lasting inroads into the *positions acquises* of the age-hierarchy. It happened most strikingly in agriculture, and in the civil service and industry where some older men emerged discredited from the Occupation and young ones took their place. It is remarkable how youthful many of the post-war pioneers were at the outset: Leclerc was twenty-three when he began his cut-price campaign in Brittany, and Planchon founded his Villeurbanne theatre at twenty-one. Today the impetus of this generation is still driving forward, in nearly every field; and many of its leaders, now around forty, are in key national positions. But their successors, now in their twenties, born into an age of greater ease and acceptance, have seldom shown the same innovating spirit. This has been even more apparent in the intellectual world. After the Liberation, many young people flocked excitedly around Sartre and Camus at St.-Germain-des-Prés, eager to revolt against their bourgeois backgrounds and help to forge a better world. This existentialist climate has since gradually dissipated.* The Sartrian disciples of those days have mostly settled down and become prosperous, and many are now leading the bourgeois lives they once denounced. Their young successors either find money-making, fast cars and hi-fi more appealing than philosophy; or else they are cynical and dispirited at the anti-bourgeois rebellion's failure to create a new society.

In the mid 1950s a few isolated and much-publicised events, vaguely influenced by existentialism, managed to sustain the impression of a generalised youthful revolt. In 1954 the eighteen-year-old Françoise Sagan, daughter of an industrialist, published her first novel, *Bonjour Tristesse*. Her sophisticated world of whisky and wealth was some steps away from the severe, intellectual *milieu* of the true existentialists; but her heroine's cool disillusion and rejection of social morality sounded a note that seemed to borrow something, however ill digested, from the ideas of Sartre. Two years later the young director Roger Vadim took a little-known actress to a modest Riviera fishing-port and there made on location *Et Dieu créa la femme*. And God-knows-who created Bardot and St. Tropez. Thousands from *une certaine jeunesse* rushed there at once. France and the world were amazed. Was this what French youth was like? Was Sagan's free-living heroine typical of French girls of eighteen? The next year, in 1958, the veteran director Marcel Carné made a film, *Les Tricheurs*, that seemed to confirm the picture. He described a *milieu* of young Parisians, bohemian 'intellectuals' and idle bourgeois students from good homes, united in the same anarchic dissipation, breaking up their parents' smart flats with wild parties, stealing and cheating and casually fornicating. According to Carné, everyone in this *milieu* is a *tricheur* (cheat) and honest feelings are taboo: in the climax of the film, bohemian slut and weak rich *fils-à-papa* do genuinely fall in love, but dare not admit it to each other and this leads to tragedy. The girl, trapped in her own depravity, cannot take the strain any more, drives off into the night in a stolen car, and crashes to her death. Another character (a nice

---

* See p. 356 (Intellectuals in disarray).

one, a sort of Greek chorus) then blames it all on society. As you can see, a sensational and contrived film, hardly a great work of art; but it did carry a certain veracity, and Carné claimed that he knew this world intimately and had drawn his portraits from life. The film caused more of a stir than any other in France for years: many pressure-groups tried to ban it, and *l'Express* gleefully published a twelve-page supplement, 'Qui Sont les Tricheurs?' Some people thought that the film's portrait was out of date and related to a St.-Germain-des-Prés of the late '40s, to the phoney existentialists who mistook liberty for licence. Others felt it was still true, of a minority. There are still some *tricheurs*, even today, just as the early Sagan novels were clearly based on experience and the crowds around the bars and beaches of St. Tropez are patently no fiction. The *tricheurs* borrowed from existentialism its permissiveness without its responsibility and took it as a cue to do just what they liked: when the young bohemian Mephistopheles of Carné's film goes into a shop to steal a record that he does not want, he claims he is performing the perfect Gidean or Sartrian *acte gratuit*. This muddled intellectual self-justification has underlain a good part of the fringe rebellions among post-war French youth—though one can hardly claim that every St. Tropez layabout is motivated by such philosophical principles.

The St. Tropez phenomenon has had plenty of post-war counterparts, in Chelsea, California, and elsewhere. What is remarkable here is its intensity in one small, picturesque seaside location. The whole affair was hardly Vadim's fault, or Bardot's: the publicists of *Paris-Match* and other such papers pounced on them while they were filming, and somehow managed to inspire a popular cult that answered a youthful need. Bardot was built into a symbol of sensualist emancipation—and the young crowds came, some innocently and some less so, to find and to worship their goddess. Of course they simply drove her away: she had bought a villa just outside St. Tropez, where she still spends part of each year, but she was soon forced to build a high wall round it, and neither she nor any other star today dares to be seen in the streets or cafés of the town, through fear of being mobbed by adoring fans. Yet the crowds still come, from every part of the world, impelled by the new religion of glamour and stardom, or simply by curiosity. I met a Dominican priest in St. Tropez who told me, 'This place is a kind of Lourdes. Young people feel a lack in their lives today, they want to be cured of their desolate yearnings, so they come here to be touched by magic and reborn. But they go away disappointed. All they find is each other.' Many of the most vicious elements in St. Tropez today are foreign, not French—the hordes of young German thugs and paederasts, the Chelseaites, the Swedes, the American beats. But the French are still there too in plenty; the girls of little more than sixteen who arrive from Paris without a penny and see how far their charms can carry them. Any summer night you can see them by the score, wide-eyed popsies with gaudy jeans, bare midriffs, and Bardot hairstyles, hanging around the modish bars like l'Escale, waiting for the next well-heeled pick-up who will let them sponge and stay a few more days.

Many of the boys and girls of this kind of milieu, in Paris or St. Tropez, come from cultured, conventional homes and have broken with their families. But they are not typical, totalling perhaps a few thousand. Many other young people today, especially students, seem to have managed to extricate themselves from old-style bourgeois morality in a less irresponsible manner; and if they are discreet, even while still living at home they can practise a good deal of Sartrian 'sincerity' in their private lives. Girls have become readier to undertake affairs before marriage, but without ceasing to be *sérieuses*. As one Parisian student told me, 'It's not that we're trying to set up counter-conventions like the *tricheurs*. We're not against our parents' morality, we ignore it. The basis of our behaviour is rejection of constraint, and within this framework we are very moral.'

Among the less intellectual teenagers, the archetype today is not a *tricheur* but a *copain*—the word means 'chum' or 'pal'. And in the 1960s it is the extraordinary pop movement of the *copains*, innocent and mildly charming but vapid, that has given a new brand-image to the whole of French youth and pushed the precocious cynicism of Sagan firmly on to the sidelines. A new generation, sipping its Coca-Colas, looks less to Bardot the sex-kitten than to Sylvie Vartan, chirpy little chum and elder sister, or to Françoise Hardy huskily leading all-the-boys-and-girls-of-her-age-hand-in-hand.

This movement began in 1959 when Daniel Filipacchi, a young disc-jockey and former *Paris-Match* photographer, launched a jazz programme on Europe Number One radio and borrowed the title of a song by Gilbert Bécaud to call it *Salut les Copains*. Instantly it was a smash-hit with teenagers, who were tired of sharing Brassens and Trenet with their elders and wanted something swinging and modern of their own, like the Americans had. Soon the programme was running for two hours nightly, using mainly American material.

Around the same period an obscure bar near the Opéra, the Golf Drouot, turned itself into a kind of teenagers' cabaret and so provided a breeding-ground for the first of France's own young pop singers. There a boy of sixteen with fair curly hair and an ugly mouth made his hesitant *début* under the name of Johnny Hallyday, singing American rock 'n' roll tunes in French. Filipacchi took him up—and a whole generation chose Johnny as their idol and self-image. French pop was born. He was followed by scores of others—besides Sylvie and Françoise (surnames are taboo among *copains*), the best known have been Richard Anthony, Claude François, Adamo, Sheila, France Gall. And in 1962 Filipacchi astutely complemented his radio show with a glossy magazine also called *Salut les Copains*, which reached and has held a sale of a million copies a month and gets 10,000 fan letters a week. Its rather similar sister monthly for girls, *Mademoiselle Age Tendre*, sells 800,000—both of them astoundingly high circulations for France.

At first the movement was highly derivative, much more so than its Liverpool equivalent. Not only did the stars borrow American tunes; many of them found it smart to adopt Anglo-Saxon names like Dick Rivers and Eddy Mitchell; Hallyday's real name is Jean-Philippe Smet. Gradually, however, the *copains* have acquired a certain French style of their own, less virile and inventive, more romantic and sentimental, than either Beatledom or American folk and rock. Some of them, including Johnny and Françoise, compose and write many of their own songs, and today probably about half the *copains*' material is home-grown and the rest imported and translated. The whole affair is basically a shrewd commercial operation by Filipacchi, who by now is one of the richest men in France. But he and his young stars can afford their mink and Ferraris just because they have managed to provide millions with an outlet of self-identification they were looking for. The tradition of modern popular songs is much older and stronger in France than in Britain, but it has, therefore, belonged to an older generation, from Piaf through to Aznavour. Teenagers resented these as their parents' idols. But their own Johnny, singing ingenuously about being sixteen and its problems, was themselves and the boy next door. At his concerts, children wave and shout hallo: 'He's young, he's gay, he's just like us,' said one girl of fourteen, 'and not at all like a real music-hall star. So we love him.' Idols and fans are all equally *copains* together, and all are *tu*: this is the carefully fostered principle of their success, and if any idol breaks the code and behaves like an aloof Hollywood star, he is finished.

Parents at first were a little anxious, as gramophone-record sales shot into scores of millions and Hallyday became the most-photographed male in France after de Gaulle. Their concern reached its height after the night of 22 June 1963, when Filipacchi staged a 'live' open-air broadcast from the Place de la Nation in Paris, and 150,000 boys and girls, twisting and rocking, surged into the square and brushed aside the police. It was the first time in French history that teenagers had displayed their solidarity in public, on this scale. Some observers saw it as a political portent, comparing it with the mass-hysteria of the Nazi rallies. A few arrests were made and an enquiry was ordered. A little damage had been done to cars and windows, but this was due simply to the weight of the crowds, and to the presence among them of a handful of hooligans. Once the fuss had blown over, it became clear that the famous *Nuit de la Nation* was really quite innocent: the kids had simply wanted to dance, and to have a look at their heroes.

Parents soon came to see there was nothing much to worry about. Filipacchi, in fact, has always been shrewd enough to steer the *copains* away from rebellious paths that might have got him into trouble. Their revolt has been purely one of music and rhythm, not of morals. The very phrase *Salut les Copains* ('Hello, Chums!') gives some idea of the *Boys' Own Paper* or *True Romance* spirit of the thing; and so harmless is the magazine that the Catholic Church has felt safely able to copy it with its own rival monthly for the teenage faithful, *Formidable*, a bit more varied and a bit less artfully glossy but otherwise much the same. Filipacchi's editor-in-chief, Raymond Mouly, a young man in black leather jacket and side-whiskers, told me: 'I suppose we've simply created a new conformism, inevitably. But there's still something zippy and fresh about us—and we needed a change from Yves Montand. What we're really doing is to prolong the age of innocence, the *âge tendre*. Life is easier than in 1945, and people have more time to live their youth.'

This belongs to a typically French romantic tradition that seems to hark straight back to Gérard de Nérval and *Le Grand Meaulnes*: adolescents playing at love, sometimes touched by melancholy and *ennui* but not by cynicism or social indignation. Browse through the brilliantly edited pages of *Salut les Copains* and you will see what these idols are like, or at least how they are presented to be. Huge snazzy colour-photos in the manner of *Un homme et une femme* show the various stars wandering hand in hand through autumn woodlands or lazing on Mediterranean beaches. Photo-articles forty pages long proclaim *Tout tout tout sur Sylvie* and *Tout tout tout sur Johnny*: that Sylvie dislikes celery and likes coloured candles, that Johnny likes hot-dogs and dislikes umbrellas. Johnny, philistine and petit-bourgeois, mad about cars and motor-bikes, is in reality much as he is made to seem; he is the perfect modern folk-hero and looks exactly like any French youth you see hanging around the streets with his *vélo* on a Sunday. Sylvie, Bulgarian by birth, is more intellectual: she used to read philosophy on the Métro before she became famous, and is known as *la collégienne du twist*. But with her tulip-mouth, her long ash-blonde curls and sturdy little figure, she projects the perfect image of the jolly bobby-soxer who's become a star by mistake; and when she bounces on to the stage of the Olympia music-hall as if it were an end-of-term concert, to trill *Ce soir, je serai la plus belle pour aller danser*, every *midinette* in the audience identifies with her. In 1965, after a long engagement, Johnny and Sylvie became Mr. and Mrs. Smet: two hundred photographers were present, yet it seemed much closer in spirit to a typical middle-class wedding than, say, to aloof Bardot marrying some foreigner in Las Vegas.

Not all the *copains* conform quite so closely to this tame bourgeois ideal. Françoise Hardy, ex-student of German at the Sorbonne, tall and languid with a spoilt, sulky temperament, has even brought a note of Grecoesque sorrow and self-doubt into some of her recent songs; there is more than a touch of Garbo about her, and she is one of the very few *copains* to have much following among maturer people as well as teenagers. But she does keep roughly in line with the Filipacchi ethic, and her *mystère* does not simmer into actual revolt. However, an intruder of a much more violent sort, calling himself Antoine, did manage to burst into the *copain* world briefly in 1966: his hair was far longer than Lennon's or Jagger's (shocking by most *copain* standards), and, instead of sweet love-lyrics, the songs he wrote and then growled at the audience were full of a bitter, socially-conscious nihilism that any intellectual beatnik might have envied. His clamorous success indicated that some French youth, at least, hankered for a stronger diet than chummery. But Filipacchi was against him, so was French adulthood; and he fizzled out.

And what will happen to the *copains*? After tiffs and reconciliations that filled all the headlines, the Smets are now parents in their twenties, growing away fast from their teenage equals. '*Adieu les copains!*' wrote *l'Exprèss* after their wedding; 'Johnny and Sylvie were *copains*. Mr. and Mrs. Smet will try to remain stars. And they will have lots more little Ferraris!' Others no doubt will take their place, but the movement may well change or fade. The *copains*' appeal has always been mainly to the less sophisticated middle teens; older or more alert ones have often preferred a more robust nourishment such as Bob Dylan or English pop. A youth in Filipacchi's office who had spent some time in London told me, 'I admit your young singers are more mature and original than ours; a group like The Animals, for instance, seem to have firm ideas about modern society. Your youth as a whole is more aggressive, creative, and non-conformist than ours. But then, they get more freedom.'

On its credit side, the *copain* cult may have fostered a kind of sweet romantic comradeship among French youth. Like British pop it has certainly helped in the struggle against delinquency; and unlike British pop it is seldom crudely hostile to real culture. Its idols have undeniable puppy-charm; and, for all the commercial wire-pulling, there has been something spontaneous and infectious about their appeal to French youth in a voice it could recognise as its own. But that voice has not proved a very inspiring one: insipid, somewhat effeminate, content to idolise a safe world of glamour and niceness. Even the melodies are not very exciting. Parents, in fact, can safely look on the *copains* as a harmless way of keeping the children out of mischief. The young things are now being allowed to throw a party on their own; but Mummy and Daddy are on the *qui-vive* upstairs.

Under this discreet parental eye, France's six million teenagers have been elaborating their own semi-private world with its own crazes, conventions, and slang—a world that is largely innocent but difficult for a non-initiate to grasp at first. Here are some examples of their slang. *Chouette, formidable* and *terrible* all mean 'super' or 'smashing'; *vachement* or *terriblement* mean 'very'; *ça chauffe* means 'things are getting hot'; *c'est du folklore*, 'it's stupid, out of date'; *dans le vent*, 'with-it'; *moins de vingt dents*, a pun meaning 'the old'; *croulant* ('crumbling'), an 'adult', a word in vogue about ten years ago but now only used by *croulants* about themselves. The notorious term *yé-yé* more or less means 'pop', and derives from French attempts to pronounce 'yeah! yeah!' in their songs. Adults often apply it pejoratively to the whole *copain* generation; teenagers themselves use it rarely, except to denote, also pejoratively, their own more *outré* elements.

When teenagers give parties on their own, they are usually informal *surprise-parties* which may sometimes develop into wilder *surboums* if *tricheurs* are around or parents well out of the way. Generally French teenage parties are noticeably sedate by London standards, at least when given (as usually happens) in parents' homes. Outside the family foyer, however, things *chauffent terriblement*, notably at one or two new Paris night-spots catering for really switched-on youth. One of these is La Locomotive, a vast rock 'n' roll club below the Moulin Rouge, banned to over twenty-fives, where the young parade their latest fashions and sit on a floor of purple glass listening to English and American rhythms. English influence is strong also at the fantastic Bus Palladium, near Place Pigalle: this was a seedy old strip-joint for tourists which in 1965 decided to get with-it by importing an English pop group and appealing to a new clientèle. Its success was unprecedented. Smarties and beatniks, typists, students, and celebrities, all flocked along to this one large darkened room where bodies swayed and jerked through the night to the strident music. The baroque church-like décor, with frescoes, aisles, and Byzantine pillars, reinforced the impression of being present at some religious rite—and several of the pale-faced, long-haired acolytes could hardly have looked more biblical. Few reporters failed to comment on this: 'It's a midnight mass in full oecumenicism,' said the *Nouvel Observateur*; 'The priest sucks his micro, the communicants sip their Coca-Cola.' But reporters have also noted how extraordinarily innocent and unerotic it all is.

La Loco and the Palladium are in the *avant-garde*, and so are some British fashion imports. Beatle hair-cuts still tend to be laughed at in public and thought effeminate, but are beginning to spread more widely. Mini-skirts and trouser-suits made a belated but successful invasion from London in 1966, and the various new Paris shops catering for teenage fashion (Vog, Dorothée Bis and the Gaminerie) are all heavily influenced by London. * Young Parisians interested in this kind of with-it-ness know that Paris can no longer make great claims to originality, and most of them are keenly aware of what is going on in London. But they get a little bored by Londoners who come and tell them how old-hat and derivative they all are.

One characteristic feature of French teenage society since the war has been the rise of the band or group. No longer expected to spend so much time with parents or relatives, young people nowadays often choose to go around in little groups of six or more, boys and girls together; frequently the relations remain platonic and fairly uncommitted, and there is less splitting into couples or 'dating' than in many Western countries. Of course, this trend has provided fertile soil for the spreading of the *copains* cult.

As for adult-organised youth activities, teenagers mainly show no great enthusiasm for them, though boy-scouting is quite popular and

* See p. 263 (Novelty and tradition in daily life).

some of the Church movements do well. The national chain of youth clubs (*Maisons des Jeunes*) might attract far greater numbers if they were better organised and had better amenities. Not that French youth moves to the opposite anti-social extreme: there is less delinquency, and certainly less drug-taking, than in many countries. Juvenile lawlessness appeared comparatively late in France, in 1959, with warring gangs of leather-jacketed youths known as *blousons noirs*. After they had swiped their bicycle chains at a number of innocent passers-by, they were severely repressed by the police, and today the gangs have largely split up and been succeeded by small groups of young professional thieves, or by sporadic hooliganism and pilfering.

Whereas in post-war Britain youth has often channelled its energies into violent self-expression, destructive or creative, in France the dominant impression left by all the varying tendencies is of a kind of docile listlessness. I do not wish to exaggerate this contrast, for the youth of the two nations also have much in common. But it does exist. The *copains* may have provided a generation with a new self-awareness, yet they seem unsure quite what to do with it. One answer to the puzzle lies in the influence of parents and school. It is true that French parents are less strict than they used to be, and are much readier to let sons and even daughters go out on their own; it is true they have grown more aware of their children's enthusiasm and needs *as children*, instead of treating them as minor adults. Often they are indulgent with pocket-money. But their offspring remain curiously under their sway.

In Parisian upper-class society, parents in recent years have resorted to various ingenious devices to keep their teenage children in check. One of the most remarkable of these is the *rallye*, a kind of exclusive dancing-club for girls of fifteen to nineteen and their carefully chosen escorts. There are some dozen of these *rallyes* in Paris today; and a boy or girl who is entered for one by his or her mother must expect to spend from four or five years in a steady round of formal parties and dances, under close parental supervision. It helps to steer the young things towards suitable marriages, and to keep them out of mischief. And astonishingly, most of the young things appear to accept this discipline, as teenagers rarely would in London.

Another reason for the French teenager's submissiveness is purely practical: the housing shortage. Emancipation from parents is not so easy when cheap furnished flats or rooms are still such a rarity: three in four of sixteen-to-twenty-four-year-olds live at home until marriage, including 54 per cent of young men of twenty-two to twenty-four. Yet even if there were no housing shortage, the picture might not change so radically. It is still considered the 'norm' to live with your parents; and very many young people, even when they do have the means to move away, prefer not to do so. This is changing, but not fast. A rich young girl I knew in Paris, who could easily have found and afforded a small flat of her own or with girl-friends, told me just before her wedding at twenty-six: 'Now at last I can get away from my mother.' In such cases, children are suffering from parents' emotional blackmail; but in millions of other cases it is simply that young French, far more than young Anglo-Saxons or Nordics, seem to remain tied to their parents by psychological cords that they find hard to cut, even when there is no parental pressure. They are still often in the grip of the kind of obsessive child–parent relationships that are such a recurring theme of modern French literature.* Perhaps this is why, when they do revolt—against parents or against society more generally—the gesture is all the more extreme, just because it has cost them so much of their inner selves.

Young people will often profess unconventional or progressive ideas in abstract, but in practice when faced with concrete situations will defer to the lead and authority of their elders. I met a twenty-year-old Sorbonne philosophy student, living with his parents in Paris, who delighted me with his mature and profound ideas about modern society and his own destiny, then surprised me by saying, 'A few young friends of mine and I have formed a local dramatic club. Luckily, my father runs it for us. You see, without him, none of us would have the right authority, we'd just quarrel.' I refrained from replying that, in England, boys much younger and stupider than he were often in charge of the discipline of large schools. But it is plain as daylight that the French school system has a large influence here. It fails to provide any training in group initiative or responsibility, and so throws the child back on parental discipline. It presses him towards an intellectual precocity that is basically conformist. And the severe and formal approach of teachers outwardly inculcates docility, while inwardly producing a kind of frustrated resentment. Perhaps it is reaction against the severity of school, or against the shadow of parents, that makes so many French teenagers behave so very badly when they escape to a different setting. In English towns such as Brighton, where they come *au pair* in the summer, they have a worse reputation for trouble-making than any other nationality. It is often hard to decide whether they are spoilt little brats or sadly deprived.

Two recent opinion surveys of teenage attitudes both give a somewhat discouraging picture. The first, carried out in 1961 among *lycéens* and apprentices by a psychologist, Yann Thireau, and an educationist, Georges Teindas, showed them as 'interested above all in securing an easy life, with lots of money'. The heroes they admired most were scientists, sportsmen, world leaders—but they seemed to envy them less for their qualities than for their style of life: 'Prince Rainier, he's got money and he's happy,' 'Churchill, he's rich,' were two replies. The second enquiry was carried out in 1962 by the Institut Français d'Opinion Publique, among a wide range of boys and girls between sixteen and twenty-four. Asked what they valued most in life, the vast majority put health and money well ahead of love, freedom, or religion. They laid immense stress

---

* See p. 240 (Novelty and tradition in daily life).

on the home, mainly as a symbol of material security; they were anxious above all to secure good, well-paying jobs, and they were confident that they would be much more prosperous than their parents. They cared little about French politics—less than a third were able to cite the names of more than two Gaullist Ministers—but they showed even less concern for old-style patriotism and *la gloire*. What mattered more to them was the Common Market and the idea of Europe. Few expressed much desire to change the basic order of society; or, if they did, they sensed a kind of powerlessness. The portrait that emerged was of an orderly and bourgeois generation, modern-minded and technocratic, anxious to feather its own nest, and idealistic mainly towards practical ends. The survey concluded: 'Rarely have we discovered signs of revolt; more often docility, or even passivity. The young accept the institutions of the adult world as they are.'

It is perhaps fortunate for France that a significant number of individuals do not fit so easily into this pattern. These are the more mature and thoughtful ones, mostly students or young graduates, many of them the kind of people who might have rallied to existentialism twenty years ago. I find their grave idealism and their integrity most impressive, and a little sad. These people *do* question society; they *do* feel concern over such things as France's cultural decline; but often they feel also a kind of impotence, an alienation from the way modern France is moving and a sense of being unable to affect it. Some of them are cowed by the existentialists' failure to transform society after the war, or by the Gaullist climate of authoritarianism. They present an aura of solitariness, and of reserve.

The Sorbonne student whose father ran his drama club seemed to typify their outlook: 'We don't feel we live in a coherent community, like you in Britain. In France, existentialism destroyed the illusion of community for us, and we've nothing to put in its place. A community is a fine idea, but it doesn't seem to work in practice: there are too many compromises and betrayals. *Enfin, on est toujours seul.* Many of my contemporaries seek an answer in Teilhardism—I prefer Kierkegaard, Nietzsche, Unamuno.' He said that he was studying philosophy and economics at the moment, and hankered to teach philosophy and go for a *doctorat*; but for practical financial reasons he would probably now concentrate on economics and go for an industrial career. He went on to criticise French parents for patronising and indulging their children instead of providing constructive guidance: 'They give us lots of pocket-money because they've no ideas to give us. They just don't know what to say. It's a catastrophe.'

This serious-minded minority, whether Catholic or agnostic, literary or more scientific, share a kind of groping idealism that they may shrug off defensively when questioned. But the list of authors they care most about can be revealing. A large number, and not only the Christian believers, are drawn to Teilhard de Chardin* and his fundamentalist

* See p. 389 (Intellectuals in disarray).

vision that seems to reconcile God and the modern scientific world. Others are influenced by Camus and especially by *La Peste*, which has sold a million copies in France: its stoical humanism seems to offer something to many young agnostic liberals who cannot accept Teilhard's theism or Sartre's contorted Marxism. Others again turn to Malraux's early novels or his philosophical books on art (but not to Malraux the Gaullist), or they search for answers in the interior universe of Proust. Among younger and rather more naïve ones, at *lycée* age, the most popular author of all is still Antoine de Saint-Exupéry, idealist and man of action, prophet— in *Citadelle* and *Terre des hommes*—of heroic virtues that make good sense to a sixteen-year-old.

These diverse writers and others have in common the possession of some questing personal *Weltanschauung* that modern serious youth finds more rewarding than books of mere narrative or description. But it may be relevant that Teilhard, Saint-Exupéry, and the young Malraux were also active men of science or adventure. Youth may have turned its back on politics and political creeds: but many of them, except perhaps an aesthetic minority, do seek practical outlets for their idealism, rather than the ivory tower. Some take part in the neo-Catholic movements of social action; many come to terms later with Gaullist technocracy, and embark on public careers. Nearly all are attracted to some degree by the new social or applied sciences. There has been a huge growth of interest among young people in anthropology, geography, psychology, sociology, and of course in film-making, most practical and documentary of the arts. Many people seek outlets abroad for their ideals of social service. Thousands go out each year to developing countries, especially in ex-French Africa, as technicians, teachers, or researchers. The Government-sponsored 'Volontaires du Progrès' scheme, equivalent of the Peace Corps or Voluntary Service Overseas, has had a good response and is often allowed as the equivalent of military service. Other young people turn to individual adventure, especially in a scientific spirit: young men like Michel Siffre who in 1963 stayed alone for thirty days at the foot of a 200-foot cave, to collect data about physical endurance; or Eric Tabarly who won the 1964 trans-Atlantic yacht race alone in his sailing-dinghy.

The decline of interest in politics, at least since the end of the Algerian war, is a self-evident phenomenon linked with Gaullism and the failures of the Fourth Republic. It might be dangerous for France in the long run: but it does have some encouraging aspects. One of these is the very striking decline in old-style nationalism and patriotism,* except among a tiny Right-wing minority of young people. De Gaulle's flag-waving leaves them cold: no longer do they stir to the sound of a military band on July 14—*tout ça, c'est du folklore*. They are less chauvinist than their elders, less insular than British youth; and most of them do believe genuinely in the ideal of a united Europe. Often I was told, in effect, 'We go to

* See p. 450 (Conclusion).

Frankfurt or Milan now as naturally as to Lyon or Bordeaux. We have no sense of frontiers any more. It's only the British whom we feel are still "different", but we wish they weren't because we like them. And we wish that European universities and degrees were integrated, so that you could study for one year in Paris and the next in, say, Munich, just as you like.'

Often I notice that when young French people talk generally about modern problems, they tend to set them in a European or world context, whereas English youth discussing the same things may relate them mainly to Britain. It suggests that the French are less insular, but also, I think, that they are less closely conscious of participating in a national community against which to set their discussions. Despite their qualities as individuals, they generally seem shy of forming their own group initiatives, or of translating their criticisms of the adult world into joint action. When they do act, it is usually for solitary ends, or by taking part in society on its terms. The exceptions are few enough to be especially striking—as when Alexis Gourvennec, aged only twenty-four, led the young Breton farmers in the 1961 artichoke wars and virtually reorganised North Finistère's agriculture. But then the farming world has for long been rather special. In the university world, I have already suggested the students' reticence at organising anything for themselves beyond discussion and protest. It was therefore heartening to visit Nancy, where in the past ten years the students have built up their own ambitious cultural organisation, now international in reputation. There have been three separate initiatives. First in 1958 a chemistry student, Jacques Laurent, founded the Centre Culturel Universitaire Lorrain which soon reached a membership of 3,000 embracing fourteen arts clubs. Then a girl at the Letters Faculty, Nicole Granger, started the idea of an annual *Nuit Culturelle*, an intensive round-the-clock arts festival, embracing everything, music, poetry, drama, debate, in one ardent and sleepless weekend. It has been hugely successful and has drawn many well-known guest stars from Paris: in 1965 all the films of Godard were shown one after the other almost non-stop for twenty-four hours! Thirdly, an amateur drama group was founded in the late 'fifties by a law student, Jack Lang, who then stayed on at Nancy as a junior lecturer, kept up his drama work, and in 1962 extended it by founding, as I have mentioned, Nancy's annual international student drama festival.

Today Mlle. Granger, now a local teacher, is still animating Nancy in conjunction with the Œuvres Universitaires. The annual guide to local cultural activities, published by the OU and the Centre Culturel, runs to over 140 pages, which may give some idea of what a swinging place Nancy now is, all through the year. The most unprecedented aspect of the situation is that this student-inspired movement has burst the bounds of the university and has now revitalised the whole cultural life of the city of Nancy, previously staid and conventional. But why has all this happened at Nancy, and not elsewhere? Perhaps climate plays a part: this is a severe Northern city, rather like its twin-town, Newcastle, without the easy distractions of sport and sun-basking that you find in the Midi. Much is due also to the strength of Lorraine local patriotism, which was a mainspring of the Centre Culturel in its early days. And the Rector, Paul Imbs, has been highly sympathetic to the new activities, lending them moral support, premises, and funds. But basically this has been a pure student venture, carried along by a few exceptional leaders and followed by the rest. It shows what French youth can do when they try.

It would not happen so easily in Paris. In the overcrowded and overwrought atmosphere of the capital, youth generally finds it harder to find a rallying-point or make an impact. Take the case of two serious-minded brothers I met, living with their bourgeois parents in Montparnasse. The elder, aged twenty-five, had a boring but lucrative job in a building firm; the younger, twenty-one, was at the Sorbonne, studying psychology. Together they had founded a 'Centre pour la Diffusion des Moyens d'Expression', a pompous title for a real attempt to do something creative. On a modest scale, they were beginning to market their own highbrow records of unusual music, to edit a roneoed intellectual magazine and run a drama group. They had also taken over a little night-bar in a side-street and were planning to run it as *une boîte pour yé-yés sages*, a place where people like themselves could meet and talk, away from their parents and from too much *copains* music. It all seemed rather impressive, but they were pessimistic to me about their progress. One said, 'Whenever we've tried to get people of our age together in Montparnasse to do anything worth while, we've met passivity. People seem interested at first, but they expect us to do it all for them. They won't share responsibility. Or else they quarrel and form into splinter groups. It's happened already with our drama circle.'

Like others I've met of their type, the brothers expressed anxiety that the French vogue for technocracy and modernism was accentuating cultural decline. They saw their own Centre as a modest attempt to fight against this, and against pop. But they struck me with their sense of isolation. They seemed to have little feeling of unity or even contact with the scores of thousands of young French people who broadly share their ideas. They said, 'Whenever you try to do anything public in France you're up against adult vested interests—whether it's in publishing, or journalism, or even in the pop music world where, after all, the *copains* are a slick adult-run commercial operation. We've found few people ready to help our Centre with money, at all disinterestedly.' Another young man said, 'In every way, whether it's to form pop groups, or go on CND marches, or publish poetry, we don't feel that we have the same liberty of movement that youth seems to have in Britain.' Their little roneoed magazines, with articles criticising the Press or literature or society, struck me as pathetic—paper-darts aimed at a world that took no notice. It is true that a few other young people, perhaps with more flair, are now succeeding as in Britain in breaking into the established commercial world: setting up their own fashion shops, pop music firms, or other such businesses. Often they have parental capital behind them. This is new and unusual in France, but is still very limited. Of course it can be argued that this type of revolution in Britain has gone much too far, and it is not the business of twenty-year-olds to try to run the country. A more serious danger is when men in their prime, at thirty-five or forty, find the way to the top blocked by stale and conservative elders in the key positions: this always used to be the problem in France, and this at least has improved radically since the war.

It is perilous to generalise about a world so elusive and constantly renewing itself as the youth of a nation, and there are plenty of human examples that may contradict everything I have written. Perhaps the central difficulty is to assess their attitude to technocracy and the modernisation of France. Many of the more serious ones, as I have suggested, accept its necessity but are suspicious of the way it is happening; they fear that it masks a great deal of social injustice, materialism, and neglect of cultural values. And so with the intensity of youth they reject modern France and all its works. Later, faced with the problem of making a career, they may come to terms with it and join in trying to influence it. This is probably easiest for people like the young neo-Catholic activists, who have a ready-made framework of idealism to belong to. Others have fewer such doubts and scruples even from the outset—such as the bright young technocrats-to-be of ENA and the *Grandes Ecoles*, who eagerly accept the challenge to help build a modern France, and the chance of combining it with a successful career. The earning of money, the getting of good and useful jobs, the acceptance of a competitive society that makes this possible: these are the primary concerns of all but a small part of French middle-class youth.

But among the important minority that does not think like this, I am left with this impression of wasted potential, of an energy and idealism failing to find positive outlets. And whose fault is it? While the young feel a sense of frustration, older people complain, 'But it's not our fault. They're so secretive, so reluctant to come forward and take part in public life. They seem to know what they don't want, but to be unable to formulate what they do want.' This *malaise* of modern youth may not be unique to France. But in France it does seem linked to certain specific factors. I think that if the school system were made more human, and if both teachers and parents were less paternalistic, youth might breathe more easily. And if that arch-paternalist, the Gaullist State, were to yield to a more democratic climate, youth might feel less impotence and isolation.

CHAPTER XI

INTELLECTUALS
IN DISARRAY

NOTHING IS MORE REVEALING of modern France than the contrast between the optimism and confidence of the average businessman, technician, or senior civil servant and the *malaise* among intellectuals. This is not solely because most intellectuals are on the Left and dislike the present régime. It also goes deeper. Many of them feel an embittered frustration at the rise of a whole new way of progress that has brushed aside their own careful theories and precepts. After the war they rebelled, with success, against bourgeois conservatism—but now the fruits of that rebellion seem to have been snatched from them and exploited for other ends. Their dreams are drowned in the hubbub of technology. Scornful of pragmatic values, ignorant of economics and out of touch with ordinary working people, they might seem almost as out of place in a modern Socialist régime as under de Gaulle. It is the whole contemporary world that they fancy has betrayed them; or have *they* betrayed it, by burying their heads in the sand?

By 'intellectuals' I mean those writers, artists, academics, and others, immersed in their own world of ideas and arguments, who have always formed a very special and recognisable caste in France, and especially in Paris. Often they have been highly vocal rather than directly influential; but always society has respected them as an honoured minority, like the holy men of India, and the word *intellectuel* has been simply a term of description like musician or sportsman, without pejorative overtones as in Britain. Today this is changing. Some of the prestige traditionally accorded to the writer or thinker is being transferred to the man of action or science; and many clever young people now shrink, as in Britain, from openly dubbing themselves as 'intellectuals'.

France no longer appears as the cultural champion of the West—and even Frenchmen will now often admit this. The economic and social resurgence of the nation has gone hand in hand with this ominous intel-

lectual and artistic decline, extending to many of the creative arts as well
as to philosophy and ideologies. The withering of the Sartrian movement
in the early 1950s has left Parisian intellectual life confused, fluid, and
with few acknowledged leaders: no wonder that so many of those serious
young students feel bereft and sceptical, as they search for a living *maître
à penser* with more spiritual nourishment to offer than the new technocratic ethos. Admittedly there are several bright spots of new and original
activity in this generally bleak picture, all of which I shall try to analyse
in the next two chapters. One is the rise of a dynamic Catholic humanism,
extending far outside intellectual circles; another, the searching and
rigorous though frighteningly pessimistic new theories of the structuralists; a third, the continued effervescence of young creative talent in the
cinema; and the growth of a new popular theatre movement, especially
in the provinces. But set these beside the present state of French painting,
music, poetry, television, journalism, radical political thinking, and the
dearth of good young novelists and playwrights.

What are the reasons for the decline? There are French historical
precedents to suggest that art and ideas flourish either under austerity (as
in the 1945 period) or in settled prosperity (as in the time of Louis XIV
or the *Belle Epoque*) but not in a period of rapid industrial transition
when the nation's main energies are elsewhere. Maybe France's culture
will re-emerge later, in a new guise, when it has shifted some of the weight
of its inhibiting classical tradition. For the moment, the crisis seems due as
much to a paralysis of outlook and expression, a stifling Parisian inbredness,
as to sheer shortage of talent.

SLUMP IN SARTRE AND NO SUCCESSOR

Like so much else in modern France, the existentialist movement was
generated during the war. It was in 1943 that Sartre brought out his key
philosophical work, *L'Etre et le néant*, though he was already well known
from his first novel, *La Nausée*, published in 1938 while he was a *lycée*
teacher at Le Havre. The Occupation, with its disruption of bourgeois
values, tempted many young thinkers besides Sartre towards a similar
kind of disenchanted humanism, so that on the Liberation he found an
immediate and sympathetic audience—and this shy, modest young school-
master, who had never seen himself as a leader of men, was startled by his
own success. For the next few years, he and groups of disciples would sit
in the St.-Germain-des-Prés cafés and discuss problems of personal responsibility, especially in relation to political action. This was the real
French existentialist movement, and it had much influence in academic
and Left-wing circles. Sartre had the brilliance and clarity to act as moral
leader for intellectuals who shared many of his ideas and feelings, especially his hatred of the bourgeois ethic that had led France into decline
in the 1930s. This was a time of high aspiration, when it seemed that social

revolution might, after all, be possible in France; and these early post-war years were a period of immense intellectual fervour and originality, amid political chaos and economic gloom—the very opposite of the situation today.

Sartre also attracted, quite incidentally, a much larger group of rather less serious young people who rarely understood his ideas but relished a philosophy that seemed to preach complete licence. The more austere of his tenets they conveniently overlooked. This parasitic movement was also the product of wartime upheaval, but has little in common with Sartre save a revolt from established morality and a liking for the same cafés. They gave the world an entirely misleading image of the existentialist as a kind of indolent beatnik, whereas Sartre and his friends in their own way have always been ascetic, hard-working, even puritanical. Sartre publicly disclaimed these feckless adolescents—some of them boys from good Passy homes who would arrive each evening in their neat suits and hurry down to the café cloakrooms to don their local uniform of jeans, lumber-jacket, and sandals.

This milieu is largely dispersed now. Many of the rebels have made peace with their backgrounds, have gone back to the provinces or suburbs to become sober lawyers or teachers. Their St. Germain haunts are infested by a motley of tourists, some of them looking for Sartre and finding each other. Juliette Greco, who was the existentialists' idol, has long since made their bohemianism respectable by moving to the *boîtes* across the river; and today the Right Bank is getting its revenge by invading St. Germain with a Champs-Elysées *chic* of boutiques and drugstores. Neo-bourgeois values of affluent arti-smartness are triumphing in Sartre's very citadel—the maggots are at the Deux Magots. It is true that the *Quartier* still has its raffish habitués, but not its old cohesion and intensity. A few years ago I met an American couple there in search of advertised *soirées existentialistes* who, when I said they'd come a decade too late, asked me, 'But what about this new movement, the Poujadists? What are their literary cafés?'

The true existentialist movement has also withered, though it has left an indelible mark on French thinking. Its end was hastened by various external factors, notably by the disillusioning political failures of the Left under the Fourth Republic, and by the luring rise of a new climate of prosperity and technocratic reform. As so often in French history, the bourgeoisie has simply shifted its ground in face of internal revolt, and has re-formed its ranks. But the existentialist movement was destroyed also from within itself—by the failure of intellectuals to pass from mental *engagement* to any kind of effective action, and by the bewildering shifts and ambiguities in Sartre's own pronouncements, both philosophical and political, since about 1950.

Existentialism, at first seized on so hopefully as a light to live by, was soon felt by many intellectuals to lead to a moral *impasse*, at least in its atheistic Sartrian form. Developing the ideas of his German precursors, Heidegger and Husserl, Sartre taught that man creates himself by his actions, for which he has freedom of choice and total responsibility; each choice is 'absurd' because there is no norm of conduct or objective moral standard, but (and here Sartre has never made himself quite clear) in the act of choosing, a man confers value on what he chooses, for himself and all mankind. Many young French agnostics warmed to the courage and humanism of this austere philosophy, which at least seemed more hopeful than determinism. But to those who searched more closely among the contradictions of *L'Etre et le néant* and *L'Existentialisme est un humanisme* (1945), this humanism began to look suspiciously like solipsism; and not everyone felt able to share Sartre's gloomy view of the impossibility of human relationships—'Hell', he wrote in *Huis clos*, 'is other people.' Existentialism had brought freedom from the bonds of convention—but was it not an empty liberty? It is significant that even Simone de Beauvoir, closest and most loyal of all Sartre's followers, seems to echo some of this feeling of deception in the anguished closing pages of the last volume of her memoirs, *La Force des choses.* * 'What have I done with my liberty?' she cries: 'The only new and important thing that can happen to me now is unhappiness. . . . My acts of revolt are discouraged by the imminence of my death and the fatal approach of decay.' This, from a woman of only fifty-five. And several French reviewers of the book commented that the feminist who once so proudly vaunted her ennobling and purposeful freedom seemed now to have been reduced to a frightened, doubting old spinster, unsure what it had all meant. Pierre-Henri Simon wrote in *Le Monde*: 'Existentialist morality, that de Beauvoir claims to have received from Sartre as a woman is marked by the man she loves, may in the end bring the thickest and heaviest clouds of that melancholy or despair which always menaces old age.' Her final astonishing sentence is, '*J'ai été flouée*': 'I've been had for a sucker!'

A more serious blow to Sartre's reputation has come, in the past fifteen years, from his subordination of existentialism to his own political obsessions in apparent defiance of logic and consistency. His Marxism, and his hatred of Right-wing oppression, are in themselves perfectly respectable. But few people can accept the logic that led him from 'absurdity of choice' to doctrinaire commitment. If man has freedom of choice, by what existentialist right does Sartre then insist that Marxism is the only 'valid' choice? Sartre has never convincingly answered this question. Since about 1951, he has increasingly neglected literature, drama, and even philosophy, and has wrapped himself up in political thought: today he asserts that Marxism is the only great philosophy of this century, and that existentialism is merely its handmaiden, taking charge of a field of humanist ideas that it had neglected. Certainly his thinking has helped to revitalise Marxism and purge it of some of its old-fashioned determinism. But, philosophically, it is not much use to anyone who is not first and foremost a Marxist.

* Gallimard, 1963.

This bourgeois son of an engineer hates the bourgeoisie so bitterly that he has taken to the most extreme and one-sided positions; this has alienated many of his milder followers. The Communist world is always right: its cruelties, or those of the FLN, are justified in the name of the anti-bourgeois struggle, while French or American excesses, however mild, are always 'fascism'. On a famous occasion in 1964 Sartre went further: he declared in *Le Monde* that in a world of starving millions, literature itself was useless and wicked if it appealed simply to a cultured minority. A writer must 'speak to all and be read by all', or else he was 'at the service of a privileged class, and like that class, an exploiter.' Several other writers, also on the Left, then retaliated. They commended Sartre's concern for humanity, but they felt he was distorting the true purpose of literature. Claude Simon, a distinguished novelist with an impeccable anti-Fascist record, accused Sartre of a sentimental, philistine neo-puritanism in subjecting literature to social utility. He suggested that Sartre's attitude, far from being genuinely democratic, rested on an unspoken contempt for 'the people' too oppressed to appreciate art.

Sartre is by no means the only French bourgeois intellectual whose devotion to the Left goes hand in hand with a large ignorance of the actual working class. De Beauvoir, for instance, describes in *La Force des choses* how, as late as 1949, she went to a meeting in Paris and 'was in contact with a popular milieu for the first time'. While Sartre espouses revolution in the name of the workers, that class itself is steadily emulating bourgeois habits and comforts—and how horrified he might be, if he ever met them. His position is a curious paradox. It is hard not to admire his concern for human suffering, or to accept it as genuinely felt. But his mind translates it on to an abstract polemical plane where it becomes distorted, and divorced from practical reality. As Maurice Cranston has written, in the best essay I know on Sartre: 'In the very intensity of his Socialism one can, I think, detect an element of what he himself calls evasion: a flight from the contradictions in his analysis of personal relations into a philosophy which does not reckon in individuals, but in masses.'*

This is the heart of the paradox: Sartre and his friends have preached that literature must be *engagée*—but in practice they have always shied away from realistic political action. Sartre prefers gestures: in 1964, in protest against Johnson's policy in Dominica, he suddenly cancelled a lecture tour of the United States, though all this achieved was the loss of a practical chance to go and support those in America who felt as he did. Politics is the art of the possible. But Sartre and his friends have always demanded utopia or nothing; they have refused to look at society squarely for what it is, or to take part in the long, impure struggle to improve it by working along with its better elements. So the technocrats have stolen the Sartrians' clothes; and the futility of most of the Sartrian gestures has

---

* *Encounter*, April 1962.

steadily isolated them from the main currents of French life, and weakened their influence even within intellectual circles.

In the '50s Sartre quarrelled and broke with one after another of his former sympathisers; first he quarrelled with Camus in 1952, then with the Sorbonne's most brilliant existentialist, Maurice Merleau-Ponty. Both these men are now dead. Camus was no great philosopher; but Merleau-Ponty was almost the only man in France qualified to do battle equally with Sartre on his own ground, as he often tried to do. His death leaves Sartre like a heavyweight champion whose muscles may go flabby with no-one to fight, with no-one clever enough to reason out his ambiguities with him. Sartre has always been harrowingly sincere and honest with himself, even when apparently distorting historical truth, and today he appears a somewhat lonely and tragic figure. As has often been said, it is the tragedy of a man with a deeply religious temperament who has killed God. And it is just because his early post-war influence was so great, and his intellectual magnetism so hypnotic, that today he has left such disarray among intellectuals throughout France. God has failed him; but he, too, is a god that failed. Today his public utterances still make headlines, but his real leadership has passed. He retains a small circle of devotees, but few of them are young. Serious eighteen-year-olds still eagerly discover his early books and find them relevant to their own problems; but they read them almost as classics, as if Sartre were as dead as Camus, Kafka, or the pre-war Malraux.

Existentialism has today merged into the air that a Frenchman breathes daily, like nineteenth-century rationalism. Few intellectuals any longer dub themselves existentialists, but all are marked by it. As a catalyst, its influence has almost certainly been positive. It is easy to forget how stifling was the French pre-war bourgeois world, the world described by de Beauvoir in *Mémoires d'une jeune fille rangée*; and she and Sartre have helped to open its windows a little. In England, the post-war movement away from this kind of conventional, restricted society (in so far as it existed) has been typically gentle and spontaneous; but in cloistered France some kind of a shock was needed, and this the existentialists provided with their violent rejection of constraint, their insistence that each individual must establish his own moral code. Nothing has been quite the same since—at least for anyone still under forty-five with some intellectual leanings. Existentialism has helped to put the young on their guard against being duped: it has generated a climate of disenchantment, at its best sceptical and honest, at its worst cynical, defeatist, and apathetic. This is the climate that youth lives in today.

In modern French sociology and criticism, in the *nouveau roman* and some of the films of the *nouvelle vague*, even in cabaret songs of the Brassens and Barbara type and in Sagan-style popular fiction, the continuing influence of existentialism is clear. Inside the philosophical world, it is still widely studied at universities, mainly as a tool for re-assessing the older philosophies: it has weakened the sterile hold of Kant and Descartes over the Sorbonne and forced a much-needed new approach to their ideas. And existentialism at least has the merit, compared with the Oxford positivist school, of appearing to be at grips with real moral problems, not merely with semantics.

But for some years existentialism left behind it a pregnant vacuum in French intellectual thought. Its fire had burned up the dead wood of bourgeois cant. Had it also killed the roots, or would new shoots break through? Throughout the '50s and early '60s the picture was mainly one of confusion: the flight continued from political idealism and the post-war ideal of *littérature engagée*, and new writers like Robbe-Grillet and Sollers took refuge in a private, asocial world of fantasy and stylistic experiment. Now in the later '60s a coherent new philosophical trend has finally emerged, much more restricted in its appeal than existentialism, but of undoubted power. It is known as 'structuralism', and its leading exponent is Claude Lévi-Strauss, who teaches ethnology at the Collège de France, next to the Sorbonne. To an extent it has grown out of existentialism and shares with it an atheistic rejection of the bourgeois view of history and morality. But whereas Sartre's philosophy sees man as the free captain of his own conscience and destiny, the structuralists regard him as the powerless prisoner of a determined system. Sartre springs from the humanist tradition, an old-fashioned moralist in a new guise: Lévi-Strauss and his friends are scientologists, using the language and methods of psycho-analysis, anthropology, and linguistic philosophy. They believe that man's thought and actions have been determined, throughout history, by a network of structures, social and psychological, where free will plays a minimal part; and that history is like a series of geological layers, each created by the pressure of the preceding one. Lévi-Strauss has applied these ideas to the study of primitive societies, past and present; Roland Barthes, the Marxist critic, uses them in the field of semantics or 'semiology', the study of the sets of signs and symbols which he believes shape our thoughts and actions; Michel Foucault applies structuralism to philosophy proper, and in *Les Mots et les choses* he argued, 'Man with a capital M is an invention: if we study thought as an archaeologist studies buried cities, we can see that Man was born yesterday, and perhaps that he will soon die.' This book, published in 1966, sent tremors well outside academic circles: for months it was a best-seller, the smart topic of party conversation whether you had read it or (more probably) not, and it even prompted full-page articles in some of the weeklies with headlines like 'Man is Dead'. Around the same time Roland Barthes was publicly taken to task by the Sorbonne literary professor Raymond Picard, and their violent quarrel about structuralism also spilled on to the popular headlines. All this went to show that French intellectuals can still, even today, steal the public limelight now and again, as in very few other countries. It also showed something of the educated public's fascinated horror at a new philosophy that made even Sartre's ideas look humane and optimistic in comparison. Sartre had killed God; the structuralists were killing Man too. For the moment their influence is largely confined to a number of *avant-garde* writers, philosophers, and scientists, and it is hard to see where it will lead. It is a symptom of the belated French post-war discovery of anthropology and the other human sciences, which they have seized on with a typical French intellectual extremism and ruthlessness.

Structuralism marks the first incursion of scientific values into the traditional domains of French intellectual life. As such, it is no more than one facet of a much wider and more important development: today the febrile little ghetto of the Left Bank finds itself increasingly challenged and circumscribed by the rise outside its walls of a new modern society with very different ideals, intent on technology, technocracy, and practical reform. And many *bona-fide* intellectuals have virtually defected to this camp, not necessarily by embracing structuralism, but simply by going to work with the reformers. Times have changed since the 1940s. The new bourgeoisie is more stable and prosperous than ever, and the bulk of the nation is absorbed in material and technical progress, or in trying to find concrete remedies for the black spots in housing, education, birth-control, marketing, and the rest. And many intellectuals have deserted their ivory towers to hitch their energies to these mundane but urgent tasks, whether by joining the Gaullists or constructively opposing them.

So today there is a most striking divorce between those intellectuals who broadly accept modern France and are helping to build it and those —still probably the majority—who reject it, remaining attached to their old ideologies or retreating into a private world of experimentation. Each group charges the other with betrayal. The 'pragmatists' are accused of compromising with a bourgeois régime, and of abandoning the hopes and ideals of an eventual victory of the Left on its terms. They include a number of economists and social scientists—younger ones like the brilliant Michel Crozier, or older ones like Raymond Aron (who twenty years ago was on the editorial board of Sartre's review, *Les Temps Modernes*!) They, in turn, charge the 'diehards' with sticking their noses in the sand and refusing to accept that conditions have changed. It is a quarrel that goes deeper than Gaullism: the successful growth of a new progress-minded society has taken the old guard by surprise and left them barking in the wrong direction. Of course there are many ramifications between the two groups, and many famous figures who do not fit easily into either: Lévi-Strauss himself, for instance. But the prototypes are blatant enough; the contrast is between Malraux building his cultural centres, and Sartre crying woe in the wilderness.

This traditional type of French intellectual, whether committed to the Left or not so political, is usually an easily recognisable species, especially on the Left Bank. Many of them hold university or *lycée* posts, or write for Left-wing journals, or combine a living out of reading for publishers, writing low-selling novels, and giving talks on the hated State radio. They generally dress drably and live modestly, in shabby, low-rent flats around the *Quartier*; they are not flamboyantly bohemian or picturesque, and they do not even spend much time in cafés any more. Though nearly all of them are bourgeois by origin, they have few social contacts, except family ones, with the despised money-making, conventional bourgeoisie. And they cling together. Nearly all have been through the precision-test of the *agrégation*, and share the Sorbonne's disdain for the rest of the world. Their capacity for semi-abstract rhetorical discussion, in a special *agrégés'* language of their own, seems inexhaustible. Recently they have come in for a good deal of heavy criticism, from various quarters—and especially from a man who is really one of themselves, a Left-wing philosophy teacher and publisher called Jean-François Revel.

In person, Revel is a mild and affable man, short, rotund, fortyish; in print, he is the wittiest and most unsparing Jeremiah of his time. In four remarkable books* he has lashed out at almost everything and everyone in modern France, and especially at the intellectual Left. 'This book is entirely negative,' he warns disarmingly at the beginning of *La Cabale des dévots*; 'those who like positive ideas shouldn't open it.' The weakness of this kind of polemicist is that he overstates his case, he attacks too many things at once and cannot be taken quite seriously. Revel is no exception: but so much *is* wrong with France that inevitably many of his shafts strike home.

He charges the intellectuals, first, with conformism: 'In the Left-wing reviews and weeklies, there is often a contrast between their political courage and their intellectual conformism. On page three, they risk police seizure,† on page seventeen they prostrate themselves before Claudel, Heidegger, or some other reactionary idol of thought or sensibility.' There is no need necessarily to share Revel's views on Claudel to agree with his main point, that most French intellectuals are scared of questioning their own basic assumptions or of getting too involved with others who share different ones. You see, they are still bourgeois beneath the skin. They live in a world of sacred cows, where the supremacy of certain accepted French authors and ideas must not be doubted—it stems back to the way they were taught Racine at the *lycée*. Revel also comments, acutely, 'Today's philosophy and literature have the function, in installing a *formalisation* of anxiety and revolt, of softening the reader's actual anxiety and revolt. By repeating every day to their placid and sated readers, "you are very distressed", they succeed in tranquillising them.' Or as a very bright *lycéenne* of eighteen told me, solemnly, 'We have a duty to be unhappy. Sartre tell us so.'

Revel castigates the notorious chauvinism‡ of French intellectuals—

---

* *Pourquoi des philosophes?* (Pauvert, 1957); *La Cabale des dévots* (the best of the four—Pauvert, 1962); *En France* (Julliard, 1965); *Contrecensures* (Pauvert, 1966).

† This was in 1962, during the FLN/OAS crisis.

‡ See p. 455 (Conclusion).

and what he calls their 'contempt for the authenticity of information' and 'great lack of interest in reality'. I have already remarked how Sartre distorts or ignores political facts to fit his own doctrines. De Beauvoir does the same: several critics noted how, in *La Force des choses*, she repeatedly charged the Fifth Republic with 'fascism' but gave de Gaulle not one word of credit for decolonising Africa or standing up to the Army and OAS. French intellectuals frequently give the impression that real life exists as grist to their own theories and not in its own right: they are afraid of peering outside the ghetto to look at the manifold changes in France, lest these do not fit in with their *idées reçues*.

Above all, Revel attacks the hallowed notion of French 'clarity'. In this instance he has found an ally in no less an organ than the *Times Literary Supplement*. In a special French number of the *TLS*, in May 1962, a now-famous front-page article suggested that the French tradition of limpid thought and clear logic, from Descartes via Voltaire to today, was now little more than a myth, and that Parisian intellectuals were today among the most abstruse and muddle-headed on earth. 'Clarity is giving place to woolly subjectivism, private symbols are posing as proofs of profundity,' said the *TLS* with a passing swipe at *L'Année dernière à Marienbad*; among the morsels it quoted to make its point was this from a prize-winning poetic passage by Michel Deguy: *

> L'homme *est* philosophique; c'est dire qu'il est philosophé par le passage au travers de son être de ce jaillissement dont la trace va s'appeler toute de suite *philosophie*, trace œuvre. La source se cache dans son propre flux; elle disparaît dans la fécondité de son sourdre. Penser c'est consentir à ce désir, qui nous constitue, de remémorer le sourdre indicible; c'est comme tenter de se convertir à la nuit d'où sort toute aube, et que les yeux, qui sont faits pour les lumineux, ne peuvent voir—tentative quasi suicidaire de gagner sur cette dérobade de l'originel pour le pressentir, recul de dos au plus près du foyer de notre être qui est abîme, perte d'être.

The *TLS* saw existentialism as one root of the trouble: 'a debased, haughty, and unscientific philosophy has invaded all thinking and all forms of expression.' Sartre himself, the article went on, was an original and courageous writer, but his imitators had abused his ideas and his language: 'He is largely responsible for the flourishing of a jargon that makes so much writing strictly unreadable, pretentious, precious, and above all, unclear.' The *TLS* called for a campaign against looseness (against vague words like *ontologie* and *dialectique* that were 'making France ridiculous') and it suggested that the linguistic purists should attack not *franglais* but highbrow obscurity as the most serious menace to pure French.

This article did no more to improve Anglo-French relations than de

---

* One of the Tel Quel group of young aesthetes: see p. 374, below.

Gaulle's veto on the British entry to the Six, a year earlier. Several Left-wing Paris papers rose in righteous fury at this assault by perfidious and uncultured Albion on sacrosanct French culture: Anne Villelaur a week later in *Les Lettres Françaises* said: 'C'est précisément pour avoir ignoré par principe et par manque d'information le contenu national de la culture française que ce numéro du *Supplément Littéraire du Times* est une trahison.' She and other critics suggested that the British are jealous of French cultural achievements and make up for our inferiority by carping. Kleber Haedens in *Le Nouveau Candide* said, 'We'd like to see one good new English novel'. But Revel, too, in *Pourquoi des Philosophes?* had been just as rude about 'clarity'. After attending a seminar on 'filmology' at the Sorbonne, he gave this summary of how the professor explained film projection: 'On peut donc considérer comme définitivement démontré par la filmologie que le passage de la réalité pelliculaire à la réalité écranique par l'intermédiaire de la réalité lenticulaire constitue une authentique promotion anaphorique.'

As the *TLS* pointed out, this epidemic is still largely confined to intellectuals. Talk to an engineer, salesman, clerk, or schoolchild, and you will usually find him a model of orderly and precise expression—and the same is true of workers and peasants, within the limits of their vocabulary and knowledge. This is the splendid legacy of French education, whatever its other failings. But why do the intellectuals deliberately tie this lucid subtlety into knots, or obscure it with word-play? Some of them, maybe, want to prove their intellectual superiority by using a clever terminology that others can't follow. Passing the *agrégation* has so convinced them of their brilliance that they feel sure anything they write must be profound. Or else, their style is a smoke-screen to hide their sheer lack of ideas. Or they are simply carried away by the Latin love of rhetoric and abstraction; in this age of experimentation, the counter-balancing French qualities of classic measure and discipline are no longer able to hold them in check.

I must not imply that all intellectuals are like this. Many real and serious writers (such as Simone de Beauvoir) are impeccably clear. Sartre may often be obscure, but he does leave the impression of struggling to express a genuine complexity of thought. Others have simply used this as an alibi for their own muddled vagueness, often allied to pomposity and lack of humour. 'French intellectuals are frequently terrified of humour,' said one critic; 'they think it's Right-wing.'

It is within a certain Parisian hard core that the various symptoms of intellectual *malaise* are most evident—at the Sorbonne, around the little reviews and a few *avant-garde* publishing-houses. This *milieu* enjoys much less of the national limelight than it did twenty years ago: it has grown more esoteric, more specialised. But it still monopolises a large part of organised intellectual society and has not lost its old arrogance and self-sufficiency. Scattered in isolation around the suburbs and provinces there are plenty of other writers, professors, thinkers, who are less pretentious and might even have something to say. But Paris seldom pays attention to them.

Outside this little Left Bank world a different climate is developing. The new participation of a number of intellectuals in reformist debate and action is throwing up new élites, closer to the British pattern. One sign of this is the recent growth of non-party economic and political study-groups such as the influential Club Jean Moulin; another, the displacement of old family business *patrons* by cultured and intellectually lively young technocrats; a third, the new keenness of students for the social sciences; and most important of all, the new Catholic ideal of militant social progress, and the support given by Christian intellectuals to the lay Catholic reform movements in agriculture and industry. As Michel Crozier has said, '*Engagement* is now more concrete, and philosophy and action have been growing closer together in the past ten years. All the new movements are marked by a need and a desire for contact across the barriers, a horror of *a priori* formulas, a passion for reforms and an ideology of participation.' In other words, this kind of intellectual is becoming more like his pragmatic British counterpart.

This trend may not in every case be quite so disinterested and idealistic, however; and it might not be right to paint too rosy a picture of young thinkers shaking themselves out of their paralysed gloom to cheer on the tractors and conveyor-belts. Looked at from another angle, pragmatic realism may sometimes appear as an opportunistic switch to a now fashionable materialist ethos. There has been no sharper portent of the changing times than the change since 1964 in the weekly *l'Express*. This used to be the very conscience of the intellectual Left, with long articles by Sartre and others on such matters as torture in Algeria. Now, though still supposedly anti-Gaullist, it has jumped smartly on to the bandwagon of technocracy and affluence, reshaped itself on the lines of *Time*, become very trend-conscious and modern minded—and definitely lowered its intellectual quality, on its literary as well as its political side. Many of its older loyalists are disgusted, and have switched to *Le Nouvel Observateur*; but clearly it appeals to a new, progress-minded, educated middle class. Only an intellectual's individual conscience can decide whether he is selling his soul in switching to the new cult of progress—France's essential salvation and her gravest danger. And the older intellectuals have only themselves to blame if they failed to provide any effective alternative, if they have let the technocrats steal the initiative and reveal their bankruptcy. For the present, the intellectuals have little choice but to follow the technocratic lead, while they regroup and readjust to the modern world. In a brilliant analysis of today's situation, Crozier writes: 'We have passed from the romantic period of the crisis, where the creative and irresponsible individual succeeded in partly breaking down the old structures [Sartre in the '40s], to the period of routine and withdrawal where the structures regain their place. If we are now in the dead period of the cycle, it is natural that the traditional-style intellectual should no longer get a hearing; the weight of social constraints has re-appeared; but it has not yet been felt long enough for there to be serious thought of revolt. . . . Such a period is naturally melancholy for the intellectual world. It easily gives an impression of retreat and decline. The illusions of the Liberation have been destroyed.' And Crozier goes on to speak of the rise of a new rationalism, and of the efforts of intellectuals to rethink their role and their attitudes, in face of a new, more fluid, more forward-looking climate. The crisis is likely to continue for some time. The old creative, turbulent, self-confident intellectual world, that made Paris the light and envy of the West, lies stricken, and is not likely to revive in its old form. It will re-emerge only by opening its eyes on a changing society, and accepting that change.

THE 'NEW NOVEL': FROM ROBBE-GRILLET'S LITTLE PUZZLES TO LE CLEZIO'S EPIC OF HELL

Since Voltaire's day the novel in France has often been closely allied to philosophy, and therefore it is not strange to find that post-war French fiction has many affinities with the various intellectual currents and anxieties of recent years, from Sartre to the structuralists. In France, as in Britain, the novel is going through a period of *malaise* and self-doubt, but the causes and the symptoms are quite different. Novelists in Britain, even the most highbrow, are in the main still loyal to a naturalistic narrative tradition that in France it is fashionable to consider outmoded; in France, the 'literary' novel (as opposed to the popular novel) is rife with metaphysical speculation and technical experiment with language and form—it is an intense, rarefied climate where every new work is potentially a poetic masterpiece but in practice more likely to be clever-clever and unreadable. You might say that the English novel has grown stale through remaining too conventional, the French novel is boldly *avant-garde* but without the leaven of genius.

There is also a striking difference between the way novelists live in the two countries, and their attitudes to society. Most of the English ones exist placidly in the provinces or the suburbs, soberly reporting on the daily scene around them. French ones rarely have so much contact with the ordinary life of the nation: whether or not they live on the Left Bank itself, their orientation is still largely towards the specialised literary milieu of the capital. Their work is much more ambitious, but often less human. Like so many French intellectuals, they seem to be motivated by a kind of anti-bourgeois complex, a passionate rejection of the bourgeoisie to which by origin they belong. This motif of French literature is not new. Flaubert strongly criticised the bourgeoisie, though he used the ordinary narrative realism of his day: yet *Madame Bovary* caused as much of a shock then as Genet or Robbe-Grillet today, and narrowly escaped being banned. Today this kind of novel has become bourgeois, that is, the bourgeoisie read and accept it: so anti-bourgeois writers have been turning to other weapons, those of *avant-garde* style and sensibility rather than social criticism. Their trump card is to write novels that the ordinary bourgeois reader won't understand or enjoy.

In the past fifty years a great revolutionary movement has developed which stems back to Proust: though in his own social life he was a bourgeois reactionary, he is still venerated as having written 'the first and greatest anti-bourgeois novel'. That is, he broke with the Balzacian tradition and concerned himself with other, private, asocial values. After the first War, other influences joined that of Proust: Joyce, Kafka, and the Surrealists led by Breton. Joyce, in fact, has probably made more impact on the alien but receptive French than on writers whose own mother-tongue he conjured with so lyrically. Between the wars the movement in France was twofold: to renovate literary style and vocabulary, which was still heavily classical, and to escape from the convention that novels must be straightforward accounts of middle-class life. Queneau and Céline stirred up literary French with a new kind of poetry drawn from colloquial speech, rather as Joyce had done with English: *Voyage au bout de la nuit* (1932), Céline's masterpiece of life-loathing, lyrical obscenity, virtually founded modern French *littérature noire* and was to have great influence on Sartre, Genet, and others. Small wonder that, in this climate, Joyce's fellow-Irish disciple Samuel Beckett decided to turn himself into a French writer. And it was in the '30s that Breton issued his famous pledge against the conventional narrative novel that has since become a war-slogan for the new novelists: 'I shall always refuse to write "la marquise sortit à cinq heures".' In order to understand modern French writers, it is necessary to realise the strength of their feelings against the nineteenth-century tradition which has been institutionalised by critics and professors and which, rightly or wrongly, they find cruelly inhibiting. So in many post-war novels you are not told whether the marchioness has gone out yet or not, or whether it is five o'clock today or yesterday, or indeed whether the marchioness is really the marchioness.

The most patent of anti-bourgeois writers, though not primarily a novelist, was of course Sartre himself. Early in his career he took up the novel as a vehicle for his philosophy, first in the metaphysical and allegorical *La Nausée* (1938), then in the more neo-realistic semi-documentary trilogy written in the '40s, *Les Chemins de la liberté*. He was followed by Simone de Beauvoir in *L'Invitée* (1943) and *Les Mandarins*, and by a number of other writers (including Genet in his own unique *genre*) who just after the war formed a kind of school of existentialist novelists. Generally they did keep to the narrative form and—except for Genet—they innovated not so much in style or language as in their ferocious Marxist moralising and their refusal to 'amuse' the reading public with what it expected—exciting plots, noble character-portrayal, and other fictional devices. The writer's duty, as they saw it, was not to invent charming stories but to set down the truth, unadorned, from the heart: induced by the rigours and verities of the Occupation, this was the era of *témoignages personnelles*. But the school fizzled out even faster than the other facets of the existentialist movement, and Sartre and de Beauvoir soon virtually gave up writing ncvels. Sartre came to realise (almost as quickly as his readers) that however urgent and original his message, his didactic approach defeated its own ends if his characters remained so flat and unconvincing. Fiction was not the right medium for him: the theatre suited him better. And today hardly anyone reads *Les Chemins* with pleasure or profit, except as the testimony of an epoch.

Albert Camus, like Sartre, brought a new questing philosophical intensity to the novel, and was much the finer stylist of the two. He was and still is more widely admired as a novelist than Sartre, and his vision of man struggling to give meaning and dignity to an 'absurd' existence—a vision more heroic and humane than Sartre's, if less intellectually rigorous—has influenced many younger writers. But Camus, too, appeared to lose faith in the novel as a form, and after *La Peste* (1947) he wrote only one more full-length novel (*La Chute*, 1956) before his death in a car accident in 1960, aged forty-six.

Parallel to Sartre and Camus, the first decade or so after the war was marked by a wide variety of different styles and approaches, showing that the traditional novel was and still is very far from dead. Many successful writers of the pre-war period were still active; among them was Jean Giono down in his native Provence, steeped in a rural world untouched by the new ideologies of the Left Bank. Younger novelists who emerged after the war frequently shared the existentialists' cynical hostility to bourgeois values but without rallying to Sartrian *engagement*. There was even a reaction against it, into a kind of hedonistic patrician egotism— witness a book like Roger Nimier's *Le Hussard bleu* (1950), or the early Sagan novels, or the work of Roger Vailland, a gifted and solitary Stendhalian figure, ex-Communist and eclectic adventurer, whose *La Loi* won the Prix Goncourt in 1957. And meanwhile, on the sidelines, largely ignored by the wider reading public, a number of other writers were pursuing some typically French aesthetic experimentations in the use of language and its inner links with reality: theorists like Maurice Blanchot, poetic surrealists like Queneau, Michel Leiris, and Jean Douassot.

This is the background against which the writers known loosely as the 'New Novelists' have emerged in the past twelve or fifteen years. More journalistic ink has flowed over the so-called *nouveau roman* than over any other literary trend in Europe since the war, and probably more than it deserves, in terms of strict achievement. It is not really a 'school' at all, for its leading exponents—Alain Robbe-Grillet, Michel Butor, Nathalie Sarraute, Claude Simon, and others—are rather different from each other and frequently quarrel and hold opposing views. They have been lumped together out of journalistic convenience, and through the smart public-relations work of their self-appointed prophet and president, Robbe-Grillet.

Yet they do have some things in common. In rejecting conventional character-portrayal and story-telling, they are in the broad line traced from Proust and Joyce via Céline, Queneau, Genet, and others. Like Sartre, they rebel against the Balzac tradition, but they go much farther than Sartre, and are even reacting against him too: Sarraute, for instance, has alleged that Sartre, Camus, Kafka, and others were using the novel as a disguised form of diary-writing, to project their own subjective hopes and fears through the thoughts of an anonymous hero, whereas the true role of the modern writer should be to portray the actual perceptible world that *is*, shorn of the author's moralising. The most obvious common feature of all the new novelists' work is an obsession with minute physical description, whether of objects or sensations. Their semi-scientific approach to literature seems to have something in common with structuralism, and their rejection of much of the normal range of human values and interests is all too clear a symptom of the post-existentialist climate.

Robbe-Grillet is the one who has taken up the most extreme position and formulated his theories the most sharply. He is an enigmatic, unclassifiable creature, utterly untypical of one's stock picture of the French writer yet hard to imagine at work anywhere except in France. Though his novels are so very dehumanised, he himself is extremely human, jolly, and relaxed; talking to him it is sometimes hard to avoid the conclusion that his whole operation might be partly a leg-pull at the expense of serious literature. 'Critics seem to have overlooked the humorous element in my books,' he once told me, 'but I laugh aloud when I read them to myself, as Kafka did at his. By far my favourite author is Lewis Carroll.' Precisely. Talking to him, or reading his books or seeing his films, one feels very much like Alice at the Mad Hatter's tea-party. 'Have some wine,' the March Hare said in an encouraging tone. 'I don't see any wine,' remarked Alice. 'There isn't any,' said the March Hare.

Now in his mid-forties, Robbe-Grillet is dapper and quizzical with thick black hair and moustache. By training and early career he is an agricultural engineer and scientist, and he took up writing almost by chance in his late twenties after being impressed by Kafka, the French surrealists, and *Brighton Rock*. He is anything but the usual Left Bank denizen, and he hates Paris literary society: he spends his time between a formal bourgeois flat in Neuilly and a country château near Caen, and his passionate hobbies are gardening, botany, carpentry, and taking his pretty young wife on skiing holidays. He even has friends who are dons at Oxford and send him rare seeds and plants for his garden. It is not the way Sartre spends his time. I have said that Robbe-Grillet is hard to imagine except in France, though from this picture you might think him more like an English eccentric *manqué*. But his literary politicking is essentially French. From the moment that *Le Voyeur* won the Prix des Critiques in 1955 and made him famous, he has set out to establish himself as *chef d'école* and to wage a vendetta against those who dare to write or admire any different kind of novel. This he does with *panache* but also with impish good humour. He enjoys flamboyant public arguments, Press conferences, and manifestos, and sometimes his books and films appear as little more than weapons in a careful strategic campaign to prove certain theories about literature and perception.

His foremost dogma is that literature must rid itself of what Ruskin called 'the pathetic fallacy', the tendency of novelists to describe physical objects emotively. According to Robbe-Grillet, mountains must not be allowed to loom 'majestically' or villages to 'nestle' in a valley, and it is better to write 'the glass is on the table' than 'reposes on the table'. He says, 'Around us, defying the onslaught of our animist adjectives, *things are there*,' and any attempt to endow the physical world with emotion is a step towards the illicit belief in God. This attitude, often known as *chosisme*, appears to have been influenced by the structuralist critic Roland Barthes, who has written warmly of Robbe-Grillet's novels and who similarly inveighs against the notion of 'the romantic heart of things'. Those novels are rich in *chosisme*—especially in their long painstaking descriptions of such things as the shape and measurements of a window (in *Le Voyeur*) or of a tropical plantation (*La Jalousie*) or the physionomy of centipedes.

But Robbe-Grillet, with apparent inconsistency, does not limit himself to *chosisme*. He denies that Man, despite appearances, has been banished from his pages in favour of Things. Although characterisation, emotion, and action in the ordinary sense barely exist, he claims that Man still holds the centre of the stage, for what *is* can be no other than what is seen or imagined (a sound Berkeleian approach), and, as he told me, his detailed descriptions 'are *passionate*, an attempt to portray the world through the obsessed eyes of my heroes: if I describe a room with five chairs in it, what I am really describing is the obsession of the looker.' In all his novels and films, the same scenes or incidents keep recurring in different guises, as if seen, remembered, or imagined by the same person in different ways. In *La Jalousie*—to my mind the best of his books—a kind of human situation does exist, a triangle of jealous husband, wife, and suspected lover, and physical objects are seen with heightened awareness through the manic gaze of the unhappy husband. It is a technique in some ways better suited to the film than the novel, and this explains Robbe-Grillet's passion for the cinema, where many directors besides himself (Antonioni, for instance, in *Blow-up*) have played the game of fudging the borderline between appearance and reality, juxtaposing contrasting images of the same scene. Robbe-Grillet said to me of his scenario for Resnais' *l'Année dernière à Marienbad*: 'What passes on the screen is the subjective struggle in the girl's mind, so the spectator can never be sure of the level of reality he is observing. The amount of furniture in the room varies according to how she is feeling. Suppose two people have a conversation—"let's go to my house in the country"—"but it will be raining"—"then we can light a log-fire". In effect they are swapping images. Screen dialogue should be like that: done in images, not words.'

How are we to assess the artistic worth of all this? On the one hand, Robbe-Grillet's great strength, in all his writing, is his sonorous and lyrical prose style that lends a dream-like fascination to many of his descriptions—and the same is true of his beautiful *mise-en-scène* in *L'Immortelle*, his first film as a director. But the effect, finally, is gratuitous and boring because there is no identifiable human impetus behind the images. Many critics have pointed out the basic contradiction in his work: on the one hand he proclaims his theory of the pre-eminence of the observable world, on the other he destroys it with a 'game of mirrors' that leaves us unable to discern what is real and what is not. 'Les choses' are not pre-eminent after all, they are the figments of human hallucination. And as John Weightman has suggested,[*] the very force of his dreamline descriptions creates a new 'pathetic fallacy' as potent as the one he campaigns against. In his most recent book, *La Maison de rendez-vous*, he appears to have become more whimsical than ever, taking the subject-matter of an ordinary thriller and playing tricks with the chronology so that the same murder keeps happening again and again in different ways: a long-drawn-out trip through the looking-glass. Robbe-Grillet claims that his books are meant to be funny: but the joke is usually such a private one (unlike the *Alice* jokes) that the effect on the reader is more often one of solemnity.

John Weightman has also analysed what he sees as Robbe-Grillet's 'religious fear of religion', his desire to purge the world of mysteries or symbols that could have any 'significance'. In all his work, and especially in his films, he first arouses our human interest and sympathy, then mockingly plants a booby-trap that snuffs it out and leaves us feeling cheated. Take *L'Immortelle*. The first half is a haunting and tender love-poem, stylised but discernibly human: a young Frenchman meets a mysterious and lovely woman in Istanbul, falls in love with her, woos her, loses her, searches for her wistfully through the eerie Turkish townscape. Then the girl equivocally reappears and equivocally dies, and for the next half-hour Robbe-Grillet treats us to an assorted battery of trick-images which firmly ram home the message that we were suckers if we took the first half of the film at all seriously, for there is no reality. Filmgoers who seek in *L'Immortelle*, or in *Marienbad*, for any deeper meaning beyond the surface beauties will seek in vain. Robbe-Grillet is at heart a scientist and an iconoclast, and he seems determined to prevent the rest of us from enjoying unscientific literary or aesthetic pleasures of the old-fashioned sort: a curious vocation for an artist.

Robbe-Grillet has stolen much of the limelight because of his sheer novelty and shock-value, and because he is so articulate and assertive,

* *Encounter*, March 1962.

always ready to give interviews or dash across the world to attend a writers' congress. Other 'New Novelists' are less colourful, but some are worth taking just as seriously. A writer often classed together with Robbe-Grillet is Michel Butor, though in fact the two have little in common beyond having brought out experimental novels at about the same time. Butor is a mild and unassuming man of about forty, formerly a *lycée* philosophy teacher: he has publicly attacked Robbe-Grillet's theories, and his own books are much less far removed from the traditional novel. He is a dedicated Proustian and his books, like Proust's, are concerned with time: they even have coherent characters and plots, of a sort, though often these are turned upside-down through Butor's obsession with the relativity of time and the time–space relationship. His best-known novel, *La Modification* (1957), takes place entirely in the mind of one character on a train-journey from Paris to Rome, with appropriate mental flashbacks. I myself prefer his earlier book, *L'Emploi du temps* (1956), with its nightmarish descriptions of Manchester where Butor had spent a year as a grammar-school teacher. The book opens with a young Frenchman beginning to write an account of his arrival in Manchester six months previously: but soon his present life becomes so fascinating to him that a second, more up-to-date thread of narrative interweaves with the first in his journal, and as life leaps ahead faster than his pen, soon there are several different accounts running parallel, and past and present are jumbled ever more closely together. The attempt to step into a new dimension of time is ingenious, and an English reader is intrigued by the horrified French-eye view of Manchester as a Kafkaesque city from which there is no escape: but, as in all Butor's books, the characters and events are a good deal less graphic than the time-theories. He is now moving away from fiction towards experimental prose that tries to explore the new time–space ratio in an age of supersonic travel. Clocks, timetables, airports, fascinate him. He once told me, 'I want each book to be like a beautiful theorem': as with Robbe-Grillet, the human heart takes second place. I do not think Butor is a great writer, but I find his conundrums more stimulating, if less finely written, than Robbe-Grillet's.

Nathalie Sarraute is different again. She is much older: a White Russian Jewish émigré to Paris, now in her sixties, who has changed her style little since her first novel over thirty years ago. She was relatively unknown until Robbe-Grillet's breakthrough gave notoriety to the experimental *chosiste* novel—and today she admits that she owes some of her public success to Robbe-Grillet, though she objects to the way he patronises her, quite unjustifiably, as his pupil. Like Robbe-Grillet she has openly and frequently condemned the moralistic novel of explicit narrative or social comment, and this has led them to be bracketed together. But her themes and subject-matter are very different from his: she is concerned not with appearance and memory, but with the living tissue of tiny, subtle sensations that she believes to make up the fabric of our lives. She admires Proust and Virginia Woolf, and uses a stream-of-consciousness technique

not so very different from theirs to depict minutely a world of psychological flickerings (*tropismes*, she calls them) which for her are the real
substance of human contact and sensibility. Her novels are difficult to
read, and not rich in outward plot or character, but within her self-imposed range she is manifestly a psychological realist, and a true poet.

Another gifted woman writer who is sometimes lumped with the 'New
Novelists' is Marguerite Duras. Her elliptical techniques of dialogue and
narrative possibly entitle her to be classed as experimental: but at heart
she is less close to Robbe-Grillet than to the *engagé* Sartrian school. Witness the difference between the two Resnais films: *Hiroshima mon amour*
with her script, and the never-never-land of *Marienbad*. She has a *colon*
background, and in several of her books she has vigorously criticised
colonial society: in *Barrage contre le Pacifique*, and in her recent impressive study of famine in India, *Le Vice-Consul*. But she is not a pamphlet-
eer: she is a very warm-blooded writer with a feeling for real people and
predicaments, and that is something to welcome in the French novel
today. In the best of her stories—*Le Square, 10.30 d'un soir d'été, Les
Petits Chevaux de Tarquinia, Des Journées entières dans les arbres*—she
portrays a rare sensitivity to atmosphere and place, the delicacy of relationships and the difficulty of communication. My only criticism is that
her books are often too slight and inconclusive, and that like many women
intellectuals of her type she is not above lapsing into women's-magazine
emotionalism.

The most powerful of all the 'New Novelists', though not the best
known outside France, is Claude Simon, who is now in his fifties but has
written all his best work in the past ten years. Even more than Butor and
Sarraute, his books recall Proust—and also Faulkner, whose influence he
freely admits. Like Faulkner he writes about violence: *La Route des
Flandres* (1961) deals with the events of 1940, and *Le Palace* (1962)
recalls his own memories of Barcelona at the outbreak of the Spanish War.
Like Proust he struggles obsessively to recapture on paper the colour and
smell of his youth; his giant sentences, sprawling over pages of baroque
metaphor, are like a very parody of Proust's. His obscurity, and his disregard for narrative, earn him a place of honour in the *nouveau roman*:
but he writes passionately, from the heart, not with chilly calculation.

There are other 'New Novelists' too: among the best known are Robert
Pinget, Claude Ollier, and Claude Mauriac (son of François). All, or nearly
all, see it as the writer's task to experiment with the links between language and consciousness rather than to depict society or tell a story; all,
or nearly all, are Left-wing in their personal sympathies, and several
including Robbe-Grillet signed the manifestos against the war in Algeria,
but not often does any hint of such views or of any topical social concern
enter their pages. Sometimes they appear to be chiefly preoccupied with
writing novels about the problems of writing novels, especially Mauriac
and Philippe Sollers. Needless to say, this inward-looking and rarified
school of literature has not found any great success with a wider public:

few of their books sell more than three or four thousand copies, except for some of the *succès d'estime* of Robbe-Grillet and Butor which have reached 60,000 or so in pocket edition. Today the *nouveau roman* appears to have passed its zenith: its new imitators are becoming fewer, and some of its leaders seem to be flagging: Robbe-Grillet has published only one novel since 1959. Students and *lycéens* rarely turn eagerly to these writers as they do, still, to Camus, Sartre, and Malraux.

What then has the 'new novel' achieved? Many critics, including some of those who are not its greatest admirers, see it as essentially a catalyst, paving the way for the future. They share the view that the French novel has grown stale under the weight of the Balzacian tradition and needs a shock renewal, even though they might not regard Robbe-Grillet as the ideal remedy. One well-known critic, Robert Escarpit, told me: 'I see the *nouveau roman* as a language laboratory or testing ground: Butor, Pinget, and Co. are doing for us what Joyce did for English. These books will have a permanent influence, but they won't last in themselves. Their role is to open a new door.' Another critic said he thought that the *nouveau roman*, with its emphasis on perception rather than morals, might prove to be the source of a 'new lyricism'. Others are less sanguine: Michel Crozier sees the *nouveau roman* as 'a critique of existentialist humanism through caricature and "the Absurd",' a shrug of despair at finding that human values do not exist and a typical symptom of the more negative aspects of the post-Sartrian void. But perhaps it is a pity that Robbe-Grillet has succeeded in stamping the whole 'movement' with his own austere and special image, for several of the others are genuinely humanists in their way.

Nearly all the 'New Novelists' are now over forty. Among the much younger writers following through the door they are said to have opened, two trends are so far discernible, one rather more encouraging than the other. The first is the emergence of an arrogant and vocal coterie of young aesthetes, led by the experimental writer Philippe Sollers. They have their own monthly review, *Tel Quel*, which champions the ideal of formal literary beauty. Their style owes something to Robbe-Grillet, whom they salute as a *maître-à-penser*, but they also claim affinities back to Valéry, Artaud, and others. Their concern is for exquisiteness of language, irrespective of content; one of their number is Michel Deguy, whose prize work I quoted from the *Times Literary Supplement* article, and he is typical of them. They have been compared to Mallarmé and his school, and they seem to have much in common with his ingrown preciosity and disregard for ideas or coarse reality. They are not especially numerous nor influential, but they are quite typical of the kind of current Left Bank intellectual effeteness that Revel and others have attacked.

Another tendency (barely yet discernible except in the case of two or three young and isolated voices) is for the kind of novel that gives vent to an aggressive personal disgust at the universe, in language that is often ferocious. They possibly owe a good deal to the *nouveau roman* in their techniques, and you can trace affinities too with Genet, Beckett, or the American beats. But more directly they are giving personal expression to the kind of *malaise* that exists among serious youth in some student and other circles. Claude Néron, a Belgian living in France, and Marcel Moreau are two names; a third was Albertine Sarrazin, a kind of female Jean Genet who wrote at first hand about an underworld of prisons, pimps, and prostitutes, and who died in 1967 at the age of thirty. These writers form no school and hold no literary theories; it may be too schematic to regard them as a trend. Much the most distinguished of them is a handsome, blond Adonis in his middle twenties who looks like a clean-living rugger captain and writes like Dante in Hell.

Jean-Marie-Gustave le Clézio is actually of British nationality. Perhaps that explains his public-school looks. He comes from Mauritius, has lived and studied in Nigeria, London, and Bristol, and now lives in Nice where he is preparing a *doctorat*. He is reserved and laconic, and tends to give anti-interviews expressing his disgust at himself and the interviewer —the opposite of Robbe-Grillet. His first novel, *Le Procès-verbal*, won the Prix Renaudot and narrowly missed the Goncourt in 1963, and was described by François Erval in *l'Express* as 'The most remarkable debut in French literature since the war.' It is on the familiar theme of a young man's search for meaning and identity, but expressed in an unusual heightened style of tormented ingenuity, with realistic settings drawn from his own experience. Then came a book of short stories, *La Fièvre*, and in 1966 his masterpiece, *Le Déluge*. This takes up the theme of his first book and lifts it on to a cosmic level while retaining the everyday settings. It is the story of a young man's nightmare odyssey through the streets of a modern city, haunted by death and decay, leading to a final expiation where, alone by the sea after days of storm, he turns his eyes to the force of the sun and blinds himself. Le Clézio marries this epic allegory of man's destiny not with the semi-abstract world of Samuel Beckett nor with the medieval past of Bergman's *The Seventh Seal*, but with the ordinary details that he finds revolting about life today, in an overcrowded city of noise, greed, and alienation. His personal hell makes the work of many of the other 'New Novelists' look like contrived doodlings. It will be interesting to see whether this youthful ferocity burns itself out, or whether his macabre vision is capable of development.

If the 'New Novel' has stolen much of the critical limelight in the past decade, this does not mean that public taste follows suit or that the traditional novel is dead. Conventional writers like Henri Troyat, Jean Lartéguy, Maurice Druon, and Gilbert Cesbron easily top the best-seller lists, with sales maybe ten or fifty times that of the average *nouveau roman*. And even among 'literary' novels, probably less than a quarter today are classifiable as *nouveaux romans*. There are still plenty of serious or ambitious new novels of narrative that deal with cherished French themes of family life and conflict, or with off-beat amorous adventures in exotic lands, or with high society. And the leading annual literary prizes which make so much difference to sales—the Goncourt, the Renaudot, the Fémina, and others—are much more often given to this kind of book than to an experimental one. When Butor's *La Modification* won the Renaudot in 1957, and then sold 100,000 copies, it was an exception. There is also a wide new vogue among the serious reading public for autobiographical *témoignages* by leading literary figures, at the expense of straight fiction which as in England has been losing some of its appeal. In this class the memoirs of Sartre and de Beauvoir have secured huge sales, and so has such a book as *La Bâtarde* by Violette Leduc, the outspoken life-story of an ageing and ugly Lesbian. And of all the prize-winning novels, the one with the highest sales since the war (around half-a-million) has been the 1959 Goncourt winner, *Le Dernier des justes* * by André Schwartz-Bart, a saga of Jewish history that in many ways is closer to documentary than to fiction.

Even the traditional novel, almost as much as the 'New Novel', shows a curious reluctance to deal squarely with the themes of modern France. Serious writers, whatever their approach to the novel, prefer to set their books in the past, or abroad, or around private subjects of love, fantasy, or childhood, rather than to analyse what it is like to live in this country today. At a time when French society is in a fascinating period of transition, the novel has virtually abdicated its classic role as chronicler of that society—and in France even the modern inheritors of that role, cinema and television, are not doing this particular job very well.† True, there are some exceptions: sharp little studies of bourgeois cupidity continue to appear, such as de Beauvoir's recent *nouvelle*, *Les Belles Images*, but one has the feeling that it's all been said before, with the same *parti pris*. The French novel remains essentially bourgeois, especially when it is trying not to be: there is virtually no equivalent of the new English school of working-class fiction (for what *that* is worth). And although a few bourgeois intellectuals have made brave attempts to penetrate the mysteries of modern working-class life (as Christiane Rochefort has in *Les Petits Enfants du siècle*) these usually lack conviction.

When a young writer does try to present the mood of modern France, it is often on a highly personal in-turned level of metaphysical allegory, as with le Clézio. And for all his qualities, he is not exactly a neo-realist. Sometimes I ingenuously ask a writer or publisher, 'France today needs her Balzac, her Flaubert, as much as ever: why is no one filling this gap?' The 'New Novelists' just laugh. Robbe-Grillet said to me, 'Flaubert and Balzac were great writers in their day, but you can't write like that now, and those who try to are bad writers. The role of the novelist today isn't to explore social values, for these already exist: it is to discover *new* values, to probe into a world where he doesn't yet know the answers.' Some

---

* English translation, *The Last of the Just*, published by Atheneum (1960).
† Or perhaps the cinema is, but obliquely.

authors, including Butor, claim that they *are* writing about real modern life but simply using new techniques. But what really seems to have happened is that, in trying to escape from the tyranny of Balzac, these writers have imposed a new tyranny, a new conformism, which is just as strong. Young writers often complain, 'After what Robbe-Grillet's done to the novel, we don't feel able to write in the traditional manner any more, or if we do, the critics won't take us seriously.' Many intellectuals, too, feel it a point of honour *not* to write the kind of readable novel which the bourgeoisie can enjoy and which therefore might encourage bourgeois complacency. Hence much of the self-conscious difficulty of modern writing.

There is therefore this gap in France between bourgeois and experimental fiction, with few writers, say, of the William Golding type in a middle position. Escarpit said to me, 'If the kind of book you're wanting doesn't happen, I think it's the fault of publishers, critics, and public as much as of writers. If anyone today wrote, say, an uncompromising realistic satire on provincial life, it would fall between two stools. The highbrows would deride it as old-hat and not what the novel is for: and bourgeois publishers and booksellers would be frightened it would offend their readers. I've tried it myself. I wrote an *engagé* novel about present-day conflicts in a small town near Bordeaux, where I live: the intellectuals ignored it, and my Catholic upper-class publisher refused to promote it.' Another Leftish writer, Daniel Anselme, told me he had much the same experience with *La Permission*, his realistic novel about the Army in Algeria—a subject of passionate interest to the French yet characteristically ignored by nearly all French fiction, and not simply because of censorship. There is little parallel to the English or American novel of social criticism: on the other hand, it is hard to imagine Claude Simon or le Clézio writing successfully in England.

This state of affairs derives partly from the special position of the writer in French society. He is publicly esteemed, his views are quoted in the newspapers much more often than in England: but generally he lives in less close contact with ordinary society than English writers from Hardy to John Brain. French novelists have tended to mix with each other in a rarefied Parisian milieu, scorning the provinces—'I was born in Amiens, but you can't *live* there,' one told me—and in extreme cases they make it almost a point of faith not to know what ordinary philistines are like. Their raw material of life is generally drawn from their own childhood memories of family crises, or from their current intrigues and *amours*. It is a world centring round the great Parisian publishing houses and the monthly and quarterly reviews, such as Sartre's *Temps Modernes* and the *Nouvelle Revue Française*. These reviews are less powerful and numerous than they used to be, but occupy a far larger place in French literary life than their English equivalents such as *Encounter*: they are given over to long prolix critiques of new books, full of abstract superlatives, and addressed essentially to other specialists. It is a world dominated by gossip and politicking over who is going to review who, and how the writers' juries will vote for the annual prizes; it is a world where the caprice of fashion plays almost as large a role, in its own highbrow way, as in the London pop scene where it is death not to be 'in'. And there is far less *va-et-vient* and easy communication than in London between this strictly literary world and the wider, less high-powered one of TV, radio, and journalism.

In the great days, until the 1930s, there was an aristocratic flavour to this literary milieu, centring round the *salons* of the great cultured families. In this way writers were in touch with at least one section of true French social life (for example Proust). Since the war the *salons* have been dying, and many intellectuals have retreated from their influence to within their own closed ranks. But today, in the '60s, a new phase is becoming apparent which might have great influence. The intellectual cliques are beginning to disperse under the impact of economic change and the new modern style of living. Some of the more successful writers, seduced by affluence, are indulging in fast cars, weekend cottages, and regular foreign travel, and are becoming less dependent on the Parisian ghetto; or else, faced with the housing shortage, they move out from their old Left Bank flats to new homes in the suburbs, just like other bourgeois. Robbe-Grillet and Butor are both typical cases: as we see from their work, it does not necessarily bring them closer to the rest of French society, but in a more oblique way it means that they are affected by the preoccupations of the age. And I think this trend is likely to develop. A few other writers have decided, like a growing number of Parisians, that the provinces might be the best place to live in after all. Le Clézio has placed on record his hatred of Paris: admittedly, Nice where he lives is not the most typical of French towns nor is he likely to be its Balzac, but I fancy that he and others are more likely to be able to realise themselves in the provinces than amid the pressures of Paris. And if there is to be a French creative revival in the arts, my guess is that it will come not from Paris but from the new intellectual life that is burgeoning in provincial towns. And against this kind of background, a French writer is much less likely to be isolated from the rest of society.

The French novel still shows a certain vitality, even if one may not always admire the expression it takes. I wish I could say the same of French poetry, which has gone into near-eclipse since the death of Eluard in 1952. The few notable French poets still alive (figures as diverse as Saint-John Perse, Francis Ponge, Henri Michaux, and Réne Char) are all over sixty. Hardly a single younger poet has made any impact, and publishers seem even more scared of marketing poetry than in England. Yet in a wider sense, poetry is very far from dead in France: the nation's modern poets are expressing themselves in prose (e.g. the strong lyrical element in many of the *nouveaux romans*, including le Clézio) and more especially in film-making.

Like many French people today, I regard cinema and literature as intimately interchangeable. Therefore it is hard to be too pessimistic about the present state of French writing when the cinema is still so flourishing—when Duras and Robbe-Grillet can turn easily and naturally from novel-writing to film-directing and back again, or when Bresson, Resnais, and Godard can give their films the density and subtlety of the novel. Whether the novel will survive as a distinct art form, or whether it will merge into cinema and disappear as epic poetry has done, is therefore a secondary consideration. For the moment, literature in France is in a period of uneasy transition and re-examination. For all the failures and preciosities of much of the *nouveau roman*'s experimentation, at least the scene is alive with a certain intensity and variety and ambition. In the last resort, and despite everything, I'm not sure that I don't prefer Robbe-Grillet to the plodding legions of grey English realists.

FRANCE'S NEW DYNAMIC:
MILITANT LAY CATHOLICISM

While intellectuals like Barthes and Lévi-Strauss have become in a sense the anti-Christian theologians of the age, the Catholics in France have been turning from theology and ritual to social action. Look closely at any of the grass-roots movements of social reform since the war, and in nearly every case you will find that some nucleus of Catholic militants has played a central part: the farming revolution led by the Jeunesse Agricole Chrétienne is the obvious example, but there are many others too, in business, industry, and trade-unionism, in the student world or among animators of the *Grands Ensembles* and even in the campaign for birth-control. In a country where the Church has tended in the past to be reactionary and integrist, this neo-Catholicism, as it is called, marks a striking change. It is much more than an intellectual trend but it does embrace a number of Parisian intellectuals, especially among those whom I described as the pragmatists involved with concrete problems.

And so one hears talk in France of a 'post-war Catholic revival'. But the term can be misleading: the revival is one of quality, not quantity. Regular church-going is still at a low ebb, the traditional influence of the parish priest has been everywhere declining, and most people in practice are quite pagan. But among those who do believe, there has been a re-examining and a sharpening of faith, and a major shift of emphasis towards Christian witness and example and away from old-style piety and ritual. This is quite largely a lay-inspired movement; but today it embraces many of the clergy too, especially the younger ones, and it has even won the qualified support of the bishops. The French hierarchy has been moving steadily to the Left since the war; and France has played as large a part as almost any country in helping to influence the new policies of the Vatican.

To anyone who knows the pre-1939 history of the Church in France, all this may seem extraordinary. Although since 1905 the State has been secular and the Church disestablished, until much more recently the hierarchy identified itself closely in practice with the ruling upper-bourgeois class, and protected its own interests by defending the social *status quo*. In rural areas, priest and gentry were natural allies. The Church was ultra-clerical, allowing little scope for lay action, and expecting its priests to be obeyed; and it inspired the bitterest anti-clericalism. The Church was also anti-temporal, concerned exclusively with spiritual, not social, welfare. And often it was nationalistic almost to the point of fascism. Many of its leaders supported Maurras's extreme Right-wing *Action Française* movement in the '30s. Many bishops even collaborated under the Occupation, or at least lifted no finger to help the Resistance. So the Catholic element in the Resistance passed into the hands of lay leaders, notably Georges Bidault, and from this there emerged after the war the new liberal Catholic political movement, the MRP.

But even in the '30s the Church was not entirely monolithic in its Right-wing stance. From early in the century several forces had been at work to 'rechristianise' the urban masses and carry the fight against Communism on to the enemy's ground. Before the war the Christian trade union (CFTC) was formed, and young workers' movements were started, the Jeunesse Ouvrière Chrétienne and the JAC itself. Then in 1943 a simple Paris priest, the Abbé Godin, published an epoch-making book, *France, pays de mission*, which for the first time openly faced up to the truth that France was no longer a Christian but a pagan country, and that the Church must alter its ways radically to meet this situation. Cardinal Suhard, then Archbishop of Paris, was deeply impressed. Soon a new *Mission de France* was active, whose priests took an oath to 'devote their life to the christianisation of the working-class'. Then in 1944 the collaborationist bishops and priests emerged discredited from the Occupation—there were even demands for them to be shot as traitors. Old-style clericalism received the heaviest blow to its prestige since Dreyfus. The way was open for the rise in influence of other bishops, the liberals. Suhard's successor, Cardinal Feltin, was a liberal; so were Cardinals Gerlier at Lyon and Liénart at Lille. In this new climate, the *Mission de France* rapidly embarked on the most dramatic Christian experiment in the world since the war: the worker-priests. Their story has been told so often that I will not repeat more than its outline. About a hundred priests turned themselves into factory-workers, sharing their lives, their jobs, their dress. The aim was partly to preach Christian example, partly to discover what the downtrodden pagan working-class was really like, and so to bridge the terrible gulf of ignorance that separated it from the bourgeois Church. And so profoundly disturbed were the priests by the sufferings of this class that many of them became heavily influenced by Marxism and began to militate in the Communist trade union. The Vatican (under Pius XII) grew worried. In vain Feltin and Liénart pleaded for the experiment to continue: the priests, they said, had *not* lost their faith, they were simply coming to terms with working-class reality. In 1954, on the orders of Rome, the movement was virtually suspended. But about one half of the priests felt so strongly that they refused to obey. They remained in their factories, some of them losing their faith and joining the Communist Party, other endeavouring in painful solitude to reconcile the Kingdom of God with the class struggle.

For several years after 1954 the intellectual leadership of the neo-Catholic movement was left in disquiet by the collapse of the worker-priest movement. Many felt that the Church had betrayed them. But the worker-priests, so it now seems, were really no more than a storm-troop spearhead that had advanced too far ahead of its supporting army and been mown down. The rest of that army has gone on steadily moving forward, more slowly but on a much wider front. And in 1965 the liberal Pope Paul gave permission for the worker-priest experiment to be tentatively resumed. By 1967, fifty such priests were back at work, but this time under closer Church discipline than before.

The dechristianisation of France is a process that has been happening gradually, as in many Western countries, for nearly a century. Although a high percentage of people still pay lip-service to Christianity through social convention (some 90 per cent are still baptised) most of them neglect it entirely except at the crucial moments of christening, marriage, and burial. In the middle classes, weekly church-going as a family status-symbol has fallen off considerably, though much more in Paris and other big cities than in small towns. At the same time the traditional role of the priest has declined, both as moral and social leader in rural parishes, and as intimate friend and counsellor to bourgeois families. Figures for attendance at Mass, after declining for several decades, now seem to have levelled off: in Paris about 14 per cent of people go to Mass each week, while in traditional Catholic rural areas like the Vendée the figure may reach 80 per cent, or fall to well below 10 per cent in industrial centres. The overall picture is clear: old-style, pious Catholicism is still slowly retreating in areas where it is strongest, while in the most heavily pagan areas a new-style Catholicism is beginning to make some progress.

This weakening of clericalism has inevitably been followed by a softening of anti-clericalism too. And so the sharpest of all the feuds that have torn France in the past century is fading away into history. In some country districts it may linger on, where villages are still ranged into two camps, behind the *curé* and the teacher; this is true especially of an area like the Brittany hinterland where the Church was most closely associated with the feudal gentry. But in many other regions the old quarrels between Rouges and Blancs are coming to seem as much a part of folklore as horse-drawn carriages or country-dancing. The younger generation aren't worried any more. And so the issue of State aid for Church schools, over which so many Third and Fourth Republic parliaments fought and bled, is dying too. Although the Gaullist régime, being loyally Catholic, has in the past decade increased the level of aid to these schools, the non-Catholic Left no longer get so worked up about it all. For them, this is one of the least of de Gaulle's sins. Under the new laws, the State pays virtually the whole of a Church school's staff salaries, and some other expenses too, depending on how much freedom each school may wish to retain. But despite the increased aid the percentage of children in Church schools has been declining steadily, especially at primary level—it moved from 20 per cent in 1959 to 17 in 1964. And the two systems, Church and State, are moving closer together. An increasing number of teachers in the Church schools are non-Christians; a growing number of Catholic families send their children to State schools (where the teaching is generally better), while many State *lycées* have Catholic almoners attached to their staff. A liberal *curé* in Rodez, a typical Massif Central country town, told me: 'A parent today chooses his school for practical reasons more than confessional ones. Or at least, he wants to be able to make the choice privately and freely, without social pressure, and without the whole thing being made into a public issue. The only people still interested in the *école laïque* debate are little pressure-groups made up of the anti-clerical teachers and old-guard priests themselves. Many of them feel it's a matter of honour to support their own type of school. But the general public couldn't care less.'

The same priest also told me: 'Younger Catholics round here have been trying to widen their faith by asking what God expects of them in their daily life and work. They are more concerned with concrete charity than with spiritual studies. They feel it's more important to aid the community than not to eat meat on Friday.' The J A C has been typical of this trend, but it is noticeable elsewhere too, and many priests now support it. Retreats, rosaries, and theological dogmas now count for less; and the new emphasis is more on economic or social sins in relation to society than on private sexual ones. In fact the opinion polls suggest that younger Catholics' attitudes to pre-marital sex and contraception are not widely different from those of non-believers. Nearly every Catholic leader I met emphasised these changes in one way or another. Jean-Marie Domenach, editor of the intellectual review *Esprit*, said, 'A young man's faith is no longer nearly so "protected" by the environment of family and parish. It has to pass through the ordeal of contact with atheism, and, if it survives, it may be more real than in the old days.' Père Cardonnel, a Dominican in Montpellier, said, 'More and more Catholic students today are faithful to Christ without the help of Catholic institutions.' And a Christian trade-union leader in Paris said, 'The Church no longer makes it so hard for a Catholic to lead an active temporal life. A young man now finds it easier to apply his faith to the world.'

And so in this new climate the Catholics have been moving to action-stations everywhere. They have been influenced by Teilhard and his optimistic world-loving, and possibly even more by Emmanuel Mounier, founder of *Esprit* and one of the most courageous early advocates of the need for the Church and all Christians to engage in improving the world. A Dominican in Paris told me, 'We're beyond the Salvation Army stage of handing out tracts. We believe in example, in working shoulder to shoulder with agnostics and touching their *bonne volonté* with our own humanism.' The immediate post-1945 generation—that of Debatisse and Leclerc—have been especially successful in pushing up into positions of influence. Besides the JAC, one should mention the influence of the Centre des Jeunes Patrons in management and labour relations; the CFDT (formerly CFTC) which, though smaller than the Communist-led CGT, is much the most intelligent and progressive of the unions; and the leading role played by neo-Catholics in the Plan and in the new political discussion-groups such as the Club Jean Moulin. 'We control a large part of the upper civil service,' Domenach told me triumphantly, as if announcing the success of some bloodless *Putsch*. Maurice Papon, for instance, former Paris Prefect of Police and now head of Sud-Aviation, is a leading authority on Teilhard. And according to one estimate, over 50 per cent of the mayors of France are now ex-JACists or ex-JOCists.

A senior Jewish technocrat told me, not unsympathetically, 'These Catholics, they're everywhere. One secret of their strength is, they've got a *réseau*, a sort of underground network, even if it's not a very unified one. And they've got such energy—they're always devoting whole evenings to their work.' The Catholic Church, which though disestablished used to be a major establishment in France, defending its own clearly defined positions, has now taken on the colouring almost of an occult lay freemasonry, a minority pressure-group that is on the offensive because it has more to gain than to lose.

The dynamic comes largely from the laity, and their relations with the Episcopate are equivocal and not easy to define. The whole movement is made up of scores of different organisations, some of them completely secular and autonomous of the Church (like the CJP and the CFDT), others formally under its ecclesiastical authority and often running into conflict with it. Equally hard to pinpoint are the attitudes of the new militants towards Gaullist technocracy. Some of them frankly support the régime and are working within its ranks to build a more humane and efficient society; others strongly oppose it and are on the Left in the classic sense, angrily aware of how little the Gaullists have done to cure social injustices. The worker-priests largely belong here, and so do several student movements. But all the militants, whatever their political views, have their activism in common: they are working, as someone said, 'to build the Kingdom of God on earth—something that the Church never used to care much about'.

The reactions of the clergy to the new trends are equally variable. Many of the older ones feel lost and *depassés* and are struggling to preserve the old order of things. There is a certain confusion among the rank-and-file clergy, many of whom feel unforceful and under-educated beside the clever lay militants, and are unsure what the role of the priesthood should be under the changed conditions. Inevitably there is some crisis of recruitment, though not as grave as had been feared twenty years ago. Many other priests are actively leading the new Catholicism—and this is true especially of the Dominicans, who are fewer in number than the Jesuits in France, but expectedly more progressive. Père Cardonnel told me: 'We are trying to deconfessionalise and declericalise the faith. We believe in a dialogue with the world; here in Montpellier we're way out ahead of the Dominican HQ in Rome. Lots of unbelievers come to my Mass, because I adapt Christ's teaching to modern life, in their own language.'

The most important factor is that the Episcopate itself, after some hesitation, has increasingly swung its weight behind the new movement and has clearly been influenced by it. Though the bishops are not so *avant-garde* as the militants, they are in advance of the rank-and-file clergy and of the older pious masses. This is not entirely a new development: as I have said, cardinals like Feltin and Gerlier were in favour of worker-priests twenty years ago, and even back in the '30s Cardinal Liénart was being denounced by the Lille *Patronat* as 'the Red bishop' because of his support for the working class. But such men used to be in a minority within the Episcopate: now they are not. During the Algerian war a number of bishops denounced Army brutalities; this is something that could never have happened in *Action Française* days. More recently they have come out against the Government in support of workers' strikes, and in 1966 they even published an official manifesto criticising the Patronat's credo of profit. As tacticians, they are now aware of the crucial need for the Church to come to terms with the challenge of Communism; as Christian humanists, they now accept that the Church must lend its weight in the fight for social justice. But their position on many matters is still *nuancé*, and many bishops are trying to steer a delicate course between two sides: after all, the Church still gains much strength from its traditional alliance with the ruling bourgeoisie, and there are plenty of senior clergy who point out the dangers of the Church, as it were, changing sides in the French class struggle. Within the Episcopate, there are forces pulling in both directions.

And how has the French working class reacted to the Catholics' new interest in them? It is a vital question to ask, but not easy to answer. Signs of progress are not great, but they do exist. Hitherto the working class identified Christianity so firmly with the bourgeoisie that in some industrial areas for a worker to admit to being a Christian was like claiming to vote on the Right, a kind of class betrayal. And the figures for Mass bore this out: in the middle classes, church-going was up to ten times as common as among workers. It is doubtful whether these figures have yet altered more than marginally. But several trade-unionists report

signs of a thaw in attitudes: workers now much more easily admit to
being Christian, or to being friends with Christians. In some districts the
worker-priests and other such ventures appear to have had some influence,
but it is hard to say how much.

There are several Leftish Catholic organisations that stress the need
for closer links between Christians and the pagan working milieu. One is
the magazine *Témoignage Chrétien*, very *progressiste*, which was up-
braided by the hierarchy not long ago for publishing an article by a
Communist leader, and for illustrating an outspoken feature on sex with
a *risqué* photo. Another body is *Vie Nouvelle*, inter-ideological rather than
purely Christian, a sort of intellectual boy-scout movement linking Catholics, Protestants, Marxists, rationalists, and others. In Montpellier one of
its leaders is Père Cardonnel, who told me how he enjoyed holding public
debates with prominent local atheists and touring the village on joint
preaching missions with a Protestant colleague. 'Young people welcome
us,' he told me, 'but many of the older bourgeois are shocked. You see,
normally in Montpellier the *haute société catholique* and *haute société
protestante* just don't mix.' Oecumenical links with France's three per
cent Protestant minority are very much in vogue among the neo-Catholics: there are numerous joint youth movements and church services, all
over France, and the Protestants have been playing their own willing
part in the *rapprochement*, especially through the influence of their
famous oecumenical centre at Taizé.

A much more remarkable new dialogue is that between Catholics and
Marxists. These are the two most dynamic ideological groups in France,
and they have a weird respect and fascination for each other. I am not
referring to the old Stalinist diehards within the Party, nor to Sartre
and his immediate circle, but to some of the thousands of other active
Marxists in France, doctors, teachers, trade-unionists, and the like, many
of them relatively open-minded and pragmatic, some Communist, some
Socialist, some without party label. Like the neo-Catholics, they are
frequently notable for their energy, their dedication, their urge towards
practical social action. And when the two of them meet, they often feel
much more common ground with each other than either has, respectively,
with old-style Catholics or with Stalinists, Sartrians, or vague liberals.
Their strange new courtship offers many striking examples in France
today, both in the field of ideological debate and of joint welfare activity.

J.-M. Domenach said to me: 'This kind of field collaboration began in
the Resistance, and with a few lapses it's gone on since, especially since
the deaths of Stalin and Pius XII. You see, it's the old-style liberals with
Alain-type ideals who just haven't been able to stay the course—Mendès-
France and Co., they've lacked the right spiritual force. But we notice
that the Marxists, like us, do have that kind of force—for good or ill.' Not
all neo-Catholics would generalise as arrogantly as this, but many of them
say much the same thing. Domenach went on, 'Whenever at grass-roots
level you find disinterested individuals actually doing voluntary social

work in France, they are nearly always Catholics or Marxists. Recently, for instance, *Esprit* ran an enquiry into handicapped children, and we found that nearly all the people helping in this field were militants of one group or other.' In the other camp, Professor Raymond Dugrand of Montpellier University told me, 'I left the Party after Hungary, but I'm still a Marxist. Today I feel more at ease with the new Catholic Left than with most CP members. Last year, for instance, some local priests and I ran a fund-raising campaign for World Famine Relief; and often Cardonnel and the CFDT invite me to join in their discussions.' In a poor district of Paris, I found Catholic and Marxist doctors working in close harmony in a pilot campaign to combat mental disease and alcoholism. In the *Grands Ensembles*, many observers have noted that the most dedicated of the 'animators' are Catholics and Marxists, who frequently get on well together. In local government, the new alliance in Grenoble between the young Catholic mayor, Hubert Dubedout, and the Marxist Left, offers another example.

When it comes to the exchange of ideas, it is not quite so easy to see what has been achieved. But at least a great deal of *bonne volonté* is displayed on both sides. Recently the Marxists have copied the Catholics' *Semaines de la Pensée Catholique* with their own similar study-conferences, *Semaines de la Pensée Marxiste*, held throughout the year in various towns. Each side invites the other to take part in these debates. On the Marxist side, the leading advocate of this kind of *rapprochement* is the Communist philosopher Roger Garaudy, who has published a number of articles and lectures in praise of Teilhard de Chardin, and who played a big part in the remarkable Christian–Marxist conference at Marienbad, Czechoslovakia, in 1967. 'The future of our age,' he said then, 'cannot be constructed either against religious believers or without them.'

But where does all this lead, intellectually? Some outsiders are highly sceptical: Barbara Bray, in a recent talk about France on the BBC Third Programme, said, 'These people are making a false synthesis of the two ideologies, based on sloppy, wishful thinking.' In strictest rationalist terms she may be right: but this seems to me less important than the positive fact that the two sides are at least able to see each other's point of view and find some common cause in the brotherhood of man. France has suffered so much in the past from the wasteful vendettas between Whites and Reds: if these two dynamic forces are now able to pool some of their ideas and energies for the common good, let us not worry too much if the synthesis is not quite intellectually coherent.

But from a strictly Christian point of view the most obvious danger is that, amid all this new secular zeal for social progress, Christ Himself may get overlooked. 'Some of the faithful complain,' a Dominican told me, 'that we priests don't talk about God any more, we talk about the housing crisis.' In serving Man, a Christian is supposed to be serving God, but he may lose sight of the wood for the trees. Many Catholics and Church leaders are acutely aware of this dilemma. 'We have gained a great deal in rejecting integrism,' said one liberal priest, 'but are we not losing the virtues of contemplation and the sense of sin?' The Episcopate, too, are worried. They have taken a bold step since the war in recognising that a Christian *per se* has temporal as well as spiritual obligations: but they are frightened, obviously, of Marxist contagion, and of the danger that the flight from orthodox piety and ritual may go too far.

The French Episcopate and the Vatican are also concerned at the decline in their own authority and discipline that has been caused by the multifarious upsurge of lay militancy. Many of the new movements, even those directly under the formal tutelage of the Church, like the *Jeunesse Etudiante Chrétienne*, have frequently been taking policies and even doctrines into their own hands. And although the Episcopate today has come willingly to accept what the French call *pluralisme*—that is, the possibility for various differing tendencies to exist within the Church— it does not want to lose its overall control of what is happening. The traditional French regard for order and hierarchy has normally been apparent nowhere so much as in the Church, and this has now been profoundly disturbed by the new effervescence.

So in the mid 1960s the Church began a careful campaign to re-assert its authority. On the orders of Rome, a ruthless and enigmatic new figure appeared on the scene: Mgr. Pierre Veuillot. He was first appointed Coadjutor of Paris in 1961, then in 1966 at the age of only fifty-three he succeeded Feltin as Archbishop of Paris and Primate of France, and a year later was made a Cardinal. By 1965 he was making his presence felt almost as much as de Gaulle. In tones of awed irony, *Le Nouvel Observateur* described this potentate as 'a technocrat of divine right, less a pastor than a prefect, a man who believes that the Church must be efficient like a business, and must be served like the State under Stalin or the Pentagon under McNamara'. This brilliant and chilly paternalist was in many ways a liberal. He was anti-integrist and clearly did not intend to undo the great work of the past twenty years; he even played a decisive role in securing the return of the worker-priests in 1965. Another of his acts was to suppress the scandalous class-distinctions in the marriage and burial services, which used to be graded according to how much you could pay for them: this did not win him friends among the older bourgeoisie. But he was also an authoritarian liberal. There were rumours of purges among those of his staff who did not get on with him. And in 1965, while he was still Coadjutor, his hand fell heavily on the unruly Jeunesse Etudiante Chrétienne. This student body had taken up an extreme Left-wing position, declaring it to be the duty of Christians to collaborate with Communists and others in helping the poor, in supporting Spanish students against Franco, in fighting Right-wing Gaullist policies, and so on. The JEC declared that the Church was still too much an ally of the bourgeoisie, and that its duty was to serve the world, not to boss it about.

Veuillot then stormed into the JEC headquarters in Paris and issued an ultimatum. He said that the Church accepted that individuals *as lay Christians* had a right to take part in this kind of temporal action—and in this he showed himself a liberal, for thirty years ago no French bishop would have allowed that this was any part of the function of being a Christian. But Veuillot then added that the JEC, being a corporate part of the Church, had no such right to implicate the Church in politics. He forced the dismissal of the JEC leaders and their replacement by others more submissive; the rebels went off and founded their own autonomous group, the Jeunesse Universitaire Chrétienne, to pursue their own ideals. No other incident since the worker-priest crisis has so clearly illustrated the dilemma of the Church in France today: how to be liberal without collapsing into anarchy, how to engage in helping the world without compromising the Kingdom of Heaven. From the Church's point of view, some resort to authoritarianism has probably been necessary: but Veuillot's own particular high-handed methods, on several different occasions, appeared to have been alienating a number of Christian leaders, and there seemed a danger that his approach might prejudice the new Catholic dynamism that has borne such fruits since the war. In February 1968, Veuillot died at the age of only 55. The Vatican will not easily find another leader with the same qualities.

Veuillot had not been hitting out only at the Left, however. The neo-Catholic movement has provoked a virulent Right-wing reaction to it within certain Christian circles, and this too has been worrying the hierarchy. The tradition of integrism will not die easily in France, and even the shadow of Maurras is still hovering: a Catholic paper like *Le Monde et la Vie* still sells 200,000 copies a month, and its pages are horrifying—long eulogies of Pétain and wartime Catholic fascists, savage attacks on Teilhard de Chardin, on worker-priest ideals, or any form of dialogue with non-believers. The well-known writer Michel de Saint-Pierre crystallised this attitude in a novel which caused some stir in 1965, *Les Nouveaux Prêtres*, a warning tract that told of a group of Paris priests who were unwise enough to take part in social action and so became defiled with Marxism. For de Saint-Pierre, the ideal priest is Vianney of Ars, the great nineteenth-century puritan who denounced every form of worldly enjoyment and demanded total piety of his flock.

This purist minority is particularly angry at recent changes in the liturgy. Mass is now generally celebrated in French, not in Latin, the priest faces the congregation when officiating, and often there is hymn-singing. In some conservative areas, the pious have marked their displeasure at all this by pointedly continuing to make their responses in Latin. The un-reconciled integrists represent only a small proportion of practising Catholics; they are fewer in number, probably, than those who can be classed as neo-Catholics. But they are vocal and well organised, and they have seriously threatened to secede from the body of the Church, just as the small Left-wing minority nearly seceded before the war. It is an indication of how far the tide has turned. In June 1966, the Episcopate openly took issue with the integrists, and placed itself clearly on the side of reform. As with all diehards, their influence will gradually fade as the older ones die.

It is possibly symptomatic of intellectual decline in France that the post-war Catholic revival has not been accompanied by the appearance of any outstanding new writers or thinkers. The earlier generation of great Catholic novelists and poets like Claudel, Péguy, Bernanos, Mauriac has had little contemporary sequel. A number of priests (Fathers Congar, Chenu, and de Lubac) have written doctrinal or philosophical works of some value; but almost all the post-war French novelists are agnostics, and among film-makers the only manifest Catholic is Bresson, now aged sixty. Domenach told me, 'I find it hard to get really good young Catholic writers for *Esprit*. We seem to be in a barren patch, intellectually. Everyone's energies have gone into activism.'

The neo-Catholic movement does have its two great *maîtres-à-penser*, but both are dead—Mounier, who died in 1950, and the towering figure of Teilhard de Chardin, who died in 1955 aged seventy-four. In France and in the world, the Teilhard cult is still of phenomenal proportions. There are those who claim that he has had more posthumous influence than any other world thinker since Marx; and Louis Armand, in an unguarded moment, even declared, 'Teilhard is certainly France's greatest gift to the world since the beginning of this century, perhaps even her sole serious contribution.' In France alone, more than a million-and-a-half copies have been sold since 1955 of the difficult, labyrinthine, abstract books of this Jesuit heretic whom the Jesuits first denounced, then eulogistically reinstated. His appeal to the ordinary lay Christian, and to many non-Christians too, is self-evident: an immensely generous and optimistic vision of the immanence of God in the modern world around us, in science, in nature, in art, and a belief in a time-conquering life-force that is built on the unity of his religious faith and his scientific convictions as a palaeontologist. An agnostic can drink at the Teilhardian fountain without having to accept the mumbo-jumbo of Christian ritual: a Christian can drink there, too, and find a spiritual justification for the modern world of science and progress that the Church itself does not really know how to give him. In the past ten years a spate of popular books on Teilhardism have appeared in France, and all have sold well. There is a certain Teilhard snobbism: in some circles, he is the *one* author you just cannot admit to not having read. And there is an anti-Teilhard snobbism, too. Many scientists object to his scientific vagueness, and many Christians to his theological woolliness; and rationalists like J.-F. Revel grow purple in the face at what they see as the sloppy wishful-thinking of young idealists eager to embrace Teilhard's portmanteau solution of life's mysteries.

And so the debate goes on. The neo-Catholics find in Teilhardism a kind of theological justification for their actions; but the rationalists allege that materialist technocracy is simply using Teilhard's ideas as a cover and a spiritual alibi. This seems to me unfair. Technocracy is necessary and inevitable; and if it carries inherent dangers, then the religious or humanist idealism of many of the technocrats is likely to be the best safeguard against them. Teilhard can give technocracy a soul. I think it is for these kind of reasons that the neo-Catholic movement is just about the most encouraging development in France since the war: it is the spiritual leaven in a materialist economic revolution. While structuralists, existentialists, and others are paralysed by their honest doubts about the meaning of life, those with some kind of religious faith are able to free their energies for helping mankind.

CHAPTER XII

ALL THE ARTS LANGUISH, SAVE ONE

———

Is FRANCE STILL 'mère des arts' and Paris still the cultural capital of the West? Some of the symptoms of sclerosis I have already traced among French philosophers and novelists can be seen also in the world of French painting and music, and even in the theatre, at least in terms of new plays if not of production. If there is one art form where I think France still leads the world it is the cinema, and most of this chapter is devoted to it. In the first section I trace the narrative of the so-called 'nouvelle vague' movement, its current economic predicament and the dangers it faces; in the second section, I consider the work of some of its leading directors, viewed as a permanent artistic achievement.

CINEMA IN BLOOM, CINEMA IN CRISIS

Françoise Sagan once told Kenneth Tynan, when asked about the new plays in Paris, 'But my generation doesn't go to the theatre any more—we go to the cinema.' It was not meant as a philistine remark, quite the reverse. The cinema has for long been intellectually respectable in France, and since the war the passion for it among younger educated people has been stronger than in any other country. Throughout Paris and the provinces, nearly ten thousand new 'ciné-clubs' have sprung up, where young people gather in a hired hall or flea-pit to watch anything from the latest Godard to an old scratched copy of *Potemkin* and then eagerly discuss it. In Paris before the war there were only two or three art-house cinemas: today there are several score, and in one of them a recent revival of Renoir's *La Grande Illusion* drew more people than had seen it in all Paris on its original run in 1938. Numerous film magazines flourish; and even the most highbrow papers devote longer articles to the cinema than to any other art, articles that are often abstruse and pretentious but at least bear witness to the public's enthusiasm.

Within narrower limits, this French intellectual devotion to films dates back almost to Méliès himself. The cinema has never had to struggle, as in England, to win acceptance beside painting or music as a major art form. In the 1920s, Cocteau was turning to film as readily as to verse, as the medium for his poetry. In the '30s, Vigo was a key figure of the *avant-garde*. And writers like Sartre, Malraux, and Robbe-Grillet have readily collaborated in film-making, or even directed films themselves. The French believe that cinema, given the right conditions, can be used just as powerfully or subtly as any other art to express a personal artistic vision, despite the incursions and pressures of a mass-entertainment industry.

This was the cinematic background from which the hundred or more young directors of the so-called 'nouvelle vague' emerged with such clamour in the late '50s—less by accident than through an explosive necessity of self-expression. A new generation had arrived that had taught itself cinema in its teens, in the ciné-clubs, *cinémathèques*, and art-houses, and grew up 'speaking cinema' as its elders spoke literature or an earlier age had lived in the language of religion. Jean de Baroncelli, film critic of *Le Monde*, wrote in 1959: 'Young creative people today have a cinematic instinct and the cinema is their first choice. Fifty years ago a young man with something to say would compose poetry, twenty years ago he would write a novel, today he dreams of making a film. Perhaps, in the eyes of some, it is the only means of expression really adapted to our epoch.' But why? The difficulties of writing a humanist novel in the present literary climate, the drawbacks of working for conformist State television—these are two obvious factors that have drawn talent towards the cinema, but they are negative ones, and even if all avenues were equally free, plenty of people would still opt first for making films. The cinema combines lyricism with documentary, to a higher degree than any other art, and this duality appeals deeply to the French. As I suggested in earlier chapters, the flight from ideologies has taken the French down two distinct paths, towards the aesthetic and towards the concrete and practical: the cinema unites the two. Location-shooting fascinates by its actuality, and the camera does not lie; but the camera is also a tool of fantasy, the perfect poetic liar. Sometimes there seems to be a narcotic, escapist element in the French film craze, as if films were a substitute for life. But in the best work of the new directors, that of Resnais for instance, imagination and reality are blended. The result is a cinema much more personal and lyrical than in Britain or the United States.

The 1930s had been a golden age, that of the great films of Clair, Carné, and Renoir. Then, after the hiatus of wartime, it seemed at first that the great days were beginning anew. Carné made one of his best films, *Les Enfants du paradis*, in 1945. Several newer talents emerged, too; and the first post-war years were at least a luminous silver age for the

French cinema, with such films as Autant-Lara's *Le Diable au corps*, Becker's *Casque d'or* and Clément's *Jeux interdits*. But as the 1950s wore on, a creeping paralysis appeared. The established directors, mostly now in their forties or over, grew steadily bankrupt of ideas and inspiration— save for one or two rare figures like Robert Bresson and the ageing Renoir. Subjects became safe and stereotyped: *policiers*, sex dramas, or costume pieces, carrying with them the stale air of the studios. Producers were scared of trusting to new talent or new themes, and the older guard of directors and screenwriters, such as Clouzot and Clément, were so firmly in the saddle that it was almost as hard as in Britain at that time for a newcomer to find a break, despite the casual fluidity of French production methods. But meanwhile France itself was changing, a new mood and style of life were emerging that the cinema seemed to ignore, and a new generation began to lose patience with the artificialities offered it on the screen. Television, too, was just making its impact, rather later than in Britain, and even the mass-audiences showed signs of fickleness and of wanting something new. Several safe-formula films went unexpectedly flop around 1957. Producers wondered whether to turn to epic spectaculars (which few of them could afford) or to try some novelty.

The new generation then proceeded to force their hand, in the most remarkable revolution in the cinema's seventy-year history. Scattered groups of young would-be feature directors were waiting their chance, working either in 'shorts', or as critics, or even essaying their own self-financed low-budget features. In the mid '50s one or two unusual films began to appear, unnoticed at first except by a select public: Astruc's *Les Mauvaises Rencontres*, for instance, and Agnès Varda's *La Pointe courte*. Then in 1956 a youngish producer, Raoul Lévy, engaged a very young *Paris-Match* journalist, Roger Vadim, to try his hand at a realistic but rarely attempted theme, the amorality of modern pleasure-loving youth, to be set on location in St. Tropez. Today, when the rest of the new wave has thundered on far beyond it, *Et Dieu créa la femme*, gaudy, slick, and cynical, looks old hat; but in the prevailing climate of Fernandel comedies and studio rehashes of Colette it was startling. It was not a great film, but it broke new ground. For almost the first time in the French cinema since the war, here was youth looking at itself with a raw directness; and instead of the traditional coquette in a man's world, *à la* Martine Carol, here was a new type of young heroine, wild, sensual, and emancipated, much closer to contemporary truth. More to the point, the film, with the aid of its gorgeous new star (Vadim's wife, Brigitte Bardot) won an immediate and fantastic commercial success, in France and throughout the world. And this at once incited other producers to look for other new talent and new real-life subjects. They did not need to look far.

A number of directors, no longer so young, had already been working for some years in documentary, helped by a generous system of Government grants and commissions. These men gladly seized the chance to make their first features, and so in 1958–9 Georges Franju, aged forty-six, directed *La Tête contre les murs*, and Alain Resnais, aged thirty-six, made *Hiroshima mon amour*. A second source of talent was the very young group of critics on the magazine *Cahiers du Cinéma*: Godard, Chabrol, Truffaut, and others. Several of them were from moneyed backgrounds, and in their passion to get started they did not wait to be invited but sank their own capital into modest features. Thus Chabrol made *Le Beau Serge* in 1958 for 480,000 francs with a legacy inherited by his wife, and thus Truffaut partly financed *Les 400 Coups* (1959), and Louis Malle (not a *Cahiers* man) made *Ascenseur pour l'échafaud* in 1957. Probably these men, and Resnais and others, would have established themselves in the end without Vadim's help; but his success certainly made it easier for them to find a market, as it did for Godard and his first feature, *A bout de souffle* (1959).

It was an exciting time to be in Paris. I remember early in 1959 attending previews of Chabrol's first two films (*Le Beau Serge* and *Les Cousins*) without having heard of him before, and enjoying the shock of a new cinema language, rather as Londoners had done in the theatre three years earlier with Osborne's *Look Back in Anger*. French cinema was back in touch with real life. Resnais and Truffaut took leading prizes at Cannes that spring, and Truffaut arrogantly declared war on the establishment directors and the whole commercial system. The gates were open. *L'Express* invented the label 'nouvelle vague', and journalists applied it indiscriminately to any new name, conveniently ignoring the wide differences between the *Cahiers* group and Resnais and his friends, or between either of them and lone-riders like Franju and Malle. Some of the new directors are genuine innovators and revolutionaries; others are simply applying an up-to-date personal style to conventional themes and subjects. But like all generalisations the label has some validity: in several ways, the new directors differ from the immediate post-war generation.

The first and most important difference lies in their devotion to what is called the 'film d'auteur', the concept of a film as a unique personal creation like a novel. This is not a new idea in France, though the new directors have carried it farther than before. Men like Clair and Renoir, not to mention Cocteau and Vigo, were making highly personal films long before the war. The French have always attached more importance than Anglo-Saxons to the director's role, and even in publicity for an ordinary commercial film, the director's name is often given as much prominence as the stars'—an honour reserved in Britain for a rare figure like Hitchcock. *Un film de Basil Dearden* or *le chef-d'œuvre de Robert Hamer* you can see in blazing neon outside French cinemas, announcing names largely unknown to their own British public. It is a custom much fairer to the man who actually *makes* the film, even if it leads to some French critics' absurd *penchant* for endowing hack foreign directors with artistic qualities they don't possess.

In the 1950s many established French film-makers had been moving away from the French tradition of director's cinema and towards the Anglo-Saxon pattern: and, although the director remained supreme once shooting started, frequently he was working from a script prepared by someone else, maybe hashed up unimaginatively from a well-known novel. The new-wave pioneers wanted to restore the pre-war purity, and more. Astruc as early as 1948 wrote a famous article, 'Le Caméra-Stylo', that came to be treated as a manifesto: 'The cinema . . . becomes bit by bit a language . . . the form through which an artist can express his thoughts or translate his obsessions, just as in an essay or novel. The film will . . . become a means of writing as supple and subtle as the written word.' In other words, first, the director should write his own script, for the film can be only *his* thoughts; next, the script itself will fade in importance, for the camera will do the 'writing' as the film is made.

Many of the new directors, notably Godard, are using just these techniques. Many of them approached their early films just as if they were first novels—the semi-autobiographical *400 Coups* is a good example. Even when they adapt from books (as Truffaut with *Jules et Jim*) they are usually careful to take little-known or banal ones which they transform completely, rather than be inhibited by scruples of fidelity like so many British films. A film must be itself, an original creation and not a copy of something else. And even those, like Resnais, who do not write their own scripts, are usually at pains to use original material and to work in close imaginative harmony with their writer.

Closely linked with the notion of *films d'auteur*, and especially with Astruc's ideas, is the new directors' insistence on *mise-en-scène*. This is often loosely translated as 'direction', but it means something more: the endowing of each film with a special aura of its own. The emphasis is thus on mood and style rather than subject-matter. In the case of the revolutionaries like Resnais or Godard, this tends towards the creation of a new film language, fragmented and elliptical in its surface detail but harmonious in its impact. Other directors are more explicit and conventional in their techniques, but no less personal in their zest for lyrical mood-building: *Jules et Jim*, Demy's *Lola*, or that highly individual bit of schmalz, Lelouch's *Un Homme et une femme*. It is a kind of film-making that the British rarely attempt, except clumsily.

Finally, these new directors have in common the fact that they came straight into features at the top: several had studied at the official French film school,* but very few had worked their way up through the usual slow, dispiriting channels of technical apprenticeship in big studios. What this lost them in experience, it added in freshness. And most of them were in their twenties, at a time when the French cinema wore a heavily middle-aged look. They arrived with anti-industry ideas on how to make films: no big stars or lavish sets, and therefore less need for concessions to

* The Institut des Hautes Etudes Cinématographiques (IDHEC).

alleged popular tastes. And for a while they got what they wanted, helped by three favourable circumstances that they would not have found so easily in the British film world.

The first of these was the French system of aid for the cinema. A select number of serious shorts and documentaries receive State grants known as *primes à la qualité*: these helped to sustain the early careers of Resnais and others, and thus did much to prepare the way for the new wave. For feature films, there are no outright grants but a number of State advances, given also on a basis of quality: a jury, made up partly of leading cultural figures, allots the loans to films of likely artistic merit, irrespective of their commercial prospects. Of course, politics enters into it too, and several worthy projects have been turned down because of their subject-matter, or because the director is *mal vu*. But on the whole the loans have gone to the good films; and in this way Resnais, Bresson, Varda, Chabrol, and others were able to take risks with commercially difficult subjects.

Next, the trade unions are much more easy-going than in Britain. There are not the same obstinate requirements about set working-hours and large minimum crews, and this makes it much easier to shoot on a low budget or to avoid having to down tools in mid-inspiration because it's time for tea. Thirdly, there are no monolithic Ranks or ABCs in France: production and distribution are haphazard, and at least in the early years of the new wave a producer or backer would trust to hunch as much as to routine assessment. Though this renders the French industry more vulnerable in time of crisis, it greatly helped independent production once the stalemate of the '50s was broken. Peter Brook, who tried in vain to make films in his own country in the '50s, easily found a backer in France to make *Moderato Cantabile* there in 1960, and in 1962 he told me: 'The star was Moreau, the script was by Duras from her own novel. The backers simply trusted our talents, they never demanded to see a written script in advance as they nearly always do in Britain. That's what I like about filming in France. We were able to improvise as we went along, and the crews were artists who shared our own creative enthusiasm, not time-serving technicians.' Matters have changed since then, for the worse in France, slightly for the better in Britain: but there is no doubt that this climate in the France of those years enabled the new wave to make its breakthrough.

Several of the first films (*Les Cousins*, for instance) were big box-office successes and easily recouped their slender costs. Producers suddenly were convinced that the public wanted novelty, and they switched from a policy of few and expensive films to one of many and cheap ones. For a while, any young hopeful with a new idea found a camera thrust in his hands: in 1959–63 more than 170 French directors made a first film, a gold-rush phenomenon without parallel in cinema history. But the boom did not last. Inevitably, few of the new directors proved to have the talent of Truffaut or Resnais. Encouraged by producers to be as 'personal' as they liked—since this was the apparent formula for success—many of the newcomers went outrageously too far. They simply made frivolous cult-films about themselves and their friends. Before long, an image formed in the public's mind of a typical new-wave film—featuring the easy-going love-lives of some group of idle, well-to-do young Parisians, full of arty camera shots and in-jokes about other films—imitations, in fact, of *Les Cousins*. The mass public soon wearied of a realism that had declined into gossip, and returned to its Bourvil comedies and Christian-Jacques period pieces. Most of the new films lost money.

In fact, apart from a few successes, the new wave has never proved a great money-spinner inside France. Several of its finest films (including *Lola* and Resnais' *Muriel*) lost money because they were over the heads of a general public, while even *Jules et Jim* had to rely mainly on exports to recover its costs. Many of the most serious directors have managed to keep going because their budgets are low and because they do have a minority following among their own generation and abroad. But despite the cinemania of students and intellectuals, the ordinary France of farm and suburb is not a great film-loving nation: the French go to the cinema less than half as often as the British, and there is little reason to suppose that ordinary public taste is much higher than anywhere else. Now that the dust has settled, many of the hack directors of the '50s are firmly back in the saddle, and with a few exceptions it is their broad comedies and lurid thrillers that head the French box-office successes. This is not to belittle the cultural achievements of the new wave, but to set them in a proper context. Cinema in France, like theatre in Britain, is something of a minority art.

Thus it is not surprising that the French film industry in the past few years has been suffering from the same economic squeezes as in other countries. Television, belatedly, has made its impact, and so have the motor-car and other rival attractions: between 1957 and 1966, annual cinema attendances fell from 411 to 232 million, and 4,000 cinemas closed. And the French industry is especially ill suited to cope with this kind of crisis. There are few big organised cinema circuits and too many small independent producers: 683 are listed, making on average one film in six years. It is precisely the opposite of the problem in Britain. And although in confident times this liberal fluidity is ideal for low-budget personal films, it leads to high costs and inefficiencies that can ill be supported in time of recession. And so today, once again, the difficult subject and the untried talent are the hardest hit, for French backers have again decided not to take gambles. The climate that in the past drew great men like Ophüls to work in France no longer, for the moment, exists: and it is symptomatic that when Roman Polanski left his native Poland for the West in 1960, he first tried and failed to get backing in France, and then found it in Britain, of all places. Mag Bodard, producer for Bresson, Demy, and Varda, told me: 'The conditions under which Brook filmed here no longer exist. Backers have become terrified of the experimental. They insist on seeing a script first. It's as bad as in Britain, and that's not the way to make a *film d'auteur*.'

The older commercial directors blame the new wave for alienating the public from the cinema, with their plotless, obscure, and facetious films. The younger directors in turn, and their producers, lay the blame on the Government—with some reason—for its heavy taxes and for very recent changes in the aid system which seem to favour routine domestic production rather than quality films for export. But whoever's fault it is, the one remedy open to film-makers is obvious: they are now turning abroad for help, and especially to America. For many years now, co-productions have been common with other European countries, chiefly Italy, and this has certainly helped to widen the markets for French films: but it has not solved the industry's basic problems, nor has the Common Market yet succeeded in creating a European film pool. Meanwhile, the giant American companies have shown themselves only too eager, as elsewhere, to increase their hold on French production and distribution by offering the backing that the French cannot find in their own country. And so, in films as in so much else, the French are now belatedly following the common European trend.

Some recent examples are notorious. For years, Truffaut looked in vain for French backing for *Fahrenheit 451*, then found it from Universal and made the film at Pinewood with English dialogue and non-French stars. United Artists financed Malle's *Viva Maria!*, and Columbia backed Vadim's *La Curée* (also with non-French stars, incongruously playing French roles). Demy's *Les Demoiselles de Rochefort* became a hybrid Franco-American spectacular. Among older directors, Clément made his flat-footed *Paris brûle-t-il?* for Paramount on a huge budget with a big starry cast portraying well-known living people, everyone, in fact, except Tati as de Gaulle.

The effects of this American backing are double-edged. There is no doubt that for some low-budget films it has its advantages, so long as the director maintains his integrity. There's a streak of the Maecenas in Columbia and United Artists, and sometimes they are genuinely glad to finance a serious inexpensive film that will later earn its passage in the American art-house market. Half a million dollars or less, for *Alphaville* or for *Le Bonheur*, is chicken-feed: both Godard and Varda have been financed by Columbia, and both of them were left entirely free to make their own modest films in their own way. But when it comes to paying for Julie Christie, or for Malle's Bardot–Moreau caper in Mexico, matters may be different. There seems to be a certain cleavage at the moment between those directors who continue to make films on their own rigorous terms, and those like Malle and Truffaut who have compromised with a commercial system they once denounced. And they have partly themselves to blame for their lack of freedom.

Malle declared in 1959: 'I am against super-productions. If there are no big stars in France, it is a sign the cinema is progressing.' But since then, he has helped to create big stars, and today he lumps two of the biggest in a very super-production! And witness the path that Demy has followed, from *Lola* via *Les Parapluies de Cherbourg* to the Americanised Rochefort film, with lavishness growing in inverse proportion to inspiration. These and other directors' new-found liking for big budgets is not only a betrayal of the ideals of the *film d'auteur*: it aggravates French production problems and forces them into the arms of American backers, with consequent risks to the films' authenticity. The artistic dangers of internationalised cinema are too well known to need repeating: by all means, let nations see each others' films as much as possible, but this does not mean we want bogus international casts and de-nationalised themes carefully geared to the tastes of a world-wide audience. This is the way the French cinema now risks being dragged.

The nouvelle vague has thus come a very long way in the space of ten short years. It has suffered heavily from economic crises that have been partly, though no more than partly, its own fault. It has often forsaken its ideals, but often too it has held to them. Its epitaph has been written many times, but it has failed to die. Above all, it has thrown up an immense diversity of new talent, which is still active and has changed the face of world cinema for ever. The economic problems are of secondary interest, save for understanding the whole: the real issue is to assess, in cultural terms, what the new directors have achieved. Just how good— or great—are their films? If the cultural vitality has sapped away from French literature and painting, do we look for it instead in the cinema?

THE NEW CINE-POETS: FRIVOLITY AND GENIUS

At the time of *Jules et Jim* and *Saturday Night and Sunday Morning*, I once imagined (*pace* G. B. Shaw and Isadora Duncan) a snatch of repartee between the two nations' young cinemas: 'Ah, François (or Jean-Luc, or Agnès), with my social-realist conscience and your lyrical camera style, what a film we could make together!' 'Yes, Karel (or Lindsay or Tony), but what if it had my social realism and your lyricism?' Since then, things have changed a little, and the British cinema has taken a few steps away from realism towards its own brand of leaden fantasy; but it still manages to keep Alfie, Darling, Joe Lampton, and the rest of our island society under some kind of fascinated scrutiny. In France, the young directors' gaze at the world around them is often so oblique that it seems they're not noticing it at all. And for this they have been criticised. Why no films on the housing shortage, the new working class, the farmers' revolt, the effects of the Algerian war? Why so many films set in the past, or abroad, or inside the director's dream-world?

There are reasons for this neglect, among them being censorship and self-censorship, or sheer frivolity and fear of involvement, and these I shall examine. But in fairness it needs to be said that the French cinema has other preoccupations, too, which the British cinema does not share. Some of the new directors are, in a sense, poets, who in earlier times might have expressed themselves through lyric poetry—and it might be as irrelevant to rebuke them for ignoring social themes as to complain that Keats never wrote about the Napoleonic wars or that Matisse painted no *Guernica*. The realism of Resnais, or of Demy's *Lola*, may not be surface social realism, but on a deeper level it is psychological realism. And though many of the new films are childishly frivolous and escapist, others in their oblique and sometimes baffling way *are* a kind of analysis of France today, at a more subtle and disturbing level than the explicit social comment of many British or American films. This is true of Godard, and, say, of Resnais' *Muriel* or Varda's *Le Bonheur*. But just as Robbe-Grillet is revolting against Balzac, so the new French cinema is reacting against the *films à thèse* of people like Cayatte, or the cosy middle-class realism of so many Gabin films.

The new directors are so diverse that this kind of generalisation is not easy, and it is best to look at the work of each in turn. First, then, the *Cahiers* group, led by Chabrol, Truffaut, Rivette, and Godard. Working together in their twenties on this magazine, they proclaimed not only their hatred of the established commercial 'system' but also their dedication to the notion of cinema *as cinema*. As their mentor, the great critic André Bazin, put it, 'the cinema is not an illustration of a scenario, it is not literature with pictures added'. This led them to postulate that brave humanist content was irrelevant to a film's greatness, just as abstract or cubist art could be as great as realistic landscape painting. A film was a unique combination of movement, light, and sound, conceived first and last in cinema terms. And this led some of them to weird critical excesses. *Bicycle Thieves* and the Gorki trilogy were ignored, and American 'B' pictures lauded; idolatry was heaped on directors like Hitchcock, Hawks, and Preminger, whose smooth commercial products you would have thought to be at the opposite pole from *Cahiers*' own art-for-art's-sake approach. Hidden virtues were found in the most unlikely films. 'The art of Hitchcock,' wrote Chabrol in a book on his Master, 'is to show us the profundity of a moral idea . . . and this leaves us with the feeling of a Unity which is the very Unity of the world, an original light which reflects on the sombre facets of Evil some of its most beautiful rays.' Much of this can only be regarded as pure tommy-rot, the *reductio ad absurdum* of a reasonable revolt against the tyranny of 'literary' cinema. Fortunately, once they got a camera between their hands, these young men generally ignored their own fanciful abstractions and came up with work that in its own way was strongly humanist.

Claude Chabrol, the first of the group to make a full-length film, is the archetype of *nouvelle vague* flair-plus-perversity. At first, his seemed one of the most powerful and original of the new talents. He shot *Le Beau*

Serge in 1958, on location in his childhood village of Sardent, near Limoges. At a time when the only peasants on French screens were harmlessly comic and Pagnolesque, here was a film that seemed near to the truth. It told a story of alcoholism and brutish decadence in one of the poorest parts of France, and for all its naïvety and sententiousness, it was clearly drawing on felt personal experience. Its raw intensity excited the critics. Next Chabrol made *Les Cousins*, about a gentle provincial student's corruption by a cynical *milieu* of young Parisian sophisticates. Again there was the nervously urgent camerawork, the rawness of style that when I first saw it reminded me of D. H. Lawrence. The mood was cool and modern. It would be common enough today, but was still rare on the screen in 1959. Even more than Vadim, Chabrol seemed to be quoting the actual voice of modern French youth, and the crowds flocked to *Les Cousins*. But after this he declined. The success of *Les Cousins* easily seduced him into the big-budget system, and his next film was a Hitch-cockian Technicolor thriller, *A double tour*, which flopped in every sense. Then came *Les Bonnes Femmes*, which I stubbornly admire though many critics have called it 'irresponsible' and 'neo-fascist'. This was a savage little study of Parisian shopgirls, their naïve dreams, their cruel defeat by life—symbolised in the closing sequence where the most sympathetic of the girls falls for a maniac who strangles her in a wood. Granted, Chabrol's picture of the girls was stylised rather than acutely realistic; yet behind his sardonic misanthropy there did seem to lurk a kind of despairing ten-derness, a typically French awareness of modern human isolation and the tragic wastage of life. Since then, he has made lots of films but few good ones: today he devotes himself mainly to off-beat anarchic thrillers with titles like *Le Tigre aime la chair fraîche* that speak for themselves. He is a born *cinéaste* and the visual surface of his films is always lively, original, and bizarre; he is also a humanist who somewhere took a wrong turning. I would not say that his films ignore French social reality: the early ones are obsessed by it, and even his recent sketch in the episodic *Paris vu par* . . . (1964) contains typically Chabrolian bitter compassion, in its portrait of a child warped by rich, beastly parents. Chabrol is perhaps the most disappointing and maddening of all the new wave's early hopes. But he is still under forty, and may yet surprise us again.

François Truffaut, like Chabrol, began his career in a blaze of humanism based on personal experience: *Les 400 Coups*, the story of a boy driven to delinquency by loneliness and unhappiness, was drawn partly from Truffaut's own childhood and his experiences in a remand home. Not only was the *mise-en-scène* masterly, but the film was a model of implied social criticism (of school, police, parental irresponsibility) without preaching any sermons. But since then Truffaut seems to have avoided themes that relate either to his own life or directly to society. He has admitted that he is not interested in dealing with 'the political and social problems of our time' and that 'the best of the permanent subjects is love'; and his more recent films like *La Peau douce* have dealt conventionally with themes of love and friendship. He is no great innovator, either in techniques or ideas, and his colossal reputation rests largely on his lyrical genius, seen at its best in the dazzling first half of *Jules et Jim* and in parts of *Tirez sur le pianiste*. As Penelope Houston has put it, 'He has the gift of making film-making look wonderfully easy, like a man running down a long, sunlit road with a camera on his hand.'* He and Claude Lelouch are two of the best examples of the new wave's film-for-film's-sake approach: men who whirl a camera compulsively, as an artist splashes paint. But these gifts can prove vulnerable. It may not be altogether fair to judge him on *Fahrenheit 451*, where, although the subject was his own choice, he was not working on his own terms and was clearly ill at ease; but apart from its inspired closing sequence of the Book Men in the snow, this film was not a success. And following the mediocrity of *La Peau douce*, it leaves one wondering if Truffaut, too, has not run out of inspiration or committed himself too imprudently to the commercial system.

Jacques Rivette has been the least prolific of the main ex-*Cahiers* directors. His first feature, *Paris nous appartient* (1960), has a number of dedicated admirers but has baffled most people and is one of the most 'difficult' of the new-wave films. Like many of them, it is set lovingly in the streets of Paris and deals with Rivette's own milieu of students, actors, and writers; but he shrouds this everyday setting in a metaphysical climate of menace and anxiety, and the film's casual Clair-like title is deceptive. Characters are mysteriously murdered or threatened with murder; there is much talk of Spain and fascism, and of some secret organisation plotting to overthrow the world. Even so, the effect is far from that of a thriller. Although there is no explicit mention of Algeria, Rivette was clearly trying to express a mood of insecurity and violence that was prevalent in Paris in 1960; and many critics praised his courageous if oblique attempt to tackle this kind of public theme. But the style of the film—deliberately flat, restrained, and elliptical, with no recourse to elegance or effects—does not entirely gel with the subject-matter, and Rivette lacked the discipline of Bresson or Resnais to make this approach really effective. *Paris nous appartient* seems to me more like the draft of a film than a finished work. Needless to say, it lost money, and it was six years before Rivette made another feature. This was an updated version of Diderot's novel *La Religieuse*, which caused a rumpus in 1966 because the Government banned it. In sum, Rivette is one of the most honest and serious of the young directors, and not at all a frivolous escapist; but he lacks creative flair. He stands at the opposite pole to his friend Truffaut.

Jean-Luc Godard, however, combines lyrical gifts with social awareness to a high and original degree. He is one of the most fascinating figures to have emerged in France since the war. And for all its quirkiness, I

---

* *The Contemporary Cinema*, p. 107 (Penguin Books, 1963).

think that his work is more relevant to the kind of place France is today, more sensitively in tune with the *air du temps*, than that of any other post-war artist or writer. Those who have heard all this before from *Sight and Sound*, or who can't stand Godard's films, may (as he might say) rejoin me six pages later.

Son of a Protestant French doctor, Godard was born in Paris in 1930 and brought up near Lausanne: he still has a Swiss passport 'to avoid French military service'. While at the Sorbonne he began to frequent ciné-clubs and write film-reviews, and so became involved with the *Cahiers* crowd and started to make cheap 16mm. shorts. His first feature, *A bout de souffle* (1959), was filmed in streets and flats with a hand-held camera for 400,000 francs, even less than *Le Beau Serge* and less than a thousandth the budget of *Cleopatra*. Not everyone found the subject or the main characters especially rewarding (Belmondo's posturing beatnik hero, Seberg's bewildered American girl); but no one was in doubt that the wry, semi-improvised, *ciné-vérité* style marked a debut more truly original than Vadim's or even Chabrol's. Godard blithely broke all the cinema's textbook rules, simply by not noticing them.

Ever since then his work has steadily matured and strengthened. While several of his friends have 'gone commercial', Godard remains resolutely outside the system. By keeping to tiny budgets, he is able to choose his own terms of style and subject, without concession. And so he goes on making as many as two or three films a year: in 1966, he was shooting two simultaneously! It is more the way a painter or poet works, erratically and compulsively by flair or mood, than according to studio routine. Individually, several of the films are very slight, barely more than notes for a film, but that is not the point: he is building up an *œuvre*, and the films in a sense all relate to each other, and add up to more than the sum of their parts. Far more than almost any other director, he has a *Weltanschauung*.

By 1968 he had made fourteen features and nine shorts. Among the best, to my mind, are *Vivre sa vie* (1962), *Alphaville* (1965) and *Pierrot le fou* (1965). The films grow steadily more way-out and individual, the prototype of *films d'auteur*. And today in France he is more talked about —and fought over—than ever. His admirers (they include Malraux and Aragon) more and more readily use the word 'genius' in print; his detractors (and there are many, including writers like Marguerite Duras) more and more loudly call him childish, woolly-minded, and facile. For *Le Nouvel Observateur*, *Pierrot le fou* was 'the finest French film ever'; for *Paris-Match* it was 'made just for a handful of fanatics. This time, he's gone *too* far.' It's said every time, and each time he goes farther.

Many people object to the casual disregard for plot and sequence, to the flippant private jokes and the audience-teasing. Others find this endearing—as when, in *Bande à part*, after the first ten minutes a narrator's voice (Godard's) mockingly résumés the action so far 'for the benefit of late arrivals.' Many critics have remarked on the fragmented, pop-art surface of Godard's films, with their sign-symbols and slogans, and he has even been called 'the Rauschenberg of cinema': some critics dislike this style and find his films too precarious and expendable, but others think it is just this quality in his work that makes it so expressive of the modern world. It is true that he can be childishly frivolous—and reaction to this can only be a matter of taste. But though he has been taken up by the highbrows and modishly exploited as one of today's cult-figures, it would be quite false to assume that he personally is in any way a modish or assertive kind of person.

In company, he is genuinely shy, even meditative, and he is not an easy person for a journalist to interview. The first time I talked to him at length was just after I had seen *Pierrot le fou*, and at first it was hard to believe that this picaresque firework of a film, all corpses and poetry, was really the work of this taciturn little man who looked like a small-town clerk. We had a café lunch of beer and salami sandwiches (his choice). No one seemed to recognise him. He chain-smoked fat yellow cigarettes and looked at me critically behind his dark glasses. He was dressed drably in a dark check suit. He had wispy hair, thin on top, and a complexion swarthy but sallow. It was hard to make him smile. I got the impression of a solitary, rather sad sort of person, utterly without 'side' or the desire to be thought fashionable or clever.

And thus he has kept a kind of purity, in the often corrupting world of the cinema. Each new Godard film, for all the private jokes and visual high spirits, strikes me as an ever sharper personal statement of horror at the way he feels modern life is going. Violence and terrorism, loneliness, confusion, the dehumanising effects of science and affluence haunt him, and out they come, Goya-like, in his anarchic yet strangely topical films, with their almost prophetic grasp of psychological changes beneath the contemporary surface. Life, like a bright light, seems to hurt and bewilder him. When someone recently asked his ex-wife, Anna Karina, why he always wore dark glasses, she said, 'It's not that his eyes are too weak. His universe is too strong.'

He sees himself as a documentarist. 'When I first started making films,' he told me, 'I knew little of life, I just copied it from other films I'd seen. Now my films are moving closer to life, I think.' It is not hard to trace this evolution. For all their *ciné-vérité* techniques, there was nothing very documentary in the ordinary sense about his first films, the anarchic *A bout de souffle*, or the amorous intrigues of *Une Femme est une femme* (1961). But his latest films have been moving away from fiction towards a kind of film essay-writing, which is how he himself regards them: *Masculin-Féminin* (1966) is little more than a series of whimsical vignettes of modern French youth, and *Deux ou trois choses que je sais d'elle* (1967) is intended as a report on life in the *Grands Ensembles*—'elle' is Paris. Godard said recently, 'A country can rarely have offered such a range of exciting subjects as France today. The choice is bewildering. I want to cover everything—sport, politics, even groceries—look at Edouard

Leclerc, a fantastic man whom I'd love to do a film about or with. You can put anything and everything into a film, you *must* put in everything.' *
And he added, teasingly, 'My secret ambition is to be put in charge of French newsreels. Each of my films constitutes a report on the state of the nation: they are news *reportages*, treated in a quirkish way, perhaps, but rooted in actuality. *Vivre sa vie* (about prostitution) ought to have been subsidised by the Ministry of Health and *Le Petit Soldat* by the Ministry of Information.' This film, about FLN-OAS terrorism, was banned in France from 1960 to 1963!

Those who dislike Godard's quirks, or take him too literally, are often annoyed that he isn't more directly *engagé* about public themes. *Le Petit Soldat* was a sympathetic portrait of a young man who happened to be working for the OAS in Switzerland; and it drove some on the Left to accuse Godard of crypto-fascism. But he isn't political in this sense. Like many of his generation, he is liberal-humanist and dislikes Gaullism but has reacted equally against Sartrian commitment. He told me, 'The film was simply trying to mirror the confusion and traumas caused by torture and terrorism, on either side. Maybe it was expressing a kind of regret that I can't feel strongly about causes, that I wasn't twenty at the time of Spain.'

It was in *Alphaville* (1965) that his attitudes to modern life emerged most explicitly. This film used a tongue-in-cheek science-fiction plot to point a *1984*-ish moral about the destruction of the soul by computers and planners. 'I set it in the future,' he said, 'but it's really about the present —the menace is already with us.' One of the *trouvailles* behind this brilliant film is that the portrait of Alphaville, soulless city of machines, was edited almost entirely from Paris location shots, filmed in modern buildings and computer centres. Lemmy Caution, secret agent and reporter for *Le Figaro-Pravda*, 'left Alphaville that night by the Boulevard Extérieur' says the narrator—and there are Eddie Constantine and Anna Karina driving along just that Paris street. At another point, the grim technocrats who rule the city are shown brain-washing their enemies 'dans les HLM's, c'est-a-dire, les Hôpitaux de la Longue Maladie', and the camera pans up a Sarcelles skyscraper. To a Paris audience, these typical Godard jokes were both funny and frightening. 'Alphaville', he told me, 'is Paris or any other modern city. I'm not against new buildings, some are nice, but I am against the destruction of emotion and thought by too much technocracy. The job of artists like me is to set ambushes for the planners. We can't hope to win—but we can delay things.'

He went on, 'the young adulterous wife in my previous film, *Une Femme mariée*, is already an inhabitant of Alphaville—woman reduced to an object by the pressures of modern life, incapable of being herself.' This film was partly about the insidious influences of advertising, which Godard admits to be one of his nightmare anxieties, as it is of several

* Reprinted from *Le Nouvel Observateur* in *Sight and Sound*, Winter 1966/67.

young French intellectuals. He said: 'The French today are suddenly waking up to the extraordinary transformations in their life and society, and they are not really adapted to it at all, they're like children.' *

In these two films and other recent ones Godard remains detached from his characters, like a reporter. *Pierrot le fou*, however, stands out from this period as much the most personal and anguished of all his work and, I think, the greatest. It is ten years ahead of its time, and was not very well understood in Britain—but Godard sees it as a turning-point in his career. A melancholy young writer (Belmondo) escapes from Paris with the girl he adores (Karina, of course) to a desperate idyll of perfection on an empty beach near Toulon. But their flight is counter-pointed with menacing scenes of anarchic violence, gangsterish murders, bloody car accidents, and reminders of Vietnam. Finally the girl betrays him, and in a climax of fierce beauty Belmondo shoots her, paints his face blue, wraps sticks of dynamite round his head, and blows himself into the clear Mediterranean sky where the film fades on an image of sun and space and voices whispering, '*Nous enfin réunis pour l'éternité*'. Godard has described it as 'a film gay and sad both at once, bound up with the violence and loneliness that lie so close to happiness today. It's very much a film about France.'

It's also very much a film about Godard. In nearly all his work, he is expressing an alarm at a transformation of the modern world that eludes his emotional grasp—or else he is haunted by a vision of some other, purer life of the past. And Pierrot is Godard with his quest, his fears, his sense of betrayal. I asked him, 'I suppose at heart you're just an old-fashioned romantic?' 'Yes, in a way. Or at least I've a nostalgia for a simple, natural life, for Rousseau's idea of *l'homme bon*, or for the kind of spontaneous gaiety and simplicity that comes into some of my films like the dance in the café in *Bande à part*. 'Are you solitary?' 'Yes, but aren't we all, today? Or rather, we no longer like solitude when we get it, as Rousseau did. It makes us anxious.'

The most personal element in *Pierrot le fou* is the role played by Karina. Godard met and married this high-spirited, unintellectual Danish girl soon after making *A bout de souffle*, and after the cinema she has been the biggest thing in his life. He created her, like Pygmalion—and she has starred in seven of his films. Several sequences in them are virtually poems about her. But soon before he made *Pierrot le fou*, she left him for the actor Maurice Ronet. It is not hard to guess what Godard felt: although they got divorced, he made her the star of three of his subsequent films, and *Pierrot* appeared as an almost embarrassing hymn of love to her. The hero is very serious, immersed in poetry and philosophy; the heroine, gay, frivolous, and bewitching, soon gets bored and can't live up to his level. It was this tug-of-war between Karina's temperament and Godard's rather solemn one that added tension to many of his films. He is now re-married, to the actress Anne Wiazemsky.

* See p. 460 (Conclusion).

When he is not filming he spends much of his time with friends on cafés off the Champs-Elysées or in Montparnasse. Often he will sit for hours and say little. Everyone remarks on his kindness and generosity, especially to hopeful younger talent. 'I've not had a holiday as such for years,' he told me. 'For me, filming is the same as holiday. I like cars,'— he was driving Karina's Alpha-Romeo—'but I don't really want money. Films are what I want. I go to see six or seven a week. I like Renoir and Bresson, and of course the Americans. And I read a lot, and look at paintings.' It is clear from his films, full of literary quotations, poetry, and references to art and other films, that he is deeply immersed in a cultural world of his own. His critics think it immature of him to parade his private tastes like this and so irritate the public. 'But why shouldn't I?' he said. 'If these are the things I care about, why shouldn't I express them in my films?'

Among film-makers, he represents an extreme example of the concept that an artist communicates by having something unique and worth expressing, and not by studying his public's requirements. He said, 'Basically I make films for the pure pleasure of filming, to satisfy an instinct as an animal goes hunting. Also I film to put together things I find interesting without having to explain them, to do a *ciné-vérité* on my own thoughts. There are two sorts of cinema—that of careful composition, and that of instinct. I'm for the latter.' He manages to stick to his own path by rejecting big studio sets and expensive stars (with occasional exceptions), so that his films do not need to reach a wide public to pay their way. *Une Femme mariée* cost 500,000 francs, one-fiftieth the budget of an average Hollywood star vehicle. He generally films only on location, and often with a tiny crew and hand-held camera. On the set, in contrast to the nonchalance of some directors, he is usually tense and absorbed—for a scene for *Pierrot le fou*, shot in a bowling-alley south of Hyères, I watched him drive his two stars over the same snatch of dialogue for fifteen separate takes in seventy-five minutes, and no-one turned a hair. And unlike nearly all other directors, he does not prepare a complete scenario in advance but writes the script daily as the film goes along: the dialogue is not exactly improvised, as is sometimes supposed, but the actors do not know until each morning's filming what lines they are to speak. In this way, he will often change the story half-way through (he films chronologically, which again is unusual); or he will work out new ideas in the middle of a shot, or down tools completely for a day if he's not in the mood. This behaviour helps to lend his films their fresh and impromptu look and it effectively removes the temptation of Hollywood contracts. He isn't even invited.

I do not claim that all his films are successful. Some are too slight, or over-self-indulgent. But he has never made a dull film. And I will defend to the last his methods and his approach to filming, for these are the most likely to produce valuable and original work. Intellectually his films are sometimes facile and muddled; but like a true artist he creates his own logic, and his films are a sensitive and true picture of the world he sees around him, France's world. Therefore I class him firmly among those intellectuals who are not in the Left Bank ghetto but are at some kind of grips with modern life. As Françoise Giroud said in her *l'Express* review of *Pierrot le fou*, 'Godard too is mad. He knows how to talk about happiness and the pain of loving. He uses spontaneously a language where words, images, and colour are integrated. Excuse me if I beg your pardon: Godard's films, I like them, even the ones I don't like.'

Of the two key figures of the new French cinema, the other is Alain Resnais, as important a revolutionary as Godard and a much more controlled and dignified stylist. The two men are totally different. Resnais is usually linked with his close friends, Chris Marker, Agnès Varda, and Henri Colpi, as a group who are somewhat older and less insolent than the *Cahiers* team, more professional in the strict sense, and more closely involved with political themes and current *avant-garde* literature. This is not to say that Resnais' films, or Varda's, are any more directly *engagés* than those of Godard or Rivette; but Resnais' work in particular has more *gravitas* than that of someone like Chabrol, or of a typical ex-*Cahiers* lightweight like Jacques Doniol-Valcroze.

Born in 1922, Resnais had made several outstanding documentaries before he stupefied the 1959 Cannes Festival with his Hiroshima love-story, sometimes regarded by critics as one of the three landmarks of world cinema, along with *Citizen Kane* and *The Battleship Potemkin*. He is a withdrawn, elusive person, even harder to interview than Godard and much more reticent about articulating his views. And this same enigmatic quality is apparent in his films. Although every one of them is marked with his own highly personal style, he prefers not to write his own scripts, and in each case has collaborated with some well-known novelist: thus it is not always so easy to tell how much in these strange films really belongs to Resnais. He confesses that he has no gift for dialogue or narrative and therefore needs the help of writers. Some of his critics go farther and suggest that he is not really very concerned about subject-matter at all. 'He appears to rejoice in the belief', says Eric Rhode, 'that he and his team can make beautiful objects out of anything. The actual world is no more than pap to feed a style.'* But I am not sure this is fair. Except for *Marienbad* (a very special case) all his films have humanist themes, and in every case he has taken an original idea, not an adaptation, and worked on it closely with a writer. Politics and ordinary social realism are clearly not his concern; but certain other themes recur, whoever his collaborator, and these are time and memory, the difficulties of identity, the erosion of love and loyalties by the chaos of modern living and the sheer passing of the years.

Hiroshima mon amour annoyed some people because it began as a

---

* *Tower of Babel*, p. 142 (Chilton Co., 1967).

film about atomic war and then turned into something quite else, a love story, or rather two love-stories linked in the mind of the heroine. They found this trivial, even in bad taste: a minor private tragedy was being exalted and a major public one ignored. Others replied that Resnais and his writer, Marguerite Duras, were suggesting that no public tragedy can be any more than a sum of private ones and were therefore deliberately contrasting the two. The debates on the film's meaning are endless, and have not been settled by Resnais' own elusive comments. What is clear is that the film's story and theme are of minor importance compared with its style—though style is a weak word for something beyond the frontiers of genius. By marvellous editing and camerawork, by the imaginative integration of image, music, and language, Resnais transmuted an unremarkable script into a work of great power and subtlety. It was the mature expression of a technique he had elaborated through the course of his documentaries and was to repeat in most of his later films: the elegiac travelling-shots, the incantatory repetition of images and phrases that has often been likened to grand opera, and the use of stream-of-consciousness flashbacks to convey, as in Proust, the actual texture and feel of memory.

Some of the same themes recurred in his next film, *L'Année dernière à Marienbad*, but this time the script, by Alain Robbe-Grillet, was beyond redemption. Duras' scenario may not have been inspired, but at least it was warm and real; Robbe-Grillet's was neither. In a baroque luxury hotel, a man meets a girl and tries to persuade her that they had a love-affair the year before; the images on the screen reflect her state of mind. Whether they *did* have the affair is immaterial: Resnais and Robbe-Grillet have given significantly different accounts of what the film is supposed to mean. For the first twenty minutes, Resnais' mesmeric *mise-en-scène* gives promise of a masterpiece; but soon, devoid of any human interest, the film lapses into repetitive and chilly boredom. It showed the dangers of Resnais' reliance on writers with a strong individuality of their own.

Muriel (1963), scripted by Jean Cayrol, returned to a much more recognisable, everyday world, and its characters were patently real—but the mood was still baffling, this time in a different way. In modern Boulogne-sur-Mer, a woman of forty meets her former lover, and a young man is haunted by memories of war service in Algeria—everything is clear, ordinary, real, yet everything is shifting, fragmentary, elliptical. Resnais in this film abandoned his usual fluid 'travelling' style for a more staccato one with short shots, broken sequences, deliberately bewildering jump cuts. The aim, so he has stated himself, was to express a certain malaise current in France in 1962, at the time of the O A S crisis, a sense of personal insecurity, of loss of identity. It was a fascinating film, hard to take in at first viewing, and probably the most personal that Resnais has made. *La Guerre est finie* (1966) was much more straightforward: again the theme was time's corrosive influence, this time not on love but on political idealism, and it showed a Spanish Left-wing agent in France in the mid '60s, weary and self-doubting in a world that was fast forgetting Guernica.

It was a warm and penetrating film on an important theme, with a good script by the exiled Spanish writer Jorge Semprun. But again Resnais left us guessing, just a bit. He beat no political drum, beyond obvious republican sympathies. Was he saying, here and in *Hiroshima*, that the age of clear-cut causes is past, and that what matters now is private tenderness? Like Godard, he appears preoccupied by the bewilderment and impermanence of modern life, and this explains their fragmented styles; but where Godard expresses his unease by a kind of instinct, Resnais would seem to be more calculating. He is a supreme poet of the cinema, and given the right kind of material can make great films. But to search amid his ambiguities for any kind of 'message' is to get lost in an endless jungle.

Agnès Varda, like Resnais, began her film career in documentary: one of the best of her early films was *Du côté de la Côte*, a highly satirical look at the Riviera made, oddly enough, as propaganda for the national tourist office. She is a slight, dark, squirrel-like woman of Greek origin, born in 1928, and in a profession dominated by men she is the world's sole distinguished female director (*pace* Miss Ono and her 365 Bottoms). She used to be a stills photographer, which may explain the strong element of formal beauty in all her film work. Like Resnais, she uses an ornate, mandarin, carefully composed style, as opposed to the free-wheeling of many of the *Cahiers* group. And, like Resnais, she is known to hold strong Left-wing views in private, while in her films she is more concerned with non-political themes. Her first feature, *La Pointe courte* (1955), a forerunner of the new wave, was a stylised study of a love-affair that paid more than lip-service to its neo-realist setting of a struggling fishing-village. *Cléo de 5 à 7* (1962) was much more realistic but still entirely personal—a tender and moving study of two hours in the life of a young Parisienne singer, with sensitive evocation of the modern daily life of Paris. Love, solitude, fear of death, the fragility of life, were beautifully woven together in a lyrical whole.

Then came *Le Bonheur* (1965), one of the strangest and most interesting of all the new-wave films. It was an intellectual attempt, so Varda admits, to analyse the concept of happiness. To explore her theme, she chose what she saw as a modern prototype of the happy simpleton: a young carpenter living joyously in a suburban villa with his pretty blonde wife and lovely babies. When he starts an even more joyous affair with another girl, his bliss is multiplied by two, until his wife (whom he still loves) goes off and drowns herself. But this proves to be no more than a passing cloud on the surface of his ecstatic amorality; the film ends, three months later, with his domestic idyll going on exactly as before, save for a new blonde wife in place of the old one. It was a shocking film in the truest sense, and was meant to be so. On the surface the style was all sweetness, with bright colours, soft smiles, and Mozart clarinet music, but this made the irony all the sharper. The result was far more disturbing than many a conventional exposé of violence or perversion.

Some audiences were outraged. Ordinary satires on bourgeois adulteries were two a penny and perfectly acceptable, but here was a film that purported to be serenading all the solid lower-class family virtues only to stick out its tongue at them. What was Varda really getting at? Some critics objected that the characters and their behaviour were so unreal that the film lost its point. But as Varda has said, realism was not her aim: it was a stylised film, and in a stylised way it conveyed brilliantly the ruthlessness of a certain kind of mindless happiness. It was also expressing Varda's own ambivalent attitude to a suburban milieu utterly remote from her own Left-Bank world. She envied these simple people, and she despised them. The screen pullulates with images of fecundity and happy domesticity—chortling toddlers, pregnant women, breasts giving suck, streetsigns like 'la Route Dorée', Renoir-like shots of girls amid flowers, all backed by the Mozart score. In its odd way, *Le Bonheur* seems very much a criticism of certain contemporary values.

The other new directors are a diverse lot. Georges Franju is another ex-documentarist, who was over forty-five when he made his first feature. He is 'new wave' only by accident of timing; in other respects he is a classic director in the mould of Becker or Carné, and his best films are sensitive and faithful adaptations of well-known novels, charged with his own somewhat old-fashioned poetic style. *Thérèse Desqueyroux* (1962), taken from the Mauriac book, is one of the finest of all French post-war films, superbly evocative of mood and landscape; but it has the feel of a film of the '30s, and I do not mean that critically.

Louis Malle, though twenty years younger than Franju and younger even than Godard, is another director who harks back to an older generation. He is an Edwardian figure, dapper and well bred, who lives and moves in upper-class formal Parisian society—rare for a film-maker—and likes staying in Edwardian hotels like the Ritz in London. Despite the stylistic modishness of many of his films—*Zazie dans le Métro*, *Viva Maria!*—he is confessedly not interested in contemporary subjects and prefers to set his films in the past or adapt them from classic novels. He is a superb master of technique, and thus was able to keep *Viva Maria!* above the level of a fatuous romp; but he lacks a defined personal style of his own, and his films are so diverse that it is not easy to see that they were made by the same man. Unlike Godard, he seems to have nothing to 'say'—save in one solitary masterpiece where the inner Malle showed through, a film totally different from all his others. *Le Feu follet* (1963), his fifth feature, was adapted from a novel of the '20s by Drieu la Rochelle, about a young alcoholic's vain search for a meaning in life, ending in suicide. Malle transposed it to his own modern Parisian milieu, and, helped by a fine performance from Maurice Ronet, made it into an exceptionally restrained and sympathetic film, Bresson-like in its concentration on the hero's inner suffering. But he depressed himself so much in the process that, Malle-like, he next hopped off gaily to Mexico to film Moreau and Bardot in their underpants. He says he regards *Le Feu follet* as a kind of expiation—his real vocation is clearly as a smooth commercial director, unashamed to use big budgets and big stars.

Roger Vadim is Malle without *Le Feu follet* but with rather more continuity of style and subject-matter. His films are suave and ornate, modishly cynical, very commercial, and not to be taken too seriously. The art of stylish seduction is his favourite subject, treated with glossy urbanity in his updated version of Laclos' *Les Liaisons dangereuses* (1959) and his remake of *La Ronde* (1964). When he tries to convey real feeling—as in *La Curée* (1966), based vaguely on Zola—it is usually so wrapped up in baroque gimmickry as to be stifled.

At the opposite pole from Vadim are the *cinéma-vérité* exponents, Chris Marker, Jean Rouch, and Mario Ruspoli, who have all chosen to remain in documentary. Most of their best work has been done abroad (in Africa or Asia) but Marker in *Le Joli Mai* (1963) and Rouch in *Chronique d'un été* (1961) have both made attempts, not entirely convincing, to apply their candid-camera techniques to life in Paris itself. Contemporary themes of a different kind can be found in the work of Alain Jessua, whose *La Vie à l'envers* (1964) dealt imaginatively with a young man's schizophrenic retreat into nihilism before the pressures of living. The splendid Jean-Pierre Mocky specialises in high-spirited satires on bourgeois hypocrisy, tinged with his own brand of comic surrealism: *Les Snobs* (1962) was an ingenious burlesque at the expense of provincial society, and *Les Vierges* (1966) a witty and subtle analysis of current French taboos about virginity. Mocky reminds me of a misanthropic Clair, or a Buñuel with less savagery but more humour.

Finally, there is what I call the charm school: a number of directors whose world is one of innocence and goodness, radiated by the camera's *joie de vivre* and untroubled by raw pain or awkward daily problems. All villains are cardboard ones; all tragedies happen safely off-stage. In truth, they form no school as such; but their kind of filming has gained ground hugely in the past five years, and appeals to the new French mood. Pierre Etaix belongs here in a way, though his more direct affinities are back with Keaton, Tati, and the early Fellini. He followed his comedy *Le Soupirant* (1962) with *Yoyo* (1965), the dream-like story of a rich man who becomes a circus clown, and then *Tant qu'on a la santé* (1966), a not-so-successful satire on the modern lack of privacy. He is a very gentle, fay young man, passionate about circuses since childhood, who has strayed into the modern French cinema from some lost pre-war world of clowns and silent films.

The true pioneer of the charm school is Agnès Varda's husband, Jacques Demy. His first feature, *Lola* (1960), was a wistful poetic reverie about a group of people in Nantes, their yearnings, their loves lost and found, their memories. It was an entirely unpretentious film, made just to please himself, and it beautifully created a private imaginative world. I think it is one of the very best of French post-war films. But since then,

Demy seems to have been seduced by the discovery that his personal
brand of make-believe has commercial possibilities. *Les Parapluies de
Cherbourg* (1964) took up the same themes as *Lola*, but the humanist
and poetic qualities were somewhat obscured by the gimmicks of arty
colour-tones and chanted dialogue. Still haunting his beloved seaports of
western France (he was brought up in Nantes), Demy next made *Les
Demoiselles de Rochefort* (1966), and by now the rot had set in: big stars,
big sets, and the result a disastrous aping of Kelly-Donen musicals with
the true Demy love-themes beginning to look mechanical.

In fact, Demy has now been replaced as *chef de file* of the charm school
by the astonishing Claude Lelouch who at the age of twenty-eight won
the 1966 Cannes Grand Prix with his *Un Homme et une femme*, the
biggest box-office hit that the new wave has ever made. It is hard to
know what to make of this film. On the one hand, it can easily be dismissed—and has been—as a middlebrow *Sound of Music*, a banal and
unreal little love-story dressed up with fashionable trimmings, and loaded
with cosy escapist schmalz. Yet it can also be regarded as the perfect
film d'auteur, for Lelouch not only invented and wrote the story himself
but acted as his own cameraman; and his authentic joy in film-making
communicates itself to the audience through the stunning photography
and *mise-en-scène*. So it is not merely a contrived commercial film; in its
way, it is a work of art. More sharply than Truffaut, Lelouch poses the
question: how important is content? If you are a lyrical genius, does it
matter that you see life in *Woman's Own* terms?

And so we are back with the question: why so little French social realism?
As this brief analysis of their work has I hope made clear, the new directors have certainly not banished Man from their work in the manner
of the most extreme 'New Novelists': love, solitude, responsibility, these
are the constant human themes of nearly all their films. But generally
the approach is oblique or semi-abstract: the French seem unwilling to
place their characters in a complete social context, as in Italian neo-realist
cinema or even a number of British and American films. Some young
directors claim they would like to tackle social themes but are dissuaded by
producers and backers. It is alleged that the public are not interested in
this kind of realism: the French are fascinated by themselves as individuals,
but are frightened of looking too closely at themselves as a society. I think
there is some truth in this. There is also the danger of Government censorship or banning, if a film deals too directly with a topic involving
Government policy or official morality; this leads producers to practise a
cautious self-censorship, rather than risk wasting their money. But sometimes these various considerations are simply an alibi for the director's
own lack of interest. When they are being candid, many of them will
admit they would rather stick to what they know and personally care
about. It is a facet of French class rigidities that virtually all of them are
bourgeois living in Paris; and just like the novelists, when they do

attempt a foray into lower-class or provincial milieux, it is rarely a success in terms of realism. Truffaut has said, 'We don't like dealing with subjects we don't know well. What point is there in filming people who are engaged eight hours a day on work they don't enjoy? There are half-a-dozen Communist directors in France, and you should ask them to make these films about working-class problems.'

I think that this lack of direct realism is a real limitation in the French cinema, and it seems to infect even the work of socially-conscious documentarists like Marker and Rouch, who are happier when filming abroad than inside France. And yet, in a different way, the French *are* trying to mirror a reality and to express a contemporary mood in their films: the questions they pose are more metaphysical and spiritual than those of the British cinema, but none the less real, and I think they go deeper. The French are not obsessed like us by the problems of community; but they are obsessed by individual solitude within community, by romantic love as a way out of solitude, by the chaos on the fringes of modern life, by the struggle for self-identity. French films today are about love, and British ones about sex; French films are about despair, and British ones about social climbing. This is true at least of the work of Resnais and Godard, and of some others too on occasions—Jessua, Varda, Rivette, early Truffaut, and Chabrol, the Malle of *Le Feu follet*. One has only to compare *Muriel* with a British film that admits its influence: Losey's *Accident*. This was about as near as the British cinema normally gets to making a real film; but it meant no more than it said, its style lacked mystery. *Muriel* cast shadows longer than itself, which the British cinema never does.

In these respects the new wave marks a break with the Clouzot-Clément post-war generation, whose films did not have this kind of personal sensitivity. But the movement is not so much revolution as renewal: a return to some of the great traditions of the pre-war French cinema. The conscious break with the past has been less abrupt than in the case of the *nouveau roman*, with which the new wave has some links but only some. Both have been influenced by existentialism, obviously, and there are some films (*Muriel* is one) where the new wave, like Antonioni, shares the new novel's *chosisme* and concern for *les temps morts*, revealing moments of silence and stillness between action. There are links, too, in the fondness of some new novelists for working for the cinema. But only in a rare untypical case like that of *Marienbad* are real personalities absent from these films as they are from many new novels. Plots may be at a discount, but not people.

Above all, the new wave has renewed the great lyrical traditions of the French cinema, which spring from Cocteau, Clair, and Vigo. *Mise-en-scène* has been the greatest achievement of the new directors, helped by some brilliant cameramen who deserve almost equal credit: Sacha Vierny working with Resnais, Henri Decaë with Chabrol and Malle, Raoul Coutard with Godard, Truffaut, and Demy, as well as Jean Rabier and others. The poetry that results from this work may in some cases be dubbed 'escapist'—but I would prefer the personal lyrical escapism of Lelouch or Truffaut to the contrived, commercialised escapism of almost any Hollywood film you care to mention.

Therefore I consider that in the past twelve years the French contribution to world cinema has been far greater than that of any other country, even Italy. And the French conception of cinema is the most likely to produce art. The new wave has had its failures by the score, and its compromises too; but the sheer diversity of talent is immense, and each year throws up some exciting new director. It is against this bright background that the relatively sombre situation of the other arts in France must be judged. The only doubt today is whether the financial crisis and American penetration will not stifle the French cinema's true self-expression.

SIX THOUSAND ACTORS IN
SEARCH OF A PLAYWRIGHT

'What marvellous actors! What terrible new plays!' wrote *l'Express* of the 1963 Paris theatre, and it is a phrase that could apply equally to almost any of the past ten seasons. As in Britain, the French theatre has changed considerably since the war, but not with the same fecundity. As in Britain, the bourgeois commercial theatre has declined at the expense of new State-subsidised repertory companies, which are attracting new types of younger audience and can afford to experiment with new kinds of drama. But the movement is less widely creative than in Britain, for it has rarely been accompanied by the appearance of new playwrights or imaginative new directors. In France, this talent has preferred the cinema.

The post-war malaise of the Parisian *théâtre du boulevard* is by now common gossip throughout Europe. These forty or so private theatres until recently did a handsome trade by providing the bourgeoisie with their staple entertainment. A 'boulevard comedy' was a clearly defined *genre*, a safe play that would amuse and gently shock, but without being too *avant-garde*—André Roussin, for instance. This kind of audience is now showing signs of disaffection: ticket prices have risen sharply, television, cinema, and travel are presenting rival claims, and the boulevard play itself has grown bankrupt in ideas and wit. A very few of these plays still manage to sustain long runs—*Fleur de Cactus*, for instance, or *Croque-Monsieur*—thus proving that the potential theatre audience is as large as ever. But they are balanced by an increasing number of flops, and the public is clearly growing more selective. Theatres are also hamstrung by a 28 per cent entertainment tax, which has forced up their admission charges and prevented them from spending money on modernisation—and so the public stays away more than ever, and receipts drop. A familiar vicious circle. I find that today there is something fusty and dispiriting about the average Paris theatre with its rickety seating, faded décor, and sour, underpaid staff.

Worst hit of all by the crisis are the handful of more serious little theatres and private managements that struggle to survive without subsidy on the fringe of the boulevard. They too suffer from high taxes and lack of good new plays, as well as from what they regard as the 'unfair' competition of the State-supported companies. A few managers have made courageous efforts recently to keep their theatres alive with a policy of serious new plays at reasonable prices: Françoise Spira at Jouvet's old theatre the Athénée, and Vera Korène at the Renaissance. But they have not found it easy. Apart from one or two obvious fashionable successes, such as *Qui a peur de Virginia Woolf?* the public for the more serious type of commercial theatre appears to be also declining. In many cases, the managements have only themselves to blame: many of the new experimental productions are pretentious, abstruse, and vacuous.

Several Paris theatres have closed in the past few years, notably the Ambigu, and others are threatened with closure. Recently, André Malraux has made gestures of dealing with the crisis. He has offered to review the tax situation, and to institute a new fund whereby successful plays would help to pay for struggling ones. The aim, apparently, is to give support for the serious small theatres. But there are fears that it might have the opposite effect—that when an experimental play does have a success, its profits will be milked to shore up failing boulevard comedies.

The three national theatres in Paris (the Théâtre de France, the Théâtre Nationale Populaire, and the much older Comédie Française) present a very different picture. Under a generous policy of subsidies, they have grown steadily more prosperous. Each is closely responsible to Malraux's ministry, and each has a director who is appointed by Malraux but allowed a free artistic hand. The TNP has had a brilliant career since the war, first under the great Jean Vilar from 1951 to 1963, and now under the scarcely less gifted Georges Wilson, who has continued Vilar's policy. It is a huge theatre, seating 2,700, and thanks to this and to a subsidy now running at over 2·6m francs a year, it has been able to carry out a policy of low prices (you can sit in the stalls for eight francs) and so play to full houses. It has built up an audience quite different from the boulevard theatres' and closer to that of the ciné-clubs: students, young intellectuals, and even some working-class people who would never dream of rubbing shoulders with Passy at an Achard comedy. The TNP has broken with the Comédie Française tradition of insistence on French classical comedy: it does indeed play the French classics, but places a larger emphasis on foreign ones, and on serious modern plays. One of its greatest post-war successes was Alfred Jarry's satire on bourgeois stupidity, *Ubu Roi*, written in 1896, but hitherto little known even in France itself. The TNP has also introduced wide new Parisian audiences to Shakespeare, Brecht, Tchekov, Osborne, and others. Every summer the company decamps with its repertoire to the Palais des Papes in Avignon, and has built this into one of the foremost annual drama festivals in Europe. Gérard Philipe, greatest of post-war French actors, worked regularly with the TNP before his death in 1960, and his performance in Corneille's *Le Cid* at Avignon will be long remembered as a supreme moment of French post-war theatre. In productions of this kind, the TNP has been able to remain faithful to the best in the French classical tradition, while extending the theatre to new popular audiences.

In 1960 André Malraux took the inspired step of inviting Jean-Louis Barrault to run a new company at the Théâtre de France, formerly the Odéon. With an annual subsidy of 2·4m francs, Barrault has carried out a policy not very different from that of Olivier in London. His public is more fashionable than that of the TNP and his *mise-en-scène* more lavish, but his choice of plays has often been as adventurous, though there are signs that his enterprise is now flagging. You may find Shakespeare's *Henry VI* in the repertoire alongside new French plays by Duras or Billetdoux; and the outstanding production of recent years has been Genet's provocative *Les Paravents*.

At the Comédie Française, the picture is not quite as bright. This State company was founded in the seventeenth century and has barely yet emerged into the twentieth. It considers itself the trustee of French classical drama, and of a certain rhetorical, stylised tradition of acting which is ill suited to modern plays. It performs the classical comedies well, in its own way, but is rarely successful with tragedies. And its regular repertoire also oddly includes a number of worthless pre-war farces, by people like Edouard Bourdet, probably because they were bought up cheap at the time and so can be played without royalties. The theatre's annual subsidy (7·5m francs) is more than that of the other two together; but it misuses this through archaic administration. And its attitude to the public is often arrogant and insulting: you are liable to be shouted at rudely as you go to buy a ticket or claim your seat. Sometimes its productions are so superb that criticism is disarmed: I shall never forget the colours and cadences of its *Cyrano de Bergerac* in 1964. And today the theatre is even beginning cautiously to essay modern drama: in 1966 it staged the French première of Ionesco's *La Soif et la faim*, and (to the delight of the Left) managed to shock its traditional dinner-jacket audiences with the scene that parodies Christian conversion. But there is still much that needs changing at the Comédie Française, and it is not the kind of French institution that lends itself readily to reform.

The post-war policy of the TNP has had a number of spontaneous counterparts in the provinces* in the remarkable new crop of regional repertory theatres. Planchon at Villeurbanne, Gignoux at Strasbourg, Dasté at St. Etienne—these and others have all been attempting like the TNP to bring serious drama at low prices to new audiences. The movement has even spread to the Paris working-class suburbs, where several

---

* See p. 160 (New life in the provinces).

little theatres have opened in the past few years at Aubervilliers, Nanterre, St. Denis, and elsewhere, as well as at Ménilmontant where the Théâtre de l'Est Parisien has the status of Maison de la Culture. Most of these provincial and suburban theatres are municipally supported; some have State subsidies too. They are building up a new pattern for drama in France, very different from the old hack provincial tours; and despite rivalry with cinema and TV, they seem to be finding audiences. Their standard of acting is not always so very high, for most leading actors prefer to live in Paris where the range of work is more varied and film and TV studios are close by. But the new provincial theatres do attract the good directors, and much of the best new experimental production is now taking place outside Paris. It is symptomatic that Antoine Bourseiller, perhaps the most distinguished of Paris art-theatre directors, should have recently given up the struggle to attract Parisian audiences and gone off to work in Aix-en-Provence.

The advantages to cultural life in France of this colonising movement are obvious enough. The dangers are that it may render harder than ever the revival of the Paris theatre, especially in terms of discovering new plays. At present the Parisian climate is not such as to encourage young writers to try their hand at new plays, or producers to risk unusual productions, except at the TNP or Odéon where outlets are obviously limited. In fact, the provinces are now playing their part in discovering or importing new plays—Gombrowicz, Obaldia, Weiss, and Pinget have all been given French premières outside Paris, and *Oh! What a Lovely War* was first performed in France by the modest little company in Nanterre. This is heroic, and a great victory for decentralisation: but inevitably it deprives some new plays of a chance to make a national impact.

Throughout France, the gravest symptom of the theatre's crisis is the lack of promising new playwrights in the past fifteen years. Take a step farther back into time, and the situation is brilliant: Genet, Ionesco, Beckett, Adamov, Sartre, Camus, Montherlant, Audiberti, Anouilh—not all of these are French, but all have written in French and lived in France, and their contribution to European theatre in the past thirty years has been colossal. But Camus and Audiberti are dead, none of the others is under fifty-five, and few are still writing for the theatre. When their work, belatedly, gets presented in London, it arrives 'like light from a burnt-out star', as Irving Wardle wrote in *New Society*, and has little relevance to the Paris theatre today. In the past few years, what new French plays has Paris seen? In 1966 there was a new Ionesco, *La Soif et la faim*, originally staged in Düsseldorf. It is a Peer-Gynt-like allegory of a man's search for self-realisation, and certainly one of his cleverest plays. Also in 1966, the superb Théâtre de France production of Genet's *Les Paravents*, which was written in 1961 and had already been seen in several countries abroad. Dealing with the usually taboo subject of Algerian colonial misery, it represents Genet's most rigorous poetic excursion into the territory of evil, obscenity, and delusion. Marguerite Duras, now in her mid-fifties, has made an interesting jump from fiction to theatre, and several of her short plays—*La Musica, La Square, Des Journées entières dans les arbres*—have been well received. But other 'New Novelists', like Robert Pinget, Claude Simon, Claude Mauriac, have not shown the same talent in their work for the theatre. And of younger playwrights, the only one with real promise is François Billetdoux, who claims to be making a much-needed bid to bridge the gulf between the bourgeois theatre of entertainment and the Beckett-Ionesco-Genet theatre of despair and the absurd. Billetdoux's *Il faut passer par les nuages,* about a woman's drift away from daily life and love into a kind of saintliness, was the triumph of Barrault's company in 1965. But there is virtually no-one else—no-one in his thirties or forties to correspond to the younger British playwrights, for what they are worth. And not only are there no heirs to the *avant-garde,* but there is no-one coming up with good new boulevard plays to take over from Anouilh and Aymé. On the boulevards, nearly all the worthwhile plays are revivals or foreign imports, like Albee and Shisgal, Osborne and Pinter; while in adapting Weiss and Hochhuth, Paris usually follows tamely a year or two behind London.

Managers complain of a lack of new plays. But young writers complain that managers do not bother to read properly the manuscripts they are sent, or that they demand the author should put up money for the production, which is frequently not possible. Young talent wanting to express itself in dramatic form has turned more readily to the cinema over the past decade. But now the cinema, too, is in crisis again and ceasing to offer such opportunities. Possibly the new provincial theatres as they strike roots into the soil of their local communities will form breeding-grounds for new regional schools of playwrights—and there are signs of this already in one or two places. I think it is fair to describe the French theatre as in a phase of transition rather than decline, and it is possible that the new pattern heralded by Vilar and Planchon will in time achieve the full creative vitality of authorship.

About modern French painting and sculpture I do not feel competent to speak. But it seems to be a truism that Paris is no longer the world's unrivalled capital of art. The world's great painters no longer flock to live there; and New York and even London have become more important as markets for dealers and galleries. Few young French painters have made any wide impact. Only in tapestry-making has there been a flourishing revival, led by the late Jean Lurçat and encouraged by State patronage.

In music, the situation is more grave than in art or theatre. André Malraux admitted in 1965 that France 'is not a musical nation', and he shows little signs of being personally interested in music or of attempting to solve the crisis; his Ministry, as all musicians complain, treats it as the poor relation of the arts. In Paris there are some good concerts and fine orchestras and soloists. But the musical life of the country as a whole

is extraordinarily formal and conservative: the thirty regional conservatoires that form the backbone of French music are run on stuffy, pedagogic
lines and shut their doors to modern music or any spirit of free enjoyment. A number of young musical people have tried to revolt against this
tradition, and to meet their needs an organisation called Jeunesse Musicale
de France has grown up which organises local concerts, usually well
patronised: but frequently it is hampered by the jealousies of established
local music societies.

So great is the prejudice of the French musical establishment against
modern music that France's great conductor-composer, the serialist
Pierre Boulez, is virtually spurned in his own country and lives in
Germany. French serialism has played an important role in modern
music: but to study it, you must go abroad! And in 1966 Boulez,
furious with Malraux's policy, declared he would no longer perform in
France.

In the world of opera, matters are scarcely better. The two national
opera-theatres in Paris have some fine singers and musicians, but are
badly administered and fail to attract a large public: the Opéra Comique
plays to 41 per cent capacity and the Opéra to 69 per cent, compared with
100 per cent audiences at La Scala, 94 per cent in Hamburg, and over
90 per cent at Covent Garden. A more vigorous and up-to-date policy
might improve these figures; but for the moment, returns are so poor that
77·5 per cent of the two opera-theatres' budgets have to come from subsidy.
There are still a number of provincial opera companies in France, far more
than in Britain, but they cannot be regarded as flourishing. Malraux has
finally begun to show concern about the position of opera in France, and
at the end of 1967 he invited no less a person than Vilar to step in and
reorganise the two Paris opera houses. Vilar, if he accepts, will face a
monumental task.

TELEVISION: THE DARKER FACE OF GAULLISM

Television has been slower to make its impact in France than in many
countries: in 1959 there were still only a million sets, and no more than
three million in 1963 compared with twelve million by then in Britain.
But today the French are catching up at least numerically: they now have
nine million sets (in Britain there are fourteen million) and two State
networks. A nation always conservative about changing its social and
cultural habits has finally caught the craze of *la télé* along with other
symptoms of modernism; and even the intelligentsia is beginning to look
less askance at this *parvenu* to *la culture française*. Until recently a
cultured family would admit to having TV only '*pour les bonnes*' or '*pour
les gosses*': but today the set will often be taken out of hiding and put in
the *salon*. And when writers of the stature of François Mauriac and Morvan
Lebesque (editor of *Le Canard Enchaîné*) employ their talents as regular

TV critics, it is a sure sign that the medium is winning intellectual respectability.

But if France has been slow to follow this path, it has not been due solely to public tastes, nor even to the inability of poorer families to afford sets. Government policy has played a large part. The State has not sanctioned the kind of competition that has galvanised British television ever since 1955, and it has never given high priority to developing the network coverage. The *Deuxième Chaîne* began transmission only in 1964, and by 1967 was still reaching only two-thirds of the country. And more important than this: if French television today is far less excitingly creative than French cinema, and less varied and dynamic than TV in Britain, the causes lie in its political subservience to the Ministry of Information. Whether we examine it as an art or as a social catalyst, everything relates back to this issue of State control. Throughout this book I have stressed that Gaullist autocracy may have benefits for France, in a number of fields. Broadcasting is not one of them.

There is nothing so new about this situation. It is simply that the Gaullists are more efficient and more ruthless than their predecessors. The Office de la Radio et Télévision Française (as it is called today) began life before the war as a branch of the Postal Ministry, and since 1939 has depended directly on the Ministry of Information. It is this basic flaw, as much as the Gaullists' exploitation of it, that causes the trouble. After the war a number of liberals made worthy efforts in Parliament to have the ORTF provided with a genuine autonomous statute like the BBC— but no Government dared part with so valuable a weapon. Ministers often alleged that the State needed the ORTF in order to balance the anti-authority tendencies of the Press. Frequently under premiers like Guy Mollet there was suppression of anti-Government views in broadcasts, or measures against hostile staff journalists. But at least in those days the heads of the ORTF outlived their masters, as in other branches of the civil service—and a few honest liberals like V. Porché (Director-General, 1946–57) and Jean d'Arcy (head of TV until 1960) were able to do something during the 1950s to build up a solid basis of good producers and programmes for the infant TV service. But when the Gaullists arrived, things changed. Tolerance of free discussion has never been their forte, and in the early 1960s they began to place their own trusted militants in the key posts of the ORTF. The noble Jean d'Arcy was sacked, and went to work for the United Nations. Then in 1964 Claude Contamine, a brilliant, bull faced toughie in his mid thirties, was moved from the Ministry of Information to be gauleiter of TV. Previously, he had helped to select each day's news-bulletin material from his desk in the Ministry: now he would be able to do so at closer quarters, more effectively.

In political debate and news coverage there had never been much pretence at what BBC and ITA know as parity. Now there was to be less than ever. The head of TV News once sought to justify this to me: 'How can you have parity in a land with so many parties? If we had a debate, say, between a Minister and the opposition, and we chose a Communist and an MRP, we'd have the Socialists and radicals up in arms for being left out. We'd have to have fifteen speakers every time, life would be impossible.' Fortunately for the Gaullists, de Gaulle himself was a brilliant TV performer and carried all before him: 'I have two political weapons,' he was once quoted as saying: 'TV and TV: TV, because I am so good at it; and TV, because my opponents are so bad.' But during the December 1965 presidential election the weapons began to rebound. This was the first real 'TV election' in France, and for the brief weeks of the campaign the Government felt obliged to open its screens to the opposition candidates. Mitterand and especially the elegant Lecanuet proved rather more telegenic than de Gaulle's usual opponents—and a public starved for years of opposition views on TV responded avidly to their addresses. This was certainly one cause of the slump in de Gaulle's vote.

After the poll, a policy struggle began in high Gaullist circles. The liberal Gaullists argued that too much State control would defeat its own ends, unless democratic elections were to be abolished too. The lesson should be learned and the screen opened to all-the-year-round political exchanges on the Anglo-Saxon model. The diehards replied this would make matters worse, and that the election campaign showed the dangers of *any* relaxation. Debré led the liberals, Pompidou the diehards. Each had his own key men in the ORTF. For several months the ORTF was, as one paper put it, 'a principal battlefield of the régime'. The liberals appeared to win a qualified victory, at least on this issue, and in 1966 one or two new programme series were introduced such as *Face à face*, in which politicians of all shades have been interviewed in depth, even the Communist leader Waldeck-Rochet. And this is still the position today. There is now a greater semblance of parity and fair play, and the ORTF has come under such criticism that it now employs a certain subtlety and avoids needling the opposition unnecessarily—when I myself took part in a French TV programme in 1967, I was *not allowed* by my producer to criticise the Communists! In place of the usual one-sided Ministerial screen interviews, some Ministers will sometimes even allow themselves to be filmed chatting to strikers.

But in a way all this is a façade. The opposition may now have a little more scope for expressing its views, but only by courtesy, not by right. And the Gaullists still closely control all programming. News material is edited to show the Government in a good light; bulletins carefully spotlight official ceremonies and statements, especially those involving the Head of State. Documentary programmes criticise the United States, or glorify French achievements. Frequently such things are not the individual producer's fault: many of them are radicals, like most creative people, but they must toe the line or else. . . . And Gaullist pressure affects almost every kind of programme. One producer filmed an objective report on the shortage of nurses: the ORTF showed it to the Ministry of Health, then banned it. Another producer filmed a sympathetic account of a priest's difficulties in a Communist district: the ORTF refused to screen it, although the Church leaders to whom it was shown approved of it. Almost every programme on a social or economic subject has to be vetted in advance by the relevant Ministry. The leading regular current-affairs magazine, *Cinq Colonnes à la une*, escapes these restrictions to a certain extent and is one of the very few programmes to be allowed a measure of autonomy; but it has to tread warily and practise a certain self-censorship. In one of its editions not long ago, one item lambasted American foreign policy, while another tackled the equally scabrous subject of Malraux's music policy and said virtually nothing.

Kow-towing to Ministers can sometimes reach comic proportions. On one occasion the ORTF hired an aircraft to fly back a special recording of a France *v.* Ireland rugby match in Dublin, because they happened to hear that Pompidou was a rugby fan and was hoping to watch it the same night. Equally, the ORTF lives in fear of the Quai d'Orsay and frequently suppresses items or programmes which it is told might not suit France's foreign interests. Therefore it is not surprising that the ORTF is reluctant to take part in any multi-national TV venture that might involve a loss of French sovereignty or a slap to French prestige. In 1965, the French boycotted the maiden Early Bird transmission because the Eurovision authorities had put a BBC, not an ORTF, producer in charge of the European end of it—and also because they objected to the name 'Early Bird'. They would have preferred 'Oiseau Matinal'. The *cause célèbre* in this domain is the history of *European Journal*. This six-nation quarterly magazine programme was pioneered by an ORTF producer in 1963: each nation would film a report on one of its neighbours and then all six would screen the results—a brilliant idea. The French thought they could dominate the project nicely. But then the BBC belatedly agreed to join in, and the French found themselves no longer dominant. And when early in 1965 the German ZDF network made a sympathetic but entirely objective film about de Gaulle's opponent, Gaston Defferre, the ORTF refused to screen it and thus broke the spirit of the whole venture. Soon afterwards the ORTF walked out of *European Journal* and left the BBC virtually to run it. It sounds like an awful warning parody of what might happen if Britain *did* join the Common Market under de Gaulle.

The dangers of the Gaullist approach to television are not only that it curbs freedom but also that it creates a bureaucracy quite unsuited to a creative medium. This is a legacy the ORTF has carried with it since pre-Gaullist days. Unlike their BBC opposite numbers, the top ORTF administrators are not broadcasters at all but men brought in from the civil service or industry—one of them worked at Simca—and few of them have experience or much understanding of programme production. A constant war rages between them and the producers, and the *malaise* is felt right round the office. Television is not the right soil for Gaullist technocracy. Added to this is the top-heavy bureaucratic organisation of the ORTF, in the worst French tradition, which has intensified over the years as TV and radio have expanded. There are 12,000 administrative and clerical members of the staff, and 250 creators: the place is still run like a sub-department of the Post Office, which is what it once was, with endless paperwork and petty regulations.* Even the BBC seems by contrast a model of flexibility. One extraordinary rule that has never been changed is that when an ORTF film team goes abroad it has to check in at the nearest French embassy to collect its living expenses! And even for his own budget the Director-General is frequently at the mercy of Ministry of Finance auditing and interference.

Contamine, during his brief but forceful three years at the ORTF, at least tried to put more order and modern efficiency into the madhouse of ORTF bureaucracy. He pruned red tape, made clerical economies, and raised producers' salaries which were formerly pegged to low civil-service scales. Yet the producers did not love him. He was a bully who lacked the human touch, and he made no secret of his philistinism and his Rightism. The producers never forgave him for the Lorenzi affair of 1965: Stellio Lorenzi was a brilliant TV director with Left-wing views, and when he took part in a strike, Contamine punished him by axing his regular programme—an innocuous historical series called *La Caméra explore le temps*—although it was a top choice with viewers. Incidents of this kind have kept recurring, and explain why even the more sensible of Contamine's reforms sometimes came to grief because he lacked the producers' confidence and they obstructed him on principle. They accused him, probably with some reason, of trying to 'depersonalise' TV programmes by easing out the arty, original creators and ensuring a safe mediocrity of product. Someone said, 'He wants to make TV like the Régie Renault—smooth production belts and no irregularities.'

Anyone visiting the ORTF's TV headquarters in the Rue Cognac-Jay, near the Eiffel Tower, will be struck by the difference in ambiance from the BBC or ITV. It is like a third-rank Ministry: sad *huissiers* in shabby uniforms, drab offices and make-shift studios, a general air of grumpiness. Probably this will improve when the planned new TV centre is completed: indeed, the mood is already somewhat brighter in the new Maison de la Radio in Auteuil. But what really needs changing is the basic ethos of the ORTF, and this will require more than new studios or the occasional interview with a Left-wing leader.

Above all, the present set-up is discouraging new recruits. The ORTF has never bothered much with a recruiting or training policy like the BBC's, and it is not surprising that the brightest talent prefers to stay away. The creative ones would rather free-lance in films or journalism, the executives go into the prestige branches of the civil service or into

* See p. 441 (Conclusion).

industry. It is precisely the opposite of the British situation, where the BBC carries high prestige and where probably too high a proportion of the country's best young brains are going into TV or journalism, at the expense of industry and public administration. A happy medium might be best. Certainly there are some creative directors at the ORTF, but on the planning and executive side the level is pretty dismal—and few of France's brilliant young *cinéastes* show much readiness to work for television even on a free-lance basis. The recruitment crisis is growing, and the ORTF will soon face a serious shortage of talent.

And so, if the quality of programmes is on balance well below that of British TV, or even of German or Italian, the reasons are obvious. The surprise is that some programmes manage to be as good as they are. But State monopoly does carry one advantage: there is no need to compete with commercial TV for audiences (except in parts of eastern France), and therefore the proportion of serious or cultural material can be kept fairly high. The ORTF buys little of the American pulp material so common on British screens, and though French quizzes and variety shows can be as banal as any, at least they are balanced by twenty to thirty hours a week (excluding schools TV) devoted to the arts, history, travel, and so on. The approach is often conformist and uninspired, and the editing sloppy by British standards, but no-one can deny the high cultural tone. French TV is didactic in the true French pedagogic manner, and takes relatively little account of audience reactions. Yet a fair section of the public—mostly the middle classes and the eager-to-learn young peasantry—does respond favourably to this spoon-feeding. And this is because some of the regular serious programmes *are* good, thanks to the talent of those who make them. Series like *Cinq Colonnes à la une* and Lorenzi's late *La Caméra explore le temps* have regularly secured the highest viewing figures of all, as if *Panorama* and *All Our Yesterdays* were to come ahead of *Coronation Street*! An arts documentary series, *Terre des arts*, has shown consistent quality; and there are two excellent regular magazine programmes for the sixteen-to-twenty-five age-group that have no British equivalent.

But in a sense these are all minority programmes. There is a split in the TV audience. The massive urban working class tend to feel that the ORTF is not for them, it is 'Parisian' and un-entertaining; and so they watch it with reluctance, or in frontier zones they switch to foreign networks or to TV Luxembourg or Monte-Carlo. In very recent years the Government has been making some efforts to woo this audience, partly for electoral reasons, partly to sugar the pill of screen propaganda: hence, a policy of *panem et circenses*, which does not oust the cultural items but increasingly supplements them. Someone said, 'We have two TVs, that of Audiberti and that of Fernandel.' A vast number of old cinema films are shown, more than 200 a year. Dramatic serials like *Belphégor*, a spoof thriller about ghosts in the Louvre, have begun to prove popular. And there is now a larger dose of variety and soap-opera. But the French have not yet shown the same flair as the British for these kinds of entertainment TV, and this is one reason why mass audiences for them have not grown more rapidly. French producers tend to look on TV drama and variety as a kind of cinema or filmed theatre, and with exceptions they have not yet learned to use the medium creatively in its own right. In a way, they are the prisoners of their cinema tradition. The one great exception has been Jean-Christophe Averty, a remarkable young man with an IDHEC training who succeeded in pioneering a new kind of variety show, surrealistic, funny, shocking, and essentially *television*. You could call him a French Ned Sherrin, save that his techniques are different. For a while in 1963–4 his series *Les Raisins verts* had a certain vogue; but many audiences found that when it came to such things as chopping up babies and selling them in butchers' shops he was upsetting their taboos too much, and Contamine eased him off the screen. Averty has since made his name in the United States, and now makes only occasional freelance appearances with the ORTF.

Yet within such limits, ORTF producers often do have rather more *artistic* freedom than they would find on the BBC—so long as they are careful not to be too controversial. That is, given a safe subject, the producer is left to get on with it in his own way, even at editing stage. Though budgets are usually tight, at least there are far fewer union restrictions than in British TV, and as in the cinema, the cameraman (often ex-IDHEC) is eager to share his producer's creative joy. Sometimes too eager: 'I wish they wouldn't all fancy they're a lot of bloody Eisensteins,' said one British producer who has worked with French crews. But at least this means that French TV, when it tries, can pull off remarkable technical feats, especially in Outside Broadcasts—witness the astonishing 'live' coverage of an ascent of Mont Blanc, back in 1959.

Despite the qualities of its film-work, however, the editing and presentation of French TV often appears old-fashioned and slapdash. Captions may come up in the wrong place or upside-down, compères practise an undisciplined verbosity, and the damsels known as *speakerines* seem to have strayed out of some Hollywood glamour film of the '30s. It is all oddly untidy for a nation supposedly so artistic, and I think it relates to that typical French insistence on form rather than detail which I referred to *à propos* of new architecture. It is also because the men at the top are not TV people and attach little importance to this kind of studio discipline. There is altogether less professionalism than on British TV, and very much less cult of the TV personality. No Robin Day or Eamonn Andrews, certainly no Frost or Muggeridge. And Pierre Desgraupes and Pierre Dumayet, who present *Cinq Colonnes* and other programmes and might be called France's Allsop and Michelmore, are quiet, rather heavy journalists in their middle years, assured and intelligent but unlikely to set the teenagers alight or bring the mobs into the streets. In short, French TV does not have the same organic connection with daily French life as in Britain. It rarely uses *vox pop* street interviews (at least not on topical subjects) and does not try to give the man-in-the-street the sense that he too is a TV performer. It remains detached, a bit impersonal, the voice of authority.

In spite of its defects, the small screen *has* of course influenced modern French life, as it has in any Western country. It has played a definite role in the reanimation of the provinces, and in breaking down the old barriers between Paris and the 'French desert': thanks partly to TV, teenage girls in the remotest country towns now quickly pick up the latest Parisian hair-styles, while peasants have had their horizons widened far beyond the nearest parish-pump and market. I would say that, despite its political distortions, the educative role of TV *has* been positive, especially in rural areas: farmers, much more than urban workers, seem to show a taste for the cultural and travel programmes. But television is inevitably having its disruptive social effects too, and these are now the subject of much analysis and discussion, just as in Britain. Educators complain, perhaps more than in Britain, that it distracts children from their homework; and there is the same teacher opposition as in Britain to the use of TV in the classroom, despite the efforts made by the Ministry of Education to provide every secondary school with at least one set and to produce twenty hours of schools' TV a week. There are also plenty of complaints that TV is destroying the French art of conversation: in cafés, people sit in the dark in front of the screen, instead of arguing. It may be a cause, too, of the decline of gastronomy. One reason why the French resisted TV for so long is that they traditionally prefer to spend their evenings talking and eating: but now *le télé-snack* is beginning to make its fateful appearance even at the French dinner table. No time to *mijoter* the casserole: *Cinq Colonnes* starts at 8.30 p.m.! Hence the lengthy opposition of so many highbrows and purists. But today they mostly admit that this battle is lost: television is here to stay, and they have switched their objections to the *étatiste* nature of French TV rather than to the medium as such.

It is hard to see the present Government, or even a future one, voluntarily relaxing its hold on French broadcasting. The best hope is for a certain liberalisation within the present *étatiste* framework. But what of the world outside? Can France remain insulated against the way that global TV is moving? We are advancing into an age of satellites and of 'live' round-the-world TV where frontiers will have no more meaning than in radio. Soon a Parisian with the right kind of set will be able to twiddle a knob and pick up maybe a dozen foreign networks as easily as the ORTF—and probably not even de Gaulle would dare to make that illegal. Already the Government has been forced to face the challenge of what are known as the 'peripheral' broadcasting stations, notably in radio but also in TV.

For a number of years, the ORTF's three radio networks have enjoyed little more than 20 per cent of the French listening audience. Most people tune in to Radio Luxembourg, Radio Monte-Carlo, the two stations in Andorra, or the powerful and popular Europe Number One with its transmitters in the Saar. These are all commercial stations, largely French-owned and backed by French advertising, and neatly dodging the State monopoly by broadcasting from just outside French soil. They are not pirates, but legally registered in their respective countries. Their forte is popular music and entertainment (e.g. Europe Number One's amazing *Salut les copains*), which the Saar station for some years combined with news-bulletins far more objective and outspoken than those of the ORTF. No wonder it drew the audiences.

The same pattern has been shaping also in television, though limited by the much shorter range of TV transmission. Télé-Luxembourg (an adjunct of the radio company) has a viewership of one million in Lorraine, at least three times as many as in Luxembourg itself: in Nancy, 98 per cent of sets are adapted to receive it. In Provence, Télé Monte-Carlo (separately owned from RMC) has been making a huge offensive and claims also a regular viewership of a million or more, from Menton to Marseille. Both these TV companies put their emphasis on variety, quiz-games, and popular films; there is virtually no culture, and within their reception zones they attract more viewers than the two ORTF networks together, especially among the working class. Foreign-based TV reaches roughly one French home in five. In German-speaking Alsace, 90 per cent of sets are adapted to one or other German *Rundfunk*. And even ITV and BBC in the Channel Islands attract a small audience in the Cotentin, around St. Malo, and as far inland as Rennes. The local paper, *Ouest-France*, publishes the British programmes; in Dinard there is a *Cercle des Amis du Channel* (Channel TV) and a holiday hotel in Carteret altered its dinner-hour so that its British summer guests could watch *Coronation Street*! There is even some French advertising on Channel TV, though the ITA does not regard this as strictly legal.

The Government has reacted to this whole situation, most astutely, by surreptitiously acquiring financial control over most of the main peripheral stations (*not* over BBC or ITV, but no doubt it would if it could). A Government-owned holding firm known as Sofirad (Société Financière de Radiodiffusion) has for some years owned 80 per cent of the shares of Radio Monte-Carlo and 97 per cent of those of the Radio des Vallées d'Andorre. Since 1962, Sofirad has extended its hold over Europe Number One too, through a series of dubious intrigues, and controls 46·8 per cent. The State's share of Télé Monte-Carlo is rather smaller, but a number of the major TMC shareholders are allies of the present Government (e.g. Marcel Dassault, whose aircraft firms are dependent on State Defence contracts). The Luxembourg company is freest from State control, and in 1966 the Luxembourg Government rejected an attempt by Sofirad to acquire a holding. Nevertheless, every one of these stations is dependent on official French goodwill in other ways: they need to keep studios and offices in Paris, and the cables between these and their transmitters belong to the French Post Office, while TMC's transmitter above Monaco is actually on French soil. It is in the interests of none of these stations to offend Paris. Therefore their programmes are not exactly outspoken: TMC screens virtually no news or political material, and even Europe Number One has muted its bulletins considerably since it virtually lost its independence in 1962. The peripheral stations' freedom is relative, and they are not such a menace to the ORTF as might appear. Moreover the Government does not altogether object to their existence, or no doubt it would have found ways of suppressing some of them completely: although they detract from the ORTF's audiences, they are also a useful source of revenue to the Treasury via Sofirad, and thus help to balance the ORTF's own deficit. And some of the more liberal Gaullists realise that it is valuable to the ORTF to face some degree of competition. Since 1964, the ORTF's France-Inter network has had a considerable face-lift in order to meet the challenge of Europe Number One: it has sharpened and liberalised its news coverage and even succeeded in winning back some of its lost audience.

Commercial broadcasting has therefore already entered France by the back door. And now it looks as if it will soon be allowed in through the front gates too, and that State TV will begin to carry advertisements. The ORTF faces a constant deficit: this was partially removed in 1966 when the annual TV-cum-radio-set licence was put up from ninety to 100 francs, but it remains an anxiety. Already for some years there has been a measure of semi-disguised publicity on TV: little films 'of national interest' exhort the public to drink more fruit juice, or eat more pasta, without mentioning brand-names, and these are paid for by the industry concerned. Now, powerful commercial interests are lobbying the Government to introduce ordinary brand advertising; and the Press is counter-lobbying, fearing that it would cut their revenue, even though British and American experience suggests the opposite. Both inside and outside the Government there are people who feel, as the BBC does, that TV should remain a public service free from the taint of commercialism; but their battle now appears lost, and the reasons are basically Treasury ones. Of course, there is little question of the Government introducing independent commercial TV on British or American lines; it will probably follow the Italian model, allowing advertisements on its own channels at certain periods. The matter is now before a special committee of enquiry, and Parliament is expected to vote on it before the end of 1968.

Meanwhile, the Government will continue to use TV as best it can, as a weapon of propaganda and also of national prestige. In October 1967 France became one of the first European countries to introduce regular programmes in colour, using the vaunted French SECAM process. But as someone said, 'The true colours of Gaullist TV are blue for the blue pencil, yellow for timidity, and red for shame.' Pressure will continue for a new and more liberal deal for French broadcasting, but is unlikely to get far under the present régime. Attempts at genuine reform are frequently foiled by the Government's skill at window-dressing. In 1964, the Gaullists under public pressure proudly introduced a new 'statute' for the

ORTF with the semblance of giving it more BBC-like autonomy. A new independent board of governors was created, with certain powers of decision. But in practice the board is appointed by the Government and does what it is told. Its chairman, Wladimir d'Ormesson, is a tired old fuddy-duddy accurately nick-named 'Va-Dormir' by the Press. Now that Contamine has been transferred to the Quai d'Orsay, a much more liberal and cultured figure has been appointed in his place as director of TV, Emile Biasini, who formerly helped Malraux to set up the Maisons de la Culture: but the Government has very cunningly subtracted the news and current-affairs programmes from Biasini's control and placed them more directly than ever under the Ministry of Information. On that front, there is little early prospect of improvement. For the longer-term future, the question is whether a post-Gaullist Government might have the courage to give any real freedom to the ORTF. Much will depend then on public opinion, and whether it can exert the kind of pressure that so rarely manages to be effective in France. This is the great weakness. A different nation would not tolerate the kind of curbs on freedom of expression that the French now accept, above all in broadcasting but also in the Press and sometimes in the arts. A nation gets the censorship that it deserves.

SIGNS OF A NEW PURITANISM

While in Britain all forms of censorship of the arts have been growing more liberal, Gaullist France has been tightening up, and not only in television. Cinema has been feeling the pinch, and even literature, traditionally so free in France. Not that it would be fair to speak of any reign of terror: France in some ways is still more free than Britain, and many of the new curbs are in practice insignificant although denounced as 'scandals' by Left-wing critics of the régime. Yet the new climate is perceptible, and it takes the form of a creeping official puritanism, most uncharacteristic of France.

Political censorship is nothing new. It has flourished from Napoleon to Guy Mollet and does so still. It was worst during the Algerian war, both before and after de Gaulle's return to power, and since then it has eased. But alongside it there is now a new kind of moral censorship which derives I think not only from the nature of the present régime but from the loosening of French society which has brought bourgeois values into open collision with traditionally free bohemian ones. Frequently the new puritanism has religious undertones, but less at the dictates of the Church hierarchy than of the old-style Catholic rearguard; and the pious and straitlaced Madame de Gaulle herself is said to be an *éminence grise* behind many of the new official measures.

In the cinema, censorship is carried out not as in Britain by the industry itself, but by the Minister of Information, who has the power to ban any film without giving reasons. In practice he usually lets himself be guided by a permanent Government committee of civil servants and moral leaders,

who besides vetting completed films also practise a kind of pre-censorship—
that is, they see each film at script stage so as to advise the producer
whether it will later get a visa. This can be a convenient way of nipping
undesirable subjects in the bud. Some directors claim they have desks
full of scripts they daren't film—say, on Communists or the police. Some
films, such as Godard's *Le Petit Soldat* have been first completed, then
banned for straight political reasons—but this kind of censorship has
eased since the end of the Algerian war. And it is certainly no worse under
de Gaulle than in earlier days: Kubrick's *Paths of Glory* was banned entry
into France in 1957 because it criticised the French Army in the Great
War. The censors also tend to prohibit the export of films they feel might
harm France's image abroad, like Vadim's *Les Liaisons dangereuses*.

The new puritanism has not yet led to visually erotic cuts on the
British model—the shots of masturbation in Bergman's *The Silence* went
by unscathed—but it does indulge in coy morality, as when Godard's *La
Femme mariée* had its title changed to *Une Femme mariée* to avoid the
implied slur on *all* French wives. It was only through the persuasion of
André Malraux, habitually more liberal either than the censors or than
his fellow Minister of Information, that the film was not banned outright.
In recent years, much the biggest fuss has been over *La Religieuse*,
Jacques Rivette's version of the eighteenth-century novel by Diderot
about a young nun's rebellion against her convents. At the pre-censorship
stage the committee advised Rivette and his producer that the film
probably *would* get a visa so long as a few discreet changes were made. So
filming went ahead. Then France's 120,000 nuns, led by their Mothers
Superior, began an impressive and skilfully organised public relations
campaign to get the film banned. They had not even read the script, but
they objected to the novel's picture of convent life, although it was a
classic on sale in every bookshop, and although Rivette was setting his
film firmly in Diderot's own epoch. Half a million petitions flooded the
Minister's desk, many of them from old-girls of convent schools. The
Hierarchy itself maintained a discreet silence, but a number of priests
openly sided with the nuns. Then the censorship committee saw the
completed film, and approved it. But the campaign against it grew in scale,
and the Government became worried for electoral reasons. On 1 April
1966, on the orders of de Gaulle, the Minister of Information, Yvon
Bourges, overruled his committee and banned the film. The liberals and
the Left at once took up their pens. Even the sober film critic of *Le Monde*,
Jean de Baroncelli, declared he was 'shattered by the gravity of this blow
to freedom of expression'. The liberal Malraux then publicly dissociated
himself from the ban, and sent the film to the Cannes festival where
it was well received as a sober treatment of an historical subject. A year
later, after the general election had passed, the ban was quietly lifted.
The most shocking aspect of the affair, so the liberals felt, was the way
the Government subordinated principles of free expression to electoral
self-interest. They also objected to the arbitrary nature of its powers.

In the theatre, there is virtually no censorship of any kind. Scripts do not have to be vetted in advance, as in Britain. If a play provokes riots or disorders, the police have the power to close the theatre, but this virtually never happens. Right-wing Catholics staged riots during *The Representative*, to induce the police to take it off; but they failed. If there are few socially controversial plays on the Paris boulevards, it is due to the public's indifference or to lack of good material, and not to the censor.

Yet literature, totally immune for more than a century, has begun to feel an official squeeze. In 1949 the Fourth Republic passed a sane and effective law aiming to protect youth against trashy pornography. In 1958, the Fifth Republic suddenly intensified this law, and extended it to cover all literature, under a decree that sidestepped Parliament. An anonymous tribunal in the Ministry of the Interior now has the power to declare any book pornographic, and there is no defence or trial. The usual penalty is *interdiction à l'affichage*—that is, the book cannot be displayed in shops, or put in a catalogue, or advertised. This may seriously affect sales. A publisher or bookseller who disobeys is liable to fines or imprisonment. And a publisher who has three books penalised in a year then has to submit all his works to the Ministry in advance of publication, and risk their seizure. Even the august house of Gallimard came near to this fate, with two books penalised in one year, one of them its translation of *The Naked Lunch*.

Why has a law aimed to protect the young been distorted like this to give the Ministry power to ban any book it dislikes? According to reports, it began when Yvonne de Gaulle found an illustrated erotic work on a bookshop counter. Her outrage gave the cue to a latent clique of puritan officials. But the law is illogical: it concerns only new books or new editions. Genet, Céline, and others equally provocative go unmolested. It is fair to say that very few new books of any value have yet suffered; but a law as fascist and arbitrary as this could easily lead to political abuses. Publishers are angry, and want to be allowed to stand fair trial for their books.

The situation is all confusion. Some officials in the Ministry are liberal, and they sabotage and countermand the work of the puritans, so it's a question of having the right contacts. 'That's France for you,' said one publisher who after having three books penalised had ignored the injunction to present the rest of his list and apparently got away with it. Some publishers are victimised, others left alone. Jérome Lindon, owner of the Leftish avant-garde *Editions du Minuit* who had eleven of his books seized by the police during the Algerian war, stated in 1965 that he felt the régime had become liberal towards literature since the end of that war and he was therefore voting for de Gaulle. Yet his friend Maurice Girodias has been savagely prosecuted, under an old law of 1881 that prescribes seizure and imprisonment for publishing books 'dangerous to public order and morals'. Girodias and his father made their name by publishing in English, in Paris, books by Henry Miller, Nabokov, and others, that in those days were not permitted in Britain or the United

States. It is an odd logic of justice that Girodias should be today penalised for books that now come out freely in London and New York, and can even be published in Paris *in French*! Genet is on sale in Paris in French, but Girodias' English translation of *Notre-Dame des Fleurs* was banned under the 1881 law. And in 1966 Girodias was sentenced to imprisonment for publishing, in English, a harmless novel by Aubrey Beardsley. The reason for this victimisation is probably that Girodias once dared to sue the Ministry of the Interior and won, and the French have not forgiven him. He is a man who enjoys twisting bigots' tails, and so gets his own twisted too. Also, it offends Gaullist pride that Paris should be 'the Charing Cross Road of Europe', a repository for Anglo-Saxon filth. His is a special case, not typical of French censorship.

Yet the fact that he is now pursued like this is a sign of how far things have changed. Sometimes the censorship is a matter of de Gaulle's personal honour. In politics, though the old-established satirical weekly *Canard Enchaîné* is allowed as a kind of licensed jester to lampoon Mongénéral, at the same time an old law has been brought out of the cupboard that holds it a crime to insult the head of state. In 1959–66 there were more than 300 convictions under this law—from the writer Jacques Laurent who criticised Mauriac's idolatry of de Gaulle, to a merchant seaman who was caught drawing a rude picture of de Gaulle on a café table. Editors have protested that, now the head of State is also head of Government, he should not be immune from criticism or even lampoon.

But the French Press as a whole is too weak and timid for its protests to be very often effective. The combined circulation of the Paris daily Press is little more than four million, and hardly any of these papers have a mass national sale: there are few powerful Press barons in France on the model of King or Thomson, the only possible exception being Jean Prouvost who owns *Paris-Match* and *Le Figaro* but whose essential commercial interests are in textiles rather than newspapers. And as the French Press with its high costs relies on some 300m francs' worth of assorted annual State subsidies to keep alive at all, it is generally careful not to offend the Government too openly. The admirably serious and fair-minded *Le Monde* is one of the few genuinely independent dailies, and its steady rise in circulation (now just about 400,000 after doubling in the past ten years) is one of the most encouraging portents on the French democratic scene; but even *Le Monde* is not always totally fearless in the subjects it tackles or the way it tackles them. There may, therefore, be direct economic and political causes for the relative weakness of the French Press, but others lie in the nature of French society itself. This is a society which accepts satire and even a measure of obscenity as kinds of licensed convention, but is frequently shocked by real social controversy and does not like looking at itself too closely. And it is because society is acquiescent and divided in this way that censorship, or self-censorship, is able to flourish as much as it does.

CHAPTER XIII

CONCLUSION

'FRANCE IS BECOMING, has already become, *another country*,' says Jean-François Revel: 'The mutations are gigantic, everything is stirring before our eyes,' says Jean-Luc Godard; 'The contrast is startling between the France of the late '40s and the new France of the '60s,' says Michel Crozier. The French, in short, believe they are living in a revolution. And peasants and provincials believe it, as well as Parisian intellectuals. The familiar France of the past is losing its power to protect them; it crumbles at their touch, and a new, unknown landscape is opening out. But what kind of France will there be, in twenty or thirty years' time? How great a price will the old France, with all her genius, have to pay to the new?

As I see it, there are three main question-marks over the future. First, will the current process of modernising the economy and administration be carried through, and will prosperity continue to increase? Second, will a more open and flexible society emerge at the same time, and will the old barriers of mistrust give way to a greater community spirit and fairer sharing of wealth and privilege? Third, can France modernise without losing her style and originality? or is much of the uniqueness of French civilisation doomed to disappear with the old France? On the first point, I am reasonably optimistic. On the second I am not too pessimistic for the long term, though the process may be slow and painful. On the third there is more doubt.

STRUCTURAL REFORM: DANGERS OF THE STATE AS NANNY

Short of a world war or other global disaster, short of a collapse of the whole Western economy, or a major upheaval inside France after de Gaulle (which I think unlikely), there is reason to hope that the transformation of the French economy will go successfully, if unevenly, forward. The French will continue to grow more prosperous, and the only doubt is whether they will do so as independent Europeans of the Common Market or increasingly as economic satellites of big American firms.

So much progress has been made in the past twenty years that it is hard to imagine a return to the old days of financial despair and commercial apathy, even under a less stable Government than the present one. Lüthy's rock is over the crest: the major industries, after a difficult period of adaptation and gathering of speed, have now built up a solid and durable rhythm. And on a wider psychological level, too, changes have taken place which would appear to be definitive, at least for the next decades: protectionism, fear of mechanisation, deliberate limitation of production, these characteristic French attitudes of the past are steadily disappearing from industry, commerce, and farming, and a new spirit is spreading. Therefore, by a natural momentum, the firms, shops and farms will continue to group together and modernise, or face extinction. The process will continue to cause hardship and bitterness to the older generation, and will still be hotly resisted for many years; but it is unthinkable that their sons should return to the old ways.

Yet there are many practical obstacles still in the way of modernisation—outdated laws and regulations, restrictive privileges, official rules and practices that inhibit expansion or give an alibi to sloth or inefficiency. These obstacles are not so great as to block overall national progress, but they are enough to slow it down and to distort it; and there might be dangers in allowing a technically advanced economy to grow up over outmoded structures, like putting too powerful an engine in a rickety car. Only the Government can impel the necessary reforms, and thus ensure that modernisation goes forward smoothly rather than chaotically. The Gaullists have in fact reformed quite a lot, as this book has shown. But more recently they have veered towards conservatism, and their handling of the economy has betrayed three areas of failure: failure to back up their reforms with adequate funds; lack of the courage to carry out other, more contentious, reforms which are urgently needed; and failure to delegate power.

Despite recent increases in the budgets for education and public works, State spending is still slanted towards prestige operations, especially de Gaulle's cherished nuclear policy. This has impeded the Government from doing more to remedy France's social injustices—grave shortage of low-cost housing, inadequate grants for students, poor hospital conditions, and old-age pensions which are still disgracefully low, though higher than in pre-Gaullist days. For all its passion for efficiency and social progress, the Gaullist régime has not displayed an over-large social conscience, and has made little effort to ensure that the nation's new prosperity is fairly spread. Moreover, the restrictions in public spending have led, in many cases, not only to injustice but to actual inefficiency: time and again the ship of reform has been spoiled for a ha'p'orth of tar, and an otherwise admirable new measure has gone off at half-cock through lack of funds for implementing it. This has been true of the SAFERs in agriculture, the ZUPs and ZADs for housing, and the Maisons de la Culture, though less true, recently, in education. Individual wealth has been allowed to outstrip the growth of public services in a way that simply frustrates the full enjoyment of that wealth: the shortage of telephones, of sports fields, of modern roads in crowded areas, are obvious examples. In France, much more than in Britain, you need to be rich in order to insulate yourself against the sheer daily inconveniences of public life. If de Gaulle's *force de frappe* is partly to blame for these shortages, so is the Government's fear of causing an outcry by increasing taxes—and this, in turn, is the public's fault, for if there is one national character trait that has barely changed yet, it is the Frenchman's rooted conviction that his neighbour, not himself, should pay the cost of public services.

The next problem is that of the structural reforms still pending. It would not be fair to minimise the efforts that the Gaullists have already made. They have had more success than any previous Government in battering a breach in the network of *positions acquises* that has strait-jacketed France for so long, and they have carried through a number of vital reforms in face of determined sectional opposition. I would list especially the Pisani agricultural measures, the extension of the TVA to commerce, the regrouping of departments and communes, the pre-fectoral changes, the Schéma Directeur for Paris, the repeal of the 1920 anti-contraception law, the Fouchet educational reforms, and several more specialised measures such as the removal of the *bouilleurs de cru*'s hereditary privileges and the transfer of Les Halles. But in a number of cases—and education and regional development provide examples—the Gaullists' high-handed approach to their public, whether teachers or local councillors, has lost them much of the co-operation that the reforms need if they are to be fully effective. What is more, other important projects still lie on the shelf because of the Government's fear of challenging the *droits acquis* of this or that section of the community. Land and property ownership provide the most flagrant instance. Here, more than any-where, social progress is held up by archaic structures; here, more than anywhere, the Government is afraid of provoking hostility—in this case, that of its own business allies. Other vested privileges still to be challenged include those of middlemen, chemists, lawyers, Paris taxi-drivers, and a variety of small trades. And within the civil service and public administra-tion itself, efficiency is held up by the dead weight of petty bureaucracy and outdated rules and routines, which the Government finds it hard to reform because of wary opposition from the *petits fonctionnaires* them-selves.

The French economy is opening out so fast, and is becoming so vul-nerable to world competition, that, as each year goes by, France can less and less afford the luxury of her quaint old weaknesses. And the implanting of modern techniques of production, planning, and marketing on top of unsuitable structures simply leads to wastage of investment and unbalance. The EDF builds splendid new power-stations, but its system of domestic tariffs and installations remains archaic. The new *marchés-gares* are fitted with teleprinters, but the middlemen's mafia is still in place. The efforts to build new flats, offices, and roads are frustrated by the nightmare of ancient laws and permits.

Some of the many problems of this kind are righting themselves, little by little, for they simply require new techniques and outlook: others are more organic and institutional, and therefore demand concrete official action. Are the Gaullists likely to act much more than they have done already and, if not, what of their successors? A Left-of-centre post-Gaullist régime, though likely to be more democratic than the present one, might also be weaker; and so it is by no means certain that in practice it would have any greater courage or ability to act. Therefore the best long-term hope might lie with European integration—or so the 'Europeans' like Monnet and Armand believe. The harmonisation of laws, taxes, transport, welfare, commerce, and education, are all ultimate goals under the Treaty of Rome, although the process of achieving them is patently a slow one. Finally, this kind of integration might well provide France with the necessary shock and incentive for breaking down the most tenacious obstacles to reform—a shock that cannot so easily come from within. In a sense, this process has already begun. Just as the lowering of Common Market tariffs has in a general way helped to modernise French industry, so, more specifically, the much-contested new T V A law has been prepared within the framework of European fiscal harmonisation and this factor has helped the Government to carry it through. Oddly, the French will accept pills sugared in Brussels more readily than those sugared by their own Government. Therefore a weaker but more genuinely Europe-minded régime in France might, in the long run, prove a more effective agent for reform than the strong but national-minded Gaullists.

The third and last problem rests on a paradox: the State has failed to make full use of its power, yet it enjoys too much power. As has often been pointed out, structural reform is peculiarly difficult in France because the State represents the toughest vested interest of all and suffers from the most insidious of structural defects, over-centralisation. This ubiquitous role of the State in France has its roots deep in royalist history and was reinforced by Napoleon. It has frequently carried advantages in the promotion of effective government and some of these it retains today, notably through the prefectoral system and centralised bodies such as the Plan. Obviously France's post-war economic recovery owes much to the lead given by a powerful body of State technocrats, while in certain public services such as railways and electricity France is a model of what intelligent centralised control can achieve. But in many sectors of national life the system is open to abuse, notably under an authoritarian régime like the present one. And even its practical assets are today becoming more questionable.

Even in certain public services, it is arguable that the State is taking upon itself more than it can properly handle: there are plenty of economists who believe that the way to solve the severe shortages of telephones, motorways, and low-cost housing is to take these things away from restrictive Ministerial budgeting, raise loans for them on the open market, and let private enterprise do the job. But the State is the victim of its own *étatiste* tradition and will not delegate. And in the sphere of relations between the State and private industry or individuals, the problem is more controversial still. When so much power and decision is in the hands of the State, private initiatives are inhibited or driven into opposition and talents and resources are under-used. This book has been full of instances, both in economic and in political or cultural affairs. The State's control of banking and finance curbs the development of Paris as a free capital market; State supervision of private firms may often restrict their spirit of enterprise and their dynamism; democratic activity in the communes and the new regions is stunted by the power of the prefects, however benevolent they may be; the bureaucracy of State education inhibits human contact between teacher and pupil; and the running of broadcasting as a Government department, even if it were used less blatantly for political ends, would still have its drawbacks compared with an autonomous B B C-type system.

The real dilemma is that, in a great many cases, the State technocrats and planners appear to be *more* vigorous, liberal, and far-sighted than private or local bodies might be. Malraux has a larger vision of civic cultural needs than the mayor of Caen; Delouvrier sees the problems of Greater Paris more clearly than a man like Berrurier; the Education Ministry's reformers are more progressive than the teachers. And if progress were left, as so often in Britain, to the groundswell of local opinion and initiative, the *esprit de clocher* might win the day. But this is a vicious circle. So long as *étatisme* remains so strong, it is bound to drive much local initiative into the role of opposition, as happens in the communes; or else it simply stunts local roots. Often I have been struck by the French citizen's sense of impotence at embarking on any co-operative public project unless it has official origin or sanction. And this is not essentially because their action would be against the law: but they would be trying to walk without Nanny. Only when the State agrees to delegate some of its own power, and to invite a more authentic local participation, will a more vigorous sense of community arise; this is especially true in regional government. Napoleonic centralisation is a waning asset under modern conditions. But it is not easy to see the Gaullists taking this kind of step: the task of their successors will be to do so without, if possible, weakening the impact of technocratic dynamism. European integration, once again, may help to bring a solution, by providing a new supra-national counter-pole to French *étatisme*.

BIRTH-PANGS OF A NEW CIVIC SPIRIT

The acceptance of *étatisme* and the tenacity of vested interests are two French traits that have their roots deep in the social character of the nation, with its bias towards clearly defined authority, routine, and hierarchy. Many Frenchmen recognise that this formal society, for all its historic virtues, is no longer ideally adapted to the more flexible conditions of today. In private conversation they will often regret the relative lack of open public debate or of the Anglo-Saxon sense of private involvement in public issues. And they know that Gaullism, though it may have aggravated this state of affairs, is also a symptom of it. Yet a new leaven is at work in society today, behind the façade of Gaullist autocracy, and it is not impossible that one day the old pattern of social harmony, built on the protective balancing of rival interests, will give place to a new pattern, more open, flexible, and trustful.

Over the centuries the French created a framework where each class, each group, each interest had its own position and privileges, many of them defined by written rules and laws, or at least by accepted custom. In a nation prone to violence and disorder, this was found to be the best way of avoiding conflict or the oppression of one group by another or by the central government. And it brought a degree of harmony and stability, although its defensive rigidity made change and progress more difficult. The role of the State was to guarantee and defend the interests of each group, even if this meant the propping up of obsolescence; hence the importance of the supreme legal body of State, the conservative Conseil d'Etat. Throughout public life, extreme importance was laid on juridical texts and defined prerogatives, so that everyone knew what was expected of him: the Code Napoléon, for instance, laid down rules even for the details of family life. It was a system that gave the individual a certain security; and, paradoxically, it left him with a good deal of freedom, so long as he kept to the basic rules. Society had found how to steer French creative individualism away from anarchy, without having to draw the reins too tight.

But the system was based also on the mutual mistrust of one group of individuals for another. A Frenchman grew up to look on his neighbour as potentially a selfish and hostile rival who might try to do him down, and laws and privileges existed to protect him against this. Those he could really rely on were limited to his family: 'In a crisis, friends don't help you but family do,' a small-town mayor once told me, and this attitude persists. Though the Frenchman would also join vigorously in association with fellow-members of his own trade or social group, this was more for mutual self-defence than out of real sentiment or civic duty. There were few organic loyalty-groupings between the unit of the family and that of the State. And even his attitude to the State was ambivalent. Though he respected its impartiality as legal arbiter, and though *la patrie* would evoke in him a feeling of patriotic duty in time of foreign menace, this sense of duty did not extend towards the State's democratic incarnation, the Government of the day. This was not to be trusted: it was elected by *les autres*, that is, other Frenchmen, and its agents, the public authorities, were to be evaded, suborned, or hoodwinked. The Frenchman's rational fear of the hostility of other sections of society was extended, rather less rationally, to the assumption that the public administration, too, was some kind of malignant rival force, operating on behalf of *les autres*.

This framework and these attitudes remain, though their force is weakening. They have been encouraged over the years by an educational system that has offered the child little practical training in leadership or sense of community, matters which were hardly considered relevant.

Today, however, a modern way of life is beginning to make nonsense of the old barriers and formalities. On the farms, on the housing estates, in the universities, new conditions are demanding a new spirit of co-operation and therefore of trust. The new economy is irked by the old practices and regulations, and by the rigid patterns of hierarchy within firms and offices which frustrate so much talent. Now a new generation is arising, more pragmatic, more tolerant, less legalistic; and new élites are trying to crack breaches in the old framework. As Crozier has pointed out,* the breaking-point has now been reached in a familiar French cycle, where society first resists change with all its force and allows an intolerably archaic situation to build up, then, under the impulse of a few dynamic individuals, it accepts complete change on every front, all at once, only to re-close its ranks when the revolution is over.

In this book I have not attempted to describe the archi-complex French legal system, nor the current attempts to reform it: these are matters for a specialist. But also in a more general sense, the attachment to legalism and to formal routine pervades almost every aspect of French public life and thought, as anyone knows who has lived in France. It is not simply that the laws and regulations themselves are ubiquitous and often abstruse; the French are also conditioned to thinking in terms of them, even when it is not strictly necessary. For instance, there is a law of 1901 which sanctions privately formed clubs and associations as being *de l'utilité publique*—and if he wants to start up a crèche, a sports centre, or a youth club, a Frenchman will not feel easy until it has been institutionalised under this law. As if to open a private crèche were an act of dangerous subversion. *Etatisme*, once again.

This spirit is now gently on the wane, in official minds and in private ones, as the new pragmatic values of technocracy gain ground. The lawyer, whose prestige in France used to be paramount, is losing position to the planner and technician; and it is significant that the Ecole Nationale d'Administration today puts the emphasis on economics rather than law,

---

* *The Bureaucratic Phenomenon*, by Michel Crozier (University of Chicago Press, 1964).

whereas the older generation of public executives received an essentially law-based training. But the *actual* texts and regulations that govern daily French life have not, except in a few cases, been altered, and this is a large part of the problem. If these were reformed, public reflexes would have some incentive to follow suit. Almost any transaction involves a maddening amount of paperwork, based on ancient regulations that have grown more complex, not less, with the accretion of the years. The lawyers grow fat on the work this brings them, and so tight is their closed shop that they are able to obstruct any moves that would reduce their profiteering: try buying a house in France, or starting a business, or getting divorced.

Even a simple matter like collecting expenses from the ORTF for a TV assignment once drove me into one of those brief fits of violent francophobia which afflict every francophile. I was told that I could not have more than the regulation 132 francs Paris daily living allowance, yet I was booked in a hotel-room that cost almost that amount: when I protested, I was made to fill in several long forms with such details as my mother's maiden name and my father's place of birth, then I was obliged to stand in queues at cash-desks and go half across Paris to another office, and only when a tolerant official deftly fiddled the rigid rule for me was I able to collect the money at all. Peter Forster in the *Sunday Times* magazine (9 April 1967) has described a similar experience: 'If you go to buy a consignment of wine at my local Co-op Vinicole in the Midi, you take your wicker bottle to the cellarman; the office girl fills in a form which you take across town to the tax-collector, who fills in another form, to establish such details as the number of your car, estimated time of arrival and departure, amount and price; then he snips it out with scissors; you sign, pay a few francs tax; go back to the Co-op, another form is filled in, you pay for the wine, you collect it. And by this time you need it.' Thousands of man-hours are wasted in France each hour on this kind of activity. The French have their own ways of cutting certain corners and circumventing some of the bureaucratic absurdities, and this is known as *le système D*. That is, everyone, even including officials, accepts that red tape can be tacitly ignored from time to time when no-one is looking, especially when it is done between pals or after a friendly *verre*. An English friend of mine with a summer villa in the South of France applied for electricity to be installed: he was told this would take years of delay and form-filling, 'but,' added the village mayor with a shrug, 'there's some old wiring stacked in the vaults of the *mairie*, and the local electrician might fix you up if you ask, but keep it quiet.' *Système D* brings human proportion into inhuman official procedures, and helps to make life workable. But it may not be the way to run a large nation's economy in a nuclear age.

The planners and technocrats are well aware of this problem, and would like to revise and simplify the official machinery. The Rueff-Armand report proposed just this; and already some improvements have been made in the complex French system of indirect taxation. But as juridical changes tend to involve the consent of the lawyers and the Conseil d'Etat, they easily become tied down in wrangling and obstruction. In their attempts to simply bureaucratic procedures, the reformers are inhibited, too, by the hostility of the *petits fonctionnaires* themselves. In a number of Ministries or public offices, bold technocratic initiative has foundered on the inability or refusal of junior staff to adapt to the changes. In a nation deeply addicted to habit, some of this is simply a failure of the older or duller ones to comprehend new routines. But it springs also from mistrust. In any office, every post or grade has its clearly defined duties and rights; and every individual fears that *he* will be the one to suffer from changes, and so he digs his heels in. Better the devil that you know.

This climate of mistrust extends also to French petty officialdom's relations with the public. A *petit fonctionnaire* will rarely give public honesty or good faith the benefit of the doubt; and a private individual will rarely believe that a public servant is on his side and trying to help him. The mask of anonymous authority stands between them, and only when, by rare effort or good luck, they make informal human contact are matters improved. A young Frenchman once told me with admiration of an incident at Dover on his first visit to Britain. He needed to make an urgent telephone-call to Paris, but had no small change and his train for London was about to leave. 'That's all right,' said the GPO operator, 'I'll put you straight through, and later, when you've got change, just put 6/3*d* in any 'phone-box and press the button.' He told me: 'It could never happen in France.' Every visitor to France has had some experience, converse to this, of French official bloody-mindedness and refusal to help in difficulty if it means the smallest departure from routine: 'Ça!— ça ne me concerne pas,' they snap scornfully from behind their *guichet*. But what the tourist does not always realise is that this is not just the French being rude again. It arises from a vicious circle of impersonal authoritarianism which pervades all official life and of which the individual in a sense is prisoner. A *fonctionnaire*, as a private person, might be friendly and helpful if approached in the right way. The same spirit colours relations between public and police. Since the end of the Algerian crisis the police *have* grown rather less officious and brutal, and have even been making official-inspired efforts to improve their image with the public. But that image is still one of the least happy in Europe. Towards the ordinary public they are often all smiles and courtesy, especially outside Paris; but if there is any kind of riot or disturbance, or if they are questioning a suspect, they can still turn very nasty. It derives partly from the Napoleonic conception of a suspect as guilty until proved innocent—the root of many French troubles.

The Rueff-Armand committee saw the damage caused by this malaise of impersonality and mistrust between public and officials: not only was it unpleasant, it also led to wasteful conflicts that impeded efficiency and progress. Their report urged that public bodies should try to personalise their employees' relations with the public—for instance, by putting name-cards on the desks and *guichets*, as in the United States. Since then a number of public offices have tried to follow along this kind of path. Uniformed young *hôtesses* with quick smiles have begun to replace the old shuffling *huissiers*. Helped by this turnover of generations, there certainly has been some improvement, mainly in the larger and more modern-minded offices; it has by no means yet spread everywhere, and I would not pretend that every post-office worker is as charming and obliging as the young heroine of *Le Bonheur*.

The real issue is the French concept of authority as something absolute, monarchic, and anonymous, and this colours relations within organisations as much as it does those with the public. In almost any office or firm, clearly defined areas of responsibility are laid down for the different grades, and the links between them are strictly formal. Michel Crozier suggests that one of the most characteristic of French traits is the fear of informal relations between subordinates and superiors: work routines and chains of command are therefore codified and formalised, in order to avoid favouritism and conflict. And so it becomes difficult for anyone in a junior position to act officially on his own initiative, for this means break-ing the codes. Crozier points out that the desire to avoid awkward face-to-face confrontations is a common facet of French society, noticeable in all work relations. He thinks that this hierarchic pattern of bureaucracy may have served France well in the past, in order to ensure smoothness and to protect the individual, but that in a period like the present it can lead to waste and strain, making it difficult to introduce modern office methods or new directives, or to put able young men of initiative where they are needed, at NCO or subaltern level. It is one reason why the bold technocratic zeal of post-war years has not always achieved its aims.

Is any new spirit of social trust and civic co-operation emerging in France? Again, one is struck by the contrast between the dynamic idealism of certain new élites and the reticence of the many—and it makes the question hard to answer. Certainly, some of the signs are positive: first, the decline in the ferocity of the old sectarian rivalries. Catholics and anti-clericals are no longer at each others' throats. Peasants are losing their suspicion of townsfolk. Poujadist opposition to big business has become less of a militant force in commerce and industry. Even working-class hatred of the bourgeoisie is being drained of some of its old bitterness as the workers steadily *s'embourgeoisent*. The disputes of local politics are today less doctrinaire than they used to be, and more concerned with practicalities: they may still be heated, but the sides are now more likely to find a common language. It is easier to convince your opponent of the wisdom of building a new road or factory than to change his views on God or Marx. The French seem to have tired of ideologies after a succession of débâcles that showed up their futility—the ideals of the Right were eroded by the War and Algeria, and those of the Left by the failures of

the Fourth Republic. And in this context, though the old rival groupings
are still largely in place, they have become less aggressive.

At the same time, élites and leaders of an entirely new kind are emerging everywhere in France. Unlike the old groups, they are essentially
concerned with helping the community as a whole, rather than with
defending this or that interest against the rest. And this is a striking
change. The neo-Catholics provide many of the most noticeable of these
new élites, but not the only ones. They include men and women of all
shades of belief, working in industry, education, social service, or public
affairs. A great many of them are technocrats in State service, men like
Lamour, de Caumont, or (until he resigned) Pisani; or they are individuals like Leclerc or Dubedout; or leaders of the birth-control movement,
or animators of the *Grands Ensembles*; or pioneers of education or popular
culture, like Marcel Bonvalet in Nancy or Gabriel Monnet in Bourges.
These are the heroes of my book, and I am not alone in thinking that they
and those like them are France's greatest hope. If a new civic spirit is
emerging in France, this is it. For all the diversity of their specialised
activities, they are working to help *everyone* to a better future, whether it
is by developing the Languedoc, cutting retail prices, legalising contraceptives, training scientists, or bringing lively culture to a dull town.

But the men and women of these elites, though they number many
thousands, are only a small minority in France; and they give the impression of fighting against great odds. Several people remarked to me, in
effect, 'Everywhere in France you find these little nuclei of dedicated
people of *bonne volonté*. They are making progress, but why do they fail
to have more impact? why do they find it so hard to carry others with
them?' Or as Peter Forster wrote in the *Sunday Times*, 'I often think
France today is a land where a few people living in the twenty-first
century are trying to pull the rest out of the nineteenth.'

In many an organisation the dynamism seems to end abruptly below a
certain level—and with it, much of the civic idealism, for the two go
hand in hand. For instance, when Pisani was Minister of Agriculture, I
was struck by the brilliance of the young team on his personal staff
(*cabinet*), and the gap between them and the bored bureaucrats at lower
échelons who tended to mismanage or even to obstruct the Minister's new
measures. In Britain, whether at official or unofficial level, one has the
impression that the load of effort and initiative is more evenly shared:
the pioneers are usually less ambitious and energetic than in France,
but the gulf dividing them from the rest is smaller, too. And although, in
industry in Britain, trade-union practices are probably a bigger obstacle to
progress than any problem is in France, yet in civic affairs there is no
doubt which country has the more developed sense of democracy.

Part of the explanation may be that French social and civic loyalties
are today in a curious period of hiatus and possibly of transition. Family
ties are weakening, and so are the old aggressive sectarian rivalries: and
frequently the individual finds no new alternative focus for his loyalties,

save that of a technocracy imposed from outside, which he may consider cold and arbitrary and which frequently does not consult his views. So, *le français moyen se replie sur lui-même*: hugging his new prosperity, he lurks behind the privacy of his new flat and new car, neither hurling brickbats at his neighbour nor joining forces with him, and warily waiting for someone else to meet the community's collective requirements. It is the drama of the *Grands Ensembles*. De Caumont in Caen, and others elsewhere, have found how hard it is to arouse civic interest on any scale. This is true, at least, in the towns. In the countryside, where the social revolution has been more dramatic, not only are resistances stronger (e.g. over *remembrement*, or *arrachement des vignes*) but a new spirit of co-operation is developing more widely too. And even on the *Grands Ensembles* we have seen signs of a thaw.

It may be unwise to be too sanguine, but I think that various economic and social trends now in progress are likely in the long term to favour the growth of a new sense of community. The interpenetration of classes, the decline of ties of kinship, and, above all, the shift to a less rigorous and possibly more humane educational ethos—these movements will continue, and will have their influence. More and more firms will be forced, by sheer economic pressure, to adapt their hierarchic routines to new methods; more and more people will travel abroad, and will pick up the outlook of more easy-going societies. The influence and spirit of the new élites will continue to spread more widely, as it has been doing. The French may come to realise that their mistrust is a defence they do not need any more, and co-operation a virtue they can no longer do without. This at least is a possibility. But there is also a danger, as Crozier has pointed out, that an old pattern may repeat itself, and that society, once it has absorbed dramatic change, will simply put up new protective barriers on different ground.

On the level of national rather than local affairs, the development of a keener sense of community and democracy will depend, clearly, on what kind of régime succeeds de Gaulle. For the present, there is the same kind of transitional hiatus as in local affairs, and even more obviously so: the old warring politics of the Fourth Republic have given way to a muzzled Gaullist calm. It is possible that when de Gaulle has gone, the old sectarian wrangles will once again dominate the brief lives of Governments. But already, behind the façade of Gaullist autocracy, a new spirit is at work, new alignments are taking place, and new élites are preparing for the future. They are exemplified by some of the new non-party politico-economic clubs and discussion·groups that have sprung up, of which the best known is the Club Jean Moulin. Named after the greatest hero of the Resistance, this club unites an important number of senior civil servants, politicians, businessmen, trade-unionists, academics, and others, who hold study conferences on modern problems in a non-party spirit. Though the club's centre of gravity is mildly Leftish, de Gaulle has not prevented his own loyalists and civil servants from taking part. He is even said to have remarked, 'It's the best way I know of getting my *hauts fonctionnaires* to work overtime.' Thus the club helps informally to aliment the Gaullist administration with new ideas from outside, even from the opposition; and at the same time it is trying to prepare a new ethos of inter-party democratic co-operation for the post-de-Gaulle future.

Within these circles, and within the committees of the Plan and the higher ranks of the civil service, there is considerable free discussion and criticism, even though de Gaulle or his Ministers will on matters of State have the last word. The Plan in particular has helped to build up a new kind of élite public opinion in France, with continual contact between technocrats and others in public and private service; and the Club Jean Moulin is in a sense an extension of this. But the essential difference from Britain is that this kind of discussion *is* confined to an informed élite in semi-private: there is not the same nation-wide forum of open public opinion. Though Gaullism has intensified this, in a sense it has always been so and derives clearly enough from the nature of French society and ordinary French attitudes to authority.

People do not have the same sense of personal responsibility for public events as in Britain, or the same feeling that the pressure of grass-roots opinion *can* influence events. And therefore they often do not even try. For instance, there is little public CND-type campaigning in France, though hordes of people, especially young ones, object to the *force de frappe*. Social injustices—such as low old-age pensions, or bad housing, or police treatment of suspects—will evoke the odd article or formal protest, but not the kind of national outcry caused, say, by the *Cathy Come Home* film or the mildest of police excesses in Britain. Many people in France feel strongly about such things, but they also feel powerless: it is up to *les autres*, the authorities, to do something about it. Hence there is little public-inspired consumer protection on the lines of the Consumers' Association. An exception to this pattern is the progress made by the campaign for birth-control: but the process has been slow, is essentially due to the work of a few pioneers, and manifestly has had difficulty in rallying grass-roots public support, not through opposition so much as reticence.

Open public discussion is naturally more difficult in a country divided by the tensions of rival groups, where debate rapidly becomes conflict. Therefore the French prefer to conduct debate through communiqués and *prises de position* (formal statements of view by bodies or individuals) rather than by chatting things over in public. The loosening-up of society might be expected to have modified this pattern; but for the moment the Gaullist régime has if anything had the opposite effect. The shackles on broadcasting, and the tameness of the provincial Press and weakness of the Paris Press, all aggravate the situation. But they are symptoms as much as causes of the relative lack of frank public discussion: a more truly democratic nation would not tolerate the kind of broadcasting system it has.

Little is likely to change outwardly under the present régime. But there are some signs that a new kind of maturity is developing beneath the surface: the Club Jean Moulin is one portent, and the election of such men as Hubert Dubedout is another. After de Gaulle, France will either return to the sectarian disputes of the Fourth Republic, or (and it seems possible) the new élites with their new approach will increasingly dominate public affairs. The nation in its new temper, more pragmatic and less doctrinaire, may then find that democracy and public spirit come more easily than they did in the hard years before the Gaullist interregnum.

FRIENDLINESS, FORMALITIES, AND FOREIGNERS

The French are not everyone's favourite people. And the British especially, whose own values and qualities are so different, often find it hard to like them. They have wit and finesse, and charm when they choose to display it. But, so it is alleged, they can also be rude, grasping, indifferent, and cruel. The French do not even like themselves very much: they can be as beastly to each other as to foreigners. Many of their personal traits are bound up inevitably with the nature of their society, and if this society is now becoming a little more open and relaxed, does it mean that the French as individuals are becoming any nicer? First, a subjective reaction. They have become nicer to *me*, I find, largely because after more than ten years of patient effort I have finally learned how to get along with them. With exceptions, I now find them stimulating, responsive, and loyal. But it has not been easy. You have to learn to accept the French on *their* terms, which means speaking good French and overcoming that English awkwardness towards foreigners that is often taken for arrogance. You have to remember that at first encounter a stranger is very often prickly, until you take the trouble to chat him up and show him you are his friend. Personally, French brusqueness has ceased to irritate me: I find it in many ways more dignified than the indiscriminate bonhomie or obsequiousness of some races. A Frenchman is charming only when he really means to be, or as a way of showing that he likes you: in his personal dealings he is frequently less hypocritical than the English. Above all, I like the French because they present a challenge: I like their alertness, their quick, cynical humour, their refusal to suffer fools gladly, and their articulateness, which makes it possible to establish immediate intellectual contact with almost anyone. But any challenge demands effort, and sometimes the French wear me out and I sigh for more easy-going company. Especially among Parisians, I grow irked by their competitive restlessness, their lack of consideration, their relentless search for individual self-fulfilment, and often by their social formality.

If there is any generalisation to be made about French niceness, it is that provincials have more of it than Parisians. So different are the two temperaments that it is usually necessary to specify this distinction; and today's complaints by foreign visitors about French rudeness and aggressivity can mostly be found to refer in practice to Parisians, or to crypto-Parisians on the Côte d'Azur. Paris has always been mercurial, anonymous, indifferent towards the weak or lonely, and today she has more than her share of modern big-city neurosis: the sheer physical problems of living there, and the malaise of past political crises and present cultural staleness, have all served to set Parisian tempers on edge. In the provinces, on the other hand, life goes at a speed the nerves can stand, and there is a new exciting feeling of living in a time of growth and renewal, which makes people more relaxed as well as more confident and cheerful.

It is Parisians who are the least inclined to be neighbourly or civic-minded. It is in Paris that motorists will most ruthlessly steal the parking-space you are just manœuvring to back into, or will tersely refuse to move their own car two feet forward to give you room to park; it is in Paris that a man can collapse groaning in the street and no one will do more than look on curiously. In 1957 Françoise Sagan had an accident on a main road just south of Paris: she was trapped beneath her overturned car, and it was many minutes before her companion could get a passing motorist (most of them Parisians) to stop and help him lift it off. As a result she nearly died. So a day or two later a Paris paper staged a dramatic-looking 'accident' near the same spot. In fifty minutes, fifty cars passed without stopping, most of them with Paris number-plates; the fifty-first, who did stop, was a farmer from a near-by village. No-one, to my knowledge, has tried a similar test in the provinces, but I doubt if the results would be so horrific. Of course, excuses can be made. Police procedures, as much as anything, inhibit samaritanism in France: if you help or bear witness in an accident, you are often held for hours for questioning and even treated as a suspect.

It is also fair to say that the Sagan incident was more than ten years ago; and, since then, I think the climate has improved a little. Tensions have relaxed and morale has lifted, especially since the end of the Algerian crisis which had filled the streets with armed police. Today people are a little more prepared to be civil and helpful to each other, even in Paris and notably in its new suburbs. In Massy I was even stopped twice within two minutes and asked if I wanted help in finding my way. And younger people, those under forty or so, are markedly more courteous and willing in France than older ones, who sometimes still seem to be marked by the strains and humiliations of the preceding thirty or so years. Worst of all are those middle-aged, middle-class Parisiennes who treat the world as their enemy. This is the opposite of the situation in Britain, where the very young are so often boorish and aggressive, and placid matrons are the readiest to help strangers with advice.

There has also been some relaxation of the social formality and ceremonial that has always been as much a feature of daily human contact as it is of the basic patterns of society. At its best, and on smart occasions, this formality can lend French social life an attractive elegance and subtlety, as in the great *salons* of the past. But ordinary daily life is not a smart occasion, and I can't help feeling that much of the time the formality induces strain and a kind of stiltedness, so that people are not making real contact with each other. It is these aspects of French civilisation that I personally find the least attractive—the endless calling of each other by titles (*Oui, Madame l'Inspectrice-Générale!*'), the insistence on etiquette, the long stylised endings to even the simplest of letters, the respect for a person's position and diplomas more than for what he is ('*Ah, Monsieur est polytechnicien!*'), and those prim social gatherings where everyone sits in starched clothes on uncomfortably elegant chairs. Though the French can be as outspoken and unconventional as anyone in the voicing of opinions and in conversation, they are oddly conventional about manners and behaving 'comme il faut' and the need to 'sauver les apparences'. A young American told *Le Nouvel Observateur* (20 April 1966): 'A French family once asked me to dinner. The hostess wanted to "montrer ce qu'est la France". She got out what remained of her wedding gifts, put the little plates in the big ones, three glasses in front of each plate. They called me "Monsieur" and, helped by heavy reinforcements of silver and of *cuisine française*, they gave me a lesson in good manners. I'd have rather had three slices of salami and been called Pat.'

The younger generation is beginning to show impatience with this approach and to set less store by titles and decorum. Today there are fewer ceremonial banquets with speeches, and more informal home entertaining. Among the new *cadres*, especially in a town like Grenoble, a new American-style openness and casualness is emerging which can be traced also in the Club Méditerranée and some other new leisure and holiday habits. Among younger, modern-minded people the trend just as in Britain is towards casual clothes, casual décor and entertainments, and what the smart advertisements call *une élégance vraiment relax*. But though they try hard, the French don't always find it easy to be spontaneously relaxed: sometimes it makes them self-conscious and they lapse back guiltily into their more natural guise of formality.

The use of christian names likewise is on the increase among younger people, though still far more restricted than in Britain or America, where the coinage has been debased virtually into meaninglessness. In France, *tu* provides an alternative step towards friendliness; and men will often call each other *tu* but stick to surnames even when they are quite close friends and especially if they have been at school or in the Army together. *Tutoiement* has now become almost universal among students and teenagers, though elsewhere it is still largely restricted to family life and male camaraderie. And though a man is today much more likely than twenty years ago to know the wife of a friend or colleague by her christian name. to call her *tu* in public would still give quite the wrong impression. Women are usually much more formal than men, even with each other. I know two professional-class married couples aged about forty where the men are firm friends and use surnames and *tu* with each other, while the wives, though they know each other quite well, say *Madame* and *vous*.

Although the French will easily strike up conversation or acquaintance with strangers, they do not make real friends lightly, and most true friendships are formed in youth or only very slowly over the years among professional colleagues. Once made, friendships between men tend to be enduring and loyal: but the reserve against breaking the ice with new friends can often lead to a chilly atmosphere, especially in office life. This follows, inevitably, from the rigid hierarchisation of French working relations. Except at senior executive level, office colleagues seldom try to meet each other socially, and casual friendship is rare between staff of differing grades. Thus the social ambience of the average French office is noticeably less bright and relaxed than in Britain or America, and this can make life lonelier for anyone who arrives to work in a new town, especially Paris, without existing friends. The most one can say is that this pattern is changing in a number of newer-style offices (those influenced by American methods or devoted to such things as PR or films) and among younger employees.

These slow mutations in the French social character are not easy to define or pin down: but a much more clear-cut change has been the decline in French insularity and old-style nationalism. This may sound an odd thing to say—it is not always the impression that France gives to the world these days, at least in her foreign policies. But de Gaulle is untypical. It is true that the French *are* mostly proud of what he achieved in the late '50s and early '60s to haul France back into the front rank of nations—how could they not be? And it is true that they share, to a degree, his resentful jealousy of Americo-British dominance. But few of them approve the intransigence of his nationalism; and only a very few, older people or diehard Right-wingers, go along with his own particular definition of French glory and grandeur. The French may still be touchy about themselves, and prickly towards foreigners; but the old ideal of *la gloire française* today means almost nothing to them. The Algerian débâcle banished that dream for ever; and today the Army has crept away humbly on to the sidelines of national life, shorn of its old prestige. When the bugles sound and the flags wave on the *Quatorze Juillet*, the nation may still, out of old habit, stand to attention with a tear in its eye; but these rituals are losing their meaning. Older people perhaps will feel nostalgic, or bitter, but few still have any illusions; and the vast majority of the young are completely opposed to this form of nationalism, whatever they may still be taught in their schoolbooks.

Instead, there is a new and genuine feeling for Europe. Opinions may vary on how far European integration ought to go, but hardly anyone, except the Communist leaders and a few on the far Right, challenges the

basic idea of the Common Market or the need for France and her neighbours to draw close together. Young people especially are losing their old
sense of frontiers, and many of them feel today towards Italians or
Germans as forty years ago, say, a Burgundian felt towards a Provençal or
a Norman—rivalry maybe, and strangeness, but also a sense of belonging
to the same community. Among a few, the most dedicated 'Europeans',
there is a kind of anti-nationalism, springing from self-disgust at past
French failures—a desire to merge their Frenchness in a new wider
identity. The average Frenchman won't go as far as this: his Europeanism
is based on the reasoned conviction, which has spread widely since the
war, that France on her own is powerless and doomed, and the only way
to preserve and extend French influence is to collaborate more closely
with others.

This is very different from the spirit in Britain, where I would say
there is less *chauvinism* than in France today but a great deal more
insularity. The French feel sharply competitive towards other countries,
sometimes jealous of them, sometimes scornful, but at least vividly
aware of their existence; the British still hardly notice them. In UNESCO
for instance, or a number of other international activities, unofficial as
well as governmental, the British tend not to be interested and the
French tend to exploit the situation for the spreading of their own
influence. International sporting or cultural events tend to be under-
reported in the British Press; in the French Press they get fuller coverage,
but with huge emphasis on the French role. All this marks a change from
pre-war days when the French, too, were enclosed behind their frontiers
or at best regarded other countries as reflections of French civilisation.
Today the French are culturally on the defensive; they are aware that
their culture has lost some of its old dominance and universality, and it
makes them prickly, difficult, sometimes arrogant. But, in the world
today, their competitive attitude may be healthier than the British one. A
Frenchman may remain convinced of the virtues of his own way of life,
but at least he regards, say, a Swede's or an Italian's as offering some
comparison. A Frenchman may feel superior to other peoples, but not
fundamentally *different*, so, when he wishes to, he can easily make contact
with them.

French public interest in the rest of the world has increased hugely
since the war, and a nation that rarely used to venture abroad is now a
nation of travellers—not only as tourists, but as explorers, exporters,
students, or technicians in backward countries. In the smallest country
towns, lectures or film-shows on *l'Iran d'aujourd'hui* or *J'ai vu vivre les
Brésiliens* will draw ready audiences. I think that the educated Frenchman
today—de Gaulle and a few intellectuals apart—has a more realistic
conception of his country's position in the world than the Englishman
has of Britain's role. For all their latent chauvinism, the French do seem
to think of themselves in terms of a wider community, not as a special
case, and in ordinary conversation on social or other problems will talk

about 'We in the West' or 'We in Europe' where an Englishman would
speak of *Britain*.

The greatest change is of course in French attitudes to Germany. Here
the ferment began immediately after the war, in shocked reaction against
the futility of three Franco-German tragedies in eighty years, and it was
greatly encouraged by an even sharper change of mood on the German
side. Today only among a proportion of older French people and French
Jews is there much residue of the old hatreds. When German NATO
troops began to be stationed in Lorraine and Champagne in the '50s there
was rarely any kind of incident; and today patriotic Nancy, despite its
heritage of war memories, is twinned with Karlsruhe. Several hundred
thousand young French and Germans visit each others' countries annually
under the auspices of the Franco-German Youth Office. Of course it is
among the new post-Hitler generation that the *rapprochement* goes
farthest—and there are older Frenchmen who are worried that the French
are once again being incautious and forgetting too easily the lessons of
the past. But this can be argued either way. I would not say that the
French today always *like* the Germans as individuals (they usually prefer
the English) but they feel respect, a kind of involvement and understanding, and a desire to work along with the better elements in Germany
to build a new future. A French Jew told me: 'You can't expect me to
like the Germans, but, rationally, I'm in favour of the *rapprochement*.
Germany and France are like man and wife: Germany raped her in
1940, but then did the honest thing and married her. It's an uneasy
marriage, but it works.'
    Relations with Germany are in many ways closer than with Britain,
and I am not speaking of Common Market economics. The British may
be preferred as individuals, but they remain a mystery. A girl *agrégée*
in Normandy told me: 'The British have more *finesse* and humour than
the Germans, but I don't feel I understand them in the same way. All those
yachting types who come to Cherbourg where I live are so aloof, they
make me uneasy. Though England is so near, I don't feel much urge to
go there. Yet I often visit countries like Italy.' A young Parisian told me:
'L'Allemand est un con, mais un bon con. Les Anglais, ils sont trop
différents de nous.' There is thus an odd paradox about attitudes to Britain
today. On the one hand, there is a fantastic vogue for things English,
especially among the young—dress, dances, pop music, slang, films, royalty.
This anglomania is not entirely new. On a much narrower scale it has
long existed among the upper classes who have considered it *de bon ton*
to import their Savile Row suits, whiskies, and nursemaids from across the
Channel, and to cultivate English *milords*. But even today when the
craze is so much more widespread it remains curiously superficial: seldom
does it relate to any deeper curiosity about what British society is really
like, or how it has changed, or how it might be relevant to France.
Socialists and liberals may cherish a wistful admiration for British justice

and democracy, but that is as far as it goes. French clichés and misconceived ideas about Britain remain stronger than British ones about France. There is the Major Thompson rolled-umbrellas-fog-and-crumpets image, which persists, and now there is the Beatles image, but between the two there is a void. And the French aren't really interested in filling the void. Britain is quaint and colourful but not 'real' to them in the way that Italy, China, America, Africa are real. Jean-Luc Godard said to me: 'British films aren't really *creative*; maybe it's because British life just isn't very interesting. A British worker seems less sympathetic than, say, an Italian worker, and I like London less than most big cities. The British are quite nice, but they're closed up, they're a special case. They've chosen to be that way.' It is a familiar French viewpoint. Britain is one of the countries with least appeal for the French at a serious level—largely, I think, because it *is* such a special case that even its best features have little validity as a model to be copied or rivalled. You can try to imitate German punctuality, or American cost-accounting, but not English self-mockery or a constitution that has nothing written down.

Yet there are other societies that fascinate the French as valid challenges to their own: the whole Communist world, Scandinavia, Israel, even Germany and Italy, and above all the United States. Here again there is a paradox. Though America's economic dominance is feared, her politics criticised (especially over Vietnam), and her naïve tourists and brash uncultured commercialism held in contempt, the French are blindly copying many of those aspects of America they affect to despise. They are mesmerised by American society as a prefiguration of what they yearn to be and dread becoming. On the more frivolous level, the copycatting of gadgets and habits is not always very different from the anglomane modes; but at the most serious level, planners and technocrats are aware that France has a great deal to learn from America, if only she can avoid copying the faults too. In short, the French want to wear American trousers but with a different colour, while British trousers simply don't fit.

Attitudes towards Russia and Eastern Europe have been evolving rapidly in recent years, perhaps more so in France than in most Western countries. De Gaulle has taken the lead in the West in *rapprochement* with the Soviet bloc; and, leaving politics aside, most liberal Frenchmen have responded quite gladly to this policy for the new social and cultural opportunities it offers. The French have always felt affinities with a part of Europe traditionally under France's cultural influence; and today they are readily forming new contacts with the more civilised elements in the peoples' democracies, just as, in the very different climate of 1956, they were second to none in their violent display of sympathy for the Hungarian rebels. You could even argue that (as in the case of attitudes to Germany) they have forgotten the past a shade too easily. Today the Frenchman is beginning to feel that Eastern Europe, like the Common Market, is part of the territory on his doorstep. A Parisian friend of mine thought nothing of motoring to Moscow for his summer holiday; student groups from such places as Wroclaw and Prague attend the Nancy drama festival as a matter of course; the Club Méditerranée hired a Russian ship for the first of its summer cruises; and, perhaps most significantly, *Salut les Copains* regularly prints fan-letters from young Czechs or Hungarians as if the unity of the European teenage world were beyond dispute. Relations with francophile Poles and Rumanians are becoming particularly warm.

As for attitudes to the *tiers monde*, it is worth noting that France spends nearly twice as much money as Britain on overseas aid (admittedly, not without strong Gaullist *arrière-pensées* of prestige). The policy has sometimes been sharply criticised by Right-wing isolationists, but is supported by most informed opinion; and I would say that individually the French are as ready as any Western people to play their part in giving help to developing countries. Many thousands of teachers and technicians are working abroad on official aid schemes, and usually there is no shortage of candidates for such posts. Many young people look on it with a sense of vocation.

Within France, coloured immigrants are accounted for largely by 520,000 Algerian workers, 60,000 Moroccans, and 40,000 Tunisians, plus a mere 45,000 Negroes and Asians. It is a small coloured population compared with Britain's, and hardly anywhere in France is colour any kind of social problem. But even if these numbers were to increase, there might well be no great rise in tension. For all their habitual social mistrust and latent chauvinism, the French are not especially colour-conscious, less so than Anglo-Saxons. There are no official bars at all: the President of the Senate, Gaston de Monnerville, is a Negro. And even at the height of the Algerian crisis, when there was widespread FLN terrorism in France, daily and personal relations between the French and the 400,000 Algerian immigrant workers remained largely free from unpleasantness. It would not be true to claim that today there is no colour bar at all: there are always a few landlords who prefer not to take North Africans, or social circles that will not readily accept them; but the problem, in so far as it exists, is essentially an economic one. The immigrants tend to have small earnings and large families, and they herd together in unhealthy shanty towns, defying resettlement.

The French have always shown tolerance towards immigrant minorities, and there is a long and honourable tradition of granting political asylum to refugee groups. The strangers are usually left peacefully alone to lead their own lives: this is the reverse side of the coin of French indifference to neighbours. There are still some large White Russian, Polish, and Spanish exile communities in France, mostly less closely integrated into their new homeland than similar groups in America or even in Britain. Newer foreign minorities have more recently come to join them, arriving not for political refuge but to find work. There are 700,000 Italians in France, 100,000 Portuguese and others, living and working beside the French with virtually no friction. If there *is* any discriminatory feeling, it is directed more towards the country's half-million Jews, who in the mass are not foreign but French! Anti-semitism in France has a long history: witness Dreyfus. A number of Frenchmen took advantage of the Occupation to carry out their own private pogroms; and more recently, Mendès-France's repeated post-war setbacks can be traced in part to anti-semitic bias against him. A recent IFOP survey found that 10 per cent of French were avowedly anti-semitic, and less than 25 per cent thought the Jews people 'like anyone else'. But then the Jews, being French, are not to be ignored in quite the same way as Algerians or Portuguese: rather, they form one of the most assertive of France's rival group interests. I would not say that anti-semitism was at all flagrant in France, and probably it is no worse than in Britain; but it exists.

If there is any last stronghold today of old-style French insularity and disregard for other nations, it is to be found among the hard-core Left Bank intelligentsia. They were brought up in the belief that French culture alone is complete and universal, and many of them stick to this belief. Just as the Sorbonne pays little attention to non-French universities and degrees, so its professors, as Revel has noted, sometimes defer as long as possible the translation into French of key works of scholarship or the scrutiny of foreign philosophies. Even French novelists and critics, passionately absorbed in their own Parisian literary rivalries, tend to turn a blinkered and bored eye on foreign writing. Invite them in a group to a party with their foreign colleagues, and they will make a few polite noises, then relapse into their own chatter. Many of them can accept foreign culture only on French terms; and the modern authors they accept most fully are the few they have managed to transmute into a French cultural context, like Faulkner and Joyce. British and French insularities are in fact at cross-purposes. In Britain, the intellectuals admire French traditional culture while the philistine upper classes are mildly anti-French; in France it is the reverse. There are plenty of exceptions to this pattern, but it is broadly true.

Today French culture is losing its universality and self-sufficiency: it is a fortress buffeted from without and starved within, and it no longer represents the full measure of man within its own harmonious whole. Many intellectuals refuse to admit this. To do so would require the humility of starting to accept another culture's terms of reference, to recognise other values as equally valid. And so they simply strengthen the barricades and narrow their front. Others, a growing number, do admit change and try to adapt to it: but it hurts their pride. Almost against their will, Parisians find themselves applauding brilliant imported plays, paintings, books, and opera. It adds to their prickly defensiveness and sometimes they take it out on the tourist, whom they suspect of patronising them. And they are forced to ask themselves the biggest question of all: what is happening to the French genius? Is Frenchness itself on the wane?

A DECLINE OF FRENCHNESS?

Modernism wears similar trappings in any part of the Western world today, as nations grow closer together and lose some of their old idiosyncrasies. And whether or not you call this process 'Americanisation', it means inevitably that much of the old picturesque Frenchness will disappear. In the old days the French had berets and bidets and the English did not, the English had pubs and the French had *bistrots*, the French had *l'amour* and the English had sport, or so it was supposed. Today it's no longer at all clear who has what, as nations copy each other fast and even the British convert to the decimal system. But this kind of change is superficial: nostalgically sad in a way, but not catastrophic. The real question to ask is whether a nation's essential genius will be lost in the process of unification. What is to be the future of this Gallic civilisation that has shed its light over Europe for so many centuries? What of the real French virtues, will these be able to adapt and survive?—a flair for style and care for quality; the honouring of individual prowess, the ethos of individual fulfilment; lucidity of thought, a passion for ideas, a certain concept of liberty, of human proportion, of harmony amid diversity; the enrichment of the present through the past. Can these last?

France is passing through a more difficult period of transition than almost any other Western country, and this demands tolerance and patience from those who love her. Not all the present symptoms are happy ones, and they have been driving many francophiles to despair. The *Corriere della Sera*, for instance, wrote in a recent supplement on French affairs, 'France is no longer the world's mirror of freedom or democracy, nor of intelligence, art, good taste, and literature.' The commonest of laments is of course for the decline of freedom under de Gaulle—the growth of censorship and official puritanism, the various encroachments of the State, the apparent endorsement by the French people of an autocratic régime. But it is worth remembering that France has passed through similar periods before, under the two Napoleons for example, and her genius survived. The French seem to find that they need these periodic bouts of authoritarian rule, and are sufficiently mature to be able to digest them. Gaullism must be regarded as no more than a phase, and no more than one facet of the many forces that are at work in France today. It is too soon to prepare an autopsy on *la liberté*.

The malaise of *la culture* and *la pensée* however seems more sinister. It has brought with it a kind of self-curtailment of freedom and a most un-French conformism of thought: the saddest aspect of the Parisian intellectual world today is its air of conventionality. Though little of this is due directly to State censorship, in a more general sense I think it *has* been influenced by the Gaullist political climate and might lighten under another régime. Benevolent autocracy is rarely the happiest background for the arts and ideas: it was the same under Bonaparte. The creative spirit is usually most vigorous either in times of oppression or austerity, or else in a secure age of freedom and wealth; and France today lies between the two.

But other causes of the cultural crisis lie deeper than Gaullism. This nation today is so absorbed in its exciting new economic revolution that its energies and aspirations are no longer so focused on the arts or literature as they were in harder or more static times. In theory, there should be enough talent available for both: there is no reason why, say, M. Armand's dedication to the Channel tunnel should preclude M. Sartre's writing a great novel. But civilisation does not work like that. France's cultural staleness is part of the staleness of the West in this age of technology and mass-media, but it appears especially severe in France in contrast to her past brilliance. It is an age that favours the disseminating of culture to new mass audiences, via theatre, TV, and education (and this is happening in France, as elsewhere). But it does not so easily favour original creative power.

The French may therefore have to wait for their socio-economic revolution to come closer to fruition before there is a creative revival. They will also need, I think, to escape a little further from the weight of their own cultural tradition, which is at once their glory and their burden. They are living on cultural capital, and it is partly because the conventional notion of culture is still so strong in France that spontaneous creativity has grown stale. It makes the educated Frenchman a civilised and erudite person, but may make it harder for him to be original. The education system has remained static and conformist far too long in its curriculum and its methods: this, as much as anything, has led to the clouding of limpid creative thought among intellectuals. The current shake-up of education may, in the long run, help to bring in a new spirit. Other factors will also help: the revival of the provinces, the slow interpenetration of classes, the growth of foreign influences. I suspect that the Parisian cultural world will gradually become less of an intense, enclosed hothouse; some of its one-time style and brilliance may be sacrificed for ever, but it might regain a sanity and fertility it has lost today.

Craftsmanship and good taste are aspects of French civilisation that have been prized alongside the arts, and these too are under assault, This is true of *cuisine* and high fashion, as of certain prestige industries like porcelain. What will happen to the French tradition of quality, in a mass-consumer age? In certain specific fields, standards are clearly being kept up, and I have confidence that some industries will continue to survive as enclaves, catering at high prices for specialised markets: a few good individual restaurants, the perfumes of Grasse and the tapestries of Aubusson, the great vintage wines, and the *haute couture* of a few Paris firms. But the issue is whether French taste and concern for quality can transplant themselves to the new mass-production world that will soon cover all but one per cent of the field. Fifteen years ago Lüthy saw the ideal of craft perfection as a major obstacle to modern efficiency. Today this problem is righting itself, but an inverse one is taking its place. So far, French factory-made consumer goods, like furniture and textiles, do not often show a very happy sense of style, though the car industry provides an exception. Style is still largely the preserve of individualism: when it comes to decorating a private villa, or renovating an old country *auberge*, or floodlighting a public building, French taste will assert itself splendidly, soaring above British taste. Yet they have not learned to apply the same flair to industrial design. It is one aspect of the French maladjustment to their hastily espoused modernism.

Another aspect of hasty, ill-digested modernism is the ubiquitous new portent of 'Americanisation', one of today's great talking-points. In the 1950s, Italy and Britain seemed much more Americanised than France, which appeared to be holding out. In the 1960s France has overtaken her neighbours. It is this glossy, restless, hedonistic new surface of French life, much of it American-inspired, that as much as anything differentiates the mood of the late '60s from the struggling, cautious, riven France of the '50s. Many thinking Frenchmen are acutely aware of the problem, and hardly a month goes by without some newspaper article on the theme, 'Are we becoming Americans?' How has it happened that the French, although so chauvinistic and superior, have suddenly begun to acquire foreign habits so fast? Does it mean they have lost their own originality?

Many of the features of the American craze are banal in the extreme—the barbecues and drugstores, the pop stars with rock 'n' roll names, the vogue for American thrillers and Westerns. In the seaside resort of Royan, there is a mock Wild West town with a railroad train that is attacked twice weekly by mock Indians, and a sheriff who greets holiday-makers with 'Hi ya, pardners, *comment ça va?*' There is the weird new Anglo-American language that has invaded all the advertisements and is now battering at the gates of daily speech. The British long ago adopted *décolleté* and *lingerie*: now the French go for *le ready-to-wear* and *le fully-fashioned*. The British on holiday enjoy *après-ski*: the Frenchman now applies *l'after-shave*. Some words are borrowed quite erroneously: the French talk about *un tennisman*, *un recordman* (one who breaks records), *un crack* (adapted from 'crack shot' but applied to anyone who excels in anything), *grand standing* (high status), and *snob* (an adjective, meaning *à la mode* or 'in'). French purists are furious at these abuses of French. A Sorbonne professor, Etiemble, wrote a famous book about it, *Parlez-vous Franglais?* He and others have suggested that French-based equivalents should be found for all the borrowings (*weekend* should always be *fin-de-semaine*) or that the words should be given French-type spellings (e.g., *beuledozère!*).

Their rage is understandable, but I think it is partly misplaced. The French language, like the whole French way of life, needs some renewal and invigoration; and if this is not to come in a civilised manner via an élite—as French culture and language were once exported to England and

Russia—then it will have to come in this vulgarian way, and be properly assimilated later. Secondly, though the *franglais*, the cowboys, and the barbecues may be fatuous and undignified, much of the more serious Americanisation that is taking place seems to me positive and necessary. If a nation is to modernise, it cannot *help* copying the Americans to some extent: they got there first, and not to take advantage of this would mean a wasteful duplication of effort. Therefore I think that such ventures as the Libby's experiment in the Gard, the introduction of Trujillo's dis-count methods or of American cost-accounting, and even to an extent the new American-style student campuses and public-relations techniques, are all steps in the right direction.

The French at least are aware of how much is at stake, in face of the American challenge. Late in 1967 the owner of *l'Express*, Jean-Jacques Servan-Schreiber, published a very remarkable book with just that title, *Le Défi Américain*, which sold more than 400,000 copies in its first three months—the highest sale *ever* recorded in France in that space of time! The author warned most powerfully that the 'technological gap' between the United States and Europe was increasing, and that unless France and her European partners, including Britain, pooled their resources and federated immediately in order to compete, Europe would either become an outright American colony or would slip into the status of a 'backward' region like South America. It was not an *anti*-American book: in fact, Servan-Schreiber wrote with sympathetic admiration of American methods and dynamism. If anything, it was anti-Gaullist and laid the blame on Gaullist policy for Europe's failure of co-operation. The author thought that although France was making stronger efforts than any other nation to meet the American challenge, these efforts were vitiated because they were too national and self-centred. The point I wish to make is not whether Servan-Schreiber is right or wrong—and possibly he exaggerates the menace— but that this particular topic should have yielded the number-one best-seller of all time and should have become *the* French talking-point in the winter of 1967–8. The French are excitedly aware, far more than the sleepy British, of the real issues facing modern technological society, as exemplified by the American breakthrough. Like Servan-Schreiber they realise that the only answer is to copy the best from America but to adapt it to French, and European, needs and traditions—and to avoid too much direct American intervention, not for narrow reasons of nationalism but in order that the European genius may be preserved and continue to play its role. From computers down to Coca-cola, the issue is the same.

For the moment there does seem to be too much blind copying, at least in the more superficial field. But it should not lead us to overlook the fact that the French *are* making their own contributions to modernism as well. I am thinking not only of the serious economic achievements—the Plan for instance, where Jean Monnet was originally inspired by the challenge of American efficiency but has built out of it something uniquely and characteristically French. I am thinking also of the flavour of ordinary modern life in France: inspired by America maybe, but with French dressing added. Just as Godard and Truffaut have borrowed the plots and conventions of cheap American gangster films and made of them something as artistically and unmistakably French as a canvas by Delacroix, so the new social institutions like the student campus, the smart housing estate or the drugstore are often less American than they appear on the surface. Take *le drugstore*: the French have borrowed an American term, and an American formula of late-closing, multi-purpose boutiques, and have turned them into a new conception whose zippiness, half vulgar and half chic, owes much more to Paris than to any Main Street chemist's. Or take the film *Un Homme et une femme*: a hero who pilots cars for an American firm, a heroine who makes Wild West films, an ethos of glossy romance that seems perilously close to the new American-inspired ideals of affluence; yet the sensibility of the film, its sheer exhilarating elegance, are products made-in-France that neither Hollywood nor the British cinema could ever begin to rival. In short the French, despite their imitativeness, despite their immature lack of certainty about the way modern life is going, still manage to bring to life certain qualities of their own that I can only call taste and sense of proportion. There is still relatively little of the public vulgarity and brash commercialism that are so evident in America and, increasingly, in Britain. I fear these may develop in France, and I think very frankly that their absence is allied to the extreme slowness of the social revolution. The price of a just democracy is often a certain measure of vulgarity.

I have referred to French sensibility and sense of proportion. One reason why they find adjustment to the onrush of modernity so traumatic is, I think, this imaginativeness: they, or at least the more thoughtful ones, are more aware than most peoples of the spiritual dangers involved, and it is a constant theme of their literature and films. While the British adapt steadily and phlegmatically to modern life, soberly concerned about practical moral issues and whether everyone is getting a fair deal, the French reaction is perhaps less mature but more sensitive. They are frenetic, dazzled, half unable to cope, and their anxieties are more personal and metaphysical, less social, than British ones. Talk to a serious-minded young Frenchman, someone like Godard, and he will tell you of his worry about the impact of advertising and publicity on the individual, about the dangers of alienation and the essential solitude of modern life. A horror of the new, mass-consumer world of noise, publicity gimmicks, and frustrated privacy has been the theme of several films from Tati's *Playtime* to Etaix's *Tant qu'on aura la santé*. Georges Perec's *nouvelle*, *Les Choses*, aroused wide discussion for its portrait of an archetypal young modern Parisian couple adrift on a sea of meaningless material aspirations. The solitude of the individual, too, has been a constant preoccupation of modern French thinking, from Sartre and Camus to the present. It recurs today in the *nouvelle vague* films, notably Godard's; in the work of le Clézio; in conversations with young people; even in pop songs like Hallyday's *Idole d'or* or Françoise Hardy contrasting her own loneliness with the comradeship of *Tous les garçons et filles de mon âge*. This concern with solitude is more than cant culled from existentialism or Marxism, though undoubtedly Sartre and others have influenced this mood. It is the way that many of the French sincerely see life, in a land where the individual counts for more than the community, and where the decline of the old ties is leaving him with a sense of isolation and of vulnerability to the new forces of science and mass-persuasion.

To be aware of these manifold problems is the first step towards solving them. But can the French succeed? Pierre Massé, when head of the Plan, told me that he thought the most crucial problem facing the French was how to borrow the good things from American civilisation without the bad, and his own Fourth Plan warned France of the dangers of copying America's *civilisation des gadgets* too thoughtlessly. A young technocrat at Lacq once told me with horror of his meeting with one of America's foremost engineers: 'He knew everything about engineering, but he knew nothing else: he was the most uncultured and incurious man I've ever met.' The French, perhaps more than any other nation in Europe, bring a vast heritage of wisdom and taste and humanism to the difficult task of preserving the best of the past in order to marry it with the future. The greater the heritage, the more difficult that process, and inevitably some things will be lost.

A while ago, France seemed to be preparing to bury her talents in a napkin; to build a bulwark around her traditions and protect them *against* the future. That policy would have spelt decay, and it has now been averted: the French have opened their eyes to the future. They now know that France *must* modernise, or go the way of the Aztecs. If some of the things we hold most precious about France appear to be lost in the process, that is sad but inevitable. Some of them may be lost for ever, some may appear in a new guise. The present revolution in France has, in many aspects, only just begun. It is a revolution which is causing changes on such a scale that it is not possible to tell what sort of a nation France will be when it is over or whether she will have the same qualities we have known. The French genius, as we knew it, is going into partial eclipse and may remain there for some time. I have faith it will finally reappear—as it has done, repeatedly, ever since Charlemagne.

CHAPTER XIV

POSTSCRIPT, JULY 1968

The uprising of May, 1968, startled everyone by its suddenness and its strength, although its causes need surprise no one who knows France today. I hope that this book will have made some of those causes clear, notably in the chapters and sub-chapters on education, television, local government, class divisions, and management: my principal regret is that I did not write more about labour relations. It was a crisis outside conventional politics; and this and the elections results seem to confirm that the crucial battles in France in the next year or two will be fought outside the framework of parliament and the parties. Therefore I still do not regret that I gave little space in this book to politics as such.

The uprising was an immensely positive and encouraging movement, for all its excesses and contradictions, for all its short-term failures, for all the new problems it has created. And I say this although I also believe that in terms of politics Gaullism is still the lesser of two evils for France: the parties of the Left have given little hope that a Popular Front government would be other than a disaster. Like many French liberals, I personally would have liked to see the Gaullists returned with a loss of their overall majority, forced to govern in coalition with the Centre and maybe the centre Left. But that was not to be. The question now is whether the Government can fulfil its election-night promise 'not to abuse the victory': the answer is uncertain, but it will be crucial.

For a few weeks in spring, half of France went joyfully and creatively mad. There were many diverse elements in that madness, and it is still too soon to assess their real significance. On the one hand, I think one should not overlook the purely theatrical element. Although with a part of themselves the French are conservative and attached to security, they also enjoy drama and action and a relief from the boredom of papa-knows-best government; and although the students and *lycéens* were certainly in earnest about their frustrations and injustices, they would not have been human had they not also relished the dramatic break from routine. One

American observer has sceptically dismissed the euphoria of May as 'the Club Méditerranée on a nation-wide scale', a kind of irresponsible holiday. I would not go nearly as far as that; but I think it is important for foreigners to remember that the ideal of 'revolution' has a very special and romantic appeal in France. And during the crisis many a Frenchman's instinct was to rally emotionally to the challenge of Cohn-Bendit without necessarily sharing his views or his aims.

With this reservation, the movement was at base a deeply serious one, involving not only students and workers but a large part of the intelligentsia and *cadres* of the nation, united in 'contesting their structures' as the French say; that is, rising up not so much against a government or a leader as against the whole outdated and fossilised network of French hierarchies and bureaucracies and therefore against the régime that had seemed to be losing interest in reforming them. It was a heterogeneous and paradoxical movement—students contesting the 'affluent society' found themselves in alliance with workers demanding a larger share in it—but it was spontaneous, and once the students had lit the flame it spread rapidly. The fires licked into the most surprising corners of the edifice of French vested interests: architects found themselves demanding of Malraux the liquidation of their 'evil' guild (see p. 210), and *Le Monde* wrote, 'Who would have thought we should live to see the day when even the chemists start contesting their own privileges?' (see p. 110).

The uprising was a crystallisation of the post-war French desire for change and modernisation that has been a constant theme of this book; or rather, it crystallised that current which does not see technocracy as the only answer but wants human solutions too. As such, the movement is irreversible. And so, as France went on holiday in July after the elections, there was a strange mood of hope that transcended the very real anxieties and disappointments. 'I am pessimistic about the short-term but hopeful for the longer term': this I was told repeatedly, *both* by reform-minded Gaullists and civil servants *and* by people on the non-Communist Left with very different views. I met few, except on the real conservative Right, who wished the uprising had never happened. A certain stalemate has been broken in French society, certain barriers have cracked, and something now *must* happen—either the Gaullists will carry out the far-reaching reforms they are promising, or there will be another uprising. In either case, there will be change.

The immediate practical problems created by the crisis are obvious enough—the setback to economic expansion, the risk of inflation and added unemployment, the threat of anarchy and of chaos in schools and universities. But its gravest legacy, it seems to me, is the danger of a repolarisation of France just at a time when the atavistic political feuds of the Third and Fourth Republics had seemed to be dying away and when some national unity is needed more than ever if reform is to be effective. The current re-awakening of interest in public issues, especially among young people, is in itself a healthy sign—but less so if it simply revives the old French tendency to fly to extremes and refuse all compromise with the opposite faction. I am not sure which I find the more depressing spectacle, the anaesthetised apolitical France of the past Gaullist decade or the current resharpening of knives. In the first years of the régime, a number of non-Gaullists of good faith collaborated with the Government and useful work was done. But one by one they dropped away, often pushed to it by Gaullist high-handedness. In local affairs, a mayor like Dubedout at Grenoble who came to power in 1965 on a strictly non-party ticket has found it increasingly hard to avoid taking sides—with the opposition. And it is symptomatic that in 1968 Jean Vilar, solicited by Malraux to undertake a reform of the State opera houses, decided he could not do so under the present régime.

There are signs that the crisis and the elections will have accentuated this trend, and that all but the Gaullist faithfuls may sink into resentful opposition. And this could be most grave for the future. Of course, as has been said a thousand times, it is essentially up to the Gaullists to reach into their hearts for an unwonted new tact and tolerance; but it is also up to non-Gaullists to 'accept the dialogue' if it is offered—and I do not think that in the past the fault has been entirely on the Gaullist side. At present, in many fields, there is often a remarkable unity of views between the two sides on what needs to be done, but intransigeance over collaboration in doing it. It is one of the oldest of French failings: civic spirit resides in consciences more than in actions. This trend of repolarisation may be temporary, and may recede as the pangs of the election period recede; if not, some of the brightest hopes of social progress aroused by the May uprising risk being dashed.

What are these hopes?

Labour relations:

The general strike had many motives, only some of which were the classic material ones: better wages and working conditions. Here it is the lowest-paid workers who have done best: the minimum legal wage has been raised by 35 per cent from its previous disgraceful level of barely two francs an hour. This is a good step forward that only the most uncontrollable inflation could wipe out; the danger however is that in some small, weak firms unable to support the new wage bills, it could have the boomerang effect of adding to unemployment. Other workers have gained some 10 to 13 per cent on average, much of which may of course be lost to inflation. They have also gained a shorter working week, and this is important in a country with some of the longest working hours in Europe. But many of them will still not be able to enjoy the same leisure evenings as British or German workers until the problems of housing and public transport have been solved, especially in the Paris suburbs (see pp. 218, 266).

It was the non-material aspirations, however, that gave this strike its particular colouring and significance. These varied from union to union and from industry to industry, but the same phrases and slogans kept reappearing—'dignité du travail,' 'contestation du pouvoir,' 'contre aliénation,' and in some cases 'co-gestion'. It was a strike against the paternalism and secretiveness of most French employers; against the boring repetitiveness of much modern factory work which leads to 'alienation'; against the rigid and bureaucratic chains of command, the refusal to delegate authority and the lack of group discussion, which characterise French industry at all levels, on the shop floor as well as between *cadres* and managers. And in many firms, the *cadres* themselves played a leading part in the revolt against *le système* from which they suffer as much as the workers. It is too early to assess the full results of this movement; much will depend on how the employers react during the months ahead and on what comes of de Gaulle's plans for 'participation'. But already it is clear that certain barriers have cracked. And in a few firms, even before the end of the strike, concessions had been won. This was especially true in the most technically advanced industries where the proportion of *cadres* and skilled technicians is highest: in the American-controlled Bull electronics factories, for instance, management agreed to set up permanent joint committees with *cadres* and workers, to review such things as the orientation of research and training and personnel policies.

The most important victory, in the unions' eyes, is the Government's agreement to pass a law giving legal status to the unions inside each firm (see p. 34). At last they will have the right to offices on the premises, and their officials will be able to use the firm's time for collecting funds, arranging meetings, and so on—just as in Britain and elsewhere. This will certainly make it easier for the unions to recruit new members. Whether their added strength will also make them more intransigeant, and will lead to a growth of labour unrest as in Britain, remains to be seen. Much will depend on the fate of the Government's other, more far-reaching plans, and here the unions are sceptical. For twenty years or more de Gaulle has nourished the dream of some kind of management/labour partnership which he calls 'participation' and which he sees as France's solution to the old dilemma between capitalism and communism. This he now intends to be his final contribution to history before he dies or retires, and he is in a hurry. It is significant that the most left-wing of all Gaullists, M. René Capitant, who broke with de Gaulle at the height of the crisis and resigned the whip, was immediately afterwards 'forgiven' and appointed Minister of Justice, charged with preparing texts on this subject. M. Capitant's ideas are very radical: he has suggested that the managing-director of a firm be elected by the workers and staff in a kind of parliament. Many people consider him a bit of a dreamer, and it is unlikely that even de Gaulle will go all the way with him. But some changes appear certain. The 1967 law obliging firms to share some of their profits with their workers, will be applied earlier (it was originally not due to yield fruit until about 1972) and probably intensified. There will also be laws obliging employers to share policy information much more fully with their staffs, and establishing a degree of co-partnership for such matters as welfare, training and promotion. This might be done through a strengthening of the existent but futile *comités d'entreprise*, or by creating new bodies.

The basic problem is that a new order cannot be produced simply by legislation; it demands also a change of heart on the part of employers and certain union leaders, notably in the CGT. 'You can't change France into a Scandinavian-type society simply by a Minister waving a wand,' a young man at the Plan told me. If there *were* a change of heart, texts would scarcely be necessary. But, so the Government argues, texts may at least encourage new attitudes and give them a framework. What are the prospects? The unions are uninterested in profit-sharing which they mostly regard as 'une tarte à la crème'—a capitalist lure to buy off the workers and weaken their solidarity. The CGT appears equally uninterested in co-partnership—this has been applied, in fact, in no Communist country except Yugoslavia—but there are signs that the CFDT and FO might accept it, if the Government can present it with tact and consult them properly. As for the Patronat, it seems to be opposed to the whole package, and the Patronat has plenty of allies within senior Gaullist ranks, which means that the path of de Gaulle and Capitant will not be an easy one. But the replacement of Pompidou by Couve de Murville indicates that de Gaulle is determined to go through with his scheme, at any cost; for the trusted Pompidou was the most powerful of the Patronat's allies.

More important is the question of how, within each firm, employers and managers have reacted to the crisis itself and to the new labour climate. The situation is still very unclear. In some older family firms there appears to be a hardening of positions, a last-ditch attempt to hold on to authority, coupled with subtle reprisals against some of the strike leaders. But the majority of employers seem to have accepted the fact that some change of style will be unavoidable: the wiser among them did not fail to note that the strike was most bitter and long in the autocratic old-style firms like Citroën, whereas the few firms with a more enlightened labour policy had little trouble, and in some such cases the strikes lasted only two or three days. The question is whether there will be any real change of heart among employers, or merely a change of tactic under duress. Since the crisis, the Patronat has been making conciliatory noises about its awareness of the need for reforms, and it is certainly true that the younger managers now pushing their way up in French firms, many of them trained in the United States, are more disposed to a new deal than the older ones. However, these young technocrats often seem to have learned American tech-niques of costing, marketing and production, rather than American styles of labour relations, generally more liberal than the French. So it is not yet quite certain how much benefit might come from a change of gener-ations.

On one principle that it regards as vital, the Patronat is determined to stand firm against the tide of reform: the right of management to final responsibility for a firm's main policy decisions. It will probably win. There is little indication that de Gaulle intends to push co-partnership to this level, while most union leaders likewise accept that any such reform would be unrealistic short of a destruction of the entire capitalist system. But many employers are scared that even a simple new deal at shop-floor level, as now proposed, might equally harm business efficiency. The experience of one or two pioneers such as Marcel Demonque of the Lafarge cement firm (see p. 34) suggests the contrary; but Demonque's kind of initiative demands the right personalities at the top, and France is short of Demonques. It will require considerable tact and goodwill on all sides—unions, bosses, Government—for the new '*co-gestion*' not to relapse into endless dispute that might, indeed, harm productivity.

How then will the unions react? They have emerged strengthened from the crisis, and this despite the fact that it was not their own officials but the rank-and-file who in most cases led the strikes. But the strikes did yield a remarkable overall solidarity among workers, despite divergences between rival unions, and this seems to have revived faith in union action among many people hitherto non-unionised. Between May and early July, union membership went up an estimated 600,000 or 20 per cent (see p. 34). Maybe, one day, the unions will become so strong in France that (especially if the CGT remains the biggest) they will be in a position to manipulate or sabotage the economy as they try to do in Britain from time to time, and this could be dangerous; but that day is still a long way off, and for the moment it is union weakness rather than union strength that in part prevents an easier labour climate in France. Whether the unions accept collaboration with the Government in applying its 'participation' schemes will depend largely on how the Government handles them, and whether they feel they have been properly consulted. Precedents are not encouraging: in 1967, the Government made some minor and necessary economies in the social services which were greeted by the unions and the Left as a ghastly scandal, largely because the Government imposed them tactlessly without proper consultation. The unions felt, and were, humiliated. Here, as with its handling of students and teachers, the new Government will be on trial, and much of the future of France will depend on it. There are signs that, if approached tactfully, the CFDT and FO might be interested in helping to work out some kind of *co-gestion*, and although the CGT will probably say no initially, it might later feel obliged to take part rather than face isolation. An FO leader told me in July, 'If the Government wants to deal with the workers' elected representatives, we shall study its proposals constructively; but we shall oppose any measures that appear to be aimed at neutralising or buying off the working class in the interests of capitalism.'

The role of the *cadres* was crucial during the strike, and a good augury for the future. In many firms they fought side-by-side with the workers, breaking down some of the hierarchic barriers that have divided them in the past. Each has gained a clearer understanding of the other's problems, and this might help towards the weakening of class divisions in France. For this was not essentially or exclusively a working-class strike like some

previous ones in France—the Communist-led strikes of 1947–48 for
instance. It was a strike against a pattern of authority which colours relations at the top of a firm as well as those much lower down, and even
within the unions themselves. One F O union leader, an engineer, told me:
'It is ourselves we need to reform, as much as the firms. In France, there is
little tradition of joint decision by discussion. Even in a trade union, what
normally happens is that the president presents a project, the delegates
vote for or against it, maybe suggesting some amendments, but it has not
been elaborated *à la base*. When I was recently elected head of my branch
of the F O, I started trying to change this. I divided people into work groups
and asked them to draw up their own projects; I also tried to modify the
hierarchy and to fight against people's innate tendency to regard me over-
deferentially as "Monsieur le Sécrétaire-Général". At first, people thought
I was "soft", nor did they know how to set about working because they'd
not been given any *ligne directrice*. But now I'm making a little progress.
Of course, it's the education system that's largely to blame for this French
attitude to authority and the lack of empirical approach to discussion and
decision-taking.'

The Patronat's insistence on the need to maintain business efficiency is
understandable, for France is entering a phase of increased international
competition while her industry is still far from fully modernised. And
unless there is an anti-capitalist revolution throughout the western
world—which is unthinkable—or unless France herself withdraws from
the capitalist fold—which is barely less inconceivable—then labour reform
must take place without prejudice to the firms' competitiveness, or the
workers will suffer in the long run along with everyone else. In fact, a
reorganisation of structures and methods of work could increase efficiency
and output at the same time that it gives the workers a much fairer deal;
but this demands a goodwill on all sides of which the French might not
be capable. In the meantime, the economy has obviously taken a knock
from the crisis in the short term. It is a knock from which however I think
it will recover: it endured worse crises, of a different kind, in the 1950s.
There has even been a tendency for both Government and Patronat to
exaggerate deliberately the likely extent of the damage in order to 'rub
the strikers' noses in it.'

The combined effects of the new wage-bills and of the weeks lost through
the strike could mean a rise in prices of at least 6 or 7 per cent by the end
of the year and an expansion rate for 1968 of about 3 per cent compared
with the 5.5 per cent forecast before May, but returning probably to 5 per
cent in 1969. The Government reacted to the crisis by imposing emergency
restrictions to combat the flight of capital and the drain on reserves,
estimated at about 10,000m francs between mid-May and early July. This
is a heavy drain, but France can just about afford it owing to the large gold
and other reserves built up since 1958. More serious are the problems of
unemployment, inflation, and a likely drop in productive investment. Un-

employment was already at about 400,000, a relatively high figure for France, at the moment of the crisis, and might well reach 600,000 by the end of the year and possibly more in 1969, due largely to attempts by firms to economise on labour in order to pay the new wage bills, and to the fact that many small firms may be pushed out of business altogether. The Government has promised to meet the unions again in March, 1969, to reconsider wages and other questions, and it risks renewed trouble if prices and the unemployment figure rise fast during the winter. It will therefore do all in its power to limit these rises; but it also faces a contrary obligation, to dissuade firms from trying to economise through cuts in their investment, for French industry is still badly equipped compared with Germany's and now risks falling further behind especially with the final removal of Common Market tariffs. Profit margins of most firms were already perilously small by American or German standards, leaving little room for manoeuvre in a situation such as this one. To meet these various demands, a budget deficit of some 10,000m francs is likely—less, it is pointed out, than in some years of the Fourth Republic.

The crucial issue is whether France decides to meet its economic crisis by measures of restriction and austerity, or by a bold expansionsim involving risks. By mid-July, most measures taken had been *ad hoc* ones to check immediate threats, and the Government had not yet revealed any longer-term policy. But unless there *is* expansionism, a danger exists of some return to the protectionist attitudes that proved so disastrous in pre-Common Market days. Given a certain courage, however, it is even possible that some of the longer-term effects of the crisis could be beneficial for the economy. It could hasten the process of modernisation by pushing smaller, less efficient firms into bankruptcy and by forcing firms to improve their methods of production and deployment of resources in order to meet the new costs. This happened successfully in Holland a few years ago, after a similar sudden increase in wages.

It is probably too much to hope that de Gaulle, even with his new-found concern for domestic affairs, will help to ease the burden on the economy by accepting any large-scale cuts in defence, especially in the nuclear programme. Conversely, it would be a grave pity if the Government *did* try to economise by making large cuts in budgets for services such as low-cost housing, hospitals, telephones, and motorways, which need all the money they can get. In fact, I think the national frustration that reached explosion-point in May was due in part, whether consciously or not, to the way in which these services have been allowed to lag behind the growth of private prosperity, thus making life so uncomfortable. Little direct mention was made of the housing shortage during the crisis; but it played its part for it, too, is responsible for the worker's 'alienation', and he would accept the drawbacks of his job more easily if he had decent transport and a decent home to come back to. But housing, at least, is no longer the 'national problem number one': since May it has been far eclipsed in urgency and gravity by another.

Education:

The most astonishing aspect of the May crisis is the new visage it has uncovered of French youth. We thought them docile and conformist, or frivolously *yé-yé*; we knew that a number were serious and idealistic, but most of these were frustrated by a sense of impotence and felt isolated not only from society but from each other (see pp. 347–353). Among those who felt this isolation, and this impotence, were the little group that met around Cohn-Bendit at Nanterre on March 22. Two months later, half the nation was at their side. It needed only this detonator, the Sorbonne revolt of May 3, for French youth to come out of its reserve and discover a solidarity and a force that were always latent but never before expressed. Across France, young people who for years had been nourishing certain hopes, certain feelings, became aware of each other for the first time. This was genuinely a kind of revolution, and French youth and French society will never be quite the same again.

But this is not to say that all French youth, or even a majority of it, shares the views of Cohn-Bendit and Jacques Sauvageot. The small extremist element in the revolt rallied wide sympathy for a while because of its daring and because of the stupid police repression against it; but in itself, it contained many unpleasant and negative aspects of nihilism, violence and irresponsibility. I met many serious students in Paris who at first were delighted by the seizure of the Sorbonne and the outburst of free debate, but later felt that the whole thing had turned sour. This is not very surprising; but if some of the revolutionaries went too far and spoilt their own cause, it does not invalidate the importance of the nation-wide movement as a whole. Youth rose up not only against the archaic and muddled education system but also against its own parents, their paternalism, and their strange mixture of over-indulgence and sheer lack of understanding. Family crises broke out 'on a scale the nation has not seen since Dreyfus,' as one paterfamilias put it. This breach in traditional French parent-child relations carries many dangers, as does any new vacuum; it also carries hope. Exactly as in industry, much will depend on how 'les chefs de famille' react.

The education system, too, has been torn apart, and cannot be patched together into the same shape as before. Whereas the Fouchet reforms touched on exams and cycles of study, now there will have to be a much more profound overhaul of methods of teaching, student-teacher relations, centralised bureaucracy, and so on—the fundamental and difficult problems, structural and psychological, that the Fouchet reforms barely tackled. But the crisis has left behind it such chaos that the application of any new measures will be harder than ever—like trying to rebuild a city that is still suffering from epidemic and incendiarism. While the factories in June went quietly back to work, the educational world was still seething, having witnessed amazing scenes that none could have believed possible in this staid milieu. Not to mention the barricades and the burning cars, there was the spectacle of the 'desanctified' Sorbonne like a cathedral in the hands of joyous pagans, with red flags and Maoist slogans stuck all over the venerable statues of the gods of French culture, Molière and others. In colleges and faculties throughout France, the same thing happened. Professors and students who in the past had hardly exchanged a word sat around in groups in sunlit courtyards discussing their joint future, or created special assemblies to declare their universities 'autonomous' in defiance of Paris. In the academic world, this was 1789. There was also the spectacle in July of *agrégatifs* committing professional hara-kiri by refusing to sit for their *agrégation* rather than compromise with the hated 'system'.

Even more surprising than the university revolt was what happened in the *lycées*, among schoolchildren, usually so quiet and orderly. A national action committee of *lycéens* (CAL) proved every bit as militant as the students. Teachers no longer dared sit at their rostra, but either fled their classrooms, or, the more liberal of them, sat for hours each day on the benches beside their striking pupils, discussing school, politics, sex, careers, life. 'I never knew my girls before, except as minds; now I know them as people,' one young woman teacher told me. *Lycéens* suddenly discovered in themselves a political and social awareness that before had been barely latent; and although many reacted stupidly, some showed a remarkable maturity. Parents, invited to take part in the *lycée* debates, were in some cases astonished to hear thoughtful and persuasive public orations from their own sons and daughters—how the babies had grown up! Other parents, worried above all that the *bac* might not take place and a precious career be jeopardised, sometimes hit back brutally. 'When some parents entered the *lycées*, we teachers had physically to prevent them from setting on their children and beating them up,' I was told in one school. Finally the *bac* did take place, in a sort of way, and the holidays began. Some *lycéens* went off quietly to the seaside with their parents, but others, filled with a new fire, embarked on strange projects—I met several, one of them only fifteen, who planned to spend the summer touring round France spreading the gospel to peasants and workers, just like the Bolsheviks after 1917! My favourite anecdote comes from a girls' *lycée* in Paris at the moment of its 'liberation' by a crowd of male invaders from a nearby boys' *lycée*: the main foyer was filled with excited schoolboys calling the girls out on strike, and in their midst was the Directrice, a tiny, round, elderly figure, totally bewildered, clutching at the jacket of a *lycéen* leader, a wild 'hippie' figure towering above her, and imploring him desperately, 'Mais non, Monsieur, je ne refuse *pas* le dialogue! Je ne le refuse pas!'

Let us hope she means what she says. It was the hostility and conservatism of the teachers that blocked some of the positive aspects of the Fouchet reforms, and reforms needed today will not succeed unless a majority of the teachers is prepared to accept them. Certainly, the crisis will have helped to change their attitudes. In many cases, it has broken the barriers of formality and aloofness that existed between students and even many of the more liberal teachers; it was as if each were afraid to make contact with the other, and now crash, bang, the contact has been forced upon them. Everywhere, pupils and professors have been discussing their problems together. But of course, there has also been a back-lash. Many professors, especially the older ones, denounced the strikes, dug their heels in, and are now struggling to redress the situation. What is even more dangerous is that many of the liberal reformist professors, who had been patiently trying for years to persuade their colleagues of the need for change, have now been abruptly *depassés sur leur gauche* by the more extremist student leaders who condemn them as 'softies'. It is the dilemma of any revolutionary situation: the liberals are squeezed in the centre. But as passions subside, it is possible that the more moderate approach will gain ground again. And it will be the task of the Government to find the right 'interlocuteurs valables' among these elements.

In every college and university, during the crisis and just after it students and teachers set about drawing up projects for reform. Millions of words were written, thousands of resolutions were passed, much of it wild and woolly verbiage; but, as the eminent educationalist Jean Capelle told me in July, 'If only one per cent of it is of any value, that will be an immense success.' Certain themes recurred in these projects: *co-gestion*, autonomy, reform of exams and curricula, and of teaching methods, especially the *cours magistrale*. The idea of *co-gestion*, whereby like workers in industry students would have a say in the running of affairs, has already been enshrined *de facto* in *commissions paritaires* in most institutions: committees created by the students and teachers themselves with equal representation for both. They do not yet have any official status, but the Government might find them hard to abolish and could usefully build on them. It is recognised—except by the more extremist students—that there are some matters, essentially academic and financial ones, that should be left to the teachers and executives; but there is a wide move for giving the students much more regular voice in such questions as the shaping of curricula, study methods, and career orientations.

Autonomy is an even more important problem. At the height of the crisis, de Gaulle himself intimated that individual universities would now be given more freedom and that constricting Napoleonic centralisation would be modified. Various unofficial projects are in the air, for a national federation of universities, for giving the universities organic links with their regions, even for abolishing the Ministry of Education. There seems to be wide agreement that, even if the finance still comes from Paris, the universities should have far more individual control over how they spend their funds and how they direct their studies and methods of selection. Linked with this is a movement, led by men like Capelle, to break down the 'ivory tower' tradition of French universities and put them into closer touch with local life. Some practical progress had already been made here, notably at Nancy and Grenoble (see pp. 124, 336), but it is slight by Anglo-Saxon standards. Why not, suggests Capelle, put professors on the boards of local industrial firms and *vice versa*? But teacher opposition to this trend is still very strong.

Projects for reform of studies and exams revolve round the students' desire, shared by many younger teachers, to do away with the didactic *cours magistrale* and the formal dissertation, and to have more group study and seminars. Fine: but where is the money to come from, short of a much more rigorous system of university entrance which the students likewise oppose and on which teachers are still very divided? There is also a move to modernise and liberalise studies such as psychology and sociology which are very badly taught in France. One younger professor told me, 'We should like to see far more interdisciplinary penetration, as you now have in Britain—but that's still taboo in France.'

In July the Ministry of Education began to send 'quaestors' around France to collect these projects, to study them, and possibly to use them as a basis for its own proposals. As I write, the Government has revealed its own intentions much less clearly here than in some other fields, such as industrial or regional reform. It is true these problems are more intractable and need more thought; but they are also more pressing. The Government faces not only the continued wariness of most teachers, as it did in the Fouchet period, but also a much more militant student opposition than before. The extreme Left-wing students represent only a small minority of the total, but they are influential because of the leading part they played in the revolt, and they want to go much farther than the Government or any teacher body. They seem deliberately to have overlooked many issues, and their policies have many contradictions. They want to abolish exams, but they have not suggested what should be put in their place to ensure that merit and hard work are fairly assessed. They want wide and easy entrance to universities, but do not say where the money will come from when student numbers swell to a million. They are indignant about lack of suitable career outlets and lack of vocational training; they also want the university to be 'une finalité culturelle' that does not worry itself with practical ends. Many of them are quite simply set on anti-capitalist revolution at all costs, and would probably boycott any reforms.

The problem for the Government therefore is to try to isolate this minority, and the diehards among professors, by appealing to the rest of the students and the more moderate teachers. I repeat: this will require more tact than any Gaullist Ministry has shown hitherto. The appointment of Edgar Faure as the new Minister of Education is possibly a hopeful sign; for although he is no great reformist, he is a skilful politician with more horse-sense than many of the younger Gaullist technocrats; and his particular qualities may be more important in the academic world than they were in his previous post, as Minister of Agriculture (see page 97). Several liberal teachers told me, 'We shall accept no imposed solution. But if the Government plays fair with us, we shall try to help.' And this dialogue is having to take place at a time of acute physical crisis, when the faculties will be flooded with those who never took their exams in the summer, and when passions and divisions are still acute after the revolt. But *now or never* is the opportunity to tear French education once and for all from its encrusted feudal encasements and reshape it to the needs of a modern society, a technological society but also a human and a just one. Something *will* happen. In education, more than anywhere, people are saying, 'I am deeply pessimistic about the short term, but for the longer term I now have new hope.'

Television:

There are two other domains where the Government will be on trial for its good intentions and for its promise 'not to abuse its victory'. One is regionalism, the other is television. In television, the strike of producers and journalists at first aroused hopes that the ORTF might now at long last gain some real autonomy and a chance of objectivity; but by the morrow of the elections those hopes had seriously receded. As I have related (pp. 420–430), resentment had been building up during the 1960s among the majority of the ORTF's staff. And the general strike in May gave them a cue for a showdown. At first the Government's clumsy handling of TV coverage of the Sorbonne riots played into their hands. It refused to let the ORTF screen any account of the first days of the riots, although the Press and commercial radio stations mentioned little else. This so angered the staff that on May 14 they forced an ultimatum on their bosses and won: they were allowed to put out a special programme including an interview with Cohn-Bendit. Soon after, when Gaullist power appeared to be crumbling, the staff staged a virtual *putsch* and for a few glorious days found themselves able to say what they liked on their screens. It did not last long. Even in their enfeebled state, the Gaullists would not permit the TV centres to be 'occupied' like the Sorbonne or the Renault works. TV was too crucial: the police or army would soon have been moved in. Rather than risk this and so lose all, the staff chose to strike, and for a month there was virtually no television in France. The producers and journalists tried to bargain with the Government for the assurance of a new autonomous statute for the ORTF, and *Le Monde* wrote that their strike 'could have even more influence on the future of French democracy than the much wider protest movements in industry and education.'

At first the Government gave signs it might yield, but from mid-June it toughened its attitude and began to take reprisals against the strikers. Their regular programmes—including nearly all the good current affairs programmes on French TV—were suspended 'indefinitely' and many producers on short-term contracts were virtually dismissed. Rumours began to circulate that the Government intended to purge the ORTF of all of its troublesome 'star' personalities (most of them non-Gaullists) and to install permanently a safe mediocrity. According to another rumour, it planned to solve the malignant problems of the ORTF by destroying it: entertainment material would be provided by free-lance companies on a commercial basis, while the Government would keep a small news and current affairs unit under its own tight control. As I write, nothing is clear. There probably *will* be a new statute of sorts (this has been promised) and

it may include a greater degree of financial autonomy for the O RT F which
at least might solve some of the problems of its bureaucracy. But there is
still little sign that the Gaullists will be any more prepared to sacrifice their
control of T V as a propaganda medium. The strike was a heroic bid for
liberty, but it seems to have failed.

Regionalism:

Although in broadcasting there seems little prospect of any waning of
étatisme, in another equally important field de Gaulle now appears to be
ready to sacrifice some Government sovereignty. Even before the crisis, in
a key speech at Lyon in March, he sketched out an idea that has now come
to the forefront: regional assemblies, locally elected, with their own local
finances and certain sovereign powers. This project, if it ever sees the light
of day, could be revolutionary for France and the first major blow in 150
years at the Napoleonic heritage of centralisation (see pp. 165–177). De
Gaulle, according to those close to him, has finally been converted to the
belief that Jacobinism is at the root of many of France's present ills, and he
wants to act fast.

The likely composition of the assemblies is not yet clear: there will
probably be direct suffrage, possibly on a collegiate rather than a party
basis—that is, with so many seats reserved for trade unionists, so many for
chambers of commerce, and so on. A new local tax will have to be created.
For some local matters, the assemblies will be entirely responsible; for
others, they will share responsibility with the Government, which will
provide the funds and lay down broad policies but leave their application
to the area involved. Over other matters, the State will retain full control.
It is thought that a number of questions that at present have to be referred
to the Ministries in Paris—the building of schools or hospitals, for instance,
or the designation of Z U P's and Z A D's—might be transferred to these assemblies. The reform might also provide a framework for university
decentralisation, by the creation of organic links between the assemblies and
the universities. Each Region would have its Prefect, who would be
responsible both to Paris and to the assembly; he would not necessarily
be drawn from the prefectoral corps. Finally, the reform would tie in with
another already before Parliament: a new Bill that provides financial
incentives to speed up the regrouping of communes into larger and more
economically efficient units.

All this may appear utopian, and there are plenty who oppose it both
within and without the Government. Some fear that if the regions became
too powerful they would threaten the unity of France. For this reason,
about twenty-one regions are likely to remain, as at present, rather than
seven or eight as has sometimes been urged for economic reasons. Other
people fear that the project would aggravate the unbalance between rich
and poor regions. This problem can probably be checked only by a careful
system of Government financing. Others wonder if de Gaulle can actually
mean such a drastic reform. Will the Government ever really dare to let so

much power out of its hands? After all the pressures have been brought to bear, after all the texts have been drafted and redrafted, will the assemblies turn out to be any more than 'CODERs améliorées' (as someone has said) and, like them, a clever piece of window-dressing? We shall have to see. On paper, this reform seems the most important of all those now planned in France; it could transform the social and political life of the nation.

Those who are close to de Gaulle report that the crisis has stirred in him a greater interest than ever before in domestic affairs, which in recent years he had so much neglected in favour of his foreign ambitions. Not all his planned reforms may be entirely realistic: he is a bit of an old-fashioned romantic, and his views on, for instance, profit-sharing, show how far out-of-touch he can be with the real desires of the people. But at least he seems to have recovered a certain radicalism, and with his huge majority he is in a position to use the votes of the Right to apply a Left-wing policy, exactly as he did over Algeria.

The crisis may therefore have supplied Gaullist reformism with a second wind which it had so obviously failed to find in the mid-1960s. Whether it will also have learned a new style is, for the moment, more doubtful. The departure of Pompidou suggests that de Gaulle will not brook any Right-wing opposition to his reforms, within his own ranks; but Couve de Murville, although he will obey de Gaulle's commands to the letter, is not a very sympathetic figure and lacks either the authority or the personal touch to give Gaullism the new image it badly needs. There are many different trends within the Government and the party, and although reformism is again à la mode it is not, alas, incompatible with arrogance. Plenty of Gaullists already believe that the huge election victory is a plebiscite to apply new measures *their* way, without discussion. And some of the early signs around election time—the handling of the TV producers on strike, the way in which university buildings were closed to the students—did not augur well. But unless the Gaullists can discover a new style, their best-intentioned reforms will be null and void and a new uprising may not be long delayed.

Finally, it seems to me that this crisis has renewed and intensified the debate among the French as to what kind of society they want to live in. And this is a positive sign. At the end of the preceding chapter, written before the crisis, I suggested that the French were becoming excitedly aware of the issues facing technological society, but that many of them, especially the young, also felt a kind of malaise at the by-products of this society. How to combine efficiency with social justice, how to modernise without losing one's soul: these are issues for many countries besides France, but the French look at them with particular intensity, and they are issues that will outlive de Gaulle. They were the issues of the May crisis, which many Frenchmen described as essentially a 'cultural revolution' rather than a social or economic one. New ideas have been bubbling to the surface in France this year. New thoughts are emerging on the role of culture and the individual in an age of science. Once again the French, who in recent years seem to have lost some of their old creative originality, might now be showing that with their imagination and sensibility they have something of their own to offer to the great argument of our times. So long, as D. H. Lawrence said in another context, as it doesn't all fizzle out in talk—or in pointless violence.

Paris and London, July 1968   J. A.

BIBLIOGRAPHY

GENERAL

J.-B. Duroselle, François Goguel, Stanley Hoffmann, Charles Kindleberger, Jesse Pitts, Laurence Wylie: *France: Change and Tradition* (Harvard University Press and Gollancz, 1963)

Janet Flanner: *Paris Journal, 1944–65* (Atheneum, 1965)

Herbert Lüthy: *France Against Herself* (Praeger, 1955)

François Nourissier: *Les Français* (Rencontres, 1967)

J.-F. Revel: *En France* (Julliard, 1965)

Alfred Sauvy: *La Montée des Jeunes* (Calmann-Lévy, 1960)

David Schoenbrun: *As France Goes* (Harper & Row, 1957)

J.-J. Servan-Schreiber: *The American Challenge* (Atheneum, 1968)

Pierre Sudreau: *l'Enchaînement* (Plon, 1967)

La France d'Aujourd'hui (31 contributors: Hatier, 1964)

Réflexions pour 1985 (preface by Pierre Massé: La Documentation Française, 1964)

ECONOMY AND INDUSTRY

François Bloch-Lainé: *Pour une Réforme de l'Entreprise* (Editions du Seuil, 1963)

David Granick: *The European Executive* (Doubleday, 1962)

Gilles Guérithault: *Guide Pratique de l'Automobile* (Arthaud, annual)

Jacques Guyard: *Le Miracle Français* (Editions du Seuil, 1965)

French Planning: Some Lessons for Britain (PEP, 1963)

AGRICULTURE

Michel Debatisse: *La Révolution Silencieuse* (Calmann-Lévy, 1963)

Michel Gervais, Claude Servolin, Jean Weil: *Une France sans Paysans* (Editions du Seuil, 1965)

Serge Mallet: *Les Paysans contre le Passé* (Editions du Seuil, 1962)

Henri Mendras: *Sociologie de la Campagne Française* (Presses Universitaires de France, 1965)

Henri Mendras: *La Fin des Paysans* (SEDEIS, 1967)

François de Virieu: *La Fin d'une Agriculture* (Calmann-Lévy, 1967)
Gordon Wright: *Rural Revolution in France* (Oxford University Press, 1964)

COMMERCE

Etienne Thil: *Combat pour la Distribution* (Arthaud, 1964)

PROVINCES

Pierre Bonte: *Bonjour, Monsieur le Maire* (La Table Ronde, 1965)
Raymond Dugrand: *Villes et Campagnes en Bas-Languedoc* (Presses Universitaires de France, 1963)
J.-F. Gravier: *Paris et le Désert Français* (Flammarion, 1958)
Olivier Guichard: *Aménager en France* (Laffont, 1965)
Paul and Germain Veyret: *Grenoble et ses Alpes* (Arthaud, 1962)

PARIS

Alain Griotteray: *L'Etat contre Paris* (Hachette, 1962)
Peter Hall: *The World Cities* (McGraw-Hill, 1966)

HOUSING

Gilles Anouil: *Les Secrets du Logement* (Editions Modernes, 1961)
Marc Bernard: *Sarcellopolis* (Flammarion, 1964)
Gilbert Mathieu: *Peut-on Loger les Français?* (Editions du Seuil, 1965)
Christiane Rochefort: *Les Petits Enfants du Siècle* (Grasset, 1961)

SOCIETY

Michel Crozier: *The Bureaucratic Phenomenon* (University of Chicago Press, 1964)
Pierre Laroque: *Les Classes Sociales* (Presses Universitaires du France, 1965)
Serge Mallet: *La Nouvelle Classe Ouvrière* (Editions du Seuil, 1963)
Laurence Wylie: *Village in the Vaucluse* (Houghton Mifflin, 1961)
Simone de Beauvoir: *The Second Sex* (Knopf, 1953)
Madeleine Chapsal: *Vérités sur les Jeunes Filles* (Grasset, 1960)
Ménie Grégoire: *Le Métier de Femme* (Plon, 1965)
Jacques Remy and Robert Woog: *La Française et l'Amour* (Laffont, 1960)
La Française Aujourd'hui, edited by Lucie Faure (*La Nef*, Oct.–Dec. 1960)
Pierre Simon: *La Contrôle des Naissances* (Payot, 1967)
Georges Perec: *Les Choses* (Julliard, 1965)
Pierre Daninos: *Snobissimo* (Hachette, 1964)
Etiemble: *Parlez-vous Franglais?* (Gallimard, 1964)
Joffre Dumazedier: *Vers une Civilisation du Loisir?* (Editions du Seuil, 1962)
Paul-Marie de la Gorge: *La France Pauvre* (Grasset, 1965)

EDUCATION, YOUTH

W. D. Halls: *Society, Schools and Progress in France* (Pergamon, 1965)
Martin Mayer: *The Schools* (Harper & Row, 1961)
André Rouède: *Le Lycée Impossible* (Editions du Seuil, 1967)
John Weightman: *The Sorbonne* (article in *Encounter*, June 1961)
Jacques Duquesne: *Les 16–24 Ans* (Le Centurion, 1963)
Françoise Sagan: *Bonjour Tristesse* (Dutton, 1955)

INTELLECTUALS, LITERATURE, RELIGION

Roland Barthes: *Critique et Vérité* (Editions du Seuil, 1966)
Maurice Cranston: *Jean-Paul Sartre* (article in *Encounter*, April 1962)
Maurice Cranston: *Sartre's Commitment* (article in *Encounter*, August 1964)
Michel Crozier: *La Révolution Culturelle* (pamphlet, 1964)
Michel Foucault: *Les Mots et les Choses* (Gallimard, 1966)
J.-F. Revel: *Pourquoi des Philosophes?* (Julliard, 1957)
J.-F. Revel: *La Cabale des Dévots* (Julliard, 1962)
Michel Butor: *Thoughts on the Novel* (article in *Encounter*, June 1963)
Bruce Morrisette: *Les Romans de Robbe-Grillet* (Editions de Minuit, 1963)
Maurice Nadeau: *Le Roman Français depuis la Guerre* (Gallimard, 1963)
John Weightman: *Alain Robbe-Grillet* (article in *Encounter*, March 1962)
Adrien Dansette: *Le Destin du Catholicisme Français* (Flammarion, 1965)
Michel de Saint-Pierre: *Les Nouveaux Prêtres* (La Table Ronde, 1964)
Réflexion Chrétienne et Monde Moderne, 1945–65 (published by le Centre Catholique des Intellectuels Français, 1966)

ARTS

Roy Armes: *French Cinema since 1946* (2 vols.: A. S. Barnes, 1966)
Jean Collet: *Jean-Luc Godard* (Seghers, 1963)
Penelope Houston: *The Contemporary Cinema* (Penguin, 1963)
Georges Sadoul: *Histoire du Cinéma Mondial* (Flammarion, 1959)
Situation du Cinéma Français (*Esprit*, June 1960)

I should also like to acknowledge my debt to *Le Monde* and its staff correspondents. Without the help of their regular coverage of French problems, I should have found this book difficult to write.

J.A.

CHRONOLOGICAL TABLE
OF EVENTS IN FRANCE, IMPORTANT OR
LESS IMPORTANT, SINCE THE WAR

Politics and Finance	*Other Events*

1945

7 MAY: Victory in Europe

21 OCT.: first General Election since the War, for the formation of a Constituent Assembly

21 OCT.: women vote for the first time in France in national politics

OCT.: renewal of the 1939 Code de la Famille, and extension of family allowances

OCT.: Sartre publishes *L'Existialisme est un Humanisme*, at the height of the existentialist movement

1946

3 JAN.: official birth of the 'Plan'

20 JAN.: General de Gaulle resigns

2 JUNE: General Election

19 SEPT.: Churchill in Zurich calls for a 'United States of Europe'

13 OCT.: the Fourth Republic's Constitution is approved by referendum

4 DEC.: official birth of the Fourth Republic

26 APRIL: nationalisation of the coal mines

1947

16 JAN.: Vincent Auriol is elected the first President of the Fourth Republic

MAY: revolt in Madagascar suppressed

5 JUNE: George Marshall, Secretary of State, proposes a new policy of American aid for Europe

NOV.: Communist-led strikes

JULY: Albert Camus publishes *La Peste*

13 NOV.: André Gide wins the Nobel Prize for literature

1948

26 JAN.: the franc is devalued by 80 per cent

APRIL: Marshall Aid begins

OCT./NOV.: Communist-led strikes, defeated by Jules Moch, Minister of the Interior

20 FEB.: Génissiat hydro-electric dam inaugurated

MAY: André Malraux publishes *Le Musée Imaginaire*

1 SEPT.: new law allows progressive unfreezing of old rents, and completely frees new rents

OCT.: Citroën brings out the '2 CV'

1949

4 APRIL: signing of the North Atlantic Treaty

MAY: Council of Europe founded, in Strasbourg

DEC. Edouard Leclerc opens his first shop, in Landerneau

— Simone de Beauvoir publishes *Le Deuxième Sexe*

1950

30 MAR.: death of Léon Blum

9 MAY: the French Government proposes a European coal and steel community on the initiative of Robert Schuman, Foreign Minister

SUMMER: Gérard Blitz founds the Club Méditerranée

1951

18 APRIL: official birth of the European Coal and Steel Community

18 JUNE: General Election: René Pleven becomes Prime Minister

16 AUG.: death of Louis Jouvet

SEPT.: Jean Vilar becomes director of the Théâtre Nationale Populaire

1952

25 FEB.: Paris becomes the headquarters of NATO

6 MAR.: Antoine Pinay becomes Prime Minister: he devalues the franc, launches a campaign against inflation

AUG.: split between Sartre and Camus

14 OCT.: le Corbusier's 'Cité Radieuse' inaugurated at Marseille

25 OCT.: opening of the Donzère-Mondragon hydro-electric dam

— Roger Planchon opens his theatre at Villeurbanne

1953

21 MAY TO 26 JUNE: longest and gravest Ministerial crisis of the Fourth Republic, following the fall of René Mayer's government

6–25 AUG.: France paralysed by strikes of railwaymen, etc.

23 DEC.: René Coty elected President of the Republic, after 13 ballots

FEB: première in Paris of Samuel Beckett's *En Attendant Godot*

29 APRIL: Henri-Georges Clouzot's *Le Salaire de la Peur* wins the Grand Prix at the Cannes Film Festival

9 AUG.: the Laniel Government reaffirms the law forbidding refusal of sale in the retail trade: victory for Edouard Leclerc

AUG.: Vinegrowers' riots in the Hérault

1954

7 MAY: fall of Dien Bien Phu, after two months' siege

18 JUNE: Pierre Mendès-France becomes Prime Minister, undertakes to resolve the Indo-China problem by 20 July

20 JULY: agreement at Geneva over Indo-China: end of the war

30 AUG.: European Defence Community treaty rejected by the National Assembly

1 NOV.: beginning of the war in Algeria: uprising in the Aurès mountains

25 JAN.: suspension of the worker-priests' movement, on Vatican orders

MAY: Françoise Sagan's first novel, *Bonjour Tristesse*, wins the Prix des Critiques

10 NOV.: Mendès-France launches his anti-alcoholism campaign

1955

5 FEB.: fall of the Mendès-France Government; Edgar Faure then becomes Prime Minister

9 MAY: West Germany becomes sovereign

3 JUNE: signing of agreements giving internal autonomy to Tunisia

20, 21 AUG.: grave disturbances in Morocco and Algeria: 768 dead

23 OCT.: the Saar votes against its European statute, and in favour of a return to Germany

16 NOV.: Sultan Sidi ben Youssef is restored to Morocco, after his Madagascan exile

6 DEC.: fall of the Edgar Faure Government

10 APRIL: death of Pierre Teilhard de Chardin

27 MAY: first experimental flight of the Caravelle, at Toulouse

MAY: Alain Robbe-Grillet's *Le Voyeur* wins the Prix des Critiques

16 SEPT.: signature of the first Conventions Collectives, at Renault (signature in the mines, 28 Dec.)

OCT.: Citroën brings out the 'DS'

1956

2 JAN.: General Election: zenith of the Poujadist movement, which wins 51 seats

1 FEB.: Guy Mollet becomes Prime Minister

6 FEB.: Guy Mollet visits Algiers, is rough-housed by the settlers

2 MAR.: France recognises independence of Morocco

20 MAR.: France recognises independence of Tunisia

20 JUNE: the 'Defferre Law' extends internal autonomy to French Africa

26 JULY: Nasser nationalises the Suez Canal

29 FEB.: new law grants third week of paid holidays

MAR.: Dr. Weill-Hallé founds the French family planning movement

MAR.: Renault brings out the Dauphine

JUNE: Albert Camus publishes *La Chute*

SUMMER: Roger Vadim and Brigitte Bardot film *Et Dieu Créa la Femme* at St. Tropez

22 OCT.: Ben Bella and four other FLN leaders captured by the French in Algeria

5 NOV.: Abortive invasion of Suez by Anglo-French forces; suppression of the Hungarian uprising

1957

25 MAR.: signature of the *Treaty of Rome*

21 MAY: fall of the Mollet Government

29 MAY: 300 Muslims massacred at Melouza, Algeria, by the FLN

11 AUG.: 'partial devaluation' of the franc by 20 per cent

8–11 APRIL: State visit of Queen Elizabeth to France

17 OCT.: Albert Camus wins the Nobel Prize for literature

OCT.: the Government abolishes the 'entrée en sixième' school examination

OCT.: Prof. B. Schwartz reforms the Ecole des Mines, at Nancy

2 DEC.: Roger Vailland's *La Loi* wins the Prix Goncourt; Michel Butor's *La Modification* wins the Prix Renaudot

DEC.: André Malraux publishes *La Métamorphose des Dieux*

1958

8 FEB.: Sakiet, in Tunisia, bombarded by the French: Franco-Tunisian crisis breaks out.

16 APRIL: fall of the Gaillard Government

13 MAY: *Insurrection in Algiers, led by the Army and settlers*

16 MAY: de Gaulle demands his return to power

1 JUNE: *National Assembly votes General de Gaulle's return to power*

28 SEPT.: Referendum on the Fifth Republic's Constitution; 'Yes' vote attains almost 80 per cent

23, 30 NOV.: General Election: crushing victory for the Gaullists

21 DEC.: General de Gaulle elected President of the Republic

27 DEC.: Pinay/Rueff financial reforms: franc devalued by 17·5 per cent

APRIL: work starts on La Défense project, Paris

OCT.: première in Paris of Marcel Carné's *Les Tricheurs*

NOV.: opening of the new UNESCO building

31 DEC.: new decrees on the creation of ZUPs and ZADs, and compulsory cleaning of house-façades

— anti-pornography laws intensified

1959

1 JAN.: first round of the tariff cuts under the Common Market

8 JAN.: Michel Debré becomes Prime Minister

16 SEPT.: de Gaulle offers self-determination to Algeria

MAR.: première of Claude Chabrol's *Le Beau Serge*

12 MAY: Air France puts the first Caravelles in service

15 MAY: the 'new wave' triumphs at the Cannes Festival: Truffaut's *Les 400*

13 DEC.: France accepts the independence of the Mali Federation

Coups and Resnais' *Hiroshima Mon Amour* win prizes; Truffaut publicly challenges the old wave

25 JULY: official opening of the Pont de Tancarville

1 OCT.: Jean-Louis Barrault becomes director of the Théâtre de France

19 OCT.: *Salut les Copains*, launched by Daniel Filipacchi during the summer, becomes a daily programme on Europe Number One

16 NOV.: André Schwarz-Bart's *Le Dernier des Justes* wins the Prix Goncourt

17 NOV.: Edouard Leclerc opens his first centre in the Paris region, at Issy.

25 NOV.: death of Gérard Philipe

30 DEC.: new law increases State aid to private schools

— opening of the Champs-Elysées Drugstore

1960

1 JAN.: introduction of the New Franc

24 JAN.: the 'barricades uprising' in Algiers, led by the settlers

13 FEB.: France explodes her first atomic bomb, in the Sahara

23 MAR. TO 3 APRIL: N. Krushchev's State visit to France

5–8 APRIL: General de Gaulle's State visit to London

SEPT.: publication of the Rueff–Armand report

4 JAN.: death of Albert Camus

11 FEB.: grave agricultural riots at Amiens

MAY: the agricultural 'orientation law' adopted by Parliament

SEPT.: the Government revises the national health service, and foils the doctors' opposition

OCT.: Marcel Bonvalet founds the Institut des Sciences de l'Ingénieur, at Nancy

NOV.: new decree limits the privileges of the home distillers

— première of Jean-Luc Godard's *A Bout de Souffle*

1961

8 JAN.: referendum in France on self-determination in Algeria: victory for de Gaulle

21 APRIL: the 'Generals' Putsch' in Algiers, led by Maurice Challe

17 OCT.: fighting in Paris between Algerian Muslims and French police: at least 60 Algerians killed

8 JUNE: the Brittany 'artichoke war': Morlaix sub-prefecture seized by the farmers

JUNE: opening of the first family-planning clinc, at Grenoble

JUNE: work begins on cleaning façades of public buildings, in Paris

AUG.: Edgard Pisani succeeds M. Rochereau as Minister of Agriculture: approval of the 'complementary law'

2 AUG.: creation of the 'District' of the Paris Region

DEC.: miners' strike at Decazeville

1962

18 MAR.: signature of the Evian agreement: *end of the Algerian war*

15 APRIL: Georges Pompidou becomes Prime Minister

20 APRIL: Raoul Salan arrested in Algiers

1 JULY: Algeria votes for independence: official end of the French occupation

2–9 SEPT.: de Gaulle's triumphant tour of West Germany

28 OCT.: referendum on the presidential election system: adoption of the principle of universal suffrage

18, 25 NOV.: General Election: new Gaullist victory

19 JAN.: maiden voyage of the liner *France*, launched at St. Nazaire

FEB.: the Government-owned Sofirad company extends its control over Europe Number One

3 MAY: *The Times Literary Supplement* attacks French 'clarity' and French intellectuals

15 JUNE: *Salut les Copains*, already a broadcast, becomes a magazine

1963

14 JAN.: de Gaulle declares Great Britain not yet ready to enter the Common Market

29 JAN.: France breaks off the Brussels talks on Great Britain and the Common Market

MAR.: miners' strike

12 SEPT.: Valéry Giscard d'Estaing launches his Stabilisation Plan

22 NOV.: assassination of President Kennedy

APRIL: opening of Caen Maison de la Culture

APRIL: Jack Lang founds the international student drama festival, at Nancy

18 JUNE: launching of the Languedoc tourist project

22 JUNE: Parisian teenagers' 'Nuit de la Nation', led by *Salut les Copains*

3 AUG.: Collèges d'Enseignement Général instituted by decree

11 OCT.: Jean Cocteau and Edith Piaf die on the same day

OCT.: première of Louis Malle's *Le Feu Follet*

NOV.: Simone de Beauvoir publishes *La Force des Choses*

NOV.: J.-M.-G. le Clézio's novel *Le Procès-Verbal* wins the Prix Renaudot

NOV.: launching of J.-C. Averty's TV programme, *Les Raisins Verts*

— Chrysler acquires control of Simca

— the Paris municipal council finally decides on the transfer of Les Halles to Rungis

1964

27 JAN.: France recognises Communist China

6 FEB.: Franco-British agreement on building a Channel tunnel

1, 2 FEB.: the Goetschel sisters win the first two places in the Slalom, in the Winter Olympics at Innsbruck

FEB.: student demonstrations at the

21 SEPT. TO 10 OCT.: General de Gaulle's tour of South America

30 OCT.: Franco-Soviet commercial agreement

1 NOV.: Common Market regulations on meat and dairy products come into force

Sorbonne, during President Segni's visit to Paris

FEB.: Etiemble publishes *Parlez-vous Franglais?*

14 MAR.: regional and prefectoral reforms; creation of the CODERs

18 APRIL: ORTF launches the second TV network

18 APRIL: A. Malraux inaugurates the Maison de la Culture, Bourges

26 MAY: Moselle Canal opened

MAY: dispute between J.-P. Sartre and Claude Simon over 'la littérature engagée'

12 JUNE: National Assembly adopts the reform of the Paris Region (creation of new *départements*)

19 JUNE: Eric Tabarly wins the transatlantic sailing race, aboard *Pen Duick II*

11 JULY: opening of Libby's factory at Vauvert (Gard)

14 JULY: Jacques Anquetil wins the Tour de France for the fifth time

22 JULY: new statute for the ORTF; Claude Contamine becomes director of TV

23 JULY: agreement between Bull and General Electric after a year of crisis

SEPT.: *l'Express* changes its format

22 OCT.: Nobel Prize for literature to J.-P. Sartre, who refuses it

OCT.: France takes eleventh place in the Olympic Games, Tokyo

1965

14, 21 MAR.: municipal elections: rise of a 'new wave' of young mayors, led by Hubert Dubedout at Grenoble

25 JUNE: Gaston Defferre withdraws as candidate for the Presidential election

JULY–AUG.: André Malraux's State visit to China

29 OCT.: Mehdi ben Barka kidnapped in Paris

6 NOV.: Parliament adopts the Fifth Plan

5 DEC.: Presidential Election, first round: de Gaulle fails to win outright majority

19 DEC.: second round: de Gaulle 55 per cent, Mitterand 44 per cent

19 JAN.: the Patronat publishes its doctrinal manifesto

FEB.: première of Agnès Varda's *Le Bonheur*

13 APRIL: wedding of Johnny Hallyday and Sylvie Vartan

APRIL: première of Jean-Luc Godard's *Alphaville*

APRIL: Mgr. Veuillot disciplines the Jeunesse Etudiante Chrétienne

18 MAY: the Patronat expels from its board the leaders of the Centre des Jeunes Patrons

19 MAY: reforms of the Baccalauréat announced

JUNE: Schéma Directeur for the Paris Region published

16 JULY: opening of the Mont Blanc Tunnel

28 AUG.: death of Le Corbusier

SEPT.: opening of the Bus Palladium, in Montmartre

14 OCT.: France wins her first Nobel Prizes for science since the War: medicine prizes for three French doctors

23 OCT.: the Episcopate, with Vatican agreement, authorises the resumption of the worker-priest movement

OCT.: opening of the Drugstore St.-Germain

21 OCT.: creation of a State oil consortium (ERAP), directed by Pierre Guillaumat

14 NOV.: Dean Zamansky demands that science students at the Sorbonne be preselected

26 NOV.: first French space satellite set in orbit

NOV.: première of Godard's *Pierrot Le Fou*

23 DEC.: Parliament adopts new Law on the extension of the Taxe sur la Valeur Ajoutée

— fourth week of paid holidays becomes law

1966

8 JAN.: Michel Debré succeeds Valéry Giscard d'Estaing as Minister of Finance; Edgard Pisani becomes Minister of Equipment and Edgar Faure Minister of Agriculture

10 JAN.: agreement between CGT and CFDT on joint union action

30 JAN.: after six months of crisis in the Common Market, compromise solution on the EEC's supranational powers

10 MAR.: France announces her decision to withdraw from NATO

11 MAY: the Six agree on final plans for an agricultural Common Market

17 MAY: general strike

20 JUNE TO 1 JULY: General de Gaulle's triumphant visit to Moscow

2 JULY: explosion of the first French hydrogen bomb

25 AUG. TO 12 SEPT.: General de Gaulle's voyage around the world

23 FEB.: merger between Lorraine-Escaut and Usinor (steelworks)

24 FEB.: university reforms announced by Christian Fouchet

MAR.: J.-M.-G. le Clézio publishes *Le Déluge*

MAR.: the Episcopate's manifesto criticises the Patronat and its doctrine of profit

1 APRIL: banning of the film *La Religieuse*

22 APRIL: Renault/Peugeot association announced

APRIL: première of Jean Genet's *Les Paravents* at the Théâtre de France

4 MAY: merger of BNCI and CNEP to create the Banque Nationale de Paris

MAY: Claude Lelouch's film *Un Homme et Une Femme* wins the Grand Prix at the Cannes Festival

20 DEC.: electoral agreement between the Communists and the Left-wing Federation

25 DEC.: ex-General Maurice Challe freed and amnestied

MAY: Pierre Boulez decides to boycott French musical life

MAY/JUNE: crisis over 'Paris Deux', which becomes 'Parly Deux'.

9 JUNE: decison to create four 'urban communities' (Bordeaux, Lille, Lyon, Strasbourg)

JUNE: Michel Foucault publishes *Les Mots et les Choses*

JULY: France does badly in the World Football Cup at Wembley

3 NOV.: Prof. Kastler wins the Nobel Prize for physics

26 NOV.: inauguration of the Rance tidal dam.

21 DEC.: Mgr. Veuillot succeeds Cardinal Feltin as Archbishop of Paris

1967

1 JAN.: Common Market regulations for fruit and vegetables come into force

30 JAN.: France frees her gold market, and lifts most of her exchange restrictions

5, 12 MAR.: General Election: Gaullist majority reduced to 3 seats

MAR.: labour unrest: strikes at Borliet and elsewhere

14 MAR.: NATO forces leave France

26 APRIL: the Government decides to ask Parliament for special powers to act by decree in social and economic matters; E. Pisani resigns in protest

17 MAY: general strike, in protest against the special powers

21 JUNE: de Gaulle condemns Israel for 'opening hostilities' against the Arab Powers

1 JULY: Common Market regulations for cereals come into force

24 JULY: de Gaulle in Montreal proclaims 'Vive le Québec libre!'

6–12 SEPT.: State visit of de Gaulle to Poland

18 NOV.: the franc does not follow the 14·3 per cent devaluation of the £

27 NOV.: de Gaulle finally rejects Britain's new bid to join the Common Market

3 FEB.: decision to raise minimum school-leaving age from 14 to 15 in October

22 MAR.: ban on *La Religieuse* lifted

MAR.: vinegrowers riot in the Midi

MAY: cuts in Social Security benefits announced

26 JUNE: agricultural riots in Brittany: 80 wounded at Redon

27 JULY: Citroën assumes control of Berliet

JULY: the Rothschild merchant bank becomes a deposit bank

1 OCT.: colour TV starts (on 2nd network)

2 OCT.: grave agricultural riots at Quimper: 280 injured

OCT.: Jean-Jacques Servan-Schreiber publishes *Le Défi Américain*

DEC.: Parliament approves Lucien Neuwirth's Bill legalising contraception

1968

3 MAY: first riots at the Sorbonne: beginning of the May Crisis

26 MAY: Grenelle labour agreements at height of the general strike: Government concedes big wage increases

30 MAY: Peak of the crisis: de Gaulle announces he will not resign, dissolves National Assembly

23, 30 JUNE: General Election: huge Gaullist victory

1 JULY: lowering of final Common Market tariffs

10 JULY: M. Couve de Murville succeeds G. Pompidou as Prime Minister

6–19 FEB.: Winter Olympic Games, Grenoble

14 FEB.: death of Cardinal Veuillot

INDEX

(Principal page-references are in italics. Book-, play- and film-titles are not indexed: see under name of author or director)

abortion, 253–4
Action Française, 380, 384
Adamo, Salvatore, 342
Adamov, Arthur, 418
advertising, 1, 12, 228–30, 264, 429
Agfa-Gevaert, 40
agrégation, 327–8, 330, 335, 362, 364, 471
Agriculture, Ministry of, 190, 444
Aillaud, 215
Air France, 18, 62, 153, 188, 292
Aix-en-Provence, 162, 418
alcoholism, 4, 136, *301–4*
Alfa-Romeo, 297
Algeria, 65; War, xiv, 16, 43, 102, 121, 175, 202, 267, 329, 350, 362n, 377, 384, 399, 405, 430–2, 442, 448, 454, 476; return of settlers, 5, 16, *140–1,* 142, 206, 278, 337; oil, 51–2; wine, 89–90
American economic challenge, *38–40,* 58–60, 61–2, 63–4, 93–5, 290, *459–61*
Americanisation, 11, 32, 109, *228–9,* 264–5, 276, 280, 398–9, 453, *458–61*
Amiens, 73, 129, 148, 156, 159, 323, 377
Anouilh, Jean, 418, 419
Anselme, Daniel, 377
Antier, Paul, 70
Antoine, 344
Antonioni, M., 370, 414

Antony, Richard, 342
Aragon, Louis, 200, 403
architecture, 188–90, 210, 214–15
aristocracy, *233–4,* 239
Armand, Louis, 19, 38, 44, 47–8, 121, 166, 174, 333, 389, 437, 457
Army, the, 233, 450
Aron, Raymond, 328, 361
art, 320, 419
Arts, 165, 182n
Astruc, Alexandre, 393, 395
Auclair, Marcelle, 263
Audiberti, Jacques, 418, 425
Auger, Mlle, 225
Autant-Lara, Claude, 256, 393
Auto-Journal guide, 276
Averty, J. C., 241, 426
Aveyron, 77–83, 143–5
Avignon, 416–17

baccalauréat, 309, *312–15,* 320, 325, 471
Bagnols-sur-Cèze, *223–5,* 239
Balkany, Robert de, 229–230
Balzac, Honoré de, 367, 369, 376–7
Bank of France, 18
banking, 36
Barbara, 359
Bardot, Brigitte, 340, 341, 342, 344, 393, 412
Barets, Jean, 210
Baroncelli, Jean de, 392, 431

Barrault, Jean-Louis, 417, 419
Barrès, Maurice, 147
Barthes, Roland, 158, 360, 370, 379
Bazin, André, 400
BBC, 421, 423–6
Beauvoir, Simone de, 244, 245, 357–9, 363, 367–8, 376
Bécaud, Gilbert, 342
Becker, Jacques, 393
Beckett, Samuel, 158, 367, 375, 418
Beeching, Dr., 47, 48
Belières, M., 82
Belmondo, J.-P., 403, 406
Bendor, island of, 292–3
Bercot, Pierre, 57
Bergman, Ingmar, 431
Berliet, 58, 152
Bernard, Marc, 213, 225, 227
Berrurier, Raymond, 184, 438
Besançon, 162
Betjeman, John, 227
Béziers, 136, 137, 153
Biasini, Emile, 430
Bidault, Georges, 15, 380
bidonvilles, 304
Billetdoux, François, 417, 419
birth-rate, rise in, *3–5,* 117, 240–1, 256
Blanchot, Maurice, 368
Blitz, Gérard, 283, 284, 287, 289–91
Bloch-Lainé, Marcel, 34
Bodard, Mag, 397
Bon Marché, le, 105

Bongrand, Louis, 264
Bonvalet, Marcel, *336–8*, 444
Bordeaux, 141, *145*, 153, 173
Borel, Jacques (writer), 240
Borel, Jacques (caterer), 274, 280
bouilleurs de cru, 302–3, 346
Boulez, Pierre, 420
Boulloche, André, 333–4
Boulogne-sur-Mer, 409
Bourdet, Edouard, 417
Bourges, *158*, 160
Bourges, Yvon, 431
Bourget, le, 182
Bourse, la, 36
Bourseiller, Antoine, 418
Brague, la, 291–2
Brassens, Georges, 359
Bray, Barbara, 386
Bresson, Robert, 379, 389, 393, 396, 407
Brest, 103, 104, 129, 133, 134, 149
Breton, André, 367
Briançon, 321
Brittany, 73–4, 95, 100–5, *131–5*, 161, 303
Brook, Peter, 396, 397
Bruel, Marcel, 75, 86
Buchwald, Art, 196
Bull, 32, 37, 39, 63–4, 465
Bundy, Otto, 94
Bus Palladium, 346
Butlin's, 282, 284, 286, 290
Butor, Michel, 368, *372*, 374, 376, 377, 378

Caen, 121, *128–30*, 131, 157–8, 159, 160, 164, 166, 172, 173, 322, 323, 332
café life, 140, 200, 221, *269–70*, 302, 356
Cahiers du Cinéma, 394, 400, 403, 410
Caisse des Dépôts, 216; *see also* SCIC
camping, 281–2, 291
Camus, Albert, 314, 320, 340, 350, 359, 368, 418, 460
Camus (builder), 210
Canacos, M., 216
Canard Enchaîné, le, 420, 433
Candilis, Georges, 138,

142, 214, 224
Cannes film festival, 394, 431
Capitant, René, 465, 466
Capelle, Jean, 472
Capte, la, 291
car ownership, 55, 261, *296–7*
Caravelle, 20, 37, *61–2*, 63, 66
Cardonnel, Père, 382, 384–6
Carné, Marcel, 340–1, 392
Caron, Christine, 294
Carrefour, 107, 108, 110
Carroll, Lewis, 369
Caterpillar, 125
Catholicism, 246, 248, 255, 256, 257, 343, 423, 430–1, 443; and education, 308, *381–2*; neo-Catholic movement, 33, 70–1, 355, 365, *379–90*, 444; links with Marxists, 222, *385–6*
Caumont, Robert de, *129–131*, 169, 170, 172, 444, 445
Cayrol, Jean, 409
Cazes, Marcellin, 144
CECA, *see* European Coal and Steel Community
Cefalù, 284, *285–8*, 289
CELIB, 133, 134
Céline, L.-F., 367, 432
censorship, 413, *430–3*
centralisation, dangers of, 88, 114–16, 148–53, 165, 166–74, 331–2, 472, 475
Centre des Jeunes Patrons, 28, 29, *32–5*, 383
Centre National des Jeunes Agriculteurs, 72–3
Cévennes, 136, 137, 139, 144
Chaban-Delmas, Jacques, 142, *145*
Chabrol, Claude, 394, 396, *400–1*
Channel Tunnel, 19, 46
Chanzeaux, 236–7
Char, René, 378
Charles-Roux, Edmonde, 264
chauvinism, see foreigners
chemists' shops, 110
Chenu, Père, 389
Chrysler, 39, 58
Church, *see* Catholicism

Citroën, 54–5, *57–9*, 129, 132, 149, 184, 297, 466
Clair, René, 392, 394, 412, 414
class barriers, 7, 75–6, 225, *230–9*, 241, 260, 288–9, 294, *309–10*, 315, 384, 467
Claudel, Paul, 362, 389
Clément, René, 230, 393, 398, 414
Clézio, J.-M.-G. le, 165, *375*, 377, 378, 461
clochards, 304–5
Clouzot, H.-G., 393, 414
Club Jean Moulin, 365, 383, 445–7
Club Méditerranée, 138, *283–91*, 449, 463
coal-mines, 49
Cocteau, Jean, 392, 394, 414
Code de la Famille, 4, 298
Cohn-Bendit, Daniel, 463, 470, 474
Collange, Christiane, 244
Collèges d'Enseignement Secondaire, 309–10, 311, 315
Colpi, Henri, 408
Colson, René, 71
Columbia Films, 398
Comédie Française, 416–17
comités d'entreprise, 33–4, 238, 466
Commissariat à l'Energie Atomique, 53, 224
Commissariat Général au Plan, *see* Plan
Commissions du Développement Economique Régional, *170–1*, 174, 184
Common Market, 7, 15, 16, *25–8*, 30, 35, 38, 40, 41, 52, 65, 107, 110, 180, 299, 328, 349, 398, 435, 437, 451, 469; in agriculture, 85, 87, 88, *90–92*, 97; and the Regions, 133–4, 142, 149
communes, 130, *166–74*, 179, 184–5, 217–18, 226, 475
Communists, 24, 140, 171–2, 216, 222, 237, 256, 380–1, 385–6, 422
Compagnie Française des Pétroles, 51
Compagnie Générale de

Télégraphie Sans Fil (CSF), 63–4, 134, 149
Compagnie Générale Transatlantique, 64
Concorde (aircraft), 7, 61–63
Confédération Française Démocratique du Travail, 24, 34, 42, 383, 466, 467
Confédération Générale du Travail, 24, 34, 42, 383, 466, 467
Congar, Père, 389
Conseil d'Etat, 439, 442
conseils généraux, 120–1, 126, 167, 170, 174
Constantine, Eddie, 405
consumer protection, 111–112
Contamine, Claude, 421, 424, 426, 430
conventions collectives, 33, 56
Corbusier, le, 138, 187, 188, 210, 214
Corfu, 284, 285, 287, 288
Corriere della Sera, 456
Cossé-Brissac, Comte de, 237
Côte d'Azur, 227, 281, 291–3, 448
Courrèges, 229
couture, 263
Cranston, Maurice, 358
Crédit Lyonnais, 151
crisis, May 1968, xiii, 462–4, 466, 469–76
Crozier, Michel, 8, 238, 282, 361, 365–6, 374, 434, 440, 443, 445
cumulards, 96

Daily Mirror, 267
Daladier, Jean, 201
d'Arcy, Jean, 421
Dassault, Marcel, 63, 428
Dasté, Jean, 160, 162, 417
Dauphiné Libéré, le 163–4
Debatisse, Michel, 71–2, 74, 75, 80, 82, 94, 95, 96–7, 383
Debré, Michel, 17, 36, 41, 44, 73, 102, 171, 235, 422
Decaë, Henri, 414
Decazeville, 144, 149
Défense, La (Paris), 183, 187–8, 208
Defferre, Gaston, 145, 423

Deguy, Michel, 363, 374
Delorozoy, Hubert, 106, 108
Delouvrier, Paul, 22, 180–183, 184, 230, 438
demography, see birthrate
Demolins, Edmond, 318
Demonque, Marcel, 34, 467
Demy, Jacques, 395, 398–399, 400, 412–13
Dépêche du Midi, la, 164
Desgraupes, Pierre, 426
design, 262, 458
Diderot, 431
District de Paris, 180, 183–6
divorce, 242
doctorat, 327
doctors, 256–7, 300–1
Domenach, J.-M., 382–3, 385–6, 389
Dorgères, Henri, 69, 70
Douassot, Jean, 368
Dreyfus, Pierre, 20, 56, 59, 60, 470
Drieu la Rochelle, 411
drinks, 261, 303
drugstores, 11, 200, 229–230, 262, 265, 278, 460
Dubedout, Hubert, 126–7, 172, 386, 444, 447, 464
Dugrand, Raymond, 139, 386
Dumayet, Pierre, 426
Dumazedier, Joffre, 265
Dunkirk, 54
Duras, Marguerite, 240, 373, 379, 396, 403, 409, 417, 418
Dutourd, Jean, 99

East Europe, links with, 453–4
Ecoles des Mines, 49; at Nancy, 336
Ecole Nationale d'Administration, 19, 129, 168, 336, 440
Ecole Normale Supérieure, 201, 334–5
Ecole Polytechnique, 19, 201, 323, 332–8
Economic and Social Council, 22, 72
education, 307–38, 468, 470–4; budget for, 43, 308; Ministry of, 124, 163, 169, 295, 307–38 passim, 427, 438, 472,

473; artistic, 320; sexual, 248, 258; technical, 315, 326; for farmers, 71, 81; and Church, 308, 381–2; and TV, 427; school holidays, 266–7, 295
Electricité de France, 23, 24, 37, 49–50, 53, 171, 190, 436
electronics industry, 63–4
Elle, 244, 251, 252, 256, 263–4, 297
Eluard, Paul, 378
Elysée Deux, 229, 235
Encounter, 358, 371, 377
Entreprise de Recherches et d'Activités Pétrolières, 52
Erval, François, 375
Escarpit, Robert, 374, 377
Espalion, 82
Esprit, 382–3, 386, 389
Essel, André, 109, 111–12
Esso, 188
Etaix, Pierre, 412, 460
étatisme, see State control
Etiemble, 264, 458
Euratom, 19, 53
Europe, idealism towards, 26, 40–1, 121, 174, 349, 350–1, 437, 450–1
Europe Number One, 342, 427–9
European Centre for Nuclear Studies, 38
European Coal and Steel Community, 26
European Economic Commission, see Common Market
European Journal, 423
existentialism, 340, 349, 355–60, 461
Express, l', 11, 218, 238, 243, 244, 264, 281, 282, 341, 365, 394, 408, 415, 459

Facel Vega, 55
Falaise, 29, 130
family, influence of, 32, 71, 234–5 239–41, 245, 282, 299, 347–8, 349
family allowances, 4, 241, 298–9
Faulkner, William, 373, 455
Faure, Edgar, 97, 473
Fédération Nationale des Achats des Cadres,

111–112, 113
Fédération Nationale des Syndicats des Exploitants Agricoles, 70, 72–5, 77, 84
Feltin, Cardinal, 380, 384, 387
Fiat, 58, 59, 60
Figaro, le, 227, 328, 433
Filipacchi, Daniel, 342–5
Finance, Ministry of, 24, 76, 101, 111, 167, 192, 209, 424
Fitzgerald, Scott, 283, 292
Flaubert, Gustave, 366, 376
Flaux, Roger de, 94–5
food, 261, *271–81,* 285–6, 427
force de frappe, 43, 53, 435–6, 446
Force Ouvrière, 34, 466, 467
Ford III, Henry, 59
foreigners, attitudes to, 277–8, 282, 350–1, 450–5
formality, 246, 271, 440–443, 448–50
Formidable, 343
Forster, Peter, 441, 444
Fortune magazine, 28
Foucault, Michel, 360
Fouchet, Christian, 308, 314, 327, 336; Fouchet reforms, 308, 325–6, 332, 333, 334, 436, 470, 471, 473
Fouquet's, 194, 200, 277
Fourth Republic, the, 15, 70, 89, 155, 180, 191, 350, 356, 432, 445, 447, 463, 469
Fraissinet, 65
France (liner), 7, 64
François, Claude, 342
franglais, 11, 228–9, 264, 274, 458–9
Franju, Georges, 394, 411
Fréville, Henri, *131–3,* 161, 226
furniture, 31, 262

Gabin, Jean, 96, 97, 400
Galeries Lafayette, 105
Gall, France, 342
Gallimard, 432
gambling, 269
Garaudy, Roger, 386
gas, natural, 50–1
Gaulle, Charles de, 5, 15–

17, 20, 21, 24, 25, 34, 39, 51, 57, 121, 126, 143, 155–6 181, 209, 235, 242–3, 250, 255, 297, 343, 382, 422, 427, 453; influence on home affairs, xiii, 6–7, 8, *43–5,* 53, 66, 150, 152, 191, 196, 430–3, *435–6,* 445–7, 456; untypical of France, xiii, 350, 405–6, 450, 469, 472, 475–6
Gaulle, Yvonne de, 243, 255, 256, 430, 432
Gaullism, 6–7, 34, 41, 130–1, 139, 159, 163, 169, 171–2, 184, 249, 316, 326, 361, 383, 422–4, 459, 462–4, 473–6
Galt, Henri, 279
General Electric, 39
General Motors, 59, 60
Genet, Jean, 289, 366–7, 375, 417, 418, 432, 433
Gerlier, Cardinal, 380, 384
Germany, friendship with, 28, 147, *452;* economic rivalry with, 4, 26, 59, 65, 259
Gide, André, 311
Gignoux, Hubert, 160, 417
Gingembre, Léon, 30–1, 106, 108
Giono, Jean, 368
Girodias, Maurice, 432–3
Giroud, Françoise, 241, 252, 408
Giscard d'Estaing, Valéry, 17, 36, 41, 333
Godard, Jean-Luc, 18, 49, 190, 220n, 249, 351, 379, 391, 394, 395, 398, 400, *402–8,* 410, 414, 431, 434, 453, 460
Godin, Abbé, 380
Goitschel sisters, 294
Gombrowicz, Witold, 418
Goncourt, Prix, 368, 375, 376
Gordon-Lazareff, Hélène, 244, 264
Goubert, Georges, *161*
Gourvennec, Alexis, 73–4, 87, 134, 351
Gramont TV, 129
Granger, Nicole, 351
Granick, David, 32

Gravier, J.-F., 88, 118–19, 121, 169
Great Britain, attitudes to, 134, *452–3;* rivalry with, 12, 60, 259
Great War, the, 4, 141, 205, 253, 431
Greco, Juliette, 356
Grégoire, Ménie, 245, 256
Grenoble, 38, 46, 101, 117, 120, *122–8,* 129, 130, 131, 142, 148, 159, 163–4, 173, 254, 280, 293, 323, 330–1, 336, 386, 449, 464, 472
Grobel, Pierre, 281
Guichard, Olivier, 120
Guillaumat, Pierre, 20, 52, 333

Habitations à Loyer Modéré, *206–8,* 210, 211, 218, 219–21, 226, 228, 405
Haedens, Kleber, 364
Hall, Peter (urbanist), 177
Halles, Les (Paris), 84, 88–9, 187, *192,* 436
Hallyday, Johnny, 339, *342–5,* 461
Hardy, Françoise, 339, 342–4, 461
Hatinguais, Mme, 311
Haussmann, Baron, 116, 177, 193
Haute Ecole Commerciale, 109
Havre, le, 130, 159, 172, 319, 355
Health, Ministry of, 255, 422
health service, 300–1
Héreil, Georges, 20, 58, *61–2*
Hirsch, Etienne, 22, 24
Hitchcock, Alfred, 394, 400
holidays, 265–6, *281–93,* *294–6*
Holman, Edward, 130–1
hospitality, 270–1
Houston, Penelope, 402
Humanité-Dimanche, l', 238
Huvelin, Paul, 33n
hygiene, 261, 263

IBM, 39, 64, 139, 148, 285

Ile-de-France, 226–7
Imbs, Paul, 352
immigrants, 304, 454
incomes policy, 42
Information, Ministry of, 405, 421, 430–1
Institut Français de l'Opinion Publique, 247n, 248, 317, 348, 455
Institut des Hautes Etudes Cinématographiques, 395n, 426
Institut des Sciences de l'Ingénieur, 336–8
Ionesco, Eugène, 417, 418
Iraqi oil, 52

Jaeger, 130
Jarry, Alfred, 416
Jazy, Michel, 294
Jessua, Alain, 412
Jeunesse Agricole Chrétienne J A C 70–2, 77, 78, 80, 172, 339, 379, 380, 382–3
Jeunesse Etudiante Chrétienne, 378–8
Jews, 455
Joliot-Curie, Fréderic, 53
Joxe, Louis, 20
Joyce, James, 367, 374, 455
Julliard guide, 276, 277, 279

Kafka, Franz, 369
Karina, Anna, 404–7
Kennedy Round, 35, 92
Kidel, Boris, 218
Killy, J.-C., 294
Kindleberger, C., 14, 23
Korène, Vera, 416
Kubrick, Stanley, 431

labour relations, 33–5, 42, 56, 129, 144, 238, 275, 464–8
Lacombe, Raymond, 78–79, 80–1, 86
Lacq, 50–1, 223, 461
Lafarge, 34, 467
Laffont, François, 142–3
Lambert, Bernard, 75–6, 95, 237
Lamour, Philippe, 120, 121, 134, 136, 137, 174, 444
land ownership, 75–7, 96–97, 153, 207–10, 436
Landerneau, 100, 102,

104; Co-operative de, 95
Landry, Adolphe, 4
Lang, Jack, 147, 165, 351
Languedoc, 90, 135–41, 153, 209
Laniel, Joseph, 89, 101
Laurent, Jacques, 351
Laurent, Jacques (writer), 433
Lebesque, Morvan, 420
Lecanuet, Jean, 209, 422
Leclerc, Edouard, 100–5, 106, 107, 109, 110, 111, 112, 113, 123, 283, 340, 383, 405, 444
Lecotteley, Jean, 328–9
Leduc, Violette, 376
Lee, Jennie, 156, 157
Lefaucheux, Pierre, 55
legalism, 440–3
Lelouch, Claude, 395, 402, 413, 415
Léon, Marcel, 73
Lettres Françaises, les, 364
Lévi-Strauss, Claude, 360, 361, 379
Levitt and Sons, 228
Lévy, Raoul, 393
Libby's, 39, 93–5, 96, 137, 459
Liénart, Cardinal, 380, 384
Lille, 146, 153, 164, 173, 384
Limoges, 46, 122
Lindon, Jérôme, 432
Lipp, café, 144, 200
living, standards of, 259–261
living, cost of, 259
Locomotive, la, 346
Lorenzi, Stellio, 424, 425
Lorient, 133, 134, 146
Lorraine, 146–7, 152
Losey, Joseph, 414
Louvel, M., 130, 172
Lubac, Père de, 389
Lurçat, Jean, 419
Lüthy, Herbert, 3, 8, 15, 30, 210, 435, 457
lycées, 218, 224, 233, 239, 307, 309–15, 316–22, 324, 327, 334, 348, 372, 382; Henri IV, 319, 471
Lyon, 27, 28, 46, 123, 127, 146, 150, 151–2, 153, 160, 161–2, 173, 247,

274, 300, 331, 475
Lyons, Joseph, 274

Mademoiselle Age Tendre, 342
Maisons de la Culture, 119, 127, 130, 156–60, 161–2, 198, 216, 269, 418, 430, 436
Maisons des Jeunes, 347
Majorca, 283
Mallarmé, Stephane, 374
Malle, Louis, 394, 398–9, 411–12
Malraux, André, 155–6, 157, 159, 160, 161, 188, 190, 197–8, 350, 361, 392, 403, 416–17 419–20, 423, 430, 431, 438, 463–4
Marie-Claire, 244, 263–4
Marcoule, 223–4
Marjolin, Robert, 22
Marker, Chris, 408, 412, 414
marriage, 235, 241–2, 244, 249
Marseille, 140, 145–6, 150, 152, 162, 173, 208, 292
Marshall Aid, 14–15
Martin, Rector, 331
Maserati, 58, 297
Massé, Pierre, 20, 24, 41, 42, 129, 328, 333, 461
Massy-Antony, 217, 218 219, 221, 225, 448
Mathieu, Gilbert, 204, 211
Mattei, Enrico, 52
Mauriac, Claude, 373, 419
Mauriac, François, 145, 165, 235, 389, 411, 420
Maurras, Charles, 380, 388
Mayer, René, 15
Maziol, Jacques, 209
Méline, Jules, 69, 73
Mendès-France, Pierre, 121, 126, 301, 303, 455
Mendras, Henri, 236, 237
Merleau-Ponty, Maurice, 359
Merlin-Gérin, 123
Mesmin, Georges, 211
Mesnil-St. Denis, le, 184, 228
métayage, 75–6, 137
Metz, 146–7
Michallon, Albert, 127

Michaux, Henri, 378
Michelin tyre firm, 23, 32, 57, 152; guide, 275, 276–7
Milhau, Prof., 137
Ministry of, see relevant Ministry
Missoffe, François, 127
Mitterand, François, 256, 422
Mocky, J.-P., 248, 412
Mollet, Guy, 421, 430
Monde, le, 126, 151, 162, 164, 204, 212, 228, 230, 292, 357, 358, 392, 431, 433, 463, 474
Monde et la Vie, le, 388
Monnerville, Gaston de, 454
Monnet, Gabriel, 158, 444
Monnet, Jean, 6, 14, 17, 20–1, 22, 24, 26, 28, 30, 40, 41, 118, 437, 459
Monoprix, 102, 103, 105, 107
Mont Blanc tunnel, 7, 46, 152
Montand, Yves, 344
Montherlant, Henri de, 418
Montpellier, 135–41, 153, 309–10, 323, 324, 329, 382, 384–6
Moreau, Jeanne, 396, 412
Moreau, Marcel, 375
Morlaix, 73–4
Moselle canal, 54, 146, 152
motorways, see roads
Moulinex, 131
Mouly, Raymond, 344
Mounier, Emmanuel, 383, 389
Mourenx, 222–3, 225
Mouvement Français pour le Planning Familial, 254–8
Murville, Couve de, 466, 476
music, 162, 320, 419–20

Nairn, Ian, 214
Nancy, 146–7, 152, 165, 172, 173, 329, 330, 336–8, 351–2, 428, 452, 472
Nanterre, 182, 188, 418, 470
Nantes, 65, 104, 146, 147, 162, 412–13

Napoleonic laws, 4, 68, 115, 168, 239, 439, 442
National Assembly, 243, 256
national parks, 84
nationalisation, 18, 20, 48–49
Néel, Prof., 117, 123, 124
Néron, Claude, 375
Neuwirth, Lucien, 256–7
Neville, John, 158, 160
New Franc, the, 16, 230
'new novel', the, 368–76
New Society, 418
newspapers, see Press
Neyrpic, 123, 124
Nice, 145, 148, 154, 165, 208, 378
Nimes, 93–4, 136, 172, 317, 320
Nimier, Roger, 367
1940, defeat in, 3, 13
Nobel prizes, 38
Normandy, 128–31
Nouveau Candide, le, 364
Nouvel Observateur, le, 164, 220n, 230, 346, 365, 387, 403, 405n, 449
Nouvelle Revue Française, la, 377

Obaldia, René, 418
Observer, The, 214
Occupation, the (1940–1944), 3, 4, 5–6, 70, 117, 136, 175, 271, 340, 355, 368, 380, 455
O E C D, 259
Office de la Radio et Télévision Française, 163, 190, 421–30, 441, 474
oil industry, 51–2
old age, 299–300
Ollier, Claude, 373
Olympic Games, 126–7, 173, 224, 293–4
Onassis, Aristotle, 65
Opéra, the, 420
Ophüls, Max, 397
Organisation de l'Armée Secrète, 140, 405, 409
Orléans, 323
Orly airport, 7, 232, 254
Ormesson, Vladimir d', 430
Ortoli, François-Xavier, 20
Ouest-France, l', 163–4, 428

overseas aid, 44, 454
overseas service, 350, 454

Panhard, 54, 58
Papon, Maurice, 383
Pari Mutuel Urbain, 269
Paris, xiv, xv, 1, 86, 88–9, 105, 130, 144, 159, 175–202, 234, 263, 277–8, 300, 304, 323, 343, 405, 470, 472, 475; problems of living in, 202, 267, 271, 281, 295, 352, 402, 447–8; centralisation on 114–19, 148–53, 165, 364, 377–8; population of, 150, 178, 181; municipal council, 179, 186–7, 192, 230, ravalement des façades, 196–8, 209; transport and parking, 180, 182, 193–6, 218; Métro, 180, 182, 188, 195, 263; slums, 179, 191; Schéma Directeur, 181–6, 188, 217, 230, 436; P A D O G, 180–1; Champs-Elysées, 200; Halle aux Vins, 191; Ile St.-Louis, 199, 277; Marais, 190, 198–9; Montmartre, 201; Montparnasse, 188–9, 200–1; St. Germain-des-Près, 200, 277–8, 340–1, 355–6; see also Défense, District, les Halles
Paris Hilton Hotel, 189
Parisien Libéré, le, 163, 288
Paris-Match, 341, 342, 403, 433
Parly Deux (Paris Deux), 230, 236
Pasteur, Louis, 37, 136
Patronat Français, 26, 32–35, 39, 42, 56, 149, 258, 296, 384, 466, 468
Paul VI, Pope, 255, 381
Péchiney, 65, 124
pensions, 299
Perec, Georges, 460
Perse, Saint John, 378
Pétain, Philippe, 69, 334, 388
Petit, Claudius, 206
Petites et Moyennes Entreprises, 30–1, 33, 102,

106
Peugeot, 29, 32, 54–5, *58–60,* 297
Peyrefitte, Alain, 325
Pflimlin, Pierre, 267
Picard, Raymond, 360
pieds noirs, see Algeria, settlers
Pierrelatte, 53
Pinay, Antoine, 15, 16, 170, 171, 173
Pinget, Robert, 240, 373, 374, 418, 419
Pisani, Edgard, 7, 20, 74, 76, 78, 93, 95, 97, 151, 209, 210, 436, 444
Pitts, Jesse, 33, 241, 318
Pius XII, Pope, 380, 385
Plan, the, 6, 9, 14, 17, *20–5,* 26, 28, 36, *41–2,* 60, 69, 72, 81, 150, 154, 212, 243, 265, 333, 383, 446, 459, 461; and the regions, 118–19, 131, 138, 159, 170
Planchon, Roger, 160, *161–2,* 340, 417, 419
Pleven, René, 133, 170, 171
Point, M., 276
Polanski, Roman, 397
police, 442
Pompidou, Georges, 34, 41, 115, 134, 202, 210, 230, 333, 334, 335, 422, 423, 466, 476
Ponge, Francis, 378
Pont-à-Mousson, 152
pop movement, 342–6
Popular Front (1936–7), 18, 69, 85
Porché, Vladimir, 421
Postes, Télégraphes et Téléphones, *154–5,* 174
Pouillon, Fernand, 208
Poujade, Pierre, 30, 99, 102, 108; Poujadism, 30, 86, 106, 108, 356, 443
Pound, Ezra, 253
prefects, 115, 119, 125, 129, 139, *166–74,* 321, 475
Press, 190, *433;* provincial, 163–4, 474
Printemps, le, 99, 105, 263
Prisunic, 102, 105, 106, 107, 216
Privezac, 77–8
Profumo, John, 250

Progrès de Lyon, le, 164
Protestants, 385
Proust, Marcel, 233, 350, 367, 373, 378
Prouvost, Jean, 433
Purina, 93, 95, 96

Queneau, Raymond, 367, 368
Queuille, Henri, 15

Rabier, Jean, 414
Radio Luxembourg, 427, 428
Radio Monte-Carlo, 427, 428
Ragon, Michel, 182, 188
railways, *see* S N C F
Rance tidal dam, 49–50
Réalités, 268
regionalism, 474–5
regions, new, 118 (map), 119, *169–70,* 181, 183
Reims, 148, 323
remembrement, 77–8
Remington Rand, 39
Renaudot, Prix, 375, 376
Renault, 18, 20, 27, 29, 34, 37, *55–60,* 129, 149, 218, 237, 295, 474
Renault, Louis, 54, 55
Rennes, *131–3,* 134, 148, 159, 160, 161, 163, 215, 226, 325, 328
Renoir, Auguste, 178
Renoir, Jean, 293, 391, 392, 393, 394, 407
résidences secondaires, 267
Resistance, *see* Occupation
Resnais, Alain, 158, 370, 373, 379, 392, 394–7, 400, *408–10,* 414
restaurants, 273–80
Revel, J.-F., 251, 362–4, 374, 389, 434
Rhode, Eric, 408
Rhône-Poulenc, 38, 65
Ricard, Paul, 292, 303
Rivette, Jacques, 400, *402,431*
Riviera, *see* Côte d'Azur
roads, *153–4,* 182, 185, 187, 193, 438, 469; accidents, 296–7
Robbe-Grillet, Alain, 360, 366, *368–74,* 376–7, 378, 379, 392
Rochefort, Christiane, 219, 376
Rochereau, Henri, 74

Rodez, 78, *144,* 382
Roman Catholic, *see* Catholic
Ronet, Maurice, 406, 411
Rothschild Bank, 36, 202, 290
Rouch, Jean, 412, 414
Rouen, 159, 323
Roussin, André, 415
Royan, 458
Rueff, Jacques, 16, 19, 25, 44, 73, 333
Rueff-Armand report, 19, 44, 110, 195, 441, 442
Rumania, 137
Rungis market, 88, 192
rural exodus, 67, 68, 73, 78–80, 116, 133, 151, 236–7
Ruspoli, Mario, 412
Russia, relations with, 60, 453–4; White Russians, 278

Sagan, Françoise, 340, 341, 342, 359, 368, 391, 448
sailing, 293
St. Chamond, 173
St. Denis, 185
St. Etienne, 120, 160, 161, 162
St.-Exupéry, Antoine de, 63, 141, 350
St. Gobain, 65
St. Nazaire, 64, 65, 133, 146
St.-Pierre, Michel de, 388
St. Tropez, 291, *340–2*
Salut les Copains, 342–5, 428, 454
Sarcelles, *212–17, 218–222,* 225, 266, 279, 405
Sarraute, Nathalie, 368, 372–3
Sarrazin, Albertine, 375
Sarrazin, Maurice, 160
Sartre, Jean-Paul, 200, 314, 328, 335, 340, 350, *355–61,* 362–4, 365, 367–9, 376, 385, 392, 405, 418, 457, 460–1
Satre, Pierre, 62
Sauvageot, Jacques, 470
Sauvy, Alfred, 4
Schuman, Robert, 26
Schwartz, Prof., 336–8
Schwartz-Bart, André, 376
scientific research, *36–8,* 53, 64, 124, 335, 357

Seberg, Jean, 403
SECAM, colour TV system, 37, 63, 66, 429
Second World War, *see* Occupation, *and* Vichy
Segni, President, 322, 329
Semprun, Jorge, 410
Servan-Schreiber, J.-J., 459
Sète, 135, 139–40
sex, *246–52*, 253–4, 287
Sheila, 342
shipping industry, 64–5
Sicily, 285–8
Siesta, la, 291–2, 297
Siffre, Michel, 350
Sight and Sound, 403, 405n
Simca, 20, 39, 55, 58, 423
Simon, Claude, 358, 368, *373*, 377, 419
Simon, Dr. Pierre, 254
Simon, Pierre-Henri, 357
Sir Winston Churchill Pub, 200, 262, 278
skiing, 123, 124, *293–4*, 319
Slavik, 262, 277, 278
social security, *298–301*
social structures, 8, 10–11, 232, *439–45*, (*see also* class barriers)
Société Centrale Immobilière de la Caisse des Dépôts (SCIC), *216–217*, 218, 223
Société Nationale des Chemins-de-Fer Français, *47–8*, 152–3, 180, 183, 218
Société Nationale des Pétroles d'Acquitaine, 50–1, 223
Sociétés d'Aménagement Froncier et d'Etablissement Rural, 76–7, 82, 97, 174, 435
Sociétés d'Economie Mixte, 18, 88, 135, 138, 188, 217
Sociétés d'Intérêt Collectif Agricole, 86–9, 96, 174
Sofirad, 428, 429
Sollers, Philippe, 360, 373, 374
Son et Lumière, invention of, 209
Sorbonne, la, 116, 191, 201, 309, 322, 323, 325, 328, 329, 330, 331, 332,

338, 359, 360, 362, 364, 455, 470, 474
Soustelle, Jacques, 335
space research, 64
Spain, 283, 409–10
Spira, Françoise, 416
sport, 269–70, *293–4*, 319
State control (*étatisme*), *17–18*, 23, 35, 36, 42, 45, 66, 115, 120, 143, 159, 163, *166–74*, 179, 218, 316, 331–2, 421–430, 437–8, 475
steel industry, 26, 53–4, 146
Stendhal, 122
Strasbourg, 146, 160, 173
structuralism, *360–1*
students, *see* universities
Sud-Aviation, 20, *61–3*
Sudreau, Pierre, 7, 20, 44, 166, 197, *209*
Suffert, Georges, 238
Suhard, Cardinal, 380
Sumé, 131
Sunday Times, 441, 444
supermarkets, 99–100, 103, *106–7*, 110
système D, 441, 465, 471

Tabarly, Eric, 350
Tahiti, 284
Taizé, 385
Tancarville bridge, 46
Tati, Jacques, 262, 398
taxation, 23, 40, *109–10*, 154, 173–4, 210, 475
Taxe sur la Valeur Ajoutée, *109–10*, 436, 437
technocrats, *18–20*, 129, 139, 168, 353, 365
Teilhard de Chardin, Pierre, 9, 349–50, 382–383, 386, 388, *389–90*
Teindas, Georges, 348
Tel Quel, 374
Télé Luxembourg, 425, 428
Télé Monte-Carlo, 425, 428, 429
telephone shortage, 81, *154–5*, 438, 469
television, 64, 75, 80, 163, 164, 241, 256, 261, 270, 312, 337, 393, *420–30*, 474–5, 476
Témoignage Chrétien, 385
Temps Modernes, les, 361, 377

theatre, *415–20*, 432; in provinces, *160–2*, 417–418
Théâtre de l'Est Parisien, 418
Théâtre de France, 416–419
Théâtre National Populaire, 159, 416–18
Thiers, 31, 72
Thireau, Yann, 348
Times, The, xiii
Times Literary Supplement, The, 363–4, 374
Toulouse, 61, 62, 135, *141–3*, 153, 159, 160, 164, 171, 208, 323, 331
Tour de France, 293
Touring Club de France, 138
tourism, 137–9, 282–3, 295–6
Tours, 105, 173
trade unions, 24–5, 33–4, 42, 72, 238, 265–6, 464–9, 475
Trappes, 181, 184, 185
Treaty of Rome, 7, 26, 243, 437, (*see also* Common Market)
Tréhard, Jo, *157–8*, 159–160
Trigano, Gilbert, 283, 290
Troquat, M. le, 250
Troyat, Henri, 375
Truffaut, François, 317, 394, 395, 398, 400, *401–2*, 413, 415, 460
Trujillo, Bernard, 106, 107, 112, 459
Tunisia, 253, 337
Tynan, Kenneth, 391

unemployment, 42, 299, 463, 468
UNESCO, 190, 451
Union Nationale des Etudiants Français, 329, 330
United Artists, 398
United Europe, *see* Europe, idealism
universities, 243, 314, *322–32*, 334–5, 472, 473, 476; provincial, growth of, 119, 123, 129, 142, 147, 149, *162–3*, 323, *330–2*

Vadim, Roger, 340, 341, 393–4, 398, 431

Vailland, Roger, 368
Valentini, Robert, 28
Valéry, Paul, 140
Van Karman, 337
Varda, Agnès, 241, 393, 396, 398, 400, 408, 410–11
Vartan, Sylvie, 342, 344–5
Veuillot, Cardinal, 387–8
Viansson-Ponté, Pierre, 126
Vichy régime, 4, 5, 14, 69, 77, 117
Vierny, Sacha, 414
Vigo, Jean, 392, 394, 414
Vilar, Jean, 416, 419, 420, 464
Villelaur, Anne, 364
Villiers, Georges, 26, 33n
vinegrowers, 89–91, 135–7
Voix du Nord, la, 164
Volkswagen, 58, 59

Volontaires du Progrès, les, 350

Waldeck-Rochet, M. 422
Wardle, Irving, 418
watch industry, 31
Weber, Dr., 147
Weightman, John, 371
Weil, Louis, 117, 124, 331
Weill-Hallé, Marie-Andrée, 254, 257
Weiss, Peter, 418, 419
Wiazemsky, Anne, 406
Wilson, Georges, 416
Wimpy bars, 200, 274
wine industry, 89–91, 135–7, 191, 302–4
Wogensky, 214
Woolf, Virginia, 372
worker-priests, 380–1
working hours, 266–9, 464

Wylie, Laurence, 236

Young Farmers, the, 6, 73, 74, 78, 81, 83, 93, 95 96–7 (see also JAC)
youth, cult of, 5, 306, 399; conformism of, 339, 345, 347–9; slang, 345–346; delinquency, 347; idealism and isolation, 349–53; new visage of, 470

Zamansky, Marc, 325
Zehrfuss, Bernard, 190
Zola, Emile, 192, 412
Zones d'Aménagement Différé, 208–9, 436, 475
Zones à Urbaniser par Priorité, 208–9, 436, 475

COLOPHON BOOKS ON EUROPEAN HISTORY

Svetlana Alliluyeva	TWENTY LETTERS TO A FRIEND, The complete text, in Russian. CN 122
J. C. Beckett	A SHORT HISTORY OF IRELAND: From the Time of St. Patrick to the Present. CN 121
Asa Briggs	VICTORIAN PEOPLE. CN 23
D. W. Brogan	THE FRENCH NATION: From Napoleon to Pétain, 1814-1940. CN 14
Louis Fischer	THE LIFE OF LENIN. CN 69
Richard Grunberger	GERMANY: 1918-1945. CN 86
R. W. Harris	ABSOLUTISM AND ENLIGHTENMENT, 1660-1789. CN 94
Alistair Horne	THE PRICE OF GLORY: Verdun, 1916. CN 107
James Joll	THE SECOND INTERNATIONAL, 1889-1914. CN 99
R. F. Leslie	THE AGE OF TRANSFORMATION, 1789-1871. CN 103
Gerhard Masur	PROPHETS OF YESTERDAY: Studies in European Culture, 1890-1914. CN 98
R. C. Mowat	RUIN AND RESURGENCE: The History of Europe, 1939-1965. CN 129
Herbert J. Muller	FREEDOM IN THE MODERN WORLD: The 19th and 20th Centuries. CN 104
Herbert J. Muller	FREEDOM IN THE WESTERN WORLD: From the Dark Ages to the Rise of Democracy. CN 36
Anthony Sampson	ANATOMY OF BRITAIN TODAY. CN 76
L. C. B. Seaman	FROM VIENNA TO VERSAILLES. CN 8
D. M. Sturley	A SHORT HISTORY OF RUSSIA. CN 90
Hugh Thomas	THE SPANISH CIVIL WAR. CN 12
J. M. Thompson	LEADERS OF THE FRENCH REVOLUTION. CN 112
J. R. Western	THE END OF EUROPEAN PRIMACY, 1871-1945. CN 116